WOMEN'S STUDIES

WOMEN'S STUDIES:
A Recommended Core Bibliography
1980-1985

Catherine R.
Loeb

Susan E.
Searing

Esther F.
Stineman

With the assistance of
Meredith J. Ross

1987

Libraries Unlimited   Littleton, Colorado

LIBRARIES UNLIMITED, INC.
P.O. Box 263
Littleton, Colorado 80160-0263

Library of Congress Cataloging-in-Publication Data

Loeb, Catherine.
 Women's studies.

 Includes index.
 1. Feminism--Bibliography. 2. Women's studies--
Bibliography. 3. Women--Bibliography. I. Searing,
Susan E. II. Stineman, Esther, 1947-   . III. Title.
Z7963.F44L63 1987   [HQ1180]   016.3054'2   86-27856
ISBN 0-87287-472-9

To our mothers:

Mary Toynton Loeb (1920-1971)
Dorothy Jean Meeks Searing, and
Patricia Lanigan Franco

CONTENTS

PREFACE AND ACKNOWLEDGMENTS

Volume one of *Women's Studies: A Recommended Core Bibliography* appeared in 1979, written by Esther Stineman with Catherine Loeb's assistance. Stineman was at that time the Women's Studies Librarian for the University of Wisconsin System, and Loeb, a member of her staff. The preface to the first volume details the many sources of support within the University of Wisconsin System for that project.

Today, Susan Searing holds the position of Women's Studies Librarian. Catherine Loeb is the senior staff member in the Women's Studies Librarian's office, and editor of *Feminist Collections* (see entry 865n). Esther Stineman is combining her women's studies background with American studies at Yale University. Together, we bring a range of expertise in interdisciplinary studies and familiarity with the body of women's studies literature to the creation of this volume. We believe that our collaborative approach — using resources in Colorado, Connecticut, and Wisconsin — has made this a stronger, richer book than any of us could have written individually.

Many people assisted us during the two years we labored on this book. Our warmest thanks go to Pamela Niebauer, staff associate for the duration of the project. She wrote many of the annotations on drama, her field of expertise, and in her grasp of the innumerable administrative details of this undertaking, proved to be an invaluable colleague.

Meredith Ross, credited on the title page, was our "third-and-a-half" collaborator, called in after the project was already underway to help us cope with the enormous number of titles in literature and the humanities. A scholar in English and women's studies, she wrote numerous annotations, inspiring us with her graceful way with words, her fresh knowledge of her field, and her cheerful approach to mountains of books.

The staff of the UW System Women's Studies Librarian were all pressed into service on the book at one time or another, especially in the final weeks as we raced toward the end of our funding period and the publisher's deadline. Alice Saben spent hours typing entries, and Christina Wagner and Ellen Mortensen verified bibliographic data and prices, and performed numerous tasks that kept the work flowing smoothly. Linda Shult contributed her expertise to our discussions with computing center staff about the project's database management program. She also composed annotations in the areas she knows best — information technology, early childhood education, and mass communications. All of these staff members cooperated to keep the daily office routines from overwhelming us as we devoted ever more time and energy to "The Book."

There are many others whom we also thank. Jurgen Patau, of the Madison Academic Computing Center, patiently explained the workings of our tailor-made database management system, and revised the program as needed. The staff of the Wisconsin InterLibrary Services (WILS) office made heroic efforts to obtain books that were not held locally; we express particular gratitude to Mary Williamson and Sylvia Adrian. Several libraries on the Madison campus rushed purchases of new titles that we requested. The Circulation unit of UW-Madison's Memorial Library cheerfully checked out truckloads of books for us, and followed up on many recalls and searches. Orlando Archibeque, Reference Librarian at the University of Colorado at Colorado Springs, checked holdings there and retrieved materials. Patricia Lanigan Franco gave bibliographic and editorial assistance. Others at the University of Wisconsin, the University of Colorado, and Yale University helped in many small but important ways.

Without the generous assistance of Susan Holte, who copyedited the manuscript and made suggestions throughout the writing process, this book would not have reached its present form. We thank her for her dedicated professionalism and her invaluable assistance in helping us realize our project.

Each of us must also thank her personal circle of scholars, friends, professional associates, and family members who shared their opinions, recommended books, and provided encouragement. Stineman thanks her family for extraordinary support during the preparation of this volume. Loeb says a warm thank you to Kristine Krozek and Robert Loeb, who attentively followed the book's progress through many long-distance letters and phone calls; to Cynthia Costello, for exceptional friendship; to the Griffeath family, for longstanding affection; and especially to David Griffeath and Robin and Brian Griffeath-Loeb. And Searing wishes to thank her colleagues in the women's groups of the American Library Association, the Librarians' Task Force of the National Women's Studies Association, the Wisconsin Women Library Workers, and the Advisory Panel to the UW System Women's Studies Librarian for their encouragement and practical advice; and Christine Jenkins and Jackie Kaplan, for their unflagging friendship and support.

This supplement was supported by a generous grant from the National Endowment for the Humanities, a federal agency that promotes the study of such fields as history, philosophy, literature, and languages. Funding from NEH made it possible to approach the project in a systematic and thorough way, with adequate staff support and travel money to bring the collaborators face to face.

In creating this supplement, our knowledge of women's studies has grown; our appreciation for feminist scholarship, in all its complexity and contradictions, has deepened. Despite the assistance of all these individuals and agencies, in a project of this scope there is still possibility for errors, both factual and evaluative. For these, we take full responsibility.

INTRODUCTION

Women's studies has changed radically in the years since Esther Stineman's *Women's Studies: A Recommended Core Bibliography* appeared in 1979. Just as the women's movement grew during this period to incorporate a more representative cross-section of women, thus broadening its concerns, so has women's studies expanded its base of scholars, and hence its range of inquiry. Diversity—of content, method, and values—characterizes feminist scholarship in the eighties, and makes it a focal point for exciting intellectual debate. Not surprisingly, the very nature of the field of women's studies is itself often at issue.

In the opinion of some scholars, women's studies is gradually giving way to "gender studies"—a recognition that the field necessarily involves women *and* men in the process of discovering a new analytic, indeed a new language in which to clarify the nature of gender differences and power relationships. In the words of historian John Faragher, it makes sense to study "women and men on the overland trail," for both sexes suffered the ordeals of the journey, and the most interesting speculations arise from observing human experience in a particular time and place as inflected by gender and sex-linked expectations.

A related development is the expansion of programs to "mainstream" feminist scholarship into the existing college curriculum. By incorporating the study of women into basic courses in the humanities, social sciences, and sciences, feminist faculty hope to move women's studies to a new stage, and to integrate women's concerns and women's values into the heart of liberal education.

Yet a separatist impulse continues to influence the field. Many scholars seek to strengthen women's studies as an independent discipline, to define and legitimize a distinct feminist theory and pedagogy. Thus we see new women's studies programs and research centers continuing to spring up on college campuses. Some argue that "gender studies" and curriculum integration represent not progress, but co-optation. Further, they assert, only within the safe, supportive structure of women's studies programs can more revolutionary intellectual explorations—in, for example, black women's studies or lesbian studies—be undertaken.

What remains undeniable, whatever one's position on the nature and future of the field, is the enormous impact feminist scholarship has had on our view of the world in the relatively short space of two decades. Coupled with this is the staggering growth in scholarly and popular publishing by, for, and about women, testifying to the vitality and remarkable vision of women's studies and the women's movement.

Such trends have markedly influenced our approaches to bibliography-building, first in the seventies and now in the eighties. With the initial volume of *Women's Studies,* covering English-language materials through mid-1979, Stineman's objective was to assemble in one source a core collection of books and periodicals to support the panoply of women's studies courses then in place; Stineman envisioned the bibliography as a sort of massive band-aid solution to the problem of collections woefully deficient in women-related scholarship. Finding an adequate number of relevant sources across the disciplines required ingenuity and perseverance.

With the second volume, extending bibliographic coverage into 1985, we faced a challenge of an entirely different order—that of winnowing a manageable "core" list of titles from the overwhelming array of publications available in nearly every field. In this list of 1,211 entries, we have been forced to be ruthlessly selective, and we have necessarily omitted many worthy books. To offset these losses, we have routinely mentioned additional related titles within our annotations, doubling the number of works to which we refer, however briefly. Consequently, many of our annotations verge on mini-bibliographic essays, clustering books on similar subjects or by the same author.

The selection process required a many-staged methodology. First, we combed reviews of English-language or translated works, both in the feminist and in the mainstream media. Comprehensive files maintained by the University of Wisconsin Women's Studies Librarian's office for the compilation of its semiannual *New Books on Women and Feminism* (see entry 865n) were a great help at this stage. The reviews afforded us a fuller picture of the shape of the literature, and enabled us to chart critical consensus on the best-written, most original, and most controversial titles. This first round of selection left us with a database of some four thousand titles, and with preliminary indexing that proved indispensable in our later efforts to compare related titles across disciplines.

We then began the long process of retrieving and examining the books themselves. We have held in our hands virtually every book described in these pages; many we skimmed, others we studied in depth. In some cases, we solicited expert outside readers. As we read, we kept in mind an array of questions. Does the book advance knowledge on women or gender? How useful is the title for a small as well as a large library, for an undergraduate, a graduate student, a librarian, a faculty member, the common reader? How might a collection be strengthened by adding the book? Many appealing books, despite their merits, did not meet our criteria.

In addition, we applied some broad guidelines to assure balance in our selection. We asked ourselves: Are women who occupy marginal positions in society adequately represented in the works cited? Are the interests of nonacademic women reflected, as well as those of academics? Have we acknowledged the international progress of women's studies by highlighting translations and studies of non-Western cultures? Have we included materials illustrating varying viewpoints on sensitive issues? In short, does our selection mirror the multiplicity of feminisms that find expression in print?

A few words about our omissions are in order. We did not feel obliged to cite all works by prolific authors, or every treatment of a popular subject, although wherever possible we strived to identify more than one useful title on a given theme. We excluded special issues of periodicals (although many important women-focused periodical titles are highlighted in their own chapter), and we cited only a handful of government documents. We did not cover the report literature accessible through such services as ERIC, or described in the bulletin *On Campus With Women* (see entry 1189). Finally, with few exceptions, we omitted reprints. Readers should be aware of the vital reprint series issued by the Virago Press and the Feminist Press; these rediscovered literary works have proven invaluable curriculum materials for women's studies courses.

Users will find works both from small women's presses and from university and trade publishers. Fortunately, the influx of mainstream publishers into the feminist marketplace of ideas has not squeezed out women's independent publishing. Both sectors of the publishing world continue to play central roles in disseminating information about women. While our five-year time period has seen the demise of pioneering feminist presses such as

Persephone Press, Daughters, Inc., and Diana Press, these losses are balanced by the birth of new publishers—Firebrand Books, Kitchen Table: Women of Color Press, Spinsters, Ink, Cleis Press, and others. And some early presses hang on, becoming more firmly established and building impressive catalogs and backlists. Among them are the venerable Feminist Press (now affiliated with the City University of New York), Naiad Press, and Virago Press. (We have listed in an appendix the addresses for small presses not covered in *Books in Print.*)

Feminist presses regularly produce pathbreaking volumes, and are often first to articulate new political issues, to showcase new literary talent, and to bring to readers writings from outside white, heterosexual, middle-class circles. Although there has been marked improvement since 1979, small press books are still slighted by the standard reviewing media. We hope that this supplement, like the first volume of *Women's Studies*, will call attention to overlooked titles. In the Periodicals chapter, we cite a number of feminist reviewing sources that will assist the reader in identifying and evaluating new small-press titles.

The substantially expanded Periodicals chapter describes nearly sixty feminist serials—literary magazines, scholarly journals, newspapers, newsletters, and art journals. Periodical literature is the cutting edge of feminist scholarship, feminist theory, and much of women's culture. We have increased our periodical listings in this volume to provide readers with a wide avenue to this lively literature.

While the format of this supplement mirrors its parent volume, we can discern some broad areas in which its content differs. Stineman's original volume emphasized pathbreaking feminist books of the seventies, but it also cited many original and reprinted titles dating back a century or more. The first practitioners of women's studies placed a high priority on the resurrection of "lost" works by women. In this supplement, we include some older materials that first saw publication after 1979—notably diaries and posthumous literary works. Overall, however, the listings have a decidedly contemporary slant.

The nascent state of women's studies dictated that the first volume include some works that took women as their subject but reflected no feminist awareness. Today, there are few topics relevant to women that have not engaged the new generation of feminist thinkers. Consequently, a stronger thematic cohesion emerges in the works covered in the supplement, a more unified sense of a body of literature informed by a feminist perspective. Increasing specialization also characterizes this maturing field of women's studies: we rejected hundreds of books that would appeal only to a small circle of experts.

The scope of women's studies is unlimited, for women participate in virtually every human endeavor. Still, we can note some shifts in the subjects that intrigue researchers and galvanize activists. Some topics that stood out in the literature of the seventies—the concept of androgyny, the processes of consciousness-raising and assertiveness training, and (alas) the E.R.A.—crop up with less frequency in the mid-eighties. Other subjects continue to inspire research and analysis—among them, violence against women, the sexual division of labor, housework, sexuality, power, socialism, political participation, and careers.

Added to the above is a host of new concerns and scholarly directions. Foremost perhaps are the "new feminisms"—the unique angles of vision articulated by black, Indian, Asian, Latina, Jewish, and lesbian American women, as well as by women in other countries. Other new topics cluster around physical and mental health: reproductive technology, eating disorders, incest, substance abuse, genital mutilation, osteoporosis, premenstrual syndrome, DES, and the appalling discrimination against older and disabled women. International issues have become increasingly important, including the impact of development on women, the effects of a world economic order, nationalism, imperialism, and the rise of a global feminist network.

Some subjects have called forth illuminating historical revisions, alongside contemporary, policy-oriented studies. Here we would single out clerical work, women in the military, right-wing women, women in the peace movement, and the lives of rural and pioneer women. Still other concepts are new since 1979—comparable worth, for example, and the gender gap in voting patterns.

In the realm of literary critical theory, one cannot miss the influence of contemporary European ideas, notably derived from the challenging writings of the "French feminists"—Kristeva, Cixous, Irigaray, Wittig, and their peers. Feminist questions have transformed current discussions of literary discourse, film, and artistic expression.

Women's studies made early inroads into the humanities and social sciences, but we now see even once-resistant fields opening up to new, feminist ways of seeing. In this volume, we include an additional chapter on science and technology, as well as a number of pioneering works in the areas of geography and ethics.

No scholar can hope to keep abreast of all the current trends in women's studies, but it is imperative that libraries represent them fairly on their shelves. Collection development influences the distribution of knowledge: people may not seek out what is not readily at hand in their libraries. Yet, librarians cannot purchase or recommend works unfamiliar to them. In this supplement, as in the original volume of *Women's Studies,* our objectives are twofold: to offer a checklist against which libraries can evaluate their holdings; and, additionally, to provide guidance to the student, the researcher, and the reference librarian.

For readers seeking further insights into the intricacies of the research process, we recommend Susan Searing's recently published guide, *Introduction to Library Research in Women's Studies* (see entry 892). Librarians responsible for ongoing collection development should consult the guide prepared by Joan Ariel and issued as a separate publication in *Choice*'s "Bibliographic Essay Series"—*Building Women's Studies Collections: A Checklist for Libraries, Research and Resource Centers, and Individual Collectors* (1986).

The subject index in this supplement, much expanded and refined from the first volume, should serve the needs of librarians and teachers who wish to refer people to appropriate reading material. We used the terminology of Stineman's 1979 volume as a working thesaurus, but have added many new terms and subdivisions, and have incorporated current usage whenever feasible.

Volume one of *Women's Studies* charted the diverse literature of a new, somewhat chaotic field; it further served a historiographic purpose of mapping major early writings by and about women. Since then, scholarship has rapidly progressed to a stage that some label "postfeminist," and that others hail as the fullest flowering of feminist thought to date. In many ways, the books described here depict the results of a social and intellectual revolution that has radically altered the way that writers, scholars, and critics from all disciplines view the world—and, perhaps most importantly, the creative and critical ways women read.

NOTES ON USING THIS BIBLIOGRAPHY

ANNOTATIONS

Annotations were composed after examining each book and considering its critical reception. We intend an annotation to convey a work's specific content, its applicability to women's studies, and its relationship to other books on similar topics. In selecting and interpreting books, we have placed ourselves in the position of general readers, not specialists. Since many of the works cited are political in content, our judgments and comments are naturally open to question or dispute. However, we prefer openly stated evaluations over such vague and unhelpful comments as "recommended" or "good source," so frequently encountered in bibliographies.

In an effort to cluster works on related topics, we mention additional sources within most entries. Many of the annotations resemble concise bibliographic essays, highlighting the best books on a subject. All works, whether accorded a main citation or referred to in an annotation to another text, are fully indexed.

BIBLIOGRAPHIC INFORMATION

The authority for all bibliographic information is Library of Congress (LC) cataloging. Entries have been verified using the OCLC database. Biographical dates for authors generally appear only when LC provides them. Though the result is an inconsistent appearance, we believe that users will prefer to have some date information than none at all.

Because of the adoption of the second edition of the Anglo-American Cataloging Rules mid-way through the period we survey — rules that mandate main entries under the most common form of an author's name (or pseudonym) — we have eliminated some sexist forms. Margaret Fuller's works, for instance, appear in this supplement under her own surname, but are listed in the first volume under her married name, "Ossoli." Any inconsistencies in this regard are, we hope, ameliorated by cross-references in the indexes.

IN-PRINT, OUT-OF-PRINT, AND REPRINTED WORKS

Each entry has been verified for in-print status using the 1985-1986 edition of *Books in Print* (*BIP*). An asterisk (*) following an entry number means that the book does not appear in the latest edition of *BIP*. For books published by university and trade presses, this generally indicates that the book is indeed no longer in print. An asterisk may also suggest, however, that the book's publisher is not indexed in *BIP*. This holds true for a number of small alternative presses, government agencies, women's groups, and the like.

We have appended a list of addresses for publishers not covered in *BIP* so that readers can make direct inquiries regarding a book's status. In cases where we questioned the information in *BIP*, we attempted to check publishers' catalogs to determine availability and price.

Out-of-print books are included for two reasons. First, we intend this bibliography as a reference guide as well as a checklist for developing library collections. Researchers need to be alerted to the full range of feminist works from mid-1979 through 1985; many titles no longer stocked in bookstores are readily available in libraries. Second, recent changes in the law discourage publishers from maintaining extensive backlists. Once the market demand for a book drops off, the title is often forced out of print. Citing the best out-of-print volumes here will, we hope, create reader interest and pressure for reprinting.

References to reprints are scant in this supplement, but they do occur. Wherever possible, we provide information about the original edition, as well as the place, publisher, and date of the reprint. In a like manner, we indicate distributors for obscure and foreign presses whenever possible.

PRICING, ISBN, AND LC NUMBERS

Generally, we have listed hardcover prices, as most libraries buy books in this format. Many of the titles cited here will also be available in less expensive paperbacks. If paperback is the *only* available format, the paperbound price is given. When we are certain that this is the case, we include the designation "pbk." ISBN and LC numbers are routinely provided to facilitate interlibrary loan and purchasing. The numbers are taken from Library of Congress records (from OCLC or Cataloging-in-Publication).

INDEXING

All works treated in this supplement — whether cited as primary entries or mentioned within an annotation — are fully indexed by author, title, and subject. The author index uses names as established by the Library of Congress. The title index includes complete titles and subtitles.

Subject indexing is derived from Stineman's first volume, but has been significantly expanded with more refined vocabulary and enriched by new words and concepts. We make frequent use of analytic subdivisions to avoid an excessive number of entries following a single term. "See" and "see also" references are employed to link related topics.

ANTHROPOLOGY, CROSS-CULTURAL SURVEYS, AND INTERNATIONAL STUDIES

Not only anthropological and cross-cultural works, but also interdisciplinary area studies, are gathered in this chapter. International studies with a specific disciplinary focus (for example, on politics, history, or education) will be found in the appropriate chapter. The books described here look at a variety of cultural and ethnic groups primarily in developing regions of the world, examining such factors as women's economic participation, women's roles in religion and the community, kinship systems, and the often deleterious effects of colonization and modernization. Ethnographic studies highlight the intersections of race, sex, age, and class in women's lives; cross-cultural studies provide valuable comparative data; and theoretical writings tackle the central puzzle of the origins of sexual inequality. These works complement others on international feminism in the Women's Movement and Feminist Theory chapter. *The Cross-Cultural Study of Women: A Comprehensive Guide,* edited by Margot Duley and Mary I. Edwards (Feminist Press, 1986), introduces both students and instructors to key theoretical perspectives and to the major topics and readings in area studies.

1. Abdullah, Tahrunnessa A., and Sondra A. Zeidenstein. **Village Women of Bangladesh: Prospects for Change.** New York: Pergamon Press, 1982. 246p. bibliog. $25.00. LC 81-19929. ISBN 0080267955.

Over the last decade, feminist scholars have looked with a critical eye at strategies for development in the Third World, showing how programs exhibiting sexist biases and ignorance of the real role of women in rural economies can severely undercut women's status and access to resources. Abdullah and Zeidenstein report here on the first four years (1974-1978) of a project designed to integrate rural Bangladeshi women in the development process. Launched by the Bangladesh Population Planning Project, and funded by the World Bank, the program, it must be noted, had a "hidden agenda" of lowering the fertility rate. The immediate strategy, however, was to create cooperatives that would expand women's economic opportunity by offering credit and training. Readers may want to compare the observations of Abdullah and Zeidenstein with those of Martha Alter Chen in *A Quiet Revolution: Women in Transition in Rural Bangladesh* (Schenkman, 1983). Working with a private, nongovernmental agency, Chen planned and administered a five-year program to organize rural Bangladeshi women into cooperatives. For additional sources on the topic, consult Nici Nelson's *Why Has Development Neglected Rural Women? A Review of the South Asian Literature* (Pergamon Press, 1979).

2. Albers, Patricia, and Beatrice Medicine, eds. **The Hidden Half: Studies of Plains Indian Women.** Lanham, MD: University Press of America, 1983. 280p. bibliog. $25.50. LC 82-23906. ISBN 0819129569.

The chief, the warrior, the hunter: these stereotypes of American Indians are drawn almost entirely from the lives of Plains Indian men, Albers contends. Plains Indian women have typically been seen through the lens of U.S./European values and experience, rendering their contributions to the community invisible. The ten papers in this volume draw upon data from ethnological, ethnohistorical, and contemporary field research; a common purpose is to ask new questions of the available data. Albers' introduction ably reviews the literature, lays bare its deficiencies, and sets forth the goals of the collection. Particularly notable are the articles by Katherine Weist, who critically examines the depiction of Plains Indian women as "beasts of burden" and "menial slaves" in nineteenth-century accounts; Janet Spector, who analyzes male/female task differentiation among the Hidatsa; Albers and Medicine, who assess the meaning of Indian women's quiltmaking; and Albers, who traces the changes in Plains Indian women's lives resulting from capitalist penetration of their communities. This collection helps fill the gap in feminist scholarship on North American native women.

3. Anker, Richard, et al., eds. **Women's Roles and Population Trends in the Third World.** London: Croom Helm, 1982. 287p. bibliog. index. $33.50. LC 81-182681. ISBN 0709905084.

Commissioned by the International Labour Office in connection with its inter-disciplinary research program on the relationship between women's roles and demographic change, the ten papers in this volume critically examine methodologies and underlying assumptions of contemporary Western research, particularly as regards: difficulties of measuring women's economic contributions; hazards of taking the household unit as the unit of analysis; assuming a common interest among household members; limitations of studying individuals or the household in isolation from the international division of labor and local class relations; failure to look at women's interpersonal power as it relates to fertility behavior; overly simplistic approaches to the relationship between women's labor force participation and fertility; and neglect of women's status as a factor shaping mortality differentials between men and women. In their introduction, editors Richard Anker, Mayra Buvinic, and Nadia H. Youssef offer a cogent analysis of the volume's theoretical, methodological, and policy implications.

4. Ardener, Shirley, ed. **Women and Space: Ground Rules and Social Maps.** New York: St. Martin's Press, 1981. 239p. bibliog. index. $25.00. LC 81-5253. ISBN 0312887337.

Ten British anthropologists join editor Shirley Ardener in exploring some of the ways in which spatial concepts and space itself are utilized to demarcate the separate and unequal domains of women and men in Peru, England, Greece, Iran, the USSR, Nigeria, and South Africa. For example, Silvia Rodgers analyzes how the allocation of space in the British House of Commons has historically spelled out in physical terms "the cultural map of political power" (p.53), and the invisibility of women in particular. *Her Space, Her Place: A Geography of Women* (Association of American Geographers, 1983), by Mary Ellen Mazey and David R. Lee, presents a succinct overview of recent studies by geographers, examining worldwide differences in female status, the diffusion of feminist reform, men's and women's varying patterns of travel and daily activity, women's relations to the landscape (including their roles in agriculture), and the design of houses and communities. Research on sex differences in environmental perception and spatial abilities is also spotlighted. The Canadian Journal *Women and Environments* has a similar focus.

5. Bendt, Ingela, and James Downing. **We Shall Return: Women of Palestine.** Westport, CT: Lawrence Hill, 1982. 129p. $16.95. LC 82-12052. ISBN 0882081543.

Swedish journalists Ingela Bendt and Jim Downing spent five months in Lebanon in 1978-1979 interviewing Palestinian women in refugee camps. They mix description, quotes from their interviews, and their own personal impressions in an account full of political passion. Viewing the mounting crisis through the women's eyes, we gain a sense not only of the oppression and resistance of stateless Palestinians, and of the exploding civil war in Lebanon, but also of the texture of these women's daily lives in a patriarchal Moslem culture. Most of the camps visited by Bendt and Downing were subsequently destroyed during the June 1982 Israeli invasion of Lebanon. Desire to return to their homeland — now Israel — fuels the Palestinian struggle. Raymonda Hawa Tawil, a Palestinian journalist living in Israel, recounts her life history in *My Home, My Prison* (Holt, Rinehart, and Winston, 1980) — from the war of 1948 through 1976, when she was placed under house arrest for writing news reports "harmful to the security of the state of Israel" (p.1). Tawil writes eloquently of her sense of oppression as a Palestinian and a woman.

6. Benería, Lourdes, ed. **Women and Development: The Sexual Division of Labor in Rural Societies.** New York: Praeger, 1982. 257p. bibliog. index. $28.95. LC 82-606. ISBN 0030618029.

The nine articles collected here analyze the impact of different development processes on rural women in India, Africa, Southeast Asia, Mexico, South America, and the People's Republic of China. In her introduction, Benería lays out the theoretical perspective undergirding the volume. First, the contributors take a critical view of the capitalist model for economic development and its impact on the status of women. Secondly, these writers give equal weight to production and *reproduction*. The sexual division of labor, it is argued, must be examined within the domestic economy as well as within the market economy; failure to do so results in gross underestimation of women's economic contributions. Together, the articles demonstrate the historical and cross-cultural variability in the sexual division of labor. *Rural Women's Participation in Development* (1980), a staff paper of the United Nations Development Programme, reports on research undertaken "to improve the United Nations system's capability to offer programming advice to governments at the project level ..." (p.1). Rural women's work and employment, health conditions, education and training, and development planning and implementation are examined in broad regional reviews. *Gender Roles in Development Projects: A Case Book* (Kumarian Press, 1985), edited by Catherine Overholt, Mary B. Anderson, Kathleen Cloud, and James E. Austin, presents technical papers and case studies developed during the first phase of a training project undertaken by members of the Harvard Institute for International Development.

7. Bennett, Lynn, 1945- . **Dangerous Wives and Sacred Sisters: Social and Symbolic Roles of High-Caste Women in Nepal.** New York: Columbia University Press, 1983. 353p. bibliog. index. $31.50. LC 83-7528. ISBN 0231046642.

Purity vs. pollution; asceticism vs. fertility — these fundamental oppositions undergird the pervasive ambivalence toward women expressed in Hindu culture, according to Bennett. Beginning with an explication of "the social, ritual, and ideological framework of Hindu culture" (p.vii), Bennett moves on to assess the ambiguous position of high-caste Nepali women. The status of Nepali women is contradictory because Hindu patrilineal ideology accords them very low rank as wives, while granting them high rank in their natal homes. In their sexual and reproductive roles, women are associated with pollution; in their consanguineal roles, they are deemed "pure." The author's fieldwork over ten years included participant observation; collection of genealogies and fertility histories; surveys of marriage patterns, ritual practices, and religious beliefs; and a series of in-depth life history interviews.

8.* Black, Naomi, and Ann Baker Cottrell, eds. **Women and World Change: Equity Issues in Development.** Beverly Hills: Sage Publications, 1981. 288p. bibliog. LC 81-9249. ISBN 0803917007.

Studies of development strategies and their impact on women should not be restricted to the underdeveloped regions of the world, Black and Cottrell assert, but must be extended to "all continents, in both fully and less industrialized economies, and in the past as well as the present" (p.7). Accordingly, the editors present material here on Singapore, Jamaica, an Acadian village in New Brunswick, Africa, the Communist countries, Britain, Sweden, Peru, India, France, and the United States. The authors of *Women and the Social Costs of Economic Development* (Westview Press, 1981) agree with Black and Cottrell that comparative examinations of development in the industrialized world will enhance understanding of Third World development. Elizabeth Moen, Elise Boulding, Jane Lillydahl, and Risa Palm studied the impact of rapid energy development on women in two Colorado towns. They found the consequences of this development to be predominantly negative for women, who shoulder most of the burden of family and community adaptation. Their evidence, they conclude, calls into question "the prevailing theory regarding the relationship between gender stratification and economic development, ... which assumes that the gender status of women will improve with development and modernization" (p.172).

9. Bossen, Laurel Herbenar, 1945- . **The Redivision of Labor: Women and Economic Choice in Four Guatemalan Communities.** Albany: State University of New York Press, 1984. 396p. bibliog. index. $46.50. LC 83-426. ISBN 0873957407.

Using quantitative and qualitative research techniques, Bossen studied the position of women in four Guatemalan communities that represent the major sociocultural and economic divisions within the society: "(1) a remote Maya farming village; (2) a modernizing sugarcane plantation; (3) a crowded urban shanty-town; and (4) a sleek urban middle-class neighborhood" (p.2). She was interested in how "changes in the larger world economic system impinge on male-female relations at the local level," and in whether "modern capitalism [is] a liberating force for women" (p.301). She concludes that changing economic and social conditions do restructure the gender division of labor, and further, that Western capitalist penetration is, if anything, associated with increasing sexual inequality in Guatemala.

10. Bourque, Susan C., 1943- , and Kay Barbara Warren, 1947- . **Women of the Andes: Patriarchy and Social Change in Two Peruvian Towns.** Ann Arbor: University of Michigan Press, 1981. 241p. bibliog. index. $18.50. LC 81-811. ISBN 0472093304.

Bourque and Warren successfully mix ethnography and theory-building in this study of two small Andean communities in Peru—one a rural trade center, the other an isolated agricultural town. The contrast between the two, with their different mix of capitalist and precapitalist relations, enables the authors to pose questions about the impact of development on rural Andean women. Guided by what they call a "social ideology perspective" grounded in class analysis, Bourque and Warren examine the range of women's social, political, and economic experience—childbirth, marriage, and family politics; the sexual division of the economy; women's positions in the agrarian class system; consciousness and participation in the patriarchal power structure; and the impact of social change and development. *Women in Andean Agriculture: Peasant Production and Rural Wage Employment in Colombia and Peru* (International Labour Office, 1982), by Carmen Diana Deere and Magdalena León de Leal, focuses more narrowly on measurement of women's agricultural contributions and on evaluation of the impact of change in agricultural production. The authors' findings demonstrate that census data underestimate women's agricultural participation and that, contrary to expectation, the family sexual division of labor has become more fluid with capitalist development.

11.   Brown, Judith K., and Virginia Kerns, 1948- , eds. **In Her Prime: A New View of Middle-Aged Women.** South Hadley, MA: Bergin and Garvey, 1985. 217p. bibliog. index. $27.95. LC 84-14671. ISBN 0897890566.

Blending two new subfields—the anthropology of women and the anthropology of aging—the thirteen contributors to this volume address developmental changes in middle-aged women's lives. Brown asserts that in nonindustrialized societies, women in middle age are often freed from social restrictions, granted greater authority over younger kin, and elevated to special status outside the household (e.g., as midwives or holy women). Matrons in industrialized societies, by contrast, realize few advantages by aging. The ethnographies in this volume describe such factors as motherhood, sexuality, public life, and menopause in a number of cultures—ranging from small-scale traditional to industrial societies.

12.   Bunkle, Phillida, and Beryl Hughes, eds. **Women in New Zealand Society.** Boston: Allen and Unwin, 1980. 265p. bibliog. index. $22.50. LC 80-67864. ISBN 0868610267.

New Zealand—or "Aotearoa" in the indigenous Maori tongue—was the first country in the world to grant women the vote, in 1893. What we know of New Zealand falls into two categories: ethnographic accounts of the indigenous Maori, written largely from a Western, male perspective; and history of the European "discovery" (colonization) and settlement. Indigenous women's history remains to be written. In Bunkle and Hughes' collection, for example, the Maori experience is represented by only one article; the experience of New Zealand women of European descent predominates in the remaining ten articles, which address a range of topics: women and politics; the New Zealand temperance movement; fertility, sexuality, and social control; women and the economy; women and the professions; educational equity; women artists; and colonial male culture, among others. The feminist monthly *Broadsheet* reflects more accurately the cultural and political diversity of New Zealand women, providing consistent coverage of Maori issues and viewpoints. Christine Dann's *Up From Under: Women and Liberation in New Zealand, 1970-1985* (Allen and Unwin/Port Nicolson Press, 1985) is a brief overview of the first fifteen years of the contemporary New Zealand women's movement.

13.   Caplan, Patricia, and Janet M. Bujra, eds. **Women United, Women Divided: Comparative Studies of Ten Contemporary Cultures.** Bloomington: Indiana University Press, 1979. 288p. bibliog. index. $22.50. LC 78-14085. ISBN 0253122155.

Nine feminist anthropologists explore the question of female solidarity in the varied cultures of Africa, China, India, Australia, England, and the Caribbean. The results are intriguing. They find female unity can be used in the interests of protecting the sexual division of labor or class privilege, as well as for feminist aims. In two instances, the conditions of women's lives are found to engender isolation and distrust rather than solidarity. In her stimulating introductory chapter, Bujra reviews recent feminist theory on production and reproduction, domestic labor, and class, drawing out of the collection's disparate case studies general conclusions relevant to these current feminist debates.

14.   Charlton, Sue Ellen M. **Women in Third World Development.** Boulder, CO: Westview Press, 1984. 240p. bibliog. index. $30.00. LC 84-2403. ISBN 0865317348.

Intended as "an advanced introduction to what development means for half the people in the world" (p.xiii), *Women in Third World Development* would be a superb text at the college level. Charlton writes clearly and sets her topic within a broad political and historical context, providing a thoughtful and thorough overview of this rapidly expanding field. She begins in Part I with an interpretation of the term *development* as "history and process," then reviews the basic contours of the contemporary international system, the pervasiveness of Western influence, women's political dependency, and current debates about development's impact on women. Part II, by far the longest section, examines in detail the question of hunger, women's roles in the food cycle, and access to credit, family planning, cash income, and training and education. In the final section, Charlton describes alternative development strategies, from the most limited to the most revolutionary; outlines major public agencies and private organizations involved in development projects; and reflects on possible meanings of "development by and for women." Footnotes and supplementary reading lists follow each chapter. *Women in Development: A Resource Guide for Organization and Action* (New Society Publishers, 1984), by the ISIS Women's International Information and Communication Service, is, as the subtitle suggests, designed more for the activist than the academic. Separately authored chapters on multinationals, rural development, health, education and communication, and migration and tourism critically summarize key issues and list international resources. A particularly fine selection of graphics and photographs helps enliven or bring the discussion to life.

15.   Chipp, Sylvia A., and Justin J. Green, eds. **Asian Women in Transition.** University Park: Pennsylvania State University Press, 1980. 262p. bibliog. $24.95. LC 79-20517. ISBN 0271002514.

The eleven articles in this collection offer a useful introduction to the expanding literature on women in Asia. The contributions are arranged geographically into three sections: East Asia (Japan, China); Southeast Asia (the Philippines, Malaysia, Indonesia); and South Asia (India, Pakistan, Bangladesh). The editors furnish brief introductions to the volume and to each section. The migration of Asian women from rural to urban areas is the focus of *Women in the Cities of Asia* (Westview Press, 1984), a collection of nineteen articles edited by James T. Fawcett, Siew-Ean Khoo, and Peter C. Smith.

16.   Eisen, Arlene. **Women and Revolution in Viet Nam.** London: Zed Press; distr. Totowa, NJ: Biblio Press, 1984. 294p. bibliog. $29.50. ISBN 0862321751.

Eisen brings the reader up to date on Vietnamese women's gains—in work, the household, health, education, social life, leadership, and culture—since 1975, when her work *Women of Viet Nam* appeared. Returning to Vietnam in 1981, Eisen concluded that her earlier views were excessively idealistic, glossing over the contradictions and difficulties faced by the country. She argues that women's progress can be appraised with accuracy only if it is seen in relation to Vietnam's legacy of war and colonialism. In Chapter 5, Eisen tackles the controversial question of the "boat people," and relates the history of Vietnam's war with Pol Pot's forces in Kampuchea (Cambodia) and with China in the North. While not blind to the limitations of Vietnamese women's advances, Eisen is persuaded of the sincerity of the regime's efforts. She views most current criticism of Vietnam as fueled by American anti-communism.

17.   Etienne, Mona, and Eleanor Leacock, 1922- , eds. **Women and Colonization: Anthropological Perspectives.** New York: Praeger, 1980. 339p. bibliog. index. $16.95. LC 79-15318. ISBN 0030525861.

In case studies of twelve societies in the Americas, Africa, and the Pacific, contributors to this volume consider the impact of European colonization on women's status. All but one of the articles were written for this volume. With ethnographic and historical detail, the authors call into question assumptions about the universality of male dominance and the benefits for women of Western-designed and -controlled "modernization." While Jean Grossholtz's study, *Forging Capitalist Patriarchy: The Economic and Social Transformation of Feudal Sri Lanka and Its Impact on Women* (Duke University Press, 1984), is much narrower in geographic focus, it will interest a broad spectrum of feminist readers because of the questions it raises concerning the "interlinking of colonialism, capitalism, and patriarchy." Tracing the history of colonial transformation in Sri Lanka (formerly Ceylon), Grossholtz poses the question: how does patriarchy change in the transition from feudalism to capitalism?

18. Gale, Fay, ed. **We Are Bosses Ourselves: The Status and Role of Aboriginal Women Today.** Canberra: Australian Institute of Aboriginal Studies; distr. Atlantic Highlands, NJ: Humanities Press, 1983. 175p. $21.00. ISBN 039102616X.

This extraordinary volume resulted from the first Australia-wide meeting of Aboriginal women, convened in Adelaide in 1980. With the help of government funding, women were brought from all parts of Australia, traditional rural communities and metropolitan centers alike. The excitement generated by this unprecedented gathering is palpable in this volume, in which the words of non-Aboriginal anthropologists and Aboriginal women mingle to create a vivid portrait and fresh interpretation of Aboriginal women's lives. Gale assured publication to any woman who wanted to express her views, in whatever form she was able to use. Thus, there is a mixture here of formal papers, transcribed (and sometimes translated) conversations, and summaries of general and workshop discussions. Many historical and contemporary photographs grace the text. The central issues are those of indigenous women the world over: land rights, preservation of culture, health care, education, economic independence. Underlying each of these is a strongly felt concern with the way European culture has progressively undermined the status of Aboriginal women relative to men. One of the anthropologists whose papers appear in this volume recently published her own monograph on the Aboriginal women of central Australia. In *Daughters of the Dreaming* (McPhee Gribble/Allen and Unwin, 1983), Diane Bell captures the vitality of Aboriginal women's lives through their active roles in ritual. Framed by feminist theory and emphasizing the pivotal importance of women's roles, Bell's work poses a challenge to received views in anthropology about Aboriginal culture.

19. Hay, Margaret Jean, and Sharon Stichter, eds. **African Women South of the Sahara.** London: Longman, 1984. 225p. bibliog. index. £5.95. LC 83-7905. ISBN 0582643732.

Hay and Stichter make the growing body of research on women in Africa more accessible to undergraduates and the general reader with this interdisciplinary collection of articles, authored by specialists in a number of fields. The focus is primarily contemporary, but set against a backdrop of precolonial and colonial history. Part I, "African Women in the Economy," includes contributions by Jeanne K. Henn and Jane I. Guyer on rural economies and by Claire C. Robertson on the urban economy. Part II, "African Women in Society and Culture," presents articles on the family (Luise White), voluntary associations (Audrey Wipper), religion and secular ideology (Margaret Strobel), literature (Deirdre LaPin), and the arts (Lisa Aronson). In Part III, "Women in Politics and Policy," Jean O'Barr writes about direct and indirect forms of women's power, Stephanie Urdang outlines women's participation in contemporary national liberation movements, and Barbara Lewis considers the impact of development policies on women. In an appendix, Stichter offers selected statistics on African women. A substantial bibliography fleshes out the volume.

20.   Hrdy, Sarah Blaffer, 1946- . **The Woman That Never Evolved.** Cambridge, MA: Harvard University Press, 1981. 256p. bibliog. index. $18.50. LC 81-2921. ISBN 0674955404.

    Cautioning feminists against seeking evidence of a lost matriarchy or even a past period of sexual harmony, Hrdy asserts that "the female with 'equal rights' never evolved; she was invented, and fought for consciously with intelligence, stubbornness, and courage" (p.190). As a feminist sociobiologist, Hrdy is in a good position to make this argument. Well-versed in the feminist literature critical of Wilsonian sociobiology, she counsels readers not to ignore the insights primatology can provide into the nature and prevalence of sexual assymetries. Her primate studies convince her that male dominance is indeed the norm, but that females exhibit a far greater variety of behaviors than many biased accounts claim — aggressiveness and competition as well as solidarity. Hrdy's well-written, scholarly study reviews available evidence from primatology on topics such as difference in male and female body size; monogamy and polygyny; female dominance, competition, and bonding; and the origins of female sexuality. Hrdy's is but one of several revisionist interpretations of evolution published between 1979 and 1982. *On Becoming Human* (Cambridge University Press, 1981), by anthropologist Nancy Makepeace Tanner, uses evidence from studies of chimpanzees, as well as from contemporary hunting and gathering societies, to argue that women's gathering activity — rather than men's hunting — was the "key innovation" in the transition from ape to human. The six original articles in *Woman the Gatherer* (Yale University Press, 1981), edited by Frances Dahlberg, work from a similar premise. By far the most wide-ranging and audacious of these recent studies is Elizabeth Fisher's *Woman's Creation: Sexual Evolution and the Shaping of Society* (Anchor Press, 1979). Clearly relishing her role as outsider-critic, Fisher roves freely among several disciplines. Like Tanner, she argues that women's inventiveness in hunting and gathering societies was critical to human evolution; it was with the transition to sedentary agricultural communities, and the discovery of paternity, that the foundations of patriarchy were established (a view Hrdy would contest). Many feminist readers will appreciate Fisher's passion, her iconoclasm, and, not least, her fluent writing.

21.   Hungry Wolf, Beverly. **The Ways of My Grandmothers.** New York: Morrow, 1980. 256p. index. pbk. $7.95. LC 79-91645. ISBN 0688004717.

    As a child, Beverly Hungry Wolf and her peers assumed that the "old ways" would die with the previous generations. Growing into adulthood, she and her husband chose to return to many of the traditional ways of their people, the Blood group of the Blackfoot tribe of Canada, and to learn all they could from their elders. This volume is a fascinating patchwork of the myths, legends, practical lore, and customs that are Hungry Wolf's heritage. She tells stories about the lives of her grandmothers (by custom, all the old women of the past); she recounts legends such as "How the Old People Say We Women Were Made"; and she shares instructions on such things as food preparation, clothing, tanning, beadwork, and preventing childbirth.

22.   Huston, Perdita, 1936- . **Third World Women Speak Out: Interviews in Six Countries on Change, Development, and Basic Needs.** New York: Praeger, in cooperation with the Overseas Development Council, 1979. 153p. $12.95. LC 78-32180. ISBN 0030521165.

In the course of interviewing nearly two hundred women in Tunisia, Egypt, Sudan, Kenya, Sri Lanka, and Mexico about their opinions on family planning, Huston found her discussion roving far from the topic at hand. This book describes the women's views on development and change, the family, women's status, health and family planning, and politics. The resulting picture does not represent a scientific sampling of women in these impoverished countries; rather, its value lies in the sense of immediacy conveyed by the women's own words. Staff of the International Center for Research on Women report the results of their content analysis of the interviews at the end of the volume.

23.   Jordan, Rosan A., and Susan J. Kalčik, eds. **Women's Folklore, Women's Culture.** Philadelphia: University of Pennsylvania Press, 1985. 245p. bibliog. pbk. $16.95. LC 84-12019. ISBN 0812212061.

Jordan and Kalčik blame sexist bias for the "lopsided orientation in folklore scholarship" (p.ix), which this intriguing collection begins to correct. The twelve studies range widely in topic and method, addressing such subjects as quilts, folktales, rag rugs, CB radio, joke-telling, and personal histories. Photographs enrich three of the pieces. One study discusses sex-role reversals in the Muslim oral tradition of Afghanistan; others reveal diverse cultures of the United States, including the lore of Mexican American women, the narratives of aged Hungarian-American women, and the life story of a Sioux woman. The compilers group the chapters into three parts: one on women in the private sphere; one on women in the public arena; and one highlighting the interrelationships between male and female worlds and views.

24.   Kishwar, Madhu, and Ruth Vanita, eds. **In Search of Answers: Indian Women's Voices from** *Manushi.* London: Zed Press; distr. Totowa, NJ: Biblio Distribution Center, 1984. 312p. $29.50. ISBN 0862321778.

In Search of Answers collects articles from the first five years of the bimonthly feminist Indian publication *Manushi: A Journal About Women and Society,* with an emphasis on the daily survival struggles of the rural majority. Madhu Kishwar's lengthy introduction establishes the context, providing an excellent overview of key issues: urban/rural differences; household labor; women's disinheritance from property rights in land and their limited access to wage labor; and activism against dowry, wife murder, and economic exploitation. Organized into six sections — "Women's Lives"; "Women's Struggles"; "Violence Against Women"; "Women's Politics"; "Letters to *Manushi*"; and "*Manushi*'s Own Struggle for Survival" — the selections are a mix of scholarly articles, journalism, letters, and personal testimony. Vivid, moving, and informative, they convey a sense of immediacy missing from most academic accounts.

25.   Lapchick, Richard Edward, and Stephanie Urdang. **Oppression and Resistance: The Struggle of Women in Southern Africa.** Westport, CT: Greenwood Press, 1982. 197p. bibliog. index. $27.50. LC 81-4267. ISBN 0313229600.

Urdang surveys the effects of apartheid on women in both rural and urban areas of South Africa and Namibia in Part I of this volume. In Part II, Lapchick looks at the role of women in the national liberation struggles of Zimbabwe, Namibia, and South Africa. *We Make Freedom: Women in South Africa* (Pandora Press, 1984), by Beata Lipman, and *Cry Amandla! South African Women and the Question of Power* (Africana, 1984), by June Goodwin, offer personal testimony by South African women themselves. Beata Lipman, a white South African journalist, returned to South Africa from exile in Britain to interview primarily black women. Lipman sets the context, but then allows the women — rural and urban workers, trade unionists, students, women in politics — to speak in their own words. One domestic worker in Johannesburg articulates the predominant experience of black women under apartheid — forcible separation from family — when she says, "We work to feed them, but we do not know our children" (p.6). A U.S. journalist, June Goodwin lived in South Africa from 1976 to 1979, having gone there determined to ferret out white as well as black perspectives on apartheid. A sense of outrage permeates Goodwin's commentary on her interviews with white liberals, pro-apartheid Afrikaners, and black women. The viewpoint of Thenjiwe Mtintso, a black resistance fighter following in the footsteps of Steve Biko, runs throughout the book. *LIP From South African Women* (Ravan Press, 1983), edited by Susan Brown, Isabel Hofmeyr, and Susan Rosenberg, collects the work of more than sixty artists, "black and white, urban and rural, old and young" (p.1). These women struggle to articulate—in photographs, poetry, artwork, stories, and other forms—the magnified separation that occurs in South Africa between colors and classes of women.

26.   Leacock, Eleanor Burke, 1922- . **Myths of Male Dominance: Collected Articles on Women Cross-Culturally.** New York: Monthly Review Press, 1981. 344p. bibliog. index. $17.50. LC 79-3870. ISBN 0853455376.

Eleanor Leacock has been a maverick in anthropology since her early days in the field: first, in questioning historical particularism (the dominant perspective in anthropology at the time she did her graduate work) and its dismissal of historical evolutionary theory; and second, in using an evolutionary perspective to strengthen her own argument that male dominance is not a historical or cross-cultural universal. Leacock's perspective is that what we know as male dominance developed along with the emergence of the world capitalist system, and was introduced into the underdeveloped world with colonization. Gathered here are articles written over a thirty-year period, organized into three sections: (1) Leacock's early work on the Montagnais-Naskapi of Labrador, and the impact of colonization on their communal, egalitarian society; (2) her writings on theories of social evolution (Engels' in particular) and women's status; and (3) critical writings on Margaret Mead, Lévi-Strauss, Steven Goldberg, and Edward Wilson. Leacock is a scholar of strong and articulate political commitment, rooted in both left and feminist movements. Her interesting preface traces the course of her intertwined personal, professional, and political development during the period covered by this volume.

27.   Lindsay, Beverly, ed. **Comparative Perspectives of Third World Women: The Impact of Race, Sex, and Class.** New York: Praeger, 1980. 318p. bibliog. index. $21.95. LC 78-19793. ISBN 0030466512.

During the highly politicized sixties and seventies, many U.S. people of color came to identify their struggles with those of the underdeveloped nations of the Third World. Lindsay attempts to support further investigation of these parallels with this collection, which offers articles on Native American, Chicana, black, and Vietnamese immigrant women in the United States, alongside studies of women in Africa, the People's Republic of China, Taiwan, Malaysia, India, the Caribbean, and Latin America. In her introduction and conclusion, Lindsay begins to develop some of the theoretical connections between women's lives in the Third World and the lives of women of color in the United States, building on the concepts of triple jeopardy (race, sex, and class), colonialism, neocolonialism, internal colonialism, and dependency.

28.   MacCormack, Carol P., and Marilyn Strathern, eds. **Nature, Culture and Gender.** New York: Cambridge University Press, 1980. 227p. bibliog. index. $34.50. LC 80-40921. ISBN 0521234913.

In 1974, feminist anthropologist Sherry B. Ortner published what was to become an exceedingly influential article. "Is Female to Male as Nature Is to Culture?" argued that women are universally associated with the concept of "nature," while men tend to be linked with the more highly valued concept of "culture," and that this opposition is a key underpinning of women's less powerful position. All eight papers in *Nature, Culture and Gender* subject this argument to careful and critical scrutiny, questioning the universality of its gender equations and of the very concepts of nature and culture themselves. The volume includes a critical overview by MacCormack, two articles on the concept of nature in the European tradition, and five case studies. The geographic coverage is unfortunately quite skewed: three of the five case studies focus on New Guinea. While the contributors to this volume are essentially specialists writing for an audience of their peers, the book's significance extends beyond anthropology into the field of feminist theory, where the relation of women to nature has been a vital topic for authors such as Susan Griffin and Carolyn Merchant (see entries 1110 and 1127). Sharon W. Tiffany and Kathleen J. Adams, both anthropologists, explore similar themes in *The Wild Woman: An Inquiry Into the Anthropology of an Idea* (Schenkman, 1985), an analysis of parallels between Western concepts of woman, the exotic, and the "primitive." Kristin Herzog tracks these stereotypes in literature in her critical study *Women, Ethnics, and Exotics: Images of Power in Mid-Nineteenth-Century American Fiction* (University of Tennessee Press, 1983).

29.* Minai, Naila. **Women in Islam: Tradition and Transition in the Middle East.** New York: Seaview Books, 1981. 283p. bibliog. index. LC 80-52405. ISBN 0872236668.

Of the Iranian revolution, Minai writes: "The whole world watched in disbelief as masses of Iranian women proudly put on the chador [veil], fought against the Westernized shah Muhammad Reza Pahlavi, and played a decisive role in bringing to power the Ayatollah Ruhollah Khomeini" (p.226). Iran's violent upheaval and women's part in it have led scholars, politicians, and the general public to question the multifaceted nature of Islam, and the role of indigenous culture in national and feminist struggles for liberation. Minai's journalistic overview of women and Islam in the Middle East and North Africa provides a readable and intelligent introduction to questions such as these. In describing the Islamic past and present, Minai addresses both progressive and restrictive traditions. In her final chapter, Minai speaks to the complex and contradictory meanings of Islamic revivalism. In *The Republic of Cousins: Women's Oppression in Mediterranean Society* (French edition, 1966; English edition, Al Saqi Books, 1983), Germaine Tillion also disputes the view that Islam is monolithically oppressive to women, finding the roots of Muslim societies' oppressiveness not in Islam but in pagan prehistory. French sociologist and journalist Juliette Minces takes a more uniformly negative view of Arab women's lives under the Islamic tradition in *The House of Obedience: Women in Arab Society* (French edition, 1980; English edition, Zed Press, 1982).

30. Ortner, Sherry B., 1941- , and Harriet Whitehead, eds. **Sexual Meanings: The Cultural Construction of Gender and Sexuality.** New York: Cambridge University Press, 1981. 435p. bibliog. index. $44.50. LC 80-26655. ISBN 0521239656.

All of the contributions to this collection fall within the tradition of symbolic anthropology; they examine cultural notions of gender — "sexual meanings" — rather than sex-role behavior or sexual status. Each of the ten essays undertakes a particular case study of gender symbolism, giving the volume a wide-ranging, if uneven, geographic coverage, including Oceania, East Africa, southern Spain, lowland South America, and native North America. Among the contributors are Marilyn Strathern, Jane F. Collier, Michelle Z. Rosaldo, and Melissa Llewelyn-Davies. In their introduction, Ortner and Whitehead outline contributors' different methodologies and attempt to tease out the theoretical implications of the volume as a whole. They conclude that "the social-cultural formations most directly bound up with conceptions of gender (and gender-related matters) are prestige structures ..." (p.25).

31.   Papanek, Hanna, and Gail Minault, 1939- , eds. **Separate Worlds: Studies of Purdah in South Asia.** Columbia, MO: South Asia Books, 1982. 317p. bibliog. index. $24.00. ISBN 0836408322.

Ten scholars contributed papers to this volume documenting the different facets of purdah — Muslim and Hindu — in Pakistan, India, and Bangladesh. Four broad themes organize the articles: purdah and sex segregation; the social structure of purdah institutions; the effects of purdah on women's political participation; and purdah and Islam. Though Patricia Jeffery's *Frogs in a Well: Indian Women in Purdah* (Zed Press, 1979) is more narrow in focus, looking at the practice of purdah in one group of Muslim families in Delhi, her discussion reflects broad familiarity with seclusion practices. Both Jeffery and the authors of *Separate Worlds* attempt to show how specific seclusion practices are related to larger social and economic factors such as class and status, and point out the contradictory nature of the institution, which bestows on women some benefits along with the more striking constraints.

32.   Randall, Margaret. **Women in Cuba: Twenty Years Later.** New York: Smyrna Press, 1981. 167p. bibliog. $19.95. LC 80-54055. ISBN 0918266157.

Author of the widely read collection of oral histories *Cuban Women Now*, Randall is a U.S. poet, writer, and photographer who lived in Cuba for many years. In these six essays, she writes about the lives of Cuban women twenty years after the revolution. In pieces on the struggle against sexism, peasant women's lives, the rights of mothers, family life, art, and the Federation of Cuban Women, Randall provides historical summaries along with current assessments. Four appendices reprint material from official Cuban sources. In *Breaking the Silences: 20th Century Poetry by Cuban Women* (Pulp Press, 1982), Randall translates the works of three generations of Cuban women writers. Appearing both in Spanish and English, the poems eloquently document the women's daily lives, emotional concerns, and political views. Norwegian-born writer Inger Holt-Seeland moved to Cuba in 1959. In *Women of Cuba* (Lawrence Hill, 1982), she describes the changes she has seen in women's lives, quoting liberally from interviews conducted with a farm worker, a student Communist Youth Party member, a high-born housewife, a university student, a factory worker, and an older black woman.

33.   Robertson, Claire C., and Martin A. Klein, eds. **Women and Slavery in Africa.** Madison: University of Wisconsin Press, 1983. 380p. bibliog. index. $22.50. LC 83-47769. ISBN 029909460X.

This collection of seventeen articles first establishes that most slaves in African slave systems were female, then moves on to evaluate possible explanations for this fact. The surprising conclusion is that the value of women slaves was based not, as is commonly asserted, on their reproductive potential, but on "a sexual division of labor which assigned much of the productive labor to women" (p.11). In a particularly intriguing article, Herbert S. Klein shows that fewer African women than men entered the Atlantic slave trade precisely because African slaveowners restricted access to the more highly valued female slave population. The second half of this volume offers case histories of the African female slave experience and studies of women as slaveowners, users, and traders.

34.   Rogers, Barbara, 1945- . **The Domestication of Women: Discrimination in Developing Societies.** New York: St. Martin's Press, 1980. 200p. bibliog. index. $27.50. LC 79-26691. ISBN 0312216270.

Rogers builds a sharply worded critique of Western-influenced development scholarship, development planning, and project implementation. In Part One, she analyzes how the sexual division of labor and the division of the world into public ("male") and domestic ("female") realms color planners' views of women's part in the development process. Part Two looks at specific development agencies, the prevailing underestimation of women's productive contributions, and the inadequacy of "women's programs" tacked onto larger development projects in response to public pressure. In her final section, Rogers assesses the effects on rural women's lives of development in Africa, Asia, and Latin America. She argues that faulty understanding of women's importance to subsistence agriculture, together with denial to women of equal standing within the family, translates into programs that undercut women's access to resources and diminish their overall status.

35.   Saadāwī, Nawāl El. **The Hidden Face of Eve: Women in the Arab World.** Edited by Sherif Hetata. Boston: Beacon Press, 1982. 212p. bibliog. $9.95. LC 81-68358. ISBN 0807067016.

A well-known Egyptian physician and feminist, Nawāl El Saadāwī opens this sharply critical profile of Arab women's lives with a chilling personal account of her own clitoridectomy at the age of six. In subsequent chapters, she unveils the grim reality of Arab preference for boy children, the sexual abuse of girls, the tyranny of virginity and "honor," illegitimacy, abortion, and prostitution. In addition, Saadāwī briefly surveys Arab women's history, views of women in Arab literature, contributions of early Arab feminists, and the status of Arab women in work, marriage, and divorce. Throughout the work, her native Egypt is the predominant point of reference. Saadāwī's "Preface to the English Edition" articulates with great clarity and force of feeling the political context within which her book should be read. It is not Islam, she argues, that is responsible for Arab women's oppression, but rather a patriarchal class system and imperialism. Islam has both progressive and reactionary tendencies; those in power both in Arab countries and in the West attempt to enlist the conservative elements in their war against revolutionary movements. Saadāwī warns Western feminists against taking Arab women's criticisms of Arab societies out of context. Two recent novels by Saadāwī are *Women at Point Zero* (Zed Press, 1983) and *Two Women in One* (Seal Press, 1986).

36.   Sacks, Karen. **Sisters and Wives: The Past and Future of Sexual Equality.** Westport, CT: Greenwood Press, 1979. 274p. bibliog. index. $29.95. LC 78-75241. ISBN 0313209839.

Building on the work of Engels, Sacks argues that gender relations in preclass societies can give us visions of how we might transform contemporary advanced capitalism. She begins with a biting critique of social Darwinist anthropology, which she defines as a world view in which "nature is an unconscious metaphor for industrial capitalist social relations" (p.3). Contesting that women have always and everywhere been oppressed, Sacks then turns her attention to societies in Africa. Evaluation of women's status in these societies must be based, in her view, on an interpretation of all aspects of women's relations to production—notably as "sisters," or equals, as well as "wives," or spouses. Sacks details women's productive relations as sisters and wives in preclass societies with a communal mode of production, preclass societies with a corporate-kin mode of production, and in class societies. While the author does place women at the center of her analysis, she concludes by advocating that productive relations *rather than* gender should be the "key analytic concept" (p.10). In *Sharing the Same Bowl: A Socioeconomic History of Women and Class in Accra, Ghana* (Indiana University Press, 1984), Claire C. Robertson studies women's evolving relationship to the means of production in Accra over the last century—from precapitalist society with a corporate-kin mode of production, through colonial capitalism, and into neocolonial capitalism.

37. Sanday, Peggy Reeves. **Female Power and Male Dominance: On the Origins of Sexual Inequality.** New York: Cambridge University Press, 1981. 295p. bibliog. index. $44.50. LC 80-18461. ISBN 0521236185.

Sanday works within both the positivist and the symbolic traditions of anthropology in this ambitious treatise. Using data drawn from the Human Relations Area Files, she examined indicators of female power and male dominance in over 150 societies from the sixth century B.C. to the present. Sanday concludes that secular power roles derive from "ancient concepts of sacred power" (p.xvi). Cultures that emphasize (female) life-giving powers and harmony with nature she refers to as having an "inner orientation," whereas to cultures emphasizing (male) life-taking powers and fear of nature she ascribes an "outer orientation." Denying the universality of female subordination, Sanday finds that male dominance tends to prevail in societies with an "outer orientation," sexual equality in societies with an "inner orientation." While she establishes a relationship between societal stress (e.g., depleting resources, migration, and colonialism) and male dominance, this is mediated, in her view, by a society's symbolic system. By contrast, in *Sex and Advantage: A Comparative, Macro-Structural Theory of Sex Stratification* (Rowman and Allanheld, 1984), sociologist Janet Saltzman Chafetz argues that "the ways in which societies organize their production activities and, to a lesser extent, their families constitute the most important factors in explaining the degree of sex stratification" (p.77). The ideological factors given primacy by Sanday are viewed by Chafetz as merely "legitimat[ing] existing structural arrangements" (p.45). Chafetz synthesizes a broad spectrum of writings, primarily by sociologists and anthropologists, in advancing a formal theory "to explain variance in the degree of sex inequality cross-culturally and historically" (p.x).

38. Sharma, Ursula, 1941- . **Women, Work, and Property in North-West India.** New York: Tavistock, 1980. 226p. bibliog. index. $25.00. LC 80-40478. ISBN 0422771201.

Sharma investigated women's role in production in two Indian villages—one where women's contributions to agriculture were minimal and the other where they were substantial. She concludes that in order to understand women's social power, researchers must look not only at the extent of women's labor, but also at their control over resources. In the two villages she studied, Sharma discovered that property ownership and the right to work for wages were almost exclusively the prerogative of men; this she takes to be a determinate factor in the villages' social restrictions on women, and in village women's dependence on men.

39. Shostak, Marjorie, 1945- . **Nisa: The Life and Worlds of a !Kung Woman.** Cambridge, MA: Harvard University Press, 1981. 402p. bibliog. index. $25.00. LC 81-4210. ISBN 0674624858.

Harvard anthropologist Marjorie Shostak spent nearly two years (1969-1971) living among the !Kung San, hunter-gatherers of the Botswana Kalahari. She came with many questions sparked by the resurgence of feminism in the United States. Her interviews with a woman named Nisa form the core of this book. Despite cultural obstacles that Shostak describes at length in her introduction, the interviews succeed in conveying a vital picture of !Kung life. Nisa speaks very frankly of the range of women's experiences: girlhood, early sexual experimentation, and later love affairs; marriage; childbirth and motherhood; death and grieving; healing rituals; and aging. Selected by the *New York Times* as one of the notable books of 1981, *Nisa* offers a striking evocation of women's lives in a hunting and gathering society that is remarkably resourceful, peaceable, and egalitarian.

40. Smith, Jane I., ed. **Women in Contemporary Muslim Societies.** Lewisburg, PA: Bucknell University Press, 1980. 259p. bibliog. $15.00. LC 78-60377. ISBN 0838722636.

In this collection of eight scholarly papers, contributors analyze Muslim women's religious lives, social and political roles, and access to property; traditional views of women in contemporary Arab Islamic literature; and women, law, and social change in Iran. *Women and Islam* (Pergamon Press, 1982), edited by Azizah al-Hibri, is a hardcover reprint of a special issue of *Women's Studies International Forum*. In nine articles, the mostly Arab contributors address Islamic images of women, Islamic "herstory," women and social change (including feminist movements) in the Muslim world, Islamic laws of divorce, virginity and patriarchy, and veiling. John L. Esposito's *Women in Muslim Family Law* (Syracuse University Press, 1982) explicates the history and development of traditional Islamic family law, describes Muslim women's lives under this law, and explores the capacity of the tradition to respond to pressures for change. Recent area studies of Muslim women include Unni Wikan's *Behind the Veil in Arabia: Women in Oman* (Johns Hopkins University Press, 1982), Carla Makhlouf's *Changing Veils: Women and Modernisation in North Yemen* (University of Texas Press, 1979), and Margaret Strobel's *Muslim Women in Mombasa: 1890-1975* (Yale University Press, 1979).

41. Smith, Robert J., 1927- , and Ella Lury Wiswell. **The Women of Suye Mura.** Chicago: University of Chicago Press, 1982. 293p. bibliog. index. $20.00. LC 82-2708. ISBN 0226763447.

John and Ella Embree (later Wiswell) spent a year in the rural Japanese agricultural community of Suye Mura in 1935. John Embree's study of community structure and economic relations, *Suye Mura: A Japanese Village*, was published in 1939 and soon became a standard source. Although Wisell's extensive notes complemented her husband's—focusing on the everyday life of the village, and especially the village women—they lay untouched for forty-five years, until Cornell anthropology professor Robert J. Smith offered to collaborate on this book. A unique source on rural women in prewar Japan, Wiswell's account is full of strikingly candid detail on subjects such as sex; birth control, pregnancy, and childbearing; relations between men and women, boys and girls; marriage, divorce, and adoption; and community ostracism. In *Haruko's World: A Japanese Farm Woman and Her Community* (Stanford University Press, 1983), Gail Lee Bernstein writes of her stay with a rural Japanese farm family during the 1970s. She focuses primarily on Haruko, the unusually forthright wife and mother, highlighting her backbreaking work life, her social world, and family tensions. Interviews, published sources, and questionnaire results flesh out Bernstein's account of community traditions and changing expectations regarding marriage, sex, drinking, generational ties, and local politics. Yet another recent ethnography is *Japanese Women: Constraint and Fulfillment* (University of Hawaii Press, 1984), in which Takie Sugiyama Lebra depicts women's lives in a small Japanese city in the 1970s, with a strong emphasis on the different stages of the life cycle.

42. Stacey, Judith. **Patriarchy and Socialist Revolution in China.** Berkeley: University of California Press, 1983. 324p. bibliog. index. $27.50. LC 82-8482. ISBN 0520048253.

Drawing on Marxism, socialist feminism, modernization theory, and studies of peasant revolutions, Stacey argues that the Chinese revolution represents not the eradication but the redistribution and democratization of patriarchy. She delineates three distinct forms of patriarchy in recent Chinese history: traditional Confucian patriarchy of the prerevolutionary period; the "new democratic patriarchy" of the mobilizing Chinese Communist Party (CCP); and "Patriarchal-Socialism" of the post-liberation era. In her view, the early CCP willingly bartered off its more radical programs for women's liberation in exchange for a consolidated allegiance from the male peasantry. In *Revolution Postponed: Women in Contemporary China* (Stanford University Press, 1985), Margery Wolf advances a slightly different interpretation. While corroborating Stacey's critical assessment of women's status in the People's Republic of China (PRC), Wolf does not accept Stacey's view that the CCP consciously "used the concepts of patriarchy to win a revolution and transform a society ..." (pp.260-261). Wolf interviewed more than three hundred rural and urban women for this study, in which she discusses marriage, family organization, domestic relations, and birth limitation. Phyllis Andors analyzes the impact on women of Chinese development policies in *The Unfinished Liberation of Chinese Women, 1949-1980* (Indiana University Press/Wheatsheaf Books, 1983). Her conclusion is that "the Chinese experience clearly shows that a commitment to female equality *cannot be simply the outcome of economic development but that it can and must shape the patterns and processes of development itself*" (p.171). Andors argues that the policies of the Great Leap Forward, the Cultural Revolution, and the post-Cultural Revolution period were most promising in this regard. In *Chinese Women Since Mao* (M. E. Sharpe, 1983), Elizabeth Croll speculates about the likely impact of the "Four Modernizations" launched in 1978.

43.   Steady, Filomina Chioma, ed. **The Black Woman Cross-Culturally.** Cambridge, MA: Schenkman, 1981. 645p. bibliog. $29.95. LC 80-17214. ISBN 0870733451.

An anthropologist, Steady has a particular interest in the African Diaspora, which she sees as providing "a framework for black unity" (p.4). She gathers in this cross-cultural anthology thirty articles on black women in Africa, the United States, the Caribbean, and South America. A majority of the pieces have been published elsewhere, and a number of these are not especially recent. In her introduction, Steady draws eight different themes from the material: African heritage; economic exploitation and marginalization; negative literary images; self-reliance as a necessary ideology; creation of survival imperatives; a less antagonistic feminism; racism, sexism, and class; and an African brand of feminism. African-born herself, Steady offes the anthology in part as a corrective to the ethnocentrism of Western feminism.

44.   Tiffany, Sharon W., ed. **Women and Society: An Anthropological Reader.** St. Albans, VT: Eden Press Women's Publications, 1979. 329p. bibliog. index. $20.95. ISBN 0920792014.

A teacher and prolific writer in the area of feminist anthropology, Tiffany gathers twelve articles originally published during the sixties and seventies in this text well-designed for classroom use. Representative articles include "A Note on the Division of Labor by Sex" and "Economic Organization and the Position of Women Among the Iroquois," both by Judith K. Brown; "The Role of Women in a Changing Navaho Society," by Laila Shukry Hamamsy; "'Sitting on a Man': Colonialism and the Lost Political Institutions of Igbo Women," by Judith Van Allen; and "Sexual Antagonism in the New Guinea Highlands: A Bena Bena Example," by L. L. Langness. Tiffany's introduction offers a thematic overview. Annotated suggestions for further reading follow each article. *A World of Women: Anthropological Studies of Women in the Societies of the World,* edited by Erika Bourguignon (Praeger, 1980), is likewise intended as a classroom text. In ethnographic accounts of women's lives in Asia, West Africa, Brazil, the Caribbean, Mexico, the U.S. mainland, and Alaska, twelve contributing anthropologists turn their attention to three broad themes: the role of women in subsistence economies; public and domestic domains; and the impact of culture change on women.

45. Urdang, Stephanie. **Fighting Two Colonialisms: Women in Guinea-Bissau.** New York: Monthly Review Press, 1979. 320p. bibliog. $16.50. LC 79-2329. ISBN 0853455112,
    Urdang reports on the revolutionary struggle for independence in Guinea-Bissau, waged over the course of twenty-five years by the African Party for the Independence of Guinea and Cape Verde (PAIGC). Urdang visited the country twice, once just before victory was achieved in 1974, and then again two years later. She found a movement committed not just to achieving independence from Portugal, but also to forging a new society in which women's liberation would be a central focus. Critical of the neocolonial development model followed by many African nations, the PAIGC was intent on devising development strategies that would favor the rural majority, women as well as men. Urdang looks with a critical eye at the movement's successes and failures, but ultimately is persuaded of PAIGC's political integrity.

46. Ward, Kathryn B. **Women in the World-System: Its Impact on Status and Fertility.** New York: Praeger, 1984. 191p. bibliog. index. $25.95. LC 84-8243. ISBN 0030697549.
    World-system theory, with its focus on enduring inequality of resources and of power between nations, helps make sense of faltering development in Third World countries. The literature has not, however, elucidated the impact of the world system on women. Working with cross-national data, Ward analyzes the relationships between foreign investment and economic dependency (as indicators of the intrusion of the world system), and women's status and fertility in underdeveloped nations. Her findings reveal that world-system penetration tends to decrease women's share of economic resources and to create conditions favoring continued high fertility. Many readers will find Ward's statistical models and analysis overly technical. But her theoretical perspective, firmly anchored in recent feminist scholarship, expands the growing discussion of women and development.

47. Weigle, Marta. **Spiders & Spinsters: Women and Mythology.** Albuquerque: University of New Mexico Press, 1982. 340p. bibliog. index. $14.95. LC 82-13611. ISBN 0826306438.
    Drawing threads from the work of folklorists, anthropologists, psychoanalysts, poets, and feminist scholars, Weigle weaves a rich tapestry of women's roles in classical, Native American, and Judeo-Christian mythology. She quotes extensively from original sources and scholarly interpretations to trace recurring motifs in folktales and myth, and she provides linking commentary, abundant footnotes, and an impressive bibliography. The lavishly illustrated sourcebook treats large themes: goddesses; guide figures; the moon, menstruation, and menopause; heroines; and origins and matriarchy. Weigel makes a distinction between the study of "women *in* mythology," women's relation to myth as constructed by male writers and male culture-builders, and "women *and* mythology," the "verbal, visual and ritual expressions women themselves hold and have held sacred and deeply meaningful" (p.285). Her concluding chapter suggests that a closer look at the stories women tell each other in private settings (the gossip and legend of "old wives' tales") may reveal a distinct and long unrecognized women's mythology.

48.* **Women in Latin America: An Anthology From** *Latin American Perspectives.*
Riverside, CA: Latin American Perspectives, 1979. 164p. bibliog. LC 79-110325.

Culled from several issues of the journal *Latin American Perspectives,* the twelve
articles in this widely cited anthology investigate the lives and struggles of Latin American
women from Marxist perspectives. The focus in Part I is "The Marxist Approach to the
Study of Women and Class Struggle"; in Part II, "Economics, Politics, and Ideology: Con-
crete Studies on Women in Latin America"; and in Part III, "The Practice of the Women's
Struggle." The contributors include Eleanor Leacock, Carmen Diana Deere, Maria Linda
Apodaca, Nancy Caro Hollander, and Margaret Randall. A related and more recent title is
Women and Change in Latin America, a collection of seventeen articles edited by June
Nash and Helen Safa (Bergin and Garvey, 1985). Nash and Neuma Aguiar open the
volume with articles on theoretical and methodological questions; then other prominent
scholars in the field take up topics such as women's contributions as producers and
reproducers, technological change and development, migration, and political action and
the state, looking specifically at Peru, Jamaica, Puerto Rico, Brazil, Bolivia, Chile, Cuba,
Venezuela, and the United States.

49. Young, Kate, et al., eds. **Of Marriage and the Market: Women's Subordination
Internationally and Its Lessons.** (2nd ed.). Boston: Routledge and Kegan Paul, 1984. 235p.
bibliog. index. pbk. $11.95. LC 84-6795. ISBN 0710202988.

Women's subordination is examined cross-culturally here in relation to involvement in
social production (Part I); the household (Part II); and kinship, sexuality, and ideology
(Part III). Editors Ruth Pearson, Ann Whitehead, and Kate Young add a fine introductory
chapter to this second edition. The twelve contributors are thoroughly conversant with
Marxist theory but critical of its economic categories. They are all active feminists, but take
issue with the prevailing ethnocentrism of feminist analysis. They find much of the literature
on women and development inadequate, tending "to isolate women as a separate and often
homogenous category" (p.x). Looking at precapitalist, feudal, neocolonial, capitalist, and
socialist societies, these authors seek to understand how gender relations are shaped by,
and in turn shape, specific socioeconomic formations. This international perspective
enables them to integrate analyses of women's domestic labor in advanced capitalist and
industrialized socialist countries with work on subsistence production in the Third World.
This volume provides an excellent theoretical framework within which to view the many
narrower area studies on women, development, and the sexual division of labor.

ART AND MATERIAL CULTURE

Books chosen for this chapter embrace many facets of women's nonliterary creative work: dance, the decorative arts, film, music, photography, painting, sculpture, and other manifestations of material culture. The emphasis is on artwork *by* women, whether consciously feminist or not; both primary and critical works receive attention. Familiar names appear—Mary Cassatt, Georgia O'Keeffe, Nadia Boulanger, Martha Graham—in books that celebrate notable women in the arts, while other studies recover the contributions of anonymous or forgotten women, from quilters and potters to hymn writers and blues singers. The image of women in the visual arts, especially film, engages a new generation of feminist critics and cultural historians whose writings appear here.

Biographical and reference works are included when they illustrate an artist's career and accomplishments. The Reference chapter contains additional filmographies, discographies, and biographical and bibliographical sources. Anthologies cited below also provide background and often extensive bibliographies on each artist covered. For feminist approaches to the literature in the arts, we point the reader toward the review articles published in women's scholarly journals. Judith Mayne's "Feminist Film Theory and Criticism" in *Signs* v.11, no.1 (Autumn 1985) is one such example.

50. Abakanowicz, Magdalena, 1930- . **Magdalena Abakanowicz: Museum of Contemporary Art, Chicago.** New York: Abbeville Press, 1982. 188p. bibliog. pbk. $24.95. LC 82-11511. ISBN 0896593231.

Polish weaver and sculptor Magdalena Abakanowicz has been a major force behind the bold experiments in fiber art in the seventies and eighties. Prepared for an exhibit at Chicago's Museum of Contemporary Art in 1982, this oversize catalog does an admirable job of conveying the effect of Abakanowicz's mammoth pieces through large photographs, many in color. The artist, even at her most abstract, refers to the human body in her works: several of her earliest three-dimensional hangings (dubbed "Abakans" by the critics) are striking in their resemblance to vulva. Throughout the volume, Abakanowicz comments on her childhood and her art in highly poetic and emotionally charged prose, while Jasia Reichardt fills in the details of the artist's career and critical reception. Unfortunately, the text provides little grist for a feminist reader.

51. Ammer, Christine. **Unsung: A History of Women in American Music.** Westport, CT: Greenwood Press, 1980. 317p. bibliog. index. $29.95. LC 79-52324. ISBN 0313220077.

Ammer surveys the achievements of women instrumentalists, composers, conductors, and teachers over the past two centuries. Once women's participation in performance was admitted, Ammer points out, their accomplishments were belittled and their seriousness questioned by labels such as "lady violinist." Even greater skepticism greeted the efforts of women composers and conductors. Discrimination against performers led to the creation of all-women orchestras and a virtual sexual apartheid in the orchestral world. In the contemporary period, Ammer finds that women musicians continue to face exclusion from the "old boy network" despite some expansion of opportunity; they are responding—as are women in other fields — by creating their own cooperative networks. Received opinion has it that the first "serious" American woman composer was Amy Beach (1867-1944). In *American Women Composers Before 1870* (UMI Research Press, 1983), Judith Tick reconstructs the history of Beach's forebears, the women who published parlor music between 1790 and 1870.

52. Anscombe, Isabelle. **A Woman's Touch: Women in Design From 1860 to the Present Day.** New York: Viking Penguin, 1984. 216p. bibliog. index. pbk. $12.95. LC 84-40262. ISBN 0670778257.

From the arts and crafts movement to the Bauhaus to the present, women's contributions to home design have been overlooked. In this illustrated book, Anscombe recovers the work of such women as embroiderer May Morris, weaver Candace Wheeler, ceramicist Adelaide Alsop Robineau, interior decorator Elsie de Wolfe, and fabric designers Phyllis Barron and Dorothy Larcher. Anscombe's survey covers England, the United States, and the Continent. Although men are credited for theoretical advances, Anscombe asserts that "the study of the lives of women designers and their pragmatic approach to design leads inevitably to a radical reassessment of the history of twentieth-century design" (p.15). She concludes, however, that women designers still "inhabit a world where women design for women" (p.197), the domestic sphere of home and fashion. Anthea Callen looks in greater depth at women's roles in the arts and craft movement in the United States and Great Britain in *Women Artists of the Arts and Crafts Movement, 1870-1914* (Pantheon Books, 1979). Callen considers class differences among Victorian craftswomen and the sexist attitudes that limited their achievements in such areas as needlework, jewelry and metal work, woodcarving, furniture design, ceramics, and book illustration and binding.

53. Arnold, Eve. **In America.** New York: Knopf; distr. New York: Random House, 1983. 207p. $35.00. LC 83-48023. ISBN 0394522354.

After twenty years abroad, photographer Eve Arnold returned to her native country to travel, interview and photograph Americans, and create this moving tribute to the diversity of American culture. Her large color photographs are crisply reproduced. Many are warm portraits of women — a tuba player in Utah, an equestrian in Rhode Island, spinners in Maine, a black housewife in South Carolina, a miner in Virginia, a prostitute in San Francisco, a Navajo matriarch in Arizona.

54.* Ashton, Dore. **Rosa Bonheur: A Life and a Legend.** New York: Viking Press, 1981. 206p. bibliog. index. LC 80-36749. ISBN 0670608130.

Rosa Bonheur (1822-1899) was enormously successful in her day as a painter of realistic animal and farm scenes. Friendly with European royalty and with Buffalo Bill, she lived an unconventional life, dressed in trousers, and was evidently a lesbian. In this beautifully designed volume, illustrated with black-and-white reproductions and many photographs of Bonheur and her surroundings and family, Ashton chronicles Bonheur's career, the artistic influences that shaped her, and the social and political upheavals that shook nineteenth-century France. One short chapter, "The Question of Sex," speculates on Bonheur's feelings about men and feminism. Rosalia Shriver provides a more concise overview of the artist's career in *Rosa Bonheur* (Art Alliance Press, 1982), with a checklist of works by Bonheur in American collections.

55. Auster, Albert. **Actresses and Suffragists: Women in the American Theater, 1890-1920.** New York: Praeger, 1984. 177p. bibliog. index. $22.95. LC 83-19253. ISBN 0030697786.

Auster begins with with a brief history of the growth of American theater and the beginning of the women's rights movement. In the early nineteenth century, actresses came mostly from theatrical families, or were poor, newly arrived immigrants; but during the 1870s and 1880s, theater-going became a more respectable activity for women, and more middle-class women became performers. Actresses were able to use their visible position to support various social causes, including women's emancipation. Auster demonstrates how three very different actresses contributed to the women's rights movement in their own ways. Mary Shaw was an overt feminist active in the club movement and the suffrage movement; Lillian Russell exploited her celebrity as an actress to promote suffrage, among other reforms; and Ethel Barrymore, with her image as "the typical American girl," advocated women's need for autonomy and self-determination. In *American Actress* (Nelson-Hall, 1984), Claudia D. Johnson analyzes the experiences of actresses in the nineteenth century, paralleling the changes in their status with the growth of the women's rights movement.

56. Bank, Mirra. **Anonymous Was a Woman.** New York: St. Martin's Press, 1979. 128p. bibliog. $19.95. LC 79-16300. ISBN 0312041853.
Growing out of a television film of the same title, this largely pictorial work "is not a scholarly documentation of our folk legacy but an illumination of the lives of the people who created it" (p.11). The color reproductions feature embroidered samplers, quilts, pastel drawings, and watercolors by American women of the Revolutionary era and the nineteenth century, accompanied by black-and-white engravings and excerpts from memoirs, instructional books, verses, diaries, and other primary sources.

57. Berg-Pan, Renata. **Leni Riefenstahl.** Boston: Twayne, 1980. 222p. bibliog. index. $14.50. LC 80-14129. ISBN 0805792759.
Best known for her Nazi films, *Triumph of the Will* (1935) and *Olympia* (1938), Leni Riefenstahl remains a controversial figure. Berg-Pan for the most part eschews analysis of Riefenstahl's politics and avoids probing her much-gossiped-about personal life. Instead, she chronicles this innovative filmmaker's thwarted career and her contributions to the development of the "ceremonial" or "ritualistic" film. Among Riefenstahl's unrealized projects is a film titled *Penthesilea,* with the fabled queen of the Amazons as its central character; in it Berg-Pan reads evidence of Riefenstahl's militant feminism.

58.* Biren, Joan E. **Eye to Eye: Portraits of Lesbians.** Washington, DC: Glad Hag Books; distr. Weatherby Lake, MO: Naiad Press, 1979. 72p. bibliog. LC 79-53946. ISBN 0960317600.
The art of Joan E. Biren (who signs herself "JEB") is familiar to readers of lesbian magazines and feminist press books. This moving collection of thirty-nine black-and-white photographs underscores the diversity — by race, age, occupation, avocation — of lesbians in the United States. Tee Corinne, another popular lesbian photographer, emphasizes a wide range of body types in her collection of erotic photos, *Yantras of Womanlove* (Naiad Press, 1982).

59. Bosworth, Patricia. **Diane Arbus: A Biography.** New York: Knopf, 1984. 366p. bibliog. index. $17.95. LC 84-737. ISBN 0394504046.
Diane Arbus's photographic studies capture images of the grotesque, the marginal, the freakish — can anyone forget her photographs of Siamese twins and transvestites? Because Arbus killed herself in 1971 when she was not yet fifty, morbid speculation persists that this search for the bizarre ultimately proved too disturbing for the photographer herself. Bosworth's slant on Arbus in this biography is that she transformed her own depression,

loneliness, and childhood isolation into art by concentrating on those shunned by society, fixing her camera's eye on those whom most people choose not to look at closely. *Diane Arbus: Magazine Work* (Aperture, 1984) gathers together in a handsome volume Arbus's riveting portraits, mainly from her commercial work of the 1960s. They give testament to her special gift, her use of irony and distortion in photographs of the farthest edges of the human spectrum.

60. Bowers, Jane, and Judith Tick, eds. **Women Making Music: The Western Art Tradition, 1150-1950.** Urbana: University of Illinois Press, 1985. 409p. bibliog. index. $21.95. LC 85-8642. ISBN 0252012046.

With the help of a dozen other musicologists, Bowers and Tick offer a brilliant sampling of the new feminist scholarship on music history. Fifteen essays, arranged chronologically, profile women composers (Barbara Strozzi, Clara Schumann, Luisa Adolpha Le Beau, Dame Ethel Smyth, Ruth Crawford Seeger) and survey women's participation in musical life in a number of countries and centuries. Among the topics are women as professional singers, female orchestras, and the influence of the church and the class structure on women's musical opportunities. From medieval cloisters to the United States in the middle of our own century, the anthology begins to restore women to Western music history.

61. Broude, Norma, and Mary D. Garrard, eds. **Feminism and Art History: Questioning the Litany.** New York: Harper and Row, 1982. 358p. bibliog. index. $28.80. LC 81-48062. ISBN 0064305252.

Although feminist scholarship in art history is advancing at such a pace that some of these seventeen essays appear dated, several others are already classics. Vincent Scully and Linda Nochlin are among the impressive contributors who define the major concerns of the field. In addition to theoretical issues, the articles address individual artists, male and female; for example, there are revisionist essays on Degas, Rossetti, and Kollwitz. The book's principal aim is to push the reader to experience canonized "high" art and marginalized "low" art from a fresh, feminist perspective.

62. Chicago, Judy, 1939- . **The Dinner Party: A Symbol of Our Heritage.** Garden City, NY: Anchor Press/Doubleday, 1979. 255p. index. $24.95. LC 78-69653. ISBN 0385145667.

Five years in the making, Chicago's monumental artwork, "The Dinner Party," celebrates "the history of women in Western civilization" (p.12). The room-sized piece consists of a triangular table with thirty-nine oversized place settings, each symbolizing a historical or mythological woman. The table rests on a porcelain floor, on which the names of 999 women are written. In this book, full-color reproductions of the ceramic plates—all handpainted, and many three-dimensional—are accompanied by biographical profiles of every woman honored. Chicago adds background on the conception and production of the exhibit, candid excerpts from her journals, and comments by the many other artists who collaborated on the project. A companion volume, *Embroidering Our Heritage* (Anchor Books, 1980), reproduces the table runners from each place setting, with detailed illustrations that show the rich variety of needlework techniques, and extensive written and visual notes on the symbols and motifs employed. Chicago continued her work with tapestry makers in her latest creation, *The Birth Project* (Doubleday, 1985). Needleworkers from around the nation participated in translating Chicago's designs to the medium of fabric; the book documents the artist's experiences in directing the collective endeavor.

63. Claghorn, Charles Eugene, 1911- . **Women Composers and Hymnists: A Concise Biographical Dictionary.** Metuchen, NJ: Scarecrow Press, 1984. 272p. bibliog. $22.50. LC 83-20429. ISBN 0810816806.

Women have played an important creative role in the area of church and sacred music, as this reference volume attests. Drawn largely from primary sources, the background presented here on 155 composers and 600 hymnists is not easily obtainable elsewhere. The entries are necessarily brief, for, as Claghorn comments, "many of the women were single or housewives...; few were noted poets" (p.vii). Samuel J. Rogal's *Sisters of Sacred Song* (Garland, 1981) provides a fuller listing of hymns (by first line) for many of the women covered by Claghorn.

64. Dahl, Linda, 1949- . **Stormy Weather: The Music and Lives of a Century of Jazzwomen.** New York: Pantheon Books, 1984. 371p. bibliog. index. $19.45. LC 83-19456. ISBN 0394535553.

"The assumption about women in jazz was that there weren't any, because jazz was by definition a male music" (p.xi). Dahl definitively puts to rest such assumptions in this well-written survey of American jazzwomen from the 1890s to the present. Not only has jazz been considered a fraternity or male club, but the instruments of jazz themselves have been sex-typed. Dahl demonstrates that the saxophone, the trumpet, the trombone, and the drums are all women's instruments, along with the more acceptably "feminine" piano and voice. Beginning with early jazzwomen such as Lil Hardin Armstrong, the blues "royalty" of the twenties (Ma Rainey, Bessie Smith, Ida Cox), and the singers of the thirties and forties (Ella Fitzgerald, Sarah Vaughan, Billie Holiday), Dahl continues her narrative right up to the present, with descriptions of contemporary feminist ensembles like Alive! She supplements the text with in-depth profiles of ten jazzwomen, brief notes on dozens more, and a lengthy discography. Two recent reference works complement Dahl's study. In *American Women in Jazz: 1900 to the Present* (Seaview Books, 1982), Sally Placksin combines biographical and historical data with interview material to create thumbnail sketches of over sixty women vocalists, instrumentalists, arrangers, producers, and composers. Narrower in scope is Mary Unterbrink's *Jazz Women at the Keyboard* (McFarland, 1983), which offers brief profiles of fifty-five jazz pianists. Sandra R. Lieb's *Mother of the Blues* (University of Massachusetts Press, 1981), is the first book-length, scholarly study of the legendary blues queen, Ma Rainey.

65. Dater, Judy. **Imogen Cunningham: A Portrait.** Boston: New York Graphic Society, 1979. 126p. $24.95. LC 79-2375. ISBN 0821207512.

Photographer Judy Dater interviewed over forty of Imogen Cunningham's closest relatives, friends, and associates and mined the artist's voluminous correspondence to compile this admiring verbal and visual tribute. Cunningham (1883-1976) was an energetic, independent, and highly individualistic photographer who excelled in a traditionally male preserve. Yet Dater concludes that "there was no conscious feminism involved. If she was devoted to any cause, it was to work" (p.11). Nevertheless, women artists have looked to Cunningham as a role model, as a brilliant photographer whose pixieish appearance belied her strong will and independence. This volume closes with sixty selected black-and-white photographs, testimony to the artistic vision and technical skill Cunningham continued to develop until her death at 93.

66. Doane, Mary Ann, et al., eds. **Re-vision: Essays in Feminist Film Criticism.** Frederick, MD: University Publications of America, 1984. 169p. bibliog. $25.00. LC 83-23366. ISBN 0890935858.

Editors Mary Ann Doane, Patricia Mellencamp, and Linda Williams introduce film criticism as a field vitalized in the last five years by the employment of new textual strategies. Drawing on the theoretical influence of Foucault and Barthes, the editors assert in the introduction that "feminist discourse on film can only be written as a counter-history, or re-vision, of the more orthodox canon." The essays that follow demonstrate the pluralistic theoretical tendencies in this enterprise. Christine Gledhill extols the value of semiotic analysis; Judith Mayne offers a feminist reading of the Hollywood "woman's film"; Mary Ann Doane attends to "masculine structures of seeing" (p.80); and Linda Williams shows how the female viewer's gaze, averted from scenes of violence in movies, attests to "her own powerlessness in the face of rape, mutilation, and murder" (p.83). Other essays by B. Ruby Rich, Kaja Silverman, and Teresa de Lauretis (author of *Alice Doesn't: Feminism, Semiotics, Cinema*, Indiana University Press, 1984) reflect on language, power, gender, and the nature of the "gaze." E. Ann Kaplan's *Women and Film: Both Sides of the Camera* (Methuen, 1983) applies theory to specific men's and women's films, American and foreign, ranging from Cukor's *Camille* (1936) to the *avant garde* film *Sigmund Freud's Dora* (1979).

67. Duncan, Isadora, 1878-1927. **Isadora Speaks.** Edited by Franklin Rosemont. San Francisco: City Lights Books, 1981. 147p. bibliog. index. $12.95. LC 81-21692. ISBN 0872861341.

Isadora Duncan is best known as the creator of modern dance and as a "free spirit" who rejected convention of all kinds. This collection of previously inaccessible essays, speeches, interviews, letters to the editor, and statements to the press shows Duncan to have been a thoughtful and articulate woman with a "consistent and practical dedication" to many radical causes, especially "the women's movement; opposition to organized religion; a new educational system; and the abolition of wage-slavery" (p.xii).

68. Erens, Patricia, 1938- , ed. **Sexual Strategems: The World of Women in Film.** New York: Horizon Press, 1979. 336p. bibliog. $15.00. LC 76-20310. ISBN 0818007060.

In the first part of this readable anthology, feminist film critics—among them, pioneers Marjorie Rosen and Molly Haskell—treat images of women in male-directed films. Essays in the second part address theoretical questions about women's cinema, trace the careers of women directors, and discuss films by women. Erens adds impressive filmographies and a good bibliography. Complementing these contemporary assessments is an unusual examination of film criticism from the 1920s on. Marsha McCreadie's *Women on Film: The Critical Eye* (Praeger, 1983) analyzes the film writings of Virginia Woolf, Simone de Beauvoir, Colette, and other luminaries, along with women primarily known as film critics, such as Pauline Kael and Judith Crist.

69.* Flack, Audrey, 1931- . **Audrey Flack on Painting.** New York: H. N. Abrams, 1981. 116p. bibliog. LC 80-20603. ISBN 0810909154.

Famed photorealist Audrey Flack here offers eleven statements on her work, ranging from "Some Notes on Art and Life," to comments on "Color" and "Line," to background on particular paintings. Among the works she highlights are *Macarena Esperanza* (1971), a depiction of an ornate saint's statue carved and painted by a seventeenth-century Spanish woman, and *Marilyn* (1977), a still life incorporating photographs of Marilyn Monroe, jars of cosmetics, fruit, an hourglass and a watch, and other symbolic objects. Flack's paintings are complex and iconographic, brilliantly colorful, and evocatively emotional. Beautifully designed, this book features full-color reproductions of many works (including sequential glimpses of works in progress) and introductory comments by Ann Sutherland Harris and Lawrence Alloway.

70.   Gold, Arthur, and Robert Fizdale. **Misia: The Life of Misia Sert.** New York: Knopf, 1980; repr. New York: Morrow, 1981. 337p. bibliog. index. pbk. $12.95. LC 80-27340. ISBN 0688003915.

A patron and muse of the arts in early twentieth-century Paris, Misia Sert (1872-1950) was a frequent model for artists such as Toulouse-Lautrec, Vuillard, Bonnard, and Renoir; her life was fictionalized by the likes of Proust and Cocteau. Gold and Fizdale, a duo-piano team, never met Misia, but the more they learned about her from contemporaries encountered on European tours, the more they "fell under [her] spell" (p.310). They recreate here the glitter of her world. Accomplished as a pianist and a critic of the arts, Misia seems to have expended more of her energy in cultivating the talents of others than in advancing her own, and, according to Gold and Fizdale, her intimate attachments were to a series of emotional tyrants. Not a feminist interpretation, this biography has been widely praised for its engrossing evocation of an exciting era in the arts.

71.   Green, Mildred Denby. **Black Women Composers: A Genesis.** Boston: Twayne, 1983. 171p. bibliog. index. $19.95. LC 81-198. ISBN 0805794506.

Blending background with commentary on selected pieces, Green spotlights five black women who composed serious music: Florence Price (1888-1953), Margaret Bonds (1913-1972), Julia Perry (1924-1979), Evelyn Pittman (b.1910), and Lena McLin (b.1929). Green emphasizes how these inventive women combined training in the classical European tradition with the black musical idiom. A brief introduction reviews the history of women in European, African, and black American music.

72.   Greer, Germaine, 1939- . **The Obstacle Race: The Fortunes of Women Painters and Their Work.** New York: Farrar, Straus, Giroux, 1979. 373p. bibliog. index. $25.00. LC 79-17026. ISBN 0374224129.

Greer terms "false" the question of why there have been no great women painters, applauding the emergence of "real questions" bordering on the sociological. Her controversial book probes for the true contribution women have made to the visual arts, delving into the seeming paucity of women's art production, the economics of pursuing artistic careers, and the acculturation process—all of which have set up formidable psychological and material "obstacles" to women artists. Greer warns against erecting a double standard that will distort women's art history; instead she advocates the recognition of "the traits of the oppressed personality"—insecurities and doubts that mark much female-produced art. Her rich historical study, replete with color illustrations, scrutinizes "the carefully cultured self-destructiveness of women" (p.327)—an obstacle that in her view has barred them from achieving excellence in the manner of Leonardo da Vinci, Titian, or Poussin.

73.   Handy, D. Antoinette, 1930- . **Black Women in American Bands and Orchestras.** Metuchen, NJ: Scarecrow Press, 1981. 319p. bibliog. index. $20.00. LC 80-19380. ISBN 0810813467.

Handy, a black flutist, provides brief biographical vignettes of more than 110 black women instrumentalists. Her scope is broad, encompassing "elite art" musicians as well as women in ragtime, vaudeville, minstrel, blues, pop, jazz, and big band. Beginning with an overview of American orchestral history, Handy goes on to cover, in sequence, orchestras and orchestra leaders, string players, wind and percussion players, keyboard players, administrators, and promising young musicians. A substantial bibliography and many photographs accompany the text.

74. Hayden, Dolores. **Redesigning the American Dream: The Future of Housing, Work, and Family Life.** New York: Norton, 1984. 270p. bibliog. index. $17.95. LC 83-9339. ISBN 0393017796.

Feminist architect Dolores Hayden has been at the forefront of the developing feminist critique of housing policy and urban design. In this work aimed at a broad audience, Hayden critically dissects the American ideal of the detached single-family dwelling. While the ideology of homeownership with its maximization of domestic consumption fueled the capitalist economy and increased workers' stake in it, the accompanying privatization intensified women's second-class status. The segregation of private housing, jobs, and social services achieved physical embodiment of the ideological separation of spheres, creating what Hayden calls "the architecture of gender." In a well-written narrative replete with interesting examples, and accompanied by numerous photographs and illustrations, Hayden not only indicts contemporary urban design, but also informs us of a multitude of experiments aimed at restructuring domestic space and domesticating urban space. She draws on the history of the turn-of-the-century domestic reform movement explored in her earlier book, *The Grand Domestic Revolution: A History of Feminist Designs for American Homes, Neighborhoods, and Cities* (MIT Press, 1981). Here Hayden reconstructs the history of "material feminism," retracing its roots both to the utopian socialists and to conservative reformers such as Catharine Beecher, examining its experiments in collective living, and revealing its failure to question inequalities of class and race and the sexual division of labor. Hayden is a contributor to two recent anthologies gathering new research in the innovative field of feminist environmental design: *New Space for Women,* edited by Gerda R. Wekerle, Rebecca Peterson, and David Morley (Westview Press, 1980); and *Building for Women,* edited by Suzanne Keller (Lexington Books, 1981).

75. Heck-Rabi, Louise, 1931- . **Women Filmmakers: A Critical Reception.** Metuchen, NJ: Scarecrow Press, 1984. 392p. index. $27.50. LC 83-20070. ISBN 0810816601.

Heck-Rabi's project encompasses the work of eleven women: Alice Guy-Blache, Germaine Dulac, and Agnes Varda (France); Leni Riefenstahl (Germany); Dorothy Arzner, Maya Deren, Shirley Clarke, Lois Weber, and Ida Lupino (United States); Muriel Box (England); and Mai Zetterling (Sweden). Several of these women—whose work spans the period from the turn of the century to the late 1970s—are still alive and active. Heck-Rabi's prose is not always compelling, but lengthy excerpts from reviews compensate to a degree for the shortcomings of her analysis. She does reveal an extensive knowledge of film, directors and screenwriters, and the literature of film criticism. Jan Rosenberg studies a younger group of women filmmakers in *Women's Reflections: The Feminist Film Movement* (UMI Research Press, 1983). Rosenberg approaches film from a sociological perspective, comparing recent feminist efforts to other American political film movements. Her book is a knowledgeable guide to the films and filmmakers of the seventies, and to the distribution channels, festivals, and information networks that have structured a market for feminist cinema.

76. Herrera, Hayden. **Frida: A Biography of Frida Kahlo.** New York: Harper and Row, 1983. 507p. bibliog. index. $21.10. LC 80-8688. ISBN 0060118431.

The life of Mexican artist Frida Kahlo (1907-1954) proves in this carefully detailed biography to be every bit as dramatic as her paintings. Kahlo contracted polio as a girl; survived a dreadful streetcar accident at age eighteen; married, divorced, and remarried the famous muralist Diego Rivera; took numerous lovers, including Leon Trotsky; translated her intense physical and emotional anguish into gripping artistic visions; and created a myth of herself that entranced an international network of artists and comrades. Overshadowed in her lifetime by the flamboyant Rivera, Kahlo is being reassessed by feminist critics, who find in her work an uncompromising, visceral depiction of a woman's reality, and in her life, a paradoxical model of devoted, suffering wife and spirited, independent woman. Herrera draws extensively on letters, journals, and interviews, blending analysis of Kahlo's oeuvre (reproduced here alongside photographs of the artist and her associates) with an account of her life. Herrera emphasizes the personal iconography of Kahlo's disturbing paintings and documents her important contributions to the revival of traditional Mexican culture. Some reviewers find fault with this approach; they object to the cursory treatment of Kahlo's active participation in communist politics, the decided reticence regarding her lesbian liaisons, and the view of her artistic accomplishments as an expression of (and only partial compensation for) her inability to bear a child. Rupert Garcia's *Frida Kahlo: A Bibliography* serves as a guide to other materials (Chicano Studies Library Publications Unit, University of California, Berkeley, 1983).

77. Hills, Patricia. **Alice Neel.** New York: H. N. Abrams, 1983. 208p. bibliog. index. $37.50. LC 82-25534. ISBN 0810913585.

Famous for her expressionistic portraits of art world celebrities, poor people, children, and her own family members and friends, Alice Neel (1900-1984) here relates her life story in language as candid and colorful as her paintings. Neel comments frankly on her friendships and loves, her attempted suicide, her leftist politics, her feminism, and her unwavering involvement with her art. To create the narrative, Patricia Hills blends materials from interviews, excerpts from public statements, comments on specific paintings, even poems and a short story by Neel. The text is closely linked to nearly two hundred photographs of Neel's works, more than half in color. Hills adds a short critical essay, addressing Neel's composition and style and highlighting her pathbreaking, sometimes shocking, achievements — for example, her unsentimental pregnant nudes and her revealing studies of couples and family groups.

78. Kallir, Jane. **Grandma Moses: The Artist Behind the Myth.** New York: C. N. Potter; distr. Crown/Galerie St. Etienne, 1982. 160p. bibliog. index. $12.98. LC 82-7683. ISBN 0517547481.

Anna Mary Robertson Moses (1860-1961) was a cultural phenomenon — a folk artist who achieved a tremendous popular following during the heydey of abstract expressionism. Moses' life, Kallir demonstrates, was of a piece with her art — unaffected, vibrant, optimistic. This lavish catalog offers nearly two hundred reproductions, many in color. Kallir's text traces the development of Moses' themes, style, and technique; her sources in popular prints and illustrations; her reception by the public and the art world; and her place in the tradition of American folk art. Moses was a role model for older women and amateur artists, as indicated by a quote from the *New York Times*: "Women everywhere have the feeling that if Grandma Moses can paint, so can they ..." (p.19).

79. Kelly, Mary, 1941- . **Post-Partum Document.** Boston: Routledge and Kegan Paul, 1983. 212p. bibliog. $29.95. LC 82-23031. ISBN 0710094957.

The Post-Partum Document (PPD), portions of which have been exhibited in the United States and elsewhere, records moments in the artist's relationship with her son from his birth to age five. Kelly mounted for display her newborn child's undershirts, stained diaper liners, first words and conversation, drawings, hand imprints, and early writings — an "archeology of everyday life" (p.xvi) — together with excerpts from her diary, a retrospective narrative, and short theoretical comments. Strongly influenced by Lacanian psychoanalysis, the PPD "is an effort to articulate the mother's fantasies, her desire, her stake in that project called 'motherhood,'" thereby replaying "moments of separation and loss ..." (p.xvii). The book presentation is strengthened by the addition of a foreword by feminist art critic Lucy Lippard, an introduction by Kelly, and four critical essays.

80.* Kollwitz, Käthe, 1867-1945. **Käthe Kollwitz: Graphics, Posters, Drawings.** Edited by Renate Hinz. New York: Pantheon Books, 1981. 146p. bibliog. LC 81-47272. ISBN 0394519485.

The works of German artist Käthe Kollwitz seem "particularly appropriate in our time in the struggle against war and for peace, disarmament, and humanitarian principles" (p.xxv). In the 132 drawings, prints, and posters reproduced in this oversized volume, the artist's commitment to socialist, feminist, and pacifist causes is powerfully expressed. Kollwitz's subjects frequently included working-class women and mothers. Feminist art critic Lucy Lippard provides a lengthy forward summarizing critical opinions of Kollwitz: some dismissed her as a sentimental propagandist, while others praised her synthesis of art and politics. Renate Hinz adds a biographical introduction, a chronology, and a bibliography.

81. Kuhn, Annette. **Women's Pictures: Feminism and Cinema.** Boston: Routledge and Kegan Paul, 1982. 226p. bibliog. index. $10.50. LC 81-21168. ISBN 0710090447.

Combining theoretical and pragmatic criticism, Kuhn's book exposes the phallocentric ideology informing male films and traces the seepage of this ideology into women's films. The bibliography is exhaustive, and the glossary of terms will bail out readers who are unfamiliar with the complex terminology of semiotics. *The Power of the Image* (Routledge and Kegan Paul, 1985) collects five recent essays by Kuhn on cinematic representation and sexuality. Mary Gentile is another author concerned with the intersection of feminism and film theory. In *Film Feminisms: Theory and Practice* (Greenwood Press, 1985), she mines the classic writings of filmmaker Sergei Eisenstein and critic André Bazin and applies their ideas to the work of contemporary women directors Márta Mészáros, Helke Sander, Yvonne Rainer, and Marlene Gorris.

82. Lange, Dorothea, 1895-1965. **Dorothea Lange: Photographs of a Lifetime.** Millerton, NY: Aperture; distr. Viking Penguin, 1982. 182p. bibliog. $9.95. LC 82-70769. ISBN 0893811009.

Dorothea Lange's photographs put the lives of America's non-elites before the public eye from the 1930s through the 1950s; they are photographs that inform and awaken conscience. Yet Lange's method was to efface herself as much as possible. Her motto was "...hands off! Whatever I photograph, I do not molest or tamper with or arrange" (p.46). This is a stunning collection of Lange's work—from "White Angel Bread Line" (1932), to the photographs taken for the Farm Security Administration during the thirties, to those documenting Ireland in the fifties. Lange's own commentary accompanies the photographs, sometimes offering insight into her artistic perspective, at other times telling the story behind a particular photograph (for example, the unforgettable "Migrant Mother"). Robert Coles writes a thoughtful introductory essay. In *Dorothea Lange and the Documentary Tradition* (Louisiana State University Press, 1980), Karin Becker Ohrn reviews Lange's life and work in relation to her contemporaries in the documentary tradition. The volume is illustrated with photographs throughout—by photographers such as Imogen Cunningham and Ansel Adams as well as Lange. Particularly noteworthy are Lange's powerful shots of Japanese evacuation and internment during World War II.

83. Lauter, Estella, 1940- . **Women as Mythmakers: Poetry and Visual Art by Twentieth-Century Women.** Bloomington: Indiana University Press, 1984. 267p. bibliog. index. $25.00. LC 83-48636. ISBN 0253366062.

Lauter's argument — that through women's poetry and art new female myths can be identified — hinges upon her belief in mythmaking as an ongoing, culturally organic process. Though she uses the terminology of Jung, she readily abandons the idea of an eternal archetype existing transhistorically. Engaging the work of poets and artists whose projects of mythmaking are quite dissimilar — Susan Griffin, Margaret Atwood, Diane Wakoski, Käthe Kollwitz, Leonor Fini, and Anne Sexton — Lauter asks, "What changes are women making in our cultural mythology?" (p.212). She speculates that myth and mythmaking, as defined in a masculinist society, have shifted in the hands of these artists who express women's identification with nature and the cosmos. In *Archetypal Patterns in Women's Fiction* (Indiana University Press, 1981), Annis Pratt, with Barbara White, Andrea Loewenstein, and Mary Wyer, use familiar archetypal models — epiphany, the journey, individuation, etc. — to open up women's fiction spanning three centuries in new and searching ways. Literature and art are not the only fertile ground for the development of archetypal theory, as Estella Lauter and Carol Schreiner Rupprecht's recent anthology demonstrates. The contributors to *Feminist Archetypal Theory: Interdisciplinary Re-Visions of Jungian Thought* (University of Tennessee Press, 1985) derive their insights from the fields of religion, literature, art, mythology, therapy, neurophysiology, and analytical psychology.

84. Lipman, Jean. **Nevelson's World.** New York: Hudson Hills Press in association with the Whitney Museum of Art; distr. Viking Penguin, 1983. 244p. bibliog. index. $75.00. LC 83-8476. ISBN 0933920334.

"There is great satisfaction in seeing a splendid, big, enormous work of art," states sculptor Louise Nevelson (p.62), and her admirers would certainly agree. This luxurious oversized volume offers photographs of the artist's monumental pieces (in both black-and-white and color), together with lucid commentary by Lipman, an appreciative introduction by critic Hilton Kramer, and many pithy pronouncements by Nevelson herself. The bulk of the volume treats her wood constructions and environments, with smaller sections on her early work, transparent sculpture, metal sculpture, and works on paper. Lipman includes a chapter on the life of the artist (b.1899) and a chronology of her career. Although the viewer might readily associate the medium, scale, and materials of Nevelson's pieces with masculine art traditions, the artist herself feels that her works "are definitely feminine ..." (p.92). By and large, however, neither Nevelson nor Lipman addresses the artist's experience as a woman. Another recent title, *Louise Nevelson: Atmospheres and Environments* (C. N. Potter; distr. Crown, 1980), catalogs an exhibit at the Whitney Museum.

85. Lipsett, Linda Otto, 1947- . **Remember Me: Women & Their Friendship Quilts.** San Francisco: Quilt Digest Press, 1985. 135p. bibliog. $29.95. LC 85-9525. ISBN 0913327042.

Pieced friendship quilts, popular in the nineteenth century, featured blocks embroidered or inked with names, dates, verses, and other inscriptions. Seven such quilts serve here as starting points for historical research. Deducing familial and friendship bonds from the quilts themselves, quilt collector Lipsett traveled to New England and the Midwest, dug in public records, and tracked down descendants of the quilt makers in order to document the women's lives in loving detail. Beautifully illustrated with color photographs of quilts, close-ups of individual blocks, and old photographic portraits, this book evokes the daily lives of ordinary nineteenth-century American women and underscores the importance they attached to their prized quilts.

86.   Lisle, Laurie. **Portrait of an Artist: A Biography of Georgia O'Keeffe.** New York: Seaview Books, 1980; repr. New York: Washington Square Books, 1981. 384p. bibliog. index. pbk. $4.95. LC 79-66083. ISBN 0671421824.

Lisle's biography begins in Wisconsin, where O'Keeffe was born in 1887 and spent her formative years. By the time she came to New York in 1918, O'Keeffe had received some formal training at the Art Institute of Chicago and had been a student and teacher in Charlottesville and Amarillo. Better known is the story of her meeting with the legendary Alfred Stieglitz, who introduced her to New York's avant garde and exhibited her early work. Lisle conveys the complexity of this alliance between two great artists, the older Stieglitz playing mentor to the young and unmalleable O'Keeffe. His photographs of her comprise some of his best work, while her impressive New Mexican works of bleached bones and scorched mesas speak of their life apart (he refused to go to New Mexico, where she spent half of every year after 1928). In this biography – unauthorized by O'Keeffe but based on impressive detective work, numerous interviews, and extensive library research – Lisle finds that "O'Keeffe planned her life so that nothing would impede her development as an artist" (p.438), not even Stieglitz, who viewed "her increasing autonomy as disloyalty" (p.246). Lisle judiciously refrains from assigning O'Keeffe's work to schools and movements. *Georgia O'Keeffe: Works on Paper,* an exhibition catalog compiled by Barbara Haskell (Museum of New Mexico Press, 1985), will surprise those familiar only with O'Keeffe's oils. Over the years the artist frequently sketched in pastels and charcoal, mastering watercolor in the pre-Stieglitz days. O'Keeffe, who died early in 1986, is the subject of two other recent books: Katherine Hoffman's *An Enduring Spirit* (Scarecrow Press, 1984), a summary of critical opinion with a fifty-page annotated bibliography, and Jan Garden Castro's heavily illustrated *The Art and Life of Georgia O'Keeffe* (Crown, 1985).

87.   Lyle, Cindy, et al., eds. **Women Artists of the World.** New York: Midmarch Associates, 1984. 148p. pbk. $12.50. LC 83-63369. ISBN 0960247645.

Midway through the U.N. Decade for Women, as women from around the globe held stormy meetings, artists from seventeen countries held their own upbeat festival in Copenhagen. Illustrated with black-and-white photographs of participants and art works, this volume – edited by Cindy Lyle, Sylvia Moore, and Cynthia Navaretta – documents that 1980 event and examines the problems and achievements of women artists in a sampling of nations. The festival involved visual artists, poets, writers, musicians, performers, dancers, art historians, and critics.

88.   Mathews, Nancy Mowll, ed. **Cassatt and Her Circle: Selected Letters.** New York: Abbeville Press, 1984. 360p. bibliog. index. $19.95. LC 83-21449. ISBN 0896594211.

Accompanied by an excellent introduction and notes, 208 letters written by Cassatt (1844-1926) and those close to her offer insight into many facets of the painter's rich career. American born and bred, Cassatt achieved a greater reputation in Europe than in the United States, and lived most of her adult life abroad. Mathews organizes the letters chronologically: Cassatt's student years abroad, 1860-1869; the years of travel and career-building, 1871-1875; her Impressionist period, 1878-1886; her mature phase, 1889-1898; and her late period, 1900-1926. The portrait revealed in the letters is that of a formidable and productive woman who set out deliberately to realize a career as a great artist. Cassatt's paintings chiefly depict women together and women with children. Her biographer Griselda Pollock (*Mary Cassatt,* Harper and Row, 1980) asserts that Cassatt's work has been largely misunderstood as romanticizing "women's sphere," when in fact the artist's project was to correct what she considered previous misrepresentations of women.

Adelyn Dohme Breeskin's monumental *Mary Cassatt: A Catalogue Raisonné of the Graphic Work* (Smithsonian Institution Press, 1979) updates her previous 1948 catalog with additional handsome reproductions and newly discovered prints.

89.* Maynard, Olga. **Judith Jamison: Aspects of a Dancer.** Garden City, NY: Doubleday, 1982. 294p. index. LC 78-1245. ISBN 0385129858.

In Part One, "Dancing," Maynard situates Judith Jamison's life and career in the context of the history of black American dance. Jamison (b.1944) joined the Alvin Ailey Theater in 1965 and has danced mostly with Ailey since. Jamison is one of the few black dancers who have reached "star" status, and she has been able to defy many dance conventions because of her fame. In Part Two, "Living," Jamison gives a first-person account of her life — growing up, dancing, being a black woman, and working with Alvin Ailey. One of the important influences on black dancers and choreographers, Katherine Dunham (b.1912) is the subject of a study by Joyce Aschenbrenner. *Katherine Dunham* (CORD, 1981) explores Dunham's career as a "self-styled dancer/choreographer/field anthropologist/political-activist/humanist" (p.ix) in the context of a changing U.S. society and Afro-American culture. In the second half of this study, Lavinia Williams presents notations and descriptions of Dunham's method and technique from 1940 to 1945.

90. Miller, Lynn F., and Sally S. Swenson. **Lives and Works: Talks With Women Artists.** Metuchen, NJ: Scarecrow Press, 1981. 244p. $17.50. LC 81-9043. ISBN 0810814587.

Interviews reveal the experiences and ideas of fifteen contemporary women artists working in varied media, including sculpture, printmaking, weaving, painting, quilting, and photography. Among them are Louise Bourgeois, Alice Neel, Faith Ringgold, and Betye Saar. Interviewer Sally Swenson probes for background on the artists' schooling and artistic development, the meaning of their work, their current interests, and their attitudes toward the women's movement and feminist art theory.

91. Mitchell, Margaretta K. **Recollections: Ten Women of Photography.** New York: Viking Press, 1979. 206p. bibliog. $30.00. LC 79-13980. ISBN 0670590789.

This beautiful book honors ten women photographers: Berenice Abbott, Ruth Bernhard, Carlotta M. Corpron, Louise Dahl-Wolfe, Nell Dorr, Toni Frissell, Laura Gilpin, Lotte Jacobi, Consuelo Kanaga, and Barbara Morgan. All were born around the turn of the century, and, as Mitchell notes in her introduction, "today they are among the distinguished elders of their profession" (p.8). Each photographer speaks of her experiences, the development of her aesthetic vision, and her feelings about her craft. The texts are followed by reproductions, fascinating in their diverse techniques and subjects. The volume concludes with chronologies of each woman's career and selected bibliographies.

92. Model, Lisette, 1906- . **Lisette Model.** Millerton, NY: Aperture, 1979. 109p. bibliog. $50.00. LC 79-3055. ISBN 0893810509.

"To understand [photographers'] 'message to the world' we need know little of their lives.... All we need to know about them is written in the images they create — naked for all to see" (p.8). Thus Berenice Abbott introduces this volume of photographs by Lisette Model. The prints are gathered here with only Abbott's brief, appreciative preface, a chronology of Model's life, and a bibliography as accompaniments. This is not a comprehensive survey of Model's oeuvre; portraits predominate, many of them from her 1937 series "Promenade des Anglais." Reviewers are divided in their critical assessment of the collection but united in the opinion that it is high time that work by this pioneer photographer be published in book form.

93. Money, Keith. **Anna Pavlova: Her Life and Art.** New York: Knopf, 1982. 425p. bibliog. index. $55.00. LC 81-47502. ISBN 0394427866.

Anna Pavlova (1881-1931) is still thought of as the epitome of the Russian classical ballerina. Yet as the many photographs in this study document, she went well beyond the convention of nineteenth-century ballet in her work as a dancer. Many thousands of people saw Pavlova dance, as she toured constantly throughout her life, beginning with the Imperial Ballet of St. Petersburg and continuing up until her death in 1931 while on tour with her own company. Drawing on a wide range of English- and Russian-language sources, Money's account achieves more objectivity than many others that rely heavily upon the Pavlova myths. Money supplements the study with a sampling of reviews, interviews, and press reports.

94. Neuls-Bates, Carol, ed. **Women in Music: An Anthology of Source Readings From the Middle Ages to the Present.** New York: Harper and Row, 1982. 351p. bibliog. index. $17.79. LC 81-48045. ISBN 0060149922.

Neuls-Bates selects excerpts from books, unpublished manuscripts, diaries, newspapers, letters, and interviews to piece together an account of women composers, performers, patrons, and educators from Chrisian antiquity to the present. Her intent is not to provide a comprehensive record but to reveal the rough contours of the history from the perspective of the musicians themselves. Liturgical singing in medieval convents, the poetry of women troubadours, Baroque compositions for the harpsichord—these are among the early musical forms depicted here. The bulk of the volume pertains to the nineteenth and twentieth centuries, documenting the artistic lives of pianist Clara Schumann, composer Fanny Mendelsohn Hensel, teacher Nadia Boulanger, conductor Antonia Brico, and contralto Marian Anderson, among others. Neuls-Bates also addresses the restrictions on women's accomplishments and includes two sections on the "woman composer question." The author's explanatory headnotes provide context for the readings.

95. Niccolini, Dianora, ed. **Women of Vision: Photographic Statements by Twenty Women Photographers.** Verona, NJ: Unicorn, 1982. 122p. $19.95. LC 82-81435. ISBN 0881010022.

Ruth Orkin, Suzanne Szasz, Sonja Bullaty, Barbara Morgan, Marcia Keegan, and Eva Rubinstein are among the New York City-based photographers represented in this handsome volume. Their work reflects "the positive and creative aspects of life" (p.9). Short statements by the artists and one-paragraph biographies precede the reproductions, some of which are in color. Because there are few collections of works by women photographers, *The Blatant Image*, a yearbook of photography and criticism by feminists founded in 1981, is of value for the study of images produced by women.

96.* O'Neal, Hank. **Berenice Abbott: American Photographer.** New York: McGraw-Hill, 1982. 255p. bibliog. LC 82-9887. ISBN 0070475512.

Transcending the coffee-table genre of art books, this exquisite collection of Abbott's photographs opens with an appreciative introduction by critic John Canaday and a lengthy account of the photographer's career by Hank O'Neal. The reproductions are in rough chronological order: "Paris Portraits," including classic shots of James Joyce, Djuna Barnes, and other notables of the twenties; "Changing New York," a major project documenting New York City in the thirties; "American People and Places," a miscellaneous group of portraits and scenes; "Science," including brilliant experimental shots of wave motion, bouncing balls, and magnetism; and "Maine," a study of the state where Abbott settled in the sixties. Unfortunately, neither Abbott's comments on the circumstances behind the images nor her notes on the technical details of certain shots shed much light on her role as one of the outstanding women in photography.

97. Orkin, Ruth. **A World Through My Window.** New York: Harper and Row, 1978. 119p. $19.95. LC 78-2153. ISBN 0060132930.

"6:00 A.M.: mist/feedings...2:00 P.M.: view/playpen time...5:00 P.M.: dusk scene/baths...10:00 P.M.: night shot/baby asleep" (p.7). Thus Ruth Orkin describes her days as a housewife and photographer in a fifteenth-floor apartment on Central Park West in New York City. This stunning collection of color photographs, all snapped from her living-room window between 1955 and 1978, captures the Manhattan skyline, the landscape of Central Park, and the movement of people and cars on the street below. The "Photographer's Notes" that conclude the volume comment on each picture and explain equipment and technique. *More Pictures From My Window* (Rizzoli, 1983) emphasizes photographs from 1979 to 1983. In the front matter and the occasional notes under the photos, Orkin shares the story of her career, her sources of inspiration (which include her painter mother), and her heartfelt love of the city she dwells in and photographs. *A Photo Journal* (Viking Press, 1981) offers a pictorial review of Orkin's career as a photojournalist and artist, with autobiographical essays complementing the photos.

98. Parker, Rozsika, and Griselda Pollock. **Old Mistresses: Women, Art, and Ideology.** New York: Pantheon Books, 1981. 184p. bibliog. $19.00. LC 81-48253. ISBN 0394524306.

Parker and Pollock counter the question, "Why have there been no great women artists?" with another question: Why is there no recognized tradition of women artists that takes into account how sex, class, culture, and ideology have set limits on their achievements? According to these art historians, it is essential to consider women artists as part of a historical process, to examine the changing material conditions under which they have worked. The exclusion of women from art academies in the nineteenth century, the paucity of women directors of museums, the invisibility or trivialization of women's art in prominent art anthologies—all serve as examples of institutionalized attitudes that result in women's art being judged "less important." The authors' examination of art history texts suggests how women artists' work has been diminished in subtle ways, labeled "feminine," "intuitive," "domestic," "soft," "passive," or lacking in "intellectual" power as compared with art produced by men. The title "Old Mistresses" (so glaringly different in its connotations from the reverent label "old masters") drives home how thoroughly masculinist is our received idea of "master"-pieces. Parker and Pollock's provocative discussion of theory and practice, accompanied by a wealth of plates, ranges intelligently over European and American, premodern and contemporary art. Parker is also author of *The Subversive Stitch: Embroidery and the Making of the Feminine* (The Women's Press, 1984), a historically grounded discussion of embroidering, "femininity," and feminist strategies of resistance.

99. Perry, Gillian. **Paula Modersohn-Becker: Her Life and Work.** New York: Harper and Row, 1979. 149p. bibliog. $19.95. LC 79-1913. ISBN 0064384217.

Paula Modersohn-Becker (1876-1907) is revered today as a precursor of the Expressionist movement, though in her brief life she was better known as the wife of a prominent German landscape painter. Accompanied by many color plates and black-and-white reproductions, Perry's text recounts Modersohn-Becker's experiences at the

Worpswede artists' colony and charts her artistic development by examining the subjects of her paintings: women, children, peasants, landscape and still life, portraits and self-portraits. Perry draws extensively on Modersohn-Becker's letters and diaries, which have since been published in a scholarly English translation — *Paula Modersohn-Becker: The Letters and Journals*, edited by Günther Busch and Liselotte von Reinken (Taplinger, 1983).

100. Peterson, Susan Harnly. **Lucy M. Lewis: American Indian Potter.** New York: Kodansha International; distr. New York: Harper and Row, 1984. 218p. bibliog. index. $49.95. LC 84-80331. ISBN 0870116851.

Rich in anthropological and historical detail gleaned from the potter and her family, this beautifully illustrated book documents Lucy Lewis's artistic achievement. Lewis creates pottery with stunning geometric and figurative painting, using traditional Acoma Pueblo techniques. Although she began her career selling clay pots along the roadside to tourists, Lewis has exhibited widely and won numerous awards. Peterson calls her an "extraordinary woman who, quietly and alone, dissolved the restraints of her society and found her individual vision" (p.143). Yet her life and her art remain intimately linked to her New Mexican mesa society and its cultural heritage.

101. Rey, Jean Dominique. **Berthe Morisot.** New York: Crown, 1982. 95p. bibliog. $9.95. LC 81-22086. ISBN 0517547090.

Using adjectives like "discreet," "understated," "delicate," and "fresh," French art critic Rey describes the creations of Impressionist Berthe Morisot (1841-1895). Rey's adulatory survey of Morisot's career emphasizes the artist's acceptance as an equal by her male Impressionist compatriots and her neglect by art critics and historians. Morisot worked in oils, pastels, and watercolors; her subjects were nearly always women and girls. The artist "endowed her models with all the charm, sensuality, and tenderness of her own vision of womanhood," Rey states, while avoiding "the trap of excessive muscularity or falsely masculine toughness" into which he claims Mary Cassatt and Suzanne Valadon fell (p.80). While Morisot's influential oeuvre awaits a feminist analysis, this volume offers fifty full-color reproductions and twenty in black and white, revealing the artist's sure vision and technique.

102. Robinson, Charlotte, 1924- , ed. **The Artist & the Quilt.** New York: Knopf; distr. New York: Random House, 1983. 144p. index. $24.95. LC 83-47775. ISBN 0394532201.

Eighteen leading women artists collaborated with sixteen skilled women quilters with the expressed intent of blurring the line between the "fine" arts and traditional crafts. Robinson, one of the originators of the project, documents the results in this handsome catalog. Among the artists were such luminaries as Alice Neel, Betye Saar, Joyce Kozloff, Miriam Schapiro, and Faith Ringgold. The needleworkers included Amy Chamberlin, Bonnie Persinger, Bob Douglas, and Willi Posey (Ringgold's mother). The designs vary greatly. Some echo the geometric pattern of traditional quilts, while others derive from abstract painting and sculpture, and thus challenged the quilters to invent new techniques. Each quilt is shown in color alongside the artwork on which it is based, with a brief commentary. Enhancing the volume are thoughtful essays by Jean Taylor Federico, Miriam Schapiro, Lucy R. Lippard, and Eleanor Munro, plus technical comments on quilt design and construction by Bonnie Persinger. *The Artist and the Quilt,* like *The Dinner Party* (see entry 62), exemplifies an exciting trend toward collaborative, feminist artmaking.

103.   Rose, Barbara. **Lee Krasner: A Retrospective.** New York: Museum of Modern Art, 1983. 184p. bibliog. index. pbk. $14.95. LC 83-62554. ISBN 087070415X.

Abstract painter Lee Krasner (b.1908) came into her own as an artist and gained critical acclaim only after the death of her husband, Jackson Pollock, in 1956. Barbara Rose's thoughtful biocritical study spotlights Krasner's experience as a woman artist, while detailing her schooling, her WPA work, her "liberation" from Cubism in the fifties, and a shift in style, content, and technique toward fuller self-expression after Pollock's fatal accident. Published in conjunction with a major retrospective exhibit, this scholarly monograph provides the definitive account of Krasner's career, 155 reproductions (many in color), a chronology, and a bibliography.

104.   Rosenstiel, Léonie. **Nadia Boulanger: A Life in Music.** New York: Norton, 1982. 427p. index. $24.95. LC 81-18811. ISBN 0393014959.

Boulanger (1887-1979) accorded Rosenstiel "many hours of personal interviews as well as access to her hitherto inaccessible personal papers" (Acknowledgments); this biography thus stands as the official account of the life of this "master teacher." Boulanger is best known as the indefatigable mentor of a huge international collection of composers, including Americans Aaron Copeland, Walter Piston, Philip Glass, and Quincy Jones. She was also accomplished as an organist, conductor, musicologist, and lecturer. She renounced composing early in life, asserting that her compositions were "useless." She also renounced marriage and motherhood as roles incompatible with the life of an artist. While recognizing Rosenstiel's prodigious research, critics fault her treatment for its surfeit of fact and detail and paucity of cogent analysis. The interviews Bruno Monsaingeon weaves together in *Mademoiselle: Conversations With Nadia Boulanger* (Carcanet, 1985) have the virtue of conveying something of Boulanger's lively intelligence and musical taste but fail to provide substantial insight into her personal life.

105.   Roth, Moira, ed. **The Amazing Decade: Women and Performance Art in America, 1970-1980.** Los Angeles: Astro Artz, 1983. 165p. bibliog. pbk. $12.50. LC 82-083532. ISBN 0937122092.

Performance art evolved in the late sixties as a new form combining theater, dance, poetry, ritual, music, and the visual arts. Arguing that the hybrid art form "was, and is, an ideal medium for...feminist statements" (p.14), Roth surveys "the amazing decade" of the 1970s in her introductory essay, dividing women's performance art into three types: autobiographical/narrative, mystical/ritualistic, and political. A freewheeling chronology follows, juxtaposing historical events, books, films, theater, and feminist and women's performance history from 1770 to 1979. The bulk of the volume is devoted to thirty-eight brief illustrated essays on performing artists, including such well-known figures as Laurie Anderson, Judy Chicago, Pauline Oliveros, and Carolee Schneemann. Three bibliographies list works on feminism, performance and women's art, and the artists profiled here. Recent books documenting the work of individual artists include Carolee Schneemann's *More Than Meat Joy*, edited by Bruce McPherson (Documentext, 1979); Laurie Anderson's *United States* (Harper and Row, 1984); and Heidi Von Gunden's *The Music of Pauline Oliveros* (Scarecrow Press, 1983).

106.   Rubinstein, Charlotte Streifer. **American Women Artists: From Early Indian Times to the Present.** New York: Avon; Boston: G. K. Hall, 1982. 560p. bibliog. index. pbk. $12.95. LC 81-20135. ISBN 0816185352.

Rubinstein surveys most well-known American women artists and many who are lesser known or anonymous. The first chapter treats the art works of American Indians, past and contemporary; other chapters follow chronologically, from "Colonial Women Artists and American Women Folk Artists" to a thorough treatment of "The Feminist Art Movement." This amply illustrated book has been used as a classroom text with considerable success. Eleanor C. Munro's earlier survey, *Originals: American Women Artists* (Simon and Schuster, 1979), delineates four major waves of American women artists, beginning with Mary Cassatt and concluding with the public art of Athena Tacha, Mary Miss, and Alice Aycock. Munro often allows the contemporary artists to speak for themselves, weaving absorbing interviews with art criticism, photographs, and plates. Based on an exhibition of the same name, *Artists in Aprons: Folk Art by American Women,* by C. Kurt Dewhurst, Betty MacDowell, and Marsha MacDowell (Dutton, 1979), highlights works produced by women in domestic environments—quilts, paintings, embroideries, and drawings. More than one hundred figures and plates accompany the text. The authors argue that "the so-called minor or decorative arts" (p.167) have evolved into a distinct genre in opposition to the male-dominated and museum-ized high art of painting and sculpture.

107. Shadbolt, Doris. **The Art of Emily Carr.** Seattle: University of Washington Press, 1979. 223p. bibliog. $45.00. LC 79-4918. ISBN 0295956879.

Emily Carr (1871-1945) is often considered a regional artist because of her focus on the indigenous people and totem figures of Victoria, British Columbia. Carr reached her full stride late in life with her "painting of dark and silent forests, monumental Indian carvings, towering trees, wild storm-tossed beaches and infinite skies, which sprang from her lifelong Pacific coast experience" (p.11). She kept a journal and recorded in detail the circumstances of many of her paintings; Shadbolt effectively incorporates journal entries into this text, which is accompanied by almost 180 photographs and reproductions. A fuller version of Carr's life is made available in Maria Tippett's *Emily Carr: A Biography* (Oxford University Press, 1979), which includes an account of Carr's creative literary ventures (she began to publish stories at age 63). Tippett's portrait, while sympathetic, suggests that Carr was a difficult woman, living in genteel Victorian poverty, caught between the demands of her painting and the need to make money.

108. Sherman, Cindy; 1954- . **Cindy Sherman.** New York: Pantheon Books, 1984. 197p. bibliog. pbk. $16.95. LC 83-43256. ISBN 0394724852.

Still in her early thirties, Cindy Sherman has met with phenomenal success in the art world. The subject of her photographs is herself, but not in the autobiographical sense of self-portraiture. Rather, she transforms herself, using makeup, costumes, wigs, and exaggerated poses. A series of black-and-white photographs from 1977 to 1980, labelled "Untitled Film Stills," presents a wide repertoire of stereotyped images of women in the fifties and sixties. More recent color shots evoke a kind of freeze-frame emotionalism, but the effect is still that of objectification, of obscuring the "real" Cindy Sherman. Feminist critics find Sherman's work unsettling. "Though the images are billed as explorations of the frontiers of female identity, their appeal is in fact misogynistic," writes Elsa Dorfman in *The Women's Review of Books* (August 1985).

109. Sherman, Claire Richter, with Adele M. Holcomb, eds. **Women as Interpreters of the Visual Arts, 1820-1979.** Westport, CT: Greenwood Press, 1981. 487p. bibliog. index. $35.00. LC 80-785. ISBN 0313220565.

It is not only as artists that women have left a mark on our visual culture, but as art historians, archaeologists, critics, museum staff, and art educators. Sherman opens this volume with three essays tracing women's contributions to art interpretation in the periods 1820-1890, 1890-1930, and 1930-1979. These are followed by twelve profiles of European and U.S. women, written by various authors. The biographies are extensively documented, and Sherman points to additional source materials in a concluding bibliography. The volume is an important advance in the restoration of women's place in art historiography. Judy K. Collischan Van Wagner turns to the present in *Women Shaping Art: Profiles of Power* (Praeger, 1984). Van Wagner interviewed nineteen art critics and gallery owners, all women who have played key roles in shaping contemporary artistic taste. Emily Genauer, Katharine Kuh, Antoinette Kraushaar, Dore Ashton, Lucy Lippard, and the others share details of their lives and careers, their opinions of artistic trends, and widely differing views of feminism and their experiences as women. Van Wagner provides full bibliographies of works by and about her subjects.

110. Silverman, Jonathan, ed. **For the World to See: The Life of Margaret Bourke-White.** New York: Viking Press, 1983. 224p. bibliog. index. $46.95. LC 82-17348. ISBN 067032356X.

Photojournalist Margaret Bourke-White (1904-1971) braved danger and discomfort to document the central events of the twentieth century, including the economic growth of the USSR under Stalin, the Dust Bowl and Southern poverty in the thirties, World War II, the liberation of Buchenwald, Gandhi's campaign for Indian indpendence, and the protest of South African blacks. Silverman's biography quotes extensively from Bourke-White's own writings, taking pains to place her hectic career in the context of recent world history but offering few insights into her personal life or her artistic vision. Some 150 photographs are reproduced, half of them previously unpublished. Fellow *Life* photographer Alfred Eisenstaedt asserts that "if she were alive today, Maggie would be in the forefront of the women's movement" (p.7); certainly this brave and passionate woman is an inspiration to all women photographers.

111. Slatkin, Wendy. **Women Artists in History: From Antiquity to the 20th Century.** Englewood Cliffs, NJ: Prentice-Hall, 1985. 191p. bibliog. index. pbk. $12.95. LC 84-11481. ISBN 013961821X.

Designed to supplement standard textbooks on Western art history, this readable overview spotlights the foremost women artists from prehistory to the present. Slatkin proceeds chronologically, describing each epoch in terms of women's lives (with attention to class differences) and prevailing art styles. She selects some forty artists for discussion in depth, all women whose work easily measures up to the standards traditionally applied to male artists. Among the earlier figures are Artemisia Gentileschi, Clara Peeters, Elisabeth Vigée-Lebrun, and Angelica Kauffman, while the modern era is well represented by Rosa Bonheur, Mary Cassatt, Paula Modersohn-Becker, Käthe Kollwitz, Sonia Delaunay, Georgia O'Keeffe, Faith Ringgold, and others. Slatkin also includes medieval embroiderers, pre-World War II photographers, and quilters. Using numerous black-and-white reproductions to illustrate her text, she frequently compares the women artists' works to those of their male contemporaries, showing how similar themes received different treatments. *In Her Own Image: Women Working in the Arts* (Feminist Press, 1980) takes a different approach to the same broad topic. Finding the usual categories of period, place, and artistic field ill-suited to a survey of Western women's art, Elaine Hedges and Ingrid Wendt divide the selections in this anthology into four thematic sections: "Everyday Use: Household Work and Women's Art"; "Becoming an Artist: Obstacles and Challenges"; "Their Own Images: Definitions and Discoveries"; and "Lend Your Hands: Women's Art and Social Change." The textbook, part of the series "Women's Lives/Women's Work," emphasizes the visual arts, crafts, and literature, although music and dance are also treated. Mixing black-and-white photographs of art works and artists, poems, stories, artists' personal accounts, brief biographies, and critical commentaries, the editors shape a vivid and multifaceted picture of women's creativity.

112. Steward, Sue, and Sheryl Garratt. **Signed, Sealed, and Delivered: True Life Stories of Women in Pop.** Boston: South End Press, 1984. 168p. bibliog. index. $20.00. LC 84-40384. ISBN 0896082415.

"Most books about 'women in rock' tell selective stories; most are glossy fanzines, papier mâché remakes of press-cuttings, press releases, and record company and magazine photographs" (p.10). In an effort to go beyond "the conventional questions of the music press" and to "[rewrite] the story from a feminist angle" (pp. 10, 12), Steward and Garratt interviewed women in the industry in Britain and the United States whose careers spanned the 1950s to the 1980s and encompassed a range of forms—"from country, jazz, salsa, soul, disco, reggae, African pop, rockabilly, to good old 7-[inch] pop" (p. 8). They spoke not only with the stars—women like Brenda Lee, Tammy Wynette, Poly Styrene, Tina Turner, Grace Jones, and Sweet Honey in the Rock—but also with women behind the scenes—factory workers, sound engineers, producers, DJ's, and the fans. For a detailed, but not feminist, history of Motown women, turn to Alan Betrock's *Girl Groups: The Story of a Sound* (Delilah Books, 1982). Among the many stars Betrock highlights are the Shirelles, Mary Wells, Patti Labelle, Leslie Gore, the Ronettes, Martha and the Vandellas, and the Supremes.

113. Stodelle, Ernestine. **Deep Song: The Dance Story of Martha Graham.** New York: Schirmer Books/Macmillan, 1984. 329p. bibliog. index. $25.95. LC 84-1261. ISBN 0028725204.

Martha Graham began her dance training in 1916, at the age of twenty-two, at the Denishawn school. She became a soloist but left Denishawn in 1923 after a period of discontent, moved to New York, and began to develop her own technique. For Graham, movement is always connected to dramatic imagery, and she used her new technique to present powerful stories, soon turning to myths as a source of material. Stodelle focuses on Graham's artistic development, bringing in relevant details of her personal life. In *Divine Dancer* (Doubleday, 1981), Suzanne Shelton gives us a biography of Graham's teacher, Ruth St. Denis. Although not a modern dancer herself, St. Denis influenced Graham and other creators of modern dance such as Doris Humphrey. St. Denis studied Indian and Oriental dance and created dance dramas with spiritual themes, stylized movement, and magnificent costumes. Shelton traces St. Denis's career from vaudeville, to her very successful years with Denishawn, to the long period after her style of dance went out of fashion.

114. Todd, Susan, 1942- , ed. **Women and Theatre: Calling the Shots.** Boston: Faber and Faber, 1984. 119p. pbk. $8.95. LC 83-5571. ISBN 0571130429.

In these remarkably forthright essays, nine women discuss their careers in contemporary British and Canadian theater. Active in traditional, experimental, and feminist theater, all these actors, writers, directors, designers, and stage managers are concerned with "how they represent their sex and its experiences in their work..." (p.9). Many also discuss the development of their ideas about the representation of women on the stage and the difficulties they encounter working with traditional plays and directors.

115. Truitt, Anne, 1921- . **Daybook: The Journal of an Artist.** New York: Pantheon Books, 1982. 225p. $14.45. LC 82-47897. ISBN 0394523989.

From 1974 to 1980, sculptor Anne Truitt kept a diary, as she struggled to come to terms with herself as an artist and to discover the "secret logic" of her life. The entries reveal both her ideas about art and the creative process and the centrality of other concerns—motherhood, health, finances, household duties. Truitt's writing is insightful and often lyric, as she recounts her past, her present, and her dreams.

116. Warnod, Jeanine. **Suzanne Valadon.** New York: Crown, 1981. 96p. bibliog. $9.95. LC 81-5412. ISBN 0517544997.

A model for Renoir, Lautrec, and others, a protégée of Degas, and the mother of Maurice Utrillo, Suzanne Valadon (1865-1938) was a talented artist in her own right. This brief biocritical study, first published in French, provides ample proof of Valadon's place in art history. Color photographs of paintings and drawings, especially female nudes, reveal a strong personality, which Warnod (who knew the artist) confirms in the somewhat rambling tale of her life.

117. Weaver, William, 1923- . **Duse: A Biography.** New York: Harcourt, Brace, Jovanovich, 1984. 383p. bibliog. index. $19.95. LC 84-4600. ISBN 0151266905.

Little known today, Eleonora Duse (1858-1924) achieved international fame as an actress in the late nineteenth century. Drawing on unpublished letters and documents, Weaver traces Duse's life from her birth into a family of professional Italian actors to her later stardom. Her naturalistic acting style and her openness toward "modern" playwrights like Ibsen won Duse the admiration of such writers and critics as George Bernard Shaw, Isadora Duncan, James Joyce, Willa Cather, and Anton Chekov. During her life, critics like Shaw contrasted Duse's natural acting style with the theatrical artificiality of her contemporary, Sarah Bernhardt (1944-1923); Bernhardt's own style and influence are examined by the eleven contributors to *Bernhardt and the Theatre of Her Time,* edited by Eric Salmon (Greenwood Press, 1984). Yet another contemporary actress was Mrs. Patrick Campbell (1865-1940), whose flamboyant, independent, fascinating life—including a romance with Shaw, for whom she played Eliza Doolittle in *Pygmalian*—is the subject of Margot Peters's *Mrs. Pat* (Knopf, 1984).

118. Wye, Deborah. **Louise Bourgeois.** New York: Museum of Modern Art, 1982. 123p. bibliog. $12.50. LC 82-60847. ISBN 0870702572.

The Museum of Modern Art mounted a major retrospective exhibit of Louise Bourgeois's painting and sculpture in 1982. This volume of plates and biocritical text is the show's catalog, and the definitive study of the artist to date. Born in 1911, Bourgeois worked first in oils, then turned to sculpture in 1949. Although she can be placed in the Surrealist and Expressionist traditions, her work is ultimately, as Deborah Wye writes, "specific, quirky, and individualistic....a strikingly poignant and authentic reminder of our humanity" (p.33). From her early paintings of the "Femme-Maison," a woman's body with a house for a head, to later overtly sexual forms in bronze, latex, and marble, Bourgeois's art work evinces a feminist sensibility, and often evokes powerful emotional responses in viewers. Wye's essay traces the artist's career through the decades from the forties to the present. A chronology of her life, a list of exhibitions, and a bibliography conclude the catalog. Only 4 of the 153 plates are in color.

AUTOBIOGRAPHY, BIOGRAPHY, DIARIES, MEMOIRS, AND LETTERS

The reading and writing of women's lives have been of particular interest to scholars in women's studies. We have included in this chapter the many genres in which women reconstruct their own lives, along with biographies, both critical and popular. Additional autobiographical and biographical works appear in other chapters, especially in Literature and Art and Material Culture, for the stories of women's lives are intimately linked to their impact on their fields of endeavor. By including personal names in the subject index, we provide access to these scattered entries.

Biographical dictionaries and indexes are located in the Reference chapter, while critical works on autobiography and biography appear in Literature: History and Criticism. Bibliographic aid is available from several directions. Anthologies listed below often contain rich bibliographies of diary sources. Narda Lacey Schwartz has identified biographical periodical articles on literary figures in *Articles on Women Writers* (ABC-Clio, 2 vols., 1977 and 1986). Those looking for a wide range of personal narratives published between 1946 and 1976 will want to check Patricia K. Addis's annotated bibliography *Through a Woman's I* (see entry 838).

119. Akers, Charles W. **Abigail Adams: An American Woman.** Edited by Oscar Handlin. Boston: Little, Brown, 1980. 207p. bibliog. index. $13.95. LC 79-2241. ISBN 0316020400.

Drawing chiefly on the Adams family correspondence, Akers contextualizes the life of Abigail Adams (1744-1818) in eighteenth-century America, where despite the gains men enjoyed as inheritors of the European Enlightenment, women experienced their political existence "only in their relationship to men" (p.32). Akers attributes Abigail Adams's influence on her husband and son—and on society at large—to her strategic assessment of the lot of eighteenth-century women: she acquiesced to the culturally encoded separation of spheres, confining her discussions of politics to the family circle. In Akers's view, Abigail wisely saw herself as a "whetstone on which to sharpen his [John Adams's] ideas" (pp.32-33), though he credits her for her knowledge of public affairs, for skill in transmitting her ideas to influential men in her circle, and for her success in preserving a private life with a public man. Akers demonstrates familiarity with the range of recent scholarship on the Adams family, including the work of such feminist historians as Joan Hoff Wilson, Nancy Cott, and Linda Kerber. The Adams' very intimate marriage is a central focus of another recent biographical study, *Dearest Friend: A Life of Abigail Adams*, by Lynne Withey (Free Press/Macmillan, 1981).

120. Alpers, Antony, 1919- . **The Life of Katherine Mansfield.** New York: Viking Press, 1980. 466p. bibliog. index. $16.95. LC 79-12088. ISBN 0670428051.

Since Alpers's first biography of Mansfield appeared in 1953, a wealth of new material has cast fresh light on the elusive writer, born in New Zealand in 1888. After schooling in London, Mansfield decided to leave New Zealand in order to live with artists and become a writer in England. During her brief, tempestuous life, she achieved both—receiving acclaim for her short stories and becoming close to many of the important literary figures of the day. Alpers stresses her love-hate relationship with both her father and New Zealand. At the crux of his interpretation is the conflict between Mansfield's passion for independence and her need for security. He also discusses her longstanding relationships with her school friend Ida Baker and her husband, the editor and writer John Middleton Murry. Alpers's project is one of restoring Mansfield to her rightful place in literary criticism, because "modern criticism has been ill-equipped to deal with [the] potential" (p.389) of a writer who died at thirty-four. In *Katherine Mansfield* (St. Martin's Press, 1981), Claire Hanson and Andrew Gurr do take Mansfield's art seriously, emphasizing the themes and technical contributions of her short stories, particularly her development of the indirect free form. Along with Alpers's biography, the appearance of some of Mansfield's unpublished writings should also dispel misunderstandings about her life and art. *The Urewera Notebook*, edited by Ian A. Gordon (Oxford University Press, 1978), contains a lode of reflections, jottings, lists, letters, and diary entries written mainly on a camping tour of New Zealand's North Island in 1907—material Mansfield drew upon in her early stories. Mansfield's sensitivity and forthrightness shine through in *The Collected Letters of Katherine Mansfield,* edited by Vincent O'Sullivan and Margaret Scott (Clarendon Press, 1984). This extensively annotated collection, the first of a projected four volumes, covers the years from 1903, when Mansfield was fifteen, to 1917, when, at twenty-nine, she was beginning to feel the effects of the tuberculosis that would eventually kill her.

121. Angelou, Maya. **The Heart of a Woman.** New York: Random House, 1981. 272p. $12.50. LC 81-40232. ISBN 0394512731.

Angelou tells her story of extraordinary accomplishment as a writer, actor, playwright, musician, singer, and activist with modesty and skill. Even as she seeks the right man to live with, she recognizes the double oppression of being black and female. Many celebrities flit in and out of Angelou's life in the fourth volume of her autobiography—Martin Luther King, Paule Marshall, Billie Holliday, Bayard Rustin, and Geoffrey Cambridge, among others. Yet, it is the story of her relationship to her son, Guy, that stands out, and her reflections on the lot of "the black mother who perceives destruction at every door" (p.36). A recent volume of her poetry that reflects the rich material of her autobiographies—love, activism, paying the bills—is *Shaker, Why Don't You Sing?* (Random House, 1983).

122. Austin, Mary Hunter, 1868-1934. **The Land of Journeys' Ending.** New York: Century, 1924; repr. Tucson: University of Arizona Press, 1983. 459p. $24.50. LC 83-1217. ISBN 0816508070.

Mary Austin's literary project, beginning with her first book, *The Land of Little Rain* (1903; repr. University of New Mexico Press, 1974), was to capture in language the essences of the West she came to know after her emigration from Illinois to California as a young woman. Many kinds of writing intervened before she set out on a journey to see and write about Arizona and New Mexico. *The Land of Journeys' Ending,* rendered in a prose style equal in grandeur to the Rio Grande and the Cliff Dwellings, records her observations in the spring of 1923. "Between Tucson and Phoenix, south of the paved road, there is a vast cactus garden I can never pass without crossing my fingers against its spell. Often in the midst of other employments I am seized with such a fierce backward motion of my mind toward it as must have beset Thoreau for his Walden when he had left it for the town" (p.129). In *Room and Time Enough: The Land of Mary Austin* (Northland Press, 1979), photographs by Morley Baer bring to life images drawn from *Land of Little Rain* and *The Land of Journeys' Ending*. Augusta Fink's succinct introduction abstracts her biography of Mary Austin, *I-Mary* (University of Arizona Press, 1983). "Withdrawn and aloof, she hid her sensitivity behind a screen of haughty detachment," writes Fink of young Mary's outward persona. Austin shielded herself by retreating into the inviolable "I-Mary" when events in her life seemed too tragic to bear. T. M. Pearce's *Literary America* (Greenwood Press, 1979) attests to Austin's wide-ranging correspondence about artistic matters and reformist politics (especially Indian rights in New Mexico) with leading artistic, political, and intellectual figures of her time—Ansel Adams, Sinclair Lewis, Herbert Hoover, and Van Wyck Brooks among them. A scholarly work linking Austin to other women writers of her period remains to be written. The Feminist Press has recently reissued Austin's auto-biographical novel, *A Woman of Genius* (1912; repr. 1985), with a new afterword by Nancy Porter.

123. Backus, Jean L. **Letters From Amelia, 1901-1937.** Boston: Beacon Press, 1982. 253p. bibliog. pbk. $10.95. LC 81-68356. ISBN 0807067024.

Backus's biography of Amelia Earhart (1897-1937) is enlivened by extensive quotations from Earhart's correspondence with her mother, newly discovered in 1975. The letters offer a glimpse into "the human side of a great woman with all her virtues and imperfections" (p.7), but they do not shed light on the sexual relationships Earhart strove to keep private, or on her mysterious disappearance while attempting a round-the-world flight in 1937. Nonetheless, Earhart fans will undoubtedly appreciate the additional window on this heroine the letters provide, and the history-making photographs accompanying the text.

124. Bateson, Mary Catherine. **With a Daughter's Eye: A Memoir of Margaret Mead and Gregory Bateson.** New York: Morrow, 1984. 242p. bibliog. $15.95. LC 84-60564. ISBN 0688039626.

Mary Catherine Bateson is the daughter of anthropologist Margaret Mead (1901-1978) and Gregory Bateson, and an anthropologist herself. Both biography and autobiography, *With a Daughter's Eye* is a moving record of her meditation on Bateson and Mead's lives—separate, together, and with her—shortly after their deaths. In her epilogue, Bateson writes of her deliberate choice to forego interviews, archival research, and rereadings of her parents' many books in preparation for writing this volume, not wanting "to remake myself as an expert instead of a daughter" (p.227). Nonetheless, the writer's detachment and the historian's concern for the record do shape Bateson's purpose here, along with her filial tenderness and regard. For example, when she discovers that her mother's intimacies extended to women (most notably, Ruth Benedict), she chooses to make the revelation public, despite a powerful sense of obligation to protect Mead's privacy. What with Mead's prodigious scholarly output, her equally prolific popular writing, and her status as a veritable household word in American culture, what we are seeing now represents only the first trickle of what will surely be a flood of future Mead studies. Jane Howard gives us a journalistic account in *Margaret Mead: A Life* (Simon and Schuster, 1984). Howard packs her tale with diverse personal anecdotes drawn from some three hundred interviews with family, friends, and colleagues of Mead. Both Howard and Bateson devote some attention to the media hoopla caused by the publication one year earlier of Derek Freeman's *Margaret Mead and Samoa: The Making and Unmaking of an Anthropological Myth* (Harvard University Press). In Freeman's work, legitimate questions about the accuracy of Mead's Samoan ethnography balloon into a virulent attack on her intellectual integrity. Readers will find a much less controversial assessment in Robert Cassidy's *Margaret Mead: A Voice for the Century* (Universe Books, 1982), which surveys Mead's writings on such topics as the American family, education, feminism, the environment, and racism.

125. Bloch, Alice. **Lifetime Guarantee: A Journey Through Loss and Survival.** Watertown, MA: Persephone Press, 1981; repr. Boston: Alyson Publications, 1983. 132p. pbk. $6.95. ISBN 0930436091.

Between February 1972 and June 1973, Alice Bloch survived her younger sister Barbara's protracted illness and death from leukemia, her father's death of liver failure, her aunt's death from cancer, and the break-up of her first lesbian relationship; Alice's mother had died when she was nine years old. Reworking her journal from that period, and drawing on her sister's notes, letters, and poems, in *Lifetime Guarantee* Bloch tries to assimilate the pain and settle old accounts so that she can continue her own life. The family crises during this period heighten her awareness both of her family roots and traditions, and of the jarring conflicts. If a Jewish identity is in part what family means to her, her new lesbian identification calls her claim on Jewish community into question. Her sister Barbara, whom she loves "almost entirely without ambivalence" (p.19), is dark and kinky-haired, while Alice is fair and straight-haired: differences in the family given weight by racism. In her novel *The Law of Return* (Alyson Publications, 1983), Alice Bloch continues to explore the tangled threads of a U.S. lesbian-feminist Jewish identity.

126. Bogan, Louise, 1897-1970. **Journey Around My Room: The Autobiography of Louise Bogan.** A Mosaic by Ruth Limmer. New York: Viking Press, 1980. 197p. bibliog. $13.95. LC 79-56279. ISBN 0670409421.

Using some autobiographical material from the original "Journey Around My Room" published by the *New Yorker* in 1933, journal and notebook entries, poetry both published and unpublished, and selections from letters, criticism, lectures, and recorded conversations, Ruth Limmer, Bogan's literary executor, here acts as a stage manager, or a gallery owner, arranging these fragments to speak of Bogan's life in the first person. Exploratory rather than documentary, Bogan's "autobiography" forces readers to content themselves with representative scenes rather than a reconstructed version of her life. In her graceful introduction, Limmer previews what we won't see in Bogan's account: the factual details of wage-earning, of traveling, of the writer's personal life, even of her career as a writer. In the chronology, Limmer tracks major places, people, and events in Bogan's life from her birth in 1897 to her death as a celebrated woman of letters in 1970. Limmer's "mosaic" is in itself a remarkable statement on the form and content of autobiography. In *Louise Bogan: A Portrait* (Knopf, 1985), Elizabeth Frank presents a detailed and sympathetic biography of a complex and often tortured woman, and demonstrates how Bogan's life illuminates her elusive, highly coded poems. For critical readings of the poetry, readers may turn to the new *Critical Essays on Louise Bogan* (G. K. Hall, 1984), a collection of reviews by Marianne Moore, Stanley Kunitz, William Meredith, Paul Ramsey, and others, edited by Martha Collins; and to Jacqueline Ridgeway's *Louise Bogan* (G. K. Hall, 1984), which analyzes Bogan's poetry and fiction chronologically, showing how she moved from early romanticism to later metaphysics and symbolism.

127.* Brittain, Vera, 1893-1970. **Testament of Youth.** New York: Macmillan, 1933; repr. New York: Wideview Books, 1980. 661p. LC 80-52677. ISBN 0872236722.

A book that electrified the young people who read it upon its publication in 1933, *Testament* chronicles the World War I period in the words of one young woman from a northern English bourgeois family. For Brittain, the war seemed at first an intrusion into her comfortable life in Buxton and her plans for college. Gradually, the idealism that carried a nation of young men to war caught up with her; she began training as a VAD in the summer of 1915. By 1918, Brittain's brother, her fiancé, and other significant young men in her life had died. Brittain herself had witnessed horrors of warfare for which neither her upbringing nor her education had prepared her. A record of the devastation the war worked upon her own life and her class, *Testament* made Brittain an acclaimed author at home and abroad, although by the time of its publication she was already established as a pacifist and feminist. Readers interested in the original diaries upon which *Testament* is based can refer to *Chronicle of Youth: The War Diary, 1913-1917*, edited by Alan Bishop with Terry Smart (Morrow, 1982). The second volume of Brittain's autobiography, *Testament of Experience: An Autobiographical Story of the Years 1925-1950* (Wideview Books), originally appeared in 1957 and was reprinted in 1981.

128. Burr, Esther Edwards, 1732-1758. **The Journal of Esther Edwards Burr, 1754-1757.** Edited by Carol F. Karlsen and Laurie Crumpacker. New Haven, CT: Yale University Press, 1984. 318p. bibliog. index. $25.00. LC 83-16958. ISBN 0300029004.

Daughter of the renowned Puritan theologian Jonathan Edwards; wife of the founder of what was to become Princeton University; mother of Aaron Burr, Jr., the second vice-president of the United States—these facts alone, one would think, would serve to distinguish the journal of Esther Edwards Burr, if its uniqueness as a Colonial woman's diary were not enough. Yet, as Karlsen and Crumpacker point out in their introduction, the document "has gone largely unnoticed by scholars and, until now, unpublished" (p.19), probably because it adds little to the existing record about these men. In the editors' view, this is precisely what makes the journal important: "It is first of all a woman's document, and its substance is domestic detail and other female concerns which have only recently been recognized as historically significant" (p.19). Written over three years in the form of letters to her intimate friend Sarah Prince, the journal offers a rare glimpse into the daily life of a woman of elite family in Colonial America.

129. Canfield, Gae Whitney, 1931- . **Sarah Winnemucca of the Northern Paiutes.** Norman: University of Oklahoma Press, 1983. 306p. bibliog. index. $19.95. LC 82-40448. ISBN 0806118148.

Sarah Winnemucca's autobiography, *Life Among the Piutes: Their Wrongs and Claims* (1883), was one of the first published works by an American Indian. Canfield's new biography is the first book-length study of Winnemucca (1844?-1891), who worked as an advocate for her people, the Northern Paiutes of the American Northwest, during the 1870s and 1880s, in the face of encroaching settlement and attacks by whites. Newspapers of the period, microfilmed records of the U.S. Bureau of Indian Affairs, and personal accounts by Winnemucca's contemporaries—in addition to Winnemucca's own autobiography—form the basis of this study, which is amply footnoted and extensively illustrated with photographs.

130. Cazden, Elizabeth, 1950- . **Antoinette Brown Blackwell: A Biography.** Old Westbury, NY: Feminist Press, 1983. 315p. bibliog. index. $16.95. LC 82-4986. ISBN 0935312005.

Cazden's is the first published biography of Antoinette Brown Blackwell (1825-1921), a major figure in turn-of-the-century U.S. feminist and social reform circles and the first woman ordained as a Christian minister in the United States. Blackwell's tenure as pastor of a South Butler, New York, parish was short-lived, as she soon came to question Congregationalist orthodoxy. She was active throughout her life as a lecturer and preacher, speaking on women's rights, antislavery, temperance, and philosophical and religious topics. Later in her life, Blackwell turned to writing, publishing works that tackled the relation of feminism to Darwinism, among other subjects. Cazden draws heavily on manuscripts, letters, and other primary sources to bring out many themes fascinating to feminist readers—for example, feminists' lack of sympathy with Blackwell's religious calling and Blackwell's intimate (very likely lesbian) relationship with Lucy Stone at Oberlin. Blackwell's correspondence with Lucy Stone has been edited and published by Carol Lasser and Marlene Merrill in a volume entitled *Soul Mates: The Oberlin Correspondence of Lucy Stone and Antoinette Brown, 1846-1850* (Oberlin College, 1983).

131. Chalon, Jean. **Portrait of a Seductress: The World of Natalie Barney.** New York: Crown, 1979. 248p. index. $10.95. LC 78-32170. ISBN 0517532646.

Chalon introduces seduction as the organizing theme of this biography: "From her birth in Dayton, Ohio, on October 31, 1876, until her death in Paris on February 12, 1972, Natalie Barney never ceased to charm and beguile" (p.1). Because of her inherited wealth and beauty, Natalie Barney, according to this biographer, lived a charmed life. In that the writer was a friend of Barney, artist Romaine Brooks, and many in their circle, these reflections become memoirs of a biographer who has little distance from his subject. Chalon's memoirs serve as one source on the lesbian writer whose literary salon in Paris flourished, with brief interruptions, for over sixty years.

132. Chernin, Kim. **In My Mother's House.** New Haven, CT: Ticknor and Fields, 1983. 309p. $14.95. LC 82-19514. ISBN 0899191673.

"'You are a writer,' she says. 'So, do you want to take down the story of my life?'" It is 1974 when Kim Chernin's mother, Rose Chernin, unexpectedly makes this proposal. The two spend the next seven years venturing into one another's lives, telling their stories as they never have before. The book that results belongs in the first half to Rose, in the second to Kim. A Jewish immigrant from Russia, Rose Chernin devoted her life fully to the Communist Party and the struggle against exploitation and injustice. She worked as an editor in the Soviet Union during the early thirties, organized California farmworkers later in the Depression, and fought deportations of foreign-born radicals during the McCarthy era. Kim was an adolescent when her mother was arrested and brought to trial as a subversive. Both mother and daughter work through layers of guilt, fear, and anger as their stories unfold. Rose anticipates censure as a mother for having given her life to political struggle; Kim fears rejection as a daughter because she cannot follow in her mother's political footsteps. Full of passion and charm, this is an extraordinarily moving book; it is also a stirring account of American radical history in this century.

133. Chesnut, Mary Boykin Miller, 1823-1886. **Mary Chesnut's Civil War.** Edited by Comer Vann Woodward. New Haven, CT: Yale University Press, 1981. 886p. bibliog. index. $40.00. LC 80-36661. ISBN 0300024592.

"There is no slave like a wife," South Carolinian Mary Boykin Chesnut protested in a feminist moment of her Civil War diaries. She herself was a member of a wealthy slave-holding family, and her journals manifest the paradox of a woman of her race and class. Perhaps no other writer of her period so vividly documents those whose daily lives she attentively observed: slaves, poor whites, soldiers, politicians, and members of the judiciary. More than the actual struggle of the Civil War, it is the personal and the political as they intersected in her own life that Chesnut records in these exceptional diaries. Woodward gives us the complete, definitive edition, based primarily on the versions Chesnut polished in the 1870s and 1880s, which were published posthumously for the first time in 1905 under the title *A Diary from Dixie*. Woodward provides introductory essays and extensive annotations, and incorporates some material from the original, unedited journals written during the sixties. *The Private Mary Chesnut: The Unpublished Civil War Diaries* (Oxford University Press, 1984), edited by Woodward and Elisabeth Muhlenfeld, makes available for the first time the complete original diaries. Together, the two editions complete the puzzle of a work many years in the writing, and many years in the scholarly editing and collating. Muhlenfeld is also a biographer of Chesnut. In *Mary Boykin Chesnut* (Louisiana State University Press, 1981), her perspective on Chesnut's journal and life is both literary—tracing major influences (Dickens, Trollope, Eliot, and Thackeray) and documenting Chesnut's efforts to teach herself the writer's craft—and political, profiling her privileged vantage point on the period as the wife of a ranking member of Jefferson Davis's government.

134. Child, Lydia Maria Francis, 1802-1880. **Lydia Maria Child, Selected Letters, 1817-1880.** Edited by Milton Meltzer and Patricia G. Holland. Amherst: University of Massachusetts Press, 1982. 583p. bibliog. index. $35.00. LC 82-8464. ISBN 0870233327.

Child was well known in nineteenth-century America as a novelist and pamphleteer, but her literary career was irreparably damaged by her outspoken support of the abolition of slavery, women's rights, and the rights of the American Indian. In the four hundred letters in this volume, Child discusses the rights of women and people of color, literary figures like Emerson and the Alcotts, and, perhaps most movingly, the strains imposed upon a marriage dedicated to the abolitionist movement. Her correspondents include Margaret Fuller, John Brown, William Lloyd Garrison, and Angelina Grimké. The editors provide a chronology of Child's life and a list of her published works, a short biographical introduction to each section, explanatory notes, and a subject index to the letters. *The Collected Correspondence of Lydia Maria Child, 1817-1880,* also edited by Holland and Meltzer (KTO Microform, 1979), makes available in microfiche 2,604 letters, of which 2,228 were written by Child. William S. Osborne's *Lydia Maria Child* (Twayne, 1980) provides a critical introduction to Child's published works: novels, domestic manuals, antislavery pamphlets, histories of women and religion, and children's books.

135. Clark, Ella Elizabeth, 1896- , and Margot Edmonds. **Sacagawea of the Lewis and Clark Expedition.** Berkeley: University of California Press, 1979. 171p. bibliog. index. $10.95. LC 78-65466. ISBN 0520038223.

Sacagawea was of great use to the white explorers of the Lewis and Clark expedition; white historians, novelists, and playwrights have immortalized (and embellished) the tale ever since. That Sacagawea's importance to Native American history may be skewed by white bias is an important point to make; it does not, however, diminish her true contributions. Biographies of Sacagawea are many. Clark and Edmonds base their account, which covers both the expedition and Sacagawea's later life, on the original journals of Lewis and Clark and recorded personal testimony, aiming to retrieve fact and dispel myth. Clark and Edmonds conclude, "It was the Missouri River, not the young Indian mother, that served as the Expedition's 'principal guide.' ... Though [Sacagawea] was not the guide for the Expedition, she was important to them as an interpreter and in other ways" (p.16).

136. Costin, Lela B. **Two Sisters for Social Justice: A Biography of Grace and Edith Abbott.** Urbana: University of Illinois Press, 1983. 315p. bibliog. index. $18.50. LC 82-21790. ISBN 0252010132.

Costin, a professor of social work, retrieves for her profession the history of two of its foremothers, Grace Abbott (1878-1939) and Edith Abbott (1876-1957). It is a fascinating story of an unusually close "partnership of ideas and action" (p.xi) between two sisters active in reform movements from the Progressive era through the New Deal. Grace is best known for her very capable administration of the U.S. Children's Bureau; Edith gained recognition as author of the pathbreaking book *Women in Industry* (1909) and for her founding contributions to the University of Chicago School of Social Service and Administration. Having begun their careers at Jane Addams' Hull House, the sisters went on to play "a major role in turning 'charity work' into a new profession" (p.vii), contributing to a range of causes including maternal and infant health, child labor legislation, advocacy for new immigrants, woman suffrage, and world peace.

137. Culley, Margo, ed. **A Day at a Time: The Diary Literature of American Women From 1764 to the Present.** New York: Feminist Press at the City University of New York, 1985. 341p. bibliog. $29.95. LC 85-13140. ISBN 0935312501.

This outstanding anthology brings together selections from the diaries of twenty-nine American women. Editor Culley bypasses the works of such famous diarists as Helen Keller and May Sarton to focus on "the life-writing of 'ordinary' American women," women who "felt their lives 'remarkable' enough to have kept a written record" (p.xii). And indeed these women are remarkable, from Abigail Abbot Bailey, an eighteenth-century wife who chronicles her struggles to put a stop to her husband's incestuous designs on their daughter; to Edith K. O. Clark, who records her experience building a cabin in the Wyoming wilderness in the early 1930s; to black lesbian poet Barbara Smith, whose 1979 journal entries, sparked by the murders of twelve black women in Boston, wrestle with racism, sexism, and homophobia in America. Culley includes a superlative primary and secondary bibliography. Where Culley chooses works from unknown writers, *Ariadne's Thread* (Harper and Row, 1982), edited by Lyn Lifshin, features selections from the diaries and journals of such famous contemporary figures as Gail Godwin, Sylvia Plath, and Denise Levertov.

138. Ditlevsen, Tove Irma Margit, 1918-1976. **Early Spring.** Seattle, WA: Seal Press, 1985. 227p. $14.95. LC 85-2091. ISBN 0931188296.

Ditlevsen is widely beloved in her native Denmark for her fiction, essays, and poetry. Alternatively painful and funny, *Early Spring* is an intelligent, moving account of growing up in pre-World War II Copenhagen. Ditlevsen has a poet's eye for metaphor — "Childhood is long and narrow like a coffin," she says at one point, "and you can't get out of it on your own" (p.26). And Tiina Nunnally's prize-winning translation captures the lilting, luminous quality of her prose. Yet Ditlevsen's subject is rarely pretty: the first part, "Childhood," portrays Vestebro, her working-class neighborhood, in all of its gritty ugliness, filled with poverty, ignorance, and fear. "Youth" is more comic than the first part, as our teenage heroine stumbles from one job and boyfriend to another. *Early Spring* concludes with a testament to the overcoming of adversity through art, as Ditlevsen escapes the confines of her upbringing and publishes her first book of poetry at age eighteen.

139. Dunbar-Nelson, Alice Moore, 1875-1935. **Give Us Each Day: The Diary of Alice Dunbar-Nelson.** Edited by Gloria T. Hull. New York: Norton, 1984. 480p. index. $19.95. LC 84-6055. ISBN 0393018938.

According to Hull, Dunbar-Nelson's diary is only the second by a black woman to be discovered, the first having been the mid-nineteenth-century journal of Charlotte Forten. Best known during her lifetime as the widow of Paul Laurence Dunbar, the first famous black poet, Dunbar-Nelson was a writer, teacher, journalist, and activist in her own right. Her diary, kept during the years 1921 and 1926-1931, yields glimpses of the Harlem Renaissance, the black women's club movement, and civil rights activity during the period. Yet, "the heart of the diary," in Hull's view, "lies in what it reveals ... about the meaning of being a Black woman in twentieth-century America" (p.19) — the complex ambivalences relating to race and class; the financial crises; the effort to maintain creativity in difficult circumstances. We also learn of Dunbar-Nelson's lesbian attachments — testimony to Hull's insistence on letting the whole woman emerge from the pages of the diary. Hull's introductions and textual notes raise provocative questions and provide needed contextualization for this landmark work.

140.   Eckhardt, Celia Morris, 1935- . **Fanny Wright: Rebel in America.** Cambridge, MA: Harvard University Press, 1984. 337p. bibliog. index. $22.50. LC 83-8571. ISBN 0674294351.

Wealthy, handsome, learned — Fanny Wright (1795-1852) arrived in the United States from England at the age of twenty-three, fleeing an unhappy childhood. With her sister Camilla, she toured the country unchaperoned, gathering material for her first book, *Views of Society and Manners in America* (1820). Literary success brought her friendships with Jefferson and Lafayette, among others. Wright's initial enthusiasm for the new American nation was later tempered as her radicalism broadened to encompass abolitionist, working-class, feminist, and sexual politics. Influenced by Robert Owen, she founded an experimental interracial community on the Tennessee frontier — a disastrous failure on many counts. Wright turned to the lecture circuit, but scandal followed her. Her assertion of sexual autonomy brought pregnancy, an unhappy marriage, withdrawal from the public sphere, and, eventually, poverty. Eckhardt sets Wright's tragic personal history against a backdrop of early nineteenth-century social history.

141.   Eliot, George, 1819-1880. **Selections From George Eliot's Letters.** Edited by Gordon S. Haight. New Haven, CT: Yale University Press, 1985. 567p. index. $25.00. LC 84-13222. ISBN 0300033265.

In this condensation of his nine-volume edition of Eliot's letters (1954-1978), Gordon S. Haight divides the letters into fourteen sections corresponding to significant periods in Eliot's life, opening each section with a short introduction. These, along with prefatory notes to many letters and an extensive subject index, make this volume accessible, useful, and fascinating to anyone interested in Eliot's views on her life and art. *George Eliot: A Centenary Tribute* (Barnes and Noble, 1982), edited by Haight and Rosemary T. VanArsdel, collects essays by several scholars covering a variety of Eliot topics along with a discussion of Eliot's biographers. *Particularities: Readings in George Eliot* (Ohio University Press, 1983), by noted Eliot scholar Barbara Nathan Hardy, is made up of essays written over fifteen years, most of them on *Middlemarch*. Hardy's essays move from early defensive arguments for Eliot's artistic merit, to later considerations of Eliot's literary form, language, and views on the imagination. A more narrowly thematic, but meticulously argued work is Suzanne Graver's *George Eliot and Community: A Study in Social Theory and Fictional Form* (University of California Press, 1984). Graver asserts that Eliot shared the nineteenth-century desire to recover a lost sense of community and tried to contribute to the creation of a new community through her writing. Graver pairs chapters on nineteenth-century social theory, including a section on the role of women, with chapters on how these theories appear in Eliot's fiction.

142. Faber, Doris, 1924- . **The Life of Lorena Hickok: E. R.'s Friend.** New York: Morrow, 1980. 384p. bibliog. index. $12.95. LC 79-91302. ISBN 0688036317.

Journalist Lorena Hickok (1893-1968) was an accomplished woman in her own right, yet it is unlikely that her biography would ever have been written were it not for her friendship with Eleanor Roosevelt. Faber's biography of Hickok raises interesting questions about the recovery of women's lives, and particularly about the special demands posed by lesbian biography. The nucleus of the work is based on some eighteen boxes of material Hickok donated to the FDR Library before her death, a collection containing more than 2300 letters from Roosevelt to Hickok. Chronicling their friendship from 1932 to 1962, the letters unquestionably establish that theirs was an intimate relationship. Yet Faber backs down from trying to define the exact nature of the friendship because she judges it unfair to place the two women "into the contemporary gay category" (pp.353-354). Lesbian historians have taken Faber to task for her "gingerly" approach. Faber does a fine job, however, in reconstructing the tough world of journalism and the career of a single woman during the 1930s. Hickok's journalistic accounts of the Depression have been collected in the volume *One Third of a Nation* (University of Illinois Press, 1981), edited by Richard Lowitt and Maurine Beasley. Readers will find additional interpretation of Hickok's relationship with Roosevelt in Joseph P. Lash's *A World of Love: Eleanor Roosevelt and Her Friends* (see entry 165).

143. Falk, Candace. **Love, Anarchy, and Emma Goldman.** New York: Holt, Rinehart and Winston, 1984. 603p. bibliog. index. $25.00. LC 83-18405. ISBN 0030436265.

"If ever our correspondence should be published, the world would stand aghast that I, Emma Goldman, the strong revolutionist, the daredevil, the one who has defied laws and convention, should have been as helpless as a shipwrecked crew on a foaming ocean" (pp.3-4). These are the words of "Red Emma Goldman" (1869-1940), written in 1911 to Chicago gynecologist and hobo Ben Reitman. Reitman was Goldman's great love (and her manager) from 1908 to 1917, years which saw some of her most active speaking and writing for the anarchist cause, and some of the most agonizing grief and depression of her lifetime caused by Reitman's infidelity. A public advocate of free love, Goldman found herself privately tormented by jealousy. After considerable reflection, Goldman chose to present only a censored version of this episode in her autobiography. Candace Falk's serendipitous discovery of Goldman's letters to Reitman opened the biographer's eyes to previously hidden dimensions of Goldman's character, and sparked the ambition to try to reconcile Goldman's private reality with her public image. Falk lets go of the larger-than-life myth of "Red Emma" to restore some of her human ambivalences and vulnerabilities in this biography which covers the entire period of Goldman's life, and quotes extensively from her unpublished correspondence. Alice Wexler's recent biography, *Emma Goldman: An Intimate Life* (Pantheon Books, 1984), delves into the Reitman correspondence and many other sources to trace Goldman's evolution as an American radical, demonstrating that the public image she projected oversimplified aspects of her political outlook as well as details of her private life. Wexler's study concludes in 1919 with Goldman's deportation. Readers seeking a more complex understanding of Goldman's political thought can now also turn to *Vision on Fire* (Commonground Press, 1983), a collection of her writings on the Spanish Civil War edited by David Porter. Finally, Alix Kates Shulman has published a new edition of her book *Red Emma Speaks: An Emma Goldman Reader* (1972; Schocken Books, 1983), with three additional Goldman essays and a new introduction by Shulman on Goldman's feminism.

144.*   Field, Andrew. **Djuna: The Life and Times of Djuna Barnes.** New York: Putnam, 1983. 287p. bibliog. index. LC 82-24140. ISBN 0399127402.

Djuna Barnes is most famous for her innovative novel *Nightwood,* a work that came out of her experience as a member of the expatriate artistic community in Europe of the twenties and thirties. Yet Barnes never achieved the fame of such peers as T. S. Eliot or James Joyce, and spent forty years as an impoverished recluse in Greenwich Village before her death in 1982. In this critical biography, Field concentrates on Barnes's childhood and early career, stressing particularly her relationship with her father and her love affair with artist Thelma Wood, which provided the basis for the lesbian relationship in *Nightwood.* Field also traces her influence on writers like Anaïs Nin and Carson McCullers. Although carefully researched, with an impressive bibliography, Field's work may prove difficult for the general reader on two counts. First, since the reclusive Barnes refused to cooperate with him, Field's accounts of her early life are often conjectural, even confusing. Second, his adopted "Barnesian" style, mixing chronological narrative, literary analysis, and flashbacks, is occasionally hard to follow. Responding to the recent resurgence of interest in Barnes, publishers have begun to issue some of her out-of-print or previously unpublished works: *Selected Works* (1962; repr. Farrar, Straus, Giroux, 1980), which includes, along with *Nightwood*, a verse drama and nine short stories; *Creatures in an Alphabet* (Dial Press, 1982), a collection of verse; *Interviews* edited by Alyce Barry (Sun and Moon Press, 1985), Barnes's "impressionistic encounters" with such contemporaries as Mother Jones; and *Smoke, and Other Early Stories* (Sun and Moon Press, 1982).

145.   First, Ruth, and Ann Scott, 1950- . **Olive Schreiner.** New York: Schocken Books, 1980. 383p. bibliog. index. $20.00. LC 80-13190. ISBN 0805237496.

Olive Schreiner (1855-1920) used the fact of her celebrity to escape the conventional role of colonial woman and wife. Her revisionist biographers, working from the writer's letters and notebooks, conclude that she paid a great price. Schreiner was apparently lonely, she suffered from asthma, and she was tortured by her slow literary production. Further, she felt alienated both in South Africa, the country that inspired her best-known fiction, and in London, the center of her intellectual life. Schreiner was unable to reconcile "sexual friendship" with intellectual friendship; her marriage remained childless and seemingly unfulfilling. The "woman question" was the predominant intellectual issue with which she struggled. Like many of her generation, she recognized the virtual servitude of blacks in South Africa, but debate about white supremacy and "native" equality was only beginning to heat up at the time of her death. Joyce Avrech Berkman's *Olive Schreiner: Feminism on the Frontier* (Eden Press Women's Publications, 1979) addresses Schreiner's work with some of these same themes in mind.

146.   Fisher, M. F. K. (Mary Frances Kennedy), 1908- . **Among Friends.** San Francisco: North Point Press, 1983. 306p. pbk. $10.00. LC 83-061393. ISBN 0865471169.

This is a delightful memoir by an author best known for her volumes on food and drink. In a series of vivid, humorous sketches, Fisher depicts her childhood in Whittier, California from 1912 to 1922. At first glance, *Among Friends* seems a scattershot collection of nostalgic anecdotes about a more innocent time. Yet there is a darker side to this world: the title refers to the status of the author's family, Irish Episcopalians who were permanent outsiders in an overwhelmingly Quaker town. Fisher's opening essay describes Whittier's polite ostracism of non-Quakers—in forty years' residence, Fisher never set foot inside a Friend's home. In addition, her descriptions of the ghettoizing of Mexican servants outside the city limits, of the town's taboo against blacks, and of its prejudice against German-Americans during World War I raise broader issues of environment, social conditioning, and tolerance. Readers entranced by Fisher's graceful, witty prose may wish to read her autobiography, *As They Were* (Knopf, 1982); *Not Now But Now* (Viking Press, 1982), a reprint of a 1947 novel with a lesbian element; and *Sister Age* (Knopf, 1983), a collection of fifteen sensitive short stories about growing old.

147. Fitch, Noel Riley. **Sylvia Beach and the Lost Generation: A History of Literary Paris in the Twenties and Thirties.** New York: Norton, 1983. 447p. bibliog. index. $25.00. LC 82-24621. ISBN 0393017133.

Daughter of a Princeton minister and his dissatisfied spouse, Sylvia Beach (1887-1962) proclaimed that her three loves were Adrienne Monnier, her lifelong companion from 1918; James Joyce, whose *Ulysses* she published in 1922; and her bookstore, Shakespeare and Company, the hangout of Hemingway, Joyce, and Gide, and a veritable hub of modernist literary activity in the 1920s. Fitch sketches Beach as victim/handmaiden of the men whose careers she advanced with maternal solicitude. Because Fitch shies away from exploring in any depth Beach's private life, preferring to dwell on her adoration of Joyce's literary powers, the readers comes away from this work with a feeling that something vital is missing. Beach's autobiography (1959), together with Fitch's well-documented account, might serve as a starting point for a more feminist analysis of Beach's complexity.

148. Frame, Janet. **An Angel At My Table: An Autobiography, Volume Two.** New York: Braziller, 1984. 195p. $12.95. LC 85-158468. ISBN 0807610429.

The first volume of Janet Frame's autobiography, *To the Is-Land* (Braziller, 1982), portrayed the happy world of her New Zealand childhood. The second volume moves on to her maturation as a writer during the 1940s and 1950s. Frame tells of the grim years of teacher training, novice writing efforts, residence in cramped and unattractive lodgings, and the tragedy of premature deaths in the family. Attempts to conform and to efface herself appear to have been behind an attempted suicide and nervous collapse in her early twenties. During forced hospitalizations, Frame was diagnosed as hopelessly schizophrenic and narrowly escaped a frontal lobotomy by winning a literary prize. Retreating into herself, she continued to write while supporting herself at menial jobs until another writer intervened and acted as mentor. In the third volume of her autobiography, *The Envoy From Mirror City* (Braziller, 1986), Frame chronicles her subsequent travels and literary growth in England and Europe. She brings to her autobiography the same lyrical gifts that distinguish her novels, the most recent of which is *Living in the Maniototo* (Braziller, 1979), a story about a woman of multiple personalities.

149. Fraser, Nicholas, 1948- , and Marysa Navarro. **Eva Perón.** New York: Norton, 1980. 192p. bibliog. index. $17.95. LC 80-29148. ISBN 0393014576.

In Fraser and Navarro's view, most writings about the mythic Eva Perón are "propaganda in the guise of biography." Their aim is to separate fact from fiction in this account based on over one hundred interviews. An actress of humble (and illegitimate) birth, Eva Perón rose to prominence in the late 1940s as an advocate for the poor, and as what some have seen as the power behind Juan Perón's presidency. She was also responsible for gaining the suffrage for Argentinian women. Her death from cancer in 1952 at the age of thirty-three intensified the adulation accorded her by the Peronist movement, such that when Juan Perón returned triumphantly to Argentina in 1973 after eighteen years in exile, it was to cries of "Evita lives!" Julie M. Taylor also analyzes the many Evita myths and their relation to Argentinian concepts of "feminine" nature in her work *Eva Perón: The Myths of a Woman* (University of Chicago Press, 1979).

150. Fuller, Margaret, 1810-1850. **The Letters of Margaret Fuller.** Edited by Robert N. Hudspeth. Ithaca, NY: Cornell University Press. 3v. bibliog. index. LC 82-22098. Vol. 1: 1983; $25.00; ISBN 0801413869. Vol. 2: 1983; $25.00; ISBN 0801415756. Vol. 3: 1984; $25.00; ISBN 0801417074.

Robert N. Hudspeth's scholarly edition of Margaret Fuller's letters is long overdue. Anticipated to run to six volumes, the complete set will make available all known letters by Fuller from 1817 through 1850. The letters represent a rich source for the recovery of Fuller's authentic personality and talents, often distorted and maligned by her contemporaries. A prolific literary critic, the first editor of *Dial*, an associate of many luminaries of her day, and author of many works, including *Woman in the Nineteenth Century* (1845), Fuller was in Hudspeth's estimation "America's most accomplished woman of letters" (p.51). Yet Hudspeth contends that she "left no masterpiece" (p.51). Some feminist critics are harshly critical of Hudspeth's assessment, among them Marie Mitchell Olesen Urbanski, who, in *Margaret Fuller's Woman in the Nineteenth Century* (Greenwood Press, 1980), deems Fuller's famous theoretical work "the intellectual foundation of the feminist movement" (p.3). In *The Achievement of Margaret Fuller* (Pennsylvania State University Press, 1979), Margaret Vanderhaar Allen engages, like Urbanski, in an effort to wrest the real Fuller from the grasp of early, denigrating contemporaries. Joel Myerson's *Critical Essays on Margaret Fuller* (Twayne, 1980) reprints reviews and essays from both the nineteenth and twentieth centuries, along with an overview of sources by Myerson and a new essay by Urbanski.

151. Gérin, Winifred. **Anne Thackeray Ritchie: A Biography.** Oxford: Oxford University Press, 1981. 310p. bibliog. index. $32.50. LC 80-49704. ISBN 0198126646.

Gérin writes an impressively researched biography of the daughter of William Makepeace Thackeray, Anne Thackeray Ritchie (1837-1919). Ritchie's literary project consisted in bringing out the collected thirteen-volume edition of her father's works and writing biographical introductions. Among the prominent literati of the day whom she counted as friends were Dickens, Tennyson, Henry James, and the Brownings. To her niece, Virginia Woolf, she was a marvel, dedicated to literary work at a time when most women confined themselves to more domestic routines. This biography illumines what Woolf admired in her aunt, who Woolf immortalized in her own novel *Night and Day* (1919).

152. Ginzburg, Eugenia Semenovna. **Within the Whirlwind.** New York: Harcourt, Brace, Jovanovich, 1981. 423p. $17.50. LC 80-8748. ISBN 0151975175.

A university teacher and loyal Communist Party member, Ginzburg was arrested by the secret police during the Stalinist purge of the late 1930s. Inexplicably she was charged with terrorism. Ginzburg's first book, *Journey into the Whirlwind* (1967), gives an account of the years between the assassination of S. M. Kirov in 1934 and her own arrest and imprisonment (1939). The present volume takes the reader into the world of Siberian slave labor camps, where Ginzburg was detained for eighteen years, separated from her two children and husband. Ginzburg's life on the prison-archipelago, familiar to readers of Solzhenitsyn's *Gulag Archipelago*, is, at its core, a journey of the soul—a nightmare of nameless terrors. Memories, poetry, and the hope of publishing the chronicle of her experiences in the camps sustain her. Released from prison for "rehabilitation" in 1955, Ginzburg died in 1977 while still in the process of reworking her reflections into this narrative and arranging for its publication.

153. Givner, Joan, 1936- . **Katherine Anne Porter: A Life.** New York: Simon and Schuster, 1982. 572p. bibliog. index. $19.95. LC 82-10626. ISBN 0671432079.

Givner seems to view Porter's life as cohering only if her fiction is read in the light of her life history, and vice versa. Though Givner interviewed Porter extensively before the latter's death in 1980 at the age of ninety, some reviewers have suggested that the biography is reductive and possibly not the definitive portrait of Porter. The author of *Ship of Fools* enjoyed a successful career as a writer. Yet she appears in Givner's work not so much as a woman of letters, but rather as a woman of exaggerated vanity, fixed on male attention, possessions, and childish gratifications. According to this account, Porter devoted herself to the literary project of fabricating her background and rewriting the misfortunes of a life marked by its share of human tragedy, failed marriages, romances, and—toward the end—ill health and senility. Enrique Hank Lopez's *Conversations with Katherine Anne Porter* (Little, Brown) appeared in 1981, also to mixed reviews. Recent critical works underscoring Porter's stature as an American writer include Jane Krause DeMouy's *Katherine Anne Porter's Women: The Eye of Her Fiction* (University of Texas Press, 1983), Robert Penn Warren's *Katherine Anne Porter: A Collection of Critical Essays* (Prentice-Hall, 1979), and Darlene Harbour Unrue's *Truth and Vision in Katherine Anne Porter's Fiction* (University of Georgia Press, 1985).

154. Glendinning, Victoria. **Edith Sitwell: A Unicorn Among Lions.** New York: Knopf, 1981. 393p. bibliog. index. $17.95. LC 80-2721. ISBN 0394504399.

Glendinning's biography of Sitwell (1887-1964) has received uniformly high marks. Sitwell comes off as an eccentric woman, passionate about her poetry and the modernist circle of artists in which she moved during the 1920s. Glendinning reengages the reader in the debate about whether Sitwell was a literary genius or merely a flamboyant, somewhat freakish literary personality. Glendinning's work poses important questions about the marginalization of women's writing, literary canonization, and the function of biography in creating a literary persona.

155.* Goreau, Angeline. **Reconstructing Aphra: A Social Biography of Aphra Behn.** New York: Dial Press, 1980. 339p. bibliog. index. $14.95. LC 80-11495. ISBN 0803774788.

Reconstructing Aphra documents the struggles of Aphra Behn (1640-1689) as a feminist and literary woman. Goreau's carefully researched account narrates the fascinating events of Behn's life. She was involved in a slave rebellion in the West Indies; worked as a spy for Charles II; spent time in debtor's prison; and was notorious as a political activist, abolitionist, and champion of sexual freedom. Behn emerges as a woman torn between a desire for independence and a need for love and social approval. Mary Ann O'Donnell's *Aphra Behn: An Annotated Bibliography of Primary and Secondary Sources* (Garland, 1986) corrects the many errors that have plagued earlier bibliographies of Behn's works, from confused titles and unidentified editions to misattributed works. O'Donnell includes a descriptive list of Behn's works published to 1700, and a definitive list of editions of her writings to 1980. Her secondary section records works from the seventeenth century to 1980.

156. Hellman, Lillian. **Maybe: A Story.** Boston: Little, Brown, 1980. 106p. $9.95. LC 80-11324. ISBN 0316355127.

Maybe straddles both "story" and memoir: although the ostensible protagonist is the author's longtime acquaintance Sarah Cameron, Hellman and her husband Dashiell Hammett are major figures in the story. The growth in Hellman's literary reputation is indicated by the recent upsurge in criticism and bibliographies about her, including *Lillian*

Hellman: An Annotated Bibliography, by Stephen H. Bills (Garland, 1979), and *Lillian Hellman, Plays, Films, Memoirs: A Reference Guide,* by Pulitzer-Prize winning biographer Mark W. Estrin (G. K. Hall, 1980). Bills's entries are divided by subject and format: biographical material; news articles and interviews; reviews of plays, screenplays, and autobiographies; scholarly books and articles; and graduate studies. Estrin's entries are arranged chronologically, allowing the reader to discern the fluctuations in Hellman's reputation through the years. Still, although his annotations are fuller than Bills's, Estrin's organization may make it difficult for the reader to locate reviews of specific works.

157. Hillesum, Etty, 1914-1943. **An Interrupted Life: The Diaries of Etty Hillesum, 1941-1943.** New York: Pantheon Books, 1983. 226p. $13.45. LC 83-47750. ISBN 0394532171.

Etty Hillesum, a Dutch Jewish student in her late twenties, began her highly acclaimed diary as part of a larger project of self-examination. The diary covers the period from 1941 to 1942, during which Nazi persecution of Dutch Jews escalated to regular deportations to the concentration camps. Yet, as J. G. Gaarlandt writes in his introduction, "Etty's diary is in the first place a journey through her inner world" (p.xi), recording her therapy and love affair with a Jungian "psychochirologist," her readings, her growing spirituality. Although she was apparently in contact with the resistance, Hillesum's response to the mounting threat was not that of an activist. Yet, she did refuse to hide or escape, or to accept any exemption. She chose to accompany the first transport of Jews to Westerbork, a deportation center, and was herself finally transported to Auschwitz, dying there on November 30, 1943. The diary, which ends October 13, 1942, is supplemented by several of Hillesum's letters from Westerbork.

158. Johnson, Joyce, 1935- . **Minor Characters.** Boston: Houghton Mifflin, 1983. 262p. $13.95. LC 82-12185. ISBN 0395325137.

The romance of the fifties Beat Generation has come down to us through the writings of Jack Kerouac, Allen Ginsberg, William Burroughs, and others; the scenes they help us to imagine are peopled most prominently by men. Johnson, who became Kerouac's lover at the age of twenty-one, tells her own story and those of some of the other women who were "minor characters" in the beat drama. It is an ambivalent retrospective view. Remembering herself at the age of twenty-two (then Joyce Glassman) — in black beat uniform, sitting at the edge of the circle of men — Johnson concludes that she does not want to let go of that young girl's sense of expectancy: "It's only her silence that I wish finally to give up ..." (p.262).

159. Kaledin, Eugenia. **The Education of Mrs. Henry Adams.** Philadelphia: Temple University Press, 1981. 306p. bibliog. index. $29.95. LC 81-9431. ISBN 0877222304.

In this feminist biography, Kaledin attempts to sort out the many elements of Marian Hooper Adams's personality and her marital relationship, as well as her relationship to her time (1843-1885). The daughter of Ellen Sturgis Hooper, a poet, and Dr. Robert Hooper of Boston, Marian Hooper (known as "Clover") married a member of one of America's foremost families. The enigma of this talented woman's life to the modern biographer has been her suicide at age forty-three, an unexpected culmination to her apparently rich life as a friend of intellectuals and artists, and a gifted photographer in her own right. Oddly, there is no mention of her in *The Autobiography of Henry Adams,* an omission that is the more peculiar in that Henry Adams pleads in that work for a fairer representation of women in history. Kaledin explores the cultural and personal reasons for Clover's inability to achieve a place in her seemingly secure world.

160. Kikumura, Akemi, 1944- . **Through Harsh Winters: The Life of a Japanese Immigrant Woman.** Novato, CA: Chandler and Sharp, 1981. 157p. bibliog. $12.95. LC 81-15534. ISBN 0883165449.

An anthropologist, Kikumura recorded her mother's life history "out of respect and admiration" for Issei (first-generation Japanese immigrant) women (p.ix). The title is taken from a Japanese proverb — "Through harsh winters/Follow springs" — and her mother's story is indeed one of harsh struggle: years of farm labor, repeated childbearing, and an unstable marriage, followed by internment in the American concentration camps of World War II. Kikumura adds her own perspective on her mother's history in an epilogue, and brief essays on the acculturation of the Japanese-American family and her research methodology in the appendices.

161. Kohfeldt, Mary Lou. **Lady Gregory: The Woman Behind the Irish Renaissance.** New York: Atheneum, 1985. 366p. bibliog. index. $19.95. LC 84-45044. ISBN 0689114869.

Although best known as a founder of the Abbey Theatre and for her association with W. B. Yeats and other Irish writers and intellectuals, Lady Augusta Gregory (1852-1932) was also a successful playwright. Kohfeldt's biography situates Lady Gregory's life and her development as a writer in the context of Irish history and social structure. Raised to be a dutiful daughter and wife, Lady Gregory did not start her public career until the age of forty, after her husband's death. She edited books on her husband's family, began her relationship with Yeats, and ultimately started writing comedies and patriotic plays. Kohfeldt discusses the plays in the context of Gregory's life and beliefs. In *Lady Gregory: An Annotated Bibliography of Criticism* (Whitson, 1982), E. H. Mikhail aims for a complete listing of works of criticism on Lady Gregory up to 1979. Divided into three sections — "Bibliographies," "Reviews of Published Books," and "Criticism on Lady Gregory" this volume includes very brief, descriptive scope notes.

162. Lamb, Patricia Frazer, and Kathryn Joyce Hohlwein. **Touchstones: Letters Between Two Women, 1953-1964.** New York: Harper and Row, 1983. 330p. $14.37. LC 81-47662. ISBN 0060149426.

Friends at the University of Utah during the fifties, when they left in 1953 Lamb and Hohlwein vowed to stay in touch. This they did, though their marriages took them to different continents. Isolated, and married to rather uncommunicative men, they poured out their feelings, questions, and ideas on paper to each other. Thousands of miles apart, they were each other's primary support through pregnancies, miscarriages, motherhood, marital estrangement, and affairs. In time they each changed and outgrew their binding, conventional marriages. The correspondence they share in this book offers an extraordinary glimpse into the interior lives of women of their generation.

163. Langer, Elinor. **Josephine Herbst.** Boston: Little, Brown, 1984. 374p. bibliog. index. $19.95. LC 83-2910. ISBN 0316513997.

Josephine Herbst (1892-1969) entered the exciting literary scene of post-World War I New York straight from Sioux Falls. Beginning her career under Mencken, Herbst married and published her first novels during the 1920s. Her trilogy — *Pity Is Not Enough* (1933), *The Executioner Waits* (1934), *Rope of Gold* (1939) — was highly regarded but has since been forgotten. During the thirties, Herbst went to Europe as a correspondent covering Paris and the break-up of the Weimar Republic, visited the Soviet Union, covered the Scottsboro case for the *New Masses,* and was one of the few women correspondents at the front during the Spanish Civil War. She was committed to the significant radical movements of the times. When anti-communism swept through the United States in the 1950s, it carried radical writers like Herbst into obscurity or worse. In her later years, Herbst was to write to friends that her "vital life" came to a halt after Spain; yet she remained committed to social protest. With the resurgence of interest in Herbst because of Langer's biography and the newly reprinted *Rope of Gold* (Feminist Press, 1984) comes a concise critical study by Winifred Bevilacqua entitled *Josephine Herbst* (Twayne, 1985).

164. Lash, Joseph P., 1909- . **Helen and Teacher: The Story of Helen Keller and Anne Sullivan Macy.** New York: Delacorte Press/Seymour Lawrence, 1980. 811p. $17.95. LC 79-25599. ISBN 0440036542.

Lash's work draws on the Helen Keller archives of the American Federation for the Blind to document the extraordinary partnership between Keller (1880-1968) and Anne Sullivan (1866-1936). The result is a fresh interpretation of Sullivan's role as teacher and friend of the gifted Keller. The biography opens in Boston at the Perkins Institution for the Blind, where Sullivan was admitted as a student in 1880, a refugee from a poorhouse. Sullivan moved to Tuscumbia, Alabama in 1887, where she took on her first and only pupil—the deaf, dumb, and blind Keller, then seven years old. Her success in breaking through to Keller, and Keller's response to "Teacher," initiated the unusual career these women were to share—traveling, living, lecturing, learning together—a career promoted by Sullivan and other leading intellectuals of the day. In exploring problems in the relationship (in particular what he terms "The Extraordinary Triangle" of Sullivan, Keller, and Sullivan's husband, John Macy), Lash addresses the conflicts arising from these women's dependency on each other, and illumines the complexity of their shared daily life.

165. Lash, Joseph P., 1909- . **Love, Eleanor: Eleanor Roosevelt and Her Friends.** Garden City, NY: Doubleday, 1982. 534p. bibliog. index. $19.95. LC 81-43383. ISBN 038517053X.

Doris Faber's biography of Roosevelt's friend Lorena Hickok (see entry 142) brings to light correspondence that suggests their relationship was intimate and very likely lesbian in character. In this volume, Lash—ER's official biographer—presents additional correspondence, striving to prove that "Hick" was only one woman in ER's circle of intimate friends, friends to whom she used "expressions of endearment as passionate as those to be found in the Hickok correspondence, equally open to many interpretations, equally suggestive, in some cases, of a physical relationship" (p.x). Lash interprets ER as a passionate woman, engulfed in a loveless marriage, who may have been drawn to other men and women, but who "disciplined" such longings by pouring herself into public service. *Mother and Daughter: The Letters of Eleanor and Anna Roosevelt* (Coward, McCann and Geoghegan, 1982), edited by Bernard Asbell, reveals another Eleanor Roosevelt. In ER's warm, epistolary style, we see a supportive, maternal, but extremely busy woman responding sometimes anxiously, many times hurriedly to her only daughter, Anna (1906-1975). That ER has come to be recognized as a perceptive prophet of our time reflects itself in the increasing appeal of her life to a mass audience. Rhoda Lerman's well-received *Eleanor: A Novel* (Holt, Rinehart and Winston, 1979) takes up ER's life from 1918 to 1921, years that saw her metamorphosis from socialite wife to committed public figure. ER's own autobiography, originally published in 1961, was reissued in 1984 by G. K. Hall. The release of Joseph Lash's two latest books was timed to coincide with the one hundredth anniversary of ER's birth. *A World of Love: Eleanor Roosevelt and Her Friends, 1943-1962* (Doubleday, 1984) is a second collection of ER's correspondence; *"Life Was Meant to Be Lived"* (Norton, 1984) is a "centenary portrait" with photographs.

Another centennial volume is *Without Precedent: The Life and Career of Eleanor Roosevelt*, edited by Joan Hoff-Wilson and Marjorie Lightman (Indiana University Press, 1984), a collection of essays by William H. Chafe, Susan Ware, Blanche Wiesen Cook, Tamara K. Hareven, and Lois Scharf, among others.

166. Longuet, Jenny Marx, 1844-1883, and Laura Marx La Fargue, 1845-1911. **The Daughters of Karl Marx: Family Correspondence 1866-1898.** Edited by Olga Meier. New York: Harcourt, Brace, Jovanovich, 1982. 342p. index. $19.95. LC 81-47302. ISBN 0151239711.

Eleanor Marx (1855-1898) has gained recognition in our day for her political and intellectual accomplishments. These letters help to rescue from obscurity the lives of her sisters. Jenny and Laura were, like Eleanor, thoughtful, politically committed women. Unlike Eleanor, however, they were also mothers, and remarkably articulate about the struggle this entailed. At home with young children, Jenny wrote to Laura in 1882: "... I hear and see nothing but the baker and butcher and cheesemonger and greengrocer. I do believe that even the dull routine of factory work is not more killing than are the endless duties of the *ménage*" (p.152). The letters mix the humdrum stuff of everyday domestic life with news and opinion on major political developments. While there is abundant suffering recorded in these pages, there is also ample affection, playfulness, and intimacy. Olga Meier, editor of the French edition, provides commentary and notes, supplemented by those of translator Faith Evans. Sheila Rowbotham's introduction places the correspondence in historical—and feminist—context.

167. Luxemburg, Rosa, 1870-1919. **Comrade and Lover: Rosa Luxemburg's Letters to Leo Jogiches.** Edited by Elzbieta Ettinger. Cambridge, MA: MIT Press, 1979. 206p. bibliog. index. $20.00. LC 79-9327. ISBN 0262050218.

"My Dear! I've been very angry with you.... Your letters contain *nothing, but nothing* except for *The Workers' Cause*, criticism of what I have done, and instructions about what I should do.... I want you to write me about your personal life. But not a single word!" (pp.7-8). Thus opens the second letter in this collection of Luxemburg's correspondence with her lover of fifteen years, Leo Jogiches. Though Jogiches and Luxemburg were also close political comrades, editor and translator Elzbieta Ettinger elects to restrict this volume to letters that illuminate their personal attachment. Luxemburg wanted a life of both political purpose and personal happiness, while Jogiches was more single-minded in his political commitment. This conflict runs through the letters, as do tensions over Luxemburg's growing prominence within the German Social Democratic Party. A selection of Luxemburg's more political letters to Jogiches and others can be found in *The Letters of Rosa Luxemburg* (Westview Press, 1978), edited by Stephen Eric Bronner. *Rosa Luxemburg, Women's Liberation, and Marx's Philosophy of Revolution* (Humanities Press, 1982), by Raya Dunayevskaya, is a serious and demanding theoretical assessment of Luxemburg's thought.

168. McCunn, Ruthanne Lum. **Thousand Pieces of Gold: A Biographical Novel.** San Francisco: Design Enterprises of San Francisco, 1981. 308p. $10.95. LC 81-68270. ISBN 093253807X.

The story of the Chinese-American pioneer woman deserves to be heard. McCunn's biographical novel chronicles the life of Lalu Nathoy (known as Polly Bemis). Sold in China by her father during a famine in the 1870s for two bags of soybeans—symbolically his daughter was his "thousand pieces of gold"—Lalu/Polly undergoes many humiliations in China and in America, including concubinage, before she finds a life of stability and fulfillment with a rugged settler named Bemis on an Idaho homestead.

169. McNaron, Toni A. H., ed. **The Sister Bond: A Feminist View of a Timeless Connection.** New York: Pergamon Press, 1985. 134p. index. $19.50. LC 85-3477. ISBN 0080323677.

Although feminists often interpret the word *sister* very broadly, McNaron limits its usage here to blood ties, noting that she found almost no literature on the subject. Most of the articles she gathers in this volume examine the relationships between well-known historical figures and their sisters: Grace and Edith Abbott; Christina and Maria Rossetti; Frances Wright D'Arusmont and Camilla Wright; Jane and Cassandra Austen; Florence and Parthenope Nightingale; Emily, Lavinia, and Susan Gilbert Dickinson; Virginia Woolf and Vanessa Bell. An additional essay analyzes poems by Denise Levertov and Adrienne Rich that focus on their sisters. In the final chapter, McNaron briefly reports the results of a small survey she conducted on contemporary women's relationships with their sisters.

170. Mebane, Mary E., 1933- . **Mary.** New York: Viking Press, 1981. 242p. $12.95. LC 80-51999. ISBN 0670459380.

Mary has been hailed as an exemplary work in contemporary black autobiography. In writing of her childhood in rural North Carolina during the thirties, Mebane confronts the self-hatred that is born of segregation in "the white world, the world that I had been taught was my implacable enemy" (p.242). *Mary, the Wayfarer* (Viking Press, 1983) continues Mebane's story, as she moves away from her rural roots to teach in Durham and elsewhere. Mebane chronicles a life of extraordinary efforts and achievements. Deftly she brings together the disparate elements of her life in the 1960s, set against the fear and exhilaration of the Civil Rights Movement gaining momentum in the South. In the final pages of the autobiography, Mebane survives rape, family violence, and her mother's death as she also attains her first literary successes. Her writing, she tells us, has saved her.

171. Menchú, Rigoberta. **I, Rigoberta Menchú: An Indian Woman in Guatemala.** Edited by Elisabeth Burgos-Debray. London: Verso; distr. New York: Schocken Books, 1984. 251p. bibliog. $19.50. ISBN 0860910830.

This is an extraordinary book, the personal testimony of a Guatemalan Quiché Indian woman, recorded and edited by a Venezuelan anthropologist living in Paris. Only twenty-three years old at the time of this narrative, Menchú had already survived unimaginable suffering—not just the poverty, malnutrition, and discrimination facing Indians in North and South America, but also the gruesome deaths of several family members at the hands of an army intent on weeding out "communists" and pacifying the indigenous population. Menchú mixes detailed description of the traditions of her people with her own history. She speaks directly to the question of women's experience at many points, perhaps most movingly in the chapter entitled "Women and political commitment: Rigoberta renounces marriage and motherhood." In *The Triple Struggle: Latin American Peasant Women* (South End Press, 1982), Audrey Bronstein presents the testimony of peasant women (mostly indigenous) from Ecuador, Bolivia, Peru, El Salvador, and Guatemala, prefaced by background information on each country. Recurrent themes are the inevitability of marriage and motherhood, poverty, lack of access to birth control (and health care in general), and the burdens of work.

172. Miller, William D., 1916- . **Dorothy Day: A Biography.** San Francisco: Harper and Row, 1982. 527p. index. pbk. $10.53. LC 81-47428. ISBN 0060657499.

Using Dorothy Day's published books, the *Catholic Worker* archives at Marquette University, and personal papers turned over to him in 1975, Miller has written a careful, very readable account of the long and unusual life of Dorothy Day (1897-1980)—Catholic convert, labor radical, pacifist, prime mover in the Catholic Worker movement, philosopher, and writer. It is problematic to see Day as a feminist, if we are to rely on her own words in a letter to a Catholic nun: "Another grotesque and horrible misery [has descended] ... on me—two of the ... women associated with our movement have come to proclaim themselves as lesbians. Scripture—St. Paul's writings—no attention is paid to that. It is 'women's lib.' And I am just not 'with it' any more, and you can imagine the desolation I feel" (p.502). A traditionalist in matters sexual in her advancing age, Dorothy Day suffered through a number of difficult relationships during the 1920s, underwent an abortion at twenty-two, and bore a daughter in common-law marriage—all this before her conversion to Catholicism. But Miller chooses not to address this paradox. In *By Little and By Little* (Knopf, 1983), Robert Ellsberg presents selections from Day's six books, her columns in *The Catholic Worker,* and other publications that reveal her passionately felt religious and social beliefs. A new reference work, *Dorothy Day and the Catholic Worker: A Bibliographical Index,* by Anne Klejment and Alice Klejment (Garland, 1986), will direct the researcher to additional works by and about Day.

173.   Modell, Judith Schachter, 1941-   . **Ruth Benedict: Patterns of a Life.** Philadelphia: University of Pennsylvania Press, 1983. 355p. bibliog. index. $30.00. LC 82-21989. ISBN 0812278747.

Modell, a feminist and an anthropologist, provides us with the first book about this foremother of anthropology since the publication in 1959 of *An Anthropologist at Work*, edited by Benedict's protégée and intimate friend, Margaret Mead. It is both an intellectual and a personal portrait that emerges from these pages. Benedict (1887-1948) came to anthropology relatively late and quite by chance, after having struggled unsuccessfully to have children and find satisfaction with her marriage. In her poetry and her journal, she recorded her efforts to make sense of her life as a woman. Having found a calling in anthropology, Benedict joined with her mentor, Franz Boas, and later her own student, Margaret Mead, to launch pioneering studies of the impact of culture on human behavior.

174.   Morgan, Janet P. **Agatha Christie: A Biography.** New York: Knopf, 1985. 393p. index. $18.95. LC 84-48678. ISBN 039452554X.

There are many biographies of Agatha Christie (1890-1976). Morgan's qualifies as the "official" biography, inasmuch as she was invited to write it by Christie's daughter and was given full access to all of Christie's manuscripts and personal papers. Despite the family's cooperative involvement, the work has been praised for its independent judgment. Morgan reveals Christie as a woman of vulnerability who greatly valued her privacy, and she uncovers the true story of what happened when Christie mysteriously disappeared in 1926. By any count, Agatha Christie's detective novels enjoy a vast readership. (Her competitors are the Bible and Shakespeare.) So it is not surprising to note the growth of secondary literature on her work. Yet, it is difficult to locate solid criticism, especially feminist criticism. The bibliography of Christie's primary and secondary works compiled by Louise Barnard is the most valuable segment of *A Talent to Deceive: An Appreciation of Agatha Christie,* by Robert Barnard (Dodd, Mead, 1980). Dennis Sanders and Len Lovallo's *The Agatha Christie Companion* (Delacorte Press, 1984) gives the Christie buff everything she wants to know and more (including the plot) about the ninety-five books Christie published during her lifetime. Russell H. Fitzgibbon approaches Christie from a popular culture perspective in his *Agatha Christie Companion* (Bowling Green State University Popular Press, 1980).

175. Mossiker, Frances. **Madame de Sévigné: A Life and Letters.** New York: Knopf, 1983. 538p. bibliog. index. $22.95. LC 83-47781. ISBN 0394414721.

Mossiker draws heavily on the extensive correspondence of Madame de Sévigné (1626-1696) with her daughter in writing this biographical study. In the preface, Mossiker acknowledges her debt "to the generations of Sévigné scholars who have built up the vast bibliography which enshrines her ..." (p.xiv), but asserts that not everything has been said about this remarkable observer of the court life of seventeenth-century France. Although conveying the famous wit and felicity of style that have made Sévigné "France's First Lady of Letters," Mossiker's selection of letters concentrates in large part on the unusually intense mother-daughter relationship, and highlights Sévigné's protofeminist character. The biography has been praised as the first in English to do justice to Madame de Sévigné.

176. Moynihan, Ruth Barnes. **Rebel for Rights: Abigail Scott Duniway.** New Haven, CT: Yale University Press, 1983. 273p. bibliog. index. $25.00. LC 83-1142. ISBN 0300029527.

Biographies of individual leaders in the frontier suffrage movement have begun to appear only recently. Abigail Scott Duniway (1834-1915), an emigrant from Illinois to Oregon during the 1850s, came to feminism from the hard experiences of a frontier wife entrapped in an unsatisfactory marriage and a life of unrelenting farm work and pregnancy. She began by writing didactic and heavily autobiographical stories and novels, and later launched her own newspaper. The *New Northwest* campaigned for suffrage but against prohibition, and addressed the experiences of frontier women from a feminist slant. Duniway's career as a writer, publisher, and tireless lecturer on women's rights on the frontier is a study in feminist issues and strategies that contrast sharply with those of her more "civilized" Eastern sisters in the suffrage cause. Moynihan wisely allows the witty, stinging prose of Duniway to frequently punctuate her analysis.

177. Murasaki Shikibu, b.978? **Murasaki Shikibu: Her Diary and Poetic Memoirs.** Edited by Richard John Bowring. Princeton, NJ: Princeton University Press, 1982. 290p. bibliog. index. $29.00. LC 81-47908. ISBN 0691065071.

This translation is of interest both as a record of the life of the great Japanese writer Murasaki Shikibu (c.1000), author of the *Tale of Genji,* and as an excellent example of a female diary from the Heian era. As translator Richard Bowring remarks, these were polished works of art: unlike men's diaries, which consisted of a series of daily entries, women's diaries comprised "records of memorable scenes interspersed with personal reflections recollected later" (p.19). Lady Murasaki served in the court of the Japanese empress, and her diary includes astute observations on life in the imperial palace. Although many of Bowring's extensive notes will interest only the advanced scholar, his format—with translation and notes on facing pages—is most convenient. The text is supplemented by a biographical sketch, along with illustrations, appendices, indexes, and a bibliography. The volume also includes a translation of Lady Murasaki's purported poetic memoirs.

178. O'Connor, Flannery, 1925-1964. **The Habit of Being: Letters.** Edited by Sally Fitzgerald. New York: Farrar, Straus, Giroux, 1979. 617p. index. $15.00. LC 78-11559. ISBN 0374167699.

In this selection of O'Connor's letters from 1948 to her death in 1964, the author's "habit of being" reveals itself in her examined Catholicism, her commitment to writing, and her attachment to the South. In the letters, she shares details of her circumscribed life in Milledgeville, Georgia, living on a farm with her mother, her beloved ducks, and the works of Catholic philosophers. "I have enough energy to write with and as that is all I have any business doing anyhow, I can with one eye squinted take it all as a blessing," she writes in March of 1953 (p.57). With her excellent ear for colorful conversation, she regales her friends in the East with amusing stories in dialect of life at the farm. Of her working habits, she cheerfully tells a friend two weeks before her death, "I'm still in bed, but I climb out of it into the typewriter about 2 hours every morning" (p.593). Robert Coles' *Flannery O'Connor's South* (Louisiana State University Press, 1980) compares O'Connor's regionalism to that of Frost, Jewett, and Hawthorne. In *Sacred Groves and Ravaged Gardens* (University of Georgia Press, 1985), Louise Hutchings Westling compares O'Connor to two other Southern women authors, Eudora Welty and Carson McCullers, focusing on their treatments of Southern womanhood. Melvin J. Friedman and Beverly Lyon Clark gather criticism from 1952 to the present in *Critical Essays on Flannery O'Connor* (G. K. Hall, 1985). David R. Farmer's *Flannery O'Connor: A Descriptive Bibliography* (Garland, 1981) attends to her work, biography, the growing body of criticism, translations, and film adaptations up to 1980. *The Flannery O'Connor Companion,* by James A. Grimshaw, Jr. (Greenwood Press, 1981), is useful for identifying characters and clustering stories by theme; Grimshaw takes an uninformed stance on issues of gender in O'Connor's work, however. In *Flannery O'Connor: Her Life, Library, and Book Reviews* (Edwin Mellen Press, 1980), Lorine H. Getz stresses O'Connor's literary theory as it appears in her book reviews. Getz has also written a thematic study of O'Connor's works, *Nature and Grace in Flannery O'Connor's Fiction* (Edwin Mellen Press, 1982).

179.* Olson, Stanley. **Elinor Wylie, a Life Apart: A Biography.** New York: Dial Press, 1979. 376p. bibliog. index. LC 78-15425. ISBN 0803723164.
    Wylie's comparatively short career as a novelist and poet has been overshadowed by a dramatic personal life that rivaled fiction itself. A Washington socialite with no literary ambitions, Wylie (1885-1928) shocked even herself when she left her first husband and child for a more attentive suitor. For this she was purged from the social register and ostracized from society at large in Washington, New York, and abroad. Miscarriages, madness, and family suicides stalked her. Invalidism was Wylie's method for coping with scandal until she left her second husband for William Rose Benét, a poet and literary critic who seriously encouraged her literary career from 1920 to 1928. Benét placed her work, solicited reviews, and effectively launched her career by introducing her to the New York literary scene of the twenties. "Her ability to convey lushness through austerity was startling" (p.184), judges her biographer. Judith Farr's analysis in *The Life and Art of Elinor Wylie* (Louisiana State University Press, 1983) finds feminist themes in both Wylie's life and her work.

180. Owen, Ursula, ed. **Fathers: Reflections by Daughters.** New York: Pantheon Books, 1985. 239p. $17.95. LC 84-22601. ISBN 0394539184.
    Contemporary literature is replete with women's searching meditations on their mothers. Fathers, on the other hand, have been the focus of more abstract analysis of their role within patriarchy. In the opinion of Ursula Owen, editor of this moving collection, there are strong taboos inhibiting daughters from recording their personal experiences with their fathers, reinforced by the pain women feel in confronting this "problematic bond, full of ambivalences and longings" (p.xi). Most of the contributors to this volume are writers, and although they are in no way a representative sample, their experiences are diverse. Mary Gordon acknowledges her lingering adoration of the father who died when she was seven, a man her adult self judges to have been either evil or mad. Adrienne Rich ponders the legacy left by a Jewish father who disavowed his Jewishness. Alice Walker confronts

the father—now dead—who never acknowledged that his daughter was a writer. Other contributions come from Grace Paley, Sheila Rowbotham, Alice Munro, Doris Lessing, and Sara Maitland, among others.

181.   Payne, Karen, ed. **Between Ourselves: Letters Between Mothers and Daughters, 1750-1982.** Boston: Houghton Mifflin, 1983. 416p. bibliog. index. $16.95. LC 83-10803. ISBN 0395339693.

Some of the letters in this collection have been published elsewhere—for example, the exchange between Anne Sexton and her daughters. Others, like Crystal Eastman's correspondence with her mother, appear to have been gathered from private collections. Mainly these women are familiar to us: Lady Wortley Montague representing the eighteenth century; Florence Nightingale, Susan B. Anthony, Queen Victoria, Calamity Jane, and Louisa May Alcott among the distinguished company of the nineteenth century. Less well known twentieth-century correspondents frequently are identified only by first name. Payne provides a brief historical essay and organizes the letters around broad themes: lesbianism, politics, death, children, reconciliation. *The Lost Tradition: Mothers and Daughters in Literature* (Ungar, 1980), edited by Cathy N. Davidson and E. M. Broner, includes twenty-four essays on the mother-daughter bond in literature—from ancient Mesopotamian and Sumerian hymns to Maxine Hong Kingston's *The Woman Warrior*—plus a bibliography.

182.   Plath, Sylvia, 1932-1963. **The Journals of Sylvia Plath.** Edited by Ted Hughes and Frances McCullough. New York: Dial Press, 1982. 370p. index. $16.95. LC 81-19435. ISBN 0385272237.

The publication of these journal excerpts came twenty years after Plath's 1963 suicide at the age of thirty. While her poetry is well known—*The Collected Poems,* edited by former husband and fellow poet Ted Hughes (Harper and Row, 1981), won the Pulitzer Prize in 1982—the journals are new material to most readers. Entries cover the period from the early fifties, when Plath was at Smith College, to her final years in England (1960-1962), when she achieved her greatest literary productivity despite the birth of two chidren and the breakup of her marriage. Even with the omissions—Hughes admits to destroying Plath's last journal—this is an intensely revealing portrait of the poet confronting the conflicting cultural messages of the period. *Ariel Ascending,* edited by Paul Alexander (Harper and Row, 1984), taps the best and most controversial of the voluminous literature about Plath. A harsh estimate of Plath by Joyce Carol Oates appears here, along with more favorable biographical and critical essays by Elizabeth Hardwick, A. Alvarez (Plath's biographer), Anne Sexton, and others. Essays in Gary Lane's *Sylvia Plath: New Views on the Poetry* (Johns Hopkins University Press, 1979) similarly reveal the fierce judgments that have settled on Plath's work, Hugh Kenner's perhaps the most scathing here, and Carole Ferrier's the most feminist. Jon Rosenblatt's *Sylvia Plath: The Poetry of Initiation* (University of North Carolina Press, 1979) warns against "views that emphasize Plath's feminism, her suicide, and her confessionalism," seeing these as "damaging to a clear and balanced reading of her work" (p.xii). Feminist critical work on Plath nonetheless grows apace. *Critical Essays on Sylvia Plath,* edited by Linda Wagner (G. K. Hall, 1984), makes a significant contribution to this new feminist criticism, with Sandra Gilbert among the essayists. In her book *Protean Poetic: The Poetry of Sylvia Plath* (University of Missouri Press, 1980), Mary Lynn Broe takes issue with "a generation of critics [who have] cramped [Plath's] full range with their cavalier use of political, psychological, and now anthropological labels" (p.191). A revisionist study that gives detailed readings of published and unpublished works, while attending to psychological and feminist issues in the Plath oeuvre, is *Plath's Incarnations: Women and the Creative Process,* by critic Lynda K. Bundtzen (University of Michigan Press, 1983).

183. Reich, Nancy B. **Clara Schumann: The Artist and the Woman.** Ithaca, NY: Cornell University Press, 1985. 346p. bibliog. index. $25.00. LC 84-45798. ISBN 0801417481.

No other woman musician has attracted the attention showered on Clara Schumann (1819-1896), virtuoso pianist, composer, teacher, and mother of eight children. Most earlier studies are hagiographic, casting Clara as saint or "priestess." Reich brings to this highly praised biography her expertise as a musicologist and a feminist perspective. Her research into new sources and her reappraisal of the old convinced her, she tells us, that Clara "is worthy of the truth" (p.9). Reich chooses an innovative form, presenting the chronological life in Part I, and developing themes from the life in Part II. Her treatment reveals Clara to have been not only the devoted and admiring wife of composer Robert Schumann, but also an ambitious woman in her own right, maintaining an active concert schedule between babies and her husband's episodes of mental illness. Joan Chissell's *Clara Schumann: A Dedicated Spirit* (Taplinger, 1983), though a less original interpretation, offers a solid introduction to the musician's life.

184. Rhys, Jean, 1890?-1979. **The Letters of Jean Rhys.** Edited by Francis Wyndham and Diana Melly. New York: Viking Press, 1984. 315p. index. $22.50. LC 83-40244. ISBN 0670427268.

Jean Rhys struggled in obscurity and poverty until the 1966 publication of her widely acclaimed novel *The Wide Sargasso Sea* made her famous at seventy-two. Rhys approved no biography before her death in 1979, and left her autobiography unfinished. Thus the publication of her letters from 1931 to 1966 is most welcome. As co-editor Francis Wyndham points out, the reader will be struck by "the impressive self-portrait that the letters reveal, and the insight they provide into the turbulent process of literary creation" (p.10). The letters are supplemented by a chronology of Rhys's early life, a publishing history of her works, extensive explanatory notes, and both subject and correspondent indexes. Rhys's growing reputation is indicated by the appearance of several critical studies of her work. Thomas F. Staley's *Jean Rhys: A Critical Study* (University of Texas Press, 1979) analyzes her novels and short stories within a biographical context. Helen Nebeker, however, rejects attempts by critics to view Rhys's fiction as autobiography in *Jean Rhys, Woman in Passage* (Eden Press Women's Publications, 1981); instead, her close readings of Rhys's five novels demonstrate their formal and thematic complexity. For additional sources, interested readers should examine *Jean Rhys: A Descriptive and Annotated Bibliography of Works and Criticism* (Garland, 1984), by Elgin W. Mellown.

185. Robinson, Phyllis C. **Willa: The Life of Willa Cather.** Garden City, NY: Doubleday, 1983. 321p. bibliog. index. pbk. $8.95. LC 82-46017. ISBN 038515254X.

Robinson revises the Willa Cather (1873-1947) we know from previous biographies, giving us less about the work and more about the life. Although Cather spent many of her early years in Nebraska and wrote novels of the Midwest, her adult life was largely spent in New York City, first as editor of *McClure's Magazine* and later as a successful novelist. Robinson does a fine job of describing the social history of the period, and refrains judiciously from reading Cather's fiction as her life. One especially admires Robinson's achievement knowing Cather's sense of privacy extended even to her correspondence: her will explicitly forbids quotation from her letters. Cather remained silent about her lifelong lesbian relationship with Edith Lewis, and carefully guarded her personal feelings from the public. "She never felt free even to dedicate a book to the friend with whom she had lived for forty years" (pp.276-277). Turning to recent criticism, *Women's Studies: An Interdisciplinary Journal* published a special issue on Cather (v.11, no.3, 1984), with essays by Adrienne Rich, Nancy Morrow, and Doris Grumbach, among others. Marilyn Arnold's *Willa Cather's Short Fiction* (Ohio University Press, 1984) takes a traditional approach to the issues of gender. *Critical Essays on Willa Cather* (G. K. Hall, 1984), by John J. Murphy, marshals a range of criticism from both Cather's contemporaries and our own. A formidably large work, Joan Crane's *Willa Cather: A Bibliography* (University of Nebraska Press, 1982) suggests the importance of Cather to American letters.

186. Rose, June, 1926- . **Elizabeth Fry.** New York: St. Martin's Press, 1981. 218p. bibliog. index. $25.00. LC 80-19857. ISBN 0312242484.

British Quaker minister, prison reformer, notable public figure, mother of eleven children—Elizabeth Fry (1780-1845) has been canonized, Rose tells us, by her biographers. Her saintly reputation took root during her own lifetime and was enhanced through the efforts of her daughters, who "carefully [removed] all trace of individuality and of human weakness" in editing her journals (Prologue). Rose returned to the original forty-four volumes of Fry's journal to research this first feminist biography and discovered therein "a far more complex and tormented human being than has ever been allowed to appear" (Prologue). What emerges in this revisionist account is the acute conflict Fry experienced— internally and with friends and family—in trying to forge a public life for herself.

187. Rose, Phyllis. **Parallel Lives: Five Victorian Marriages.** New York: Knopf; distr. New York: Random House, 1983. 318p. bibliog. index. $16.95. LC 83-47785. ISBN 0394524322.

Rose takes as her subjects Jane Welsh and Thomas Carlyle, Effie Gray and John Ruskin, Harriet Taylor and John Stuart Mill, Catherine Hogarth and Charles Dickens, George Eliot and George Henry Lewes. Engagingly written, her study plumbs the private lives of these five famous couples, raising insistent questions about the role of power and the nature of equality within marriage—questions that illuminate the shape of relationships in our own times as clearly as those of the Victorian era. Rose characterizes marriage as "a subjectivist fiction with two points of view," within which "a struggle for imaginative dominance" is waged (p.7). Her analysis is simultaneously political and literary. Eliot and Lewes (whose union was never formalized legally) are revealed as the happiest pair, but Rose picks as her heroine feisty Jane Carlyle, who achieved a kind of equality in marriage through the "perpetual resistance, perpetual rebellion" documented in her diaries (p.270).

188. Rudnick, Lois Palken, 1944- . **Mabel Dodge Luhan: New Woman, New Worlds.** Albuquerque: University of New Mexico Press, 1984. 384p. bibliog. index. $19.95. LC 84-7415. ISBN 0826307639.

Luhan (1879-1962) has been portrayed by previous biographers as merely a culture carrier, her life little more than a succession of artists, lovers, and husbands. Rudnick's biography traces Luhan's life from her gilded-age roots in Buffalo, as the daughter of wealthy and unaffectionate parents; through her sojourn in Europe, when she was exposed to post-impressionism; to her years in New York, where her Fifth Avenue salon was the gathering place of radicals, writers, and artists; to her final years in Taos as high priestess of an art colony. Rudnick introduces Luhan as a woman who "wanted to be the artist-as-god, but ... ended up playing the more traditional female role of the artist-of-life" (p.xii)—a collector of recognized men in every field, perhaps her most famous conquest having been D. H. Lawrence. Luhan remained at the center of American high culture throughout her lifetime. Rudnick gets past the anecdotalized Luhan and succeeds in contextualizing her both as a representative American woman of her time and class and as an individual woman whose writings suggest her exceptional nature.

189. Sarton, May, 1912- . **Recovering: A Journal.** New York: Norton, 1980. 246p. $14.95. LC 80-15155. ISBN 0393014029.

Poet and novelist, in her later years Sarton has received considerable recognition for her journals. *Recovering* was written during a year of writer's block, recovery from a mastectomy, unfavorable criticism of her work, and the loss of her lifelong companion to senility. Full of literary friendships and gardens and moments of conviviality, the journal also exposes the underbelly of literary success: insecurity, fear of aging, financial worries. Sarton's prose remains consistently optimistic and brisk in *At Seventy* (Norton, 1984), bringing the reader up to date on the writer's life in Maine through 1982. Writing, observing nature, giving poetry readings, and taking pleasure in her life are the things that preoccupy Sarton, but with characteristic candor she also reflects upon growing old and experiencing the deaths of cherished friends. A critical assessment of the autobiographical writings and other published works appears in one section of *May Sarton: Woman and Poet,* edited by Constance Hunting (National Poetry Foundation/University of Maine at Orono, 1982), with a particularly fine essay by Carolyn Heilbrun on earlier Sarton memoirs. Sarton's most recent novel, *The Magnificent Spinster* (Norton, 1985), features a young lesbian novelist who is attempting to render in fiction the life of a favorite spinster schoolteacher. The poems in *Halfway to Silence* (Norton, 1980) likewise explore the nature of love between women, along with other familiar Sarton themes.

190. Schilpp, Madelon Golden, and Sharon M. Murphy. **Great Women of the Press.** Carbondale: Southern Illinois University Press, 1983. 248p. bibliog. index. $27.50. LC 82-19574. ISBN 0809310988.

Schilpp and Murphy select eighteen women—some obscure, some well known—who contributed in some significant way to publishing, editing, and/or journalism in the United States. The biographical sketches stretch from colonial times to the near present (no living person is included). Among the women profiled are Elizabeth Timothy, who inherited her husband's press to become the first woman newspaper publisher on this continent; Mary Katherine Goddard, the first publisher of the Declaration of Independence; Anne Newport Royall, chronicler of the Jackson era and early traveling reporter; Elizabeth Meriwether Gilmer (early twentieth-century advice columnist Dorothy Dix); and photojournalist Margaret Bourke-White. Several full-length biographies of women journalists have appeared recently, including: *Virago! The Story of Anne Newport Royall (1769-1854)* (McFarland, 1985), by Alice S. Maxwell and Marion B. Dunlevy; *Right in Her Soul: The Life of Anna Louise Strong* (Random House, 1983), by Tracy B. Strong and Helene Keyssar; *Ida Tarbell: Portrait of a Muckraker* (Seaview/Putnam, 1984), by Kathleen Brady; and *Buying the Night Flight: The Autobiography of a Woman Foreign Correspondent* (Delacorte Press/Seymour Lawrence, 1983), by Georgie Ann Geyer.

191. Schwarzer, Alice, 1942- . **After the Second Sex: Conversations with Simone de Beauvoir.** New York: Pantheon Books, 1984. 120p. pbk. $5.95. LC 83-22880. ISBN 0394724305.

Schwarzer's collection of interviews ranges widely over de Beauvoir's life (1908-1986), including her writing and her relationship with Jean-Paul Sartre, revealing an intellectual feminist and pacifist who attempted to enjoy life while working against the oppression of others. Five early unpublished stories, highly autobiographical in content—*When Things of the Spirit Come First* (Pantheon Books, 1982)—illuminate the young de Beauvoir's notion of her own destiny. *Adieux: A Farewell to Sartre* (Pantheon Books, 1984) offers additional insights into the Sartre/de Beauvoir relationship. De Beauvoir goes at her task of documenting Sartre's pensées with deadly seriousness; she is reticent and self-effacing regarding her own intellectual contributions to his career. In *Simone de Beauvoir* (Tavistock, 1985), Mary Evans finds puzzling the dearth of feminist criticism of de Beauvoir. She herself argues that the values upheld in de Beauvoir's work — independence, autonomy, and self-realization — are "precisely the values ... that have done much to produce the very subordination of women that de Beauvoir attacks" (p.xvi). Carol Ascher's *Simone de Beauvoir: A Life of Freedom* (Beacon Press, 1981) — "part biography, part literary criticism, part political and personal commentary" (p.3) — does not hesitate to challenge the privileged status of de Beauvoir as feminist theorist. Ascher carries on an imaginary discourse with de Beauvoir, writing reproachfully, in a discussion of *All Said and Done,* "Sometimes it seems you think you can escape *every* trap life sets out for others" (p.111). Ascher's self-conscious work pioneers a new feminist form of biography, one in which the subject eludes objective coherence. Among more traditional studies of de Beauvoir are Terry Keefe's *Simone de Beauvoir: A Study of Her Writings* (Barnes and Noble, 1983); Anne Whitmarsh's *Simone de Beauvoir and the Limits of Commitment* (Cambridge University Press, 1981); and Judith Okely's *Simone de Beauvoir* (Virago Press, 1986). The forthcoming special issue of *Yale French Studies* on de Beauvoir will gather a range of criticism and commentary, as well as a 1984 interview by the issue's editor, Hélène Wenzel.

192. Shelley, Mary Wollstonecraft Godwin, 1979-1851. **The Letters of Mary Wollstonecraft Shelley.** Edited by Betty T. Bennett. Baltimore: Johns Hopkins University Press. 2v. bibliog. index. LC 79-24190. Vol. 1: 1980; $35.00; ISBN 0801822750. Vol. 2: 1983; $32.00; ISBN 0801826454.

A projected three-volume work, this edition will include more than thirteen hundred letters, several hundred never before in print. Beginning with Mary Shelley's elopement and her association with the Romantic literary movement, the letters richly document daily life in the early nineteenth century, Shelley's labors as her husband's editor, her devotion to her son, and contacts ranging from American reformer Frances Wright to Lord Byron. Betty T. Bennett's meticulous editing and research underscore the unfairness of the role most critics have assigned to Mary Shelley, whose own considerable literary accomplishments have been "overshadowed by the fame of her husband, Percy Bysshe Shelley (1792-1822), and her parents, William Godwin (1756-1836) and Mary Wollstonecraft (1759-1797)" (p.xi). Contributors to *The Endurance of Frankenstein: Essays on Mary Shelley's Novel* (University of California Press, 1979), edited by George Levine and U. C. Knoepflmacher, reexamine Mary Shelley's literary legacy. In two notable essays, Kate Ellis decodes a radical feminist message in *Frankenstein* (1818), and Ellen Moers writes about the female Gothic.

193. Sicherman, Barbara. **Alice Hamilton: A Life in Letters.** Cambridge, MA: Harvard University Press, 1984. 460p. bibliog. index. $25.00. LC 83-26521. ISBN 0674015533.

Gracefully weaving correspondence and commentary, Barbara Sicherman traces the life and accomplishments of pioneering industrial toxicologist Alice Hamilton (1869-1970). Hamilton was a physician, a resident of Hull House for a decade, an outspoken crusader for occupational safety and other reforms, and the first woman appointed to the Harvard medical faculty. Another Harvard first was astronomer Cecilia Payne-Gaposchkin (1900-1979), the first woman to be appointed as full professor. Katherine Haramundanis edited and added to her mother's memoir, "The Dyer's Hand," in *Cecilia Payne-Gaposchkin: An Autobiography and Other Recollections* (Cambridge University Press, 1984). The account speaks honestly of years of discrimination, and Payne-Gaposchkin concludes that being a woman in science "is a tale of low salary, lack of status, slow advancement ... a case of survival, not of the fittest, but of the most doggedly persistent" (p.227).

194.   Simon, Kate. **Bronx Primitive: Portraits in a Childhood.** New York: Viking Press, 1982. 179p. $13.95. LC 81-52675. ISBN 0670192392.

Simon evokes the closely circumscribed world of the Jewish neighborhood in the Bronx where she grew up in the pre-World War I years. "Our suburbs, our summer country homes, our camps, our banks and braes, our America the Beautiful, our fields of gaming and dalliance and voyeurism, were in Crotona Park, whose northern border fronted on Tremont Avenue" (p.3), writes Simon of the immigrant experience. Though Simon's story of coming of age has many humorous moments, her adolescence is not without its horrors. When a family friend takes her to the movies and molests her, she realizes that telling her parents is unthinkable. "When I got upstairs I could say to my parents, yes, it was a good show and a good picture; yes, I had enjoyed myself very much; yes, I had thanked him; yes, Mr. Silverberg was very nice to take me" (p.162). By the end of this candid memoir, Simon takes stock of her status as a young woman, her brain "busily clicking observations about power and vanity, theirs and mine, and yet knowing nothing ..." (p.175).

195.   Slone, Verna Mae, 1914- . **What My Heart Wants To Tell.** New York: Harper and Row, 1979. 143p. index. pbk. $1.95. LC 78-31688. ISBN 0060805102.

"I guess my scribblings are like my crazy quilts, without any form or unity. The more I write, the more I remember.... Our young folks have lost so much without ever knowing they had it to lose" (p.59). Slone's "crazy quilt" of tales about Appalachian mountain people is offered to her grandchildren as their inheritance. Slone writes to honor her father, and to correct prevalent distortions of mountain life. She tells of births and deaths; growing and preserving food; special occasions like "eating around the fire" or "molassie stir-offs." There is a strong sense throughout of the fortitude of women, and the comfort of ties between them.

196.   Spalding, Frances. **Vanessa Bell.** New Haven, CT: Ticknor and Fields, 1983. 399p. bibliog. index. $22.95. LC 83-4967. ISBN 089919205X.

Surprisingly, this is the first full-length biography of the painter Vanessa Bell, Virginia Woolf's older sister and the emotional center of the Bloomsbury group. Spalding's careful, exhaustive account describes Bell's well-known love life, revealing the pain hidden beneath her apparently serene bohemianism. An art critic, Spalding also presents cogent analyses of Bell's paintings, many of which accompany the text, and finds in them considerable artistic merit — although Bell herself, dependent upon the opinions of others, thought little of them. Like Bell, Vita Sackville-West is best known in relation to Virginia Woolf, yet was important in her own right. Victoria Glendinning's authorized biography, *Vita* (Knopf, 1983), emphasizes Sackville-West's aristocratic heritage, her devotion to literature, and her unorthodox marriage to Harold Nicholson. Sackville-West's personality appears more directly in *The Letters of Vita Sackville-West to Virginia Woolf* (Hutchinson, 1984), edited by Louise DeSalvo and Mitchell A. Leaska. The volume includes all of Sackville-West's letters to Woolf from 1922 up to Woolf's 1941 suicide, plus selections from Woolf's replies. The letters document the fluctuations in their relationship, from initial infatuation, to sexual involvement, to enduring friendship. Sackville-West's prose demonstrates an acid wit, a descriptive flair, and a gift for dramatization not always apparent in her published works.

197.* Stanley, Julia Penelope, 1941- , and Susan J. Wolfe, 1946- , eds. **The Coming Out Stories.** Watertown, MA: Persephone Press, 1980. 251p. LC 79-27073. ISBN 0930436032.

In her foreword to Stanley and Wolfe's anthology, lesbian poet Adrienne Rich describes "coming-out" as not only "that first permission we give ourselves to name our love for women as love, to say, I AM A LESBIAN, but also the successive 'comings-out' to the world ..." (p.xiii), while the editors refer to "an on-going process of self-definition and self-education" (p.xx). All these meanings and more are reflected in the forty-one first-person accounts, which range in style from the prosaically confessional to the lyric. Stanley and Wolfe provide little interpretation, letting the stories speak for themselves. In contrast, Margaret Cruikshank's quite similar collection, *The Lesbian Path* (1980; rev. ed. Grey Fox Press; distr. Subterranean, 1985), groups its thirty-five pieces under headings such as "Young Lesbians," "Struggles," "Public Lives," and "Adventures." Ruth Baetz also takes a topical approach in *Lesbian Crossroads: Personal Stories of Lesbian Struggles and Triumphs* (Morrow, 1980). Extracts from interviews are skillfully interwoven to convey the variety of lesbian experience and the many "crossroads" lesbians face in affirming their identity to themselves, to those closest to them, and to the world at large.

198. Stanton, Elizabeth Cady, 1815-1902, and Susan B. Anthony, 1820-1906. **Elizabeth Cady Stanton/Susan B. Anthony: Correspondence, Writings, Speeches.** Edited by Ellen Carol DuBois. New York: Schocken Books, 1981. 272p. bibliog. index. $17.95. LC 80-27603. ISBN 0805237593.

DuBois presents in chronological order public and private documents and letters of two great suffragists. Although Stanton and Anthony collaborated closely during their activist careers, they did not always see eye to eye on how to achieve suffrage—or even on what constituted the major issues in the debate. DuBois is intent on establishing Stanton and Anthony's separate identities. She chooses "Stanton's speeches, to emphasize her power as a political orator, and the passionate and militant character of her thought ... [and] documents that [stress] Anthony's contributions as an organizer, and her ability to draw out women's anger and commitment to the Cause" (pp.xiv-xv). One-third of the documents DuBois draws from unpublished archival material. Other sources include newspaper articles and printed documents of the day. DuBois writes exemplary introductions and notes. Stanton's radicalism, and the feisty independence on which it was based, are also the focus of Elisabeth Griffith's recent biography, *In Her Own Right: The Life of Elizabeth Cady Stanton* (Oxford University Press, 1984). Judged the best Stanton biography to date by several reviewers, the study strives to reconstruct the real woman from archival sources scattered and mutilated as part of a posthumous effort to "whitewash [her] into respectability" (p.xvi).

199.* Stone, Lucy, 1818-1893, and Henry Browne Blackwell, 1825-1909. **Loving Warriors: Selected Letters of Lucy Stone and Henry B. Blackwell, 1853-1893.** Edited by Leslie Wheeler. New York: Dial Press, 1981. 406p. index. LC 81-957. ISBN 080379469X.

Judging from the correspondence gathered here, Lucy Stone and her husband, Henry Browne Blackwell, enjoyed an extraordinary companionate marriage strengthened by their mutual interest in women's rights, abolition, and reformist causes. Stone, a successful orator on the antislavery and suffrage lecture circuit, insisted upon keeping her birth name and retaining control of her own money. Blackwell, a businessman and brother of physician Elizabeth Blackwell, eagerly embraced the suffrage cause as the core of their marriage. Together they worked on the organizing of the American Woman Suffrage Association and founded and edited *The Woman's Journal* (ultimately bequeathed to their only child, Alice Stone Blackwell). Wheeler provides a wealth of information in headnotes and references to these letters, which illumine the love and understanding between two noted activists and offer insights into important movements, associations, and figures in nineteenth-century reformist America.

200. Strouse, Jean. **Alice James: A Biography.** Boston: Houghton Mifflin, 1980. 367p. bibliog. index. $15.00. LC 80-22103. ISBN 0395277876.

Alice James (1848-1892) was the fifth and last child of Mary and Henry James, Sr., and the only girl. The family that produced novelist Henry James and psychologist William James confronted in their daughter Alice a permanent invalid from adolescence until her death at age forty-three. Like so many women of her period, Alice James lacked systematic education. Her entrée into larger intellectual circles was contingent upon her brothers or marriage, and she seems to have scorned all suitors and rejected marriage. Instead, she maintained a longstanding "Boston marriage" with her faithful companion Katharine Peabody. Strouse's consistently acclaimed biography examines the historical, cultural, and familial influences that shaped the life of this brilliant but neurotic woman. Alice's diary, begun three years before her death, has been described by *New York Times* critic John Leonard as a work of "shimmering intelligence." Now her letters are also available, published under the title *The Death and Letters of Alice James* (University of California Press, 1982), edited by Ruth Bernard Yeazell.

201. Thomas, Sherry. **We Didn't Have Much, But We Sure Had Plenty: Stories of Rural Women.** Garden City, NY: Anchor Books, 1981; repr. San Francisco: Spinsters, Ink, 1984. 185p. pbk. $5.95. LC 80-956. ISBN 0385149514.

After a short introduction detailing her methods and her responses to the rural women she interviewed, Thomas lets the voices of twelve women speak unimpeded. Thomas's expert editing and her sure hand with dialect make these oral histories a delight — from Irene Nixon, a black Georgian field hand in her nineties, to Alice Tripp, a middle aged political activist in Minnesota. In *Heartwomen: An Urban Feminist's Odyssey Home* (Harper and Row, 1982), we accompany Sandy Boucher as she observes and listens to women on her travels through eastern Nebraska and Kansas. More limited geographically than Thomas's story-gathering, Boucher's search for her roots nevertheless finds women in many walks of life and from a wide range of backgrounds. With farmers and town-dwellers, whites and women of color, waitresses and academics, traditionalists and mavericks, Boucher experiences a sense of community and becomes reacquainted with aspects of herself.

202. Thurman, Judith, 1946- . **Isak Dinesen: The Life of a Storyteller.** New York: St. Martin's Press, 1982. 495p. bibliog. index. $19.95. LC 82-5573. ISBN 0312437374.

In her readable, award-winning biography of the Danish writer Karen Blixen (pen name Isak Dinesen, 1885-1962), Thurman invites the reader to speculate on the subtext of her subject's rich and productive life. Daughter of a syphilitic father whom she adored, Blixen ironically married a syphilitic herself. Their married life as coffee farmers in East Africa provided material for *Out of Africa* (1938; repr. Modern Library, 1983), her best-known book. "As one of the greatest feudal overlords in the country" (p.128) — yet also an advocate for her "Natives" — Blixen found her position paradoxical. In Anne Born's translation of her *Letters from Africa, 1914-1931* (University of Chicago Press, 1981), the reader finds Blixen referring to "the Natives" in terms we would now consider patronizing, patiently discussing at one moment her servants' ignorance in the culinary arts, then turning around in another letter to express fury at the racism of women "who go in terror of their boys" (p.25). Thurman's biography, together with the letters, render a life of complexity, and anguished personal relationships. Blixen's analysis of her creative life and habits in *Daguerrotypes and Other Essays* (University of Chicago Press, 1979) reminds us that storytelling sustained her.

203. Tristan, Flora, 1803-1844. **Flora Tristan's London Journal, 1840.** Charlestown, MA: Charles River Books, 1980, 259p. $20.00. ISBN 0891820248.

Flora Tristan, nineteenth-century feminist and socialist, documented the public and private spheres of Victorian society using tools today employed by sociologists and ethnographers. Her major journalistic and literary themes—drawn from her own experiences and extensive travels—center on the welfare of women and the conditions of the working classes. In the *London Journal* (*Promenades dans Londres*), Tristan addresses both the touristic and the sociological: essays on prisons, prostitutes, factories, and infant schools flow from her pen along with pieces on the Ascot races, London's climate, and a visit to Parliament. In one chapter, she challenges the "abject servitude" and "revolting inequalities" (p.191) imposed on English women, and quotes at length from Wollstonecraft's *A Vindication of the Rights of Woman* (1792), which she terms "an undying work" (p.203). In 1982, Virago Press published the first English translation of the 1842 popular edition, with an illuminating introduction by translator Jean Hawkes. Tristan's *The Worker's Union* was also recently translated into English for the first time (University of Illinois Press, 1983).

204. Wagenknecht, Edward, 1900- . **Daughters of the Covenant: Portraits of Six Jewish Women.** Amherst: University of Massachusetts Press, 1983. 192p. bibliog. index. $17.50. LC 83-3562. ISBN 0870233963.

Wagenknecht offers well-written vignettes of the work and more particularly the characters and personalities of six Jewish women who intrigue him "as individuals" (p.vii): Rebecca Gratz (1781-1869), active in Jewish philanthropy and religious education; Emma Lazarus (1849-1887), Zionist and writer, best known for her poem engraved on the Statue of Liberty; Amy Levy (1861-1889), poet and novelist; Lillian D. Wald (1867-1940), pacifist and leader in the social settlement movement; Emma Goldman (1869-1940), anarchist and feminist; and Henrietta Szold (1860-1945), Zionist founder of Hadassah and, in Wagenknecht's opinion, "the greatest woman in my book" (p.viii). Bibliographies and notes follow the six profiles.

205. Warner, Marina, 1946- . **Joan of Arc: The Image of Female Heroism.** New York: Knopf; distr. New York: Random House, 1981. 349p. bibliog. index. $19.95. LC 80-2720. ISBN 0394411455.

Warner presents a feminist analysis of Joan of Arc (c.1412-1431)—the person and the legend. Drawing on records of Joan's trial and defenses written by her supporters, Warner argues that the factors leading to her rise and fall were not merely political, but religious and social as well. Her countrymen accepted her because of her virginity and knightliness, yet they saw her androgynous dress, mystic visions, and rejection of Church authority as evidence that she was an insubordinate heretic—even a witch. Warner also outlines the verbal and visual transformations of Joan's legend from the fifteenth century to the present. A more narrowly historical, but extremely detailed account of Joan's battles, trial, and execution is Frances Gies's *Joan of Arc: The Legend and the Reality* (Harper and Row, 1981).

206.* Warner, Sylvia Townsend, 1893- . **Letters.** Edited by William Maxwell. New York: Viking Press, 1983. 311p. index. LC 81-69971. ISBN 0670427292.

Warner's interests seem to have been as boundless as her prose was impeccably precise. The letters, in the words of her editor, "offer a running report on her life — on the weather, the annual arrival of gypsies, flowers blooming in the garden, ... the creatures of the river, often in flood, that flowed past her house, the pleasures of travel, politics, ..." and so on (p.xvi). Yet Warner, who numbered among her correspondents many from the Bloomsbury group, was a private person, and wished to leave out of her published correspondence love letters to her companion, Valentine Ackland. *Scenes of Childhood* (Viking Press, 1982), her memoirs, is engaging for its irreverence and odd juxtapositions — the chapter "My Father, My Mother, the Butler, the Builder, the Poodle, and I" is one example of Warner's approach to her privileged childhood. With the appearance of *Collected Poems* (Viking Press, 1983), many of Warner's unpublished poems can be read for the first time, and her forgotten poetry from out-of-print editions rediscovered. The volume also includes an intriguing essay on "Women as Writers" (1959). *Collected Poems* was edited by Claire Harman, as is a newer volume of Warner's poetry entitled *Selected Poems* (Viking Press, 1985). Stories collected by Susanna Pinney in *One Thing Leading to Another and Other Stories* (Viking Press, 1984) — some never before published, others not previously in book form — represent work from the 1940s to 1978, when Warner died.

207. Webb, Beatrice Potter, 1858-1892. **The Diary of Beatrice Webb.** Edited by Norman Ian MacKenzie and Jeanne MacKenzie. Cambridge, MA: Belknap Press of Harvard University Press. 4v. bibliog. index. Vol. 1: 1982; $25.00; LC 82-9158; ISBN 0674202872. Vol. 2: 1983; $25.00; LC 83-63; ISBN 0674202880. Vol. 3: 1984; $25.00; LC 84-391; ISBN 0674202899. Vol. 4: 1985; $25.00; LC 85-7681; ISBN 0674202864.

Born to a liberal, well-to-do family, beautiful, intelligent — Beatrice Webb might have made a conventionally successful marriage for herself. Indeed, as the first volume of her diary makes clear, she came close to doing just that, falling in love with a famous radical politician who, in her words, expected from his wife "intelligent servility" (vol. 1, p.102). Yet Webb painfully cured herself of this passion and forged a career as a social investigator and advocate for the poor. Well established in her work by the time she met Sidney Webb, she married him to cement their professional collaboration. The Webbs went on to write many books together; to found the London School of Economics and the radical journal *New Statesman*; and to wield great influence as Fabian socialists in British national politics. The four volumes of her diary offer an intimate view of Webb from the age of fifteen to the year of her death. Frequently caricatured in the press of her day as an "unnatural" or "masculine" personality, Webb was a woman of strong emotions, intellectual ambitions, and antifeminist views. Nonetheless, as editors Norman and Jeanne MacKenzie point out, her diary shows "how much her struggle to find herself was ... a woman's struggle in a man's world" (p.xx). In *The Apprenticeship of Beatrice Webb* (University of Massachusetts Press, 1985), Deborah Epstein Nord strives to debunk early caricatures of Webb and to reconstruct a more complete picture of her personality and lengthy career.

208. Welty, Eudora, 1909- . **One Writer's Beginnings.** Cambridge, MA: Harvard University Press, 1984. 104p. $10.00. LC 83-18638. ISBN 0674639251.

In these wonderful essays, Welty ambles through the childhood that shaped her writerly experience: daily life in Jackson, Mississippi; old family stories; visits to Ohio and West Virginia; books she read and loved; attitudes of the adults around her. When Welty recounts her mother's reminiscence of her own father's death at thirty-seven, it could be

Welty's own childhood experience, so deft is her translation of her mother's numbed shock and grief. Welty's first story, "Death of a Traveling Salesman," appeared in 1936; this story and thirty-eight others have been gathered in *The Collected Stories of Eudora Welty* (Harcourt, Brace, Jovanovich, 1980). All but two appeared in previously published collections. Taken together, these stories give a sense of Welty's virtuosity with the short story form, demonstrating her lyrical talents as well as her fine comedic ear. Michael Kreyling has written a perceptive study of many of the stories entitled *Eudora Welty's Achievement of Order* (Louisiana State University Press, 1980). A goodly range of Welty criticism is represented in *Eudora Welty: Thirteen Essays,* edited by Peggy Whitman Prenshaw (University Press of Mississippi, 1983). The essays are drawn from the 1979 volume, now out of print, entitled *Eudora Welty: Critical Essays.* Prenshaw has also edited Welty interviews in *Conversations with Eudora Welty* (University Press of Mississippi, 1984). Elizabeth Evans' small guide, *Eudora Welty* (Ungar, 1981), proves useful and readable. Though bibliographies exist—the most recent is Bethany C. Swearingen, *Eudora Welty: A Critical Bibliography, 1936-1958* (University Press of Mississippi, 1984)—a more authoritative, current listing is needed.

209. Williams, Selma R. **Divine Rebel: The Life of Anne Marbury Hutchinson.** New York: Holt, Rinehart and Winston, 1981. 246p. bibliog. index. $14.95. LC 80-20109. ISBN 0030558468.

Daughter of a prominent English clergyman who weathered the winds of religious change, Hutchinson (1591-1643) "gravitated toward nonconformity" as a young woman. Williams' biography traces her movement toward radical doctrine. Hutchinson found Familism compelling because it valued the "superiority of the spirit over the letter of the Bible" (p.45) and rejected the necessity of an academically trained clergy. It was her doctrinal dispute with John Cotton—whom she had admired in England and followed to New England—that finally sparked her public investigation and trial. Hutchinson threatened Cotton and colonial Governor John Winthrop in her role as a woman interpreter and teacher of biblical text. Williams skillfully uses primary documentation to back up a careful analysis of the theological points of dispute, never losing sight of the human, daily element in her subject's story. Hutchinson was a woman of formidable intellectual force despite marriage, a large family (fifteen children), and her work as a midwife and herbalist.

210. Wilson, Emily Herring. **Hope and Dignity: Older Black Women of the South.** Philadelphia: Temple University Press, 1983. 200p. $19.95. LC 82-19437. ISBN 0877222266.

The history of black Americans, Maya Angelou asserts in her foreword to this volume, compels us to ask the question: How and why did they survive? While the fact that writer Emily Wilson and photographer Susan Mullally are white might have called the success of their project into question, in Angelou's judgment the oral histories and portraits they have gathered do "[offer] some answers to the question of Black survival" (p.xii). Wilson interviewed some fifty older black women from North Carolina. In this volume, she presents brief narratives (six to eight pages) by twenty-seven women, and even briefer biographies of twenty more. Among the women are gospel singers, midwives, a painter, an editor, teachers, and a stockbroker. Where Wilson and Mullally document the diversity of Southern black women's experience in this century, others have recorded the stories of individual women in greater detail. *Lemon Swamp and Other Places: A Carolina Memoir* (Free Press, 1983) is the product of collaboration between Karen Fields, a young Brandeis professor, and her ninety-year-old grandmohter, Mamie Garvin Fields. The germ of the memoir was a packet of letters Mamie Fields gave to her granddaughters in the early 1970s describing her history and that of her home—Charleston, South Carolina—from the 1890s. In *I Am Annie Mae: An Extraordinary Woman in Her Own Words* (Rosegarden Press, 1984), Annie Mae Hunt, a black Texas woman in her seventies, vividly recalls family members who knew slavery; adolescence and sex education; her attitudes toward men; years of poverty, field work, and domestic labor; her thirteen pregnancies; and, finally, a contented old age of political activism and independence. Editors Ruthe Winegarten and Frieda Werden arrange the material gracefully into short chapters, punctuated at frequent intervals by family and historical photographs. The oral history of Bessie Jones, a Georgia singer who has devoted her career to preserving the black spiritual tradition, is recorded by John Stewart in *For the Ancestors: Autobiographical Memories* (University of Illinois Press, 1983).

211. Wollstonecraft, Mary, 1759-1797. **Collected Letters of Mary Wollstonecraft.** Edited by Ralph M. Wardle. Ithaca, NY: Cornell University Press, 1979. 439p. bibliog. index. $37.50. LC 78-15641. ISBN 0801411645.

In 1794, Mary Wollstonecraft wrote to American speculator Gilbert Imlay, her lover and father of her first child, "You know my opinion of men in general ... systematic tyrants.... When I am thus sad, I lament that my little darling ... is a girl" (p.273). The Wardle collection begins with a lengthy biographical introduction to Wollstonecraft, author of the classic feminist tract *Vindication of the Rights of Woman* (1790). Wollstonecraft's letters map a perplexing and productive life that included marriage to philosopher William Godwin, an intellectual giant of the day. Wardle's careful notes and appendices supplement the self-portrait that emerges from the letters. Barbara H. Solomon and Paula S. Berggren's sampler of Wollstonecraft's work, *A Mary Wollstonecraft Reader* (New American Library, 1983), includes selected passages from *Vindication* and excerpts from her fiction, nonfiction, and tracts on women's education. Another primer contextualizing Wollstonecraft's work biographically and historically is Moira Ferguson and Janet Todd's *Mary Wollstonecraft* (Twayne, 1984). More theoretical than the above books, Mary Poovey's *The Proper Lady and the Woman Writer: Ideology as Style in the Works of Mary Wollstonecraft, Mary Shelley, and Jane Austen* (University of Chicago Press, 1984) attends to the tensions between eighteenth- and nineteenth-century gender roles and writing as manifested in the characters these three women created.

212. Young-Bruehl, Elisabeth. **Hannah Arendt: For Love of the World.** Edited by Oscar Handlin. New Haven, CT: Yale University Press, 1982. 563p. bibliog. index. pbk. $14.95. LC 81-16114. ISBN 0300026609.

In this definitive biography of Hannah Arendt (1906-1975), one of the century's greatest political philosophers, Elisabeth Young-Bruehl draws connections between the events in Arendt's life—her Jewish girlhood in Germany, her brilliant university studies, the interest in Zionism that forced her to flee Hitler's regime, her years as a refugee in France, her eventual settlement in the United States—and her individualistic (and often controversial) theories on power, violence, totalitarianism, revolution, and justice. Although Arendt did not specifically address women's issues, many of her ideas, such as those on violence and totalitarianism, will be of interest to feminists. For analyses of Arendt's political philosophy, see *Hannah Arendt: The Recovery of the Public World* (St. Martin's Press, 1979), edited by Melvyn Hill; *Into the Dark: Hannah Arendt and Totalitarianism* (Temple University Press, 1980), by Stephen J. Whitefield; and *Hannah Arendt: Politics, Conscience, Evil* (Rowman and Allanheld, 1984), by George Kateb.

BUSINESS, ECONOMICS, AND LABOR

The works in this chapter overwhelmingly concern women's experiences in the workforce. Among the recurrent themes are causes of and remedies for occupational sex segregation, the historical and present role of women in labor unions, the struggles for equal employment opportunity, and the special needs of working mothers. Scholars have examined women in all occupational strata—management, the professions, industry, skilled trades, and clerical work—as well as women's unpaid labor as homemakers and volunteers. Studies of some occupational groups will be found in other chapters—for example, women in the health professions in Medicine, women artists in Art, lawyers in Law, scientists in Science. Larger economic issues and theories also appear in the Business chapter, including recent treatments of the feminization of poverty, women on the "global assembly line," and comparable worth. No single bibliography addresses all these issues, but such guides as Judith Leavitt's *Women in Management* (see entry 880), Mary Drake McFeely's *Women's Work in Britain and America from the Nineties to World War I* (see entry 882), and Martha Jane Soltow and Mary K. Wery's still useful *American Women and the Labor Movement, 1825-1974: An Annotated Bibliography* (2nd ed., Scarecrow, 1976) provide access to the current and historical literature on women and work.

213.* Adams, Carolyn Teich, and Kathryn Teich Winston, 1946- . **Mothers at Work: Public Policies in the United States, Sweden, and China.** New York: Longman, 1980. 312p. bibliog. index. LC 79-18670. ISBN 0582280648.

Adams and Winston bring a needed comparative focus to the study of public policy and parenting. Focusing on "the career limitations women face because of their family roles," the authors first survey social policies for working families in the United States, Sweden, and the People's Republic of China, looking at maternity benefits, family planning, child care, housework, and family assistance. They go on to investigate women's politics and feminist strategies in the three countries, the impact of national economic policy, and government intervention and change. A narrower but more exhaustive approach is taken by Sheila B. Kamerman, Alfred J. Kahn, and Paul Kingston in *Maternity Policies and Working Women* (Columbia University Press, 1983), which offers a systematic survey of maternity policies and provisions in the United States. In *Public Policy and the Family: Wives and Mothers in the Labor Force* (Lexington Books, 1980), Zaida I. Giraldo also confines her analysis to the United States, but with a broader focus on policy implications of changing family forms. Her book is composed of four sections: current trends in the United States family; tax policy and the dual-income family; state equal rights legislation; and the impact of employment on family life in the United States.

214. The Bank Book Collective. **An Account to Settle: The Story of the United Bank Workers (SORWUC).** Vancouver: Press Gang, 1979. 127p. pbk. $3.25. ISBN 0889740127.

It all began one afternoon when a bank teller in Vancouver refused to do involuntary unpaid overtime because she needed to pick up her child at the daycare center. Sister workers rallied to the cause, and the incident grew into a full-blown effort to organize Canadian bank employees. Written by a collective of clerical workers, this slim volume gives a stirring account of the unionizing venture, which faced the determined opposition of not just the banking industry, but also of segments of organized labor.

215. Berch, Bettina. **The Endless Day: The Political Economy of Women and Work.** New York: Harcourt, Brace, Jovanovich, 1982. 212p. bibliog. index. pbk. $11.95. LC 81-85461. ISBN 0155179500.

This concise little volume may well be one of the undiscovered classics of feminist pedagogy; it appears to be a superb text for the undergraduate student or the "common reader," especially those who find orthodox economics intimidating and/or obscurantist. Berch presents a readable summary of current research on women and work, including historical perspectives, statistics on labor force participation and sex segregation of occupations, household work, childbearing, government remedies, the corporate woman, trade unions, and cross-cultural comparisons. Each chapter concludes with footnotes and a brief evaluative discussion of additional readings. The book's strength lies in its demystifying explications of competing perspectives. Berch is meticulous but critical in her explanation of neoclassical economic theories. Another text designed for the undergraduate classroom is *Women at Work*, by Mary Frank Fox and Sharlene Hesse-Biber (Mayfield, 1984). Fox and Hesse-Biber cover the sex segregation of occupations, income inequality, work socialization, economic theory, law, minority women, dual-worker families, and specific occupations (clerical, blue-collar, professional, and managerial).

216. Buvinić, Mayra, et al., eds. **Women and Poverty in the Third World.** Baltimore: Johns Hopkins University Press, 1983. 329p. bibliog. index. $32.50. LC 82-8992. ISBN 0801826810.

Editors Mayra Buvinić, Margaret A. Lycette, and William Paul McGreevey have selected papers for this collection from presentations made at a 1978 workshop convened by the International Center for Research on Women. The volume aims to furnish policymakers and implementers of development projects with data on "women's contribution to the economy of poor households, and the extent of women's poverty" (p.ix), through international surveys and case studies of the Philippines, Malaysia, Peru, Nigeria, Guatemala, and Brazil. Poverty is analyzed here at the family and local levels; relations between rich and poor nations do not enter the picture. Contributing scholars come primarily from the field of economics, and several serve on the staffs of the Rand Corporation and the World Bank. Most of the analysis is highly technical; the general reader and the undergraduate student will find the introductory overviews and the concluding assessments most accessible.

217. Card, Emily. **Staying Solvent: A Comprehensive Guide to Equal Credit for Women.** New York: Holt, Rinehart and Winston, 1985. 224p. bibliog. index. $15.95. LC 84-4537. ISBN 0030629543.

Card, a financial advisor and architect of the 1974 Equal Credit Opportunity Act, has written a primer for women on establishing and using credit. In clear language, Card covers the history of sex discrimination in credit, and legal problems and solutions.

218. Catalyst, Inc. **What To Do With the Rest of Your Life: The Catalyst Career Guide for Women in the 80s.** New York: Simon and Schuster, 1980. 626p. bibliog. pbk. $11.95. LC 79-26653. ISBN 0671250701.

Any woman entering (or reentering) the world of paid employment can benefit from the materials prepared by Catalyst—a nonprofit national organization that provides a clearinghouse and support services for career women. *What To Do With the Rest of Your Life* describes a wide range of career fields, outlines educational requirements and job options, and provides checklists and exercises to aid the reader in assessing her skills and interests. Other Catalyst titles include *Marketing Yourself: The Catalyst Women's Guide to Successful Resumes and Interviews* (Putnam, 1980), *When Can You Start?: The Complete Job-Search Guide for Women of All Ages* (Macmillan, 1981), *Making the Most of Your First Job* (Putnam, 1981), and *Upward Mobility* (Holt, Rinehart and Winston, 1982).

219. Cook, Alice H., et al., eds. **Women and Trade Unions in Eleven Industrialized Countries.** Philadelphia: Temple University Press, 1984. 327p. bibliog. index. $34.95. LC 83-17946. ISBN 087722319X.

Thirteen original articles are collected by editors Alice H. Cook, Val R. Lorwin, and Arlene Kaplan Daniels in this volume documenting continuities and divergences in women's trade union experiences in Denmark, West Germany, Finland, France, Great Britain, Ireland, Italy, Japan, Norway, Sweden, and the United States. The case studies look at women's labor force participation, sex segregation of the labor force, representation of women in unions and union leadership, and workplace issues such as wages, training and apprenticeship, seniority, and shorter work weeks. There is a mix here of the dismal history of male-dominated unions and their hostility to women, on the one hand, and of women's continuing fight for representation, on the other. The eightieth birthday of Alice Cook—social worker, labor educator and organizer, foreign service officer, and professor—was the occasion for a 1983 conference whose proceedings are gathered in *Women Workers in Fifteen Countries*, edited by Jennie Farley (ILR Press, 1985). Fourteen scholars of different nationalities report on the status of women workers in the USSR, China, Yugoslavia, Japan, Israel, Great Britain, France, West Germany, Sweden, Switzerland, Italy, the United States, and the low-income countries. In her afterword, Cook reviews the discouraging findings, advocating that researchers "put scholarship in the service of activism ..." (p.179). Patricia A. Roos analyzes data from twelve countries in North America, Western Europe, and Asia in *Gender and Work: A Comparative Analysis of Industrial Societies* (State University of New York Press, 1985). She finds the United States pattern of occupational sex segregation replicated throughout her sample, and demonstrates that marital status does not account for sex differences in occupational attainment.

220. Davies, Margery W. **Woman's Place Is at the Typewriter: Office Work and Office Workers, 1870-1930.** Philadelphia: Temple University Press, 1983. 217p. bibliog. index. $27.95. Lc 82-13694. ISBN 0877222916.

Davies renders a carefully drawn account of the feminization and proletarianization of office work in the late nineteenth and early twentieth centuries. Prior to the Civil War, most offices were small and personal in atmosphere; they were populated by businessmen and their male clerks, who were in essence apprentices expecting to climb the ladder as their careers progressed. As capitalist enterprises expanded toward the end of the nineteenth century, growing demand for office workers met up with a ready supply of literate female labor. Simultaneously with the induction of women into office work, executives increasingly sought to rationalize the labor process, applying the principles of "scientific management." By 1930, the clerical labor force was almost exclusively female, and was barred from upward mobility. The typewriter and other office machinery were not responsible, Davies argues, for the degradation of office work during this period. Rather, it was a changing political economy stamped with a strongly patriarchal character that proletarianized office work, and it was the simultaneous feminization of the clerical work force that masked this fundamental transformation.

221. Dex, Shirley. **The Sexual Division of Work: Conceptual Revolutions in the Social Sciences.** New York: St. Martin's Press, 1985. 234p. bibliog. index. LC 85-8301. ISBN 0312713495.

"We simplify by dealing only with men. Married women have the same class positions as their husbands. Unmarried women will here be ignored." Taken from a 1953 text on the American class structure, this passage (quoted p.143) expresses an androcentric world view shared by much of the literature in industrial sociology and labor economics that Dex critically reviews here. "The traditions," she asserts, "can be criticised for their reliance upon common stereotypes about women, treating women as a problem, for their reliance upon false assumptions and for just plain ignorance" (p.8). Dex aims not simply to document these failings, but also to survey the "conceptual revolutions" brought about by feminist scholarship on women's employment and unemployment, career choice, occupational segregation, domestic labor, pay inequity, class, deskilling, and the reserve army of labor. Although intended as a text for undergraduate students in Britain and the United States, Dex's study will probably prove challenging for readers not already acquainted with the scholarship and issues she discusses.

222.* Easton, Susan, et al. **Equal to the Task: How Workingwomen are Managing in Corporate America.** New York: Seaview Books, 1982. 238p. bibliog. LC 81-52073. ISBN 0872237524.

Businesswomen Susan Easton, Joan M. Mills, and Diane Kramer Winokur bring a healthy dose of skepticism to the burgeoning self-help literature for aspiring women managers. Critical of books that coach women on how to fit into the male-defined world of business, the authors encourage women to be themselves, to be realistic, and to work to make the corporate world more accommodating. Their book is based on their interviews with thirty-five women managers working in diverse settings. They organize their findings into eight chapters based on women prototypes—e.g., the assimilated woman, the autocratic woman, the alienated woman—and one chapter on "the ambivalent man," "the men who hired, worked with, and married the executive women we were writing about" (p.xiii). The proceedings of a 1982 conference designed to answer students' questions about careers in management are reproduced in *The Woman in Management: Career and Family Issues* (ILR Press, 1983), edited by Jennie Farley. At the conference, Juanita Kreps spoke of "Women in a Changing Economy," Betty Lehan Harragan advised her audience on how to "jockey for position," and Rosabeth Moss Kanter offered comments on "moving up in a high tech society." In addition, eight businesswomen shared their personal experiences with juggling careers and family. Farley adds a brief bibliographical essay and a thoughtfully annotated bibliography to the volume.

223. Eisenstein, Sarah. **Give Us Bread, But Give Us Roses: Working Women's Consciousness in the United States, 1890 to the First World War.** London: Routledge and Kegan Paul, 1983. 207p. bibliog. index. pbk. $10.95. LC 83-4538. ISBN 0710094787.

Unfortunately, Eisenstein did not live to complete the full work she envisioned. What we have here is one previously published essay providing the rough outline of her projected study, and the working drafts of the study's first three chapters, edited by her husband Harold Benenson. Benenson writes an introduction tying the disparate parts together, while Nancy Cott's afterword situates Eisenstein's highly original approach within the context of contemporary women's labor history. Using working-class women's own writings as well as prescriptive literature and reports by observers, Eisenstein sought to understand the impact of bourgeois ideals of womanhood on working-class women's consciousness at the turn of the century, without (in Cott's words) "either sacrificing or idealizing the integrity of working women's point of view" (p.163). Connected with this is Eisenstein's exploration of the ways working women assimilated their newfound independence while maintaining ties to older cultures of family, ethnicity, and class. Dedicated to Eisenstein, Meredith Tax's *The Rising of the Women: Feminist Solidarity and Class Conflict, 1880-1917* (Monthly Review Press, 1980) looks at women's activism during the same period. Tax first discusses efforts to unionize women workers in Chicago in the 1880s and 1890s. She then examines the work of three national organizations—the Women's Trade Union League, the IWW, and the Socialist Party—between 1900 and World War I. Case studies of two of the mass strikes of the period and a brief theoretical summary conclude the volume. Tax recreates this period in fictional form in her novel *Rivington Street* (Morrow, 1982).

224. Epstein, Cynthia Fuchs, and Rose Laub Coser, eds. **Access to Power: Cross-National Studies of Women and Elites.** London: Allen and Unwin, 1981. 259p. bibliog. index. $12.50. LC 80-40676. ISBN 0043011187.

The outgrowth of a 1976 conference, this volume brings together fourteen articles on political and economic elites in the United States and selected European countries. In the introduction, Epstein synthesizes some theses common to the various articles: women cluster at the bottom in sex-role-appropriate positions; women as well as men are influenced by sex-role stereotypes; intervention at the state level can make a difference; women need expanded access to education and other opportunities; home responsibilities limit women's careers. Though recent changes are slight, Epstein takes heart from the fact that "the direction of change is constant" (p.14). Co-editor Coser makes a gloomier assessment, finding that "like sediment of a good wine, [women] have sunk to the bottom" (p.16).

225. Fernandez, John P., 1941- . **Racism and Sexism in Corporate Life: Changing Values in American Business.** Lexington, MA: Lexington Books, 1981. 359p. bibliog. index. $31.50. LC 80-8945. ISBN 0669044776.

Fernandez reports findings from his survey of over four thousand Native American, Asian, black, Hispanic, and white male and female managers from twelve large companies. The study revealed that some managerial concerns exist independently of age, race, and sex. These pertain to the shift in values that divides "old guard" managers from "new breed" managers; younger managers express higher expectations of job satisfaction and overall quality of life. The study also showed substantially different perceptions by race and sex regarding the efficacy of affirmative action. The book is packed with easily comprehended tables separating out managers' reactions by age, sex, and race. Among women, blacks are most critical of their work situations, Asians least critical. White men are most disgruntled with affirmative action, viewing it as undercutting the "fair-merit system" they assume existed in the past. After analyzing the data, Fernandez offers his own solutions to "the race, sex, and value-system problems that will confront corporations in the 1980s" (p.xxi).

226. Finch, Janet. **Married to the Job: Wives' Incorporation in Men's Work.** Boston: Allen and Unwin, 1983. 182p. bibliog. index. $18.95. LC 82-16435. ISBN 0043011497.

Finch expanded a Ph.D. dissertation on wives of clergy into this theoretical and empirical overview of wives' incorporation into their husbands' work. Part I details the ways in which men's work structures their wives' lives. Part II surveys the variety of contributions women make to their husbands' work. In Part III, Finch strives to make sense of the phenomenon from women's point of view. She concludes that women cooperate with the processes of incorporation (a) because they have few alternatives, and (b) because it can in fact be in their interest to do so. This second reason rests on the assumption that women as a rule gain higher class status and economic rewards from vicarious association with their husbands' work than they do from their own. Finch's discussion draws heavily on both British and United States feminist scholarship, situating the specific issue in the larger context of feminist theory of domestic labor, marriage, and women's oppression.

227. Foner, Philip Sheldon. **Women and the American Labor Movement.** New York: Free Press. 2v. bibliog. index. Vol. 1: 1979; $29.95; LC 79-63035; ISBN 0029103703. Vol. 2: 1980; $29.95; LC 80-753; ISBN 0029103800.

Foner is an unusually prolific historian, with more than forty books to his credit. This prodigious, two-volume account of United States women's labor history is encyclopedic in scope. Volume I, "From Colonial Times to the Eve of World War I," opens with the female indentured servants and black slaves who labored in the colonies, and continues with the story of the first factories, early trade unions' hostility to women workers, the Knights of Labor, the American Federation of Labor, Socialist Party women, the National Women's Trade Union League, key strikes at the turn of the century, and the Wobblies. Volume II, "From World War I to the Present," takes in women's work during the world wars, the militancy of the thirties, District 1199 of the National Union of Hospital and Health Care Employees, the farmworkers' struggle, the contemporary women's movement, and the Coalition of Labor Union Women. Foner works with a broad definition of labor history, encompassing resistance and strikes by unorganized women workers, and wives' support of men's labor struggles, as well as traditional union history. However, his opus is more a compendium of facts than a theoretical interpretation. One learns a vast amount about what women have done, very little about their thoughts and motivations. A one-volume, abridged version of this work is available under the title *Women and the American Labor Movement: From the First Trade Unions to the Present* (Free Press, 1982).

228.* Fuentes, Annette, and Barbara Ehrenreich. **Women in the Global Factory.** New York: Institute for New Communications; Boston: South End Press, 1983. 64p. bibliog. LC 84-162494. ISBN 0896081982.

In this brief pamphlet, Ehrenreich and Fuentes explain in the clearest possible language how contemporary multinational production is altering the international division of labor. In their initial chapter, they summarize how corporations are moving labor-intensive jobs to those Third World countries where they buy the cheapest (generally *female*) labor. In subsequent chapters, they zero in on the situation of women on "the global assembly line" in East Asia, in Mexico's *maquiladoras* (offshore assembly plants), in Central America, Korea, and the Philippines, as well as in the garment sweatshops of New York City and in California's Silicon Valley. *Women, Men, and the International Division of Labor* (State University of New York Press, 1983), edited by June Nash and María Patricia Fernández-Kelly, covers similar territory, but in far greater detail and for an academic audience. The eighteen articles in the collection are organized thematically into four sections: global accumulation and the labor process; production, reproduction, and the household economy; labor flow and capital expansion; and case studies in electronics and textiles. Not all of the articles focus exclusively on women. Editor Fernández-Kelly, who contributes an article to the collection on the Mexican *maquiladoras,* is also author of a monograph on this topic: *For We Are Sold, I and My People: Women and Industry in Mexico's Frontier* (State University of New York Press, 1983).

229. Gold, Michael Evan. **A Dialogue on Comparable Worth.** Ithaca, NY: ILR Press, 1983. 111p. bibliog. $14.00. LC 83-8508. ISBN 0875460984.

Seeking to alleviate salary inequities associated with occupational sex segregation, comparable worth is an exceedingly controversial idea. It raises questions not just about the rights of men and women but also about the role of the "free market" in our society. Both proponents and opponents of comparable worth are given voice in Gold's book, in which a fictitious advocate and critic battle out the issues in a mock debate. Arguments for both sides are concise, elegantly presented, and carefully footnoted by Gold. The debaters wrangle over interpretation of the earnings gap, methods of job evaluation, the consequences of comparable worth, and legal and labor issues. Gold is true to his goal of presenting the strongest possible case for each side. Readers at all levels are likely to appreciate his careful and entertaining delineation of the issues. Those seeking an overview of current scholarship on comparable worth can turn to Helen Remick's collection, *Comparable Worth and Wage Discrimination: Technical Possibilities and Political Realities* (Temple University Press, 1984). Fifteen articles written by scholars, attorneys, and activists consider the historical and cultural context of comparable worth, technical issues in job evaluation, methods of assessing wage discrimination, and legislation and litigation. Some of the contributors are familiar as authors of their own studies in the field, among them Donald J. Treiman, Heidi I. Hartmann, Barbara R. Bergmann, Joy Ann Grune, Ronnie Steinberg, and Alice H. Cook. Treiman and Bergmann both contribute to *Comparable Worth: New Directions for Research* (National Academy Press, 1985), a collection of papers edited by Heidi I. Hartmann. In *Comparable Worth: The Myth and the Movement* (Westview Press, 1984), Elaine Johansen analyzes the issue for an audience of political scientists. For a handy annotated guide to literature on comparable worth through 1982, see *Equal Pay for Work of Comparable Worth* (American Library Association, 1982), compiled by Catherine Selden and others.

230. Goldberg, Roberta. **Organizing Women Office Workers: Dissatisfaction, Consciousness, and Action.** New York: Praeger, 1983. 152p. bibliog. index. $28.95. LC 82-18907. ISBN 0030632870.

Seeking to understand the nature of consciousness among women office workers, Goldberg undertook an intensive case study of Baltimore Working Women, an affiliate of the national organization "9 to 5." She utilized participant observation, open-ended interviews, and a small-scale survey to investigate members' dissatisfactions at work, and whether they attributed these dissatisfactions more to their specific jobs or to their experiences as women. Distinguishing three types of consciousness among the women she studied—job consciousness, feminist consciousness, and class consciousness—Goldberg theorizes that the first two combine to create a gender-specific class consciousness, contending that "much of what has been taken to be indicative of class consciousness is, in fact, male-specific class consciousness" (p.139). In *9 to 5: The Working Woman's Guide to Office Survival* (Penguin Books, 1983), Ellen Cassedy and Karen Nussbaum, founders of 9 to 5, speak directly to the working woman, offering counsel on salaries, health hazards, automation, family issues, and retirement. Helpful exercises, glossaries, and questionnaires break up the text, and an office worker's "Bill of Rights" concludes the volume.

231.   Harragan, Betty Lehan. **Knowing the Score: Play-by-Play Directions for Women on the Job.** New York: St. Martin's Press, 1983. 207p. index. $10.95. LC 83-9794. ISBN 0312458703.

Harragan, author of the best-selling *Games Your Mother Never Taught You* (1977), takes a no-nonsense approach to career advancement and fulfillment on the job. Here she reproduces her question-and-answer columns from *Savvy* and *Working Woman* magazines on difficult bosses and coworkers, strategies for promotion, salaries and expense accounts, sexual harassment, and other practical concerns. In several places she reports reader response to the columns and expands upon her original advice.

232.   Heim, Kathleen M., ed. **The Status of Women in Librarianship: Historical, Sociological, and Economic Issues.** New York: Neal-Schuman Publishers, 1983. 483p. bibliog. index. $35.00. LC 82-7887. ISBN 0918212626.

The fourteen scholarly papers in this watershed collection range thematically from the history of librarianship and library education to current studies of the salaries, ranks, and mobility of men and women librarians. Heim has carefully balanced a variety of methodologies, including reviews of the literature, analysis of archival sources, experimental research, oral history, and survey research. Whereas earlier studies often blamed individual women for their low professional status (pointing to lack of career commitment or unwillingness to relocate), this volume debunks such accusations and lays bare the fact of sex discrimination. Editor Heim is co-author of two other important contributions: *Career Profiles and Sex Discrimination in the Library Profession*, with Leigh S. Estabrook (American Library Association, 1983); and *On Account of Sex: An Annotated Bibliography on the Status of Women in Librarianship, 1977-1981*, with Katharine Phenix (American Library Association, 1984). The latter includes a concise essay on the women's movement within librarianship during the period covered by the bibliography. Also of interest is Betty Jo Irvine's *Sex Segregation in Librarianship: Demographic and Career Patterns of Academic Library Administrators* (Greenwood Press, 1985).

233.   Henry, Fran Worden. **Toughing It Out at Harvard: The Making of a Woman MBA.** New York: Putnam, 1983; repr. New York: McGraw-Hill, 1984. 253p. pbk. $6.95. LC 83-24885. ISBN 0070293244.

Henry entered the Harvard Graduate School of Business Administration at the age of thirty-two, already a successful career woman and a feminist. In this revealing book, she recounts her grueling two years at the "B School"—the numbing emphasis on quantitative methods, the intense competition, and the endemic sexism. Her women's support group proved crucial to her academic survival. Although she exposes and condemns the "fast track" values that underlie the business curriculum, she concludes that her experiences were ultimately empowering. In *Women Like Us* (Morrow, 1985), journalist Liz Roman Gallese profiles six women MBAs from Harvard's class of 1975, taking an in-depth look at their careers and private lives. Yet another insider's account of high-level corporate life, and its rewards and pitfalls for women, can be found in Mary Cunningham's memoir: *Powerplay: What Really Happened at Bendix* (Linden Press/Simon and Schuster, 1984).

234.   Jensen, Joan M., and Sue Davidson, 1925- , eds. **A Needle, A Bobbin, A Strike: Women Needleworkers in America.** Philadelphia: Temple University Press, 1984. 304p. bibliog. index. $29.95. LC 83-24338. ISBN 0877223408.

Unusually thorough and lucid volume and section introductions turn this anthology's nine separately authored articles into a coherent social history of the needle trades. The first section, "Needlework as Art, Craft, and Livelihood Before 1900," documents how the invention of the sewing machine undermined women's needle crafts. Section Two, "The Great Uprisings: 1900-1920," provides stirring accounts of major unionizing efforts and strikes in Rochester, Chicago, Cleveland, and New York. Articles in Section Three, "Inside and Outside the Unions: 1920-1980," consider the role of Dorothy Jacobs Bellanca in the Amalgamated Clothing Workers of America, the two-year strike at the Farah Manufacturing Company in the early seventies, and New York's Hispanic garment workers in the 1980s. A feminist perspective shapes the text throughout, demonstrating how and why it is that sewing has continued to be women's work, though transformed from a home-based craft into an exploitative multinational corporate enterprise. Two additional titles add to our knowledge of the increasingly international character of the garment industry: *The Lace Makers of Narsapur: Indian Housewives Produce for the World Market* (Zed Press/Lawrence Hill, 1982), by Maria Mies; and *Of Common Cloth: Women in the Global Textile Industry* (Transnational Institute, 1983), edited by Wendy Chapkis and Cynthia Enloe.

235. Johnson, Laura Climenko, with Robert E. Johnson. **The Seam Allowance: Industrial Homework in Canada.** Toronto: The Women's Press, 1982. 135p. bibliog. pbk. $7.95. LC 82-209898. ISBN 088961072X.

Popular conception has it that industrial homework is a thing of the past, banned by legislation passed in the thirties. This slim volume makes it abundantly clear that homework is alive and well in Canada, where homeworkers are predominantly immigrant women with young children. For employers, homework is a strategy for remaining competitive in a market flooded by foreign imports. Dismantling the factory and farming out work dramatically cut overhead costs and wages. Most homeworkers earn the minimum wage or less and receive no benefits; in addition, they assume overhead costs—purchase and maintenance of equipment, utilities, etc. Working conditions are highly stressful, due to piecework rates, health hazards of working at home, and, for many of these women, the competing demands of work and children. Johnson interviewed fifty homeworkers in the Canadian garment industry. Her carefully researched study vividly describes homeworkers' working lives; excellent photographs graphically portray the cramped conditions in which these women labor. Robert E. Johnson adds a chapter on the origins of industrial homework. This is a powerful book documenting a form of labor abuse of increasing dimensions—not just in the garment industry, but also in home knitting, jewelry making, and clerical work. While Johnson is emphatic in rejecting any depiction of homeworkers as small-time businesswomen, there are those who believe an entrepreneurial approach to work at home can be successful. Two recent books on this topic are *The New Entrepreneurs: Women Working From Home* (Universe Books, 1980), by Terri P. Tepper and Nona Dawe Tepper, and *Women Working Home: The Homebased Business Guide and Directory* (2nd ed., WWH Press; distr. Rodale Press, 1983), by Marion Behr and Wendy Lazar.

236. Kahn-Hut, Rachel, et al., eds. **Women and Work: Problems and Perspectives.** New York: Oxford University Press, 1982. 327p. bibliog. index. $9.95. LC 81-14025. ISBN 0195030338.

For this introductory text on women and work, editors Rachel Kahn-Hut, Arlene Kaplan Daniels, and Richard Colvard have selected seventeen articles published in the journal *Social Problems* between 1975 and 1981. Some of the work will strike the researcher in the field as dated. However, the editors' intent is to use these articles to open up questions and illustrate competing perspectives on the subject for students. They divide the volume into four major sections: "Women and the Division of Labor: Limiting Assumptions"; "Home Work and Market Work: Systematic Segregation"; "Invisible Work: Unacknowledged Contributions"; and "Women and the Dual Economy: Continuing Discrimination." The editors' introductions present key issues and raise questions for discussion. In a final section, the editors give a very cursory overview of liberal, Marxist, and radical feminism. *The Economics of Women and Work*, edited by Alice H. Amsden (St. Martin's Press, 1980), is likewise designed for the student. Amsden brings together eighteen articles published in a variety of journals between 1962 and 1978, dividing them into three sections: "Market Work, Homework and the Family"; "Job Segregation by Sex and Women's Lower Pay"; and "Women's Employment and the Economy." Amsden's thoughtful introduction familiarizes students with the four viewpoints represented in the volume: neoclassical, institutional, Marxist, and radical.

237. Kaminer, Wendy. **Women Volunteering: The Pleasure, Pain, and Politics of Unpaid Work From 1830 to the Present.** Garden City, NY: Anchor Press, 1984. 237p. bibliog. index. $25.95. LC 84-3119. ISBN 0385184239.

Feminists have in some instances judged volunteering as yet another example of women's exploitation. Kaminer's intent here is to sort out the contradictions of volunteer work, as well as her own ambivalences. The heart of the book consists of profiles of contemporary volunteers, drawn from Kaminer's interviews with an "unscientifically mixed sample of women" (p.51). The profiles are preceded by a brief history of women's volunteerism from the 1830s through the 1920s, and of its relation to middle-class social and political activism. Not strong in treating class issues, Kaminer's discussion does bring out the many sides of volunteering: as a form of empowerment as well as exploitation; as a vehicle for social change as well as simple service; as a community obligation as well as a leisure pastime.

238. Kessler-Harris, Alice: **Out To Work: A History of Wage-Earning Women in the United States.** New York: Oxford University Press, 1982. 400p. bibliog. index. $22.50. LC 81-11237. ISBN 0195030249.

Lavishly praised by many critics, this book seems destined to become the standard history of U.S. wage-earning women. Kessler-Harris makes creative use of a wealth of sources both primary and secondary, synthesizes the most recent research from women's history, and offers her own original interpretations of the material. Moreover, while her focus is confined to wage-earning women, she is at all points interested in the relationship between women's wage labor and the family. Kessler-Harris traces the historical movement from the colonial household economy to wage labor; the stranglehold of the sex-segregated marketplace; the ironies of the movement for protective labor legislation at the turn of the century; and the "radical consequences of incremental change" in our own epoch, as wage-earning women become a majority. Social, economic, and ideological forces all enter into her interpretations of the sweeping changes of the last three centuries, as do the distinct effects of class, ethnicity, and race. *Out To Work* is, in Kessler-Harris's words, "both parent and child" of her book *Women Have Always Worked: A Historical Overview* (1981), written for the Feminist Press series "Women's Lives/Women's Work." Designed for the college or high school classroom, this text is less comprehensive in historical detail than *Out To Work*, but enlarges the focus to include nonwaged labor such as homemaking and reform work.

239. Kornbluth, Joyce L., and Mary Frederickson, eds. **Sisterhood and Solidarity: Workers' Education for Women, 1914-1984.** Philadelphia: Temple University Press, 1984. 372p. bibliog. index. $29.95. LC 84-8734. ISBN 0877223289.

Nine essays by historians and labor educators profile innovative programs for women workers' education, from 1914 to the present: the Women's Trade Union League Training School for Women Organizers; the International Ladies' Garment Workers' Union programs; industrial programs of the YWCA; the Bryn Mawr Summer School for Women Workers; and several more. Each essay is supplemented by documentary material—essays, poems, plays, oral histories, and photographs. In the final chapter, Lyn Goldfarb records the memories of four pioneers in the early workers' education movement: Alice Cook, Esther Peterson, Marguerite Gilmore, and Larry Rogin. In these interviews, as in the balance of the anthology, feminism is an explicit focus. Contributors to the volume include Robin Miller Jacoby, Alice Kessler-Harris, and Barbara Mayer Wertheimer. Wertheimer herself edited an anthology on the topic, *Labor Education for Women Workers* (Temple University Press, 1981), which is packed with practical information on program design, teaching techniques, curriculum, and fundraising for contemporary labor education.

240. Lloyd, Cynthia B., 1943- , and Beth T. Niemi, 1942- . **The Economics of Sex Differentials.** New York: Columbia University Press, 1979. 355p. bibliog. index. $29.00. LC 79-9569. ISBN 0231040385.

This volume represents a comprehensive review of the neoclassical economic literature on sex differentials (through 1979). The orthodox approach to labor market analysis begins with the assumption that each individual makes economic decisions based on an unrestricted set of choices. While Lloyd and Niemi adopt the orthodox emphasis on choice, they also draw on the concepts of segmented labor markets and discrimination to argue that "men and women do face different opportunities in both the market and nonmarket sectors" (p.3). Using this perspective, the authors examine the economics of labor supply; education, training, and occupational selection; earnings and unemployment; discrimination; and law and policy-making.

241. Lopata, Helena Znaniecka, 1925- , et al. **City Women: Work, Jobs, Occupations, Careers.** New York: Praeger. 2v. bibliog. index. LC 84-15933. Vol. 1: 1984; $31.95; ISBN 0030692466. Vol. 2: 1985; $51.95; ISBN 0030692474.

City Women reports on a large-scale study carried out in Chicago from 1975 to 1979. The title notwithstanding, urban experience per se is not a major focus here. The project interviewed some 1880 women representative of seven occupational groups: service workers; blue-collar workers; clerical workers; sales workers; homemakers; managers, administrators, and officials; and professional and technical workers. In volume one, *America,* Lopata presents an up-to-date review of the literature on each of these seven occupational groups, as well as on the history of women's work in the United States. Coauthors Lopata, Debra Barnewolt, and Cheryl Allyn Miller summarize the findings of the Chicago study in volume two, titled *Chicago.* Although lacking any strong theoretical perspective, the study provides a wealth of data detailing the backgrounds, work histories, role conflicts, and work attitudes of women in specific occupational groups. Both volumes are marred by clumsy writing. Lopata previously investigated the lives of widows in the Chicago area. She reports her findings in *Widowhood in an American City* (Schenkman, 1973) and *Women as Widows: Support Systems* (Elsevier North Holland, 1979).

242. Maresca, Carmela C. **Careers in Marketing: A Woman's Guide.** Englewood Cliffs, NJ: Prentice-Hall, 1983. 211p. index. $16.95. LC 82-21482. ISBN 0131151398.

Maresca's handbook is required reading for the ambitious female business student. Although much of the information on marketing practices and strategies for career development applies equally to men and women, chapters on balancing work and family and coping with success speak specifically of women's experiences. Maresca blends practical advice on self-presentation, interpersonal relations, and organizational politics, with admonitions such as "Don't be afraid to think like a woman" (p.164) and "Don't overembrace the male model" (p.165), reflecting her belief that the influx of women into marketing is reshaping the field for the better.

243. Matthaei, Julie A. **An Economic History of Women in America: Women's Work, The Sexual Division of Labor, and the Development of Capitalism.** New York: Schocken Books, 1982. 381p. bibliog. index. $29.50. LC 81-84111. ISBN 0805238042.

Appearing in the same year and covering much the same territory, Matthaei's book and Alice Kessler-Harris's *Out To Work* (see entry 238) are bound to be compared. Like Kessler-Harris, Matthaei paints in broad strokes the historical transformation of women's work in the United States from colonial times to the present. Their treatments differ significantly, however. While Kessler-Harris plumbs her sources and constructs her account with the historian's eye for detail and the unexpected contradiction, Matthaei — a Marxist economist — shapes her material with a more theoretical purpose in mind. Furthermore, where Kessler-Harris restricts her inquiry to the wage-earning woman, Matthaei's overriding interest is in the impact of capitalism on the sexual division of labor — as expressed in waged and unwaged labor, at home and at the factory or office. Matthaei's interpretation has alternately been criticized for subordinating historical evidence to the theoretical argument, and praised for forging a provocative and original synthesis. The sexual division of labor in the post-World War II era is the focus of Ann Game and Rosemary Pringle in *Gender at Work* (1983). In case studies of whitegoods manufacture, banking, retailing, computing, nursing, and housework in the Australian context, the authors seek "to develop an understanding of the relationship between gender, the labour process, and technological change" (p.15).

244. Meehan, Elizabeth M. **Women's Rights at Work: Campaigns and Policy in Britain and the United States.** New York: St. Martin's Press, 1985. 253p. bibliog. index. $27.50. LC 84-15997. ISBN 0312887930.

Meehan gives a comparative historical account of equal employment policies in the United States and Britain. She finds some parallels in the stories, due to cross-fertilization of feminist ideas and the influence of United States civil rights experience on British policymaking. Yet Meehan finds differences, too, in the two countries' movements for legislative reform, and in their resulting policy implementation and enforcement — differences she roots in distinctive American and British politics, economics, and institutions. More extensive international comparisons can be found in *Sex Discrimination and Equal Opportunity: The Labour Market and Employment Policy*, a collection of articles comparing Sweden, the United Kingdom, the United States, and West Germany, edited by Günther Schmid and Renate Weitzel (St. Martin's press, 1984), and *Equal Employment Policy for Women: Strategies for Implementation in the United States, Canada, and Western Europe,* edited by Ronnie Steinberg Ratner (Temple University Press, 1980).

245. Milkman, Ruth, 1954- , ed. **Women, Work, and Protest: A Century of U.S. Women's Labor History.** Boston: Routledge and Kegan Paul, 1985. 333p. bibliog. index. $14.95. LC 84-27732. ISBN 0710099401.

In her preface to this exciting collection, Ruth Milkman surveys the scant research on women in the U.S. labor movement. Early feminist revisionism, she argues, essentially tried to compensate for gaps and blindspots in the literature. As such, it was largely descriptive and, to a certain degree, distorting. The articles collected here attempt to go beyond description to pinpoint the specific historical circumstances favoring women's militancy, and to explain the nature of male unionists' opposition. Among the fourteen original essays are "Bread Before Roses: American Workingmen, Labor Unions and the Family Wage," by Martha May; "The Women of the Colorado Fuel and Iron Strike," by Priscilla Long; "Problems of Coalition-Building: Women and Trade Unions in the 1920s," by Alice Kessler-Harris; "Survival Strategies Among African-American Women Workers: A Continuing Process," by Rosalyn Terborg-Penn; "'I Know Which Side I'm On': Southern Women in the Labor Movement in the Twentieth Century," by Mary Frederickson; "Women and the United Automobile Workers' Union in the 1950s," by Nancy Gabin; and "Women Workers, Feminism and the Labor Movement Since the 1960s," by Ruth Milkman.

246.* Neugarten, Dail Ann, and Jay M. Shafritz, eds. **Sexuality in Organizations: Romantic and Coercive Behaviors at Work.** Oak Park, IL: Moore, 1980. 166p. bibliog. index. LC 80-20737. ISBN 0935610146.

Though addressed to managers, and focused more on organizations than on women, this collection offers a handy introduction to the literature on sexual harassment of working women. In their overview, the editors distinguish romantic from coercive relationships and discuss the problems of defining sexual harassment and determining responsibility. The seventeen articles look at the nature of sexual harassment and its context, responses of organizations, and legal issues. Among the contributors are: Jennie Farley; Catharine MacKinnon (author of *Sexual Harassment of Working Women: A Case of Sex Discrimination* [Yale University Press, 1979], excerpted here); Peggy Crull; and Constance Backhouse and Leah Cohen (authors of *The Secret Oppression: Sexual Harassment and Working Women* [1978; Prentice-Hall, 1981], excerpted here). Missing from the roster is Lin Farley, one of the original organizers on this issue and author of *Sexual Shakedown: The Sexual Harassment of Women on the Job* (McGraw-Hill, 1978).

247. Nieva, Veronica F., and Barbara A. Gutek. **Women and Work: A Psychological Perspective.** New York: Praeger, 1981. 177p. bibliog. index. $29.95. LC 81-2713. ISBN 0030557615.

Nieva and Gutek present a review of empirical and theoretical literature on women and work through 1979. Though their discussion embraces studies from several disciplines, they come at the material from a psychological perspective. "Our learned bias is to study the individual woman, her choices, decisions, behaviors, and problems" (p.vii). Women's work experience outside the realm of paid employment is excluded from consideration, as are the experiences of "women in unions, poor and disadvantaged women, and working women outside of the industrialized Western world" (p.vii). The literature review covers the following topics: the context of women's work; women's career choices; factors affecting women's decision to work; combining work and family life; integrating women into the workplace; the evaluation of women's performance; women and leadership; views of women's achievements; organizational rewards for women; and approaches to change.

248. Reskin, Barbara F., ed. **Sex Segregation in the Workplace: Trends, Explanations, Remedies.** Washington, DC: National Academy Press, 1984. 313p. $22.95. LC 84-8342. ISBN 0309034450.

Most of the papers in this collection were originally presented at a 1982 workshop convened by the National Research Council. Both literature reviews and presentations of original research are included, augmented by the remarks of workshop commentators.

Reskin divides the volume into three sections: "Extent, Trends, and Projections for the Future"; "Explaining Segregation: Theoretical Perspectives and Empirical Evidence"; and "Reducing Segregation: The Effectiveness of Interventions." Two articles make comparisons by sex and race.

249. Roby, Pamela. **Women in the Workplace: Proposals for Research and Policy Concerning the Conditions of Women in Industrial Service Jobs.** Cambridge, MA: Schenkman, 1981. 138p. bibliog. index. $15.50. LC 80-24605. ISBN 0870731726.

Roby laments the paucity of research on women in blue-collar, industrial, and service jobs, noting that what little research there is tends to focus "on how to increase [the women's] productivity rather than on how to improve their own and their families' well-being" (pp.1-2). In this slim volume, Roby first provides a brief survey of the literature, 1890-1970, then proposes a research and policy agenda in five areas: wages and working conditions; work, training, and promotion opportunities; living conditions; attitudes of blue-collar women; and unions. Roby urges the government to provide fuller documentation of the specific conditions of "ethnic, Third World, young, aged, and handicapped women as well as women who face multiple discrimination" (p.4).

250. Sacks, Karen Brodkin, 1941- , and Dorothy Remy, 1943- , eds. **My Troubles Are Going to Have Trouble With Me: Everyday Trials and Triumphs of Women Workers.** New Brunswick, NJ: Rutgers University Press, 1984. 263p. bibliog. $29.00. LC 83-23079. ISBN 0813510384.

Sacks and Remy selected and organized the fifteen articles in this collection to bring out two major themes: "what capitalism has done to women's work, and how women resist and do *for* each other" (pp.1-2). Sacks' introduction provides the context for the collection, addressing recent trends such as multinational corporate expansion, United States industry's migration from the Northeast and Midwest to the Southeast and Southwest, the rise of the service industry and decline of manufacturing, and the current economic crisis. Articles in Part I explore the relationship between the family and capital. Part II focuses on the impact of new technology on women's work, with articles on the meat-packing industry, retail sales, word processing, legal secretaries, librarians, and hospital ward clerks. Contributors to Part III depict resistance strategies of women workers throughout the "global factory"—from a Providence, Rhode Island jewelry factory, to Silicon Valley, to the *maquiladoras* of Mexico. Among the contributors are Susan Porter Benson, Leigh S. Estabrook, María Patricia Fernández Kelly, and Louise Lamphere.

251. Sealander, Judith. **As Minority Becomes Majority: Federal Reaction to the Phenomenon of Women in the Work Force, 1920-1963.** Westport, CT: Greenwood Press, 1983. 201p. bibliog. index. $29.95. LC 82-15820. ISBN 0313237506.

Sealander gives an account of federal responses to women workers from the founding of the Women's Bureau to the passage of the Equal Pay Act; the Women's Bureau itself is her primary focus. "The Women's Bureau, the core of the federal program for female workers until the 1960s, was a Progressive legacy steeped in the Progressive idea that women workers needed a government advocate to help keep them fit for present or future domestic obligations" (p.5). Particularly interesting is her analysis of the contradictions faced by women bureaucrats in their dual status as "outsiders" advocating for women workers and as "insiders" with a stake in the bureaucracy and the economic status quo.

252. Shaw, Lois Banfill, ed. **Unplanned Careers: The Working Lives of Middle-Aged Women.** Lexington, MA: Lexington Books, 1983. 149p. bibliog. index. $22.00. LC 82-47925. ISBN 0669057010.

This book utilizes data from the National Longitudinal Survey of the Work Experience of Mature Women (NLS), a survey of nearly four thousand black and white women in the United States. The women were thirty to forty-four years of age at the time of the first interview in 1967; several additional interviews were obtained over the next ten years. The sample studied here represents "'women in the middle,' the generation caught between the old norms of devotion to family and new ideas about independent and active work lives ..." (p.1). (The work attachment, marriage patterns, and fertility behavior of the younger set of women interviewed for the NLS study are analyzed in *The Employment Revolution: Young American Women in the 1970s,* edited by Frank L. Mott [MIT Press, 1982].) Contributors examine the data with respect to: problems of labor market reentry; causes of irregular employment; "traditional" vs. "nontraditional" employment; the relationship between attitudes toward women's employment and women's labor force participation rates; and economic consequences of poor health, widowhood, separation, and divorce. Eileen Appelbaum also draws on the NLS dataset in *Back to Work: Determinants of Women's Successful Re-entry* (Auburn House, 1981). Appelbaum worked with two subsamples: women who interrupted their employment for three or more years following marriage or childbirth, and women who stopped work for less than three years. It is unfortunate that Appelbaum eliminated black women from her analysis; she did so, ironically, because very few of them fit the pattern of the first sample—a fact worthy of study in itself. Appelbaum's key finding is easily predicted: longer interruptions of employment are associated with greater economic costs. *Women Returning to Work: Policies and Progress in Five Countries* (Allanheld, Osmun, 1980), edited by Alice M. Yohalem, places these issues in an international context. Four separately authored articles detail the status of women reentering the labor market, and government policy towards reentry, in West Germany, France, Sweden, the United Kingdom, and the United States.

253. Sokoloff, Natalie J. **Between Money and Love: The Dialectics of Women's Home and Market Work.** New York: Praeger, 1980. 299p. bibliog. index. $37.95. LC 80-17101. ISBN 0030552966.

Sokoloff critically reviews theoretical frameworks within mainstream and radical sociology that seek to explain women's disadvantaged position in the labor market: the theory of status attainment; the theory of dual labor markets; Marxist theories of monopoly capitalism; early Marxist feminism; and later Marxist feminist theories of patriarchal capitalism. Building on her critique of these theories, Sokoloff develops her own perspective, which rests on the idea of a dialectical relationship between women's status in the home and in the labor market.

254. Wallace, Phyllis A. **Black Women in the Labor Force.** Cambridge, MA: MIT Press, 1980. 163p. bibliog. index. pbk. $5.95. LC 80-14175. ISBN 0262730634.

Black women differ significantly from white women in their occupational distribution and their lifetime work histories. In this concise little volume, Wallace pulls together a wealth of data attesting not only to these differences, but to the differences among black women themselves. Many tables drawn from United States government documents support the text's discussion. Difficult as it is to locate good research on black women workers, it is considerably more difficult to find scholarship on other women workers of color. Sources that do exist are often hard to access. *With Silk Wings: Asian American Women at Work,* by Elaine H. Kim with Janice Otani, is one example. Published in 1983 by Asian Women United of California, the book lacks the "hard data" of Wallace's study, but is valuable for the fifty-two profiles it presents—twelve in depth—of Chinese-, Filipino-, Japanese-, and Korean-American women workers: administrators, attorneys, researchers, physicians, journalists, judges, and more. The slim volume concludes with a brief historical essay on Asian women in the United States.

255.   Wallace, Phyllis Ann, ed. **Women in the Workplace.** Boston: Auburn House, 1982. 240p. bibliog. index. $24.95. LC 81-12775. ISBN 0865690693.
   The research gathered in this volume illustrates, in the judgment of editor Phyllis Wallace, "that, although women are becoming an increasing share of the labor force, they continue to face poorer opportunities than men" (p.xiii). The collection surveys affirmative action progress, career outcomes for women and men MBA's, apprenticeship opportunities, sex differences in managerial career advancement, women in white-collar and blue-collar jobs, and the role of corporate employers in improving women's job opportunities. The nine contributors are all social scientists, most of them affiliated with MIT, Wellesley College, or the Conference Board. The eight contributions to *The Subtle Revolution: Women at Work*, edited by Ralph E. Smith (1979), are all based on original research by members of the Urban Institute (which also published the volume). Six researchers investigate women's status in the labor market, unemployment and work schedules, women's employment and the family, and changes in the federal income tax system and social security.

256.*   Walshok, Mary Lindenstein. **Blue-Collar Women: Pioneers on the Male Frontier.** Garden City, NY: Anchor Press/Doubleday, 1981. 310p. bibliog. index. LC 81-43069. ISBN 038517845X.
   Walshok, a sociologist, interviewed 117 women from San Francisco, San Diego, and Los Angeles from 1975 to 1977. Among the women were "welders, carpenters, mechanics, forklift operators, and cable splicers, as well as women working in dozens of other skilled blue-collar jobs previously closed to them" (p.xvii). Walshok discusses the women's family backgrounds, work role identities, on-the-job experiences, work relationships, and the meaning of work in their lives, frequently drawing quotations from the interviews to underscore her points. Her findings dispel popular stereotypes about blue-collar women's backgrounds, confirm the existence of harassment on the job, and reveal these women to be risk takers who express greater job satisfaction than do blue-collar men or white-collar women. Jean Reith Schroedel, author of *Alone in a Crowd: Women in the Trades Tell Their Stories* (Temple University Press, 1985), conducted lengthy oral history interviews with twenty-five diverse women working in Seattle-area aerospace, shipbuilding, maritime, forestry, and other trades. The first-person accounts are arranged into five thematic sections: feminism, occupational safety and health, race, unions, and family. These lively stories reveal both the stress associated with the women's "outsider" status and the confidence the women gained by doing their jobs well and earning a better wage. Some recent case studies of women in "nontraditional" occupations include Elaine Pitt Enarson's *Woods-Working Women: Sexual Integration in the U.S. Forest Service* (University of Alabama Press, 1984); *Women and Wilderness,* by Anne LaBastille (Sierra Club Books, 1980); *Women of Steel: Female Blue-Collar Workers in the Basic Steel Industry*, by Kay Deaux and Joseph C. Ullman (Praeger, 1983); *Breaking and Entering: Policewomen on Patrol,* by Susan Ehrlich Martin (University of California Press, 1980); and, with a historical focus, Angela V. John's *By the Sweat of Their Brow: Women Workers at Victorian Coal Mines* (Croom Helm, 1980). *Tradeswomen: A Quarterly Magazine for Women in Blue-Collar Work* addresses issues of concern to women currently employed in "nontraditional" jobs.

257.   Weiner, Lynn Y., 1951- . **From Working Girl to Working Mother: The Female Labor Force in the United States, 1820-1980.** Chapel Hill: University of North Carolina Press, 1985. 187p. bibliog. index. $17.95. LC 84-7276. ISBN 0807816124.

Weiner's primary interest is the demographic shift over the past 150 years from a predominantly single to a largely married female labor force. She traces the history of the changing population of women workers, along with concomitant shifts in ideology. In the nineteenth century, the entrance of white, native-born, single women into the labor force provoked a reaction fueled by racist concerns about these women's future motherhood. As married women workers became the norm in our own century, debate began to center on the welfare of working women's children. Weiner's account reveals "the cultural lag between new patterns of labor force behavior and traditional ideas of domesticity" (p.9) and the changing social policies that accompanied these trends. This cultural lag notwithstanding, women's labor force participation is "the most effective predictor of the traditionality of sex-role behaviors and attitudes," argue sociologists Joan Huber and Glenna Spitze in *Sex Stratification: Children, Housework, and Jobs* (Academic Press, 1983), a report on survey research conducted in 1978.

258.   Werneke, Diane. **Microelectronics and Office Jobs: The Impact of the Chip on Women's Employment.** Geneva: International Labour Office, 1983. 102p. bibliog. pbk. $11.50. LC 83-168772. ISBN 9221032787.

Werneke's small volume is the most comprehensive study so far on this timely topic. Werneke first explores the overall impact of the new technology on job structure and employment, then zeroes in on women's jobs, which are concentrated in information-handling sectors. The heart of the study is an examination of the effects of microelectronics on labor displacement, work content, and work organization in North America, Europe, and Australia. Some of Werneke's specific examples are taken from *Women and the Chip: Case Studies of the Effects of Informatics on Employment in Canada,* by Heather Menzies (Institute for Research on Public Policy, 1981), itself a very solid work on the topic. G. L. Simons' *Women in Computing* (National Computing Centre, 1981) looks at attitudes affecting women's employment in the computing field. *Your Job in the Eighties: A Woman's Guide to New Technology,* by Ursula Huws (Pluto Press, 1982), discusses the impact of microtechnology on a variety of "female" occupations, but with a nonacademic, union-organizing focus. *Office Automation: Jekyll or Hyde?,* edited by Daniel Marschall and Judith Gregory (Working Women Education Fund, 1983), is an eclectic collection of papers by academics, consumer advocates, and government and industry representatives. For a nitty-gritty, very readable and empowering guide to how a computer works and what it can and cannot do, turn to Deborah L. Brecher's *The Women's Computer Literacy Handbook* (New American Library, 1985). Another good popular work is *Computer Confidence: A Woman's Guide,* by Dorothy Heller and June Bower (Acropolis Books, 1983).

259.   Westwood, Sallie. **All Day, Every Day: Factory and Family in the Making of Women's Lives.** Urbana: University of Illinois Press, 1985. 259p. bibliog. index. $21.95. LC 84-23989. ISBN 0252011910.

Westwood spent a year (1980-81) as a participant observer on the shop floor of a British hosiery company she calls "StitchCo." She came to this study not just with the ethnographer's desire to describe, but with the hope of testing socialist-feminist theory on the interaction of patriarchy and capitalism against the reality of factory and home. Westwood describes in vivid detail and readable style women's shop floor culture: how it both resists patriarchal management and reinforces patriarchal conceptions of womanhood; and how it nurtures sisterhood and solidarity among workers. Asian immigrants from East Africa constituted a significant segment of the workforce of StitchCo, and Westwood is consistently attentive to issues of race as well as of sex and class.

260. Yeandle, Susan. **Women's Working Lives: Patterns and Strategies.** New York: Methuen, 1984. 232p. bibliog. index. pbk. $15.95. LC 84-16250. ISBN 0422789607.

Although based on a small-scale study of employed women in Kent, England, Yeandle's volume shows broad familiarity with recent United States and British literature, both empirical and theoretical. After some preliminary remarks on the history of women's labor, Yeandle discusses her subjects' work patterns and how the employment strategies they devise are shaped by the labor market and the social relations of household work. Quotes from her interviews punctuate her own analysis, and each of the three major chapters ends with the full story of one woman's working life. The relationships of home and work, and of patriarchy and capitalism, give underlying structure to the study. *Work, Women and the Labour Market,* edited by Jackie West (Routledge & Kegan Paul, 1982), examines women's employment in contemporary Britain through case studies of the clothing industry, factory work, clerical work, Asian women sweatshop workers, West Indian migrant workers, working-class housewives, and unions.

261. Yohalem, Alice M. **The Careers of Professional Women: Commitment and Conflict.** Montclair, NJ: Allanheld, Osmun, 1979. 224p. bibliog. index. $16.50. LC 77-10187. ISBN 0876638213.

Yohalem reports the findings of a longitudinal study of the careers of 226 graduates of Columbia University. The women were intially surveyed in 1963, when they were in their late thirties or early forties; a follow-up questionnaire was administered in 1975. The study attempted to measure the impact on career commitment of such factors as marital status, motherhood and size of family, husbands' attitudes, and career choice. It also questioned the women about their perceptions of discrimination and conflicts between work and family. The major finding was that "the career commitment of this group of women was variable in intensity, but was rarely extinguished" (p.190). Not surprisingly, "it was primarily the presence of children that acted as a brake upon careers" (p.191).

EDUCATION AND PEDAGOGY

Books on a range of themes appear in this chapter: histories of women's education; studies of women's roles in education (as students, teachers, administrators); innovative sourcebooks on feminist pedagogical methods; studies of sex discrimination and sexual harassment in academia; strategy manuals for achieving sex equity at all levels of schooling; and assessments of women's studies' impact on the undergraduate curriculum. *Women's Studies Quarterly* (see entry 1211) updates these listings with articles on women's studies content and classroom process; the newer *Feminist Teacher* (see entry 1169) also provides inspiration. The microfiche ERIC files continue to offer access to report literature, while several bibliographies (see entries 895 and 899) serve as guides to older writings. Further writings on the philosophy and politics of feminist education can be found in the chapter titled Women's Movement and Feminist Theory.

262.* Acker, Sandra Sue, 1944- , et al., eds. **Women and Education.** London: Kogan Page; New York: Nichols Publishing, 1984. 358p. bibliog. index. ISBN 0893971766.
Together with co-editors Jacquetta Megarry, Stanley Nisbet, and Eric Hoyle, Acker brings together twenty-three articles in this thematic volume of the *World Yearbook of Education*. Primary, secondary, and higher education, as well as vocational training and adult education, are all treated. Part One offers theoretical perspectives on women's education from the angles of philosophy, psychology, sociology, and sociolinguistics. Part Two presents case studies from the Third World, Australia, England, Malaysia, Jamaica, the United States, Wales, Canada, and Scotland. Part Three looks at the education of women in the context of other social institutions—the family, the labor force, religious tradition, and the new technology—in articles focused on the Soviet Union, Egypt, and Sweden. Part Four examines policies and strategies for change in social and educational systems. The fifth part is an extensive bibliography, selectively annotated. The contributors are largely British and American scholars, yet the volume is unrivaled in its international scope.

263.* Balbo, Laura, and Yasmine Ergas. **Women's Studies in Italy.** Old Westbury, NY: Feminist Press, 1982. 63p. LC 82-7644. ISBN 0935312056.
In this brief report, Balbo and Ergas assess the evolution of Italian women's studies. Free classes organized by trade unions have been central to the spread of feminist studies in Italy, while universities and research centers have played a secondary role. The report includes listings of research projects and courses. The Feminist Press intended this work to be the first in a series of monographs on international women's studies, but no further volumes have appeared. The Press did, however, issue a short-lived journal, *Women's Studies International*, and continues to offer coverage of feminist education worldwide in *Women's Studies Quarterly* (see entry 1211).

264. Biklen, Sari Knopp, and Marilyn B. Brannigan, eds. **Women and Educational Leadership.** Lexington, MA: Lexington Books, 1980. 268p. bibliog. index. $27.50. LC 79-7748. ISBN 0669032166.

Sexual inequality is evident in the administrative ranks of educational institutions at all levels. This interdisciplinary anthology examines the causes of male dominance in education and possible models for increasing female leadership. Biklen's introduction reviews the literature on the topic and poses questions about the semiprofessional status of teaching, the forms and extent of sex discrimination, and the constraints on women in their work lives. The sixteen papers address the nature of leadership, historical perspectives on women administrators, obstacles to achievement (both institutional and psychological), and new models for boosting women's participation.

265. Bowles, Gloria, and Renate Duelli Klein, eds. **Theories of Women's Studies.** Boston: Routledge and Kegan Paul, 1983. 277p. bibliog. index. pbk. $9.95. LC 82-19512. ISBN 0710094884.

Originally published in two parts by the Women's Studies Program at the University of California, Berkeley, this anthology provides a framework for discussing the theory and practice of women's studies. Among the topics scrutinized here are the autonomy/integration debate, the status of women's studies as a distinct discipline, methodologies for feminist reasearch, and women's studies as a strategy for social change. Bowles, Duelli Klein, and Taly Rutenberg contribute a selected annotated bibliography. Other essayists include Dale Spender, Sandra Coyner, and Shulamit Reinharz.

266. Bunch, Charlotte, 1944- , and Sandra Pollack, eds. **Learning Our Way: Essays in Feminist Education.** Trumansburg, NY: Crossing Press, 1983. 334p. $22.95. LC 83-15182. ISBN 0895941120.

The twenty-six essays in this anthology reflect progress in educational experimentation from the mid-1970s to the mid-1980s. Part I, focused on existing institutions, examines not only women's studies programs on college campuses but also innovative educational projects in a prison and an urban neighborhood. Part II describes a number of feminist programs outside formal institutions — some successful, others not. Several perspectives are offered on Sagaris, a short-lived institute in Vermont, and Califia, an ongoing southern California "community." Other pieces analyze antiracism education for white women, a "feminist chautauqua" in rural Montana, home-based movie production, and programs for women artists, writers, planners, and architects. The topic of educational alternatives for women has rarely been treated in print, and the bringing together of so many inspiring examples in one volume is unprecedented. In Part III, questions of theory, methodology, and pedagogy are addressed by leaders in women's studies and the feminist movement — Charlotte Bunch, Nancy Schniedewind, Michelle Gibbs Russell, Evelyn Torton Beck, Jan Zimmerman, Betty Powell, and Elizabeth Kamarck Minnich.

267. Culley, Margo, and Catherine Portuges, eds. **Gendered Subjects: The Dynamics of Feminist Teaching.** Boston: Routledge and Kegan Paul, 1985. 284p. bibliog. index. $24.95. LC 84-18079. ISBN 071009907X.

The application of feminist principles to the classroom situation, declare the editors of this pathbreaking anthology, "far from reductive or doctrinaire, contains the potential for reconstructing and revitalizing the ways in which knowledge is acquired, sanctioned and perpetuated" (p.2). Some of the essays are classic statements from the early and mid-1970s, while others are new; although narrowly focused on college teaching, they tackle a range of theoretical issues and pedagogical strategies. Certain themes recur in many of the twenty-three pieces: the question of authority (of teacher and/or text); the legitimation of emotion and personal experience as co-equal to reason and intellect in the learning process; and the effects of race, gender, class, sexual preference, and political differences in the classroom context. Contributors to this inspiring collection include Adrienne Rich, Janice G. Raymond, Helene Keyssar, Judith McDaniel, Nancy Jo Hoffman, Nancy K. Miller, Susan Stanford Friedman, Mary Helen Washington, and John Schilb.

268.   DeSole, Gloria, 1937- , and Leonore Hoffmann, 1929- , eds. **Rocking the Boat: Academic Women and Academic Processes.** New York: Modern Language Association of America, 1981. 129p. bibliog. pbk. $12.50. LC 81-14030. ISBN 087352330X.

When they conceived *Rocking the Boat*, editors DeSole and Hoffmann were both tangled in legal actions against their academic institutions. This slim book, which "falls somewhere between the action handbook and the documentary" (p.ix), presents eight case histories of women faculty members who challenged negative decisions on questions of appointment, equal pay, tenure, or promotion. Four appended essays discuss the career consequences of involvement in women's studies, court rulings on peer review, the failure of affirmative action at one large university, and networking on campus. The MLA has sponsored several other volumes on women's concerns, among them *Stepping Off the Pedestal: Academic Women in the South* (Modern Language Association of America, 1982), an anthology of personal and historical accounts with a bibliographical essay. Patricia A. Stringer and Irene Thompson are the editors.

269.   Dziech, Billie Wright, 1941- , and Linda Weiner. **The Lecherous Professor: Sexual Harassment on Campus.** Boston: Beacon Press, 1984. 219p. bibliog. index. $16.95. LC 82-73960. ISBN 0807031003.

Their title notwithstanding, Dziech and Weiner intend not to titillate, but to enrage. The authors restrict their study to harassment of female students by male faculty because all available evidence suggests this form to be the most prevalent and damaging. Based on information and anecdotes gathered from some four hundred students, faculty, administrators, and alumni nationwide, men as well as women, their indictment of the abuse of power by male faculty is relentless, and sharpened by the personal testimony scattered throughout the work. Dziech and Weiner dissect the specific conditions prevailing within the academy that may facilitate or encourage harassment; debunk the myths of the coed; speculate on the motivations of the offenders; and consider the responsibility of women faculty. In their final chapter, they offer recommendations for collective action to students, faculty, parents, administrators, and deans and department heads. Included in the appendices are Title VII guidelines on sexual harassment and several policy statements and guides to legal remedies. *Sexual and Gender Harassment in the Academy: A Guide for Faculty, Students, and Administrators* (1981), written by Phyllis Franklin, et al., and published by the Modern Language Association of America, is a concise source on the topic.

270.   Fisher, Jerilyn, and Elaine Reuben, eds. **The Women's Studies Service Learning Handbook: From the Classroom to the Community.** College Park, MD: National Women's Studies Association, 1981. 281p. pbk. $2.00.

Community service outside the classroom is a vital mode of feminist learning. This handbook addresses the planning, evaluation, and joys and pitfalls of field experiences in women's studies. Faculty, supervisors, and student interns share their experiences and opinions. They present models for service learning programs, cite print and media resources, and provide numerous sample syllabi and forms.

271. Hoffman, Nancy. **Woman's "True" Profession: Voices From the History of Teaching.** Old Westbury, NY: Feminist Press; New York: McGraw-Hill, 1981. 327p. bibliog. index. $17.95. LC 80-23329. ISBN 0912670932.

As part of the "Women's Lives/Women's Work" series, this volume assembles written and visual primary sources on women teachers in the United States. From the autobiography of Emma Willard, founder in 1821 of the Troy Female Seminary, to turn-of-the-century arguments for unionization and equal pay, these documents speak eloquently of women's roles in education. Selections are grouped in three parts: "Seminary for Social Power: The Classroom Becomes Woman's Sphere"; "A Noble Work Done Earnestly: Yankee Schoolmarms in the Civil War South"; and "Teaching in the Big City: Women Staff the Education Factories." Hoffman provides an introduction to each part and short notes before the selections. Polly Welts Kaufman's *Women Teachers on the Frontier* (Yale University Press, 1984) employs the diaries and letters of pioneering teachers to strip away the stereotype of "the schoolmarm from the East" who, under the auspices of the National Board of Popular Education, traveled to the western frontiers to live and work in the mid-nineteenth century. Kaufman's introduction analyzes these teachers' motivations and their experiences at work and in their new communities.

272. Horowitz, Helen Lefkowitz, 1942- . **Alma Mater: Design and Experience in the Women's Colleges From Their Nineteenth-Century Beginnings to the 1930s.** New York: Knopf, 1984. 420p. bibliog. index. $25.00. LC 84-47506. ISBN 0394534395.

Women's colleges are the subject of this history—the "Seven Sisters" (Mount Holyoke, Vassar, Wellesley, Smith, Radcliffe, Bryn Mawr, Barnard) and by way of contrast, Sarah Lawrence, Bennington, and Scripps. Horowitz examines changes in architecture, curriculum, and campus governance. These key elements, she demonstrates, "serve as vivid emblems of how Americans once perceived college women and how women students, alumnae, and faculty came to perceive themselves" (p.354). Horowitz's analysis highlights the visions of the colleges' founders, the development of a student peer culture (often at odds with societal prescriptions of femininity), and the increased professionalism and autonomy of female faculty. The text is illustrated with photographs of college buildings and campus life.

273. Howe, Florence. **Myths of Coeducation: Selected Essays, 1964-1983.** Bloomington: Indiana University Press, 1984. 306p. $35.00. LC 84-47702. ISBN 0253339669.

Howe, an early proponent of women's studies and founder of The Feminist Press, here presents nineteen selected essays, all but two previously published. Among the classic texts reprinted here are "Mississippi's Freedom Schools: The Politics of Education," "Why Educate Women?," "Sex-Role Stereotypes Start Early," and "Women and the Power to Change." Many of the essays were written as lectures; the topics span the future of women's colleges, images of women in American literature, feminist teaching methods, and the growth and future of women's studies. Howe blends historical and literary research, personal anecdotes, impassioned feminism, and apt quotations from literary sources in a straightforward style that makes her enlightening ideas readily accessible.

274.* Howe, Florence, and Paul Lauter. **The Impact of Women's Studies on the Campus and the Disciplines.** Washington, DC: National Institute of Education, Program on Teaching and Learning, 1980. 132p. bibliog. LC 80-602566.

This volume is one in a series of seven reports presenting a state-of-the-art overview of women's studies at the start of the 1980s. The other titles in the "Women's Studies Monograph Series" are: *The Effectiveness of Women's Studies Teaching* (Nancy M. Porter and Margaret T. Eileenchild); *The Relationship Between Women's Studies, Career Development, and Vocational Choice* (Christine E. Bose and Janet Priest-Jones); *Re-entry Women Involved in Women's Studies* (Blanche Glassman Hersh); *Women's Studies as a Catalyst for Faculty Development* (Elizabeth Ness Nelson and Kathryn H. Brooks); *Women's Studies Graduates* (Elaine Reuben and Mary Jo Boehm Strauss); and *Women's Studies in the Community College* (Allana Elovson). Each report reviews the pertinent literature and makes recommendations for policy and further research. An eighth monograph on minority women in women's studies, although listed in the other volumes, was never published.

275. Kelly, Gail Paradise, and Carolyn M. Elliott, eds. **Women's Education in the Third World: Comparative Perspectives.** Albany: State University of New York Press, 1982. 406p. bibliog. index. $44.50. LC 82-789. ISBN 0873956192.

The sixteen research papers collected in this volume reveal a pattern of female "undereducation" in the developing countries of Asia, Africa, and Latin America. Starting from the premise that "the social and economic outcomes of women's education are shaped by sex-gender systems that place women in subordination to men" (p.4), the authors document factors affecting access to education, issues in educational practice and curriculum content, and the effects of schooling on women's work and family roles. Many of the studies rely heavily on quantitative analysis. Elliott and Kelly add a concluding chapter sketching directions for future research, and an excellent bibliography of works in English, French, and Spanish, arranged by topic.

276. Komarovsky, Mirra. **Women in College: Shaping New Feminine Identities.** New York: Basic Books, 1985. 355p. bibliog. index. $19.95. LC 84-45307. ISBN 0465091989.

Komarovsky seeks to ascertain how undergraduate women cope with the rapidly changing status of women and how college affects their attitudes and aspirations. At an unnamed women's college, a sample of entering freshmen in 1979 replied to a set of questionnaires, and some were then interviewed. The data-gathering was repeated in their sophomore and senior years. Extracts from interviews and student diaries enliven this case study. Part I examines the transition to college: how students become integrated into the campus community and how their self-concepts and relations with family and peers are transformed. Part II centers on students' attitudes toward gender roles, as reflected in their plans for careers, marriage, and motherhood. Part III looks at interpersonal relationships between women and men.

277. Langland, Elizabeth, and Walter Gove, eds. **A Feminist Perspective in the Academy: The Difference It Makes.** Chicago: University of Chicago Press, 1983. 162p. $17.00. LC 82-17520. ISBN 0226468747.

Nine leading academicians thoughtfully assess the theoretical and methodological implications of the new feminist scholarship on their disciplines. The authors of these engaging essays are: Patricia Meyer Spacks on literary criticism; Nancy S. Reinhardt on theater; Rosemary Radford Ruether on religious studies; Carl N. Degler on American history; Nannerl O. Keohane on political science; Nancy S. Barrett on economics; Judith Shapiro on anthropology; Janet T. Spence on psychology; and Cynthia Fuchs Epstein on sociology. All point to inroads made by feminist analysis, but most conclude that the lasting influence is thus far minimal. These collected pieces were first published as a special issue of *Soundings*, vol.64, no.4. For additional viewpoints on this question, see *Men's Studies Modified* (entry 283). Collections such as these continue the work of the trailblazing anthology *The Prism of Sex: Essays in the Sociology of Knowledge* (University of Wisconsin Press, 1979), edited by Julia A. Sherman and Evelyn Torton Beck. A classic assessment of male bias in scholarship, the volume presents critiques of history by Nancy Schrom Dye and Jane Tibbetts Schulenberg; of literature by Catharine R. Stimpson, Susan Sniader Lanser, and Evelyn Torton Beck; of psychology by Carolyn Wood Sherif; of sociology by Dorothy E. Smith; of philosophy by Kathryn Pyne Parsons; and of political science by Jean Bethke Elshtain and Virginia Sapiro. These influential scholars "examine the assumptions and question the questions" (p.5) of their academic disciplines, thus charting a course for feminist inquiry in the eighties.

278.   Perun, Pamela J., ed. **The Undergraduate Woman: Issues in Educational Equity.** Lexington, MA: Lexington Books, 1982. 433p. bibliog. index. $33.50. LC 80-8596. ISBN 0669043044.

"The intent of this book," states Perun, "is to initiate a comprehensive examination into the processes and settings of undergraduate education for women" (p.7). Presenting a state-of-the-art overview of research and theory as of 1980, the seventeen contributions draw on several disciplines. The volume is divided into four sections: Part I, "Historical and Recent Trends in College Attendance by Women"; Part II, "The Precollege Years: Issues of Access and Selection"; Part III, "The College Experience: Issues of Growth and Change"; and Part IV, "College and Beyond: Issues of Outcomes and Achievements." *The Undergraduate Woman* is addressed to administrators, faculty, and counselors, who will also find inspiration in Karen Bogart's compendium, *Toward Equity: An Action Manual for Women in Academe* (Project on the Status and Education of Women, Association of American Colleges, 1984). Bogart profiles some 150 exemplary programs that promote sex equity in postsecondary education. In an introductory section titled "The ABCs of Change," educators who have themselves served as catalysts for institutional change share their strategies and insights in thirteen short essays.

279.   Rich, Sharon Lee, and Ariel Phillips, eds. **Women's Experience and Education.** Cambridge, MA: Harvard Educational Review, 1985. 301p. bibliog. index. pbk. $15.95. LC 84-081321. ISBN 0916690199.

From a half-century of the prestigious *Harvard Educational Review,* Rich and Phillips managed to cull only ten articles that specifically address women's education. Among these, however, are such important pieces as Marcia Westkott's "Feminist Criticism of the Social Sciences," Maxine Baca Zinn's "Employment and Education of Mexican-American Women," and Carol Gilligan's two germinal pieces, "In a Different Voice: Women's Conceptions of Self and Morality" and "Woman's Place in Man's Life Cycle." Articles by Robert Ulich and Ordway Tead, both writing in the forties, convey male attitudes toward women's education that were liberal in their time but now sound staunchly traditional. Excluded from this anthology are articles by, but not about, women, and pieces that address women's experiences solely as wives and homemakers. Instead, the editors flesh out the collection with seventeen book reviews, many of them substantial pieces in their own right.

280.   Sadker, Myra Pollack, and David Miller Sadker, 1942- . **Sex Equity Handbook for Schools.** New York: Longman, 1982. 331p. bibliog. $18.95. LC 81-8213. ISBN 0582282608.

A very practical guide to identifying and combatting sexism in elementary and secondary schools, the *Sex Equity Handbook* also overviews research on sexism and examines how sex bias affects children's development. Chapters one to four include exercises for adults/teachers, while chapters five to six contain lesson plans adaptable to various age groupings from K through 12. A substantial resource directory lists organizations, publishers, and government agencies that distribute sex equity materials. *Equal Their Chances: Children's Activities for Non-Sexist Learning,* by June Shapiro, Sylvia Kramer, and Catherine Hunerberg (Prentice-Hall, 1981), is another how-to guide, presenting both discussion of sexism in elementary-level curriculum areas and related ungraded lesson plans.

281. Schuster, Marilyn R., and Susan R. Van Dyne, eds. **Women's Place in the Academy: Transforming the Liberal Arts Curriculum.** Totowa, NJ: Rowman and Allanheld, 1985. 328p. bibliog. $24.95. LC 84-27566. ISBN 084767407X.

Under the rubric of "curriculum integration," "gender balancing," or "mainstreaming," projects to incorporate feminist scholarship into the basic college curriculum have sprung up, prompting several new how-to books. Schuster and Van Dyne's anthology provides a framework for understanding the context and process of gender balancing. The eighteen essays are grouped in three sections: "Curriculum Transformation: Redefining the Core" (six theoretical pieces); "Faculty Development: Models for Institutional Change"; and "Classroom Consequences." The final section presents field-tested guidelines for the redesign of syllabi, plus a discipline-specific bibliography of sources for classroom use and teacher preparation. Betty Schmitz's *Integrating Women's Studies Into the Curriculum* (Feminist Press, 1985) is even more pragmatic. Schmitz reveals the nuts and bolts of managing a curriculum development project, profiles ten campuses in the Northern Rockies Program on Women in the Curriculum, and provides a national directory of similar projects. An excellent annotated bibliography covers general works on women's studies and curriculum integration, methodologies for evaluation, course revision models, feminist periodicals, reference works, and other materials. Additional resources for curriculum development include *Toward a Balanced Curriculum: A Sourcebook for Initiating Gender Integration Projects,* edited by Bonnie Spanier, Alexander Bloom, and Darlene Boroviak (Schenkman, 1984), and *Toward Excellence & Equity: The Scholarship on Women as a Catalyst for Change in the University,* by JoAnn M. Fritsche (University of Maine at Orono, 1985). The former presents the proceedings of a 1983 conference, supplemented by brief reports on revised courses, unannotated bibliographies, and project descriptions. The latter is a detailed handbook, addressed to faculty, administrators, and professional staff who must mobilize campus support. Teachers and librarians involved in such projects should also consult *Integrating Women's Studies Into the Curriculum: An Annotated Bibliography,* by Susan Douglas Franzosa and Karen A. Mazza (Greenwood Press, 1984).

282. Solomon, Barbara Miller, 1919- . **In the Company of Educated Women: A History of Women and Higher Education in America.** New Haven, CT: Yale University Press, 1985. 298p. bibliog. index. $25.00. LC 84-19681. ISBN 0300033141.

"This book is a history, not of institutions but of generations of women: those who hungered for education, those who fought for it, and those who took it for granted" (p.xvii). Solomon views higher education in the United States through a feminist lens, never losing sight of the social, cultural, and economic circumstances that shaped women's lives. She traces women's struggles for access to institutions, the dimensions of their collegiate experiences, the effects of education upon their life choices (and on society as a whole), and the complex interactions between feminism and women's educational advancement. The comprehensive narrative draws on a wealth of published and archival sources from Abigail Adams' time to the present. In her conclusion, Solomon is cautiously optimistic that coeducation, in concert with the contemporary women's movement, will continue to expand women's opportunities for learning and employment.

283. Spender, Dale, ed. **Men's Studies Modified: The Impact of Feminism on the Academic Disciplines.** Oxford: Pergamon Press, 1981. 248p. bibliog. $33.00. LC 80-41818. ISBN 008026770X.

Spender argues that men, heretofore the primary producers (and subjects) of knowledge, create and sustain a "men's studies" curriculum that is passed off as universal. By challenging such ingrained notions as the value of objectivity and the use of the generic "man," feminist scholarship has begun to rattle the foundations of the academic disciplines. The fifteen essays gathered here document the varied effects of such challenges and the long road ahead for feminists who dream of a transformed academy and a new politics of knowledge. The contributors are: Mercilee M. Jenkins and Cheris Kramarae on linguistics; Annette Kolodny on literary criticism; Sheila Ruth on philosophy; Jane Lewis on history; Helen Roberts on sociology; Joni Lovenduski on political science; Carol P. MacCormack on anthropology; Beverly M. Walker on psychology; Marianne A. Ferber and Michelle L. Teiman on economics; Helen Baehr on media studies; Dale Spender on education; Katherine O'Donovan on law; Mary Ann Elston on medicine; Ruth Hubbard on biology; and Kathy Overfield on the physical and natural sciences. For additional viewpoints, see *A Feminist Perspective in the Academy* (entry 277).

284.* Stockard, Jean, et al. **Sex Equity in Education.** New York: Academic Press, 1980. 238p. bibliog. index. LC 80-10082. ISBN 0126715505.

Of the limited number of scholarly works on sex inequities at the elementary and secondary school levels, Stockard's is probably the most comprehensive and useful. Part I examines sex-role inequities experienced by both students and teachers, reviews the literature on sex differences in student performance, and overviews sex segregation in the education profession. Part II explores possibilities for change, evaluating the psychological context, sex discrimination law, and the influence of the women's movement. Appendices provide experiential exercises to complement each of the chapters. More limited in scope and less accessible to a broad readership is *Gender Influences in Classroom Interaction*, edited by Louise Cherry Wilkinson and Cora B. Marrett (Academic Press, 1985). This nicely arranged selection of conference papers examines a range of factors affecting the differential performance of males and females at the elementary level, including peer interaction, subject matter, race, preschool influences, and teacher-student interaction. Dale Spender's *Invisible Women: The Schooling Scandal* (Writers and Readers; distr. Norton, 1982) is an excellent feminist overview of sexism in education. Though grounded in British school experience, Spender's findings and radical arguments for change are quite applicable to the United States.

285. Thomas, Martha Carey, 1857-1935. **The Making of a Feminist: Early Journals and Letters of M. Carey Thomas.** Edited by Marjorie Housepian Dobkin. Kent, OH: Kent State University Press, 1979. 314p. $18.00. LC 79-88605. ISBN 0873382323.

Editor Dobkin asserts that M. Carey Thomas "was certainly the most compelling and dramatic figure among pioneer leaders in higher education for women" (p.1) and "raised as many hackles as any feminist before or since" (p.19). Thomas was the first dean of Bryn Mawr College and its second president. Dobkin has assembled a chronological selection of Thomas's journals and letters, which reveal her strength of will, indomitable spirit, and often unorthodox ideas. Dobkin fills in the details of Thomas's life from her birth in 1857 to her appointment at Bryn Mawr in 1884. She goes to great lengths trying to refute the commonly held notion that Thomas was a lesbian. A foreword by Millicent Carey McIntosh (Thomas's niece) and an appendix that collates the autobiographical fragments Thomas left behind round out the volume. Other recent studies of pioneering women educators include Elizabeth Alden Green's *Mary Lyon and Mount Holyoke: Opening the Gates* (University Press of New England, 1979) and *Three Who Dared*, by Philip S. Foner and Josephine F. Pacheco (Greenwood Press, 1984). The latter profiles Prudence Crandall, Margaret Douglass, and Myrtilla Miner, all champions of education for black children before the Civil War.

286.   Thompson, Irene, and Audrey Roberts, eds. **The Road Retaken: Women Reenter the Academy.** New York: Modern Language Association of America, 1985. 152p. bibliog. $27.50. LC 84-19091. ISBN 0873523407.

Twenty-five women scholars contribute personal accounts of reentering the academic world as students and teachers after interrupting their educations for five years or more. All faced difficulties in graduate school, in finding jobs, and in balancing the demands of career and family. Aware of the dearth of materials by or for such women, the editors intend "that these experiential and factual chronicles will serve as both history and inspiration to all reentry women ..." (p.3).

287.   Thompson, Jane L. **Learning Liberation: Women's Response to Men's Education.** London: Croom Helm, 1983. 207p. bibliog. index. pbk. $14.75. LC 83-124343. ISBN 0709924399.

Many adult and continuing education programs serve women students, yet few books present a feminist analysis of their organization and impact. Thompson, a Britisher, combines a scathing indictment of conventional adult education with an inspiring report on an interdisciplinary course for working-class women in Southampton. She traces the history of schooling for girls and the theory and practice of adult education in Britain, grounding her vision of women-centered education in the politics of liberation. In the United States, the spotlight is on the "returning" or "nontraditional" student, who pursues a college degree after interrupting her education for a number of years. Surprisingly, there are few book-length studies of this phenomenon as well. Aimed at policymakers, Carol Kehr Tittle and Elenor Rubin Denker's *Returning Women Students in Higher Education* (Praeger, 1980) discusses the key factors—institutional, psychological, and social—affecting women's educational reentry. The authors provide case studies of programs and individual students, but unlike Thompson they fail to examine the curriculum or to offer a broader analysis of women's interactions with the educational system. Women contemplating a return to college should peruse Pamela Mendelsohn's *Happier by Degrees* (Dutton, 1980). Supportive in content and tone, the sourcebook answers questions about admissions, financial aid, career choice, familial attitudes, and campus life.

288.   Vartuli, Sue, ed. **The Ph.D. Experience: A Woman's Point of View.** New York: Praeger, 1982. 144p. bibliog. $23.95. LC 81-17797. ISBN 0030600367.

In tones that range from introspective and self-confident to cautionary and bitter, this uneven collection recounts the experiences of eleven women graduate students at Ohio State University. The personal stories touch on many aspects of doctoral study: deciding to pursue an advanced degree; struggling through comprehensive exams; writing a dissertation; surviving in a predominantly white male institution; coping with physical and emotional stress; building support networks; balancing school with relationships and family; being an older woman in a Ph.D. program; and job hunting. Despite the strain, all the writers confess (some more enthusiastically than others) that the process was worth it.

HISTORY

The preponderance of American and British studies cited in the History chapter reflects the trend in English-language scholarship in women's history. While the period from the nineteenth century to the present continues to dominate feminist historical inquiry, interest in earlier periods is growing. We have selected some semiautobiographical, diary, and documentary accounts for this chapter—including anthologies of primary sources—but the emphasis is on historical analysis and method. A few topics have garnered particular attention in the past five years, as evidenced in the clusters of works we cite within entries. Among the subjects that preoccupy feminist historians are race relations, Victorian mores, the World Wars and the interwar period, reform movements, early feminism, and women's experiences in the American West and South. Historical studies within other disciplines will be found in the appropriate chapters—e.g., histories of women's labor force participation and activism in Business, of women's education in Education, of women's contributions to religion in Religion, and of the contemporary women's movement in Women's Movement and Feminist Theory. Two reference tools mentioned elsewhere in this volume will lead users to major resources in history: volume two of *Women in American History: A Bibliography* (see entry 873) and *Women's Studies: A Bibliography of Dissertations 1870-1982,* compiled by Gilbert and Tatla (see entry 868). *Signs* (see entry 1195), a mainstay of journal literature for women's studies, periodically summarizes the state of the art in the discipline in review essays that critique and assess trends.

289. Anderson, Judith, ed. **Outspoken Women: Speeches by American Women Reformers, 1635-1935.** Dubuque, IA: Kendall/Hunt, 1984. 258p. pbk. $14.95. LC 84-80377. ISBN 084033298X.
Historians and students of rhetoric will find valuable source material in this volume, which reprints speeches by forty American women reformers—from Anne Hutchinson's testimony in her 1637 trial for religious heresy, to Mary McLeod Bethune's 1933 celebratory address, "A Century of Progress of Negro Women." Anderson introduces each document with a short biography. In addition to the champions of women's rights—Susan B. Anthony, Charlotte Perkins Gilman, and Alice Paul, for example—the reader encounters Jane Addams, Dorothea Dix, Mary Baker Eddy, Elizabeth Gurley Flynn, Angelina Grimké, Sojourner Truth, Frances Willard, and other courageous and impassioned speechmakers. In *Index to American Women Speakers, 1828-1978* (Scarecrow Press, 1980), Beverly Manning creates a bibliographic key to over three thousand speeches from a 150-year period. Manning has diligently mined published proceedings, anthologies, documentary histories, congressional hearings, and periodicals. Among the themes addressed are the suffrage movement, the contemporary women's movement, education, employment and economic rights, abortion, and the E.R.A. Full citations are provided under the names of the speakers, with indexes to titles and subjects.

290.   Anderson, Karen, 1947- . **Wartime Women: Sex Roles, Family Relations, and the Status of Women During World War II.** Westport, CT: Greenwood Press, 1981. 198p. bibliog. index. $27.50. LC 80-1703. ISBN 0313208840.

Anderson portrays the effects of the Second World War on women in three war-boom cities—Detroit, Baltimore, and Seattle. Changes in women's work and domestic lives were major, striking "at the roots of the fundamental divisions between the social roles of women and men" (p.154). Nonetheless, Anderson concludes, the war did not ultimately net women a higher status in the labor force; nor did it substantially undermine patriarchal values. Similar conclusions are reached by Penny Summerfield regarding the British experience in *Women Workers in the Second World War: Production and Patriarchy in Conflict* (Croom Helm, 1984). In an important new study of the United States in the 1940s, *The Home Front and Beyond* (Twayne, 1982), Susan M. Hartmann qualifies Anderson's assessment to some degree, finding in the forties decade "seeds of change which worked a deeper transformation in women's consciousness, aspirations, and opportunities a generation or so later" (p.215). Hartmann's is a well-documented survey of women's changing labor-force participation in wartime and reconversion; women's education; women in the armed forces, in politics, and under the law; and "the unshaken claim of family." In *Creating Rosie the Riveter: Class, Gender, and Propaganda During World War II* (University of Massachusetts Press, 1984), Maureen Honey analyzes fiction and advertising in the *Saturday Evening Post* and *True Story* to demonstrate how the media accommodated to the propaganda aims of a government eager for women workers during the war. Adapted from the film documentary of the same name, *The Life and Times of Rosie the Riveter* (Clarity Educational Productions, 1982), by Miriam Frank, Marilyn Ziebarth, and Connie Field, adds a vivid pictorial record to the growing social history of women workers during World War II.

291.   Aptheker, Bettina. **Women's Legacy: Essays on Race, Sex, and Class in American History.** Amherst: University of Massachusetts Press, 1982. 177p. bibliog. index. pbk. $9.50. LC 81-23137. ISBN 0870233645.

Daughter of communist parents (her father is the well-known historian Herbert Aptheker), leader of the 1960s' Free Speech Movement in Berkeley, member of the national staff of Angela Davis's defense committee—Bettina Aptheker comes to her material with the deep political commitment of a veteran activist. She writes here on abolitionism and women's rights, woman suffrage and the campaign against lynching, W. E. B. Du Bois and women's emancipation, black women in the professions from 1865 to 1900, black and white women's domestic labor, and the Moynihan report. Her frame of reference is both Marxist and feminist in these essays which seek to uncover the historical foundations of solidarity and tension between black and white women.

292.   Badinter, Elisabeth. **Mother Love: Myth and Reality: Motherhood in Modern History.** New York: Macmillan, 1981. 360p. bibliog. index. pbk. $8.95. LC 81-8193. ISBN 0025046101.

In a foreword that places this work for the U.S. reader, Francine du Plessix Gray notes that *L'Amour en plus* (the French original) "has been a greater *succès de scandale* in France than any feminist tract of the past decade ..." (p.ix). The subversive heart of Badinter's book is her emphatic repudiation of the existence of the "maternal instinct" and her reference to historical examples of maternal indifference or neglect to prove her point. Most starkly, she describes the late eighteenth-century practice among middle- and upper-class urban French women of farming out their infants to wet nurses in the countryside, under whose appallingly negligent care over half of them died before the age of two.

Badinter, a professor of philosophy at the École Polytechnique in Paris, traces the transition over two centuries from maternal indifference to the oppressive idealization of mother love. Her own idea is parenthood adopted by conscious choice, and shared equally by mother and father. In *Inventing Motherhood: The Consequences of an Ideal* (Schocken Books, 1983), British psychiatrist Ann Dally first covers similar ground in a sketchy historical survey of "Changing Motherhood," then meditates on the psychological fall-out from the contemporary idealization and isolation of mothers. Catherine M. Scholten also reconstructs the historical movement toward a more isolated and idealized childbearing and childrearing experience in her posthumously published work entitled *Childbearing in American Society: 1650-1850* (New York University Press, 1985).

293.   Banner, Lois W. **American Beauty.** New York: Knopf; distr. New York: Random House, 1983. 369p. bibliog. index. $20.00. LC 82-47838. ISBN 039451923X.

Drawing from diaries, autobiographies, novels, travelers' accounts, and fashion magazines and other prescriptive literature, Banner writes an intriguing exploratory social history of changing styles of beauty in the United States between 1800 and 1921. She discerns four major models: the "steel-engraving lady" of the antebellum period; the postbellum "voluptuous woman"; the Gibson girl of the 1890s; and the Mary Pickford-type in the teens. "Why such changes in the standards of beauty occurred," Banner writes, "is a complex issue in the interaction of class, women's changing expectations, social modernization, medical points of view, and other factors" (p.5). One persistent theme running through this account is the conflict between feminism and fashion. Another feminist treatment of the subject is *Face Value: The Politics of Beauty*, by Robin Tolmach Lakoff and Raquel L. Scherr (Routledge and Kegan Paul, 1984). Lakoff and Scherr review the history, psychology, and politics of beauty, working from the thesis that beauty is "an instrument of political control" that serves to separate "woman from woman, women from men, and race from race ..." (p.277).

294.   Basch, Norma. **In the Eyes of the Law: Women, Marriage, and Property in Nineteenth-Century New York.** Ithaca, NY: Cornell University Press, 1982. 255p. bibliog. index. $22.50. LC 82-2454. ISBN 0801414660.

Basch places married women's property reforms (exemplified by a series of New York state laws enacted between 1848 and 1862) in the broader context of nineteenth-century U.S. feminism. Her carefully documented study relies on primary legal materials and antebellum popular literature, as well as recent secondary sources in legal history, social history, and women's studies. She finds that legislative reforms failed to guarantee equality to married women, largely because of the conservative pull of common law tradition. Contemporaneous reforms in Great Britain, which culminated in the Married Women's Property Act of 1882, are described in *Wives and Property,* by Lee Holcombe (University of Toronto Press, 1983). Dorothy Stetson's *A Woman's Issue: The Politics of Family Law Reform in England* (Greenwood Press, 1982) takes a wider view of parliamentary debate and action on marriage reform from the 1850s to the 1970s, using a political scientist's framework.

295.   Bauer, Carol, and Lawrence Ritt, eds. **Free and Ennobled: Source Readings in the Development of Victorian Feminism.** New York: Pergamon Press, 1979. 317p. bibliog. index. $40.00. LC 78-41265. ISBN 0080222722.

Drawing on books, periodical articles, official reports, speeches, and the transactions of reform societies, Bauer and Ritt bring to life the struggles of nineteenth-century British feminism and its opposition. Extracted here are the words of such influential writers as Sarah Stickney Ellis, John Ruskin, Frances Power Cobbe, Emily Davies, Bessie Rayner Parkes, and Millicent Garrett Fawcett. In ten topical sections, the editors treat the Victorian image of womanhood and its perpetuation by science, law, and the Chuch; the emergence of feminism; women's roles in social reform; education; employment; women's legal status; and the debates over suffrage. The volume closes with a lengthy bibliographic essay, citing both primary and secondary sources, and an index. Patricia Hollis's *Women in Public: The Women's Movement, 1850-1900* (Allen and Unwin, 1979), another documentary sourcebook, is also limited to British sources. Hollis covers some important figures omitted by Bauer and Ritt (e.g., Annie Besant, Florence Nightingale) in thematic sections treating paid work, education, law, public service, and politics, among other topics. The volume lacks a bibliography and index.

296.   Becker, Susan D. **The Origins of the Equal Rights Amendment: American Feminism Between the Wars.** Westport, CT: Greenwood Press, 1981. 300p. bibliog. index. $29.75. LC 80-23633. ISBN 0313228183.

Becker's work is part of a "new wave" of women's history that seeks to revise the prevailing view that U.S. feminism faded after the ratification of the Nineteenth Amendment (see also Scharf and Jensen, entry 357). At the center of Becker's account of the interwar period is the National Women's Party (NWP), which introduced militant tactics into the U.S. suffrage battle during the teens and sponsored the Equal Rights Amendment in 1923 under the leadership of Alice Paul. Becker analyzes the differences between the NWP "equalitarian feminists" and the "social feminists" of the period. While both groups strove for the economic independence of women, they parted when it came to protective legislation, which the NWP saw as discriminatory and the social feminists saw as advantageous for women. Becker attributes the limited success of the NWP in part to its narrow economic focus on work as Everywoman's liberation, and its neglect of issues connected with marriage and motherhood. Yet she credits the organization with "[keeping] feminism alive during the interwar years, [alerting] women to the legal and economic discriminations against them, and ... [preventing] many of these discriminations from becoming worse" (p.279).

297.   Beddoe, Deirdre. **Discovering Women's History: A Practical Manual.** Boston: Pandora Press, 1983. 232p. bibliog. index. pbk. $7.95. LC 83-8131. ISBN 0863580084.

Beddoe aims her advice at amateur researchers and study groups, rather than professional historians. Although firmly rooted in the modern British historical context, her handbook can offer encouragement to U.S. students, for whom no similar guide has yet appeared. Organizing her ideas by topic—the image of women, education of girls, waged work, family life, sexuality, and politics—Beddoe recommends primary and secondary sources and suggests possible lines of inquiry.

298.   Berkin, Carol Ruth, and Mary Beth Norton, eds. **Women of America: A History.** Boston: Houghton Mifflin, 1979. 442p. bibliog. index. pbk. $17.50. LC 78-69589. ISBN 0395270677.

Berkin and Norton, prominent historians, solicited fifteen original essays for this introductory text organized by chronological period. The editors' volume and section introductions highlight major themes, trace new trends in the literature, and preview the essays to follow. Each section begins with a biographical profile of a woman "whose life illuminates especially well the status of women in her own day" (p.xv). Among the volume's essays are: "Women's Lives Transformed: Demographic and Family Patterns in America, 1600-1970" (Robert V. Wells); "The Founding of Mount Holyoke College" (Kathryn Kish Sklar); "Chinese Immigrant Women in Nineteenth-Century California" (Lucie Cheng Hirata); "The Academic Prism: The New View of American Women" (Rosalind Rosenberg); "Woman's Place Is in the War: Propaganda and Public Opinion in the United States and Germany, 1939-1945" (Leila J. Rupp); and "Tomorrow's Yesterday: Feminist Consciousness and the Future of Women" (Sara M. Evans). Documents accompany most essays. Linda K. Kerber and Jane De Hart Mathews attempt a similar overview in their anthology *Women's America: Refocusing the Past* (Oxford University Press, 1982). The editors reprint essays and documents selected to cover four periods (1600-1820, 1820-1880, 1880-1920, 1920-1980) and four themes (economics, politics, biology, ideology). Writers whose work is excerpted here include Anne Firor Scott, John Mack Faragher, Barbara Mayer Wertheimer, Carroll Smith-Rosenberg, David M. Katzman, Alice Kessler-Harris, Blanche Weisen Cook, and William H. Chafe. These texts are well designed for the undergraduate classroom, although they both reflect the deficiencies of the literature in their neglect of the lives of America's native women.

299. Berkin, Carol Ruth, and Clara M. Lovett, 1939- , eds. **Women, War, and Revolution.** New York: Holmes and Meier, 1980. 310p. bibliog. index. $34.50. LC 79-26450. ISBN 0841905029.

Berkin and Lovett sort the eleven articles in this collection into three thematic sections, providing short introductions for each. The three articles in Part I look at women's mobilization in revolutionary Paris, Nazi Germany, and the United States shipyards during World War II. Each of the articles considers the expectations raised and promises made to women during national crises. Articles in Part II assess the postrevolutionary status of women in the United States, France, the Soviet Union, China, and Cuba, pointing out discrepancies between stated revolutionary ideals and observed reality. Articles in Part III focus more narrowly on one particular wartime and postrevolutionary role for women—"Patriotic Motherhood"—as it was articulated in France after 1789, Italy after the Risorgimento, and in U.S. women's peace and preparedness movements during World War I.

300. Blair, Karen J. **The Clubwoman as Feminist: True Womanhood Redefined, 1868 to 1914.** New York: Holmes and Meier, 1980. 199p. bibliog. index. $34.50. LC 79-26390. ISBN 084190538X.

In reconstructing the history of women in nineteenth-century America, feminist historians have devoted the lion's share of their attention to the radical minority, the suffragists. In Blair's opinion, "these studies ... leave us with a partial veiw of resistance among nineteenth-century women in incarceration in the home" (p.3). Like the Woman's Christian Temperance Union (the other large-scale nineteenth-century women's movement), the women's club movement represented middle-class women's "struggle to leave the confines of the home without abandoning domestic values" (p.4)—a brand of what Blair terms "Domestic Feminism." Blair recounts the history of early clubs like New York's Sorosis and the New England Woman's Club in Boston, the grass-roots literary clubs that subsequently popped up in many states, and the General Federation of Women's Clubs established in 1890. She documents the friendship, intellectual stimulation, confidence, and organizing skills the clubs provided to their members. Though conservative by comparison with the suffrage movement, the club movement offered women a bridge between the safe, but suffocating confines of domesticity and the uncharted territory of the public world.

301.   Bordin, Ruth Birgitta Anderson, 1917- . **Woman and Temperance: The Quest for Power and Liberty, 1873-1900.** Philadelphia: Temple University Press, 1981. 221p. bibliog. index. $27.95. LC 80-21140. ISBN 087722157X.

Following the repeal of Prohibition, historians as well as the general public tended to view the temperance movement only in its antilibertarian and moralistic dimensions. While historians have revised this perspective in the last two decades, reinstating temperance to its rightful place as part of the American reformist tradition, they have paid scant attention to women's part in the movement. Feminist historians of the 1970s, too, scarcely mentioned the movement, drawn more to the radicalism of the suffragists. Bordin's is the first substantial scholarly study of the Woman's Christian Temperance Union (WCTU) and the only contemporary feminist profile of WCTU leader Frances Willard. Bordin is interested in why temperance attracted so many nineteenth-century women — far more than suffrage. She sees the WCTU as having offered women a respectable outlet for their public commitments and energies, as well as a stepping stone to participation in other reformist causes. In *The Politics of Domesticity* (Wesleyan University Press, 1981), Barbara Leslie Epstein looks at the temperance movement and earlier evangelical revivals as outgrowths of the distinctive women's culture born of the separation of public and private spheres accompanying industrialization. She finds in both evangelism and temperance expressions of "a popular women's consciousness of difference from, and antagonism to, men" (p.1), culminating in the "protofeminist politics" of the WCTU. Nancy A. Hardesty's *Women Called to Witness: Evangelical Feminism in the Nineteenth Century* (Abingdon Press, 1984) also links women's revivalism (including its manifestation in the WCTU) with emergent feminism. A recent and more narrowly focused study of the temperance movement is *"Give to the Winds Thy Fears": The Women's Temperance Crusade, 1873-1874* (Greenwood Press, 1985). Author Jack S. Blocker, Jr., takes issue with many of the conclusions of Bordin and Epstein.

302.   Bridenthal, Renate, et al., eds. **When Biology Became Destiny: Women in Weimar and Nazi Germany.** New York: Monthly Review Press, 1984. 364p. bibliog. $27.50. LC 84-18969. ISBN 0853456429.

Editors Renate Bridenthal, Atina Grossmann, and Marion Kaplan — all from German-Jewish families touched by the Holocaust — have selected eleven articles and two personal narratives for this collection with the aim of bringing feminist perspectives to bear on "the classic and unavoidable questions that all historians ask of German history: What went wrong? ... How was Auschwitz possible?" (p.xii).. The result, judges Linda Gordon in the *Women's Review of Books*, is "the best women's history anthology on any subject ... in at least five years." In essays on the Weimar Republic (1917-1933) and Nazi Germany (1933-1945), contributors begin to unravel some of the complexity of women's experience: from the outright advocacy of Nazi women, to the unwitting complicity of feminists who embraced a "separate spheres" ideology, to the resistance of women on the Left. Alongside the elitism of women's groups, the volume documents the class divisions and sexism within the Left that facilitated the Nazi victory. The contributors are, in addition to the editors: Claudia Koonz, Elisabeth Meyer-Renschhausen, Amy Hackett, Karin Hausen, Annemarie Tröger, Gisela Bock, and Sybil Milton. The editors provide a historical overview and headnotes to each piece. Two recent titles fill in the checkered history of German social democracy from the Empire to the Third Reich: *Reluctant Feminists in German Social Democracy, 1885-1917,* by Jean H. Quataert (Princeton University Press, 1979), and *A Conflict of Interest: Women in German Social Democracy, 1919-1933,* by Renate Pore (Greenwood Press, 1981).

303. Buhle, Mari Jo, 1943- . **Women and American Socialism, 1870-1920.** Urbana: University of Illinois Press, 1981. 344p. bibliog. index. $21.95. LC 81-719. ISBN 0252008731.

Buhle, who researched a vast array of primary sources, rewrites the history of turn-of-the-century American socialism, bringing into focus both the rich cross-fertilization and the persistent tensions between feminism and socialism. In doing this, Buhle lays out the very different perspectives of native-born Populist and immigrant camps within the socialist movement. It was within the former tradition that women advocating suffrage and women's right to labor found the most congenial setting; the immigrant sector, by contrast, distrusted feminist aspirations as "bourgeois" and reflected conservative notions of women's "place." Buhle brings to light women's efforts to bridge the gap between mainstream feminism and socialism, and the resulting broadening of both movements as they fought campaigns for suffrage, labor, and sexual reform. Buhle expands her focus in *Women and the American Left: A Guide to Sources* (G. K. Hall, 1983), covering the period from 1871 to 1981. Arranging the bibliography chronologically, she cites histories and general works, autobiographies and biographies, books and pamphlets on the "woman question," periodicals, and fiction and poetry. Her lengthy annotations provide invaluable guidance to the researcher. Buhle also contributed a chapter to the reader *Flawed Liberation: Socialism and Feminism* (Greenwood Press, 1981), edited by Sally M. Miller. The seven essays in the collection fill in the history of women activists within the American Socialist Party. Miller is coeditor, with Philip S. Foner, of *Kate Richards O'Hare: Selected Writings and Speeches* (Louisiana State University Press, 1982). "Red Kate" was a socialist and feminist whose career "exactly paralleled the rise and fall of the Socialist Party of America" (p.11).

304. Chambers-Schiller, Lee Virginia, 1948- . **Liberty, A Better Husband: Single Women in America: The Generations of 1780-1840.** New Haven, CT: Yale University Press, 1984. 285p. bibliog. index. $22.50. LC 84-3524. ISBN 0300031645.

Chambers-Schiller has written a feminist history of American spinsterhood from 1780 to 1840, based on research on the lives and writings of more than one hundred white, mainly Protestant and native-born Northeastern women, daughters of the middle and upper classes. In the postrevolutionary era, Chambers-Schiller asserts, the ideology of Republican Motherhood gave way not just to the Cult of Domesticity, but also to a complementary Cult of Single Blessedness. She looks to the reasons why some women of the period, despite overpowering social pressure, rejected marriage and articulated ideas of independence and vocation in its place, achieving freedom at the cost of social stigma and personal stress. Their legacy was similarly contradictory: while they "broke ground for the descendants," their challenge to traditional roles also sparked an antifeminist backlash in the twentieth century (p.9). A fine companion study is Martha Vicinus's *Independent Women: Work and Community for Single Women, 1850-1920* (University of Chicago Press, 1985). Looking at two generations of single women in England, Vicinus documents how they revolted against societal accusations of their "redundancy," channeling a passion for meaningful work into the building of woman-controlled, residential institutions— church communities, training facilities for nurses, women's colleges and boarding schools—and ultimately into the suffrage struggle. Like Chambers-Schiller, Vicinus adeptly brings out the paradox of these women's achievements, demonstrating that the newly created vocations that offered them the radical alternative of independence conformed at the same time to narrow Victorian precepts of proper feminine callings.

305. Clinton, Catherine, 1952- . **The Other Civil War: American Women in the Nineteenth Century.** New York: Hill and Wang, 1984. 242p. bibliog. index. $17.95. LC 84-525. ISBN 0809074605.

Clinton synthesizes the new scholarship on nineteenth-century U.S. women's history in this well-written overview. It is a graceful fusion Clinton achieves, although as she laments in her preface, many gaps remain, particularly in the research on women of color, poor women, and lesbians. Clinton writes her narrative chronologically, highlighting the impact of industrialization; the separation of spheres; women's participation in reform movements, including temperance, abolitionism, and suffrage; struggles over educational and professional opportunities; campaigns around health, sexuality, and reproduction; and the frontier and immigration experience. A bibliographic essay rounds out the volume. Readers can get a feel for the texture of nineteenth-century middle-class women's lives in the United States from *The Light of the Home,* by Harvey Green with the assistance of Mary-Ellen Perry (Pantheon Books, 1983). Drawing from the substantial collection of Victoriana at the Margaret Woodbury Strong Museum in Rochester, New York, the amply illustrated volume describes day-to-day routines and household objects associated with housework, childcare, fashion, home decorating, leisure activities, and more. Jeanne Madeline Weimann's *The Fair Women* (Academy Chicago, 1981), subtitled "The Story of the Woman's Building, World's Columbian Exposition, Chicago 1893," is a fascinating account of how a group of women organized to create a display celebrating the achievement of nineteenth-century women in the arts, industry, science, and reform.

306. Clinton, Catherine, 1952- . **The Plantation Mistress: Woman's World in the Old South.** New York: Pantheon Books, 1982. 331p. bibliog. index. pbk. $7.95. LC 82-3549. ISBN 0394516869.

Concerned to challenge both sexist interpretations of Southern history and what she calls the Northern "regional chauvinism" of women's history, Clinton mines a wealth of primary sources to reconstruct the lives of Southern white plantation women. She concedes that "one cannot equate the plight of the plantation mistress with the brutal dehumanization of slaves" (p.15) but finds that white slaveowners used similar tactics to exclude both from spheres of power. A central argument here is that "sex is as critical a factor for understanding social relations in the South as race" (p.xv). Two other recent works seek to challenge the conventional picture of Southern womanhood. Suzanne Lebsock writes a history of free black and white women in the antebellum South in *The Free Women of Petersburg: Status and Culture in a Southern Town, 1784-1860* (Norton, 1984). Her central thesis is that women's status can change for the better in the absence of organized feminism. Moving to the twentieth century, Jacquelyn Dowd Hall profiles the life of Jessie Daniel Ames and the efforts of the Women's Campaign Against Lynching in her work *Revolt Against Chivalry* (Columbia University Press, 1979). Interested in questions of consciousness, Hall attempts to explain how "ordinary middle-class [Southern] white women confronted such explosive issues as rape, lynching, and interracial sex" (p. ix).

307. Cott, Nancy F., and Elizabeth H. Pleck, eds. **A Heritage of Her Own: Toward a New Social History of American Women.** New York: Simon and Schuster, 1979. 608p. bibliog. index. $11.95. LC 79-19565. ISBN 0317051601.

Many of the twenty-four previously published essays in this collection are classics in the field, authored by such well-known historians as Mary Beth Norton, Gerda Lerner, Carroll Smith Rosenberg, Johnny Faragher, Eugene D. Genovese, Alice Kessler-Harris, Blanche Wiesen Cook, and Linda Gordon. Cott and Pleck have made an effort to include scholarship on American women who are not of white middle-class background, but their anthology still reflects the discipline's neglect of the experience of American Indian women. In their introduction, the editors summarize the themes and approaches of the new women's history. Published a year later, *Women's Experience in America: An Historical Anthology* (Transaction Books, 1980), edited by Esther Katz and Anita Rapone, overlaps somewhat, with five of its sixteen articles duplicating pieces found in the Cott and Pleck volume. *Clio Was a Woman: Studies in the History of American Women,* edited by Mabel E. Deutrich and Virginia C. Purdy (Howard University Press, 1980), collects papers and proceedings of the Conference on Women's History held in Washington, D.C., in 1976, with Anne F. Scott, William H. Chafe, Andrea Hinding, Linda K. Kerber, Susan M. Hartmann, and Mary P. Ryan among the contributors.

308.* Davis, Marianna W., ed. **Contributions of Black Women to America.** Columbia, SC: Kenday Press, 1982. 2v. bibliog. index. LC 82-80761.

Intended as a corrective to the usual (white) accounts of women's achievements, this work represents the most complete overview to date of the accomplishments of black American women. Volume One covers the arts, media, business, law, and sports; Volume Two treats civil rights, politics and government, education, medicine, and the sciences. Each section has its own author, consultant, and editors. These volumes can be used for quick reference and as guides to further reading, thanks to the name indexes and bibliographies in each section.

309. Degler, Carl N. **At Odds: Women and the Family in America From the Revolution to the Present.** New York: Oxford University Press, 1980. 527p. bibliog. index. pbk. $11.95. LC 79-17438. ISBN 0195026578.

Degler's ambitious project is to contextualize the place of women in the emergence of the modern American family. He falls short of his stated objective of canvassing American history from the Revolution to the present, for he is chiefly interested in the nineteenth century. Degler argues that modern family values are "at odds" not only with feminism, but with individualism itself. Among the changes that Degler credits as being most significant in creating the modern family are the emergence of companionate marriage; planned limitation of the number of children (resulting in increasingly child-focused, nuclear families); and the doctrines of "separate spheres" and the "Cult of True Womanhood," designating to women the role of primary caretaker both of the family and the home. Degler relates these major trends to changing personal and sexual relationships within the family; social movements including Social Purity, the women's club movement, the labor movement, and suffrage; and women's employment both within and outside the home.

310. Dublin, Thomas, 1946- . **Women at Work: The Transformation of Work and Community in Lowell, Massachusetts, 1826-1860.** New York: Columbia University Press, 1979. 312p. bibliog. index. $26.00. LC 79-10701. ISBN 0231041667.

Dublin is interested in "the human impact of early industrial capitalism in the United States, particularly as it was felt by women" (p.12). He focuses here on the textile industry in Lowell, Massachusetts in the first half of the nineteenth century. During this period, New England underwent transition from a preindustrial to an industrial economy. Factory textile production displaced household manufacturing, undercutting women's source of livelihood in the home but opening up new opportunities for single women in the mill towns. By mining the uniquely rich records of the Hamilton Manufacturing Company of Lowell, Dublin is able to document empirically the changes in structure and wages in the industry between 1820 and 1860 and the transformation of the workforce as native-born women workers were gradually replaced by Yankee and immigrant women. Dublin sympathetically portrays mill workers' strikes and other collective action, as well as their efforts to create a new culture in changed circumstances. *Farm to Factory: Women's Letters, 1830-1960*, edited by Dublin (Columbia University Press, 1981), makes available a collection of largely unpublished letters written by mill workers and their families.

311. Dudden, Faye E. **Serving Women: Household Service in Nineteenth-Century America.** Middletown, CT: Wesleyan University Press; distr. Scranton, PA: Harper and Row, 1983. 344p. bibliog. index. $19.95. LC 83-1263. ISBN 0819550728.

In this well-written and creatively researched study of household service from 1800 to 1890, Dudden draws a distinction between the early "peculiarly American form of service" known as "help," or "hired girls," and the later "domestic service," modeled on the European servant tradition. Her study, which omits Southern service (slave and free) from consideration, sets the transition from "help" to domestic service within the context of the transformation of work and household during industrialization, documenting the experience of both the server and the served. While the tradition of "help," once lost, became overly romanticized in the popular imagination, Dudden does show it to have been a less onerous and demeaning form of employment than domestic service was to become. Yet, she notes, "for employers the change in service represented a gain in time, energy, and human possibilities" (p.240), and many feminists "used other women to achieve their own freedom," unable to "see it as ironic that feminism was underwritten by the household labors of domestic servants" (p.241). Household service has only recently become a focus of historical research. David Katzman's *Seven Days a Week: Women and Domestic Service in Industrializing America* (Oxford University Press, 1978) was, in Dudden's words, "the pioneering modern social history of the subject" (p.3). Katzman fills in the period from 1870 to 1920, during which domestic service changed from a live-in to a live-out occupation. His work, which does incorporate material on the South, is especially valuable for its history of the shift from native-born to immigrant to black servants, and for its attention to the corrosive nature of the mistress-servant relationship. Linda Martin and Kerry Segrave's *The Servant Problem: Domestic Workers in North America* (McFarland, 1985) profiles domestic service in North America from the 1940s to the present. A new sociological study based on interviews and participant observation is Judith Rollins' *Between Women: Domestics and Their Employers* (Temple University Press, 1985).

312. Dye, Nancy Schrom, 1947- . **As Equals and As Sisters: Feminism, the Labor Movement, and the Women's Trade Union League of New York.** Columbia: University of Missouri Press, 1980. 200p. bibliog. index. $17.50. LC 80-16751. ISBN 0826203183.

Concentrating on the New York Women's Trade Union League's work in New York City during the first two decades of this century, Dye's study documents the unique achievements and difficulties of this early effort at cross-class organizing among women. Founded in 1903 by social reformers and settlement house residents, the New York WTUL set out to recruit working-class women into unions. In this the League was at first phenomenally successful, particularly with women in the garment trades. By 1913, however, the organization had lost faith both in the union movement and in women workers, and it confined its efforts thereafter to lobbying for legislative reform. Dye adeptly brings out the internal contradictions of the organization. On the one hand, the WTUL offered unprecedented opportunities for leadership to women workers such as Rose Schneiderman, Leonora O'Reilly, and Pauline Newman, and strengthened working-class members in their confrontations with the sexist male-dominated unions. On the other hand, the wealthy WTUL members were not free of classist bias, their egalitarian ideals notwithstanding, and cross-class sisterhood was not easy to achieve.

313. Engel, Barbara Alpern. **Mothers and Daughters: Women of the Intelligentsia in Nineteenth-Century Russia.** Cambridge: Cambridge University Press, 1983. 230p. bibliog. index. $32.50. LC 82-14611. ISBN 0521251257.

Radical women in late nineteenth-century Russia, Engel states, "added a moral dimension to revolutionary politics seldom seen before or since" (p.203) and an altruism rooted in the traditional Orthodox Christian ideal of women's moral superiority. Paradoxically, religious values became the rationale for rebellion against the traditional family-centered role, and led many women to extreme acts of heroism and self-sacrifice in the cause of social justice. Engel tells the stories of novelists, nihilists, populists, and terrorists, adding a chapter on women medical students, who found a more acceptable channel for their idealistic impulses. Women involved in radical politics addressed the "woman question," but as Linda Harriet Edmondson demonstrates, it was the liberal feminist movement that succeeded in increasing women's access to higher education and professional employment. Edmondson's *Feminism in Russia, 1900-1917* (Stanford University Press, 1984) traces the origins of Russian feminism, the founding of its major organizations, the influence upon it of Western women's rights movements, and its increasing factionalization after the 1905 revolution. Rose L. Glickman studies the working class in the prerevolutionary period, and its relation to feminism, in *Russian Factory Women: Workplace and Society, 1880-1914* (University of California Press, 1984). Biographies provide another approach to the history of women's political activism in Russia, notably Jay Bergman's *Vera Zasulich* (Stanford University Press, 1983) and two studies of the USSR's most famous female revolutionary: Barbara Evans Clements's *Bolshevik Feminist: The Life of Aleksandra Kollantai* (Indiana University Press, 1979) and Beatrice Farnsworth's *Aleksandra Kollantai: Socialism, Feminism, and the Bolshevik Revolution* (Stanford University Press, 1980).

314. Evans, Sara, 1943- . **Personal Politics: The Roots of Women's Liberation in the Civil Rights Movement and the New Left.** New York: Knopf, 1979. 274p. bibliog. index. pbk. $3.95. LC 78-54929. ISBN 0394419111.

In this gracefully written and stirring account, Evans documents the birth of the contemporary women's liberation movement in the civil rights movement and the New Left, based on extensive interviews with women veterans of these movements and research of their papers. White radicals gained skills in grass-roots organizing from their work in the South with the Student Non-Violent Coordinating Committee (SNCC). As SNCC's orientation moved from integration to black power, white radicals left the organization and applied their skills to community organizing projects and anti-war work, building up New Left organizations like Students for a Democratic Society (SDS). In both the civil rights movement and the New Left, women gained a sense of their political efficacy, found strong women role models, and identified with the prevailing democratic ideology. Evans traces the spark that ignited the second wave of feminism to the contradiction between these women's expectations of equality and their actual marginality in these movements. A different angle on women's experience in the civil rights movement is provided in *Selma, Lord, Selma* (University of Alabama Press, 1980), which records Sheyann Webb and Rachel West Nelson's memories of their girlhood participation in Selma voter registration drives.

315. Everett, Jana Matson. **Women and Social Change in India.** New York: St. Martin's Press, 1979. 233p. bibliog. index. $35.00. LC 79-9740. ISBN 0312887310.

Indian women have a long history of activism, little known to Western feminists. Everett's study is badly written and shows its origins in a Ph.D. dissertation. Nevertheless, it may be recommended for its broad historical sweep, covering women's movements in India from the late nineteenth through the mid-twentieth century and their links to the nationalist movement. Providing a more contemporary focus, Gail Omvedt's *We Will Smash This Prison! Indian Women in Struggle* (Zed Press, 1980) is a personal account based on the author's interviews and observations of feminist political ferment in India in the mid-seventies. *The Extended Family: Women and Political Participation in India and Pakistan* (South Asia Books, 1981), edited by Gail Minault, brings together eleven scholarly papers on Indian and Pakistani women's activism before and after independence.

316. Faderman, Lillian. **Surpassing the Love of Men: Romantic Friendship and Love Between Women From the Renaissance to the Present.** New York: Morrow, 1981. 496p. bibliog. index. $18.95. LC 80-24482. ISBN 068803733X.

Marshaling a wealth of literary and biographical sources, Faderman sets out to prove her controversial thesis that romantic friendship between women, "the love that had no name" (p.154), has constituted a proto-feminist lesbianism in Western culture from the Renaissance to the present. Faderman claims a host of literary names for her argument: Mary Wollstonecraft, Margaret Fuller, George Eliot, Emily Dickinson, Alice James, Sarah Orne Jewett, and Willa Cather. These are women whose lives exemplified, in Faderman's words, "a refusal to fulfill the male image of womanhood or to bow to male supremacy" (p.413). In his *Gay/Lesbian Almanac* (Harper and Row, 1983), Jonathan Ned Katz takes a very different, but equally illuminating, approach to lesbian history. Focusing on the early American colonies (1607-1740) and the modern United States (1880-1950), he analyzes and excerpts a wealth of primary sources, including sodomy laws, letters, medical reports, theater and book reviews, newspaper stories, fiction, photographs, and cartoons. Lesbian-relevant references are visually coded. Katz's general introduction on the theory and methods of gay and lesbian history, and his overviews for the two periods, are lucid guides to this emerging field.

317. Faragher, John Mack, 1945- . **Women and Men on the Overland Trail.** New Haven, CT: Yale University Press, 1979. 281p. bibliog. index. $31.00. LC 78-10290. ISBN 0300022670.

Closer examination of the primary accounts of pioneer women has revived and revised American Western studies. Faragher's work dismisses as myth the idea that the pioneer woman of the 1840s and 1850s was freed of gender constraints by the radical task she confronted. Faragher finds she often went reluctantly on the trek West, forced to follow father, spouse, or brother because of the limited options available to independent women. Once on the road, her normal, backbreaking domestic routine expanded to include unaccustomed campsite chores. At journey's end, a traditional sexual division of labor reasserted itself. In *Frontier Women: The Trans-Mississippi West, 1840-1880* (Hill and Wang, 1979), Julie Roy Jeffrey argues that the records left by literate frontier women tend to underscore their heroism and resourcefulness and fail to analyze their lack of alternatives. Her sources suggest that the West offered no more liberating vistas to women than the East had. In *Westering Women and the Frontier Experience, 1800-1915* (University of New Mexico Press, 1982), Sandra L. Myres draws from the diaries of Mexican, black, and Anglo women to debunk the popular stereotypes—"sun bonnet saints" and "gentle tamers"—so marketable in Eastern fiction and artwork of the period; yet she, too, heroizes her subjects. Myres disaffiliates herself from "feminist historians" (p.2) and in her book *Ho for California!: Women's Overland Diaries from the Huntington Library* (Huntington Library, 1980), she contends that stereotypes such as "trail drudge, reluctant companion, and overworked helpmate" were created by feminist historians. In the journals and diaries of five women headed for California, Myres finds evidence of a leisure that she claims permitted women to observe the scenery and reflect on their experience. Yet she concedes that marital, educational, and class status colored each woman's perspective. Myres appends a valuable bibliography of manuscript and published journals as well as related secondary sources. Glenda Riley's *Frontierswomen: The Iowa Experience* (Iowa State University Press, 1981) reconstructs the bleak life of pioneer women isolated on farms, finding them to be a cohesive group despite the distances that separated them. In another book, *Women and Indians on the Frontier, 1825-1915* (University of New Mexico Press, 1984), Riley makes a case, based on diaries, letters, and journals, that white women often maintained friendly relations with Indians, though they had difficulties with other minorities.

318. Ferguson, Moira, ed. **First Feminists: British Women Writers 1578-1799.** Bloomington: Indiana University Press; Old Westbury, NY: Feminist Press, 1985. 461p. bibliog. $25.00. LC 84-42838. ISBN 0253322138.

"Was there ever any so abused, so slaundered, so railed upon, or so wickedly handeled undeservedly, as are we women?" (p.59). These are the words of Jane Anger, written in 1589 to counter a misogynist tract. Little is known about Anger, or about many of the other twenty-seven early British feminists whose writings are excerpted by Ferguson. Those who *are* familiar to us include Aphra Behn, Mary Astell, Anne Kingsmill Finch, Countess of Winchilsea, and Mary Wollstonecraft. The period Ferguson covers begins with the earliest known English feminist writings and ends "where many excellent modern anthologies start" (p.xi), encompassing the transition from a feudal-agricultural to a bourgeois-industrial society. Early British feminism is also Katharine M. Rogers' focus in *Feminism in Eighteenth-Century England* (University of Illinois Press, 1982). Drawing on a rich variety of sources, Rogers evaluates the liberating effects of rationalism, sentimentalism, and radicalism, considers the significance of the novel's emergence, and looks to women's self-perceptions in order to define the nature of eighteenth-century feminism. Not just feminist, but a full range of eighteenth-century views on women are represented in Bridget Hill's anthology of excerpts from courtesy books, novels, and contemporary history and travelogues, entitled *Eighteenth-Century Women* (Allen and Unwin, 1984). Hill furnishes introductions and notes to contextualize the many snippets collected here, voicing opinion on topics such as female perfection and chastity, education, marriage, crime, poverty, domestic servants, and protest. For background on the period from 1500 to 1800, readers can turn to Mary Prior's collection of seven scholarly articles, *Women in English Society* (Methuen, 1985).

319. Foley, Helene P. **Reflections of Women in Antiquity.** New York: Gordon and Breach, 1981. 420p. bibliog. index. $42.00. LC 81-13352. ISBN 0677163703.

Most of the fifteen essays gathered here originally appeared in a special issue of *Women's Studies* (1981). Represented are major figures in this developing field—Sarah B. Pomeroy, Marylin B. Arthur, and Froma I. Zeitlin, among them—writing on a range of topics: the socioeconomic roles of women in Mycenaean Greece; the *Iliad*; Sappho; Herodotus's *Histories*; Aristophanes's *Thesmophoriazousae*; the literacy of Greek women; women in Roman Egypt; Virgil's *Aeneid*; and more. Foley views the *Women's Studies* issue as a "sequel" to two special issues published in 1973 and 1978 by the classical journal *Arethusa*, recently combined in book form under the title *Women in the Ancient World: The Arethusa Papers*, edited by John Peradotto and J. P. Sullivan (State University of New York Press, 1984). The Arethusa collection offers both in-depth critical studies—for example, Helen P. Foley's "'Reverse Similes' and Sex Role in the *Odyssey*"—and historical surveys such as Marylin B. Arthur's "Early Greece: The Origins of the Western Attitude Toward Women." An undergraduate syllabus and a comprehensive bibliographic essay (through 1981) by Sarah B. Pomeroy round out the volume. *Black Women in Antiquity,* edited by Ivan Van Sertima (Transaction Books, 1984), gathers eleven articles on Ethiopian and Egyptian queens and goddesses, the black woman in ancient art, and African women conquerors and courtesans. The articles originally appeared in a thematic issue of the *Journal of African Civilizations.*

320. Fout, John C., 1937- , ed. **German Women in the Nineteenth Century: A Social History.** New York: Holmes and Meier, 1984. 439p. bibliog. index. $39.50. LC 83-18596. ISBN 0841908435.

In his introductory chapter, "Current Research on German Women's History in the Nineteenth Century," Fout surveys the development of this growing field. The collection's sixteen essays demonstrate the breadth and eclecticism of on-going research. Among the topics covered here are: girls' education in the Bavarian reform era; the literary socialization of women writers in the *Vormärz* period (1815-1848); women's political opposition prior to 1848; German women writers and the 1848 revolution; the impact of agrarian change on women's work and childcare in early-nineteenth-century Prussia; domestic industry; and women's role in the German working-class family. Fout concludes the volume with a lengthy English-language bibliography on European and U.S. women's history.

321. Fraser, Antonia, 1932- . **The Weaker Vessel.** New York: Knopf; distr. New York: Random House, 1984. 544p. bibliog. index. $19.95. LC 84-47751. ISBN 0394513517.

A biographer of Mary Queen of Scots, Charles II, and Cromwell, Fraser turns her attention in this lavishly detailed and illustrated study to the lives of women in seventeenth-century England. Though she finds numerous examples of female strength and courage in this period, especially during the Civil War, she concludes that the century did not improve women's lot overall; restrictions that eased during wartime intensified once again with the Restoration. Nonetheless, the seventeenth century did give rise to some of the first articulations of feminism, documented by Hilda L. Smith in *Reason's Disciples* (University of Illinois Press, 1982). Smith studies twelve seventeenth-century feminists, among them, Margaret Cavendish, Duchess of Newcastle, Bathsua Makin, and Hannah Woolley, who wrote mainly about women's education; Mary Astell and Elizabeth Elstob, who raised broader questions about women's status; and poets Anne Winchilsea, Lady Mary Chudleigh, Elizabeth Singer Rowe, and Sarah Fyge Egerton. For background on the "woman question" in Renaissance England, readers can consult Katherine Usher Henderson and Barbara F. McManus's *Half Humankind: Contexts and Texts of the Controversy About Women in England, 1540-1640* (University of Illinois Press, 1985).

322. Giddings, Paula. **When and Where I Enter: The Impact of Black Women on Race and Sex in America.** New York: Morrow, 1984. 408p. bibliog. index. $15.95. LC 84-60089. ISBN 0688019439.

Giddings's narrative history of black women in the United States has received extravagant praise from critics as a pathbreaking synthesis and fresh interpretation for the general reader. Making substantial use of a variety of primary sources, and using black women's own words whenever possible, Giddings traces the active roles of black women in confronting racism and sexism and in shaping U.S. history. In the first section, Giddings depicts black women's efforts to redefine themselves in the postbellum period, focusing particularly on the contribution of Ida B. Wells to the anti-lynching campaigns, and of

Mary Church Terrell to the black women's club movement. Part II delineates the period from World War I to World War II, and black women's responses to wartime employment, postwar unemployment, the Great Depression, migration northward, and the Garvey movement. The activism of Mary McLeod Bethune is highlighted here. In her final section, Giddings writes of black women's pivotal roles in the civil rights and women's liberation movements, and of their confrontations with black men's sexism and white women's racism. Jacqueline Jones, historian at Wellesley, covers the same period in her meticulously researched and elegantly written book *Labor of Love, Labor of Sorrow: Black Women, Work, and the Family from Slavery to the Present* (Basic Books, 1985). Two major themes unite the work: the "cultural distinctiveness of black community life and the attempt by black working women to subordinate the demands of their employers to the needs of their own families" (p.9). Jones aims to provide "a much needed corrective to the northeastern-urban bias" (p.8) of the new women's history, devoting one-half of the study to the experience of slave, rural, and working-class women in the South, 1830-1915.

323. Gorham, Deborah. **The Victorian Girl and the Feminine Ideal.** Bloomington: Indiana University Press, 1982. 223p. bibliog. index. $20.00. LC 82-47944. ISBN 025336258X.

Gorham examines how the middle-class ideals of femininity and family shaped the lives of English girls in the nineteenth century. She begins by comparing the realities of Victorian homes and schools to the prevailing images of girlhood, then analyzes advice literature of the period and its changing prescriptions for the rearing of daughters. The final chapters present biographical sketches of fourteen girls, organized to highlight the shifting ideals and realities from early-, mid-, and late-Victorian times. In *Girls Growing Up in Late Victorian and Edwardian England* (Routledge and Kegan Paul, 1981), Carol Dyhouse studies the socialization of working-class and middle-class girls between 1860 and 1920. She considers family, schooling, and girls' organizations as all being instrumental in the education of girls for feminine, domestic roles. She concludes by discussing nineteenth-century theories of adolescent girlhood and feminist responses to them. Joan N. Burstyn, in *Victorian Education and the Ideal of Womanhood* (Barnes and Noble, 1980), analyzes the opposition to women's higher education in nineteenth-century England.

324. Greenwald, Maurine Weiner, 1944- . **Women, War, and Work: The Impact of World War I on Women Workers in the United States.** Westport, CT: Greenwood Press, 1980. 309p. bibliog. index. $27.50. LC 80-540. ISBN 0313213550.

Building on case studies of the railroad, streetcar, and telephone industries, Greenwald situates the sweeping changes of World War I in the context of social and economic transformations underway since the Civil War, particularly "the development of hierarchical work arrangements and fragmentation of the labor process" (p.242). Women gained access to wider employment opportunities and higher wages during the war, generally along lines of race—white women replacing white men, and black women filling in for white women and black men. Women's entrance into "nontraditional," "male" occupations sparked men's hostility, coinciding as it often did with the dilution of craft skills by management. Cooperation and solidarity between male and female workers thus were limited, Greenwald finds, to occupations where rigid sex segregation was maintained. Greenwald concludes, "While the war emergency enhanced labor's bargaining power and secured women workers new opportunities, the war's end revealed the entrenched strength of management and the relative weakness of women workers against managerial rationalization strategies, on the one hand, and the hostility of male workers, ... on the other" (p.243). Gail Braybon's study of Britain, *Women Workers in the First World War* (Croom Helm/Barnes and Noble, 1981), likewise finds that the war produced few fundamental or lasting changes.

325. Harris, Barbara Jean, 1942- , and JoAnn K. McNamara, 1931- , eds. **Women and the Structure of Society: Selected Research From the Fifth Berkshire Conference on the History of Women.** Durham, NC: Duke University Press, 1984. 305p. bibliog. index. $37.50. LC 84-1599. ISBN 0822305585.

This volume represents a selection from papers presented at the fifth Berkshire Conference on the History of Women, held in 1982; it is only the second such anthology to come out of the highly respected Berkshire conferences. The range of topics here is broad and eclectic, as is the geographic coverage, but Harris and McNamara create a theoretical overlay based on the concept of social structure. They divide the eighteen articles into five sections according to whether the pieces depict women as defined by, adapting to, eroding, or confronting old structures, or articulating new structures.

326. Hawks, Joanne V., and Sheila L. Skemp, eds. **Sex, Race, and the Role of Women in the South: Essays.** Jackson: University Press of Mississippi, 1983. 140p. bibliog. $15.00. LC 83-10356. ISBN 0878051902.

This collection gathers six papers originally delivered at a 1982 symposium sponsored by the University of Mississippi, supplemented by a bibliographical essay. The essays are: "Women's History and the Revision of Southern History," by Jean E. Friedman; "The Public Role of Southern Women," by Martha H. Swain; "Black Women in a Southern City: Washington, D.C., 1890-1920," by Sharon Harley; 'Southern Literary Women as Chroniclers of Southern Life," by Anne Goodwyn Jones; "Historians Construct the Southern Woman," by Anne Firor Scott; and "Sisters Under Their Skin: Southern Working Women, 1880-1950," by Dolores E. Janiewski. Janiewski has also authored a book-length study of how race, class, and sex shaped labor activism during industrialization in the South. Entitled *Sisterhood Denied* (Temple University Press, 1985), the work details the history of black and white women's incorporation into urban industry in Durham, North Carolina between 1860 and 1940.

327. Hellerstein, Erna Olafson, et al., eds. **Victorian Women: A Documentary Account of Women's Lives in Nineteenth-Century England, France, and the United States.** Stanford, CA: Stanford University Press, 1981. 534p. bibliog. index. $35.00. LC 79-67770. ISBN 0804710880.

Hellerstein and her co-editors, Leslie Parker Hume and Karen M. Offen, have assembled a rich, evocative collection of primary materials by and about Victorian women from all walks of life. The volume draws on an impressive range of documents: diaries, letters, advice manuals, medical and legal records, case studies, government inquiries, and the published findings of nineteenth-century social scientists. French sources are translated. The editors organize the contents by the stages of a woman's life, providing lengthy introductions by leading scholars to each major division. "The Girl" highlights childhood experiences, including education, socialization, religious training, play, child labor, and health. "The Adult Woman: Personal Life" covers courtship, marriage, sexuality, and motherhood, among other topics. In addition to the full spectrum of paid labor, "The Adult Woman: Work" treats household management, philanthropy, and social reform. The final section, "The Older Woman," highlights menopause, aging, and death. By making the life cycle the organizing principle, the editors spotlight the centrality of biological determinism to Victorian ideology. Primary texts drawn from the literary and popular press are blended with insightful commentary in *The Woman in Question: Society and Literature in Britain and America, 1837-1883* (Garland, 1983). In this three-volume set, co-authors Elizabeth K. Helsinger, Robin Lauterbach Sheets, and William Veeder reveal many facets of Victorian public opinion about gender roles.

328. Hume, Leslie Parker. **The National Union of Women's Suffrage Societies, 1897-1914.** New York: Garland, 1982. 253p. bibliog. index. $37.00. LC 81-48371. ISBN 082405167X.

Historians of the suffrage movement in England have focused rather exclusively on the activities of the militant Women's Social and Political Union. Contemporary feminists have been no less intrigued by the legacy of the militant suffragettes, who broke with Victorian dictates of proper feminine behavior—and legal restrictions—to heckle Parliament, organize demonstrations, engage in stone throwing and arson, and risk arrest, imprisonment, and forcible feeding. In this careful study, Hume resurrects the history of the much larger National Union of Women's Suffrage Societies (NUWSS), which claimed in excess of fifty thousand members by 1914. The NUWSS maintained propriety and respectability as it went about the business of lobbying for suffrage reform. Although Hume concedes that it was the Great War that turned the tide in favor of woman suffrage, she credits the NUWSS with laying the groundwork.

329. Jensen, Joan M. **With These Hands: Women Working on the Land.** Old Westbury, NY: Feminist Press; New York: McGraw-Hill, 1981. 295p. bibliog. index. pbk. $9.95. LC 80-13944. ISBN 0912670908.

Despite the dearth of written records left by rural women, Jensen has unearthed a riveting selection of documents—letters, journals, oral histories, novels, and poetry—framed by her concise introductions and headnotes. The sources reveal the diversity of U.S. rural women: Native American women, the first farmers of the continent; Euro-American women on early nineteenth-century farms; black women in the slave South; women on "the last frontier" at the turn of the century; agrarian reformers; women who joined this century's exodus to the cities, and those who tenaciously remained on the land. A concluding photo essay presents documentary photography from the Depression. In *The Invisible Farmers: Women in Agricultural Production* (Rowman and Allanheld, 1983), Carolyn E. Sachs strives to correct both historical and contemporary distortions of rural women's contributions to United States agriculture, and to reveal the patriarchal reality underlying the often idealized family farm. Her work falls into three parts: a historical survey, from the subsistence farms of the seventeenth and eighteenth centuries to the commercial farms of today; a discussion of her own findings about contemporary Midwestern farm women; and an analysis of how sexism in U.S. agriculture shapes development strategies exported to the Third World.

330. Johnson, Kay Ann. **Women, The Family, and Peasant Revolution in China.** Edited by Philip S. Foner. Chicago: University of Chicago Press, 1983. 282p. bibliog. index. $25.00. LC 82-24748. ISBN 0226401871.

Johnson has written an interpretive history of changing marriage and family policy in rural China from the prerevolutionary period through 1980. Based on literature from the social sciences as well as Johnson's own field research, the study finds that the Chinese Communist Party (CCP) has consistently given economic reform and development higher priority than reform of marriage and family. This assessment agrees with that of Judith Stacey in *Patriarchy and Socialist Revolution in China* (see entry 42). In *The Politics of*

Marriage in Contemporary China (Cambridge University Press, 1981), Elisabeth Croll uses documentary sources and interview material to study changes in urban and rural marriage from 1950, when the first communist marriage law was instituted, to the present. Bobby Sui's *Women of China* (Zed Press, 1982) looks at an earlier period, investigating the impact of European, U.S., and Japanese imperialism on Chinese women from 1900 to 1949. Mary Sheridan and Janet W. Salaff's *Lives: Chinese Working Women* (Indiana University Press, 1984) helps to flesh out the changes in China during this century with the detail of lived experience. Life histories from prerevolutionary China, the People's Republic (PRC), and Hong Kong and Taiwan are presented, along with several essays on method. The PRC stories were originally recorded by Chinese fieldworkers to serve as inspirational tales of "model Chinese women"; the balance of the histories were written by Western scholars.

331. Jones, Mary Harris, 1843?-1930. **Mother Jones Speaks: Collected Writings and Speeches.** Edited by Philip S. Foner. New York: Monad Press; distr. Pathfinder Press, 1983. 724p. bibliog. index. $35.00. LC 83-60486. ISBN 0913460885.

Historian Philip Foner, editor of this collection, chastises feminist scholars who have overlooked Mother Jones, or written that the tireless labor activist was unsympathetic to the plight of working women. "The truth is that Mother Jones was a fighter for the working class everywhere" (p.30). The speeches, letters, newspaper clippings, and interviews Foner has marshaled from myriad sources to trace Mother Jones's fearless career as a labor organizer speak mainly of her work with miners. Yet these sources also evidence her support of women workers (textile, garment, and needle trades), the Women's Christian Temperance Union, child labor laws, suffrage, and the wives of miners. Mother Jones came to socialism and began organizing at the age of fifty, continuing to inspire workers with her bombastic oratory up until the end of her long life. Edward M. Steel has recently edited a sizeable collection of Jones's letters, *The Correspondence of Mother Jones* (University of Pittsburgh Press, 1985).

332. Kaledin, Eugenia Oster. **Mothers and More: American Women in the 1950s.** Boston: Twayne, 1984. 260p. bibliog. index. $15.95. LC 84-15656. ISBN 0805799044.

The decade of the fifties—the era of McCarthyism, Sputnik, civil rights organizing, and affluence—is commonly assumed to have ensnared women in lives of intensified domesticity. Kaledin's goal is to modify "the dominant myth of [women's] victimization" (Preface). Thus, the author retrieves from relative obscurity the accomplishments of women in education, politics, literature, science, and art, finding early traces of the feminism that would explode into view during the 1960s. Reviewers have faulted Kaledin for taking a "great women" approach to history in her effort to belie popular conceptions of the period, in the process losing sight of the lives of the majority of women and biasing the work toward the experience of the white middle-class (although Kaledin does devote one chapter to black activists, artists, and athletes). In *Only Halfway to Paradise: Women in Postwar Britain, 1945-1968* (Tavistock, 1980), Elizabeth Wilson seeks to understand whether feminism was in fact "dormant" in postwar Britain, as is popularly assumed.

333. Kealey, Linda, 1947- , ed. **A Not Unreasonable Claim: Women and Reform in Canada, 1880s-1920s.** Toronto: The Women's Press, 1979. 233p. bibliog. $9.95. LC 80-466542. ISBN 0889610525.

The turn-of-the-century Canadian women's reform movement was essentially "North American in character" (p.3), Kealey argues, sharing many characteristics with contemporaneous U.S. reform efforts. Restless middle-class women were drawn into reform through philanthropic and church activities. As in the United States, the radical impulse of the Canadian reform effort was undercut by class, race, and ethnic prejudice, as well as by the ideology of "maternal feminism," which justified women's public role on the basis not of natural rights but of moral superiority deriving from motherhood. Maternal feminism and its critics, the women's movement in Quebec, the suffrage movement, women doctors, campaigns to reduce infant and maternal mortality, the Women's Christian Temperance Union, child emigration, and British female immigration are the topics taken up in the anthology. Carol Lee Bacchi's perspective on the turn-of-the-century Canadian women's movement is very similar to Kealey's in *Liberation Deferred? The Ideas of the English-Canadian Suffragists, 1877-1918* (University of Toronto Press, 1983).

334.   Kelly, Joan, 1928-1982. **Women, History, and Theory: The Essays of Joan Kelly.** Chicago: University of Chicago Press, 1984. 163p. bibliog. index. $18.00. LC 84-2558. ISBN 0226430278.

Joan Kelly's essays underscore both the magnitude and the tragic foreshortening of her achievement. One of the pioneers of the new women's history, Kelly died of cancer in 1982 at the age of fifty-four; several feminist colleagues pulled this volume together posthumously, with manifest love and respect. Kelly's widely cited essay "Did Women Have a Renaissance?" explores how a woman-centered perspective transforms our view of the period. In "The Social Relation of the Sexes: Methodological Implications of Women's History," Kelly outlines how a feminist vantage point revises traditional historical periodization, categories of social analysis, and theories of social change. Her classic essay "The Doubled Vision of Feminist Theory" demonstrates her commitment to developing a Marxist-feminist theory that overcomes inherited dualisms such as public vs. private and theory vs. practice. "Early Feminist Theory and the *Querelle des Femmes*" attempts to establish the existence of a 400-year-old tradition of European feminist thought prior to the French Revolution. The final essay, "Family and Society," is drawn from the volume *Household and Kin* (see entry 1059).

335.   Kennedy, Susan Estabrook. **If All We Did Was to Weep at Home: A History of White Working-Class Women in America.** Bloomington: Indiana University Press, 1979. 331p. bibliog. index. $20.00. LC 78-20431. ISBN 0253191548.

Over the last decade, feminist scholarship and the women's movement have called for a recognition of *difference*—of race, ethnicity, religion, sexual preference—as a crucial source of conflict and creativity among women. Focusing on white working-class women, Kennedy might well have explored their experiences in a multicultural context. She bows out of this responsiblity, however, limiting her scope, she says, on "practical rather than conceptual" grounds (p.xvi): the subject is vast, the field new. She surveys white working-class women's history from the colonial period to the 1970s, making her sources more fully available in *America's White Working-Class Women: A Historical Bibliography* (Garland, 1981). In *Wage-Earning Women: Industrial Work and Family Life in the United States, 1900-1930* (Oxford University Press, 1979), Leslie Woodcock Tentler, like Kennedy, excludes the experience of women of color, and even discounts ethnicity as an important factor (pp.4-5). In a study of women factory workers in major industrial cities of the East and Midwest, Tentler puts forward the controversial argument that employment in the early twentieth century was for working-class women not a form of emancipation but "an ultimately conservative aspect of socialization ... toward conventional maturity" (p.2).

336.   Kinnear, Mary, 1942- . **Daughters of Time: Women in the Western Tradition.** Ann Arbor: University of Michigan Press, 1982. 228p. bibliog. index. pbk. $13.50. LC 82-11152. ISBN 0472080296.

This slender but ambitious volume seems designed to serve as a corrective to androcentric courses in "Western Civilization." Kinnear sets out to describe, analyze, and assess "the roles of women at various times in Western history" (p.2) in chapters on early civilization, Greece, Rome, early Christians, the Middle Ages, the Renaissance and the Reformation, the Enlightenment, the French Revolution, women's work in the eighteenth and nineteenth centuries, sexuality and reform in the nineteenth century, socialism, fascism and World War II, and contemporary trends. Although Kinnear demonstrates familiarity with recent feminist scholarship, the book's structure adheres rather closely to conventional periodization.

337. Kleinbaum, Abby Wettan. **The War Against the Amazons.** New York: New Press/McGraw-Hill, 1983. 240p. bibliog. index. $18.95. LC 82-7781. ISBN 0070350337.

The Amazons bring to mind the vision of an autonomous, self-sufficient community of women warriors, a vision that has galvanized feminist (and especially lesbian-feminist) utopian thought. Kleinbaum's argument is that Amazon myths have been created by men as a vehicle for the affirmation of maculine might: the Amazons existed in order that they might be conquered by men. Kleinbaum surveys men's writing about the Amazons from Herodotus to the present, noting along the way the few women writers who have appropriated the myth for their own purposes (Christine de Pizan, Charlotte Perkins Gilman, Monique Wittig). Like a hand-me-down garment, the myth is, she concludes, "not a perfect fit for the feminist" (p.219), yet its subversive elements nonetheless make it worth retaining.

338. Kolodny, Annette, 1941- . **The Land Before Her: Fantasy and Experience of the American Frontiers, 1630-1860.** Chapel Hill: University of North Carolina Press, 1984. 293p. bibliog. index. $28.00. LC 83-10629. ISBN 0807815713.

In *The Lay of the Land: Metaphor as Experience and History in American Life and Letters* (1975), Kolodny looked to frontier literature by men to determine the nature of male fantasies of the land. She discovered recurrent erotic imagery in which the land was cast as virgin or mother waiting to be conquered. The women's imagery Kolodny analyzes in the present volume contrasts sharply, associating the frontier with a domestic garden and its prosaic delights. Kolodny mines a host of sources, including emigrants' guides and promotional literature, to raise important questions about women-constructed myths of the frontier over a two-century period. She focuses in detail on a diverse group of popular writers—Mary Rowlandson, Mary Jemison, Mary Austin Holley, Eliza Farnham, Margaret Fuller, and Caroline Kirkland among them—whose material ranges from the captivity narrative to the domestic novel.

339. Laska, Vera, ed. **Women in the Resistance and in the Holocaust: The Voices of Eyewitnesses.** Westport, CT: Greenwood Press, 1983. 330p. bibliog. index. $29.95. LC 82-12018. ISBN 0313234574.

The Holocaust is frequently equated exclusively with the annihilation of the Jews, the Resistance with the heroism of men. These are two popular misconceptions Laska hopes to correct in this collection of eyewitness accounts of the experiences of women—Jews and Gentiles; homosexuals; political prisoners; Gypsies—in the Resistance, in the concentration camps, and in hiding during World War II. Herself a Resistance fighter and a survivor of the camps, Laska gathered these stories primarily from other published sources, and sets each in its historical and geographic context. We learn of women's bravery working with the underground in Czechoslovakia, Denmark, Norway, the Netherlands, Greece, France, and Germany; we read sickening descriptions of women's fate in Auschwitz, Ravensbrück (the largest women's camp), Terezín, and Bergen-Belsen; and we hear of the women who survived in hiding. To say this is difficult reading is to state the obvious. Laska has provided us with a document of historic importance. Her introduction and epilogue, footnotes, and bibliography of nonfiction works in several languages will guide the reader interested in further pursuit of the topic. Two related works are Margaret L. Rossiter's *Women in the Resistance* (Praeger, 1986), an account of women's clandestine bravery in France during World War II; and Kevin Sim's *Women at War: Five Heroines Who Defied the Nazis and Survived* (Morrow, 1982).

340. Lefkowitz, Mary R., 1935- , and Maureen B. Fant, eds. **Women's Life in Greece and Rome.** Rev. ed. Baltimore, MD: Johns Hopkins University Press, 1982. 294p. bibliog. index. $9.95. LC 82-7756. ISBN 0801828651.

Designed for classroom use, this primary source anthology makes available in translation "the kinds of materials on which historians of women in the ancient world must base their work" (p.xv). These materials include both familiar texts by Hesiod, Juvenal, Aristotle, Sappho, and the like, and more obscure sources such as papyrus letters, dedicatory and funerary inscriptions, and medical documents. Lefkowitz and Fant omit widely available literary texts and mythological documents. Divided into two parts, "Greece" and "Rome," the anthology arranges the sources topically: "Poets"; "Wives, Daughters, Friends"; "Accomplishments"; "Daily Life"; and so on. This volume supersedes the editors' earlier reader, *Women in Greece and Rome* (1977); the revised edition features new introductions and notes, and additional documents on women's occupations, legal status, and religious life. Sixteen of Lefkowitz's essays on women in antiquity (primarily ancient Greece) are gathered in *Heroines and Hysterics* (St. Martin's Press, 1981).

341. Lerner, Gerda, 1920- . **The Majority Finds Its Past: Placing Women in History.** New York: Oxford University Press, 1979. 217p. bibliog. index. $19.95. LC 79-14048. ISBN 0195025970.

These twelve essays, written over a period of ten years, document the exciting birth of the new women's history. As her fascinating autobiographical introduction reveals, Lerner came to the history profession late in life—she was forty-six when she completed her Ph.D.—but she pioneered the feminist revision of the discipline, teaching her first course in women's history as a middle-aged undergraduate in 1963. Lerner's personal history as a wife, mother, and political activist gave her a perspective unusual for an academic, and she was among the first feminist scholars to question the early feminist emphasis on sisterhood, cautioning that "generalizations about the oppression of women are inadequate unless qualified by factors of race and class" (p.xxviii). Three of the essays gathered here grew out of Lerner's research in black women's history. All of the essays reflect her continuing effort to better define the questions and methods of women's history, and the nature of its challenge to the priorities, categories, periodization, and values of traditional history. Lerner's *Teaching Women's History*, a pamphlet published by the American Historical Association in 1981, offers pedagogical guidance to teachers of women's history, especially at the college level, and stands as the best comparative bibliographic survey of the field.

342. Lewis, Jane E. **Women in England 1870-1950: Sexual Divisions and Social Change.** Bloomington: Indiana University Press, 1984. 240p. bibliog. index. $25.00. LC 84-48437. ISBN 0253366089.

Surveying the period from the late 1800s through World War II in England, Lewis concludes that "there was no simple progressive erosion of the boundaries between male and female worlds" (p.xi); real advances in women's life circumstances (for example, the falling birth rate) were often accompanied by retrogressive ideological developments (e.g., a revised cult of domesticity). In Part I, Lewis traces changes in working-class and middle-class families, marriage, and motherhood. In Part II, she reviews trends in women's employment during the period. Three other recent titles take up topics covered by Lewis in greater detail. In *Fair Sex: Family Size and Structure in Britain, 1900-39* (St. Martin's Press, 1982), Diana Gittins evaluates possible explanations for the significant decline in working-class family size in England early in this century, proposing women's work histories, use of birth control, and power within the marriage as key factors. Sheila Jeffreys has written a revisionist history of feminist campaigns around sexuality and "social purity" in the late nineteenth century, and the ideology of "sexual revolution" early in the twentieth century in *The Spinster and Her Enemies: Feminism and Sexuality 1880-1930* (Pandora Press, 1985). And Elizabeth Roberts recreates something of the texture of working-class women's lives during the period in *A Woman's Place: An Oral History of Working-Class Women, 1890-1940* (Basil Blackwell, 1984).

343.* Light, Beth, 1952- , and Alison L. Prentice, 1934- , eds. **Pioneer and Gentlewomen of British North America 1713-1867.** Toronto: New Hogtown Press, 1980. 245p. bibliog. index. ISBN 0919940153.

This documentary collection is volume one of the series "Documents in Canadian Women's History," edited by Alison Prentice. The focus here is predominantly on British and American settlers of what is now Canada; French-Canadian and native women, though not excluded, do not receive substantial attention. The documents — letters, diaries, records of associations, court records, drawings, photographs, and more — are arranged thematically into sections on growing up and education; courtship; marriage, the work of wives, separation, widowhood, and old age; women in public life; and law, community pressure, and public opinion regulating the roles and status of women. The editors provide introductions and notes throughout. *Canadian Women on the Move, 1867-1920* (New Hogtown Press/Ontario Institute for Studies in Education, 1983), edited by Beth Light and Joy Parr, is volume two in the series, and follows a similar format. Two recent works have highlighted Canadian women's frontier experiences: *The Last Best West: Women on the Alberta Frontier 1880-1930* (Eden Press Women's Publications, 1984), by Elaine Leslau Silverman; and *The Embroidered Tent: Five Gentlewomen in Early Canada* (Anansi, 1982), by Marian Fowler. Students of Canadian history should also consult *True Daughters of the North: Canadian Women's History: An Annotated Bibliography,* compiled by Beth Light and Veronica Strong-Boag (Ontario Institute for Studies in Education, 1980).

344. Lucas, Angela M. **Women in the Middle Ages: Religion, Marriage, and Letters.** New York: St. Martin's Press, 1983. 214p. bibliog. index. $25.00. LC 82-42578. ISBN 0312887434.

Lucas concentrates on the history of women in England from the fifth to the fifteenth century. Her sources include legal documents, theological, philosophical, and medical treatises, and sermons and homilies, as well as such familiar materials as *The Canterbury Tales.* The book is organized in three parts: "Women and Religion"; "Women and Marriage"; and "Women and Letters." Christine E. Fell, Cecily Clark, and Elizabeth Williams slice off a narrower period of English history in *Women in Anglo-Saxon England: The Impact of 1066* (Indiana University Press, 1984). Their illustrated text draws on written and archaeological sources to chronicle daily life, sex and marriage, family and kinship, manor and court, religious life, and the lives of Viking women, both before and after the Norman Conquest. Suzanne Fonay Wemple's *Women in Frankish Society* (University of Pennsylvania Press, 1981) explores women's roles in the family and the church in Merovingian and Carolingian societies, 500 to 900 A.D. In *The Lady & the Virgin* (University of Chicago Press, 1985), Penny Schine Gold examines archetypal images of women in twelfth-century France. Balancing these geographically limited studies, Shulamith Shahar's *The Fourth Estate: A History of Women in the Middle Ages* (Methuen, 1983) attempts an ambitious overview of women's status across Europe. Reviewers have found the work disorganized and repetitious, though impressive in its scope and creative use of sources. Shahar's choice of title underlines her contention that medieval women formed a unique social class, alongside the men who were "Worshippers, Warriors, and Workers" (p.1).

345. Macías, Anna. **Against All Odds: The Feminist Movement in Mexico to 1940.** Westport, CT: Greenwood Press, 1982. 195p. bibliog. index. $29.95. LC 81-6201. ISBN 0313230285.

A historian specializing in the Mexican independence period, Macías presents a carefully documented and well-written account of Mexican feminism from 1890 to 1940. Women in Mexico did not achieve the vote until 1953. Mexican feminists faced formidable opposition from the powerful Catholic Church, men in government, the press, and the general culture of *machismo*. Political and class differences, and the extreme poverty of the majority of Mexican women, further hampered the efforts of feminist organizers. Macías's account of women's participation in the Mexican Revolution, and of the distinctive contributions of Yucatán and two of its revolutionary governors, documents the uniqueness of the Mexican context.

346. Marcus, Jacob Rader, 1896- . **The American Jewish Woman: A Documentary History.** New York: Ktav Publishing House; Cincinnati: American Jewish Archives, 1981. 1047p. bibliog. index. $35.00. LC 81-1966. ISBN 0870687522.

Marcus, an eminent historian of the American Jewish experience, has gathered 177 primary documents by and about Jewish women in the United States. Ranging from 1737 to 1980, these comprise letters, autobiographical writings, organizational reports, new accounts, opinion pieces, and other materials. The massive volume, itself a significant contribution to women's history, is designed to accompany Marcus's monograph *The American Jewish Woman, 1654-1980* (Ktav Publishing House/American Jewish Archives, 1981). Although not feminist in perspective, Marcus's chronological narrative serves as a crucial first step in the rediscovery of American Jewish women's history. Marcus concludes with an analysis of "The Women's Revolt and the American Jewess" and a peek at the future. Other studies of Jewish women's history include *Consecrate Every Day: The Public Lives of Jewish American Women, 1880-1980,* by June Sochen (State University of New York Press, 1981), which was faulted by reviewers for uninspired writing and reliance upon secondary sources in its treatment of Jewish women workers, activists, volunteers, and writers; and *Written Out of History: Our Jewish Foremothers,* by Sondra Henry and Emily Taitz (2nd ed., Biblio Press, 1983), an international compendium of the lives of outstanding Jewish women.

347. Margolis, Maxine L., 1942- . **Mothers and Such: Views of American Women and Why They Changed.** Berkeley: University of California Press, 1984. 346p. bibliog. index. $19.95. LC 83-12639. ISBN 0520049950.

Mothers and Such is a synthetic work traversing largely familiar ground: the history of women's changing circumstances as workers and as mothers, and of corresponding ideas about womanhood, in the United States over the last two centuries. An anthropologist, Margolis interprets this history from the perspective of cultural materialism, looking "to the productive and reproductive modes in a given society in order to account for its structural and ideological components ..." (p.3). She utilizes prescriptive literature of the period as an index of "ideological trends," confining her study to the middle-class, mainly white women this literature addressed. Margolis's perspective leads her to emphasize the persistent lag between evolving reality and cultural ideals, the latter seen as after-the-fact adjustments to the former. Thus, in her view, "the women's movement was ultimately a *result,* rather than a *cause* of women's massive entry into the labor force" (p.4).

348. Möbius, Helga. **Woman of the Baroque Age.** Totowa, NJ: Allanheld, Osmun; Montclair, NJ: Schram, 1984. 203p. bibliog. index. $35.00. LC 82-18496. ISBN 0839002831.

One hundred sixty-four illustrations, many of them color plates, accompany this survey of women's lives in the seventeenth and eighteenth centuries. Allegorical and realistic art of the period, as well as clothing and furniture, reveal much about prevailing attitudes towards women of all classes — from aristocrats like Madame de Pompadour to working peasants. Möbius takes into consideration the social, economic, religious, political, and cultural changes in this "age of extreme contradictions" (p.7), devoting chapters to women in the home, women's work, education, witches and saints, powerful women, women artists, and ladies' clothes. The text is translated from the German.

349. Murray, Janet Horowitz, 1946- , ed. **Strong-Minded Women: And Other Lost Voices From Nineteenth-Century England.** New York: Pantheon Books, 1982. 453p. bibliog. index. $22.00. LC 81-48231. ISBN 0394504593.

Murray's title is rather misleading. What she has collected here are short excerpts by both women and men about Englishwomen's lives in the nineteenth century. Further, far from all being "lost voices," many of the anthologized writers are well-known figures — Harriet Taylor Mill, Elizabeth Gaskell, and George Eliot, to name a few. The volume is a fascinating and entertaining patchwork of writings on the ideals of womanhood, woman's sphere (domestic life and marriage), education, work, and prostitution. The reader will encounter, among others, William Rathbone Greg pondering the question, "Why Are Women Redundant?"; Charlotte Brontë counseling her friend Ellen Nussey to relinquish the expectation of passionate marriage; Helena Swanwick describing her uncontained delight as a new student at Girton College, Cambridge; and Sybil Marshall recalling her mother's description of what it was to be a farmer's maid. Murray's editing, introductions, and headnotes make the volume a pleasure to read for the specialist and nonspecialist alike.

350. Newton, Judith L., et al., eds. **Sex and Class in Women's History.** Boston: Routledge and Kegan Paul, 1983. 270p. bibliog. $9.95. LC 82-25006. ISBN 0710095295.

Focusing primarily on women in Britain and the United States in the nineteenth century, this anthology draws its articles from the respected journal *Feminist Studies.* The essays are: "Class and Gender in Victorian England" (Leonore Davidoff); "Freud's Dora, Dora's Hysteria" (Maria Ramas); "Servants, Sexual Relations and the Risks of Illegitimacy in London, 1801-1900" (John R. Gillis); "Free Black Women and the Question of Matriarchy" (Suzanne Lebsock); "The Power of Women's Networks" (Mary P. Ryan); "'The Men Are as Bad as Their Masters ...': Socialism, Feminism and Sexual Antagonism in the London Tailoring Trade in the 1830s" (Barbara Taylor); "One Hand Tied Behind Us: A Review Essay" (Christine Stansell); "Examining Family History" (Rayna Rapp, Ellen Ross, and Renate Bridenthal); and "The Doubled Vision of Feminist Theory" (Joan Kelly). Editors Judith L. Newton, Mary P. Ryan, and Judith R. Walkowitz provide a brief introduction.

351. Norton, Mary Beth, ed. **Liberty's Daughters: The Revolutionary Experience of American Women, 1750-1800.** Boston: Little, Brown, 1980. 384p. bibliog. index. $15.00. LC 79-25245. ISBN 0316612510.

Norton draws on women's private writings as well as selected government records in her investigation of the impact of the Revolutionary War on American women. She argues that the war "had an indelible effect" (p.xv) but concedes that its legacy was ambiguous. The war did not bring women equality in the public sphere, nor did it enable them to abandon the private realm. Rather, it granted a new significance to women's age-old domestic duties, attributing a *public* importance to women's roles as wives and mothers. Norton sees this new recognition of women's roles as an advance over their status in preindustrial days, which she emphatically does not believe constituted a "golden age" of equality. Norton organizes her text not chronologically but thematically: Part I examines "the constant patterns of women's lives" before and after the Revolution, while Part II looks to new trends arising in the revolutionary and postrevolutionary periods. In *Women of the Republic: Intellect and Ideology in Revolutionary America* (University of North Carolina Press, 1980), Linda K. Kerber arrives at similar conclusions about the war's impact, but voices them in a more critical tone. While the ideology of "Republican Motherhood" "... [appeared] to reconcile politics and domesticity ... it could be used to mask women's true place in the polis: they were still on its edges" (p.12). Kerber looks to the war's impact on coverture, dower rights, and divorce as specific indices of women's status during the period. *The Way of Duty: A Woman and Her Family in Revolutionary America* (Norton, 1984), by Joy Day Buel and Richard Buel, Jr., profiles the life of Mary Fish (1736-1818), a Connecticut housewife, affording a glimpse into how one woman experienced the revolutionary era.

352. Pomeroy, Sarah B. **Women in Hellenistic Egypt: From Alexander to Cleopatra.** New York: Schocken Books, 1984. 241p. bibliog. index. $16.95. LC 84-3122. ISBN 0805239111.

Pomeroy, a pioneer in the field of feminist antiquity studies, turns her attention here to Greek and Hellenized Egyptian women in Ptolemaic Egypt (331-31 B.C.). She mines the rich evidence of Egyptian papyri, along with literary and archaeological sources, to determine the role of both elite and non-elite women in the colony's economy, finding that "the status of women in Ptolemaic Egypt was higher than that of women in Classical Greece. At the top level, some queens managed to wield more power legitimately than any Roman woman" (pp.xviii-xix). The status of elite women in Rome is the focus of Judith P. Hallett's *Fathers and Daughters in Roman Society* (Princeton University Press, 1984). Drawing on literary sources—mostly written by men—Hallett argues that "filiafocality" (the structural importance of the father-daughter relationship in the elite family) lay the foundation for the power and influence of Roman women. In *The Reign of the Phallus: Sexual Politics in Ancient Athens* (Harper and Row, 1985), Eva C. Keuls studies classical Athens in the Periclean Age (480-430 B.C.). Keuls looks to history, myth, ritual, and drama to develop her thesis that Athenians lived under the sway of "a pronounced phallicism ... a combination of male supremacy and the cult of power and violence" (p.13). Numerous photographs of vase paintings starkly illustrate the phallus-worship and misogynistic sexual relations Keuls analyzes at length.

353. Riemer, Eleanor S., and John C. Fout, 1937- , eds. **European Women: A Documentary History 1789-1945.** New York: Schocken Books, 1980. 258p. bibliog. index. $17.50. LC 79-26373. ISBN 0805206442.

Aiming to "reveal what women themselves were doing, saying, and thinking, the factors that affected their lives, and the motivations that lay behind their actions" (p.xiii), Riemer and Fout assemble fifty-three historical documents on four broad themes: women and work; women's politics; women and the family in modern society; and woman and her body. Sources from England, France, Russia, Austria, Italy, Germany, Holland, Switzerland, Sweden, and Belgium appear here, many of them translated into English for the first time. The editors' introductions and commentary provide sociohistorical background. The documents, which reflect primarily middle- and lower-class experiences, include extracts from books, periodical articles, official government publications, reports commissioned by voluntary associations, letters, and speeches.

354. Robertson, Priscilla Smith. **An Experience of Women: Pattern and Change in Nineteenth-Century Europe.** Philadelphia: Temple University Press, 1982. 673p. bibliog. index. $39.95. LC 81-9315. ISBN 0877222347.

Thoroughly researched, this monumental and well-written study explores many aspects of women's lives in England, France, Germany, and Italy between 1815 and 1914. Robertson draws on a rich variety of sources to describe, first, the laws, customs, and social conventions of the times, and second, the rebellious women who defied the norms. Attitudes toward love, marriage, sexuality, housekeeping, and unmarried women are compared among the four countries in Part I, "The Pattern." In Part II, "Breaking the Pattern," Robertson offers vignettes of early feminists who ventured into the public spheres of education, career, and political and social action. The study is limited to middle- and upper-class women—those who left written evidence, who could exercise options in their lives, and who were in positions to influence the course of events. For them, Robertson argues, feminism became a means of asserting individuality. Thus they rejected socialism, the one political philosophy that advanced the equality of men and women, because it championed collective control rather than personal autonomy.

355. Rosenberg, Rosalind, 1946- . **Beyond Separate Spheres: Intellectual Roots of Modern Feminism.** New Haven, CT: Yale University Press, 1982. 288p. bibliog. index. $30.00. LC 81-15967. ISBN 0300026951.

Rosenberg reconstructs the little-known history of women social scientists in turn-of-the-century America. These were women who, having gained a foothold in higher education, used their (precarious) positions and knowledge to subject Victorian ideas about the nature of the sexes to scientific scrutiny, formulating theories about intelligence, personality development, and sex roles. In a work that combines intellectual history, the history of science, and biography, Rosenberg shows how these women's intellectual subversion drew on "the skepticism of the infant fields of psychology, sociology, and anthropology" (p.xviii) and gathered support from young and iconoclastic male scholars. She also discloses something of the personal costs paid by these pioneers. For a study of feminism's impact on the beginnings of social science, as well as on nineteenth-century reform movements, readers can consult William Leach's *True Love and Perfect Union: The Feminist Reform of Sex and Society* (Basic Books, 1980). Focusing on mid-nineteenth-century feminism, Leach demonstrates that the movement's concerns reached well beyond the demand for suffrage, encompassing a critique of romantic love and sexual secrecy, and advocacy of marital reform, coeducation, and women's economic independence.

356. Rothman, Ellen K., 1950- . **Hands and Hearts: A History of Courtship in America.** New York: Basic Books, 1984. 370p. bibliog. index. $19.95. LC 83-45261. ISBN 0465028802.

Rothman's is an ambitious study of courtship in white, Protestant, middle-class, heterosexual America over the course of a century and a half. Drawing on reminiscences, diaries, and letters of 350 women and men living in the settled North, Rothman attempts to define courtship ideology, feelings about courtship, and actual courtship behavior during three periods: 1770-1840; 1830-1880; and 1870-1920. She presents a brief overview of the past sixty years in an epilogue. It is not the changes over the course of time that surprise the reader, but the continuities—for example, in the degree to which couples, not parents, have assumed prerogative over the decision to marry, and in the prevalence of premarital sexual expression. Liberal quotations from Rothman's sources enliven her narrative.

357. Scharf, Lois, and Joan M. Jensen, eds. **Decades of Discontent: The Women's Movement, 1920-1940.** Westport, CT: Greenwood Press, 1983. 313p. bibliog. index. $35.00. LC 81-4243. ISBN 0313226946.

The experience of women in the United States during the interwar period has, until recently, received little attention. According to popular wisdom, the "first-wave" women's movement was simply lost from view following the achievement of suffrage. Historians are now looking at this period more closely, informed by a new set of feminist questions; Scharf and Jensen's reader provides an introduction to this new scholarship. Contributors map the shift in employment opportunities and popular ideology from the halcyon days of the flapper and the "new woman" to the retrenchment of the Depression—and the impact of this shift on feminism. A wide range of topics is represented, including the experience of Chicana and black women workers; international feminism, black feminism, and socialist feminism; the "new womanhood" as inscribed in the movies of the 1920s; and the American housewife between the wars. Among the contributors are Estelle B. Freedman, Mary P. Ryan, Ruth Schwartz Cowan, and Rosalyn Terborg-Penn. Coeditor Scharf contributes an excerpt from her monograph *To Work and to Wed: Female Employment, Feminism, and the Great Depression* (Greenwood Press, 1980). In this study, Scharf paints the Depression as a period of loss for women despite gains in employment, with 1920s' feminist assertions of women's right to work overwhelmed by the resurgence of conservative family ideology. Yet another contributor to the Scharf/Jensen collection, Winifed D. Wandersee, advances a different perspective in *Women's Work and Family Values, 1920-1940* (Harvard University Press, 1981). Wandersee argues that rising economic aspirations underwrote women's increasing entrance into the labor market, aspirations that were "the result of new family values with respect to consumption, standard of living, and the role of women and children in the family" (p.3). In her view, the ideology that justified women's employment in terms of family needs rather than personal autonomy served not just conservatives' but also women's purposes.

358. Schlissel, Lillian, ed. **Women's Diaries of the Westward Journey.** New York: Schocken Books, 1982. 262p. bibliog. index. $16.95. LC 80-54143. ISBN 0805237747.

Literary scholars and historians have turned to Western Americana collections in recent years to explore a rich source of primary materials written by the nineteenth-century women who accompanied husbands, fathers, and brothers on the trail West. Lillian Schlissel samples 104 women's diaries, discovering that while for men the trip West signaled adventure, for women it represented domesticity under duress. Schlissel's revisionist reading suggests that the lives of pioneer women were marked by disruption of the life cycle, intensified subjugation to men, and, frequently, tragedy. The second half of Schlissel's book presents four of the original diaries. In *Read This Only To Yourself: The Private Writings of Midwestern Women, 1880-1910* (Indiana University Press, 1982), Elizabeth Hampsten concentrates on the correspondence and private writings of "ordinary" women pioneers living on the agrarian frontier. Both Anglo and minority women's experiences are represented in Cathy Luchetti and Carol Olwell's *Women of the West* (Antelope Island Press, 1982), a study drawing on letters, diaries, and oral histories. Over one hundred photographs amply illustrate the diversity of women pioneers. In *Pioneer Women: Voices from the Kansas Frontier* (Simon and Schuster, 1981), Joanna L. Stratton delves into files of memoirs gathered by her great-grandmother, a newspaper editor. Stratton analyzes the reminiscences spanning the years from 1854 to 1890, her synthesis sometimes drowning out her speakers' voices. *Following the Drum: A Glimpse of Frontier Life,* by army wife Teresa Griffin Vielé (1858; repr. University of Nebraska Press, 1984), represents the first published woman's account of military life in the trans-Mississippi West, according to editor Sandra Myres. Vielé records moments from her personal life, along with colorful sketches of her surroundings, politics, life in the military, and the Indian and Mexican inhabitants of Texas. Susan Shelby Magoffin's diary, *Down the Santa Fe Train and Into Mexico,* edited by Stella M. Drumm (University of Nebraska Press, 1982), tells of her venture into Mexican territory with her trader hsuband at the time of the Mexican War. A considerably later record of the frontier experience takes shape in Elinor Pruitt Stewart's *Letters of a Woman Homesteader* (1914; repr. Houghton Mifflin, 1982), a work recently brought to the screen as the movie *Heartland*. Stewart shows considerable storytelling talent as she recounts through her letters her difficult but adventurous life on a Wyoming ranch from 1909 to 1913.

359. Schwarz, Judith. **Radical Feminists of Heterodoxy: Greenwich Village 1912-1940.** Lebanon, NH: New Victoria Publishers, 1982. 110p. bibliog. index. pbk. $6.95. LC 81-85702. ISBN 0934678057.

Although many of its members attained prominence as individuals, the Heterodoxy club, which flourished in Greenwich Village from 1912 to 1940, had virtually slipped from history when Judith Schwarz first discovered its existence in 1976. Intrigued, even "possessed," Schwarz set about to reconstruct the history of this remarkable women's club, which met for lectures, discussion, and friendship on a weekly basis for almost thirty years. More than one hundred women became members during the club's lifetime — among them, Charlotte Perkins Gilman, Elizabeth Gurley Flynn, Mable Dodge Luhan, Rose Pastor Stokes, and Crystal Eastman. The women were a politically active, independent, and "unorthodox" (their word) group. During this period, Greenwich Village was a mecca for radicals and "bohemians," and we are beginning to learn more about the talented women among them. Blanche Wiesen Cook has gathered Crystal Eastman's feminist writings in a volume entitled *Crystal Eastman on Women and Revolution* (Oxford University Press, 1978). The writings of Mary Heaton Vorse, another member of Heterodoxy, have recently appeared in a volume entitled *Rebel Pen* (Monthly Review Press, 1985). Edited by Dee Garrison, the collection brings together Vorse's labor journalism from 1912 through 1959, along with selections from her writings on women. In *"Friend and Lover"* (Horizon Press, 1982), Virginia Gardner strives to correct the many distortions of the life of Louise Bryant, the feminist wife of John Reed; Bryant's career in journalism took root in the Greenwich Village of the teens among the socialist writers of *The Masses*.

360. Scott, Anne Firor. **Making the Invisible Woman Visible.** Urbana: University of Illinois Press, 1984. 387p. bibliog. index. $29.95. LC 83-17962. ISBN 0252011104.

The articles, reviews, and lectures gathered in this volume secure Scott's status as a "grandmother" (her term) of the new women's history and, in particular, as a pioneer in the feminist revision of Southern white women's history. In Part I, Scott presents a number of biographical essays, profiling women such as Jane Franklin Mecom (Benjamin Franklin's sister), Emma Willard (founder of the Troy Female Seminary), and Jane Addams (founder of Hull House in Chicago). Part II collects some of her writing on the South, including "The 'New Woman' in the New South," an early essay prefiguring much of her later work. Women's voluntary associations are the focus of the two articles in Part III, while lectures on women's history, women's education, and other topics comprise Part IV. Scott's scholarship is first-rate. Not content to let the work stand on its own merits, however, Scott adds an exceptionally candid and thoughtful introduction, "A Historian's Odyssey," which—together with her reflective section introductions and headnotes—places the collection itself in historical context, inviting the reader to ponder with her the evolution of her life, her work, and of the new women's history.

361. Seller, Maxine Schwartz, 1935- , ed. **Immigrant Women.** Philadelphia: Temple University Press, 1981. 347p. bibliog. index. $29.95. LC 80-21756. ISBN 0877221901.

"Using documents written by immigrant women themselves, or by others who knew them intimately, *Immigrant Women* offers ... a woman-centered perspective on American immigration history" (p.5). Speeches, memoirs, government reports, oral histories, short stories, novel excerpts, and scholarly articles are arranged in eight thematic sections: "Why They Came"; "Surviving in a New Land"; "Work"; "Family"; "Community Life"; "Education"; "Social Activists"; and "Daughters and Granddaughters." Together, the collection represents the experiences of women from Europe, Asia, Latin America, and elsewhere, from 1820 to the present. Some of the writers are well-known—e.g., Anzia Yezierska, Mother Jones, Emma Goldman, Rose Schneiderman, Paule Marshall, and Golda Meir—while others are more obscure. A bibliographical essay concludes the volume. The history of Irish immigrant women in the nineteenth century receives in-depth treatment from Hasia R. Diner in *Erin's Daughters in America* (Johns Hopkins University Press, 1983). In *Immigrant Women in the Land of Dollars: Life and Culture on the Lower East Side 1890-1925* (Monthly Review Press, 1985), Elizabeth Ewen documents the lives of first- and second-generation Jewish and Italian women immigrants to Manhattan's Lower East Side.

362. Sievers, Sharon L. **Flowers in Salt: The Beginnings of Feminist Consciousness in Modern Japan.** Stanford, CA: Stanford University Press, 1983. 240p. bibliog. index. $22.50. LC 82-60104. ISBN 0804711658.

Rapid industrialization and Westernization came to Japan with the Meiji Restoration in 1868, and were accompanied by the beginnings of feminist activism. In a history of the period between the Restoration and World War I, Sievers depicts ideological debate about women's "place"; women's activism, and the Meiji opposition; the early push for suffrage; women's position in the textile industries; women's participation in the socialist movement after 1900; and the founding of *Seitō,* magazine of the "new" women. *The Hidden Sun: Women of Modern Japan* (Westview Press, 1983), by Dorothy Robins-Mowry, is designed as a comprehensive textbook. Beginning with brief background material on traditional Japan and the modernization period, the volume is primarily devoted to a profile of women's lives in post-war Japan. Robins-Mowry's perspective reflects her history as a foreign service officer in the U.S. Information Agency. For more specialized treatments, see *Working Women in Japan: Discrimination, Resistance, and Reform* (New York State School of Industrial and Labor Relations, 1980), by Alice H. Cook and Hiroko Hayashi, and *Political Women in Japan: The Search for a Place in Political Life* (University of California Press, 1981), by Susan J. Pharr.

363. Slaughter, Jane, and Robert Kern, 1934- , eds. **European Woman on the Left: Socialism, Feminism, and the Problems Faced by Political Women, 1880 to the Present.** Westport, CT: Greenwood Press, 1981. 245p. bibliog. index. $29.95. LC 80-23553. ISBN 0313225435.

Ten essays profile radical women active on the European Left, highlighting their attempts to integrate commitments to socialist and feminist politics. The women are a diverse group, including well-known figures such as Clara Zetkin, Alexandra Kollontai, and Angelica Balabanoff; lesser-known women such as Spanish anarchist Federica Montseny; and even a contemporary, Ulrike Meinhof, of the German Baader-Meinhof group. *Clara Zetkin: Selected Writings* (International Publishers, 1984), edited by Philip S. Foner, collects many writings and speeches in which Zetkin articulates her socialist-feminist perspective. Foner provides a biographical essay and extensive notes. One might add to the group profiled in the Slaughter and Kern volume Louise Michel (1830-1905), a French revolutionary and feminist whose memoirs recently appeared in English for the first time under the title *The Red Virgin* (University of Alabama Press, 1981), edited and translated by Bullitt Lowry and Elizabeth Ellington Gunter.

364. Smith, Bonnie G., 1940- . **Ladies of the Leisure Class: The Bourgeoises of Northern France in the Nineteenth Century.** Princeton, NJ: Princeton University Press, 1981. 303p. bibliog. index. $29.00. LC 81-47157. ISBN 0691053308.

Feminist critics of classic Marxism have frequently called attention to the contradictions that arise when women are assumed to be of the same class standings as their husbands. In this work based largely on interviews, Smith goes beyond simple documentation of the different economic positions of nineteenth-century French bourgeois and bourgeoises to articulate "the substances and meaning of the domestic universe" bourgeois women inhabited (p.7). In her view, domesticity was not a trap set to ensnare women in trivial pursuits outside the arenas of power. Rather, Smith argues, bourgeois women themselves embraced and embellished the domestic life, transforming it into an independent culture that represented "the last bastion of a preindustrial, traditional, or premodern world view" (p.214). In *Housewife or Harlot: The Place of Women in French Society 1870-1940* (St. Martin's Press, 1981), James F. McMillan finds that the doctrine of separate spheres governed the lives of French women during the period of the Third Republic, not even appreciably modified by the cataclysm of the First World War.

365. Smith-Rosenberg, Carroll. **Disorderly Conduct: Visions of Gender in Victorian America.** New York: Knopf; distr. New York: Random House, 1985. 357p. bibliog. index. $19.95. LC 84-48821. ISBN 0394535456.

In "Hearing Women's Words," her opening essay, Smith-Rosenberg outlines the central theoretical and methodological trends in women's history. To set the stage for the pieces that follow, she also charts her own intellectual odyssey. This new essay, together with her now-classic "The Female World of Love and Ritual," constitutes Part One of the volume. Part Two focuses on the Jacksonian era, offering essays on the myth of Davy Crockett, the American Female Moral Reform Society's campaign against prostitution, and women's part in the religious revivals of the Second Great Awakening. Part Three looks at the latter half of the nineteenth century, examining Victorian medical attitudes toward puberty and menopause, analyzing the social causes and meanings of female hysteria, and interpreting the rhetoric of the anti-abortion movement. Finally, in "The New Woman as Androgyne," Smith-Rosenberg links the challenge that single, educated, economically autonomous women posed to the bourgeois social order at the turn of the century, to attacks on lesbianism from the emerging field of sexology. Smith-Rosenberg's fluid writing, scrupulous documentation, and provocative theories reaffirm her position as a leading explicator of the relationships of gender, class, and culture in nineteenth-century America.

366. Sowerwine, Charles. **Sisters or Citizens? Women and Socialism in France Since 1876.** New York: Cambridge University Press, 1982. 248p. bibliog. index. $29.95. LC 81-7692. ISBN 0521234840.

Sowerwine focuses primarily on the period of the Third Republic (1870 to 1940), during which "both feminism and socialism developed in their definitive forms, ... the alliance between them was sought and then rejected, and ... the socialist women's movement began and ended" (pp.3-4). He attributes the failure of the French feminist/socialist alliance to the class loyalties of bourgeois feminists, on the one hand, and to socialists' failure to champion women's rights, on the other. This part of the story has a familiar ring to those acquainted with the similar divisions between feminists and socialists in the United States and elsewhere. What demands explanation is the question of why France, often considered the birthplace of modern feminism, failed to enact woman suffrage until 1945. This question is a central preoccupation of a recent study, *Women's Suffrage and Social Politics in the French Third Republic* (Princeton University Press, 1984), by Steven C. Hause with Anne R. Kenney. The authors depict French feminists as caught between "the collectivist visions of Catholics, socialists, and radicals alike" (p.281). Patrick Kay Bidelman details the early origins of the French feminist movement in his work *Pariahs Stand Up! The Founding of the Liberal Feminist Movement in France, 1858-1889* (Greenwood Press, 1982).

367. Spencer, Samia I., 1943- , ed. **French Women and the Age of Enlightenment.** Bloomington: Indiana University Press, 1984. 429p. bibliog. index. $35.00. LC 83-48403. ISBN 0253324815.

Nineteenth-century interpretations of French women's lives during the previous century underlined the exceptional independence and influence of the female élite—some approvingly, some with dismay. Contemporary feminist scholars, by contrast, have emphasized the substantial contraints operating on eighteenth-century French women's lives. This collection of twenty-seven essays was planned as a first step in reconciling these two opposing interpretations. Spencer divides the volume into seven thematic sections: "Women and Political Life"; "Women and Society"; "Women and Culture"; "Creative Women and Women Artists"; "The Philosophes: Feminism or Antifeminism?"; "Portrayal of Women in French Literature"; and "Portrayal of French Women in Other European Literatures." Germaine Brée contributes a preface, and Elizabeth Fox-Genovese, the introduction.

368. Sterling, Dorothy, 1913- , ed. **We Are Your Sisters: Black Women in the Nineteenth Century.** New York: Norton, 1984. 535p. bibliog. index. $22.50. LC 83-11469. ISBN 0393017281.

"While [nineteenth-century] white women were hampered by the bonds of 'true womanhood' and told that their sphere was the home," Sterling writes, "the black woman was enslaved" (p.x). Sterling confines her documentary history of black women to the period from 1800 to the 1880s, omitting material available elsewhere—for example, in Gerda Lerner's pathbreaking *Black Women in White America* (1972). Slave narratives and other first-person testimony, letters, excerpts from diaries and autobiographies, and newspaper accounts, powerful in their sense of immediacy, flesh out our picture of the varied lives of nineteenth-century black women—enslaved and free, Northern and

Southern. Sterling sorts the documents chronologically into chapters, and topically within chapters, her own commentary providing historical background and continuity of narrative. The final chapter excerpts the diaries of four black women from the first free generation. A bibliography and source notes complete the volume. Sterling is also the author of *Black Foremothers: Three Lives* (Feminist Press, 1979), which profiles Ellen Craft, Ida B. Wells, and Mary Church Terrell.

369. Strasser, Susan, 1948- . **Never Done: A History of American Housework.** New York: Pantheon Books, 1982. 365p. bibliog. index. $22.00. LC 81-48234. ISBN 0394510240.

"The history of housework," as Strasser amply illustrates, "provides a description of fundamental changes in American daily life as the economy developed ..." (p.7). Her survey of women's domestic duties in the nineteenth and twentieth centuries and the technologies that transformed them draws on a variety of sources, including mail-order catalogs, government surveys, accounts by foreigners, women's magazines, and manuals on household management. Chapters early in the book treat food preparation, home heating and lighting, laundry, and garment production, among other chores, while later chapters focus on consumerism, "labor-saving" devices, and the present-day lives of wives and mothers employed outside the home. In between, Strasser examines the ideas of Catharine Beecher and Melusina Peirce, who glorified the homemaker's role; of Christine Frederick, one of the founders of modern home economics; and of Charlotte Perkins Gilman, the visionary theorist. Over a hundred black-and-white photographs offer further documentation. In *More Work for Mother: The Ironies of Household Technology from the Open Hearth to the Microwave* (Basic Books, 1983), Ruth Schwartz Cowan takes up several of the same themes. Her chronological overview reinforces her assertion that domestic labor has become "industrialized." Cowan argues that technological advances, while ameliorating the physical strains of housework, have paradoxically increased the demands on women's labor.

370. Taylor, Barbara, 1950- . **Eve and the New Jerusalem: Socialism and Feminism in the Nineteenth Century.** New York: Pantheon Books, 1983. 394p. bibliog. index. $19.45. LC 82-19007. ISBN 0394527666.

Taylor achieves a fresh reading of familiar history in this highly praised study of the British Owenite movement of the 1830s and 1840s. The Owenite socialists advocated the abolition of all forms of social hierarchy, sexual as well as class-based, and formed their own communities to actualize these goals. Briefly successful, the movement ultimately foundered as its working-class base of support fell apart. Termed "utopian" socialists by Marx, the Owenites came to be viewed as "primitive" by comparison with later "scientific" socialists. Taylor rejects this distinction, arguing that the Owenite ideals, while premature in the early 1880s, have a meaning that transcends their time. She unearths new evidence about the Owenite women, demonstrating that their views on sexual freedom and marriage diverged significantly from those of the men (which became identified with Owenite thinking in general). Despite these gender differences, the Owenites stand out in contrast to the later "scientific" socialists in not subordinating the "woman question" to the class struggle; in Taylor's view, feminism has been the inheritor of these ideals.

371. Thomis, Malcolm I., and Jennifer Grimmett. **Women in Protest 1800-1850.** New York: St. Martin's Press, 1982. 166p. bibliog. index. $25.00. LC 81-21290. ISBN 0312887469.

Historians have not accorded a very significant role to women in protest movements; where women's activism has been investigated and recognized, it has typically been in protests linked with domestic concerns, such as food riots. Skeptical that the historical record was complete, Thomis and Grimmit sought evidence of the full range of women's social and political protest in early nineteenth-century Britain. In this book they report their findings not just on food riots, but also on women's part in protests against evictions, enclosures, and the poor laws; on women's labor protests and their participation in the working-class Chartist movement; and on the many independent female reform societies that cropped up during the period. A concluding chapter looks to the history of crossdressing among male protesters for clues as to "the supposed role of real women in social protest as well as the pretending men" (p.138).

372. Ulrich, Laurel Thatcher. **Good Wives: Images and Reality in the Lives of Women in Northern New England, 1650-1750.** New York: Knopf; distr. New York: Random House, 1982. 296p. bibliog. index. $17.50. LC 81-18589. ISBN 039451940X.

Sources for a history of colonial women are few and far between. According to Ulrich, there were "no female diaries written in New England before 1750 and few female letters" (p.5). Ulrich turned to family papers, male diaries, and court, probate, and church records to create this well-written narrative. Her goal is to recover the reality hidden beneath the normative ideals of colonial womanhood. A woman in early New England was almost universally a wife, yet, Ulrich discovers, she was "simultaneously ... a deputy husband, a consort, a mother, a mistress, a neighbor, and a Christian" (p.9). Ulrich presents her account thematically in three sections based on "role clusters": "Bathsheba" (economic life); "Eve" (sex and reproduction); and "Jael" (the intersection of religion and aggression). Lyle Koehler has tapped a similar set of primary sources in researching his provocative book *A Search for Power: The "Weaker Sex" in Seventeenth-Century New England* (University of Illinois Press, 1980). Rejecting revisionist claims that Puritanism was a liberating force for women, he seeks to document the severity of seventeenth-century male dominance. He surveys the range and prevalence of female deviance—from murder and infanticide to adultery, depression, and suicide—concluding that these deviant behaviors should be viewed as instances of nascent feminism. Ulrich finds Koehler's study "marred by a curiously polemical style and by what sometimes appears as deliberate distortion of evidence" (p.281).

373. Van Kirk, Sylvia. **"Many Tender Ties": Women in Fur-Trade Society in Western Canada, 1670-1870.** Norman: University of Oklahoma Press, 1983. 301p. bibliog. index. $21.50. LC 82-40457. ISBN 0806118423.

"The early historical development of Western Canada was based upon a close economic partnership between Indian and white and extensive intermarriage. It is unfortunate that, in terms of its racial ties, the early world of the fur trade became 'a world we have lost'" (p.242). In this social history of Canadian fur-trade society, Van Kirk delineates changing sexual and racial relationships over two centuries. Early traders typically formed families with native women. As the children of these unions matured, "half-breed" women were sought after as wives. Van Kirk documents how the eventual arrival of white women contributed to the increasing stratification of this unique society, as racial and class distinctions took on ever greater meaning.

374. Walkowitz, Judith R. **Prostitution and Victorian Society: Women, Class, and the State.** New York: Cambridge University Press, 1980. 347p. bibliog. index. $34.50. LC 79-21050. ISBN 0521223342.

The Contagious Diseases Acts, first passed in 1864 and finally repealed in 1886, attempted to control veneral disease among British soldiers by empowering special police in garrison towns and ports to register prostitutes and to force them to undergo medical examinations and treatment. Led by Josephine Butler, the Ladies National Association vigorously agitated for repeal, arguing that the C.D. Acts deprived poor women of their rights, sanctioned male vice, and enforced a double standard of morality. Walkowitz scrutinizes the repeal movement, paying attention to class and gender conflict and coalition. In a related work, *Policing Prostitution in Nineteenth-Century Paris* (Princeton University Press, 1985), Jill Harsin mines a wealth of archival sources to reveal how government regulation controlled French prostitutes' lives. Two studies look at prostitution on the American frontier during the same period. In *Gold Diggers and Silver Miners* (University of Michigan Press, 1981), Marion S. Goldman examines prostitution on Nevada's Comstock Lode in the boom years of the 1860s and 1870s. She traces the economic and ideological links between the world of the prostitutes and the larger business community. *Daughters of Joy, Sisters of Misery* (University of Illinois Press, 1985), by Anne M. Butler, details the sordid, unstable, and impoverished lives of prostitutes in the American West between 1865 and 1890. Meticulously documented and rich in anecdote, Butler's work revises the stereotype of the glittering dance-hall girl, and demonstrates the role prostitutes played in building the social institutions of the West. Moving into the twentieth century, Ruth Rosen surveys prostitution in the United States from 1900 to 1918 in *The Lost Sisterhood* (Johns Hopkins University Press, 1982). Rosen documents how the near-hysterical Progressive attacks on prostitution and "white slavery" led to reforms that curtailed prostitutes' already limited economic and personal choices. She argues that the brothels offered both an enticing economic alternative and a sense of community to poor and immigrant women.

375.*   Ward, Margaret. **Unmanageable Revolutionaries: Women and Irish Nationalism.** London: Pluto Press, 1983. 296p. bibliog. index. £5.95. LC 83-146572. ISBN 0861047001.

The conflicting allegiances felt by contemporary Irish women in the nationalist and feminist movements inspired Ward's research into the past. She seeks to recover the forgotten history of women's contributions to Irish nationalism, as well as to investigate the feminist struggles waged by women within and outside the nationalist movement. She highlights three organizations: the Ladies' Land League (1881-1882), mobilized so women might take the place of imprisoned nationalist men; Inghinidhe na hEireann (1900-1914), formed because women were excluded from all other nationalist groups; and Cumann na mBan (1914-   ), an organization relegating women to a subordinate role in the nationalist struggle. Ward finds that unity between nationalist and feminist women was rarely achieved.

376.   Ware, Susan, 1950-   . **Holding Their Own: American Women in the 1930s.** Boston: Twayne, 1982. 223p. bibliog. index. $15.00. LC 82-6215. ISBN 0805799001.

"In general, women survived the 1930s in far better shape than has previously been suggested" (p.200), argues Susan Ware in this contribution to the Twayne series "American Women in the Twentieth Century." The series provides excellent decade-by-decade history texts. The scope of this volume is broad, encompassing employment, education, feminism and social reform, women on the Left, literature and the fine arts, and popular culture. The tone is upbeat, in striking contrast to other recent feminist interpretations of the era. (See, for example, Lois Scharf's *To Work and to Wed,* mentioned in entry 357.) While granting that women faced layoffs and unemployment during the thirties, their lives, Ware asserts, "were probably less disrupted ... than were men's" (p.198). Trying to make ends meet, women regained some of their productive functions within the household. In the world of work, "women as a group often fared better than men," although they "continued to be shunted into low-paying, low-status jobs ..." (p.199). Feminism, Ware concludes, did not die during the period. Ware takes the same revisionist tack in *Beyond Suffrage: Women in the New Deal* (Harvard University Press, 1981), which profiles the accomplishments of a New Deal network of twenty-eight professional women, among them Grace Abbott, Mary Anderson, Molly Dewson, Frances Perkins, Eleanor Roosevelt, and Rose Schneiderman. For a glimpse of how women at the lower end of the socioeconomic spectrum fared during the Depression, readers can turn to Julia Kirk Blackwelder's *Women of the Depression: Caste and Culture in San Antonio, 1929-1939* (Texas A&M University Press, 1984), which makes careful distinctions in women's experience along lines of race, ethnicity, and class.

377.   Windschuttle, Elizabeth, ed. **Women, Class and History: Feminist Perspectives on Australia, 1788-1978.** Auckland, New Zealand: Fontana, 1982. 604p. bibliog. index. pbk. $13.95. ISBN 0006357229.

Twenty-five papers document the vitality of the women's history field in Australia. There is much here to fascinate the reader from outside Australia. For example, those familiar with the saga of the Pankhursts in England will be intrigued to learn about their "lost daughter," Adela Pankhurst Walsh, banished by her family to Australia in 1914. Other topics include the colonial exploitation of Aboriginal women; women's organizations, from the anti-war Women's Peace Army (1915-1919) to the anti-labor Women's Guild of Empire (1929-1940); women writers in the interwar period; and labor struggles in health care, the meat industry, and "white collar" occupations. An index adds cohesiveness to the collection. In *Uphill All the Way: A Documentary History of Women in Australia* (University of Queensland Press, 1980), Kay Daniels and Mary Murnane make available a sampling of the primary sources. The editors emphasize two major themes: "the active response of women to their conditions and the class relationship between women" (p.xii). Theirs is not a history of the famous and the elite, but rather of exiled British convicts and "undesirables," displaced Aborigines, ordinary mothers and workers, prostitutes, and professional women.

378.   Woloch, Nancy. **Women and the American Experience.** New York: Knopf, 1984. 567p. bibliog. index. $19.00. LC 84-746. ISBN 0394535154.

Drawing primarily from the scholarship of the past two decades, this introductory text surveys women's experience in the United States from the seventeenth century to the present. Each period is presented as a set of paired chapters, the first describing an event or profiling an individual in some detail, the second providing a historical overview. For example, Woloch tells the story of the shirtwaist strike of 1909 in Chapter 9 and then goes on in Chapter 10 to fill in the background on working women's history during the period from 1860 to 1920. The text is amply illustrated, and each pair of chapters is followed by a thoughtful review essay on additional sources.

LANGUAGE AND LINGUISTICS

The books cited below reflect issues in both theoretical and applied linguistics. They range from manuals on nonsexist English usage, to empirical research on male and female communication styles. Feminist scholars study language from many perspectives; consequently, additional relevant works fall into other chapters. The Literature: History and Criticism chapter, for example, spotlights analyses of literary discourse, while the Religion and Philosophy chapter treats images of women in the language of worship. Readers are advised to consult the periodical literature as well. *Women and Language* (see entry 1206) provides leads to recent publications and works in progress, while bibliographies (see entry 877) point to older materials.

379.   Frank, Francine Harriet Wattman, 1931- , and Frank Anshen, 1942- . **Language and the Sexes.** Albany: State University of New York Press, 1983. 130p. bibliog. index. $24.95. LC 83-24141. ISBN 0873958810.

Addressing the general reader, linguists Frank and Anshen explore the interplay of language and sexism. They devote chapters to names, sex differences in speech, how men and women address and describe each other, derogatory and stereotpyed terms, and proposed reforms. Although they draw illustrative examples from history and from other languages, they are primarily concerned with current English usage. The book ends with suggestions for research projects and guidelines for nondiscriminatory language use. This is a concise, lively introduction to several key areas in feminist linguistic research.

380.   Kramarae, Cheris. **Women and Men Speaking: Frameworks for Analysis.** Rowley, MA: Newbury House, 1981. 194p. bibliog. index. $14.95. LC 80-16802. ISBN 0883771799.

Because research on gender and language has mushroomed, this attempt to survey recent findings and place them in theoretical frameworks is a much-needed step forward. Kramarae fits evidence about male and female language use into theories of social structure and gender interaction. She chooses four theoretical vantage points: the "muted group" thesis, based on the work of anthropologists Shirley Ardener and Edwin Ardener; the "reconstructed psychoanalysis" of Jacques Lacan and Cora Kaplan; the framework of "speech styles" developed by social psychologist Howard Giles; and a "strategy model" adapted from recent British and American anthropological approaches. In a more recent study, *Feminism and Linguistic Theory* (Macmillan, 1985), Deborah Cameron seeks to demystify current ideas about the relationship of language, culture, and society by outlining key concepts in semiology, structuralism, psychoanalysis, and sociolinguistics. She identifies three areas of feminist investigation — sex differences in language use, sexism in language itself, and women's "alienation" from language — and concludes by advocating a "radical linguistic practice" (p.162).

381. Mayo, Clara, et al., eds. **Gender and Nonverbal Behavior.** New York: Springer-Verlag, 1981. 284p. bibliog. index. $28.00. LC 81-9067. ISBN 0387906010.

The thirteen papers in this anthology—jointly edited by Clara Mayo, Alexandra Weiss, and Nancy M. Henley—review past research on various aspects of sex differences in nonverbal behavior, report new findings, and point to theoretical implications and areas requiring further study. Among the topics addressed are gender patterns in touch, space, gaze, and movement; androgyny and nonverbal communication; the role of socialization and other factors in the acquisition of nonverbal skills. For a more thorough review of existing data, see *Nonverbal Sex Differences*, by Judith A. Hall (Johns Hopkins University Press, 1984). Hall systematically draws together the vast research literature on gender differences in nonverbal behavior, analyzes it statistically, and evaluates significant theories and hypotheses. She looks at accuracy of judgment of nonverbal messages, and accuracy of expression, plus specific sources of cues: face; gaze; interpersonal distance and orientation; touch; body movement and position; and voice.

382. McConnell-Ginet, Sally, et al., eds. **Women and Language in Literature and Society.** New York: Praeger, 1980. 352p. bibliog. index. $35.95. LC 80-20816. ISBN 0030578922.

Sally McConnell-Ginet is a linguist, Ruth Borker an anthropologist, and Nelly Furman a literary critic. As the editors of this anthology, they contribute the three essays that constitute the first part, "Views From and To the Disciplines," surveying conceptual frameworks for the study of social and literary discourse from a feminist perspective. Part II, "Men's Power, Women's Language," presents five essays by others that "advance our understanding of the subtle and varied interactions between social power, language, and gender" (p.57). Part III, "Language in Women's Lives," has six pieces on women's speech, the politics of naming, and women's writing, emphasizing "a multiplicity of contextual factors affecting and affected by language," including "education, economic activities, membership in social groups, physical environment, political ideologies, and historical period" (p.137). Part IV, titled "Reading Women's Writing," features seven articles on literature. Cheris Kramarae, Wendy Martyna, Howard Giles, Annette Kolodny, Nancy K. Miller, and Jane Gallop are among the contributors to this volume. Throughout, they illuminate theoretical and methodological concerns; the anthology is therefore an excellent introduction to a variety of scholarly perspectives on the study of women and language.

383. Miller, Casey, and Kate Swift. **The Handbook of Nonsexist Writing: For Writers, Editors, and Speakers.** New York: Lippincott, 1980. 134p. index. $10.53. LC 79-26851. ISBN 0690018827.

"At a deep level, changes in a language are threatening because they signal widespread changes in social mores," state Miller and Swift. "At a level closer to the surface they are exasperating" (p.3). The generic use of "man," the "pronoun problem," gratuitous modifiers (such as lady attorney or male nurse), the feminization of inanimate objects, trivializing constructions—all are exposed and remedied in this concise handbook. With sensible examples of reworded sentences and preferred terms, and engaging tidbits of linguistic history, this guide eases the exasperation of anyone seeking to communicate in graceful, unbiased prose.

384. Morahan, Shirley, 1945- . **A Woman's Place: Rhetoric and Readings for Composing Yourself and Your Prose.** Albany: State University of New York Press, 1981. 308p. bibliog. index. $34.50. LC 81-4802. ISBN 0873955498.

Speaking in the first person in this unique textbook for college composition classes, Morahan poses frequent questions and "writing tasks" to her readers. She uses sample essays by such writers as Adrienne Rich, Tillie Olsen, Virginia Woolf, and Mary Wollstonecraft to illustrate basic points of definition, grammar, outlining, and revising. Two chapters are devoted to collaborative research and writing.

385. Smith, Philip M., 1953- . **Language, the Sexes and Society.** New York: Basil Blackwell, 1985. 211p. bibliog. index. $34.95. LC 84-14489. ISBN 0631111115.

At the center of this volume is the presentation of Smith's original empirical data, demonstrating a correspondence between a speaker's self-image and the degree of masculinity or femininity attributed to him/her by the listener. The findings also point to a correlation between listeners' perceptions and their own gender identity. Smith surrounds this statistics-laden chapter with a thorough survey of the literature on the representation of the sexes in language, male-female speech patterns, methods of measuring masculinity and femininity, and the use of language to regulate interactions between men and women.

386. Spender, Dale. **Man Made Language.** 2nd ed. Boston: Routledge and Kegan Paul, 1985. 250p. bibliog. index. pbk. $9.95. LC 80-40877. ISBN 0710203152.

Arguing that language is a crucial factor in our construction of reality, Spender exposes the "male-as-norm" assumption in the operation of language and its role in perpetuating the patriarchal order. After critiquing previous research on language and sex (most of which she finds poorly designed and/or hopelessly biased), Spender proceeds to explore women's silence and invisibility within the male meaning system, the notion of "the dominant and the muted" in mixed-sex conversation, male fear of "woman talk," the power of consciousness-raising, the relationship of language and reality as revealed in research on the generic use of "man," the politics of naming, and women and writing.

387. Thorne, Barrie, et al., eds. **Language, Gender, and Society.** Rowley, MA: Newbury House, 1983. 342p. bibliog. index. $15.95. LC 82-22537. ISBN 088377268X.

Eight years after their groundbreaking volume *Language and Sex. Difference and Dominance,* sociolinguist Barrie Thorne and psycholinguist Nancy Henley are joined by speech communication specialist Cheris Kramarae to produce a second anthology. Like its predecessor, the present volume features a hefty annotated bibliography. Although selective, it is the most thorough guide available to published materials on gender marking and sex bias in language structure and content, stereotypes and perceptions of language use, sex differences and similarities in language use, conversational interaction among men and women, genre and style, children and language, language varieties in American English, and nonverbal aspects of communication. The ten papers that precede the bibliography follow a similar outline of topics, beginning with a survey of recent research by the editors. Other pieces address sex bias (the "he/man approach" and the "pronoun problem"), rural black women's linguistic options and choices, female intonation, women and men in conversational interactions, genre and style in women's writing, and men's speech to young children.

388. Vetterling-Braggin, Mary, ed. **Sexist Language: A Modern Philosophical Analysis.** Totowa, NJ: Rowman and Littlefield, 1981. 329p. bibliog. pbk. $7.95. LC 80-26263. ISBN 0822603535.

Viewing the feminist call for language reform from the standpoint of logic and philosophical principle, the contributors to this volume make a unique contribution to studies on women and language. The twenty-three essays are grouped thematically. They define sexist language, debate the moral significance of using sexist language, address specific examples (the generic "he," terms for sexual intercourse, and titles such as "Miss" and "Mrs."), and compare sexist and racist language use in terms of content and impact. Vetterling-Braggin provides short introductions to each section, delineating the areas of agreement and disagreement among the authors.

LAW

Feminists continue to push for legal reforms, and lately the number of women practicing law has risen sharply. Not surprisingly, the literature on women's legal rights has ballooned. We include in this chapter several books critical of the criminal justice system, both past and present, which demonstrate feminist concern over the application of the law, as well as its spirit. Specific legal issues—e.g., abortion, woman-battering, job discrimination—are covered in materials listed here, as are women's roles in the legal professions. We also highlight several excellent general handbooks on women's legal rights, aimed at lay readers. The Periodicals chapter cites several law reporters and professional journals devoted to women (see entry 1171). For bibliographic guides, see entry 844.

389. Adler, Freda, ed. **The Incidence of Female Criminality in the Contemporary World.** New York: New York University Press, 1981. 275p. bibliog. index. $42.50. LC 81-2495. ISBN 0814705766.

Laden with charts and graphs, this anthology is valuable for its multinational perspective on women and crime. The contributors write knowledgeably of the situations in their home countries—the United States, the Netherlands, Finland, Norway, England and Wales, Germany, Poland, Hungary, Nigeria, Egypt, Argentina, Venezuela, India, and Japan. Although female crime is on the upswing in the United States (a fact Adler attributes to the increased opportunities and strains in a society moving toward sexual equality), most other nations have not registered such striking increases.

390. Chapman, Jane Roberts. **Economic Realities and the Female Offender.** Lexington, MA: Lexington Books, 1980. 234p. bibliog. index. $26.50. LC 79-3785. ISBN 0669035157.

Aware that nonviolent, economically motivated crimes make up the largest category of crimes women commit—including theft, fraud, prostitution, and drug dealing—Chapman posits that the increase in female criminality in recent years stems not from the impact of the women's movement, as some have hypothesized, but from increasing poverty and unemployment. In the second half of her study, she examines innovative programs for socioeconomic rehabilitation of women offenders. Programs fall into three basic categories, emphasizing vocational skills, parenting, and preparation for independent living. Chapman builds a strong case for women offenders' legal right to such programs, but admits that implementing them widely will require fundamental changes in the criminal justice system.

391. Curry, Hayden, and Denis Clifford. **A Legal Guide for Lesbian and Gay Couples.** 3rd ed. Berkeley, CA: Nolo Press, 1985. 257p. bibliog. index. pbk. $17.95. ISBN 087337004X.

Aimed at lay readers, this practical guide covers such matters as living-together contracts, finances, real estate, children, and estate planning. Sample contracts, powers of attorney, wills, and other legal documents are provided. The revised edition of *The Rights of Gay People* (Bantam Books, 1983), prepared by the American Civil Liberties Union, looks not only at couple-related questions, but also at laws governing employment, immigration, housing, public accommodations, and freedom of speech. A state-by-state review of criminal statutes regarding homosexuality and a list of legal assistance groups are appended. Law students and practitioners who require more detailed information on applicable laws and precedents can consult *Sexual Orientation and the Law* (Clark Boardman, 1985), a comprehensive looseleaf treatise edited by Roberta Achtenberg for the progressive National Lawyers Guild.

392. Datesman, Susan K., and Frank R. Scarpitti, eds. **Women, Crime, and Justice.** New York: Oxford University Press, 1980. 376p. bibliog. pbk. $8.95. LC 79-18791. ISBN 0195026764.

"Female criminality has often ended up as a footnote to works on men that purport to be works on criminality in general," complains Dorie Klein (p.71) in her perceptive literature review. Datesman and Scarpitti strive to right this wrong by assembling some of the best writings from the 1970s, when the topic of women and crime began to receive long-overdue attention. The section on the etiology of female crime explores such factors as sex role conditioning, broken homes, and the women's liberation movement. Another group of papers exploring patterns of crime treats violent acts, organized crime, heroin addiction, prostitution, and girl gangs. A third section examines the criminal justice system and finds evidence of sex discrimination in sentencing, paternalism, unequal protection for boys and girls in juvenile court, and inadequate services for incarcerated women, especially mothers. The editors bracket these studies with a lucid statistical analysis of the extent and nature of female crimes and a statement on the hotly debated question of the relation between women's emancipation and women's crime.

393. Davidson, Sue, ed. **Justice for Young Women: Close-up on Critical Issues.** Tucson, AZ: New Directions for Young Women, 1982. 141p. bibliog. pbk. $5.50. LC 82-7848. ISBN 0960869603.

"The contradictions in the position of the average young woman who runs afoul of the law are glaring: she is simultaneously a victim and an offender," contributor Meda Chesney-Lind pointedly states (p.10). Most girls who tangle with the criminal justice system are "status offenders," guilty of disobeying authorities, running away, being sexually active—acts that are labeled criminal only because the perpetrators are minors. The six articles in this anthology relate female delinquency to the broader situation of women in contemporary society. The opening piece is a first-hand account—"Listen to Me: A Female Status Offender's Story." The other articles treat nineteenth-century reform schools, recent research on female delinquency, adolescent prostitution, incest, and advocacy programs.

394. Epstein, Cynthia Fuchs. **Women in Law.** New York: Basic Books, 1981. 438p. bibliog. index. $18.50. LC 80-68954. ISBN 0465092055.

Epstein follows the careers of women lawyers in the United States from their choice of the legal profession, through law school, and into a variety of practices. Separate chapters recount the experiences of lawyers in government, public interest law, feminist firms, husband-wife partnerships, Wall Street firms, law professorships, and the judiciary, among other options. The final chapters focus on personal and family issues. The text is liberally sprinkled with excerpts from interviews. Epstein concludes that women can succeed in law today only by following a career pattern set by (and for) men, but that as more and more women work as lawyers, the legal profession will itself change, for the betterment of both women lawyers and their clients. Ronald Chester's study, *Unequal Access: Women Lawyers in a Changing America* (Bergin and Garvey, 1985), is a more focused account of the careers of women who attended law school in the 1920s and 1930s, based on oral histories. Female networking has been — and Chester cautions, must continue to be — the surest means for women lawyers to achieve their potential.

395.   Freedman, Estelle B., 1947- . **Their Sisters' Keepers: Women's Prison Reform in America, 1830-1930.** Ann Arbor: University of Michigan Press, 1981. 248p. bibliog. index. $20.00. LC 80-24918. ISBN 0472100084.

Freedman's well-documented historical study begins by analyzing the ideas, motives, and activities of white, middle-class women who worked on behalf of female prisoners in the nineteenth century. The middle section recounts the establishment of separate women's reformatories between 1870 and 1910 and provides glimpses of the women administrators and inmates who populated them. The final chapters assess a shift in the Progressive Era, away from hereditarian explanations of criminal behavior and toward an acceptance of environmental and economic causes. Ironically, the new theories had little effect on prison training programs, which continued to emphasize domestic skills. After examining the legacy of "separate but equal" prisons in her concluding chapter, Freedman compares the earlier reformers, who wanted to uplift and rehabilitate the individual fallen woman, to their Progressive successors, who favored social services to prevent women from entering a life of crime, and to contemporary feminists, who, by eliminating racism and sexism and allowing economic and sexual autonomy for all women, would end the need for women's prisons. In a study that complements Freedman's, Barbara M. Brenzel mines the archives and case histories of the State Industrial School for Girls in Lancaster, Massachusetts. Her book is titled *Daughters of the State: A Social Portrait of the First Reform School for Girls in North America, 1856-1905* (MIT Press, 1983). Nicole Hahn Rafter likewise draws on first-hand accounts, prison records, legislative documents, and other primary sources in her impressive historical overview — *Partial Justice: Women in State Prisons, 1800-1935* (Northeastern University Press, 1985).

396.   Hevener, Natalie Kaufman. **International Law and the Status of Women.** Boulder, CO: Westview Press, 1983. 249p. bibliog. index. $22.00. LC 82-20298. ISBN 0865319243.

Hevener has assembled twenty-three international treaties and other legal instruments specifically concerning women adopted by the United Nations between 1945 and 1980. For each she provides a brief background section, the text of the document, and a table of nations that have ratified it. Her excellent introductory analysis splits the agreements into three categories: "protective" provisions prohibiting women from certain activities; "corrective" provisions designed to improve the treatment of women; and "non-discriminatory" provisions, which treat women and men identically. The Convention on the Elimination of All Forms of Discrimination Against Women, adopted in 1979, illustrates progress in current international consensus toward the nondiscriminatory approach.

397.   Jones, Ann, 1937- . **Women Who Kill.** New York: Holt, Rinehart and Winston, 1980; repr. New York: Fawcett Columbine, 1981. 408p. bibliog. index. pbk. $5.95. LC 80-12329. ISBN 0449900584.

Jones contends that "women who kill find extreme solutions to problems that thousands of women cope with in more peaceable ways from day to day" (p.14), and that nearly half the women who commit murder do so in self-defense. Her thoroughly researched study examines murder cases in the United States from the colonial times to the present, including instances of infanticide, revenge on rapists, and murders of husbands and lovers. She considers questions of motivation, as well as the perpetrators' treatment by the courts and the larger community. In recent years, the mass media have spotlighted the plight of battered women who kill their husbands. Faith McNulty's *The Burning Bed* (Harcourt, Brace, Jovanovich, 1980) recounts the chilling experiences of Francine Hughes, who was acquitted after killing her tormentor. Helen Yglesias's novel *Sweetsir* (Simon and Schuster, 1981) treats the same theme.

398. Kanowitz, Leo. **Equal Rights: The Male Stake.** Albuquerque: University of New Mexico Press, 1981. 197p. bibliog. index. pbk. $9.95. LC 81-52056. ISBN 0826305954.

Kanowitz, a professor of law and specialist in sex discrimination, advocates male support for the Equal Rights Amendment and the women's movement in general, because, as he demonstrates, "males are *direct* victims, along with women, of a system that arbitrarily assigns roles on the basis of sex" (p.12). Two rather legalistic chapters trace judicial precedents for the doctrine of "benign" sex discrimination in such areas as protective labor law, while other chapters assess the impact of the E.R.A. and the failed strategies for ratification. In the latter discussion, Kanowitz criticizes the boycott of unratified states, anti-pornography "vigilante tactics," and the conflation of the struggle for equal rights with the denigration of homemakers, gay liberation, and the pro-choice movement. Many of these opinions are echoed by other, more strident proponents of men's rights; Kanowitz is exceptional for his focused attention on law and legal routes to social reform.

399. Lefcourt, Carol H., ed. **Women and the Law.** New York: Clark Boardman, 1984. various pagings. bibliog. index. $75.00. LC 84-11150. ISBN 0876324413.

Dubbed the "Best New Law Book of 1984" by the Association of American Publishers, this annually updated looseleaf volume is aimed at attorneys, judges, and other legal professionals. Although replete with case citations and references to statutes, the text is clearly written and accessible to the general reader. Experts contribute sections on comparable worth, sexual harassment, homemakers' economic rights, child support, child custody, prenuptial and marital agreements, artificial insemination, battered women, rape, birth trauma, and infant formula marketing. Appendices emphasize practical information, including lists of organizations, bibliographies, sample complaints and contracts, and reference materials for use in trials.

400. Mann, Coramae Richey, 1931- . **Female Crime and Delinquency.** University: University of Alabama Press, 1984. 331p. bibliog. index. $30.00. LC 82-16052. ISBN 0817301445.

Mann presents a balanced and well-organized overview of current theory and practice regarding female miscreants. She discusses data on the extent and nature of female crime, critiques various theories of causation, and examines the workings of the law, the courts, and the correctional system. Throughout she pays equal attention to juveniles and adults, and her final chapter on "the most forgotten female offenders" highlights the plight of incarcerated mothers and women on Death Row. Her epilogue calls for a unisex theory of crime and delinquency and identifies many areas for further research and reform. Readers intrigued by the theoretical questions should turn to Eileen B. Leonard's exceptionally articulate survey, *Women, Crime, and Society* (Longman, 1982), for a deeper look at existing theories—anomie theory, labeling theory, differential association, subcultural theory, and Marxism—and a glimpse of how a new, feminist approach to criminology might be constructed.

401. Milbauer, Barbara, in collaboration with Bert N. Obrentz. **The Law Giveth: Legal Aspects of the Abortion Controversy.** New York: Atheneum, 1983. 363p. bibliog. index. $21.95. LC 82-45184. ISBN 0689113129.

The Law Giveth opens with the chilling tale of the real woman behind the famous *Roe* v. *Wade* Supreme Court case that legalized abortion in the United States. Gang raped, "Jane Roe" was forced by her poverty to continue the ensuing pregnancy and give up the child for adoption. Chance brought her into contact with two feminist attorneys intent on challenging the constitutionality of abortion laws; determination to spare other women her experience led her to lend herself to the case. Milbauer's aim in this clearly written book is to familiarize the layperson with abortion law, past and present. The chronology documents the landmark cases of *Roe* v. *Wade* and *Doe* v. *Bolton,* as well as some of the estimated 144 statutes and regulations passed by several states in the aftermath of *Roe* in an effort to chip away at the legality of abortion. Among the issues the survey brings to light are the right to privacy, the question of fetal viability, abortion and public aid, parental consent, maternal health and life versus fetal life, and the Human Life Bill. Recent developments are placed in context in a chapter that briefly traces the history of abortion and birth control in the United States.

402. Nicholas, Susan Cary, et al. **Rights and Wrongs: Women's Struggles for Legal Equality.** 2nd ed. Old Westbury, NY: Feminist Press, 1986. 87p. index. pbk. $7.95. LC 86-2461. ISBN 0935312420.

Designed as a supplementary text for the school classroom, *Rights and Wrongs* serves equally well as a quick and readable introduction for more advanced students who lack grounding in the principles and history of United States law. Joint authors Susan Cary Nicholas, Alice M. Price, and Rachel Rubin cover four major areas: the Constitution; marriage; employment; and control over women's bodies. The authors highlight past and current reforms and point out many areas where full sexual equality has yet to be achieved. The volume appears in the series "Women's Lives/Women's Work" and has been thoroughly revised to reflect legal changes since the first (1979) edition.

403. Niles, Gayle L., 1944- , and Douglas H. Snider, 1946- . **Woman's Counsel: A Legal Guide for Women.** Denver, CO: Arden Press, 1984. 240p. bibliog. index. pbk. $8.50. LC 84-11161. ISBN 0912869046.

"The law is complex and constantly changing," note attorneys Niles and Snider on the first page of their handbook; this is reflected in a steady stream of updated legal guides for women. The latest, *Woman's Counsel,* is a readable introduction to basic rights, obligations, and legal procedures. Topics of special concern to women are covered — among them divorce, child custody, sex discrimination, sexual harassment, rape, battering, and credit — along with basic advice on attorney selection, jury duty, small claims court, traffic court, arrest, searches, and wills. Also noteworthy is the revised edition of *The Rights of Women,* by Susan Deller Ross and Ann Barcher (Bantam Books, 1983), one of a series of inexpensive paperback handbooks from the American Civil Liberties Union. Using a question-and-answer format, the authors present a staggering amount of information on constitutional rights, employment discrimination, education, the mass media, crimes, juvenile delinquency, reproductive rights, divorce and related issues, name changes, and sex discrimination in such areas as housing, daycare, military service, and jury duty. Appendices furnish charts of state laws and directories of resource organizations. Among other helpful titles are *Everywoman's Legal Guide* (1983; Doubleday, rev. ed., 1985), a collection of chapters by legal experts, edited by Barbara A. Burnett; and the specialized *A Woman's Legal Guide to Separation and Divorce in All 50 States* (Scribner, 1985), by Norma Harwood.

404. O'Connor, Karen, 1952- . **Women's Organizations' Use of the Courts.** Lexington, MA: Lexington Books, 1980. 157p. bibliog. index. $25.00. LC 79-2275. ISBN 0669030937.

O'Connor explains how special-interest groups use three strategies to influence public policy at the Supreme Court level: publicity-oriented litigation; outcome-oriented litigation; and *amicus curiae* (friend of the court) briefs. The National Woman Suffrage Association and the National Consumers' League offer, respectively, historical examples of the first two tactics, while current women's groups frequently favor *amicus* briefs or a combination strategy. Here O'Connor distinguishes several organizations active on the legal front and spotlights the Women's Rights Project of the American Civil Liberties Union. She analyzes each approach in terms of nine "success factors," which include longevity of the effort, staffing, financing, publicity, and coordination with other interest groups.

405. Rafter, Nicole Hahn, 1939- , and Elizabeth Anne Stanko, 1950- , eds. **Judge, Lawyer, Victim, Thief: Women, Gender Roles, and Criminal Justice.** Boston: Northeastern University Press, 1982. 383p. bibliog. index. pbk. $10.95. LC 82-2285. ISBN 0930350294.

The editors contend that gender roles and societal expectations continue to have a major impact on theory and practice in the fields of victimology, criminology, and the criminal justice professions. The volume's introduction dissects the stereotypical images of women and shows how they have resulted in differential treatment. The sixteen papers, all by research specialists or professors, reinforce the editors' point that gender roles are responsible for a "commonality between women on opposite sides of the law" (p.22). The papers are grouped according to their focus on women as victims, as offenders, as defendants and prisoners, and as practitioners and professionals. In *Women in the Criminal Justice System* (Praeger, 1980), Clarice Feinman studies women criminals, correction officers, police officers, lawyers, and judges, using the madonna/whore stereotype as her organizing motif.

406. Sachs, Albie, and Joan Hoff Wilson. **Sexism and the Law: A Study of Male Beliefs and Legal Bias in Britain and the United States.** New York: Free Press, 1979. 257p. bibliog. index. $15.95. LC 78-63402. ISBN 0029276403.

Sachs and Wilson convincingly demonstrate that sexism has been equally endemic in the legal systems of Great Britain and the United States, despite the fact that British judges are seen as interpreters of the will of Parliament, while American judges operate as guardians of the Constitution. In Part I, "The Male Monopoly Cases," the authors examine decisive court cases in the struggle of women to be recognized as "persons" or "citizens" referred to in laws. Other parts treat historical developments in family law, women's entrance into the legal profession, and progress toward legal equality in the 1960s and 1970s.

407. Tong, Rosemarie. **Women, Sex, and the Law.** Totowa, NJ: Rowman and Allanheld, 1984. 216p. bibliog. index. $22.50. LC 83-16001. ISBN 0847672301.

Seeking answers in feminist theory more often than in legal opinion or precedent, Tong asks "why different kinds of women have suffered in different sorts of ways at the hands of Anglo-American law for the same reason: their sexuality" (p.1). She examines pornography, prostitution, sexual harassment, rape, and woman-battering in successive chapters, while two final chapters explore black and lesbian perspectives on all five problems. Tong lucidly outlines traditional legal viewpoints and analyzes the pro's and con's of various reforms proposed by feminists. The tone is fair-minded and cautionary.

Throughout Tong recognizes the limits of the law in altering cultural attitudes about female sexuality, especially in pluralistic Western society, but she nevertheless affirms the necessity of legal reform.

408.* United States. Department of Labor. Women's Bureau. **A Working Woman's Guide to Her Job Rights.** Washington, DC: U.S. Government Printing Office, 1984. 56p.

This succinct guide explains the legal rights of women in the paid labor force under federal law. The chapter titled "Getting the Job" covers employment services, apprenticeship and training programs, and discrimination in hiring. "On the Job" treats a number of concerns, including minimum wages, overtime pay, pay equity, maternity leave, sexual harassment, unemployment benefits, occupational safety, union activities, and tax credits for child care. The final chapter, "After Retirement," discusses social security and pensions. Addresses of federal and state agencies are appended, along with sample complaint forms. In *Yes You Can: The Working Woman's Guide to Her Legal Rights, Fair Employment, and Equal Pay* (Prentice-Hall, 1984), Emily B. Kirby goes into greater detail to help women recognize illegal employment practices and devise strategies for redress.

409.* United States Commission on Civil Rights. **Under the Rule of Thumb: Battered Women and the Administration of Justice.** Washington, DC: United States Commission on Civil Rights, 1982. 100p. bibliog.

In 1980 the Commission on Civil Rights conducted research and hearings on law enforcement and battered women. The findings point to serious failings on the part of police, prosecutors, courts, and diversion programs such as counseling and mediation. The recommendations insist that woman beating be treated as seriously as any violent assault, and that state and federal governments play a stronger role in supporting shelters and social services.

410. Weisberg, D. Kelly, ed. **Women and the Law: The Social Historical Perspective.** Cambridge, MA: Schenkman, 1982. 2v. bibliog. index. LC 82-843. Vol. 1: $18.95; ISBN 0870735861. Vol. 2: $18.95; ISBN 0870735926.

With this collection, Weisberg seeks to ameliorate the "remarkably ahistorical" state of current scholarship on women and the law. Addressing a range of theoretical issues, places, and periods, the articles bridge the disciplines of law, history, and sociology. Twenty-three articles are organized into five thematic sections, each opening with a short introduction and closing with a list of suggested readings. Volume I focuses on women and the criminal law, while volume II explores the topics of property and family and concludes with essays on women in the legal profession.

411. Wortman, Marlene Stein, ed. **Women in American Law. Vol. 1: From Colonial Times to the New Deal.** New York: Holmes and Meier Publishers, 1985. 421p. bibliog. index. pbk. $19.75. LC 83-22527. ISBN 0841907536.

Wortman encourages historical research on women and the law in the United States by assembling over 160 documents, organizing them by period and topic, and adding lengthy interpretive headnotes. Her choices include legal materials (judicial cases, statutes, administrative rulings, legal treatises, contracts, wills, and legislative reports) as well as nonlegal materials that illustrate the changing cultural images of women and the social reality of their lives. Among the latter are newspaper articles, essays, speeches, government reports, advertisements, and letters, often presented in condensed or excerpted form. The basic arrangement is chronological, with sub-units for major topics: Marriage and Property; Family Roles; Occupational Choice; Crime and Deviance; and Protection v.

Equal Rights. Although Wortman relies on existing collections of primary sources rather than unearthing new documents, she greatly eases the research task of legal historians, while aiding nonspecialists with a glossary of legal terms and a fifteen-page bibliography. Volume 2 will extend coverage to the present.

LITERATURE

Works in this section are grouped under the following subheadings: fiction, poetry, drama, essays, literary history and criticism, and mixed genres. This last category covers multigenre works by single authors as well as collective volumes. Included are both translated works and literature originally written in English. Our list foregrounds a number of contemporary writers who did not show up in the first volume, and often relies on anthologies to represent important contributions of lesser-known authors. Although works expressing a feminist viewpoint outnumber other titles, we have selectively included literature by major women writers who disavow any links with feminism. Important reprints, now available through the Feminist Press, Virago, and other publishers, are seldom cited, although we recommend them highly.

The last decade has seen the emergence of a strong, theoretical feminist literary criticism. In the subchapter on literary history and criticism, we have tried to include most particularly anthologies and general overviews that suggest the liveliness and pluralism in feminist literary studies. A critical study of a particular author, however, is usually mentioned under a primary work by the author; and we have taken special pains to cover bibliographies of works by and about individual writers.

Because of the benefits to the user of clustering materials by and about an author, we have in most cases chosen one important work and mentioned other works within that annotation. In a few cases, when letters or an autobiography are the major source, other literary works by the author and criticism about her find their place in the Autobiography chapter.

We encourage users to browse through the Periodicals chapter for literary journals and review media covering fiction and poetry. Bibliographies of works by and about lesbians, Hispanics, working women, Canadian writers, blacks, and other subgroups often appear in periodicals, as do reading lists narrowly focused on periods, national literatures, and specific themes. Check the reference chapter for more general bibliographies on writers and genres.

DRAMA

412. Chambers, Jane, 1937-1983. **Last Summer at Bluefish Cove.** New York: JH Press, 1982. 107p. $25.00. LC 81-86655. ISBN 0935672044.

This warm, funny play takes place during Lil's last summer at Bluefish Cove, a lesbian beach colony where a group of friends has spent many summers together. They want this summer to be special, because Lil is dying of cancer. Eva — recently divorced and on her own for the first time in her life — has mistakenly rented one of the cottages on the cove. At first, Eva is confused by the women's relationships, and they do not trust her; but over the course of the summer, she and Lil become lovers. Eva learns to enjoy her life without men, while Lil learns to accept Eva's love and her own need for Eva. Chambers has also written *My Blue Heaven* (JH Press, 1981).

413. Churchill, Caryl. **Plays: One.** New York: Methuen, 1985. 320p. pbk. $5.95. LC 85-186277. ISBN 0413566705.

Caryl Churchill is an innovative English playwright whose plays deal with controversial issues of gender, class, and race. *Plays: One* collects five of her six plays: *Owners, Traps, Vinegar Tom, Light Shining in Buckinghamshire,* and *Cloud Nine.* Act One of *Cloud Nine,* one of her best-known plays, takes place in nineteenth-century colonial Africa, Act Two in Britain in 1980. Many of the female characters are played by male actors, and vice versa, which points up one theme of the play—the arbitrariness of sexual stereotypes. The same characters appear in both acts, having aged only twenty-five years in the interim. With this device, Churchill explores the transformation of the self under changing circumstances. Churchill has also written *Fen* (Methuen, 1983), *Softcops* (Methuen, 1984), and *Top Girls* (Methuen, 1982).

414.* France, Rachel, 1936- , ed. **A Century of Plays by American Women.** New York: Richards Rosen Press, 1979. 223p. bibliog. LC 78-12347. ISBN 0823904725.

Editor Rachel France has brought together twenty-three one-act plays—many of them unavailable elsewhere—from the turn of the century to the mid-1970s. Although France rejects the notion that "women, as a group, have a unique point of view, or special sensibilities," she sees this volume as an attempt to "bring women authors into the critical mainstream of American drama" (p.16). The plays in this volume were written for little theaters all around the country, from New York's famous Provincetown Players, to the San Francisco Mime Troupe, to smaller regional groups like Minneapolis's At-the-Foot-of-the-Mountain feminist ensemble. Among the better-known authors represented here are Susan Glaspell, Djuna Barnes, Edna Ferber, and Gertrude Stein. The plays are concerned not only with "women's" issues like the suffrage movement, economic equality, and lesbian relationships, but also with more general themes like racism, anti-Semitism, and class struggle; and they range in form from Barnes's eerie, enigmatic *Three from the Earth* (1919) to Joan Holden's feminist parody of Victorian melodrama, *The Independent Female* (1970). France includes a short biography of each playwright and a supplemental list of twentieth-century women's drama. *Plays by American Women: 1900-1930,* edited by Judith E. Barlow (Applause Theatre Books, 1985), includes five plays which "in one way or another, protest against the positions women are forced to occupy" (p.xxxi): Rachel Crothers's *A Man's World* (1909); Susan Glaspell's *Trifles* (1916); Zona Gale's *Miss Lulu Bett* (1920); Georgia Douglas Johnson's *Plumes* (1927); and Sophie Treadwell's *Machinal* (1928).

415. Gems, Pam. **Piaf.** Oxford: Amber Lane Press, 1979. 111p. pbk. $6.95. ISBN 0906399068.

French singer Edith Piaf (1915-1963) is the subject of Gems's most successful play, produced both on Broadway and in the West End in 1980. Refusing to romanticize the performer, Gems portrays Piaf as a woman unwilling to conform to stereotypes of femininity or celebrity—who experienced acute loneliness as a consequence. Gems uses an episodic structure to explore the conflict between Piaf's public life and image and her private needs. Similar in structure and theme, Gems's Queen Christina (St. Luke's Press, 1982) presents the complex life of the famous nonconformist Swedish ruler. Queen

Christina (1626-1689) was raised to govern Sweden as a man; yet as an adult she was expected to maintain a feminine image, marry, and bear sons. Christina elected instead to abdicate the throne and leave her country.

416. Henley, Beth. **Crimes of the Heart.** New York: Viking Press, 1982. 125p. $12.95. LC 81-24026. ISBN 0670247812.

Henley's hilarious and moving Pulitzer Prize-winning play opens with Lenny, the oldest McGrath sister, trying to make her birthday wish on a single candle stuck in a cookie. The three McGrath sisters are to be reunited after five years, not to celebrate Lenny's thirtieth birthday but because the youngest sister, Babe, has just shot her husband, Zackery. Babe says she shot him because she "didn't like his looks," but the middle sister, Meg, finally learns that Zackery had been beating Babe and then threatened her young lover. Meg has flown home from Hollywood, where she has supposedly been trying to start a singing career but has actually been working in a dog-food factory following a nervous breakdown. Together the sisters face pleasant and painful memories and push each other on into the future. Henley has also written *The Wake of Jamey Foster* (Dramatists Play Service, 1983) and *The Miss Firecracker Contest* (Doubleday, 1985).

417. McDermott, Kate, ed. **Places, Please! The First Anthology of Lesbian Plays.** Iowa City: Aunt Lute Book Company, 1985. 209p. pbk. $8.95. ISBN 0918040051.

This is the first anthology of lesbian plays published in the United States. Three are one-act plays: Julia Willis's "Going Up," a comedy about two women stuck in an elevator; Mariah Burton Nelson's "Out of Bounds," a realistic drama about homophobia and athletic competition; and Ellen Gruber Garvey's "Soup," a painful study of a disintegrating relationship. The other four selections are full-length dramas: Terry Baum and Carolyn Myers's "Dos Lesbos," a comic series of sketches and songs on lesbian life; Sarah Dreher's "8x10 Glossy," a dramatic monologue spoken by a middle-aged woman to her dying lover; and Dreher's "Ruby Christmas," a complex, compassionate family tragedy about class differences, mother-daughter relationships, and male privilege. Each play is preceded by a production history, author's notes, and editor's comments. McDermott also includes brief biographies of the playwrights.

418. Miles, Julia. **The Women's Project: Seven New Plays by Women.** New York: Performing Arts Journal Publications and American Place Theatre, 1980. 372p. pbk. $9.95. LC 80-81997. ISBN 0933826079.

The Women's Project was established by Julia Miles at The American Place Theatre in response to statistics showing that from 1969 to 1975 only six percent of playwrights and seven percent of directors working in nonprofit theaters were women. This anthology is a collection of seven of the plays presented in rehearsed readings, studio productions, or full productions from 1978 to 1980. Perhaps the best known of these plays is Rose Leiman Goldemberg's *Letters Home,* based on the letters of Sylvia Plath and her mother. *Killings on the Last Line* by Lavonne Mueller explores the lives of nine women in a Chicago factory. The effect of the civil rights movement on an upper-class black family is the subject of Kathleen Collins's *In the Midnight Hour.* Also included are Joyce Aaron and Luna Tarlo's *Acrobatics,* Penelope Gilliatt's *Property, Separate Ceremonies* by Phyllis Purscell, and *Signs of Life* by Joan Schenkar. The book ends with a chronology of readings and productions presented by The Women's Project. Miles has also edited *The Women's Project 2* (Performing Arts Journal Publications, 1984), with plays by Kathleen Collins, Lavonne Mueller, Carol K. Mack, Terry Galloway, and Paula Cizmar. *New Plays by Women* (Shameless Hussy Press, 1979), edited by Susan LaTempa, is another recent anthology of seven mostly one-act plays. While not all of these plays focus on feminist issues, most offer good roles for women.

419.   Morgan, Fidelis, ed. **The Female Wits: Women Playwrights on the London Stage 1660-1720.** London: Virago Press, 1981. 468p. bibliog. $14.95. LC 81-140855. ISBN 0860682315.

In *The Female Wits*, Morgan presents five works by Restoration playwrights Aphra Behn, Catherine Trotter, Mary Delarivier Manley, Mary Pix, and Susannah Centlivre. In addition to the plays, which have previously been difficult to obtain, Morgan provides brief biographies of these and other Restoration playwrights, compiled from unpublished and some previously unstudied documents. Morgan also includes *The Female Wits,* an anonymous satirical attack on women playwrights; a chronology of plays and historical and theatrical events; and a checklist of plays. In *Women Playwrights in England* (Bucknell University Press, 1980), Nancy Cotton provides plot summaries and biographies of playwrights from the Middle Ages to 1750. She starts with a discussion of Renaissance noblewomen who wrote closet dramas as private entertainments for friends, and then moves on to the Restoration women whose plays were published and produced in public — and the sometimes virulent attacks these productions provoked. Cotton includes a chronology of plays to 1750.

420.   Norman, Marsha. **'Night, Mother.** New York: Hill and Wang, 1983. 89p. $13.95. LC 83-10834. ISBN 0809073617.

First produced in 1982, *'Night, Mother* won the 1983 Pulitzer Prize for drama. In this play, Norman explores the problematic relationship between Jessie and her mother. One night, Jessie announces to her mother that she is going to commit suicide, and as her mother tries to dissuade her they discuss their relationship, the past, Jessie's run-away son, her ex-husband, and Jessie's overwhelming sense of being alone. For Jessie, suicide is her assertion of control over her own life. In Norman's first play, *Getting Out* (Avon Books, 1980), Arlene, just out of prison, is haunted by "Arlie-girl," her former rebellious self. Arlene is determined to start her life over, although to do so she also has to fight against the people in her life — her mother, a prison guard, and her former pimp — who try to tell her how to live.

421.   Sarraute, Nathalie. **Collected Plays.** New York: Braziller, 1981. 107p. pbk. $5.95. LC 78-7111. ISBN 0807609404.

Originally published in French, the present volume contains "It Is There" (1980), "It's Beautiful" (1975), "Izzum" (1973), "The Lie" (1967), and "Silence" (1967). Each of the plays has been staged. In the more recent *Childhood* (Braziller, 1984), an attempt to reflect on the process of writing and the reconstruction of events through specific texts recalled from childhood, Sarraute demonstrates her skill in employing her feminized version of dialogic. The world of *Childhood* is ruled by words. Sarraute's obsession with words is the subject of Valerie Minogue's study of her first five novels, *Nathalie Sarraute and the War of the Words* (Edinburgh University Press, 1981). Minogue's title emphasizes Sarraute's struggle to use the power of words to express both a preverbal psychological reality and the fluidity of experience. Similarly, in *The Novels of Nathalie Sarraute: Towards an Aesthetic* (Rodopi, 1981), Helen Watson-Williams argues that Sarraute has shaped her novels to capture in language the psychic states hidden beneath words. Gretchen Rous Besser's *Nathalie Sarraute* (1979) is a basic Twayne introduction to the author's novels and plays through 1979.

422. Sayers, Dorothy Leigh, 1893-1957. **Love All: A Comedy of Manners; Together With Busman's Honeymoon: A Detective Comedy.** Edited by Alzina Stone Dale. Kent, OH: Kent State University Press, 1984. 226p. bibliog. $19.95. LC 84-9746. ISBN 0873383044.

This is the first publication of Sayers's *Love All,* produced in 1940, a feminist statement in the form of an enjoyable drawing room comedy. The novelist Godfrey Daybrook leaves England to go to Italy with his actress-mistress, Lydia Hillington, a woman he finds more exciting and inspiring than his homemaker wife. In his absence, Godfrey's wife becomes a famous playwright under the pseudonym of Janet Reed, and Lydia leaves Godfrey to audition for one of Janet Reed's plays. When Godfrey returns to England, he discovers that both women are now more interested in their work than in him. *Love's All*'s theme of women finding fulfillment in their careers is still relevant. *Busman's Honeymoon,* written by Sayers in collaboration with Muriel St. Clare Byrne, is about the honeymoon of her most famous character, Lord Peter Wimsey, and Harriet Vane.

423. Shange, Ntozake. **Three Pieces.** New York: St. Martin's Press, 1981; repr. New York: Penguin Books, 1982. 142p. pbk. $5.95. LC 82-9870. ISBN 0140481702.

Shange uses theater to explore the direct emotional and aesthetic impact of words, movement, and music. In addition to creating poetic effects, Shange works to break down racial and gender stereotypes by creating her own myths and history. In order to do this, she takes language apart, "leaving us space to literally create our own image" (p.xii). In these three plays—*Spell #7, Boogie Woogie Landscape,* and *A Photograph*—she explores questions of identity and relationships through poetry, music, and movement. Shange's collection of poems, *From Okra to Greens: A Different Love Story* (Coffee House Press, 1984), was developed from theatrical works first performed in 1978.

424. Shultis, Elizabeth C. **Seneca Falls 1848: All Men and Women Are Created Equal.** Seneca Falls, NY: Elizabeth Cady Stanton Foundation, 1984. 39p. bibliog. $3.00. LC 85-160279.

Although somewhat pedantic, this play provides a useful introduction to the first women's rights convention in Seneca Falls, New York in 1848. The play focuses on Elizabeth Cady Stanton and, through her commentary as a narrator and scenes with her father and her husband, gives a sense of her development as an equal rights activist. The last section of the play is a reenactment of the convention itself, with parts of speeches by Stanton, Lucretia Mott, and Frederick Douglass, the presentation of resolutions, and the response of those in attendance.

425. Wandor, Michelene, ed. **Plays by Women.** London: Methuen, 1982-1985. 4v. bibliog. Vol. 1: pbk. $8.50; ISBN 0413500209. Vol. 2: pbk. $8.50; ISBN 0413510301. Vol. 3: pbk. $8.50; ISBN 0413543005. Vol. 4: pbk. $8.95; ISBN 0413567400.

In her introduction to the first volume of this anthology, Michelene Wandor gives a brief history of women playwrights in England, arguing that the content of theater has traditionally been male-defined. In 1985, her introduction to the fourth volume points out, women playwrights still represent only seven percent of plays produced in England. Wandor's anthologies bring well-deserved and needed exposure to both well-known and lesser-known playwrights, most of them English. The plays gathered in Volume One are *Vinegar Tom,* by Caryl Churchill; *Dusa, Fish, Stas and Vi,* by Pam Gems; *Tissue,* by Louise Page; and *Aurora Leigh* by Wandor. Volume Two includes *Rites,* by Maureen Duffy; *Letters Home,* by Rose Leiman Goldemberg; *Trafford Tanzi,* by Claire Luckham; and *Find Me,* by Olwen Wymark. Volume Three contains *Aunt Mary,* by Gems; *Red Devils,* by Debbie Horsfield; *Blood Relations,* by Sharon Pollock; and *Time Pieces,* by

Lou Wakefield and the Women's Theatre Group. Volume Four collects Churchill's *Objections to Sex and Violence,* Grace Dayley's *Rose's Story*, Liz Lochhead's *Blood and Ice,* and Alison Lyssa's *Pinball.* Wandor has also edited *Strike While the Iron Is Hot* (Journeyman Press, 1980), an anthology of three plays about women written and produced by collective theater groups in England. In *Understudies* (Methuen, 1981), Wandor analyzes sexual politics in contemporary English theater and surveys feminist and gay theater in the 1970s.

426. Warren, Mercy Otis, 1728-1814. **The Plays and Poems of Mercy Otis Warren: Facsimile Reproductions.** Compiled by Benjamin Franklin V. Delmar, NY; Scholars' Facsimiles and Reprints, 1980. 384p. in various pagings. $60.00. LC 80-16625. ISBN 0820113441.

Although Warren's plays have questionable dramatic value, they are important historically, both as a document of the times and because Warren was one of the few early American women of letters. Her plays were meant to be read rather than performed, and were first published in newspapers, usually in excerpted form. The conflict between good and evil, respectively represented by the American patriots and British soldiers, is the theme running through the plays and much of her verse. The first collection of Warren's plays, this facsimile edition includes an introduction with plot summaries and commentaries, and a bibliography of commentary on her plays and poems.

ESSAYS

427. Flanner, Janet, 1892-1978. **Janet Flanner's World: Uncollected Writings 1932-1975.** Edited by Irving Drutman. New York: Harcourt, Brace, Jovanovich, 1979. 368p. index. pbk. $8.95. LC 79-1820. ISBN 015645971X.

This volume brings together Janet Flanner's uncollected essays, letters, and pieces written for *The New Yorker* from 1931 to 1976—journalism that comprises, in the opinion of William Shawn, "political, social, and cultural history of the first order" (p.xiv). Flanner's much-admired prose ranges over subjects as disparate as the Mona Lisa and the Olympic Games. Flanner frequently wrote profiles of women; Sylvia Beach, Margaret Anderson, Alice B. Toklas, and Colette are among her subjects here. Many consider Flanner's style poetic, likening her to Marianne Moore because of her fondness for the idiosyncratic, her ear for eccentric rhythms, and her gift for the *double entendre,* honed to an exquisite edge from living and working in Europe for many years. *Darlinghissima* (Random House, 1985) collects Flanner's letters to her lover, Natalia Danesi Murray, written between 1944 and 1975. In the letters, Flanner discusses current events and paints vivid portraits of such contemporaries as Carson McCullers, Kay Boyle, and Nancy Cunard.

428. Goodman, Ellen. **At Large.** New York: Summit Books, 1981. 245p. $12.95. LC 81-8816. ISBN 0671433067.

Pulitzer Prize-winner Ellen Goodman here assembles her syndicated columns from 1979 to 1981, in which she reflects on a broad range of experiences and issues, always refusing "to separate the public from the private, the humorous from the serious" (p.16). Among the topics she addresses in her short, breezy essays are "having it all" ("Superwoman, Supertired"); clerical work ("Being a Secretary Can Be Hazardous to Your Health"); reentry woman workers ("A G. I. Bill for Mothers"); marital rape ("Rape: A

Crime of Violence, Not Sex"); biological sex differences ("Designer Genes"); and communication between women and men ("'What Are You Thinking?' 'Oh, Nothing'"). Goodman's fans will also enjoy her first collection, *Close to Home* (Simon and Schuster, 1979), and her latest, *Keeping in Touch* (Summit Books, 1985).

429.   Janeway, Elizabeth, 1913- . **Cross Sections: From a Decade of Change.** New York: Morrow, 1982. 320p. $14.95. LC 82-3485. ISBN 0688010245.

Janeway introduces her collection of essays and reviews with an optimistic survey of recent years. Her sense of the second wave of feminism is that it is a "highly creative" response to world events, but she cautions women to opt for "trust instead of hostility, commonality instead of polarization" (p.26). Janeway can come down hard on issues that displease her—for example, feminist interest in the occult. Janeway's topics here range from prostitution and Victorian society to technology, witches, career identity, middle age, and incest. In *Powers of the Weak* (Knopf, 1980), Janeway attempts an examination of the nature of power from the point of view of the powerless—the working class, blacks, children, women—concluding that power is a social relationship shaped by both the powerful and the weak.

430.   Lorde, Audre. **Sister Outsider.** Trumansburg, NY: Crossing Press, 1984. 190p. bibliog. $17.95. LC 84-1844. ISBN 0895941422.

"The question of separatism is by no means simple. I am thankful that one of my children is male, since that helps to keep me honest. Every line I write shrieks there are no easy solutions" (p.78). This quote comes from the essay "Man Child: A Black Lesbian Feminist's Response," one of fifteen selections drawn together here, representing eight years of Audre Lorde's nonfiction writing. The courage to stare fear and conflict in the face distinguishes Lorde's approach to politics and relationships, whether she is entreating Mary Daly to engage in critical dialogue about the racism in her work ("An Open Letter to Mary Daly") or herself engaging with the question of black men's misogyny ("Sexism: An American Disease in Blackface"). Even when confronting what is seemingly an entirely personal matter—breast cancer—Lorde chooses public revelation to exorcise terror ("The Transformation of Silence into Language and Action"). Several of the pieces included here have become classics—for example, "Poetry Is Not a Luxury" and "Uses of the Erotic: The Erotic as Power." Lorde's remarkable writings on her battle with cancer have been published separately as *The Cancer Journals* (Spinsters, Ink, 1980). *Zami: A New Spelling of My Name* (1982; repr. Crossing Press, 1983) is an account of Lorde's growing up, the child of Grenadian immigrants. Having spent her childhood in the shadow of her powerful mother, Lorde discovered her love for women in early adulthood, and lived the life of a "gay girl" in the Greenwich Village of the fifties. It is the women in her life that Lorde credits with nurturing her own strength, and she recreates them in *Zami* with startling intensity.

431.   O'Reilly, Jane. **The Girl I Left Behind.** New York: Macmillan, 1980. 220p. pbk. $5.95. LC 80-7833. ISBN 0020232403.

O'Reilly brings together, in slightly revised form, articles written and published in popular magazines during the seventies. In a light and chatty tone, laced with frequently barbed wit, these pieces address mainstream issues of feminism: socialization and coming of age as a woman; mothers and daughters; romance, work and love, and love and sex; housework; childcare; employment; power and the "Establishment"; and life as a feminist.

432.   Rule, Jane. **A Hot-Eyed Moderate.** Tallahassee, FL: Naiad Press, 1985. 242p. $13.95. LC 84-22831. ISBN 0930044592.

Canadian writer Jane Rule has a loyal readership, especially among lesbian feminists. This collection brings together nearly fifty short essays, including pieces on the practice of writing, lesbian and gay life, and profiles of artists and writers. Rule's latest works of fiction are *Contract With the World* (Harcourt, Brace, Jovanovich, 1980; repr. Naiad Press, 1982), *Outlander* (Naiad Press, 1981), and *Inland Passage and Other Stories* (Naiad Press, 1985). Naiad Press is also reprinting Rule's earlier works.

433. Russ, Joanna, 1937- . **Magic Mommas, Trembling Sisters, Puritans and Perverts: Feminist Essays.** Trumansburg, NY: Crossing Press, 1985. 119p. bibliog. $16.95. LC 85-4147. ISBN 0895941643.

The six essays reprinted in this slender volume revolve around the theme of sexuality. Unflinchingly personal, "Not For Years But For Decades" explores Russ's gradual acceptance of her lesbian identity and her multifaceted fantasies. "Power and Helplesssness in the Women's Movement" is a bitingly sarcastic delineation of the roles played by "magic mommas" and "trembling sisters" within the feminist movement. The remaining essays deal with pornography and sexual freedom, as Russ cuts through the rhetoric of the "puritans" and the "perverts" to bring a sharp theoretical vision to some of the toughest issues dividing feminists today.

434. Sontag, Susan, 1933- . **A Susan Sontag Reader.** New York: Farrar, Straus, Giroux, 1982. 446p. $17.95. LC 82-9259. ISBN 0374272158.

Tutored as she has been by the likes of Benjamin, Barthes, Levi-Strauss, Canetti, and Simone Weil, Susan Sontag does not wear the label of feminism easily. Philosophical discourse is her method; style, her subject. In these selections from *The Benefactor* (1963), *Against Interpretation* (1966), *Death Kit* (1967), *Styles of Radical Will* (1969), *I, etcetera* (1978), *Under the Sign of Saturn* (1980), and *On Photography* (1977), among other books, the reader is introduced to Sontag's central project: the examination of modernism and its permutations under the lens of French formalism. Specifically, Sontag analyzes the iconography of our time: film, photography, material culture, pornographic texts. Her passion for truth in ideas should be of great interest to feminists who work in the abstract critical tradition of French feminism. Missing from this volume, by its nature selective, is an excerpt from *Illness as Metaphor* (1978).

435.* Willis, Ellen. **Beginning to See the Light: Pieces of a Decade.** New York: Knopf; distr. New York: Random House, 1981. 320p. LC 80-22890. ISBN 0394511379.

Willis's essays from the late sixties through the seventies show her to be a clear-eyed observer. She feels strongly about feminist issues, rock music, her Jewish heritage, and human relationships, and defends her positions with cool intelligence, sensitivity, and humor. What interests her is the cultural current below the surface of American life and media events. In essays on the family, abortion, and pornography, Willis manages to retain her individual writerly voice while acknowledging her intellectual debt to the women's liberation movement and radical feminist politics.

FICTION

436. Adams, Alice. **To See You Again: Stories.** New York: Knopf; distr. New York: Random House, 1982. 304p. $13.50. LC 81-15621. ISBN 0394523350.

Reviewers regularly comment that women writers are "deft" observers of the social scene. This is certainly true of Alice Adams. "Snow" exposes the insecurities of a man, his girlfriend, his daughter, and her lover spending an idyllic skiing holiday together. Only the father stays pleasantly in control. "Greyhound People" plots a hopeful, maybe even adventurous future for a woman whose major excitement is riding the bus. Other stories describe with precision marriages and affairs, usually unhappy, among people who attend Harvard, submit articles to the *Yale Review*, or teach philosophy at Berkeley. Each ends with the familiar, delicious Alice Adams irony. Reminiscent of Mary McCarthy's *The Group, Superior Women* (Knopf, 1984) traces the lives of five Radcliffe women who become friends in the early 1940s, and over the next forty years define for themselves what it means to be "a superior woman." Careerism, lesbianism, ageism, mothers and daughters, and feminism figure prominently in Adams's interpretation of the contemporary American social scene. Adams's most recent collection of short stories is *Return Trips* (Knopf, 1985).

437. Adler, Renata. **Pitch Dark.** New York: Knopf; distr. New York: Random House, 1983. 144p. $12.95. LC 83-48133. ISBN 0394503740.

Pitch Dark could be a post-modernist version of Henry James's *Wings of the Dove,* Kate Ennis substituting for Kate Croy rethinking her relationship to James's Morton Densher. Journalist Kate Ennis's story takes us through the soul-searching self-analysis of leaving a lover. Moving tentatively through the dark of Kate's uncertainty, Adler, like an archaeologist, strips away layers of facade to reveal Kate's family, her background, her tastes, her past. Kate's is a chatty, manic consciousness that will not be stilled. Conversations reconstructed from the past with her married lover, Jake, dredge up opinions from Kate the Narrator on everything from Nabokov to Wittgenstein, from Flannery O'Connor to childhood summers at the tennis court. Adler's prose, beautiful and haunting, eerily parallels the tale she tells: out of language we attempt to make sense of the "pitch dark" that is memory wedded to experience. In Adler's fine first novel, *Speedboat* (1976), she employed the same distinctive voice.

438. Allen, Paula Gunn. **The Woman Who Owned the Shadows.** San Francisco: Spinsters, Ink, 1983. 213p. pbk. $8.95. LC 83-50233. ISBN 0933216076.

In this stunning first novel, Allen, who describes herself as "Laguna Pueblo/Sioux/ Lebanese-American," writes of Ephanie, an Indian woman of mixed blood. Hers is a double bind. As a colonized people, the American Indians have had their identity appropriated by whites: "the people would never return to the old ways.... The dreams had been colonized" (p.160). Yet even among her own people, Ephanie is an outsider, a half-breed. In a form as complex, fragmented, and atemporal as the workings of memory and the unconscious, the novel traces Ephanie's internal and external journey of self exploration. Interspersed with accounts of her childhood, marriage, friendships, and childbearing are Indian legend and ritual. Ephanie achieves her identity by delving into painful memories, and through encounters with the maternal spirits of creation. In the end, it is a circular movement, in which she comes back to herself, redefined. Allen is also the author of several volumes of poetry, including *Shadow Country* (American Indian Studies Center, University of California, 1982), a series of lyrics (accompanied by James Trujillo's striking paintings) in which the poet herself undertakes a similar journey toward self-definition.

439. Allende, Isabel. **The House of the Spirits.** New York: Knopf, 1985. 368p. $17.95. LC 84-48516. ISBN 0394539079.

Allende is a Chilean writer who was forced into exile in Venezuela after the assassination of her uncle, President Salvador Allende. Her novel resembles Gabriel García Márquez's *One Hundred Years of Solitude* both in its structure — family chronicle — and in the "magic realism" of its rich detail. Unearthly characters and incidents like Rosa the Beautiful, with her green hair and golden eyes, are presented matter-of-factly, while realistic events and objects take on a fantastic quality. Yet *The House of Spirits* is a woman's tale, dedicated to "my mother, my grandmother, and all the other extraordinary women of this story." Its central characters—the passionate, violent patriarch Esteban Trueba and his clairvoyant wife Clara—are modeled on Allende's own grandparents. In the end, the narrator explains the meaning of the history she has reconstructed from fifty years of Clara's diaries—"Clara wrote them so they would help me now to reclaim the past and overcome terrors of my own" (p.368).

440.   Atwood, Margaret Eleanor, 1939- . **Bodily Harm.** New York: Simon and Schuster, 1982; Hastings-on-Hudson, NY: Ultramarine, 1982. 266p. $15.00. LC 81-18370. ISBN 0671441531.

Atwood defines the body politic in a novel about a woman whose life is a succession of physical violations and invasions. Rape, mastectomy, and imprisonment become the metaphors for the psychic amputations Atwood's main character Rennie passively awaits. Rennie reminds us of other Atwood protagonists—women who believe they cannot control their own lives, until a major crisis forces them to recognize and confront the roots of their powerlessness. In the bleak collection *Dancing Girls and Other Stories* (1977; repr. Simon and Schuster, 1982), the Canadian writer represents the anesthetized lives of disempowered, insecure women who commit their spirits and bodies to men unable to return love. *Life Before Man* (Simon and Schuster, 1979) is an intricate novel depicting two years in the lives of three interconnected characters—wife, husband, and husband's lover. The tale speaks to the feeling of isolation that can permeate even the most convoluted relationships. Atwood astonishes us with the range of women's lives she evokes—mothers, writers, graduate students, college teachers, landladies, madwomen—as she urgently establishes in fiction the details of daily life.

441.   Azpadu, Dodici. **Saturday Night in the Prime of Life.** Iowa City: Aunt Lute Book Company, 1983. 95p. pbk. $5.95. ISBN 0918040037.

This small, spare novel touches on lesbian love, family relationships, and the tensions between immigrants and their Americanized children. Lovers Neddie and Lindy find their twenty-six-year-old relationship threatened when Neddie's Sicilian mother Concetta seeks reconciliation with the daughter she rejected thirty years ago. Moving back and forth between Neddie's home in California and Concetta's in New York, the novel vividly portrays the hopes, expectations, and resentments that tie family members together, leading to a disturbing yet utterly believable finale. In her somber novel *Goat Song* (Aunt Lute Book Company, 1984), Azpadu modifies the conventions of Greek tragedy to chronicle the rise and fall of several lesbians in San Francisco. Like the ancient tragedies, *Goat Song* ends in a scene of cathartic violence—here, an act of protest against patriarchal brutality.

442.   Bambara, Toni Cade. **The Salt Eaters.** New York: Random House, 1980. 295p. $9.95. LC 79-4806. ISBN 0394507126.

In this highly acclaimed first novel, Bambara—a short-story writer and anthologist of black and women's writings—depicts the psychic healing of black activist Velma Henry following a suicide attempt. The story begins at an infirmary, where Minnie Ransom, healer and spiritualist, enlists the psychic power of both the community and a spirit guide in her attempt to pull Velma out of her withdrawn disillusionment. Interspersed with scenes of the healing session are flashbacks through the eyes of a number of characters which establish the personal and political betrayals that have led Velma to try suicide. The novel ends with Velma's recovery, as she rises reborn from "a burst cocoon" (p.295). *The Salt Eaters* mingles realistic portraits of political activism with spiritualism and astrology; and it includes astute observations on both race and gender issues, particularly on the relationships between men and women in "the Movement." Throughout, Bambara stresses the need for an empowering kinship between women.

443. Barker, Pat. **Union Street.** New York: Putnam, 1982; repr. New York: Ballantine Books, 1984. 265p. pbk. $3.50. LC 83-9723. ISBN 0345315014.

Barker's highly acclaimed first novel is a stark portrait of working-class women's lives in a decaying city of Britain's industrial northeast. Kelly, a prepubescent child of the streets, is brutally raped by the man who has been shadowing her wanderings; Dinah is an aging prostitute; Iris, coming from even grimmer origins, is determinedly cheerful and maternal on the surface but fights a private depression. Barker devotes a chapter each to these and four other Union Street women. Her style is spare, and she is skilled at finding the precise word. Her evocation of the pressures and constraints of working-class women's lives can be painful to read, as when she depicts a young pregnant woman struggling through a supermarket with two toddlers in tow. Barker's second novel, *Blow Your House Down* (Putnam, 1984), also received extravagant praise. Set in the same industrial landscape, the novel again focuses on a series of women, in this instance prostitutes whose lives are threatened by a psychopath on the loose.

444. Beattie, Ann. **The Burning House: Short Stories.** New York: Random House, 1982. 256p. $12.95. LC 82-5292. ISBN 0394524942.

Beattie's people are an unhappy lot, strung out on Valium, abandoned by lovers, mourning the past, and dreading the future. In one story in this third collection of Beattie's short fiction, a woman counsels her husband's homosexual lover; in another, an affluent family marks the drowning death of a son, coping with drugs and alcohol, scrapping among themselves. A master of super-realism, Beattie sketches in a few details and renders a lifetime. When she turns her attention to domestic details, it is the ugly underside of domesticity she reveals, as in her novel *Falling in Place* (Random House, 1980). Here the husband and wife remain married, though he lives with his alcoholic mother, commuting to the city where he works and sees his mistress. The teen-aged daughter and young son constantly bicker at home, ending in an accidental shooting. Family dinners, vacations, picnics are joyless events because everyone would rather be somewhere else with someone else. In Beattie's vision of modern life, nothing coheres; every character moves in the slow motion of a nightmare—passively out of control. In *Love Always* (Random House, 1985), a group of "creative types" gathers in Vermont to vacation—an advice columnist for an upscale shelter magazine, her lovers, and her niece, Nicole, a teenage TV soap opera actress. Beattie choreographs their Vermont summer in typical, dissonant fashion by adding another writer working on a novel of the soap and a designer pressed to go into production on a Nicole doll. This is a world where fame is fast fleeting, where the creative idea of the moment must be commodified before it sours.

445. Birtha, Becky, 1948- . **For Nights Like This One: Stories of Loving Women.** East Palo Alto, CA: Frog in the Well, 1983. 107p. pbk. $4.75. LC 82-21087. ISBN 0960362843.

Birtha is a black lesbian whose stories often revolve around relationships between black and white women. The complexities of women's love inform these tales. In "Babies," Sabra and Lurie are split apart when Lurie wishes to adopt a child in spite of Sabra's belief that motherhood is inherently oppressive; in "Next Saturday," Jennifer's fear of expressing her growing love for her talented violin student Kacey causes her to stand by silently as Kacey plunges into self-destruction; in "We Used to Be Best Friends," Francie's friendship with Kelly is threatened when Kelly admits that her feelings have grown into love. Birtha's style is simple and her stories occasionally schematic, yet they touch on emotional dilemmas rarely portrayed in fiction.

446. Blais, Marie-Claire, 1939- . **Anna's World.** Toronto: Lester and Orpen Dennys, 1985. 176p. pbk. $9.95. ISBN 0886190584.

Blais is a Canadian whose stunning, lyrical, densely packed novels have garnered numerous awards, as well as comparisons with Virginia Woolf, Henry James, and Franz Kafka. In the original French, *Anna's World* won the 1983 Prix de l'Académie Française. It is the story of a teenager drifting in a modern world devoid of human values or passion—her heart was "neither cool nor blazing, it was empty ..." (p.1). After wandering through the Caribbean drug scene, Anna returns to Canada, "back to a human story in which tears would flow, endless, bitter and violent" (p.160), and accepts as her heritage the fragility of her own life in the nuclear age. In the end, Anna rejects both aimless hedonism and past love, choosing instead "the roads of her cold conscience" (p.176). Since 1960, Blais has written nearly twenty novels and plays, along with one volume of poetry, *Veiled Countries/Lives* (originally 1964; English translation by Michael Harris, Signal Editions, 1984).

447. Bombal, María Luisa, 1910-1980. **New Islands and Other Stories.** New York: Farrar, Straus, Giroux, 1982. 112p. $12.95. LC 82-9762. ISBN 0374221189.

This slim volume includes five tales written in the 1930s and '40s by the late Chilean novelist María Luisa Bombal, whose works have long been out of print in the United States. Four of the stories concern women who try in vain to escape from their barren, unfulfilling lives in patriarchy through imaginative fantasy or union with nature. Throughout, the author parallels the psychic landscapes of her characters with the natural landscape surrounding them; in the novella "The Final Mist," for example, the narrator's despairing realization that her love affair was only a fantasy, and that she is left with only her correct, loveless marriage, coincides with the moment when "the fog settles over everything like a shroud" (p.47). Bombal, whose haunting, poetic style has evoked comparisons with Virginia Woolf and Kate Chopin, is highly regarded in her own country; and this collection begins with a brief but enthusiastic preface by Jorge Luis Borges.

448. Bowen, Elizabeth, 1899-1973. **The Collected Stories of Elizabeth Bowen.** New York: Knopf, 1981. 784p. bibliog. $20.00. LC 80-8729. ISBN 0394516664.

Bowen is recognized as an elegant prose stylist in the manner of Henry James or Virginia Woolf. In his introduction to all seventy-nine of Bowen's stories, spanning her very early work in the teens to the postwar fiction, Angus Wilson remarks upon Bowen's "deeply romantic" interpretation of love, "central and without the *froideur* that, in Virginia Woolf's novel, is destroying Clarissa Dalloway's life" (p.9). To support the point that Bowen, like the romantics, achieves many of her most successful fictions in stories that recall childhood (her own and others'), Wilson looks to "Charity," "The Jungle," "Coming Home," and "The Visitor." For feminist readers, a typical Bowen character is the young woman brought under the domination of her husband—"Joining Charles" and "The Shadowy Third," two examples. Hermione Lee's *Elizabeth Bowen: An Estimation* (Barnes and Noble, 1981) traces Bowen's stylistic roots to both her Anglo-Irish background and European literary modernism, and analyzes her themes in light of her biographical circumstances and mid-century social concerns. *Elizabeth Bowen: A Bibliography*, by

J'nan M. Sellery and William O. Harris (Humanities Research Center, University of Texas at Austin, 1981), provides complete and well-indexed descriptive entries on Bowen's writings. Also listed, but not annotated, are studies about Bowen.

449.   Boyle, Kay, 1902- . **Fifty Stories.** Garden City, NY: Doubleday, 1980; repr. New York: Penguin Books, 1981. 648p. pbk. $7.95. LC 81-7361. ISBN 0140059229.

Journalist, novelist, poet, autobiographer—Boyle stands as one of the virtuosos of the American short story. Because Boyle has lived abroad during much of her lifetime, the stories are usefully grouped chronologically and geographically: "Austrian Group 1933-1938"; "English Group 1935-1936"; "French Group 1939-1966"; and so on. The subjects of Boyle's fiction reflect her international perspective. Critic David Daiches writes the appropriate introduction. *This Is Not a Letter and Other Poems* (Sun and Moon Press, 1985) is a sequence of verse addressed to, or composed in honor of, friends of Boyle's—among them, Beckett and Joyce. Boyle's literary and political essays, dating from 1927 to 1984, are collected for the first time in *Words That Must Somehow Be Said* (North Point Press, 1985). In the words of editor Elizabeth S. Bell, these essays further reveal the writer who "has used her voice to make known the cries of the socially, emotionally, and politically voiceless" (p.xiii).

450.   Bradley, Marion Zimmer. **The Mists of Avalon.** New York: Knopf, 1983. 876p. $16.95. LC 82-47810. ISBN 0394524063.

In this ambitious historical fantasy, Bradley has rewritten the story of King Arthur from a feminist perspective. By placing the Round Table in the context of ancient Britain's historical struggle between matriarchal goddess-worship and patriarchal Christianity, Bradley alters the story's character relationships, plot motivation, and—ultimately—meaning. Morgaine le Fay, the witch-villainess of the traditional tale, becomes the novel's heroine, a pagan priestess whose efforts to maintain religious pluralism in Britain are undermined by Queen Gwenhwyfar, the product of a repressive, intolerant Christian upbringing. Thus, the Arthurian tragedy becomes not the estrangement of Arthur and Lancelet, or the loss of the Round Table's male fellowship, but the enmity between Morgaine and Gwenhwyfar and the destruction of the pagan community of women at Avalon. Bradley's feminism informs her other works of fantasy and science fiction as well, especially her series about the planet Darkover. In the more recent works in the series—particularly *Thendara House* (DAW Books, 1983) and *City of Sorcery* (DAW Books, 1984)—Bradley compares the lives of women in traditional (patriarchal) Darkovan society, in the Terran colony on Darkover, and in the Society of Free Amazons. *Warrior Women* (DAW Books, 1985) is a tale of a community of women struggling to break free of an oppressive, patriarchal society. Martin H. Greenberg has selected sixteen of Bradley's stories written between 1954 and 1980—several from the Darkover series—for inclusion in *The Best of Marion Zimmer Bradley* (Academy Chicago, 1985).

451.   Brantenberg, Gerd, 1941- . **Egalia's Daughters: A Satire of the Sexes.** Seattle, WA: Seal Press, 1985. 269p. $15.95. LC 85-22191. ISBN 0931188350.

This satiric dystopia became a best-seller when it was published in Norway in 1977. The country of Egalia is an oppressive matriarchy, where *wim* wield economic, political, cultural, and sexual power, while *menwim* can hold only low-paying jobs, or else become "housebounds" responsible for childcare—as is only natural, the *wim* point out, since "after all, it is *menwim* who beget children" (p.9). When Petronius Bram argues that *menwim* should stop concentrating on curling their beard hair and look at their dependent condition, he becomes the leader of a fledgling "masculist" movement fighting the establishment for *menwim's* rights. Brantenberg's ironic role reversals become predictable after a while; still, her satire is deft, funny, and provocative.

452.   Brown, Rita Mae. **Southern Discomfort.** New York: Harper and Row, 1982. 249p. $14.37. LC 81-47683. ISBN 0060149280.

In her earlier comic novels, Brown wrote about characters who refused to contain their passions within conventional heterosexual marriage — and got away with it. Hortensia Banastre, heroine of *Southern Discomfort*, also defies convention, but here the novel, despite its fast and often funny tone, approaches tragedy. Hortensia is a wealthy Southern society matron of the 1920s who falls in love with a young black boxer, Hercules Jinks, and secretly bears him a daughter. Brown emphasizes the fundamental innocence of their love, yet it results, through a tangle of intrigue and revenge, in two deaths, and it leaves their mixed-race daughter Catherine wondering about her place in society. Brown's latest novel, *Sudden Death* (Bantam Books, 1983), is a *roman à clef* about a lesbian relationship between a college professor and a tennis pro, yet it is also an effective exposé of the commercialism and hypocrisy of women's professional tennis.

453.   Brown, Rosellen. **Civil Wars: A Novel.** New York: Knopf, 1984. 419p. $16.95. LC 83-48866. ISBN 0394534786.

Two white, left-wing veterans of the civil rights struggle are bringing up their children in a black neighborhood of Jackson, Mississippi in 1979. Jessie and Ted Carll met and romanced each other during the voter registration campaigns of the 1960s. Teddy, a Southerner and a renegade from the beliefs of his family, still retains a romantic dream of subversive, if not revolutionary action fifteen years later as a textbook salesman. Jessie, a teacher in an alternative school, has come to terms with her youthful, romantic radicalism, replacing idealism with irony and pragmatism. When Teddy's sister and brother-in-law (bigoted Mississippians) die in a car crash, the liberal Carlls fall heir to the two Tyson children, yanked out of their Birmingham environment to live with the "nigger lovers." The orphaned cousins' presence in the Carll household provides the material for Brown to shape a fiction dealing with Northern and Southern politics and history, adolescence, and moral self-consciousness. Brown's *Tender Mercies* (Knopf, 1978) similarly spoke of her preoccupation with the South.

454.   Bruner, Charlotte H., ed. **Unwinding Threads: Writing by Women in Africa.** Exeter, NJ: Heinemann, 1983. 208p. pbk. $6.00. LC 83-17175. ISBN 0435902563.

An exemplary anthology, *Unwinding Threads* assembles a wide range of writers from western, eastern, southern, and northern Africa, carefully contextualizing the work historically and geographically. Each geographical section explains the relative scarcity of published women writers in the region — often due to women's exclusion from educational and political institutions. Not surprisingly, many of the stories deal with women's oppressed status, although most of the writers come from backgrounds of comparative privilege. It is a pleasure to read selections from Mable Dove Danquah, Adelaide Casely-Hayford, Mariama Bâ, Buchi Emecheta, Martha Mvungi, Charity Waciuma, Olive Schreiner, Miriam Tlali, Bessie Head, and Marguerite Amrouche, among others.

455.*   Bulkin, Elly, 1944- , ed. **Lesbian Fiction: An Anthology.** Watertown, MA: Persephone Press, 1981. 295p. bibliog. LC 81-12194. ISBN 0930436113.

Collected in *Lesbian Fiction* are short stories by contemporary lesbian writers on themes such as motherhood, old age, Southern life, sexual relationships, work, illness, family bonds, and racism. The editors have chosen work representative of different racial, ethnic, class, and regional realities. Two important essays written by editor Elly Bulkin delineate the scope and goals of the project. With Joan Larkin, Bulkin also co-edited *Lesbian Poetry* (Persephone Press, 1981). Among the poets appearing in this collection are: Elsa Gidlow, May Sarton, Adrienne Rich, Audre Lorde, Paula Gunn Allen, Judy Grahn, Irena Kepfisz, Marilyn Hacker, Susan Griffin, Pat Parker, Minnie Bruce Pratt, Olga Broumas, Jan Clausen, and Cherríe Moraga. Like *Lesbian Fiction, Lesbian Poetry* contains suggestions for using the volume in the classroom. Margaret Cruikshank's *New Lesbian Writing: An Anthology* (Grey Fox Press; distr. Subterranean, 1984) presents poetry by Martha Courtot, Marilyn Hacker, Karen Brodine, and Suniti Namjoshi, among others. The prose section reflects new and rediscovered works by deceased writers not anthologized elsewhere (e.g., Reñée Vivien), along with contemporary selections from writers such as LindaJean Brown, Elsa Gidlow, Barbara Deming, and Mary Meigs. With an eye to making this a teaching and reference source, Cruikshank appends a selected bibliography covering 1980 through 1983. Jane Rule's essay, "Lesbian and Writer: Making the Real Visible," suggests the theoretical angle that makes Cruikshank's anthology cohere. Also of interest is *The Reach and Other Stories: Lesbian Feminist Fiction* (Onlywomen Press, 1984), the first such anthology to be published in Great Britain. Lilian Mohin and Sheila Shulman are its editors.

456.. Butler, Octavia E. **Wild Seed**. Garden City, NY: Doubleday, 1980; repr. New York: Pocket Books, 1981. 256p. pbk. $2.75. LC 79-7596. ISBN 0671430661.

Science fiction has traditionally been the province of white men. The protagonists of Butler's novels, however, are black women who negotiate the obstacle course of racial and sexual oppression in their movement toward autonomy. *Wild Seed,* a "prequel" to Butler's earlier novels about Patternist society, features such a heroine. In seventeenth-century Africa, Anyanwu is a 300-year-old female immortal who is a healer and oracle. She meets the 4000-year-old male immortal Doro, a patriarchal dictator intent on breeding a race of telepaths. Doro persuades Anyanwu to travel with him to colonial America, where his ruthless exploitation of her as a breeder and slave parallels the slaveholding society around them. The story of Anyanwu's struggles with Doro elucidates the origins of Patternist society and marks her personal growth. Anyanwu survives as a strong black woman — one who strives for freedom but accepts the necessary restraints of an imperfect world.

457. Calisher, Hortense. **The Collected Stories of Hortense Calisher.** New York: Arbor House, 1984. 502p. pbk. $9.95. LC 84-70362. ISBN 0877956022.

This volume brings together thirty-six of Calisher's stories, covering almost two decades (1948-1967) and combining three earlier collections. In his introduction, John Hollander observes that Calisher combines the prose romance tradition of Hawthorne and Melville with the social analysis of James, Wharton, and Fitzgerald to "celebrate the powers of moral imagination" (p.xvi). Ranging from the quasi-autobiographical realism of her accounts of middle-class Jewish life in Manhattan, to the surrealism of "Heartburn," a story about a man who insists he has swallowed a newt, Calisher's tales are characterized by a dense, moving lyricism, and satisfy her own definition of the short story as "an apocalypse, served in a very small cup" (p.xix).

458. Cameron, Anne. **Daughters of Copper Woman.** Vancouver, British Columbia: Press Gang, 1981. 150p. pbk. $7.95. ISBN 0889740224.

In lyric, spellbinding prose, Anne Cameron recounts the myths and oral history of the native women of Vancouver Island. The slim volume opens with the chilling "Song for the

Dead," a record of Indian deaths from diseases introduced by white settlers, and then reveals the myths that until now have been the unrecorded and carefully guarded knowledge of the secret Society of Women. Through a series of short episodes, Cameron weaves an inspiring tale of the descent of humankind from the self-reliant Copper Woman. Midway through the book the scene shifts to the present, and the reader meets Granny, a wise old Nootka woman and member of the Society of Women. Granny's tales include horrific accounts of exploitation and suppression of Northwest Indians by the Spanish and English, and of blood Indian revenge; a sweet folktale of an Indian maiden beloved of a female bear; explication of the central role of female clowns in Nootka culture; and revealing snippets of her own and her family's histories. Author Cameron states that present-day members of the dwindling Society gave her permission to share their stories with other women, provided their identities and their rituals remained a secret. "A secret can die, sometimes," she has Granny declare. "And a secret can kill sometimes. But a book, maybe some women will read it and they'll Know" (p.142).

459. Chase, Joan. **During the Reign of the Queen of Persia.** New York: Harper and Row, 1983. 215p. $13.41. LC 82-48680. ISBN 0060151366.

Two sets of sisters, Celia and Jenny, and Katie and Anne, form the collective "we" that narrates this lyrical and moving first novel. The four cousins spend their summers together on an Ohio farm, where their grandmother, nicknamed the "Queen of Persia," rules her family of five daughters and four granddaughters, treating the men of the family as unimportant, even dangerous, intruders. The girls run free, living in their imaginations. Over the course of the novel, a number of painful events pull the young women back into reality; yet their world on the farm remains an insular one, and maintains its hold on each of them, even into adulthood.

460. Chen, Yuan-tsung, 1932- . **The Dragon's Village.** New York: Pantheon Books, 1980; repr. New York: Penguin Books, 1981. 285p. pbk. $5.95. LC 80-27463. ISBN 0140058117.

Chen relives China's 1949 Revolution using the character Ling-ling as her autobiographical, youthful alter ego. The cherished, well-educated niece of her upper-class guardians in Shanghai, Ling-ling becomes part of the Revolution after her aunt and uncle flee from the communists to Hong Kong. Like the others who remain behind, Ling-ling is swept up into the revolutionary agenda of land reform in Northwest China's Gansu Province. Chen addresses the disorganization and ambiguity of revolutionary enterprise forthrightly. Most poignant in this narrative is Ling-ling's realization of the cultural differences that separate her from the peasantry and her further realization that revolution, though at times exhilarating, is inevitably bound up in bureaucracy, dogmatism, and intra-party conflict. Ling-ling brings us face to face with the pain and poverty of the Chinese peasants, especially the landless, oppressed women, but the book speaks most eloquently about the situation of an individual woman—Ling-ling—exposed to a reality from which she had been protected by her prerevolutionary class status. The author, who spent twenty years intermittently working with cadres in the countryside to organize the peasants and help them in their cooperatives, has lived and worked in the United States since 1972.

461. Chute, Carolyn. **The Beans of Egypt, Maine.** New York: Ticknor and Fields, 1985. 215p. $15.95. LC 84-8840. ISBN 0899193145.

Chute's first novel received considerable attention when it appeared because the author's background—that of a small rural, poor, Maine family—mirrors the story she tells. Chute's Bean clan of Egypt, Maine bears comparison with Faulkner's Snopeses of Yoknapatawpha for the violence of their lives. For women, life in Egypt is a hard lot; incest, rape, pregnancy, poverty, and abuse are simply treated as incidents in daily life. Earlene Pomerleau, the improbable Fundamentalist heroine, is either a tragic or comic character, depending on how she is interpreted. The author has a keen ear for dialect. Chute has repeatedly stated that her motivation for writing *The Beans* has nothing to do with changing Earlene's miserable lot; rather, Chute's effort seems directed towards transcribing the conversations and experiences of poor white Americans.

462. Colette, 1873-1954. **The Collected Stories of Colette.** Edited by Robert Phelps. New York: Farrar, Straus, Giroux, 1983. 605p. $19.95. LC 83-16449. ISBN 0374126291.

Thirty-one of the one hundred stories in this collection appear in English for the first time, while twenty-nine others are newly translated. Readers will find a familiar lyrical Colette, a master storyteller whose tales have defied genre classification. The arrangement of these stories—confusing as it is—makes Joan Hinde Stewart's *Colette* (Twayne, 1983) indispensable as a reference tool. *Colette: The Woman, The Writer,* edited by Erica Mendelson Elsinger and Mari Ward McCarty (Pennsylvania State University Press, 1981), was published to mark the one hundredth anniversary of Colette's birth (1973). Elaine Marks writes an introduction celebrating "new directions in Colette criticism" informed by semiotics and feminism. The contributors to the volume deconstruct Colette as both reader and writer, as lesbian and married woman, as "enchantress and illusionist," in complex essays addressed to her genesis as a writer, to gender/genre issues in the text, and to the production of her writing. The scholars represented here include Françoise Mallet-Joris, Donna Norell, and Christiane Makward. Joanna Richardson's biography, *Colette* (F. Watts, 1983), portrays an earthy, pragmatic Colette making her way through the difficult apprenticeship of writing, vacillating between a career in the theater, the straight and gay worlds of Paris during the 1920s, marriages, and love affairs.

463. Conlon, Faith, 1955- , et al., eds. **The Things That Divide Us.** Seattle: Seal Press, 1985. 191p. pbk. $7.95. LC 85-8290. ISBN 0931188326.

"Only by writing and talking of our differences can we begin to bridge them," declare editors Faith Conlon, Rachel da Silva, and Barbara Wilson (p.12). All fifteen stories in this moving collection revolve around points of diversity and conflict between women—racism, lesbianism, class barriers, anti-Semitism, and the generation gap, among other themes. Some, like Barbara Neely's "Sisters" and Janice Mirikitani's "Survivor," poignantly trace the lines of division that separate the characters, while others, like Robin Becker's "In the Badlands" and Becky Birtha's "Her Ex-Lover," portray at least tentative reconciliation.

464. Cooper, J. California. **A Piece of Mine.** Navarro, CA: Wild Trees Press, 1984. 124p. pbk. $7.95. LC 84-051985. ISBN 0931125006.

This is the first book published by Alice Walker and Robert Allen's Wild Trees Press. In her foreword, Walker applauds Cooper's work for its "strong folk flavor," comparing her to Langston Hughes and Zora Neale Hurston. Cooper's narratives, straightforward as they seem, reveal painful and complex truths about human interaction and survival, centering on the characters of spunky women. In "Who Are the Fools?" Cooper profiles the existence of Mr. and Mrs. Rembo with immediacy and economy. "Mr. Rembo also tore up his wife's Bible books and laughed at her as she would struggle to retrieve them. He would pull her down in bed on Sunday mornings, when she was going to church, to have sex, when he wasn't too hung over and sick from being drunk. Her only relief was when he went to his job as a night watchman" (p.20). Mr. Rembo's fate is the electric chair, a conclusion characteristic of many of these stories in which simple characters come to violent endings, leaving the reader with disturbing questions about the deceptively direct meaning and method of Cooper's work. Cooper has a particularly good ear for dialogue, deriving perhaps from her experience as a playwright. For her 1978 play "Strangers," Cooper was honored as Black Playwright of the Year.

465. Danly, Robert Lyons, 1947- . **In the Shade of Spring Leaves: The Life and Writings of Higuchi Ichiyō, A Woman of Letters in Meiji Japan.** New Haven, CT: Yale University Press, 1981. 355p. bibliog. index. $28.50. LC 81-50434. ISBN 0300026145.

Winner of the American Book Award in Translation, this sensitive, scholarly study introduces Western readers to Japan's greatest woman writer of the modern era. Higuchi Ichiyō died in 1896 at the age of twenty-four, leaving behind a sixty-volume diary, some four thousand poems, over twenty short stories, and numerous essays. The first half of this study is a literary biography of a writer who "gave her life the shape and meaning of a work of art" (p.viii). In the book's second section, Danly translates and annotates nine of Ichiyō's most representative stories, tales of the innocence of childhood and the bitterness of growing up. Throughout, Danly stresses Ichiyō's debt to Japan's literary tradition. Yet, he argues, Ichiyō reworked this tradition in her tales so that they "have more in common with the modern novel (Proust or Joyce, for example) than many of the self-consciously 'modern' works" of her day (p.133).

466. de Pizan, Christine, ca. 1363-ca. 1431. **The Book of the City of Ladies.** New York: Persea Books, 1982. 281p. bibliog. index. $17.95. LC 82-331. ISBN 0892250619.

Perhaps the most important work of the medieval scholar and aristocrat Christine de Pizan, *The City of Ladies* (*Livre de la cité des dames*) was first published in 1405. The work demonstrates Christine's facility in using allegory, trope, and other literary conventions of her day to support the education of women and a host of other feminist issues prominent in the *quarelle des femmes* of the fifteenth century. Medea, Xanthippe, Minerva, and Queen Blanche emerge as her intellectual and heroic precursors in the utopian city she creates, a setting inhabited by scores of ordinary and extraordinary women. Although questioning Christine's version of history and mythology, Marina Warner, in her foreword to this widely praised translation, reads *City* as "a determined and clear-headed woman's attempt to take apart the structure of her contemporaries' prejudices; a reasoned but fierce counter-assault against baiting by the male" (p.xvii). Readers will note that the last translation of this work was published in 1521; thus, the inaccessibility of the book itself epitomizes the exclusion of women from intellectual life Christine sought to illuminate in her text. Feminist scholars have recently focused on Christine as a figure comparable to recognized male medieval writers and scholars. Christine's *The Treasure of the City of Ladies: Or, the Book of the Three Virtues* has also finally been translated for the English-speaking reader by Sarah Lawson (Penguin Books, 1985). Edith Yenel's admirable *Christine de Pisan: A Bibliography of Writings By Her and About Her* (Scarecrow Press, 1982) updates the state of Pizan scholarship by documenting biographical, literary, and bibliographic sources, including publications in English, French, German, Dutch, and Italian. Charity Connon Willard's long-awaited scholarly biography, *Christine de Pizan: Her Life and Works* (Persea Books, 1985), contextualizes and summarizes Christine's career.

467. Desai, Anita, 1937- . **Clear Light of Day.** New York: Harper and Row, 1980. 183p. $12.45. LC 80-7603. ISBN 006010984X.

Many themes are played out in this intense, vivid novel of contemporary India. The setting is a family reunion in Old Delhi; the "events" of the novel are confined claustrophobically to conversations between the siblings, and reinvoked memory. Desai interweaves past and present, retelling the same stories from different points in time. One sister, Bim, remained in the family home, taking care of her alcoholic aunt and her retarded brother, Baba. Tara escaped through marriage to an Indian diplomat and a life of international travel. Raja, absent from the actual reunion but a strong presence nonetheless, abandoned Bim and Baba soon after Tara to pursue dreams of heroism embodied for him in the tradition of Urdu poetry and the person of a wealthy Moslem Sahib. The bloodshed of partition, religious antagonism, class differences, post-colonial adjustment — these are all evoked in the novel, yet only as viewed in the distance from the window of the decaying family home. Paralysis and stagnation vie with impulses toward independence, freedom, and change as these characters wrestle with the hold of history, family, and culture from their contrasting positions as men and women. Desai's latest novel, *In Custody* (Harper and Row, 1984), explores the world of a would-be Urdu poet.

468.   Dinesen, Betzy, ed. **Rediscovery: 300 Years of Stories By and About Women.** New York: Avon Books, 1982. 196p. pbk. $3.50. LC 82-90369. ISBN 0380607565.

Though some readers may have difficulty grasping the organizational principle behind Dinesen's collection — she chooses to organize the stories thematically based on a woman's life cycle, a decision the table of contents fails to make clear — students, teachers, and common readers alike will applaud the editor's selection of fiction, much of it difficult to find in smaller libraries. Among the twenty-two authors represented here are Aphra Behn, Dorothy Richardson, Janet Frame, Kate Chopin, Mary Wilkins Freeman, June Arnold, Willa Cather, and Sara Orne Jewett.

469.   Doerr, Harriet. **Stones for Ibarra.** New York: Viking Press, 1984. 214p. $14.95. LC 83-47861. ISBN 0670192031.

Hope, remembrance, and fate are persistent themes in this extravagantly praised first novel, published by Doerr at the age of seventy-three. Dubbed crazy by their friends, Sara and Richard Everton give up their California home and livelihood to claim the adobe home and flooded mines abandoned by Richard's grandfather during the 1910 Mexican Revolution — in their minds, the other-worldly images of faded photographs. Even as they successfully recreate elements of the past (an elegant home, a productive mine), they are brought face to face with the future in the form of Richard's diagnosis of leukemia. Yet they persevere — whether blindly or courageously, it's not altogether clear. In this meeting of two cultures, we see the North American couple through the puzzled eyes of the Ibarra townspeople, whose own poignant stories we learn along with Richard and Sara. Doerr has a remarkable gift for the stark yet persuasive image, and a rare economy of style.

470.   Drabble, Margaret, 1939- . **The Middle Ground.** New York: Knopf, 1980. 277p. $10.95. LC 80-7630. ISBN 0394512243.

Drabble writes with the eye of an anthropologist, describing everyday life in Britain with scrupulous attention to detail. Kate Armstrong, the protagonist of this novel, is a journalist who began writing with a feminist slant before the second wave. At forty, she "looks at the component parts of her life — her children, her ex-husband, her ex-lover, her work, her parents — and doesn't know what to do or to think about any of them" (p.13). In other words, she is experiencing a "mid-life crisis." By the end of this comic novel, Kate is planning a party. She seems to have gained back her equilibrium and to welcome the unknown: "Anything is possible, it is all undecided" (p.277). In Kate's taking on the aura, in fact, of a sort of contemporary, careerist, quirky Mrs. Dalloway, Drabble seems to be confronting Woolf's fictional problem: the coherent representation of a woman's fragmented day. *Critical Essays on Margaret Drabble,* edited by Ellen Cronan Rose (G. K. Hall, 1985), provides a useful introduction to Drabble and to criticism of her work. Rose notes Drabble's surprising "resistance to feminism in its ideological manifestations" (p.12). One contribution to this collection is a hefty bibliography; another is an interview with Drabble by Diana Cooper-Clark. Mary Hurley Moran's *Margaret Drabble: Existing Within Structures* (Southern Illinois University Press, 1983) and Joanne V. Creighton's *Margaret Drabble* (Methuen, 1985) also offer thoughtful critical interpretation of Drabble's work.

471. Duras, Marguerite. **The Lover.** New York: Pantheon Books, 1985. 117p. $11.95. LC 84-26321. ISBN 0394545885.

This austere, haunting novel by one of France's preeminent women writers has achieved both critical and popular success, perhaps because of the universality of its themes: erotic love and death. The narrator, a French writer in her sixties, seeks to understand the meaning of an episode that took place when she was a teenager living in Saigon. In the midst of genteel poverty and family strife, the narrator became involved in a scandalous affair with a rich, older Chinese man. In a series of flashbacks, she describes her obsessive sexual encounters with the man, who resembles the exotic and forbidden lover of fantasy; she recalls her family's unspoken acquiescence in her lucrative disgrace; and she considers the emotional consequences of the relationship. Intense and disturbing, this is a beautiful work.

472. Elgin, Suzette Haden. **Native Tongue.** New York: DAW Books, 1984. 301p. pbk. $3.50. ISBN 0879979453.

Native Tongue demonstrates the possibilities open to feminists for using science fiction to explore the concrete implications of theoretical concerns—in this case, the problem (popular among continental feminists) of the relationship between language, cognition, and behavior. In the novel, twenty-third century America is an absolute patriarchy where women have no legal rights. Extensive interplanetary trade has necessitated the development of a caste of linguists to communicate with aliens. A group of female linguists rebel against their oppression by creating a separate women's language, Láaden, which constructs reality in a radical new way and thus becomes an instrument of liberation. Elgin's characterization is often two-dimensional; and—though a linguist herself—Elgin does not portray the new language in much detail in the novel. Still, her depiction of female bonding is strong, and her underlying concept of a separate language is compelling.

473. Emecheta, Buchi. **The Joys of Motherhood.** New York: Braziller, 1979. 224p. $8.95. LC 78-24640. ISBN 0807609145.

Throbbing with the rhythms of daily life, this novel of motherhood in Nigeria serves as an eloquent metaphor for the struggles of that country against colonialism, as well as for its delivery, kicking and screaming, into the post-World War II world of threatening modernity. Nnu Ego, the courageous mother of this story, whose many children bring her both joy and torment, becomes a vital presence for the reader, rendered as she is in simple, economic prose. Emecheta's two autobiographical novels about a Nigerian woman's struggle to bring up a family in London have been published in one volume as *Adah's Story* (Allison and Busby, 1983). In *Double Yoke* (Braziller, 1983), Emecheta's heroine must choose between becoming a traditional wife and mother or a university-educated career woman—and possibly losing touch with her African roots. *The Rape of Shavi* (Braziller, 1985) is a parable about the cultural imperialism and corruption that occur when Englishmen stumble upon the imaginary African kingdom of Shavi.

474. Enchi, Fumiko, 1905- . **Masks.** New York: Knopf, 1983. 141p. $11.95. LC 82-48726. ISBN 0394509455.

A daughter-in-law and mother-in-law, each widowed, struggle to find out the truth about each other in this complicated tale by one of Japan's foremost feminist writers. Yasuko, the daughter-in-law of an elite, scholarly family, ponders her dead husband's feelings toward his poet/mother, Mieko, "a woman of extraordinary abilities" (p. 34) who now threatens to take over Yasuko's life—whether erotically or intellectually and spiritually is not clear. Enchi's intricate unraveling of a family scandal initiates the Western reader into the family lives of Japanese scholars. Although many of the stylistic techniques of this novel may seem strange to the Westerner, the bitterness between the two women as observed by two male friends holds our attention and suggests possibilities for a feminist critique.

475. Erdrich, Louise, 1954- . **Love Medicine.** New York: Holt, Rinehart and Winston, 1984. 275p. pbk. $13.95. LC 84-3774. ISBN 0030706114.

In her depiction of three generations of Chippewa Indians on a North Dakota reservation, Erdrich creates a panorama of North American Indian life in this century. Six characters share the narration with Erdrich, jumping back and forth through time between 1934 and 1984. The women are the residing strength of the novel, suffering fewer casualties than the men in a world of crumbling Indian tradition and intensifying white domination. Yet the men are drawn sympathetically, and the novel's central themes—reservation vs. the city; tradition vs. change; land, culture, and alienation—are played out in the lives of all Erdrich's characters, strong as well as weak. This is a dense, intricately woven tale, with many beautifully evoked moments. Erdrich is also a poet, whose work was recently gathered in a collection entitled *Jacklight* (Holt, Rinehart and Winston, 1984).

476. Fairbairns, Zoë. **Benefits.** New York: Avon Books, 1983. 214p. pbk. $2.95. LC 82-90809. ISBN 0380631644.

The right-wing FAMILY party comes to power in a future, economically troubled Britain, and with it comes legislation designed first to make traditional motherhood compulsory, then later, as the economic crisis worsens, to control which women will be mothers. Fairbairns succeeds in showing both the points of conflict and the potential areas for alliance between FAMILY women and radical feminists. Fairbairns' later novel, *Stand We At Last,* (Houghton Mifflin, 1983), is a family saga dramatizing the lives of a family of women from the mid-nineteenth century into the 1970s.

477. Fox, Paula. **A Servant's Tale.** San Francisco: North Point Press, 1984. 321p. $16.50. LC 84-060679. ISBN 0865471649.

The language Fox uses to tell the tragic story of a servant employs such reserve and distance that the narrative evolves into a cultural critique. Fox never allows her narrator Luisa to lapse into solipsistic reflection. Simply, Luisa, the daughter of a servant and her master's son, tells the facts of her own illegitimate birth on the Caribbean island of San Pedro. These two eventually marry, though Luisa's father, disinherited and in poverty, despises his wife, who can never know or share what he has known. Exchanging one bad set of circumstances for another, Luisa and her family emigrate when revolution threatens their island, and settle in a New York barrio. Luisa knows her fate before leaving her native island: "The United States was a great hole to the north which would swallow me" (p.83). Supporting her family by working as a servant in Forest Hills, she becomes the dispassionate witness of a life of servitude she cannot escape because of material circumstances beyond her control.

478.   Freeman, Mary Eleanor Wilkins, 1852-1930. **Selected Stories of Mary E. Wilkins Freeman.** Edited by Marjorie Pryse. New York: Norton, 1983. 344p. bibliog. $27.50. LC 82-21179. ISBN 0393017265.

Freeman's regional perspective as a New England writer in postbellum America was until recently interpreted as cloistered, domestic, and lacking in power and authority. Critics now find that her small fictions encompass a world of discovery and liberation. This volume includes the stories from *A Humble Romance* (1887) and *A New England Nun* (1891), her most successful collections. Freeman supported herself by her writing, and her literary output was prodigious, as is apparent from the recently published collection of her letters, *The Infant Sphinx,* edited by Brent L. Kendrick (Scarecrow Press, 1985). Her stories foreground cheerful, practical women—many of them spinsters—whose salvation often resides in refusing or delaying marriage. The most famous, "A New England Nun," is about a woman who decides after fifteen years of courtship not to trade her serenity for "coarse masculine presence in the midst of ... delicate harmony" (p.118). A useful source for comparison and contrast of nineteen New England women writers, almost all familiar, is *The Writing Women of New England, 1630-1900: An Anthology*, edited by Arlen Gilman Runzler Westbrook and Perry D. Westbrook (Scarecrow Press, 1982). The collection begins with Anne Hutchinson's examination by the General Court of Massachusetts and ends with a story by Alice Brown (1856-1948), who, like her contemporary Freeman, earned her living by writing.

479.   Gaskell, Elizabeth, 1810-1865. **Elizabeth Gaskell: Four Short Stories.** Edited by Anna Walters. Boston: Pandora Press, 1983. 122p. pbk. $5.95. LC 82-22289. ISBN 0863580017.

The last ten years have witnessed renewed interest in Gaskell, a writer who used her fiction to criticize Victorian economic and social institutions. As Anna Walters points out in her introduction, the four stories in this volume "still constitute a challenge to established values" regarding love, marriage, and motherhood (p.21). Gaskell's heroines are plain, unromantic, and working class; three of them are unmarried. The tales are typically Victorian in their sentimentality, yet radical in social viewpoint: in two tales, for example, the heroines reject convention to set up households with other women. Gaskell also writes sympathetically of the plight of the "fallen woman." Gaskell's views on women's roles and other subjects appear clearly in *Elizabeth Gaskell: A Portrait in Letters* (Manchester University Press, 1980), edited by J. A. V Chapple and John Geoffrey Sharps. The editors alternate background text with representative letters that show Gaskell to be intelligent, witty, and humane. Although some of the explanatory material is inadequate, the arrangement of the letters by topics such as "marriage," or "family life" is helpful. In *Elizabeth Gaskell* (Twayne, 1984), Coral Lansbury begins with a short biography and chronology of the author's life, then presents close readings of her works, emphasizing Gaskell's interest in women's issues. Lansbury's annotated bibliography of selected secondary sources is especially useful.

480.   Gilchrist, Ellen, 1935- . **Victory Over Japan.** Boston: Little, Brown, 1983. 277p. $15.45. LC 84-11307. ISBN 0316313033.

We care about many of the raucous women characters of Ellen Gilchrist's collection, which won the 1984 American Book Award for short fiction. In the first story, the young Rhoda enthusiastically participates in a playground paper drive in Seymour, Indiana, when "strange, confused, hush-hush" news arrives that the bomb has been dropped on Japan. In the second story, in which the now fourteen-year-old Rhoda has been relocated to Clay County, Kentucky, Gilchrist humorously speculates about evangelism and adolescent passion. Called a practitioner of the "New Regionalism," Gilchrist shows an uncanny gift for entering the characters she creates, whether they be the teenaged Rhoda or the narrator-maid of "Traceleen's Diary." Some of these characters made their debut in Gilchrist's first book, *In the Land of Dreamy Dreams* (Little, Brown, 1981). Gilchrist's *tour de force* as a Southern writer—like that of her precursor, Flannery O'Connor—is to imagine believable regional characters that astonish and entertain us, perhaps because they transcend stereotypes.

481. Gilman, Charlotte Perkins Stetson, 1860-1935. **The Charlotte Perkins Gilman Reader: "The Yellow Wallpaper" and Other Fiction.** Edited by Ann J. Lane. New York: Pantheon Books, 1980. 208p. $10.95. LC 80-7711. ISBN 0394510852.

In her introduction to these selections from Gilman's fiction—including the well-known novella *The Yellow Wallpaper* (originally 1892), *Herland* (a utopian novel), and numerous stories from Gilman's periodical *The Forerunner*—editor Ann Lane contextualizes Gilman's career. Gilman's heroines shun passivity, break out of patterns of subordination, and take charge by making choices. Her fiction addresses the utopian feminist issues of her day—for example, the kitchenless house in "The Cottagette"; middle-class women who escape the domestic sphere by turning their homes into businesses, in "An Honest Woman"; or experienced women bonding with the inexperienced in "Turned." The formulaic, careless style of Gilman's fiction, Lane points out, is attributable to the deadlines of its production; the plots are often thinly disguised autobiography. Mary A. Hill's highly regarded biography (*Charlotte Perkins Gilman: The Making of a Radical Feminist, 1860-1896,* Temple University Press, 1980) ends with the celebrity years, prior to the appearance of Gilman's controversial *Women and Economics* (1898). Hill discovers the formative issues in Gilman's early life and depicts with sympathy her decision to leave husband and child to pursue a career of writing, editing, and lecturing on women's issues. (Marriage and motherhood had brought Gilman to a state of nervous collapse.) In *Charlotte Perkins Gilman* (Twayne, 1985), Gary Scharnhorst places Gilman squarely in the center of reformist America in the late 1890s, his analysis of the social movements of her day neatly complementing Hill's reconstruction of the private Gilman. His chronologically and thematically arranged study underscores just how prodigious Gilman's output as a writer was. Scharnhorst is also compiler of *Charlotte Perkins Gilman: A Bibliography* (Scarecrow Press, 1985).

482. Godwin, Gail. **A Mother and Two Daughters.** New York: Viking Press, 1982. 564p. $16.95. LC 81-65286. ISBN 0670490210.

With her fifth novel, Godwin has achieved that rare combination of critical acclaim and popular success. The death of Leonard Strickland acts as a catalyst for three women who must renovate their lives: Nell, his wife, who faces life without Leonard's support; Cate, their rebellious older daughter, who is pushing forty, unmarried, and pregnant, and who has just lost her teaching job; and Lydia, heretofore the conventional daughter, who leaves her husband and returns to school, seeking independence. In this graceful, generous work, Godwin focuses on the tangled, prickly relations between the women, ultimately presenting a healing vision of community. Godwin's *The Finishing School* (Viking Press, 1985) is also about a female relationship—in this case, between a lonely fourteen-year-old girl and an eccentric, aristocratic older woman. It is a dark, fascinating story, filled with ancient secrets, family obsessions, and mutual betrayal.

483. Gómez, Alma, 1953- , et al., eds. **Cuentos: Stories by Latinas.** New York: Kitchen Table: Women of Color Press, 1983. 241p. pbk. $7.95. LC 83-202778. ISBN 0913175013.

Editors Alma Gómez, Cherríe Moraga, and Mariana Romo-Carmona argue that U.S. Latinas have been silent for too long—both because of the illiteracy and passivity expected of women in Latin cultures and because of the insecurity imposed by biculturalism, which leaves them "caught between two languages, two political poles" (p.xi). The stories in *Cuentos* break this silence, communicating the cultural differences as well as the common realities of Latinas' lives. Furthermore, *Cuentos* validates the experience of biculturalism linguistically by including works written in Spanish, English, Spanglish, and Tex-Mex. The stories are divided into three sections: tragedies of women whose passions are denied legitimate outlet and who end up deranged, sick, or senile; growing-up tales; and stories of women who challenge the traditional values of Latin culture, especially its heterosexual bias. In the semi-autobiographical poems of *Emplumada* (University of Pittsburgh Press, 1981), California Chicana Lorna Dee Cervantes addresses many of the same issues, especially the problem of language and identity: "Mama raised me without language./I'm orphaned from my Spanish name" (p.41).

484.   Gordimer, Nadine. **July's People.** New York: Viking Press, 1981. 160p. $10.95. LC 80-24877. ISBN 0670410489.

The dilemma faced by white South African moderate and Marxist intellectuals haunts Gordimer, who gives such characters no solace in her fiction. In *July's People*, the liberalism of a white South African family is put to the test when in the wake of civil war, they commit their destiny to their former servant, July, who hides them in his homeland. Deprived of every empowering accoutrement, Maureen, the central character, is forced to recognize her own role as a citizen in a society scarred by apartheid. As she and her husband become the wards of their former servant, the masters realize that their former dependent hated them all along and exercises a similar system of benevolent tyranny now that roles are reversed. Of greater interest for its attention to female character development is the story of Rosa Burger, the orphaned daughter of two white anti-apartheid activists, told in *Burger's Daughter* (Viking Press, 1979). Rosa's mother and physician father, martyrs to the cause, left her a legacy of radicalism, a network of friends espousing Marxist solutions to apartheid, and memories of her own childhood surrounded by activists to whom trials, imprisonment, house arrest, and banning constituted the natural order of things. Rosa's life is circumscribed by her revolutionary roots, asserting Gordimer's point—that institutionalized racism ultimately ensnares the entire society in positions of dominance and subordination. This theme predominates in Gordimer's short story collections as well; her two most recent volumes are *A Soldier's Embrace* (Viking Press, 1980) and *Something Out There* (Viking Press, 1984).

485.   Gordon, Caroline, 1895- . **The Collected Stories of Caroline Gordon.** New York: Farrar, Straus, Giroux, 1981. 352p. $17.95. LC 80-28675. ISBN 0374126305.

In an appreciative introduction to this collection, Robert Penn Warren measures Gordon favorably against Henry James's criterion of "solidity of specification" in fiction. Gordon's women are superb—in stories like "One Against Thebes," a Southern child's recollection of her Aunt Maria, and "All Lovers Love the Spring," in which the female narrator, an aging spinster, constructs for the reader her perceptions of Fuqua, Kentucky as the luscious Southern spring unfolds. In *Caroline Gordon as Novelist and Woman of Letters* (Louisiana State University Press, 1984), Rose Ann C. Fraistat examines Gordon's beliefs about the function of art in society, relating them to the concerns and style of her novels. In *The Southern Mandarins* (Louisiana State University Press, 1984), Gordon's letters to Sally Wood (who edited the volume) from 1924 to 1937 provide insights into the obstacles Gordon faced—poverty, family strife, sponging acquaintances, and marital strains—in her quest for her own creative voice. The conflict between Gordon's roles as artist and wife/mother is epitomized in the letter in which she explains that she has spent two days sewing a dress for her daughter: "I love to sew but you can't sew very well and have any kind of prose style" (p.116).

486.   Gordon, Mary. **The Company of Women.** New York: Random House, 1980. 291p. $12.95. LC 80-5284. ISBN 0394505085.

Gordon turns the novelist's lens on a group of women whose friendship centers around their Catholic faith and a priest they greatly admire, Father Cyprian. Felicitas, a young woman who comes of age in the 1960s at Columbia, believes at the outset that the lives of her mother's friends are "bankrupt." Yet when she gives birth to her own illegitimate daughter, these women gather around her. Felicitas brings up her daughter in a communal environment with her mother's friends, retired on a farm with their beloved Father Cyp. As much absorbed by the guilts associated with Catholicism as by the spiritual security the Church holds out to true believers, Gordon manages to persuade us that there is both constraint and freedom in these women's lives. Gordon continues to ponder the meaning of faith in contemporary women's lives in *Men and Angels* (Random House, 1985), a work in which the feelings of a mother for her children are evoked with extraordinary intensity.

487.   Grumbach, Doris. **Chamber Music.** New York: Dutton, 1979. 213p. $8.95. LC 78-13033. ISBN 0525079203.

Doris Grumbach, whose criticism of music and books often appears in *The New Yorker* and the *New York Times Book Review*, uses a widow's memoirs as a fictional device in this novel about a woman who spends her active life nurturing her invalid husband, a noted American composer at the turn of the century. His death releases her to find a life of compatibility, fulfillment, and ardor with her friend and her husband's former nurse, Anna Baehr. "To tell you what we had together that night, and during all the nights and days that filled the next twelve years: how difficult it is to find words to hold it all, to capture the quality of close, understanding comradeship, to place inexpressible love into public phrases," our narrator records (p.167). Why does she write this extraordinary memoir of her unhappy marriage and subsequent joyous affair? — "... because I am freed by my survival into extreme old age, and because I write in the air of freer times" (p.5). In another historical novel, *The Ladies* (Dutton, 1984), Grumbach fictively recreates the story of the "Ladies of Llangollen." Eleanor Butler and Sarah Ponsonby, both from privileged Welsh families, eloped and established a refuge called Plas Newydd, where they lived solitarily but contentedly from the mid- to late-eighteenth century, receiving the likes of Wordsworth and Walter Scott. Grumbach writes with dry wit and takes many comic liberties with her eccentric subjects.

488.   Guy, Rosa. **A Measure of Time.** New York: Holt, Rinehart and Winston, 1983. 365p. $16.95. LC 82-15461. ISBN 0030576539.

Opening in 1926, when young Dorine Davis leaves Montgomery, Alabama for the promise of Harlem, and closing nearly thirty years later, *A Measure of Time* paints a panoramic portrait of black life in the rural South and urban North. What holds the book together is its narrator: a sort of black Moll Flanders, Dorine is a gutsy, earthy, fiercely determined woman who propels herself from small-time thief and swindler to successful businesswoman. Although Dorine's picaresque adventures expose her to constant racial and sexual abuse, she does not allow herself to be defeated. As the book ends, the era of Rosa Parks, Malcolm X, and Martin Luther King has arrived; the world of big timers who walked the Harlem streets "in their cutaways, their top hats, vests, twirling their canes like batons of gold" is vanishing (p.364). "Who would tell their tales," Dorine laments, "when those buildings finally crashed down to bury their memories?" (p.364). In telling Dorine's story, Guy assures that a glittering period in black history will live on.

489. Hanson, Katherine, 1946- , ed. **An Everyday Story: Norwegian Women's Fiction.** Seattle, WA: Seal Press, 1984. 249p. $16.95. LC 84-14096. ISBN 0931188210.

Hanson's introduction to this particularly fine collection sketches the history of the feminist novel in Norwegian literature, beginning in 1854 with Camilla Collett's pioneering novel, *Amtmandens Døttre*. The fiction included here explores such traditional themes as girlhood, marriage, female oppression in society, and feminine psychology. Some of the writers will be familiar — for example, Sigrid Undset (1882-1949), author of the trilogy *Kristin Lavransdatter* (1920-22), who received the Nobel Prize. Other, more contemporary writers, such as Bjørg Vik (b.1935), Tov Nilsen (b.1952), and Karin Moe (b.1945), introduce present-day concerns in Norwegian writing. For example, Moe's first book, *Kjønnskrift* (1980), shows the influence of current French feminist theory relating language to gender, emulating Hélène Cixous and others who write in a consciously "feminine" manner.

490. Holley, Marietta, 1836-1926. **Samantha Rastles the Woman Question.** Edited by Jane Curry. Urbana: University of Illinois Press, 1983. 235p. bibliog. index. $14.95. LC 82-13482. ISBN 0252010205.

Though compared favorably to Mark Twain, Marietta Holley is little known among contemporary readers. Suffrage, temperance, and other movements of the late nineteenth century sparked the inspiration for her enormously popular character Mrs. Samantha Allen, a Christian Methodist wife who spurns feminist extremism while espousing a moderate view on "the woman question." Samantha has a gift for getting to the heart of the matter. In a battle of wits with her ridiculous spouse, Josiah, she replies to his taunting: "... you think that for a woman to stand up straight on her feet, under a blazin' sun, and lift both her arms above her head, and pick seven bushels of hops, mingled with worms and spiders, into a gigantic box, day in, and day out, is awful healthy, so strengthenin' and stimulatin' to wimmin, but when it comes to droppin' a little slip of clean paper into a small seven by nine box, once a year in a shady room, you are afraid it is goin' to break down a woman's constitution to once" (p.27). Curry's careful notes render Holley's text accessible to the modern reader and describe other volumes of the "Samantha" series.

491. Hsiao, Hung, 1911-1942. **Selected Stories of Xiao Hong.** Beijing: Chinese Literature; distr., San Francisco: China Books, 1982. 220p. pbk. $3.95. ISBN 0835110494.

Translator Howard Goldblatt comments in his introduction that Xiao Hong, author of three novels and numerous short stories between 1935 and 1941, was "revolutionary in her desire to expose the cruelties in a male-dominated 'feudalistic' society" (p.8). The writer also anticipated the Communist Revolution in her dissection of class conflicts in China. Six of the nine stories in this volume have female protagonists; almost invariably tragic, the tales show women confronting, and generally defeated by, rigid sex and class traditions. In "The Death of Wang Asao," a woman dies in childbirth after her landlord has murdered her husband and beaten her; in "The Bridge," a wet nurse realizes that although she suckles both her master's son and her own, the boys are separated by a chasm of class distinctions; in "Hands," a young girl enters school hoping to learn enough to teach her family, but because of her stained hands — evidence of her work as a dyer — she is ostracized and forced to leave school. Xiao Hong's touching, evocative tales present a stark portrait of the experience of Chinese women—"a lifetime of tears, a never-ending flow" (p.18). One woman writer whose career has in many ways paralleled that of Xiao Hong is her younger contemporary Ding Ling (1904-1986). A political activist and supporter of the 1949 revolution, Ding Ling became one of Communist China's most influential writers, yet fell victim to Mao's Cultural Revolution—only to be rehabilitated in 1979. Yi-tsi Mei Feuerwerker's *Ding Ling's Fiction* (Harvard University Press, 1982) is an outstanding, scholarly analysis of the interplay between ideology and form in Ding Ling's narratives.

492. Hulme, Keri. **The Bone People.** Baton Rouge: Louisiana State University Press, 1985. 450p. $17.95. LC 85-12937. ISBN 0807112844.

When Keri Hulme's *The Bone People* won Britain's prestigious Booker Award for fiction in 1985, nearly everyone—including the author—was astonished. For Hulme is not only a New Zealander (and no New Zealander had ever even made the Booker shortlist), but also a woman, a Maori, and, at the age of thirty-eight, a first-time novelist. *The Bone People* is the story of an encounter among three individuals—a woman who lives alone in an isolated tower she built for herself, a speechless child, and the child's abusive foster father. To those outside the culture of New Zealand's indigenous people, it is an unfamiliar world, imbued with "Maoritanga" (Maori spirit and culture). The novel was repeatedly rejected by New Zealand and British publishers before it was taken up by a feminist publishing group, the Spiral Collective.

493. James, P. D. **The Skull Beneath the Skin.** New York: Scribner, 1982. 328p. $13.95. LC 82-5981. ISBN 0684177730.

P. D. James has begun to be recognized as a writer whose work challenges—and even breaks apart—the boundaries of detective fiction. In this novel, James deliberately employs the most hackneyed of mystery plots: the isolated British house party at which (of course) a murder takes place. Yet *The Skull Beneath the Skin* is remarkable for two reasons. First, it marks the long-awaited return of Cordelia Gray, detective-heroine of James's delightful 1972 novel, *An Unsuitable Job for a Woman*. Second, the depth and empathy of James's characterization transform an otherwise conventional detective story into a sensitive exploration of the human experience of death, which is always present yet always hidden: the skull beneath the skin. James's *Innocent Blood* (Scribner, 1980) is a more experimental, symbolic work that doesn't even pretend to be a conventional mystery. Here, orphan Philippa Palfrey's search for her natural parents leads her into a nightmare of forgotten crimes—rape, child murder, incest. As Philippa is forced to reassess and accept her blood relationships, she must reassess her own identity as well.

494.* Jhabvala, Ruth Prawer, 1927- . **How I Became a Holy Mother, and Other Stories.** New York: Harper and Row, 1976; repr. New York: Penguin Books, 1981. 267p. ISBN 0140048294.

Jhabvala has received her share of criticism for writing about an India that exists only for Westerners. She is captive to India's immensity, her beauty, her contrasts between rich and poor, yet she cannot come to terms with the powerlessness of Indian women, a subordination crossing caste and class lines. In an apologetic introduction to this collection, Jhabvala gives readers some insight into her experience as the German-born, Polish, Jewish wife of an Indian. Middle-class Indian women figure prominently in the stories, often treated with contempt by their husbands in marriages lacking companionship or equality. The title story follows the misadventures of Katie, a young Englishwoman wandering from ashram to ashram in search of an Indian refuge for her restless spirit. Jhabvala spares neither Katie nor the gurus her gentle laughter. (Because of its recognition of the color barrier separating Europeans from Indians, a related text is Sarah Lloyd's autobiographical *An Indian Attachment* [Morrow, 1984].) In contrast to her earlier work, Jhabvala's *In Search of Love and Beauty* (Morrow, 1983) strikes a harsher, more decadent tone. The main character, Leo, is an obese, bisexual sponger, whose center for psycho-spiritualism has drawn in three generations of affluent German immigrant families — and made Leo wealthy in the process. The search for "The Meaningful Encounter" takes place this time in the less exotic setting of New York City.

495. Kessler, Carol Farley, comp. **Daring to Dream: Utopian Stories by United States Women, 1836-1919.** Boston: Pandora Press, 1984. 266p. bibliog. index. pbk. $8.95. LC 84-5827. ISBN 0863580130.

Comprising six short pieces and excerpts from ten novels, *Daring to Dream* presents feminist utopias written by U.S. women from 1836 to 1919. The selections take a variety of forms and represent several strands of nineteenth-century feminism, from the evangelical to the communitarian traditions. Interestingly, in their portraits of non-sexist societies, most of the works dwell not on women's voting or property rights but on reforming or eliminating the institution of marriage. Often moralistic and sometimes negligible as literature, these pieces nonetheless provide fascinating evidence of the imaginative leaps taken by nineteenth-century women. Paul M. Gaston describes an actual turn-of-the-century utopian community in *Women of Fair Hope* (University of Georgia Press, 1984), chronicling the personal and intellectual journeys of three of its women members. *Women in Search of Utopia: Mavericks and Mythmakers* (Schocken, 1984), edited by Ruby Rohrlich and Elaine Hoffman Baruch, is an interdisciplinary, cross-cultural look at women's utopias of the past, present, and future. The thirty-three selections include studies of ancient, non-patriarchal cultures and modern communitarian experiments; essays on political organizations, language, and technology; and poetry and dramatic pieces by Marge Piercy, June Jordan, Audre Lorde, and Ntozake Shange. Unfortunately, the selections are so brief as to provide only the most rudimentary introduction to these intriguing areas of study, and the editors' preliminary essays fail to establish a theoretical framework capable of pulling the diverse pieces together. *Women and Utopia* (University Press of America, 1983), edited by Marleen Barr and Nicholas D. Smith, presents essays on women and utopian writing, including studies of both well-known authors like Ursula K. Le Guin and Doris Lessing and relative unknowns like Elizabeth Stuart Phelps.

496. Kincaid, Jamaica. **Annie John.** New York: Farrar, Straus, Giroux, 1985. 148p. $11.95. LC 84-28630. ISBN 0374105219.

This beautifully written novel is set on the Caribbean island of Antigua. Annie's growing-up story is punctuated by her ambivalence toward the separation from her mother that comes with adulthood. The novel opens when Annie is ten, secure in her mother's love. This oneness is shattered when Annie's mother no longer allows her daughter to dress like her — since, she explains "you just cannot go around the rest of your life looking like a little me" (p.26). In her teens, Annie alternates between dependence and rebellion, viewing her mother as "a person I did not recognize" (p.27). Mother and daughter come together in the final scene, as seventeen-year-old Annie is leaving home for school in England. The ten first-person stories in *At the Bottom of the River* (Farrar, Straus, Giroux, 1983) are also drawn from Kincaid's Caribbean background. Sensuous and shimmering, these are tales of mothers and daughters, men and women, mountains and rivers, dreams and identity.

497. Kingston, Maxine Hong. **China Men.** New York: Knopf, 1980. 308p. $13.95. LC 79-3469. ISBN 0394424638.

As Kingston's 1976 *The Woman Warrior* transcended genre to mythically explore the writer's female ancestry, *China Men* successfully collapses autobiographical, fictive, and mythic forms to trace her male ancestry. Beginning with the father—a teacher despised by his students, who fail to grasp the importance of his message—Kingston links this story to that of her gentle brother caught up in the Vietnam War. This youngest brother is ineffectual as a fighter because he has no appetite for killing and is unable to tell his story, the story his sister translates for us.

498. Kogawa, Joy. **Obasan.** Boston: D. R. Godine, 1982. 250p. $14.95. LC 81-20094. ISBN 087923430X.

In clear, evocative, and restrained prose, Kogawa retrieves through this first novel the submerged history of Japanese Canadians: immigration and assimilation through successive generations; forceable relocation as "enemy aliens" during World War II; loss of Japanese relatives to the war and the atomic bombs; the effort to survive and preserve dignity and heritage. For narrator Naomi Nakane, the past is hazy and replete with unexplained gaps. Her mother never having returned from a trip to Japan in 1941, Naomi has been raised since the age of five by her uncle and aunt (Obasan), who confront the grief of their past with silent stoicism, protecting Naomi and her brother from some harsh truths. Growing into adulthood, Naomi becomes more intimate with her Aunt Emily, an activist who has openly fought her family's victimization for years and who shares scrapbooks, letters, and her journal with Naomi. "'You have to remember,' Aunt Emily said. 'You are your history. If you cut any of it off you're an amputee ... Denial is gangrene'" (pp. 49-50). When her uncle dies, Naomi returns to Obasan to find her even further sunk into silence. Yet memories shaken loose by this loss and by Emily's prodding urge Naomi to break the silence and reconstruct her past, seeking "the freeing word." *Obasan* received the Canadian Authors' Association prize for best prose fiction of 1981. Earlier collections of poetry by Kogawa include *A Choice of Dreams* (1974) and *Jericho Road* (1977).

499. Koppelman, Susan, ed. **Between Mothers & Daughters: Stories Across a Generation.** Old Westbury, NY: Feminist Press, 1985. 293p. pbk. $8.95. LC 84-13562. ISBN 0935312269.

Between Mothers and Daughters is one of a series of short-story collections edited by Susan Koppelman. In her preface to the series, Koppelman documents the under-representation and misrepresentation of stories by women in the literary canon. She sees it as her task to retrieve from obscurity works which—because of the gender of their authors or the "inappropriateness" of their subject matter—have been neglected. *Between Mothers and Daughters* includes eighteen stories, from the 1840s to the 1980s. Some of the authors—Fannie Hurst, Tillie Olsen, Joanna Russ—are familiar; others, like Caroline W. Healey Dall and Alice Brown, have only recently been rediscovered. The stories vary in style, theme, and literary quality; yet all focus on the complex relationships between mothers and daughters. Other collections edited by Koppelman are *Old Maids* (Pandora Press, 1984), nineteenth-century stories about (and often by) unmarried women; and *The Other Woman* (Feminist Press, 1984), nineteenth- and twentieth-century tales of "women—both wives and other women—who love adulterous men" (p.xvii).

500.   Leffland, Ella. **Rumors of Peace.** New York: Harper and Row, 1979. 389p. $10.95.
LC 78-20209. ISBN 0060125721.
     As this novel opens, eleven-year-old Suse Hensen is living a comfortable, unexamined existence in Mendoza, a northern California town that is "as familiar and absolute as my face" (p.2). Suddenly, the Japanese attack Pearl Harbor; upon America's plunge into World War II, and Suse's entry into adolescence, nothing is familiar anymore. Leffland juxtaposes the details of adolescent life — school, parties, dresses, boys — against screaming headlines and blackout drills. As the novel progresses, Suse, like her country, must confront her ignorance and prejudices.

501.   Le Guin, Ursula K. **The Compass Rose.** New York: Harper and Row, 1982. 273p.
pbk. $3.50. LC 81-48158. ISBN 0060149884.
     Representing Le Guin's work at its political and moral best, "The Diary of the Rose" — one of twenty stories from the last two decades gathered here — tells of a young woman psychiatrist who unwittingly becomes a participant in torturing political dissidents. In another story, "Sur," the narrator recalls how in 1909 nine South American women undertook a secret expedition to the as-yet-undiscovered continent of Antarctica. The adventure empowers the women to name mountain peaks — but "not very seriously, since we did not expect our discoveries to come to the attention of male geographers" (p.269) — and to confront untamed nature. Le Guin no longer writes on the fringes of feminist science fiction. She has mastered the language, plot nuances, and science-fiction color that readers of the genre demand. To this she adds her substantial knowledge of the social sciences, especially history. In her utopian novel, *The Eye of the Heron* (Harper and Row, 1983), Le Guin's problem is to refrain from moralizing. A plot in which the space colonists include a group of pacifists and a group of war-mongers (remember *Lord of the Flies*) and suspense attendant upon a woman's efforts to dialectically bring about compromise constitute the philosophical guts of the novel. Le Guin wrestles with the complex moral problem of freedom in two other recent novels: *Malafrena* (Berkley Books, 1979) and *The Beginning Place* (Harper and Row, 1980), the latter a novel of adolescent development lacking the author's usual high literary quality. In her latest work, *Always Coming Home* (Harper and Row, 1985), Le Guin imagines a future-tense autobiographical account of a California visionary.

502.*   Lessing, Doris May, 1919- . **The Diaries of Jane Somers.** New York: Vintage Books, 1984. 501p. LC 84-17245. ISBN 0394729552.
     In 1983 and 1984, Lessing published *The Diary of a Good Neighbour* and *If the Old Could* ... under the name Jane Somers. Her dual purpose, she later explained, was to ensure that her work was reviewed on its merits and to highlight the difficulties faced by unknown writers trying to break into print. Rejected by Lessing's London publisher, "Jane Somers's" novels were eventually published, received mildly favorable reviews, and vanished after selling only a few copies. Vanished, that is, until Lessing revealed the hoax and republished them together in one volume under the title *The Diaries of Jane Somers.* Janna, the protagonist of *The Diary of a Good Neighbour,* is a selfish, pampered writer who is forced to acknowledge her limitations through an unlikely friendship with Maudie, a poor but feisty old woman. *If the Old Could* ... chronicles Janna's romance with Richard and examines her relationships with other women. The works appear to be little more than sensitive, realistic novels, akin to Lessing's early works, but for one complication — Janna's real name, we learn, is Jane Somers. With this information, and with their new title, *The Diaries of Jane Somers,* the two novels begin to echo the dizzying, metafictional pyrotechnics of Lessing's 1962 postmodern masterpiece, *The Golden Notebook.* In *The*

Good Terrorist (Knopf, 1985), the ever-unpredictable Lessing satirizes her own most common concerns—women and politics. Pursuing an unrequited love for the despicable Jasper, Alice joins a left-wing terrorist group. Yet her role there, as her mother acidly observes, is a traditional one: "'... you spend your life exactly as I did. Cooking and nannying for other people. An all-purpose female drudge'" (p.329).

503. Loewenstein, Andrea Freud. **This Place.** Boston: Pandora Press, 1984. 440p. pbk. $6.95. LC 84-11326. ISBN 0863580394.

"This place" is "Redburn Prison," a "liberal" prison for women based on the Framingham Correctional Institution outside Boston, where novelist Andrea Freud Loewenstein taught writing. Though priding itself on its reputation as a "model institution," Redburn is a world of sharp divisions and (not always) suppressed violence. Our view of Redburn is filtered through the experiences of four women, whose voices alternate throughout the novel. Ruth, director of mental health at the prison, is for the first time unsure of her role as therapist, as gradually acknowledged lesbian stirrings unleash a profound emotional "coming-out" that unsettles all parts of her life. Candy, a Redburn inmate, emerges as a kind of soul-mate of Ruth, whose life was turned in very different directions by less fortunate circumstances. Sonya is Redburn's new art therapist, and an open lesbian; her flamboyant disregard for the divisions of prison life acts as a catalyst for both astonishing creativity and predictable violence. Telecea, a black woman, is the resident madwoman/visionary, the focal point of the book's climax. Loewenstein succeeds in creating absorbing fiction out of the grim world of prison life. Her work brings alive the issues of racism, class, and lesbianism, while also forging convincing characters whose lives show there are no easy answers.

504. Lord, Bette Bao. **Spring Moon: A Novel of China.** New York: Harper and Row, 1981. 464p. $15.34. LC 78-20210. ISBN 0060148934.

Spring Moon, an intelligent and beautiful heroine, emerges as the central figure of this best-selling historical novel set in mainland China. Two historical threads bind the novel: the changes in woman's status in upper-class Chinese Mandarin families from the turn of the century to the Cultural Revolution, and the larger social, political, and military upheavals in China from 1892 to 1972. Lord's China encompasses principally Shanghai, Soochow, and Peking in this work, which continues in the poetic strain of her earlier *Eighth Moon* (1964; repr. Avon Books, 1983). The incestuous love story between Spring Moon and her uncle at the heart of the novel compels the reader, while the violence of the Cultural Revolution casts the darkest shadow over this tale. Perhaps it is because in its zealotry the Cultural Revolution disregarded the need many Chinese harbor for old traditions and for family—imagined as poetic, beautiful, and cherished by this Chinese-American novelist.

505. Lurie, Alison. **Foreign Affairs.** New York: Random House, 1984. 291p. $15.45. LC 84-42657. ISBN 039454076X.

In this witty, intelligent, and beautifully plotted novel, Lurie alternates love affairs of two Americans who happen to be in London at the same time. Vinnie Miner, a professor of children's literature, is "fifty-four years old, small, plain, and unmarried" (p.3) and dogged by self-pity. Her colleague, Fred Turner, is a strikingly handsome, young eighteenth-century scholar trying to recover from a broken marriage. Each falls in love in London. Vinnie's philosophy of self-preservation—"why shouldn't she look out for herself? Nobody else will" (p.5)—is tested as she becomes involved in an increasingly serious relationship with the unsuitable Chuck Mumpson, a boorish and uneducated but essentially decent

Oklahoma sanitary engineer. In the end, Vinnie's conviction that she is not meant for love proves sadly self-fulfilling. Fred's misery takes on a new twist as he falls desperately in love with the beautiful but erratic actress Rosemary Radley; in several scenes, he plays the role of a Henry James innocent awed by Rosemary's fast-track London set. Lurie is the author of seven other novels written over the last twenty years.

506.* Madden-Simpson, Janet, ed. **Woman's Part: An Anthology of Short Fiction By and About Irish Women 1890-1960.** Dublin: Arlen House; New York: Boyars, 1984. 223p. LC 85-116726. ISBN 0905223330.

Editor Janet Madden-Simpson has collected stories written between 1890 and 1960 by fifteen Irish women, among them Edith Somerville, Katharine Tynan, and Mary Lavin. Seeking to redress the "equation of Anglo-Irish literature with a record of masculine perceptions" (p.1), Madden-Simpson has chosen well-written tales that explore previously unrecorded aspects of Irish women's lives. The stories range from "Virgin Soil," a nineteenth-century tale by George Egerton (Mary Chavelita Dunne) about a young girl who is destroyed due to her utter ignorance of the physical side of marriage, to Geraldine Cummins's "The Tragedy of Eight Pence," a modern tragicomedy about a woman who tries to keep her invalid husband from learning that his death will leave her penniless. The male bias that Madden-Simpson detects in Anglo-Irish criticism is abundantly clear in *Woman in Irish Legend, Life, and Literature,* edited by S. F. Gallagher (Barnes and Noble, 1983). Although it seeks to address feminist concerns, this collection of nine essays considers only one woman writer — Anna Parnell, sister of Charles Stewart Parnell. Still, the essays do examine the legendary manifestations of Ireland as a female — as goddess, princess, old crone, or devouring sow — and present useful analyses of the works of Shaw, Yeats, Synge, O'Casey, and Joyce.

507. Marshall, Paule, 1929- . **Praisesong for the Widow.** New York: Putnam, 1983. 256p. $13.95. LC 82-13215. ISBN 0399127542.

Avey Johnson discovers a lost part of herself when she abandons her cruise ship vacation to immerse herself in a native ritual on the Caribbean island of Carriacou. Marshall's premise is that white culture has polluted the sixty-two-year-old widow's spiritual self; Avey must literally vomit up her middle-class identity before she can participate fully in the black community celebration. The novel fuses dream and recollection as the troubled Avey recalls the ecstasy and rage of early married life with Jay, and their struggle to get ahead. Also dominating her memory are the powerful figure of her great-aunt Cuney and her narrative of the slave rebellion at Ibo Landing. We are given to believe that Avey's unconsciousness teems with images of white injustice she has tried to submerge as she and her family clutched at some received version of "The American Dream." *Reena and Other Stories* (Feminist Press, 1983) is important for Marshall's autobiographical essay "From the Poets in the Kitchen," in which she pays tribute to her literary precursors — the community of Barbados housewives in New York — who cleaned house for a living and whose ambition it was to buy a brownstone. She remembers these women as poets who "talked — endlessly, passionately, poetically, and with impressive range" (p.5). The stories, preceded by autobiographical notes, reveal Marshall's struggle as a writer and as a black woman.

508. Martinson, Moa, 1890-1964. **Women and Appletrees.** Old Westbury, NY: Feminist Press, 1985. 216p. bibliog. pbk. $8.95. LC 85-6898. ISBN 0935312382.

With this novel, first published in Sweden in 1933, the Feminist Press inaugurated a new series of international feminist classics. Martinson was a popular journalist and novelist who rose from illegitimacy and poverty; the novel reflects her working-class background. The enduring friendship of Sally and Ellen is a central theme, played out against the brutal depiction of the harsh struggle to survive in the slums and the countryside. Translator Margaret S. Lacy, who has retained Martinson's conversational tone, adds a biocritical afterword.

509.   Mason, Bobbie Ann. **Shiloh and Other Stories.** New York: Harper and Row, 1982, 247p. $12.45. LC 82-47541. ISBN 0060150629.

Mason writes about contemporary relationships between men and women, inspired by the rhythms of speech and culture of her native Kentucky. In one of these stories, "The Rooker," Mary Lou delves under the fears of her recluse husband, a craftsman who seldom leaves the house. Her epiphanic discovery of her husband's fear of women makes her "so sick and heavy with her power over him that she wants to cry" (p.33). This collection dwells on the themes of people burying themselves alive in marriage, smothered by the lack of breathing space in intimate relationships, and of the strength of women and the vulnerability of men. The stories are steeped in references to current movies, television shows, fast food, and Southern rock. What Mason may be saying about commodification and women's lives in traditional environments opens this text to feminist critics in provocative ways. The author has recently published a first novel entitled *In Country* (Harper and Row, 1985), which deals with the legacy of Vietnam.

510.   Miner, Valerie. **Blood Sisters: An Examination of Conscience.** New York: St. Martin's Press, 1982. 206p. $11.95. LC 82-5536. ISBN 0312084617.

Miner delineates the issues of women involved in social, class, and national upheavals through the relationship of two first cousins—Beth, a terrorist working in London to undermine British control in Northern Ireland, and Liz, a California radical feminist. Women's liberation is Liz's dominant preoccupation during the years 1974 to 1976, whereas for Beth, national liberation takes precedence. Though these characters confront separate realities, Miner's point appears to be precisely that only by engaging differences can anything like a dialectic occur. Politics is a compelling subject for Miner, who in *Movement: A Novel in Stories* (Crossing Press, 1982) scrutinizes the political choices of Susan Campbell, a photojournalist and wife of a draft resister fleeing to Montreal during the mid-1970s. Miner's two other novels combine political themes with mystery. Professor Nan Weaver is accused of murdering a male colleague because of their disagreements over feminist politics in *Murder in the English Department* (St. Martin's Press, 1983). In *Winter's Edge* (Crossing Press, 1985), the warm friendship between two older women is undermined by political tensions, intrigue, and violence sparked by a hotly contested election in San Francisco's Tenderloin district.

511.   Morante, Elsa, 1916- . **Aracoeli.** New York: Random House, 1984. 311p. $17.45. LC 84-42524. ISBN 0394535189.

Morante, one of Italy's most renowned novelists, speaks here through the voice of Emanuele, a middle-aged Italian homosexual driven by his unhappy existence and haunting memories to undertake a pilgrimage to Andalusia in search of the spirit of his long-dead mother, Aracoeli. Memory, dreams, and fantasies are densely interwoven in this beautifully written novel, which draws heavily on the nightmarish legacy of European fascism. Morante's earlier masterpiece, *History* (1977; repr. Vintage Books, 1984), is a wrenching tale of one woman's frantic struggle to survive and to protect her son amidst the devastation of Mussolini's Italy.

512.   Morrison, Toni. **Tar Baby.** New York: Knopf, distr. New York: Random House, 1981. 305p. $14.95. LC 80-22821. ISBN 0394423291.

In Morrison's fourth novel, the Caribbean home of retired Philadelphia businessman Valerian Street is disrupted by the arrival of Son, a black American fugitive. Son's jarring effect on the household is seen through the eyes of the Streets, their loyal black cook and butler, and the servants' niece Jadine, a Sorbonne-educated model who becomes Son's lover. In this richly textured, often symbolic work, Morrison dissects the power relationships between blacks and whites, servants and masters, women and men. In particular, she stresses the problem of identity: for blacks, who must create their own mythology to counteract white stereotypes; and for women, who learn that they must look to themselves for completeness.

513.   Muller, Marcia, and Bill Pronzini, eds. **She Won the West: An Anthology of Western and Frontier Stories By Women.** New York: Morrow, 1985. 372p. $17.95. LC 84-20789. ISBN 0688047017.

Muller and Pronzini's anthology brings together stories of fourteen recognized Western writers of the twentieth century—Mary Hunter Austin (1868-1934), Mari Sandoz (1901-1966), Gertrude Atherton (1857-1948), and Willa Cather (1873-1947), as well as more contemporary women. The work here is of uneven quality, as Atherton and Austin's inclusion demonstrates. Though contemporaries, these writers were hardly in the same league—Atherton a best-selling writer of romantic fiction, Austin often called a Western Thoreau. Both, however, are usually inaccessible for comparison because their fiction remains out of print, a problem this anthology remedies to a small extent. Short introductions to each author are, in the main, inadequate. Atherton, Austin, Sandoz, and Cather are joined by Helen Eustis, Juanita Brooks, Leslie Silko, and others in *Westward the Women: An Anthology of Western Stories by Women* (Doubleday, 1984). Editor Vicki Piekarski speculates that until recently our idea of winning the West excluded a women's perspective, which may account for the relative obscurity of Western fiction by women.

514.   Munro, Alice. **The Beggar Maid: Stories of Flo and Rose.** New York: Penguin Books, 1979. 210p. pbk. $4.95. LC 79-63809. ISBN 0394506820.

Award-winning Canadian author Alice Munro places her female characters in the part of the world she knows best, small-town southwestern Ontario. Central to this collection are Rose and her sharp-tongued stepmother Flo, whose relationship and sharing of stories—exaggerated family legends, local gossip, events of their past and present lives—link the ten pieces. "Royal Beatings" explores the theme of family violence and its reverberations in the community. "Privilege" is the tale of Rose's public schooling—sexual education in the outhouses, fights in the coatrooms, a crush on an older girl. Naturalistic details of small-town poverty abound. Yet, as Rose understands, "Learning to survive, no matter with what cravenness and caution, what shocks and forebodings, is not the same as being miserable. It is too interesting" (p.29). Rose leaves the town of West Hanratty behind, marrying (and later divorcing) a wealthy man, becoming a mother and well-known actress. Still she remains inextricably tied to her family, her community, and her working-class background; the later stories dip again and again into the past. Munro's more recent collection, *The Moons of Jupiter* (Knopf, 1983), also explores the theme of family. In both books, Munro effortlessly and realistically delineates her women characters as they struggle with uneasy loves and friendships. Louis K. MacKendrick gathers ten critical articles and an interview with Munro in *Probable Fictions: Alice Munro's Narrative Acts* (ECW Press, 1983).

515. Murdoch, Iris. **The Philosopher's Pupil.** New York: Viking Press, 1983. 576p. $17.75. LC 82-45901. ISBN 0670551864.

Murdoch has never been read for her feminist message. Nonetheless, she is one of the most gifted contemporary novelists. Readers are unlikely to encounter a more classic marital squabble than that between Stella and George McCaffrey in *The Philosopher's Pupil.* Ineffectual windshield wipers and a "malignant rain" conspire to sustain the furious scene, which opens Murdoch's saga of the wealthy McCaffreys, and the incursion into their lives of the brilliant philosopher Rosanov. The unpleasant atmosphere between Stella and George is typical of the relationships between men and women throughout the novel. Whether Murdoch is describing the highway at night, a room's furnishings, or the town spa, no detail is extraneous. In *Iris Murdoch: Work for the Spirit* (University of Chicago Press, 1982) — perhaps the most important, if traditional, critical work — Elizabeth Dipple praises Murdoch for the "courage to insist on the almost intolerable demands of excellence," and argues that she puts correspondingly high demands on the reader (p.1). Dipple does not offer a feminist critique of Murdoch, however.

516. Naylor, Gloria. **The Women of Brewster Place.** New York: Viking Press, 1982. 192p. $14.95. LC 81-69969. ISBN 0670778559.

Winner of the American Book Award for the best first novel, *The Women of Brewster Place* is more accurately a group of short stories tracing the separate lives of seven black women who settle on Brewster Place, a forgotten, dead-end city street. Each has come to Brewster Place for her own reason — a mother whose resources have been exhausted by a wayward son; a middle-class college graduate from the affluent black neighborhood, Linden Hills, who has taken on an African name and the task of organizing the neighborhood; two lesbians seeking retreat from the prying eyes of a busier neighborhood; a mother of an expanding brood of uncontrollable children. Many of the stories are sad, a few improbable. When men enter these narratives, Naylor chooses to represent them negatively. This may cause problems for some critics, especially those who identify black feminist agendas as quite different from the concerns of white feminists. In Naylor's book all the women are courageous, all the men wimps. Naylor's second novel, *Linden Hills* (Ticknor and Fields, 1985), is an allegorical exploration of the world of the black middle class.

517. Oates, Joyce Carol, 1938- . **A Bloodsmoor Romance.** New York: Dutton, 1982; repr. New York: Warner Books, 1983. 651p. pbk. $3.95. LC 82-2416. ISBN 0446308250.

Beginning with *Bellefleur* (Dutton, 1980) — a saga of amazing complexity characterized by myth, violent historical romance, fantasy, and melodrama — Oates turned her novelist's eye to the nineteenth century. In the present work, she takes the reader back to Bloodsmoor, Pennsylvania of the 1870s, again using romance as her literary vehicle, and sprinkling the tale with bits of feminist social history of the period. Using the device of a gossipy Victorian narrator, Oates limns the details of the lives of the Zinn family, especially the five unmarried Zinn sisters. The destinies of the women characters include marriage, a balloon abduction, elopement, sexual "transformation," occultism, the theater, escape from tyrannical husbands, and a life of science with father. Oates playfully employs her narrator's voice to feign the conventional reactions of the day to the sisters' fates, while Oates herself clearly wants these sisters to make choices independent of the institutions that contrain them, chiefly marriage. The author taps her prodigious knowledge of American literature, especially that of Emerson, Alcott, Hawthorne, and Twain, copiously borrowing and parodying when it serves her narrative purpose. Another period piece churned out of the Oates fiction factory is *Mysteries of Winterthurn* (Dutton, 1984), a parody of turn-of-the-century detective fiction, featuring grisly murders of women. After these three historical novels, Oates is once again electing a contemporary setting for her fiction, most recently with *Last Days* (Dutton, 1984), her twelfth short-story collection, and the novel *Solstice* (Dutton, 1985), a disturbing evocation of friendship between women.

518. Oates, Joyce Carol, 1938- . **A Sentimental Education: Stories.** New York: Dutton, 1980. 196p. pbk. $4.95. LC 80-36767. ISBN 0525199505.

"Only in parable, in myth, can tragedy be transcended," writes Oates in her critical volume *Contraries* (Oxford University Press, 1981). Beginning with a tale of a wealthy older woman who takes a narcissistic, idle young man for her lover after her longstanding marriage dissolves, Oates's stories make parabolic the ordinary tragedies of contemporary life in affluent American society. Women in these jarring tales are brutalized in many ways; it is arguable that they transcend their separate tragedies. Critics often have made the point that Oates's preoccupation is the ugliness of modernity, that her isolated characters are types who move convulsively through time and events overwhelmed by violence, out of control, unable to make sense of their own lives or of those around them. Joanne V. Creighton's perceptive treatment of Oates's work up to 1979, *Joyce Carol Oates* (Twayne, 1979), and Linda Wagner's *Critical Essays on Joyce Carol Oates* (G. K. Hall, 1979), a collection of reviews and essays, each address this. Oates herself writes the preface to the latter volume, terming many of her critics and reviewers "ideal readers." Oates's interest in the human drama is also evident in her poetry, recently gathered in *Invisible Woman: New and Selected Poems, 1970-1982* (Ontario Review Press; distr. Persea Books, 1982). In "Honeymoon," for example, she conjures the image of "My face in the frame of your fingers./Bedsheets writhing like snakes," only to add the ironically subversive lines, "It is all very casual./It is all very domestic" (p.24).

519. O'Brien, Edna. **A Rose in the Heart.** Garden City, NY: Doubleday, 1979. 287p. pbk. $8.95. LC 78-18563. ISBN 0385143494.

Chosen by *The New York Times* as one of the best books of 1979, *A Rose in the Heart* proves once again that Edna O'Brien has an unerring eye and ear for the grim details of the ordinary lives of women. The title story, "A Rose in the Heart of New York," grapples with familiar O'Brien themes, notably the paradox of family ties and family knots, and conflicted realities steeped in Irish Catholicisim. O'Brien's characters present themselves as convincing, sympathetic human beings, as a result of carefully crafted prose and writerly sensitivity to human afflictions. The author's mastery of dialogue, economy of phrase and detail — in short, her use of the absolutely appropriate language — astonishes and seduces us to enter into her fictive garden. In her 1982 collection of tales, *Returning* (Penguin Books), O'Brien introduces us to former classmates, relatives, friends, and authority figures from her girlhood. The title for *A Fanatic Heart* (Farrar, Straus, Giroux, 1984), a collection of twenty-nine stories gathered from the *New Yorker* and previously published collections, comes from Yeats's "Out of Ireland we have come/Great hatred, little room/Maimed us at the start./I carry from my mother's womb/A fanatic heart." These stories of women reflect this fiercely held Irish tradition.

520. Ozick, Cynthia. **Levitation: Five Fictions.** New York: Knopf; distr. New York: Random House, 1982. 157p. $11.50. LC 80-7997. ISBN 0394514130.

Though Ozick would eschew the label "feminist writer," having expended considerable critical ink in deriding this categorization, notably in *Art and Ardor: Essays* (Knopf, 1983), she undoubtedly stands as one of the most important writers of fiction and brilliant critics of our time. In these five stories Ozick is at her best, unmasking her characters so that they show us what is true and intelligent about them (though her skill is so great, they seem to unmask themselves). With beauty and economy of language, she weaves Jewish myth and experience into these six loosely connected tales. Clearly Ozick loves her characters, even the most ridiculous among them. And she sometimes gently, often trenchantly, insists on our seeing the humor and pathos of Jews and Jewishness in sentences that point to an American concept of cultural pluralism in which her characters tread water for survival. Ozick admires intelligence above all and is quick to note how others make an idol of it. In *The Cannibal Galaxy* (Knopf, 1983), she creates a character who makes a fetish of his own child's intelligence only to find that ironically his step-daughter, seemingly a slow child, is an artist, while his own progeny's fate is to slog around in the swamps of mediocrity.

521.   Paley, Grace. **Later the Same Day.** New York: Farrar, Straus, Giroux, 1985. 211p. $13.95. LC 84-26072. ISBN 0374184097.
Written over the last ten years, the stories in Paley's beautifully wrought collection are a wide-ranging, vibrant, humorous group, in which women — young and old, poor and middle-class, pacifist, feminist, intellectual and anti-intellectual — speak about their experiences in American society. In "Listening" — the story of a couple's longstanding, easy relationship — one senses that Paley has found her stride. Men's stories of women, Faith chides Jack, are "your falling-in-love stories, your French-woman-during-the-Korean-War stories, your magnificent-woman stories, your beautiful-new-young-wife stories, your political-comrade-though-extremely-beautiful stories ..." (p.203). For Paley, however, writing as a woman contains the calculus of gender, race, and class. Her characters (many of whom appear in several pieces) are complex and authentic; the personal and the political are inextricably intertwined in their lives and observations. In the final pages of the volume, Paley reminds the reader (and herself) that she has not told all. In a sudden burst of feeling, Cassie accuses her friend Faith (the narrator) of leaving out her "woman and woman, woman-loving life" in these tales of heterosexual women (p.210). Faith asks for forgiveness, but Cassie (Paley's writerly conscience) lovingly declares, "I'll watch you like a hawk. I do not forgive you'" (p.211). Honesty and empathy are the hallmarks of Paley's fiction.

522.*   Perrin, Ursula. **Old Devotions.** New York: Dial Press, 1983. 264p. LC 82-9663. ISBN 0385276567.
"I don't want my drawers poked into, my closets opened. My inner space, too, I like to protect a bit," confesses the narrator midway through this novel about female friendship, disastrous marriages, death at an early age, and life on the other side of forty (p.148). Perrin constrasts the lives of two women, former roommates at an Eastern college whose paths diverge: Isabel, a writer and the narrator of the story, is divorced and probingly analytical about the relationships she has chosen and those that have chosen her; Morgan, the nurturant personality, has chosen marriage and maternity in suburbia. Perrin manages to take the ordinary material of human lives and transform it into an extraordinary fiction, the central theme here the fidelities and infidelities of entwined lives. Perrin plots the perilous course of female friendship resumed as a necessary but painful journey toward self-knowledge.

523.   Pesetsky, Bette. **Author From a Savage People.** New York: Knopf, 1983. 197p. $12.95. LC 82-48731. ISBN 0394530330.
In this dark satire, ghostwriter May Alto goes off the deep end when one of her clients wins the Nobel Prize and she realizes the extent to which she has languished in obscurity while men have taken credit for her work. When the client, Quayle, explains to May that he

hired her merely as a "technician," her fury boils over: "Quayle, that book is mine. Never mind whose name is on the cover. You wrote not one line, not one word, not one period, one comma, not even your own name. My book, my words, my ideas" (pp.106-107). Furthermore, May has proof of her authorship — she has woven stories of her dead relatives into every book she has ever ghostwritten. From this point on, May is determined to get hers — she wants Quayle's money, his fame, his life — and Pesetsky pulls out all the stops in her fantasy of an obsessed woman's quest for vengeance. Pesetsky's deadpan, fragmented style also serves her well in her first book, *Stories Up to a Point* (Knopf, 1981), in which her woman narrators reflect on their disappointments as wives, lovers, mothers, friends.

524.   Petesch, Natalie L. M. **Soul Clap Its Hands and Sing.** Boston: South End Press, 1981. 206p. $20.00. LC 81-51386. ISBN 0896081192.

Natalie Petesch is the author of the well-received feminist novel *The Odyssey of Katinou Kalokvich* (1974; repr. Motheroot, 1980). In this volume, ordinary people try to cope with an existence that sometimes seems overwhelming. Like the Yeats poem from which she takes her title, most of Petesch's sixteen vignettes feature elderly protagonists: poor, infirm, and unwanted, they struggle to meet daily loneliness and humiliation with dignity. In "Shopping," a woman saves heating money by spending her days in stores, looking at goods she will never buy; in "Lunching with Tenney," an old man, alienated from his family, faces the solitude of retirement. Petesch offers us other characters as well: a middle-aged woman whose husband has just left her for one of his students; a victimized waitress in an ice-cream parlor; a Turkish immigrant. Still, her often bleak world is softened by a glimmer of hope, and although they all make some statement, these moving, beautifully written stories rise well above mere political tract. Readers may also wish to look at Petesch's latest novel, *Duncan's Colony* (Swallow Press/Ohio University Press, 1984), a tense political fable about eight people waiting for nuclear apocalypse.

525.   Phelps, Elizabeth Stuart, 1844-1911. **The Story of Avis.** Edited by Carol Farley Kessler. New Brunswick, NJ: Rutgers University Press, 1985. 278p. bibliog. $25.00. LC 84-27538. ISBN 0813510988.

Avis Dobell is an ambitious, dedicated painter when she meets and marries Philip Ostrander. Phelps depicts in minute detail the disastrous effect of the marriage on Avis's creativity: Philip abandons his original promise to support Avis's artistic endeavors, and she is soon bogged down in the mundane concerns of domesticity and motherhood. Less polished in style and structure than Chopin's *The Awakening, The Story of Avis* (first published in 1877) nevertheless presents an equally radical critique of women's traditional roles. Editor Carol Farley Kessler's introduction and notes provide social and biographical background, and she includes four contemporary reviews of the novel, along with an essay by Phelps entitled "The True Woman." Phelps's novel *The Silent Partner* (Feminist Press, 1983), a realistic portrait of industrialism, stresses the bonds between women that cross class lines. Kessler's full-length study, *Elizabeth Stuart Phelps* (Twayne, 1982), explores "the opposing impacts upon Phelps's life and novels of a conservative Protestant socialization ... and a liberating women's movement that urged women, in Phelps's words, to 'dream and dare," (Preface).

526.   Phelps, Ethel Johnston. **The Maid of the North: Feminist Folk Tales from Around the World.** New York: Holt, Rinehart and Winston, 1981. 176p. bibliog. $10.95. LC 80-21500. ISBN 0030568935.

"The traditional folk and fairy tales in this collection, as in my earlier book of tales [*Tatterhood and Other Tales,* (Feminist Press, 1978)], have one characteristic in common:

they all portray spirited, courageous heroines. Although a great number of fairy and folk tale collections are in print, this type of heroine is surprisingly rare," writes Phelps (p.ix). Central characteristics of women subjects Phelps searched for in gathering these tales—cleverness, amiability, resourcefulness, cooperativeness, and courage—appear to be more readily found in heroines from Britain and northern Europe, a factor that accounts for the skewed selection. African, Japanese, Persian, and American Indian tales are outnumbered here by the English, Celtic, German, and Scandinavian. These twenty-one stories, elegantly illustrated by Lloyd Bloom, serve the juvenile reader as well as the folklorist.

527.   Phillips, Jayne Anne. **Black Tickets.** New York: Delacorte/Seymour Lawrence, 1979. 265p. $8.95. LC 79-12353. ISBN 0440007089.

Phillips's narrative voice, jagged and raw, speaks in these thirty short stories of the eroticism, prostitution, and pornography that for many constitute daily life in the urban environment. Some may notice a resemblance between Henry Miller's post-modernist style and Phillips's unrelenting eye for the ugliness of life on the street and her ear for the language of America's "have-nots." *Machine Dreams* (1984) is Phillips's latest work.

528.   Pym, Barbara, 1913-1980. **A Few Green Leaves.** New York: Dutton, 1980. 250p. $13.95. LC 80-18905. ISBN 052510450X.

In the last of her novels, completed before her death in 1980, Pym imagines the character of Emma Howick, an anthropologist who comes to an Oxfordshire village to do an ethnography. Pym's readers will be familiar with the widows, spinsters, and rectors who have been humorously and sensitively evoked in earlier novels, many recently reprinted. Shy and retiring, Pym's characters come to us stripped of the veneer of modernity. Perhaps this is why some of Pym's work has escaped us until quite recently; fortunately, she was unable to turn out the trendy, formula fiction the publishing world deemed saleable. Pym stopped writing for fifteen years after her publisher rejected a novel about a librarian's "unsuitable attachment," the title of the now rediscovered work (Dutton, 1982). Other previously unpublished Pym novels seem to be turning up by the day. *Crampton Hodnet* (Dutton, 1985) is a recent discovery featuring archetypal Pym protagonist Barbara Bird. Pym's sister, her literary executor, has pieced together a map of sorts to Pym's world, *A Very Private Eye: An Autobiography in Diaries and Letters* (Dutton, 1984). Chronicling the years from 1932, when Pym was at Oxford, to 1980, when she died from cancer, the diaries illumine an unsuccessful writer's life. Supporting herself by working as an editor, in her free time Pym wrote about women like herself, unmarried observers of the daily scene around them. Apparently this life suited her, as both the autobiographical writings and fiction of Pym sparkle with English wit, humor, and, perhaps paramount, hope for the human condition.

529.   Robinson, Marilynne. **Housekeeping.** New York: Farrar, Straus, Giroux, 1981. 219p. $10.95. LC 80-24061. ISBN 0374173133.

Ruth and Lucille, abandoned as youngsters by their mother (a suicide), lived with their grandmother until she died, then with two maiden great-aunts who finally fled from their responsibility to the girls. Their mother's sister, Sylvie, finally arrives to look after them, but her odd behavior makes the girls fear she too will leave them. The story is set in isolated Fingerbone, Idaho; the sense of place and atmosphere is powerfully evoked in Ruth's narration. *The New York Times Book Review* termed this first novel "an extraordinary performance."

530.   Salmonson, Jessica Amanda, ed. **Amazons II**. New York: DAW Books, 1982. 239p. pbk. $2.95. ISBN 0879977361.

Amazons II is a sequel to the 1979 collection *Amazons!* (DAW Books), also edited by Salmonson. The twelve fantasy tales in this volume, by both women and men, concentrate on women warriors—their societies, religious practices, and mythologies—and present alternative visions to the usual swashbuckling sword and sorcery fare. Authors include well-known figures like Jo Clayton, Tanith Lee, and F. M. Busby, along with many lesser-known writers. Salmonson's introduction provides a historical overview of the woman warrior tale. *Asimov's Space of Her Own* (Dial Press, 1983), edited by Shawna McCarthy, brings together twenty science-fiction stories and two poems by women. The interest of the stories varies: some specifically address women's issues, while others are merely adventure tales. Ursula K. Le Guin, Pamela Sargent (editor of the excellent *Women of Wonder* anthologies), and Connie Willis are among the authors represented here. Well-known science-fiction writer Marion Zimmer Bradley has edited *Sword and Sorceress II* (DAW Books, 1985), an anthology of heroic fantasy by both men and women featuring female protagonists.

531.   Santmyer, Helen Hooven, 1895-1986. **"... And Ladies of the Club."** Columbus: Ohio State University Press, 1982. 1344p. $35.00. LC 81-22401. ISBN 081420323X.

Perhaps more a social history than a novel, *"... And Ladies of the Club"* records an era (1868-1932) when the Waynesboro, Ohio Women's Club provided an acceptable opportunity for educated women to gather and to hold discussions outside the home. Some of the novel takes place during the prelude to suffrage, associationism, temperance, and other social movements historians now argue were tentative steps toward women's equality, cloaked under the safe banner of domesticity and valorization of family. Santmyer's loving attention to decoration, clothing, customs, religion, and politics—in short, to every detail of material life—distinguishes this best-selling novel. Santmyer has created a group of middle-class white women in strokes of realism Howells would have applauded. The plot sags under the heft of sheer detail at times, but for evocation of time and place, Santmyer's effort has no equal.

532.   Schneider, Nina, 1913- . **The Woman Who Lived in a Prologue**. Boston: Houghton Mifflin, 1979. 479p. pbk. $3.95. LC 79-18595. ISBN 0380599817.

Schneider's style recalls that of her Jewish literary precursor, Anzia Yezierska (c.1880-1970). Using a first-person narrative, Schneider creates the delightful Ariadne Arkady, her septuagenarian heroine embarking on the project of writing her autobiography, a journey through memory. As in Yezierska's novel/autobiography, the father and mother engage in constant battle over Ariadne's body and mind. "My father had the heroism to resist death of the spirit; my mother, of the flesh. Together, my parents might have made one hero" (p.15). Schneider has a keen ear for dialogue and makes use of hyperbole toward the same literary ends as Yezierska, but Schneider's background and the story she tells are unique. Schneider was sixty-seven when she wrote this first novel.

533.   Segal, Lore Groszmann. **Her First American**. New York: Knopf, 1985. 287p. $15.95. LC 84-43067. ISBN 0394536274.

Ilka Weissnix, a twenty-one-year-old Jewish refugee from Vienna, wants to discover the "real" America. On a barstool in Nevada, she meets Carter Bayoux, a middle-aged black intellectual whose self-destructive impulses are exceeded only by his immense self-confidence and charm. "I'm a wonderful teacher," proclaims Carter (p.16)—and indeed he is, becoming an unlikely Pangloss to Ilka's latter-day Candide. Carter shows Ilka the ins and outs of American culture, and he teaches her about love and friendship in the process. In this marvelously funny, poignant novel, Segal—herself a Viennese refugee—presents a love affair between a larger-than-life American hero and a European innocent abroad, a black man and a Jewish woman, with true compassion for the intricacies and the contradictions of human relationships.

534. Shange, Ntozake. **Sassafrass, Cypress & Indigo: A Novel.** New York: St. Martin's Press, 1982. 224p. $10.95. LC 82-5565. ISBN 0312699719.

Best known as a poet and dramatist, Shange has written a first novel that reads like poetry. The three title characters are the daughters of Hilda Effania, a black weaver. The sisters are named after their mother's favorite dyes for fabrics; and Shange has structured the novel so that it resembles a weaving, alternating the stories of Sassafrass, an artist, Cypress, a dancer, and Indigo, a young spellcaster. Shange incorporates a number of literary forms into her work, including prose narrative, dream sequences, recipes (for magical spells along with more mundane dishes like "Hilda's Turkey Hash"), letters, poetry, and drama. The subject of the novel is announced in the first line—"Where there is a woman there is magic"—and the author explores the ways in which women embody, or create magic, often drawing on African and Afro-American folklore. Shange presents a powerful portrait of black culture, female creativity, and family bonding, especially in the figure of Hilda Effania. Readers may also be interested in *Betsey Brown* (St. Martin's Press, 1985), about a middle-class black family in the 1950s; and *A Daughter's Geography* (St. Martin's Press, 1983), poems for her daughter.

535. Sinclair, Jo, 1913- . **The Changelings.** New York: McGraw-Hill, 1955; repr. Old Westbury, NY: Feminist Press, 1985. 352p. bibliog. pbk. $8.95. LC 85-6875. ISBN 0935312404.

This important novel was first published in 1955, but has long been out of print. Set in a midwestern, mostly Jewish, working-class neighborhood in the early fifties, it documents the destruction caused by racism, class and ethnic antagonism, and sexual hierarchies. As upwardly mobile residents flee to the suburbs, those left behind in the neighborhood find a scapegoat in the blacks—*die schwartze*—who are moving in. The novel's many subplots come together in the friendship between Judy Vincent, a thirteen-year-old Jewish tomboy, and Clara Jackson, a black girl. In her portrait of the community's breakdown, Sinclair presents a scaring indictment of Jewish bigotry, not only against blacks but against gentiles as well. Yet she concludes on a note of hope, bequeathing the future to Vincent, Clara, and the other "changelings" who "leave behind that narrow corner of our stranger parents, our frightened elders" (p.304).

536. Spark, Muriel. **The Only Problem.** New York: Putnam, 1984. 179p. $14.95. LC 83-26203. ISBN 0399129871.

Why has Harvey, the millionaire scholar, deserted his wife Effie to meditate and write his tome about the sufferings of the biblical Job? "I couldn't stand her sociological clap-trap," he says at one point in this invigorating novel. Spark's characters speculate on the nature of suffering, love, and comfort, but "the only problem" may be that all is futility—and that nobody really suffers. If there were a contemporary version of Job's wife, it would be Effie and women like her, dependent upon the whims of men like Harvey. In *Loitering With Intent* (Coward, McCann and Geoghegan, 1981), Fleur Talbot—an alter ego, perhaps, for Spark—ponders the nature of artistic creation. *The Stories of Muriel Spark* (Dutton, 1985) conjoins Spark's first two collections, plus uncollected pieces.

Though a few of the tales are rough or insubstantial, the majority demonstrate the author's characteristic liveliness and astringency. Social realist, post-modernist, Catholic novelist — Spark has been labeled all of these. Ruth Whittaker examines Spark's novels and the sources that nourish her in *The Faith and Fiction of Muriel Spark* (St. Martin's Press, 1982), as do the several contributors to *Muriel Spark: An Odd Capacity for Vision*, edited by Alan Bold (Barnes and Noble, 1984).

537.   Spencer, Elizabeth. **The Stories of Elizabeth Spencer.** Garden City, NY: Doubleday, 1981; repr. New York: Penguin Books, 1983. 429p. $15.95. LC 79-6601. ISBN 0385156979.

In the thirty-three stories in this volume, written between 1944 and 1977, Spencer's settings range from Italy to the West Indies. Yet her most compelling stories take place in the rural Mississippi of her childhood — for example, "The Little Brown Girl," about a white child who longs for an imaginary black playmate; "Prelude to a Parking Lot," the tragicomic history of a working-class family; or "A Christian Education," about a child's rebellion against her parents' strict Sabbath rules. Like fellow southerners William Faulkner, Flannery O'Connor, and Eudora Welty, Spencer shows a strong sense of place, and of how the past impinges on the present. Although at first glance her tales appear to be little more than polished mainstream fiction, complexity, mystery, and awe lurk beneath the surface of everyday events. Welty's highly laudatory foreword praises Spencer's "finely shaded perceptions" and her "cool deliberateness to pull no punches" (p.xix).

538.   Stafford, Jean, 1915- . **The Collected Stories of Jean Stafford.** New York: Farrar, Straus, Giroux, 1969; repr. New York: Dutton, 1984. 463p. pbk. $10.95. LC 83-72961. ISBN 052548101X.

This volume assembles thirty of Stafford's short stories, most of them originally published in *The New Yorker*. The stories are arranged in geographic groupings, portraying Americans in Europe, in Manhattan, in their wanderings, and in the Rocky Mountains of Stafford's childhood. In her preface, Stafford pays homage to Mark Twain and Henry James, "who are two of my favorite American writers and to whose dislocation and whose sense of place I feel allied"; her stories blend Twain's sardonic viewpoint with James's gentler dissection of social manners. Stafford, however, stresses the experience of women — mothers, daughters, wives — caught up in the emotionally sterile landscape of postwar America. Throughout, the stories are distinguished by the cool, intelligent precision of her language. Wanda Avila's *Jean Stafford, A Comprehensive Bibliography* (Garland, 1983) lists and annotates Stafford's numerous books, short stories, articles, and book reviews, as well as critical and biographical works about her.

539.   Stimpson, Kate. **Class Notes.** New York: Times Books, 1979; New York: Avon Books, 1980. 225p. pbk. $8.95. LC 78-58172. ISBN 0812907949.

Stimpson, founding editor of the major United States women's studies journal *Signs*, and a moving force in feminist scholarship as a professor, writer, and lecturer, turns her formidable talents to the novel. Hers is a "fable" of coming to womanhood in the fifties. Harriet's epiphany occurs when she realizes that "despite taboos, despite the pain the taboos nurtured, despite the bite of her mind against itself as it sought a reunion with the body, she was happier with women than with men" (p.224).

540.   Sullivan, Ruth, ed. **Fine Lines: The Best of Ms. Fiction.** New York: Scribner, 1981. 271p. $12.95. LC 81-8857. ISBN 0684171430.

Reading these stories is like tracking the second wave of the women's movement from 1971 to 1981. Writers included are Hilma Wolitzer, Jane Shapiro, Doris Lessing, Lynda

Schor, Alice Walker, Joyce Thompson, Meghan B. Collins, Sally Gearhart, Frenchy Hodges, Fanny Howe, Mary Gordon, Margaret Atwood, Mary Heaton Vorse, Ingeborg Bachmann, and Margaret Drabble. They write a range of feminist fictions from futuristic fantasy to fairy tale, from stories about parents to those about lovers. Several of these stories, notably Alice Walker's "Advancing Luna—and Ida B. Wells," explore female friendship.

541.   Tanaka, Yukiko, and Elizabeth Hanson, eds. **This Kind of Woman: Ten Stories by Japanese Women Writers, 1960-1976.** Stanford, CA: Stanford University Press, 1982. 287p. $25.00. LC 81-51332. ISBN 0804711305.

The emergence of recognized women writers who deal with contemporary changes in family life and the diverse roles of women in Japanese society has created new literary trends in Japan. This book's strong introduction should assist Westerners in understanding the complexity of traditional expectations of female passivity and servitude as represented in recent literature. Phyllis Birnbaum's collection *Rabbits, Crabs, Etc.: Stories by Japanese Women* (University of Hawaii Press, 1982) includes some of the same influential contemporary writers—Kōno Taeko and Fumiko Enchi, for example—though Birnbaum chooses to translate different stories from those included in Tanaka and Hanson. Still more stories by twentieth-century Japanese women writers surface in Noriko Mizuta Lippit and Kyoko Iriye Selden's *Stories by Contemporary Japanese Women Writers* (M. E. Sharpe, 1982). The historical introduction in this collection will prove useful to those unfamiliar with the work of Uno Chiyo, Tomioka Taeko, and Takahashi Takako—three of the dozen writers represented.

542.   Tyler, Anne. **Dinner at the Homesick Restaurant.** New York: Knopf; distr. New York: Random House, 1982. 303p. $13.50. LC 81-13694. ISBN 0394523814.

Critics compare Tyler to Southern precursors Flannery O'Connor, Carson McCullers, and Eudora Welty. Like them, she writes fiction of exceptional precision. Her characters are rooted in Southern cities; only the lost migrate north. In *Dinner,* her ninth novel since 1962, Tyler plays with the plight of the deserted mother, left to deal with three children in the post-World War II era of valorized family. Proud and self-sufficient Pearl makes up a story about the absence of her traveling salesman husband and works as a grocery store clerk to support Cody, Ezra, and Jenny. The most calculating and cold child, Cody, remembers Pearl's lack of tenderness with the least mercy, while Ezra, who ultimately shoulders the responsibility for their mother, is least critical. Tyler's novel explores the drama and mystification of remembered childhood, the guilts of remembered motherhood. It is about family friction, but also about working toward family cohesion. In *Morgan's Passing* (Knopf, 1980), seemingly simple snapshots of family life, upon closer look, reveal complex portraits of the beautiful and terrible in ordinary lives lit by the glaring intimacy of marriage and family life. Tyler's most recent novel is *The Accidental Tourist* (Knopf, 1985).

543.   Vivien, Renée, 1877-1909. **The Woman of the Wolf and Other Stories.** New York: Gay Presses of New York, 1983. 122p. pbk. $6.95. LC 83-80806. ISBN 0960472436.

Renée Vivien is the pseudonym of Pauline Mary Tarn, an American expatriate who was a member of Natalie Barney's lesbian coterie in turn-of-the-century Paris. Though prolific, Vivien has been unfamiliar to United States audiences because until recently her works were available only in French. *The Woman of the Wolf* is the first translation of her stories into English. Vivien's persistent irony lends interest to these slight, highly stylized lesbian fairy tales, as she repeatedly inverts traditional expectations: biblical villainesses like Vashti and Lilith become heroines; male narrators unknowingly undercut their own authority; the tale of Prince Charming receives an unexpected lesbian twist. Karla Jay's introduction discusses Vivien's major themes, particularly the importance of bonds between women. These themes are apparent as well in *At the Sweet Hour of Hand in Hand* (Naiad Press, 1979), a volume of lesbian love poetry. Though marred by a sentimentality absent from the stories, the poems are nonetheless of historical interest.

544.   Walker, Alice, 1944- . **The Color Purple.** New York: Harcourt, Brace, Jovanovich, 1982. 245p. $11.95. LC 81-48242. ISBN 0151191530.

Winner of the American Book Award and the Pulitzer Prize, *The Color Purple* blends black, feminist, and lesbian themes. Walker chronicles the struggle of Celie, a poor, nearly illiterate, Southern black woman, to achieve independence and self-respect. Raped by her stepfather and abused by her husband, Celie exists in a state of passive numbness until she meets blues singer Shug Avery. Celie's emotional and sexual relationship with Shug and her bonding with other female characters give her the strength to begin a life of her own. The story is told in a series of letters from Celie to God, and between Celie and her sister Nettie, a missionary in Africa. The epistolary mode allows the reader to observe Celie's growth as her body and spirit are healed. Walker presents a probing and often painful analysis of male-female and black-white relationships; yet she allows her characters the possibility of change, and grants them an almost fairytale happy ending that underscores the redemptive power of love. Many of these same concerns reappear in the thirty-six essays, speeches, and letters of *In Search of Our Mothers' Gardens: Womanist Prose* (Harcourt, Brace, Jovanovich, 1983). To Walker, a "womanist" is a black feminist. Accordingly, the title essay and several others stress the position of the black woman, especially the black woman artist. Walker also discusses the civil rights movement and nuclear warfare; her artistic models (among them Zora Neale Hurston, Jean Toomer, and Flannery O'Connor); and her own experiences as a black woman writer. The anger that surfaces only occasionally in these essays is more apparent in the overtly political short stories of *You Can't Keep a Good Woman Down* (Harcourt, Brace, Jovanovich, 1981), tales of rape, abortion, and male-female estrangement. Walker is also the author of several volumes of poetry, including *Good Night, Willie Lee, I'll See You in the Morning* (Dial Press, 1979) and *Horses Make a Landscape Look More Beautiful* (Harcourt, Brace, Jovanovich, 1984).

545.   Washington, Mary Helen, ed. **Midnight Birds: Stories by Contemporary Black Women Writers.** Garden City, NY: Anchor Press/Doubleday, 1980. 274p. pbk. $4.50. LC 79-7627. ISBN 038514878X.

Ntozake Shange, Toni Cade Bambara, Shirley Anne Williams, Gayle Jones, Alexis Deveaux, Frenchy Hodges, Paulette Childress White, and Alice Walker contribute to the second volume of fiction on diverse themes by black women compiled and introduced by Washington. Washington notes: "In the writing of black men, women are almost always subordinate to men.... The quest of the black man to achieve manhood has always inspired the highest respect, but the equivalent struggle of the black woman has hardly been acknowledged — except by black women writers" (p.xv).

546.   Weldon, Fay. **The Life and Loves of a She-Devil.** New York: Pantheon Books, 1983. 241p. $13.45. LC 84-7070. ISBN 0394539206.

Weldon's ninth novel is an outrageous satire on the modern craze for self-improvement. Ruth is an average, if ugly, housewife in the suburb of Eden Grove. However, after her husband Bobbo deserts her for petite, beautiful romance novelist Mary Fisher, Ruth vows revenge. She dumps her children on the lovers and spends years covertly harassing them, eventually contriving to have Bobbo imprisoned for embezzlement. Meanwhile, Ruth has amassed a fortune and has embarked upon a program of plastic surgery which transforms her into a replica of Mary. In the novel's finale, Ruth achieves a perfect, if horrifying, revenge. This intricately plotted work abounds with Weldon's caustic wit and polished prose. Weldon has also written *Puffball* (Summit Books, 1980), a comedy about marriage, pregnancy, and fidelity; *Watching Me, Watching You* (Summit Books, 1981), eleven short stories and a novella; and *Letters to Alice on First Reading Jane Austen* (Taplinger, 1985), an epistolary novel in which "Aunt Fay" writes to her niece about the life and work of Jane Austen in order to convince her that literature *does* matter.

547. West, Jessamyn, 1907-1984. **The State of Stony Lonesome.** San Diego: Harcourt, Brace, Jovanovich, 1984. 184p. $12.95. LC 84-12882. ISBN 015184903X.

This is the last novel of Jessamyn West, who died in 1984. Though not on a par with some of her earlier frontier books, critics have judged *Stony* to possess much of the familiar West charm and narrative craft. The theme, too, is a recurrent one—a young girl's coming of age. On the eve of her marriage, Ginerva Chalmers and her uncle Zen nostalgically recall in a series of flashbacks the evolution of their relationship, tinged with suppressed eroticism, through Ginerva's growing-up years in California of the 1920s. In *The Life I Really Lived* (Harcourt, Brace, Jovanovich, 1979), West creates the character of Orpha Case, a successful novelist looking back on her past.

548. Wilson, Barbara Ellen, 1950- . **Ambitious Women: A Novel.** Argyle, NY: Spinsters, Ink, 1982; repr. Seattle: Seal Press, 1985. 228p. pbk. $7.95. LC 85-22060. ISBN 0931188369.

Over the last few years, Barbara Wilson has written several works of popular fiction that are not only fun to read but also feature good writing, strong characterization, and thoughtful analyses of the social, moral, and political dilemmas facing feminists. *Ambitious Women* is a novel about three Seattle working women. Allison and Holly, partners in a print shop, and Magda, a writer for a radical newspaper, find their lives drastically altered when Allison is accused of harboring a fugitive terrorist. Wilson devotes one section of the novel to each woman's perspective, exploring how the three confront such issues as running a feminist business, being a single mother, and coming out as a lesbian, as well as judicial inequities, political violence, and violence against women. Wilson's *Murder in the Collective* (Seal Press, 1984) is a delightful whodunit that neatly blends a murder mystery, Filipino politics, details of the printing business, and a lesbian love story. Wilson is also the author of three volumes of short stories, including *Thin Ice* (Seal Press, 1981) and *Walking on the Moon* (Seal Press, 1983).

549. Wilson, Harriet E., 1808-ca.1870. **Our Nig: Or, Sketches From the Life of a Free Black, In a Two-Story White House, North: Showing That Slavery's Shadows Fall Even There.** Edited by Henry Louis Gates. Boston: Geo. C. Rand and Avery, 1859; repr. New York: Vintage Books, 1983. 140p. bibliog. pbk. $10.95. LC 82-49197. ISBN 0394715586.

In his superb introduction, Henry Gates establishes that Harriet E. Adams Wilson stands as "probably the first Afro-American to publish a novel in the United States ... and ... one of the first two black women to publish a novel in any language." Given this distinction, *Our Nig* would seem unlikely to be overlooked as it has been in the black literary tradition. The novel takes up the subjects of miscegenation and of white, Northern racism—both taboo topics in the liberal North of the period, which preferred to focus its righteous attention on the slave-owning South. Careful research into the life of Wilson has proven that the book is largely autobiographical. The tensions between fiction and autobiography, Gates speculates, provide the clue to the suppression of the text. Gates sees Wilson as the inventor of an entirely new form fusing slave narrative with those conventions of the sentimental "women's novel" germane to her project. Frado, an indentured servant living in New England, finds a voice for herself, learns to read, and, hence, creates herself as a *subject. Our Nig* thus represents a major step beyond contemporary representations of blacks in nineteenth-century literature.

550. Wolf, Christa. **A Model Childhood.** New York: Farrar, Straus, Giroux, 1980. 407p. $17.50. LC 80-13601. ISBN 0374211701.

What begins as the novelist's excursion back into her childhood in Nazi Germany, using an autobiographical form, becomes a deconstruction of the process of memory itself. East German novelist Christa Wolf (*Divided Heaven* [1965; repr. Adler's Foreign Books, 1981]; *Quest for Christa T* [1971; repr. Farrar, Straus, Giroux, 1979]; *No Place on Earth* [Farrar, Straus, Giroux, 1982]) has been compared to Virginia Woolf, whose modernist interest in stream of consciousness and memory she emulates. If Christa Wolf's writing is at its core about the artist in search of freedom, novels like *A Model Childhood* and *No Place on Earth* (whose protagonists are male and female early nineteenth-century poets) pose imprisonment as a function of language and gender. Tied as we are to concepts like "model childhood," Wolf's project appears to be the dangerous one of testing the limits of "the prison house of language." In *Cassandra: A Novel and Four Essays* (Farrar, Straus, Giroux, 1984), the title character is also a prisoner: the scorned prophetess of the Trojan War condemned to die for telling the truth. In a stream-of-consciousness portrait of Cassandra's ideas and memories at the moment before her death, Wolf presents the war not as a matter of honor or glory, as it is in Homer's *Iliad,* but as the ignoble outcome of patriarchal greed and arrogance. The novel is accompanied by four essays on Wolf's experiences in modern Greece.

551. Wolff, Cynthia Griffin, ed. **Classic American Women Writers: Sarah Orne Jewett, Kate Chopin, Edith Wharton, Willa Cather.** New York: Octagon, 1980. 406p. bibliog. $23.00. LC 80-81107. ISBN 0374987114.

Wolff's introduction addresses the issue of the restricted canon in American literature, which until the 1960s and 1970s went virtually unnoticed. The work of nineteenth- and early twentieth-century women writers was excluded from anthologies and syllabi or treated condescendingly. Selected short stories by Sarah Orne Jewett, Willa Cather, Kate Chopin, and Edith Wharton are published in this useful anthology that also includes chronologies and bibliographies for each author.

552. Yezierska, Anzia, 1885-1970. **The Open Cage: An Anzia Yezierska Collection.** Selected by Alice Kessler-Harris. New York: Persea Books, 1979. 262p. $12.95. LC 78-61060. ISBN 089255035X.

Yezierska's writings belong to the new realism in literature practiced by immigrant writers of the 1920s. Writes Alice Kessler-Harris, editor of this edition: "She is the precursor of a generation of Jewish immigrants whose written language is English, but who breathed and lived in Yiddish. From a historical perspective, the stories carry us back into the collective experience of a mass migration as it settled into the soul of America" (p.xii). Stories in this volume fall into four thematic categories: Dreams, Struggle, Success, Old Age. "The Fat of the Land," included here, launched Yezierska's modest literary career when it was named the "best story of 1919" after publication in *Century.* Yezierska's daughter, Louise Levitas Henriksen, contributes an illuminating afterword to this edition.

Persea Books has also reissued a 1920 collection of Yezierska's stories, *Hungry Hearts and Other Stories* (1985), adding to it three previously uncollected stories. *Anzia Yezierska,* by Carol B. Schoen (Twayne, 1982), traces American influences on Yezierska's writing (Emerson, Whitman, William James); discusses her relationship with John Dewey, her literary mentor; and critically examines her novels, short stories, and nonfiction.

HISTORY AND CRITICISM

553.   Abel, Elizabeth, ed. **Writing and Sexual Difference.** Chicago: University of Chicago Press, 1982. 315p. bibliog. index. pbk. $8.95. LC 82-11131. ISBN 0226000761.

Growing out of a special issue of the journal *Critical Inquiry,* this volume examines how "gender informs and complicates both the writing and the reading of texts" (p.1). Aside from a study of fiction by Mahasveta Devi, a Bengali writer, Abel's collection stands as a white women's project. Most of the essays are theoretical rather than practical, and many employ a French-inspired critical methodology, as when Mary Jacobus uses Luce Irigaray to read George Eliot. Essays by Elaine Showalter, Susan Gubar, and Judith Kegan Gardiner address general problems of "difference"; those by Margaret Homans, Nina Auerbach, and Catharine Stimpson tackle Wordsworth, Freud, and lesbian novels, respectively, each addressing the ingenious strategies seized upon by women readers and writers to radically subvert male-defined literary forms. The essays in *Gender and Literary Voice* (Holmes and Meier, 1980), edited by Janet Todd, consider the question, "Is there a distinctive female style/tone/content?" (p.1). The contributors, among them Joyce Carol Oates, Marilyn Butler, and Judith Wilt, analyze works ranging from the love poetry of Christine de Pizan to Lisa Alther's *Kinflicks.* In *The Voyage In: Fictions of Female Development* (University Press of New England for Dartmouth College, 1983), Elizabeth Abel has collaborated with Marianne Hirsch and Elizabeth Langland to gather sixteen fine essays viewing the female *Bildungsroman* from a variety of perspectives. The list of fictions analyzed here represents nineteenth- and twentieth-century; American, British, and European; lesbian, male, female, and feminist-created works.

554.*   Ammons, Elizabeth, ed. **Critical Essays on Harriet Beecher Stowe.** Boston: G. K. Hall, 1980. 307p. bibliog. index. $18.50. LC 79-17596. ISBN 0816182604.

Collected in this first volume of criticism on Harriet Beecher Stowe (1811-1896) are chronologically arranged reviews and essays, chiefly on *Uncle Tom's Cabin.* The pieces range from George Sand's sentimental praise to Elizabeth Ammons's critical essay centering on Stowe's moderate feminism. Stowe's championing of the sensational Lord Byron affair has motivated one critic, Alice Crozier, to suggest that "Byron is the single greatest literary and imaginative influence on the writings of Harriet Beecher Stowe, and this despite her very considerable debt to Scott and, somewhat less, to Dickens" (pp.195-196). William Dean Howells, perhaps the most powerful literary figure of her era, remembered Mrs. Stowe as "gracious," as well as "very motherly" and "divinely sincere." Ammons's book, a delight for the literary historiographer, conveniently assembles materials that might otherwise elude Stowe scholars.

555.   Ammons, Elizabeth. **Edith Wharton's Argument With America.** Athens: University of Georgia Press, 1980. 210p. bibliog. index. $17.00. LC 79-48000. ISBN 0820305138.

By placing Wharton's major and minor works of fiction from the 1890s to the 1930s within a sociopolitical context, Ammons demonstrates that they critique those aspects of society that Wharton (1862-1937) believed enslaved women, particularly the ideology of romantic love and marriage. She also discusses Wharton's retreat into a conservative idealization of motherhood after World War I, and her later movement toward a matriarchal religion. Wendy Gimbel's *Edith Wharton* (Praeger, 1984) is a narrower but more detailed study, which focuses a psychoanalytic and feminist lens on Wharton's exploration of women's selfhood in patriarchal society. Combining biographical data with close readings of *The House of Mirth, Ethan Frome, Summer,* and *The Age of Innocence,* Gimbel argues that Wharton moves toward granting her heroines a sense of identity based on "that precarious balance between the needs of the self and those of society" (p.19).

556. Andreas-Salomé, Lou, 1861-1937. **Ibsen's Heroines.** Edited and translated by Siegfried Mandel. Redding Ridge, CT: Black Swan Books, 1985. 155p. $20.00. LC 85-28668. ISBN 0933806280.

A friend and confidante of Friedrich Nietzsche, Rainer Maria Rilke, and Sigmund Freud, Lou Andreas-Salomé was one of the most controversial intellectual women of her time. She knew and understood better than many middle-class women how difficult and dangerous was the path for the woman who sought intellectual and erotic transcendence within the confines of Victorian society. Mandel has produced the first translation of Salomé's portraits of Ibsen's women—Nora, Mrs. Alving, Hedwig, Rebecca, Ellida, and Hedda—accompanied by a biographical essay that contextualizes Salomé's literary life within her time. As the only woman critic of Ibsen's plays when they were actually produced, the revival of her essays signals an important event in Ibsen studies and Victorian studies.

557. Ascher, Carol, 1941- , et al., eds. **Between Women: Biographers, Novelists, Critics, Teachers, and Artists Write About Their Work on Women.** Boston: Beacon Press, 1984. 469p. $29.95. LC 83-70651. ISBN 0807067121.

In eloquent, provocative, and often moving essays, twenty-five women writers, scholars, and artists examine the strong bonds they feel with the women who are their subjects. Each author discusses why she chose her subject, and how her identification with her subject has affected her work and personal life. Sara Ruddick (co-editor of the volume, along with Carol Ascher and Louise DeSalvo) calls her essay "Learning From Virginia Woolf," while Yi-Tsi Mei Feuerwerker's piece on Chinese writer Ding-Ling is subtitled "(In Quest of Myself)." Two common themes emerge from these diverse sketches. First, there is general agreement that rather than distancing herself from her subject, the author should put herself into her writing. Second, these writers view rigid distinctions between fiction and nonfiction as counterproductive; after all, as Alexis Kate Shulman argues, "biography and autobiography are no less fictions than novels are" (p.8). Although *Between Women* could use an illuminating introduction or conclusion to tie the essays together, it offers intriguing insights into how women's creativity is affected by the experience of other women's lives and works.

558. Auerbach, Nina. **Woman and the Demon: The Life of a Victorian Myth.** Cambridge, MA: Harvard University Press, 1982. 255p. bibliog. index. $17.50. LC 82-9298. ISBN 0674954068.

Auerbach subverts the myth of the stunted Victorian stay-at-home to reveal the nineteenth-century woman in a heroic light: "My aim in this book," she writes, "is to become the Frankenstein of this seeming monster, reconstructing her outcast grandeur from paintings, from essays, from the buried structures of literary texts, and from the letters and memoirs that hint at the shapes of past lives" (p.9). Psychoanalysis is

Auerbach's tool; Dante Gabriel Rossetti, Edward Burne-Jones, and their school, her visual texts; and *Trilby, Dracula,* and popular magazines, among her literary sources. She uses these to reveal "the Victorian woman's power ... as central, not marginal" (p.219). Auerbach's bold articulation of the Victorian angel/demon, old maid, and fallen woman myths will change our conception of Victorian womanhood, enabling us to ask important feminist questions about both nineteenth-century and contemporary literature and society. In *Romantic Imprisonment* (Columbia University Press, 1985), Auerbach extends her interest in outcasts to include actresses, orphans, and renegades as well as ordinary women, and provides sympathetic essays on Austen, Dickens, Browning, and Lewis Carroll.

559. Barickman, Richard, et al. **Corrupt Relations: Dickens, Thackeray, Trollope, Collins, and the Victorian Sexual System.** New York: Columbia University Press, 1982. 285p. bibliog. index. $27.50. LC 82-4534. ISBN 0231052588.

Through persuasive readings of fictions by Dickens, Thackeray, Trollope, and Collins, *Corrupt Relations* brings to light ambivalence about feminism expressed in the works of these canonized Victorian male authors. Indeed, Richard Barickman, Susan MacDonald, and Myra Stark argue that "because these authors inherit a dominant rather than a dependent role — both as authors and in their more ordinary social roles — they are driven to explore and expose the abuses of that power to a degree that no woman of the period did" (p.242). In *Dickens and Women* (J. M. Dent, 1983), Michael Slater provides a thorough, intelligent analysis of the personal and cultural anxieties about women that found their way into Dickens's art. Ambivalence is also the focus of Shirley Foster's *Victorian Women's Fiction: Marriage, Freedom, and the Individual* (Barnes and Noble, 1985). In the novels of Dinah Mullock Craik, Charlotte Brontë, Elizabeth Sewell, Elizabeth Gaskell, and George Eliot, Foster finds both a high regard for the ideal of marriage and a condemnation of its often ugly reality for Victorian women. In *Love and the Woman Question in Victorian Literature: The Art of Self-Postponement* (Barnes and Noble, 1983), Kathleen Blake examines the work of Christina Rossetti, George Eliot, Charlotte Brontë, George Gissing, Thomas Hardy, and Olive Schreiner from a feminist perspective.

560. Bataille, Gretchen M., and Kathleen Mullen Sands. **American Indian Women: Telling Their Lives.** Lincoln: University of Nebraska Press, 1984. 209p. bibliog. index. $18.95. LC 83-10234. ISBN 0803211597.

Bataille and Sands trace the evolution of Indian women's autobiography as it has moved from oral to written tradition, commenting on the impact of mediation by recorder-editors on the earlier narratives, and contrasting Indian women's narratives with other forms (e.g., slave narratives). They go on to analyze in greater detail several notable autobiographies: *Papago Woman,* by Marie Chona; *Mountain Wolf Woman; A Pima Past,* by Anna Moore Shaw; *Me and Mine,* by Helen Sekaquaptewa; and *Halfbreed,* by Maria Campbell. A final chapter speculates on future narratives by Indian women. The volume concludes with a fifty-page annotated bibliography of Indian women's autobiography and biography, selected ethnographic and historical studies, contemporary literature and criticism, and additional resources. There is some overlap of coverage with Rayna Green's bibliography (see entry 69), but approach and perspective differ significantly in the two volumes: where Bataille and Sands examine the material primarily for its literary merit, Green is more concerned with evaluating the material's accuracy from an Indian perspective. Researchers will want to work with both books.

561.* Bell, Roseann P., et al. **Sturdy Black Bridges: Visions of Black Women in Literature.** Garden City, NY: Anchor Press/Doubleday, 1979. 422p. bibliog. LC 77-16898. ISBN 0385133472.

The eclecticism of this major anthology, evidenced by its inclusion of black women writers working in many genres and representing several cultures (the United States, Africa, and the Caribbean), recommends it as a reference and teaching tool. Critics comment on specific authors and their works (Ama Ata Aidoo, Phillis Wheatley, Alice Walker, Zora Neal Hurston), while interviews with Toni Cade Bambara, Ann Petry, Toni Morrison, and others yield insights of a personal and reflective sort. The creative segment offers the primary texts: work by twenty-five authors, including Bessie Head, Paule Marshall, Mari Evans, Nikki Giovanni, Sonia Sanchez, Nathaniel Johnson, and Margaret Danner. The bibliographies of specific American, African, and Caribbean writers are selective but strong. Still other bibliographic listings cover the literature from a historical, sociological, and literary perspective up to the mid-1970s. *Conjuring: Black Women, Fiction, and Literary Tradition,* an anthology edited by Marjorie Pryse and Hortense J. Spillers (Indiana University Press, 1985), features criticism on Jessie Redmon Fauset, Ann Petry, Margaret Walker, Paule Marshall, and Toni Cade Bambara, among others. The importance of Mari Evans's *Black Women Writers (1950-1980): A Critical Evaluation* (Anchor Press/Doubleday, 1984) lies more in the treatment of less well-known contemporary writers—Gayl Jones, Alice Childress, and Carolyn Rodgers, for example—than in its essays on those more widely recognized. Several recent studies have focused on individual black women authors, including *Lorraine Hansberry: Art of Thunder, Vision of Light* (1979), a special memorial issue of *Freedomways* edited by Jean Carey Bond; *Lorraine Hansberry* (Twayne, 1984), by Anne Cheney; *Jessie Redmon Fauset* (Whitston, 1981), by Carolyn Wedin Sylvander; and *Gwendolyn Brooks* (Twayne, 1980), by Harry B. Shaw.

562. Bernikow, Louise, 1940- . **Among Women.** New York: Harmony Books, 1980; repr. New York: Harper and Row, 1981. 296p. bibliog. index. pbk. $4.95. LC 79-24733. ISBN 0060908785.

Bernikow looks at women's relationships with and images of each other—as mothers, daughters, sisters, friends, and lovers—in folk and popular culture. She scrutinizes frequently dissected intimacies such as those between Virginia Woolf and Katherine Mansfield, the Brontë sisters, and Sylvia Plath and her mother, as well as analyzing women's ties in folktales such as "Cinderella." Critical response to this work was lukewarm to negative, faulting Bernikow for attempting too much, and for failing to offer persuasive evidence for her arguments.

563. Boumelha, Penny. **Thomas Hardy and Women: Sexual Ideology and Narrative Form.** Sussex: Harvester Press; Totowa, NJ: Barnes and Noble, 1982. 178p. bibliog. index. $28.50. LC 81-22903. ISBN 0389202592.

Tess Durbeyfield, Bathsheba Everdene, Sue Bridehead—Thomas Hardy (1840-1928) has long been associated with his female characters. Yet, as Penny Boumelha points out in her introduction to this intelligent and well-documented study, critics have been divided between those (usually men) who remark on Hardy's unusual understanding of women, and those (usually feminists) who decry his entrapment in conventional notions of woman's role and character. Boumelha examines Hardy's fiction in relation to turn-of-the-century ideologies about sexual difference and the nature of women. She also analyzes Hardy's formal experimentation in relation to aesthetic ideologies of the time—particularly the experimental "New Woman" fiction of women novelists. In close readings of *The Woodlanders, Tess of the d'Urbervilles, The Return of the Native,* and *Jude the Obscure,* Boumelha argues that "the radicalism of Hardy's representation of women resides ... in their resistance to reduction to a single and uniform ideological position" (p.7).

564. Brown, Lloyd Wellesley, 1938- . **Women Writers in Black Africa.** Westport, CT: Greenwood Press, 1981. 204p. bibliog. index. $27.50. LC 80-1710. ISBN 0313225400.

This excellent study presents serious critical analyses of the works of five authors: Bessie Head, Ama Ata Aidoo, Efua Sutherland, Flora Nwapa, and Buchi Emecheta. Brown argues persuasively that the five write from a distinctive "women's perspective," even as they share with male writers such thematic concerns as conflicts between African and Western values, or rural and urban lifestyles, post-colonial changes, and societal upheaval. In *The Sociology of Urban Women's Image in African Literature* (Rowman and Littlefield, 1980), Kenneth L. Little presents a useful overview of the female "types" found in the works of some thirty African authors; but he also advances the dubious hypothesis that these fictional works provide a sociologically accurate portrait of the roles of African women. Complementing Little's study are the eighteen essays in *Ngambika: Studies of Women in African Literature,* edited by Carole Boyce Davies and Anne Adams Graves (Africa World Press, 1986). Treating a variety of works by men and women, the essays examine the "female presence" in African literature. The writers stress a redefinition of women's roles as portrayed in literature, moving from Little's male-centered categories, such as girlfriend or mistress, to women-centered categories such as prophet, heroine, or martyr.

565. Chinoy, Helen Krich, and Linda Walsh Jenkins, eds. **Women in American Theatre: Careers, Images, Movements: An Illustrated Anthology and Sourcebook.** New York: Crown Publishers, 1981. 370p. bibliog. index. $4.95. LC 80-16786. ISBN 051753729X.

This anthology begins by looking beyond conventional theater to events and rites "done primarily for community and family bonding" (p.ix). Essays in this first section discuss the rituals of Native American Indians, the use of ritual in the Woman's Crusade and Women's Trade Union League, and the exploitative rituals of beauty pageants. The next three sections discuss women's contributions to American theater as actresses, playwrights, critics, designers, and producers. Included are both famous women such as Eva Le Gallienne and Lillian Hellman, and women whose achievements are less well known. In the section "Images," essays on melodrama, creative drama, Susan Glaspell's play *Trifles,* and on black women in plays by black playwrights, the focus is on the images of women portrayed on stage. The section titled "Feminist Theatre" includes an interview with playwright Megan Terry, in addition to essays on three feminist theater companies and two feminist plays. The "Sourcebook" provides a list of plays by some seven hundred women, a list of resources for tracking down further information on these plays, and a feminist theaters index. The "References and Resources" section cites books, periodical articles, dissertations, and nonprint works—an excellent starting place for further research.

566. Christ, Carol P. **Diving Deep and Surfacing: Women Writers on Spiritual Quest.** Boston: Beacon Press, 1980. 159p. bibliog. index. pbk. $7.95. LC 79-51153. ISBN 0807063630.

Following an introduction that describes the ways in which stories shape our experience, Christ presents close readings of works by Kate Chopin, Margaret Atwood,

Doris Lessing, Adrienne Rich, and Ntozake Shange, arguing that their protagonists undergo the stages of a woman's spiritual quest — from the sense of nothingness, through mystical identification with nature or other women, to a new naming of self and reality that overcomes traditional dualities. In her final chapter, Christ shows how these same themes appear in other areas of women's culture, including music, art, and ritual. Christ highlights the spiritual dimension of works that usually have been examined only in their social aspects, while further demonstrating their common concerns as women's literature. In *Lilith's Daughters: Women and Religion in Contemporary Fiction* (University of Wisconsin Press, 1982), Barbara Hill Rigney examines revisionist representations of traditional Judeo-Christian archetypes — Christ, Mary, Eve, and the Garden — in thirty novels by fifteen contemporary women authors. Rigney argues that the protagonist in feminist literature moves beyond traditional religion toward existential freedom and responsibility.

567. Christian, Barbara, 1943- . **Black Feminist Criticism: Perspectives on Black Women Writers.** New York: Pergamon Press, 1985. 261p. bibliog. index. $29.95. LC 84-22805. ISBN 0080319564.

This volume collects seventeen of Christian's essays, written between 1975 and 1984. Several essays address broad themes — for example, images of black women in Afro-American literature, black women poets, and the writings of African women. Other pieces analyze and evaluate the works of individual authors such as Audre Lorde, Paule Marshall, Ntozake Shange, Alice Walker, Toni Morrison, Gloria Naylor, and Buchi Emecheta, stressing the themes of selfhood, motherhood, and female relationships. Because it includes essays adapted from a variety of sources, *Black Feminist Criticism* does suffer from repetition, and the volume as a whole goes over ground already covered in Christian's *Black Women Novelists: The Development of a Tradition, 1892-1976* (Greenwood Press, 1980). Nevertheless, it is clear why Christian is one of this country's foremost black feminist critics: she insists not only on placing black women writers within a tradition distinct from either black men or whites, but also on reading literature as a part of its social, economic, and historical context. Several other critics have also published thematic studies of fiction by and about black American women. In *No Crystal Stair* (Pilgrim Press, 1984), Gloria Wade-Gayles looks at such writers as Ann Petry, Dorothy West, Paule Marshall, Toni Morrison, and Alice Walker to illuminate "the impact of racism and sexism on the reality of black women in white America" (p.xxii). Employing a clear theoretical framework and well-defined terms, Wade-Gayles uses history, psychology, and sociology to read literature, and draws on literature to illuminate social reality. She finds in these fictional works four levels of female consciousness: acceptance of traditional roles, hopelessness, challenge, and wholeness. Trudier Harris's *From Mammies to Militants: Domestics in Black American Literature* (Temple University Press, 1982) analyzes the evolving image of the domestic in fiction by black men as well as black women through 1970. Carole McAlpine Watson's *Prologue: The Novels of Black American Women, 1891-1965* (Greenwood Press, 1985) discusses broad characteristics of fiction by black American women, and compares these novels to mainstream American fiction. The strong point of the volume may be its annotated bibliography, which includes fifty-eight novels by black women.

568. Clausen, Jan. **A Movement of Poets: Thoughts on Poetry and Feminism.** Brooklyn, NY: Long Haul Press, 1982. 54p. bibliog. pbk. $3.25. ISBN 0960228411.

A poet herself, in this extended essay Clausen asks searching questions of the feminist movement about its relationship to feminist poetry and poets. According to Clausen, the feminist movement hampers poets by not giving their work serious attention, and by expecting poetry by feminists to be "politically correct" and useful. She reviews the history of feminist poetry and calls for a greater commitment to poetry and for greater intellectual freedom for feminist poets. Clausen has also tried her hand at fiction recently, publishing a collection of short stories, *Mother, Sister, Daughter, Lover* (Crossing Press, 1980), and a novel, *Sinking/Stealing* (Crossing Press, 1985). Both of these works explore the everyday lives of lesbian feminists, with a strong focus on the experience of co-parenting in a lesbian relationship.

569. Conley, Verena Andermatt, 1943- . **Hélène Cixous: Writing the Feminine.** Lincoln: University of Nebraska Press, 1984. 181p. bibliog. index. $16.95. LC 83-23600. ISBN 0803214243.

Cixous is best known to American audiences for her manifesto "The Laugh of the Medusa," which both embodies and calls for a new woman's writing—*l'écriture féminine.* Her belief that social revolution can occur only through a revolution in language has led her to disrupt traditional syntax and play with the linguistic signifier in her works, making them difficult both to comprehend and to translate. Conley examines Cixous's writings chronologically—from her early revolt against the limits of fiction, through the beginnings of her theory of *l'écriture féminine,* to her elaboration of a psychoanalytic basis for that theory—and concludes with a 1982 interview. Throughout, Conley stresses Cixous's belief in the importance of language itself; her attempt to traverse literary boundaries, as she combines theory with poetry; and her desire to "revalorize 'women' who had been repressed and forgotten" in masculine discourse (p.125). In particular, Conley argues, Cixous's career demonstrates a consistent equation of "death with the masculine and life with the feminine" (p.16)—thus Cixous's emphasis is on the stasis, rigidity, linearity, and "lack" in masculine writing, as opposed to the dynamism, freedom, roundness, and "presence" she finds in feminine writing. Conley admirably conveys the joy and vitality of Cixous's writing. Still, although she tries valiantly to clarify Cixous's relationship to such continental theorists as Hegel, Heidegger, Bataille, Freud, Derrida, and Lacan, Conley's language is often as difficult as their own. More seriously, in her attempt to portray Cixous as a "feminist" to American readers, Conley fails to address serious inconsistencies in Cixous's theories (her ambiguous distinction between social and biological gender, for example) and obfuscates Cixous's involvement in controversies among French feminists.

570. Crump, Rebecca W., 1944- . **Charlotte and Emily Brontë: A Reference Guide.** Boston: G. K. Hall. 2v. index. LC 82-1097. Vol. 1: 1982; $29.00; ISBN 0816179530. Vol. 2: 1985; $32.00; ISBN 0816186723.

This promises to be the authoritative bibliography of the two most famous Brontë sisters. Volume I presents a comprehensive annotated list of secondary studies from 1846 to 1915, with an extensive cross-referenced index. When completed, Crump's bibliography will supersede Anne Passel's *Charlotte and Emily Brontë: An Annotated Bibliography* (Garland, 1979). Of the many critical studies of the Brontës, two merit individual mention. In *Emily Brontë* (Blackwell, 1985), James Kavanagh applies Marxist, psychoanalytic, and poststructuralist approaches to *Wuthering Heights*, seeing in it a conflict between patriarchal law and Oedipal desire. John Maynard's *Charlotte Brontë and Sexuality* (Cambridge University Press, 1984) traces Brontë's successful attempt to present a vision of sexual awakening in her novels, a vision that links sexuality with independence and integrity. In *Emily Brontë: The Artist as a Free Woman* (Carcanet, 1983), Stevie

Davies explores the connections between Brontë's life, her poetry, and *Wuthering Heights,* stressing recurrent themes. Davies's book is marred by the lack of an index, a flaw shared by Barbara and Gareth Lloyd Evans's otherwise immensely useful work, *The Scribner Companion to the Brontës* (1982). In a clear, readable format, the authors bring together a wealth of background information on the Brontë family: a chronology of events; character sketches of family members; synopses, commentary, character lists, and glossaries for both the unpublished works of the Brontë children and the published works of Anne, Charlotte, and Emily; excerpts from contemporary reviews; and information on places associated with the Brontës. *The Poems of Charlotte Brontë* (Basil Blackwell, 1984) is a new annotated and enlarged edition of the Shakespeare Head Brontë edited by Brontë scholar Tom Winnifrith.

571. Donovan, Josephine, 1941- . **Sarah Orne Jewett.** New York: Ungar, 1980. 165p. bibliog. index. $12.95. LC 80-5334. ISBN 0804421374.

Donovan's treatment of Jewett (1849-1909) begins with a short biographical portrait of the New England writer who never claimed more for her works than that they were "little sketches." Donovan gives us insight into the material that most interested Jewett—bonding between women; tensions between city and country life; the pull between comic and tragic. Always, according to Donovan, Jewett engaged in "personal advocacy of a kind of individualistic feminism" (p.74). Donovan expands on this theory at length in *New England Local Color Literature: A Women's Tradition* (Ungar, 1983), examining Jewett along with four other writers—Harriet Beecher Stowe, Rose Terry Cook, Elizabeth Stuart Phelps, and Mary E. Wilkins Freeman—and widow Annie Fields, Jewett's lifelong companion. Donovan looks at the achievements of these literary figures, singly, as well as assessing what they, as a group, contributed to women's realism and the female literary tradition. Jewett has begun to receive the attention that critic F. O. Matthiessen and novelist Willa Cather predicted for her during the teens and twenties. In *Critical Essays on Sarah Orne Jewett,* edited by Gwen L. Nagel (G. K. Hall, 1984), both her contemporaries— William Dean Howells and Horace E. Scudder, for example—and present-day scholars praise Jewett's precise craftsmanship. Louis A. Renza uses one of Jewett's stories to engage issues of canon, feminism, and regionalism in literature, in *"A White Heron" and the Question of Minor Literature* (University of Wisconsin Press, 1984).

572. Draine, Betsy, 1945- . **Substance Under Pressure: Artistic Coherence and Evolving Form in the Novels of Doris Lessing.** Madison: University of Wisconsin Press, 1983. 224p. bibliog. index. $20.00. LC 82-70556. ISBN 0299092305.

Draine refuses to judge the novels of Doris Lessing (b.1919) by their ideological content, since, she asserts, "there has been no radical change in her basic themes" over the last thirty years: "Lessing's unchanging subject is itself change—in the individual and the collective consciousness" (p.xiii). Instead, Draine examines the dialectic of evolving form in Lessing's major novels, from the tragedy of *The Grass Is Singing* to the science fiction of *Canopus in Argos,* arguing that Lessing's "moments of artistic triumph are very often moments of upheaval—moments in which the 'perfected' forms are broken by the intrusion of new and unexpected imperatives" (p.xv). Other critics have studied Lessing's work from a number of angles. Roberta Rubenstein, in *The Novelistic Vision of Doris Lessing* (University of Illinois Press, 1979), examines Lessing's understanding of the nature of consciousness, emphasizing her use of symbolism and Sufi mysticism. The eight contributors to *Notebooks, Memoirs, Archives: Reading and Rereading Doris Lessing,* edited by Jenny Taylor (Routledge and Kegan Paul, 1982), work within a feminist framework and stress Lessing's involvement in British intellectual and political life. Lorna Sage, in *Doris Lessing* (Methuen, 1983), finds the colonial experience central to Lessing's identity as a writer. Dee Seligman's *Doris Lessing: An Annotated Bibliography of Criticism* (Greenwood Press, 1981) provides a complete annotated listing of primary and secondary material up to 1978.

573. DuPlessis, Rachel Blau. **Writing Beyond the Ending: Narrative Strategies of Twentieth-Century Women Writers.** Bloomington: Indiana University Press, 1985. 253p. bibliog. index. $27.50. LC 83-49512. ISBN 0253367050.

DuPlessis presents a challenging analysis of how twentieth-century women writers have revised the conventions of romance fiction. The traditional romance plot ends with the heroine's personal and social success (marriage) or failure (death); in either case, heterosexuality, sexual hierarchies, and female domesticity are reaffirmed. DuPlessis blends feminist, Marxist, and psychoanalytic theory as she examines the writings of a variety of British, American, and Canadian women – among them, Olive Schreiner, H. D., Virginia Woolf, Zora Neale Hurston, and Adrienne Rich. She elucidates the ways in which these authors have written "beyond the ending" of romance in their works, including nonerotic relationships among characters, women's quest plots, female *Künstslerromanes,* revisionary mythopoesis, speculative fiction, and the use of a collective protagonist. In *Women Writing in America: Voices in Collage* (University Press of New England, 1984), Blanche H. Gelfant also looks at how twentieth-century women writers have sought alternatives to dominant literary forms. As her title suggests, Gelfant celebrates diversity, evident in her choice of subjects, who include Meridel LeSueur, Jean Stafford, Grace Paley, Willa Cather, and Margaret Mitchell.

574. Eagleton, Terry, 1943- . **The Rape of Clarissa: Writing, Sexuality, and Class Struggle in Samuel Richardson.** Minneapolis: University of Minnesota Press, 1982. 109p. bibliog. index. $25.00. LC 82-243008. ISBN 0816612048.

Eagleton looks at Samuel Richardson's eighteenth-century masterpiece, *Clarissa*, from structuralist, feminist/psychoanalytic, and Marxist perspectives. He argues that "the genuinely subversive effects of *Clarissa* ... far exceed its author's intentions" (p.ix). In particular, Clarissa's death reveals the patriarchal complicity of interest between her bourgeois family and the aristocratic Lovelace. Other scholars have presented similar rereadings of Richardson, stressing the ways in which eighteenth-century sexual, religious, economic, and political conflicts converge on the battleground of Clarissa's body; among them are Terry Castle, in *Clarissa's Ciphers: Meaning and Disruption in Richardson's "Clarissa"* (Cornell University Press, 1982), and Rita Goldberg, in *Sex and Enlightenment: Women in Richardson and Diderot* (Cambridge University Press, 1984). Other feminist critics have begun to explore the rise of the novel in the eighteenth century. In *Women, Letters, and the Novel* (AMS Press, 1980), Ruth Perry argues that eighteenth-century women's preoccupation with romantic love, apparent in the popularity of the sentimental novel, resulted from their political and economic disempowerment in the new market economy. Janet Todd, in *Women's Friendship in Literature* (Columbia University Press, 1980), explores the conflict between marriage and female friendship in French and English novels from Richardson to Austen.

575. Elbert, Sarah. **A Hunger for Home: Louisa May Alcott and Little Women.** Philadelphia: Temple University Press, 1984. 278p. bibliog. index. $24.95. LC 83-4824. ISBN 0877223173.

This intelligent biography places Alcott within the traditions of nineteenth-century feminism and social reform to provide enlightening analyses of her life and writings. Elbert traces the events of Alcott's childhood – the disastrous failure of her father Bronson's communal experiment at Fruitlands, dreary poverty, the constant moves from house to house—that led to her passion for domesticity. Yet Elbert also highlights Alcott's desire for individuality and achievement. Resolved to supplant her improvident father as the family breadwinner, she never married, instead becoming a best-selling writer who campaigned for social reforms and served as a volunteer nurse during the Civil War. Elbert argues that Alcott's inner conflicts reverberate throughout her writings, especially *Little Women:* "It was precisely her ability to communicate this tension between domesticity and feminism that explains her enduring popularity as a writer for women" (p.3). In *The Alcotts* (C. N. Potter; distr. Crown, 1980), Madelon Bedell focuses on the contrast between Bronson Alcott's brilliant, idealistic impracticality and his wife Abby May's domestic capability and intelligent, committed social activism. Alma J. Payne's *Louisa May Alcott, A Reference Guide* (G. K. Hall, 1980) surveys the critical reaction to Alcott's work from 1854 to 1980, while *Critical Essays on Louisa May Alcott* (G. K. Hall, 1984), edited by Madeleine B. Stern, provides excerpts of selected reviews and essays—by authors ranging from Alcott's contemporary, Henry James, to present-day feminist critic Judith Fetterley.

576. Ferguson, Marjorie. **Forever Feminine: Women's Magazines and the Cult of Femininity.** Brookfield, CT: Gower, 1983. 243p. bibliog. index. $15.00. LC 83-149. ISBN 0435823019.

Using three British magazines as case studies, with comparisons to such U.S. publications as *Cosmopolitan, Ms.,* and *Good Housekeeping,* Ferguson explores how women's magazines have both reflected and reinforced stereotyped female roles. She concludes that although the surface message has changed to include independence and has broadened female roles, this medium continues to define women as women, separate from but in relation to men, and in need of suggested norms for behavior. *The Soap Opera* (Sage Publications, 1983) studies another mass medium aimed largely at women. Authors Muriel G. Cantor and Suzanne Pingree examine the soaps thoroughly, from definition and history to content, audience demographics, and effects on behavior.

577. Ferlazzo, Paul J., ed. **Critical Essays on Emily Dickinson.** Boston: G. K. Hall, 1984. 243p. bibliog. index. $32.50. LC 83-18635. ISBN 0816184631.

Scholarship on Dickinson is developing into a small industry. Ferlazzo's collection contains appraisals of Dickinson by diverse critics: William D. Howells writes of her poetry from the perspective of a male critic in the early 1890s; Allen Tate evaluates her in the 1950s from the standpoint of a poet and New Critic; Adrienne Rich writes in the mid-1970s from still another slant—that of a feminist and woman poet. *Feminist Critics Read Emily Dickinson,* edited by Suzanne Juhasz (Indiana University Press, 1983), includes, among others, essays by such major Dickinson critics as Sandra Gilbert, Barbara Antonina Clarke Mossberg, Joanne Feit Diehl, and Margaret Homans. Juhasz presents an extensive feminist analysis of Dickinson's celebrated "withdrawal" in *The Undiscovered Continent: Emily Dickinson and the Space of the Mind* (Indiana University Press, 1983). In her controversial study *Dickinson, The Anxiety of Gender* (Cornell University Press, 1984), Vivian Pollack combines biography and criticism, arguing that Dickinson's verse of victimization is the literary symptom of her "crisis of sexual identity." In *The Only Kangaroo Among the Beauty: Emily Dickinson and America* (Johns Hopkins University Press, 1979), Karl Keller contextualizes Dickinson in the social, intellectual, and cultural movements of her period. David T. Porter in *Dickinson, The Modern Idiom* (Harvard University Press, 1981) claims Dickinson for modernism and post-modernism, following a trend in recent literary criticism that has artfully done the same for Emerson, Thoreau, and other nineteenth-century writers. Other studies of Dickinson are *Lyric Time: Dickinson and the Limits of*

Genre (Johns Hopkins University Press, 1979), by Sharon Cameron; *Dickinson and the Romantic Imagination* (Princeton University Press, 1981), by Joanne Feit Diehl; *Emily Dickinson: When a Writer Is a Daughter* (Indiana University Press, 1982), by Barbara Antonina Clarke Mossberg; and *Emily Dickinson: A Voice of War* (Yale University Press, 1984), by Shira Wolosky. Joseph Duchac's *The Poems of Emily Dickinson: An Annotated Guide to Commentary Published in English, 1890-1977* (G. K. Hall, 1979) remains important as a historical guide to criticism and commentaries—textual, interpretive, and biographical.

578.* Fleischmann, Fritz, 1950- , ed. **American Novelists Revisited: Essays in Feminist Criticism.** Boston: G. K. Hall, 1982. 419p. bibliog. LC 82-6097. ISBN 0816190455.

The purpose of this volume, according to editor Fritz Fleischmann, is to present "a coherent rethinking of American literary history" (p.2) by examining eighteen major American novelists—thirteen men and five women—from a feminist perspective. Many of the essays, which look at writers from the eighteenth century to World War II, are fairly conventional (albeit well-executed) studies of how women are portrayed in each author's fiction; but a few writers push their analyses further—for example, Nina Baym in a piece on Nathaniel Hawthorne, and Rolande Ballorain on Mark Twain. Other recent works that present feminist perspectives on the largely male American fictional canon include Joyce W. Warren's *The American Narcissus: Individualism and Women in Nineteenth-Century American Fiction* (Rutgers University Press, 1984), which examines Cooper, Emerson, Thoreau, Melville, Twain, and James; and Peter Schwenger's *Phallic Critiques: Masculinity and Twentieth-Century Literature* (Routledge and Kegan Paul, 1984), which includes discussions of Hemingway, Mailer, and Roth. The two male authors who have received the most attention from feminist critics, however, are not American at all—James Joyce and D. H. Lawrence. *Women in Joyce*, a collection of essays edited by Suzette Henke and Elaine Unkeless (University of Illinois Press, 1982), is complemented by Bonnie Kime Scott's *Joyce and Feminism* (Indiana University Press, 1984). Lawrence's views on women are the subject of Hilary Simpson's *D. H. Lawrence and Feminism* (Northern Illinois University Press, 1982) and Judith Ruderman's *D. H. Lawrence and the Devouring Mother* (Duke University Press, 1984).

579. Franklin, Benjamin, 1939- , and Duane Schneider. **Anaïs Nin: An Introduction.** Athens: Ohio University Press, 1979. 309p. bibliog. index. $20.00. LC 79-10635. ISBN 0821403958.

Franklin and Schneider argue that "Nin was too long neglected, and she has been praised to excess recently for the wrong reasons. Her greatest value is as a legitimate cicerone through the female psyche" (p.294). This comprehensive introduction examines Nin's fiction and criticism as well as her famous *Diary.* The authors conclude that Nin's novels, which the public rejected, represent an ambitious attempt to portray the psychological complexity of female characters. The *Diary,* while it "simulates sincerity and authenticity" (p.292), presents a stylized portrait of Nin's persona, who functions as its main character. Still, the *Diary* is "frequently as engaging in its intensity and richness as the fiction is not" (p.293). In *Anaïs Nin* (Twayne, 1984), Nancy Scholar looks at Nin's entire corpus, but concentrates on the *Diary,* both as an art form in itself and as the genesis of the fiction. Since 1982, Harcourt, Brace, Jovanovich has published volumes 2-4 of Nin's *Early Diary,* covering the years 1920-1931.

580. Garner, Shirley Nelson, 1935- , et al., eds. **The (M)other Tongue: Essays in Feminist Psychoanalytic Interpretation.** Ithaca, NY: Cornell University Press, 1985. 388p. bibliog. $39.50. LC 84-17560. ISBN 0801416930.

As editors Shirley Nelson Garner, Claire Kahane, and Madelon Sprengnether note in their excellent introduction, current feminists approach Freud "less as the founder of a science that provides a key to psychic mysteries than as a theorist of the imagination engaged in a lifelong study of the relationships among psyche, language, and symbol" (p.15). At the same time, however, feminists recognize "the fault lines in his representation of femininity" (p.17). Focusing on the role of the mother in the Oedipal and pre-Oedipal stages, the contributors to this volume — among them, Jane Gallop, Annette Kolodny, and Susan Rubin Suleiman — examine points of conflict and consensus between psychoanalysis and feminism. Four essays confront Freud directly; five provide feminist psychoanalytic readings of literary classics by male authors; and seven scrutinize texts by such female authors as George Sand, Doris Lessing, and Virginia Woolf. The volume provides a provocative introduction to feminist and psychoanalytic approaches to literary theory and literary texts.

581. Gilbert, Sandra M., and Susan Gubar, 1944- , eds. **Shakespeare's Sisters: Feminist Essays on Women Poets.** Bloomington: Indiana University Press, 1979. 337p. bibliog. $25.00. LC 78-9510. ISBN 0253112583.

In their introduction, Gilbert and Gubar state that the purpose of this volume is to "revise our inherited notion of literary history" by tracing the "outlines of a distinctively female poetic tradition" (p.xxiv), and by examining the achievements of women poets "in relation to all those patriarchal social strictures, all those obstacles that discourage women from attempting the pen" (pp.xv-xvi). To that end, nineteen outstanding essays by feminist critics analyze the work of fifteen women poets: Jane Lead, Anne Bradstreet, and the Countess of Winchelsea from the seventeenth and eighteenth centuries; Emily Brontë, Elizabeth Barrett Browning, Christina Rossetti, and Emily Dickinson from the nineteenth century; and Edna St. Vincent Millay, H.D., May Swenson, Gwendolyn Brooks, Sylvia Plath, Denise Levertov, Adrienne Rich, and Muriel Rukeyser from the twentieth century. There are also general essays on the forms of women's poetry and the tradition of Afro-American women poets. Although *Shakespeare's Sisters* doesn't clearly identify what is distinctively "female" about women's poetry, it does point to the existence of a matrilineal succession of poets.

582. Gould, Jean, 1909- . **American Women Poets: Pioneers of Modern Poetry.** New York: Dodd, Mead, 1980. 322p. bibliog. index. $14.95. LC 79-25670. ISBN 0396078281.

Jean Gould's twofold purpose is "to show not only the important role played by outstanding women in the evolution of modern poetry, but also to give a sense of the struggle waged by these women for equality of treatment in the arts" (p.xiii). Some of her figures — e.g., Emily Dickinson, Amy Lowell, H.D., and Gertrude Stein — have been the focus of so many scholars that Gould is pressed to produce new material on them. Her volume nonetheless serves as a handy and readable introductory source on these poets, as well as on Amy Lowell, Sara Teasdale, Elinor Wylie, Marianne Moore, Edna St. Vincent Millay, Louise Bogan, and Babette Deutsch. In a similar work, *Modern American Women Poets* (Dodd, Mead, 1984), Gould uses the interview technique to explore the lives and work of most of the outstanding women poets of our times: Muriel Rukeyser, Denise Levertov, Elizabeth Bishop, Mary Swenson, Jean Garrigue, Sylvia Plath, Anne Sexton, Maxine Kumin, Gwendolyn Brooks, Adrienne Rich, Ruth Whitman, Jean Burden, Isabella Gardner, Audre Lorde, Marge Piercy, Freya Manfred, Carol Muske, and Nikki Giovanni.

583.   Greene, Gayle, 1943- , and Coppélia Kahn, eds. **Making a Difference: Feminist Literary Criticism.** New York: Methuen, 1985. 273p. bibliog. index. $22.00. LC 85-11427. ISBN 0416374700.

The nine essays in this superb collection provide a clear overview of the theories, methodologies, trends, and disputes in contemporary feminist criticism. In their introduction, Greene and Kahn describe the complementary efforts of feminist scholarship in anthropology, history, and literature. The remaining essays look specifically at feminist literary criticism. Sydney Janet Kaplan surveys attempts to delineate a women's literary tradition, and discusses the debate between Annette Kolodny's "playful pluralism" and Elaine Showalter's monolithic "gynocritics." Nelly Furman illustrates how differing modes of feminist criticism relate patriarchal culture to language. Ann Rosalind Jones elucidates the theories of leading French feminists. Judith Kegan Gardiner discusses the relationship between feminism and psychoanalysis. Cora Kaplan looks at the split between liberal and socialist feminists. Bonnie Zimmerman considers the achievements, problems, and future of lesbian criticism. Susan Willis demonstrates the possibilities of feminist criticism of works by black women writers. And Adrienne Munich calls for serious feminist study of male-authored works. Each essay includes a lengthy bibliography. The trends discussed in Greene and Kahn's volume are evident in several collections of feminist criticism. *Women Writing and Writing About Women* (Croom Helm/Barnes and Noble, 1979), edited by Mary Jacobus, gathers essays on nineteenth- and twentieth-century fiction, poetry, and film, by such critics as Showalter, Kaplan, and Gillian Beer. *Be Good, Sweet Maid* (Holmes and Meier, 1981), edited by Janet Todd, brings together selections from eight years of the journal *Women and Literature,* covering the romantic, Victorian, modern, and contemporary periods. *Theory and Practice of Feminist Literary Criticism* (Bilingual Press, 1982), edited by Gabriela Mora and Karen S. Van Hooft, divides its eighteen essays into three groups: theoretical approaches; critical applications to works by women; and critical applications to works by men. Most of the authors discussed are Spanish or Spanish-American, and five of the essays are written in Spanish, one in French.

584.   Halperin, John, 1941- . **The Life of Jane Austen.** Baltimore, MD: Johns Hopkins University Press, 1984. 399p. bibliog. index. $25.00. LC 84-9741. ISBN 0801823358.

Halperin assesses Austen (1775-1817) as "a tough-minded woman, who did not bend or bow easily under affliction" (p.350). She died of consumption at an early age, after a career of enormous literary productivity. In their grief over her death, Halperin claims, the family mystified Austen's life, practically ignoring the fact of her literary career and sanctifying her in saccharine eulogies. Halperin's biography, the first on Austen for over half a century, is important as a revisionist portrait of Austen. But readers who expect Halperin to arrive at feminist insights may be disappointed by some of his pronouncements about Austen's deviation from the eighteenth-century role of the family woman. Luckily, Susan Morgan, though not a biographer, acts as a corrective to some of Halperin's unfortunate moments. Of the extensive critical literature around, her book *In the Meantime: Character and Perception in Jane Austen's Fiction* (University of Chicago Press, 1980) is highly regarded by scholars, as is Julia Prewitt Brown's *Jane Austen's Novels* (Harvard University Press, 1979). Janet Todd's edited volume of essays, *Jane Austen: New Perspectives* (Holmes and Meier, 1983), assembles the work of major Austen critics: Margaret Kirkham, David Spring, Jane Nardin, Nina Auerbach, David Monaghan, and Avrom Fleishman, to name a few. David Gilson's widely praised *A Bibliography of Jane Austen* (Oxford University Press, 1982) remains the standard bibliography, listing criticism and biography from 1813 to 1978. Look to Gilson for editions of Austen's works, and to Barry Roth's *An Annotated Bibliography of Jane Austen Studies* (University Press of Virginia, 1985) for over one thousand references to criticism appearing between 1973 and 1983.

585. Hannay, Margaret P., ed. **As Her Whimsey Took Her: Critical Essays on the Work of Dorothy L. Sayers.** Kent, OH: Kent State University Press, 1979. 301p. bibliog. index. $20.00. LC 79-10933. ISBN 0873382277.

In this group of essays about her work, it becomes clear that Sayers (1893-1957), known to the world at large as a mystery writer, pursued her other specialties — fiction, translation, drama, and philosophy — with ardor. Indeed, the particular virtue of this volume lies in the attention it gives to Sayers's diverse intellectual projects. P. D. James writes in her foreword to James Brabazon's biography *Dorothy L. Sayers* (Scribner, 1981) that Sayers might have been disappointed to learn that her reputation as a scholar has been dwarfed by her fame as the creator of the detective Lord Peter Wimsey. Brabazon struggles to bring Sayers into clear focus, but despite his speculations about her unacknowledged illegitimate son, her personal life remains an enigma. Several smaller, useful studies of Sayers exist: Mary Brian Durkin's *Dorothy L. Sayers* (Twayne, 1980); Dawson Gaillard's identically titled critical assessment of the detective fiction (Ungar, 1981); and Nancy Tischler's *Dorothy L. Sayers: A Pilgrim Soul* (John Knox Press, 1980), a study that seriously considers the problems Sayers faced as a woman writer and intellectual. Ruth Tanis Youngberg's *Dorothy L. Sayers: A Reference Guide* (G. K. Hall, 1982) provides annotations for many additional works about her.

586. Hartman, Joan E., and Ellen Messer-Davidow, eds. **Women in Print.** New York: Modern Language Association of America, 1982. 2v. bibliog. LC 82-3596. Vol. 1: $22.50; ISBN 0873523369. Vol. 2: $22.50; ISBN 0873523385.

The MLA's Commission on the Status of Women in the Profession sponsored these two volumes. The first assesses areas ripe for feminist research in language and literature, offering eleven pieces that "fall into three categories: fundamental tasks of scholarship — bibliography, archival research, and linguistic analysis; women's literature of special concern to feminists — lesbian, black, and working-class; and national literatures — German, Russian, Hispanic, French, and British" (p.3). The second volume presents twelve viewpoints on "Establishment Publishing" and four on "Alternative Publishing," covering such subjects as university presses, publishing abroad, reprints, textbooks, anonymous manuscript reviewing, and feminist journals and book publishers.

587. Heilbrun, Carolyn G., 1926- , and Margaret R. Higonnet, eds. **The Representation of Women in Fiction.** Baltimore: Johns Hopkins University Press, 1983. 190p. bibliog. pbk. $6.95. LC 82-12685. ISBN 0801829291.

The provocative essays in this volume testify to the diversity and sophistication of feminist criticism. Three are based on the thematic/contextual tradition of Anglo-American feminist criticism: Susan Gubar's piece on the influence of ideologies of motherhood, childbirth, and fertility on women writers; Jane Marcus's critique of patriarchy in Virginia Woolf's works; and Mary Poovey's study of Jane Austen's *Persuasion*. The other three essays use the language and analytical techniques of French structuralism and poststructuralism. Elizabeth Ermath argues that women in fiction challenge the social consensus, thus catalyzing plot; J. Hillis Miller uses George Meredith's Clara Middleton as an example of the fragmentation of a female character; and Nancy K. Miller gives George Sand's *Valentine* a critical reading in order to define the "female plot." In *The Fallen Angel* (Bowling Green State University Popular Press, 1981), Sally Mitchell analyzes Victorian attitudes toward women by examining the image of the unchaste woman in British fiction from 1835 to 1880. Sheila Delaney's *Writing Woman* (Schocken Books, 1983) is a fascinating scholarly study of women as characters in, and writers of, fiction, ranging from Chaucer's Wife of Bath to Marge Piercy.

588. Henderson, Katherine Usher. **Joan Didion.** New York: Ungar, 1981. 164p. bibliog. index. $13.95. LC 80-53705. ISBN 0804423709.

Didion (b.1934) was one of the fifties' "silent generation" of students who observed rather than protested war and social injustice. This generation equated protest with an inability to face up to what Didion termed the "meaninglessness which was man's fate" (p.7). Henderson outlines Didion's most important concerns as humanism, self-discovery, and honesty. Didion writes about modernity's empty materialism, the family in flux, and the meaninglessness of movements towards social and economic progress, according to Henderson's analysis of *Slouching Towards Bethlehem* (1968), *Play It As It Lays* (1970), *A Book of Common Prayer* (1977), and *The White Album* (1979). Didion's later books — *Salvador* (Simon and Schuster, 1982), a nonfiction account of a two-week trip to El Salvador rendered in meticulous, flat, journalistic prose, and *Democracy* (Simon and Schuster, 1984), a novel — indicate a movement toward more politicized material. *Democracy*'s journalistic narrative traces the subordinated, empty life of Inez, who serves as hostess, fundraiser, tireless campaigner, and photo-opportunity — all for the career of her senator husband. As Inez moves away from her husband's life into another world of helping refugees in Kuala Lampur, something like a vision of hope and meaning creeps into Didion's world view. Other recent critical studies include *Joan Didion: Essays and Conversations* (Ontario Review Press, 1984), edited by Ellen G. Friedman, and Mark Royden Winchell's *Joan Didion* (Twayne, 1980).

589. Hickok, Kathleen. **Representations of Women: Nineteenth-Century British Women's Poetry.** Westport, CT: Greenwood Press, 1984. 277p. bibliog. index. $29.95. LC 83-13029. ISBN 0313238375.

Hickok explores images of women not only in the work of nineteenth-century Britain's three major women poets — Emily Brontë, Elizabeth Barrett Browning, and Christina Rossetti — but also in the poetry of some thirty-five minor women writers. Hickok analyzes how these authors portray women in the roles of daughter, wife, mother, fallen woman, spinster, working woman, or "new woman," showing the most popular poets to be fairly conservative, and guilty of stereotyping. Still, she argues, "a cautious tradition of subtle protest" (p.8) did emerge. Although Hickok's findings are unsurprising, this comprehensive study lays the groundwork for future research. The book includes a biography of each minor poet and an excellent selected bibliography.

590. Holledge, Julie. **Innocent Flowers: Women in the Edwardian Theatre.** London: Virago Press, 1981. 218p. bibliog. index. pbk. $7.95. LC 81-139074. ISBN 0860680711.

Women's theater in the Edwardian period — 1908 through the 1920s — is the worthy project Holledge takes on. First, she writes a social history of prominent actresses — Ellen Terry, Mrs. Stirling, Jane Crow, and others — largely from their interviews and autobiographies. Because actresses had no union and often no theatrical reputation when they entered the profession, they were frequently unable to support themselves. Unmarried actresses often found that the public treated them with disrespect; husbands of married actresses seldom respected their careers; divorced actresses became social pariahs. Some actresses became feminists. In the second part of her book, Holledge introduces the Actresses' Franchise League and its primary movers. Founded in 1908, the AFL "succeeded in breaking down the delineation between amateur and professional theatre" (p.72) and eased the way for suffragists to present plays at fairs and other suffrage gatherings. The third part of Holledge's work focuses on Edith Craig's important role as a director of the Pioneer Players. The illegitimate daughter of Ellen Terry, Edy was born into a theater tradition. In the final segment of the book, three texts of AFL Edwardian plays are reproduced: "Jim's Leg," by L. S. Phibbs (1911); "Mrs. Appleyard's Awakening," by Evelyn Glover (1913); and "10 Clowning Street," by Joan Dugdale (1913). Each of these propaganda plays thematizes the suffrage issue.

591. Homans, Margaret, 1952- . **Women Writers and Poetic Identity: Dorothy Wordsworth, Emily Brontë, and Emily Dickinson.** Princeton, NJ: Princeton University Press, 1980. 260p. bibliog. index. $26.50. LC 80-7527. ISBN 0691064407.

"How does the consciousness of being a woman affect the workings of the poetic imagination?," asks Homans at the outset of this pathbreaking work of criticism. Reacting against those critics (Hélène Cixous, for one) who celebrate the essential "feminine," Homans maintains that "usage and context create symbols" (p.4). While gender definitions are never static, they nevertheless are reified by transmitted cultural beliefs and codified into language. Homans reads Dorothy Wordsworth's, Emily Brontë's, and Emily Dickinson's works as texts, "while at the same time finding a language for evaluating the literary effects of the author's femininity" (p.9). In her treatment of Dickinson, for example, Homans argues that the poet thought of herself first and foremost as a woman writer—a subversive rhetorician whose language inverts or eliminates masculine dominance. One of the more innovative feminist literary critics, Homans writes carefully—but her thesis could elude those unfamiliar with recent literary theory.

592. Jardine, Lisa. **Still Harping on Daughters: Women and Drama in the Age of Shakespeare.** Sussex, England: Harvester Press; Totowa, NJ: Barnes and Noble, 1983. 202p. bibliog. index. $28.50. LC 83-3888. ISBN 0389203874.

Traditional Shakespeare criticism has viewed the Renaissance as a time of great advances for women, and early feminist critics agreed that Shakespeare's women characters were representations of female power. Recent feminist Shakespeareans, however, have disputed both notions. Lisa Jardine examines the ideological context of Shakespeare's plays, demonstrating that the attitude of his audience toward women was ambivalent at best. Working from a variety of perspectives—historical, psychoanalytic, and New Critical—the seventeen essays in *The Woman's Part: Feminist Criticism of Shakespeare* (University of Illinois Press, 1980), edited by Carolyn Lenz, Gayle Greene, and Carol Thomas Neely, explore Shakespeare's relation to the patriarchal order: the extent to which his plays depict patriarchal structures; the relation between his male and female characters; stereotypes about his women characters; the relationship between gender and genre; and his division of experience into male and female spheres. The last two points have received full-length studies of their own. In *Comic Women, Tragic Men* (Stanford University Press, 1982), Linda Bamber asserts that Shakespeare's comedies portray women as powerful and nurturing, while in the tragedies they are absent or destroyed. Marilyn French, in her deliberately polemical work *Shakespeare's Division of Experience* (Summit Books, 1981), claims that Shakespeare's drama reflects the cultural polarization of experience into masculine and feminine principles. She argues that while the later plays show a movement toward appreciation of feminine qualities, Shakespeare retained his fundamental belief in masculine superiority. Coppélia Kahn's *Man's Estate* (University of California Press, 1981) is a psychoanalytic examination of male identity in Shakespeare's drama.

593.* Jelinek, Estelle C., ed. **Women's Autobiography: Essays in Criticism.** Bloomington: Indiana University Press, 1980. 274p. bibliog. LC 79-2600. ISBN 0253191939.

This collection of essays is important to feminist studies for its range of critical theory on women's autobiography, an area too long neglected. Jelinek suggests that the literary criteria applied to male autobiography—"orderliness, wholeness, or a harmonious shaping" of events—are "often not applicable to women's autobiographies" (p.19). The volume includes essays on English and Afro-American autobiography, general theoretical articles on the autobiographical form, and analyses of specific autobiographers: Gertrude Stein, Lillian Hellman, Elizabeth Cady Stanton, Harriet Martineau, Anaïs Nin, Maya Angelou, and Maxine Hong Kingston. Among the stronger essays in this volume are: Annette Kolodny's close reading of Kate Millett's *Flying*, and Patricia Meyer Spacks' essay on the autobiographical self. The gap between "the personal and the public" (p.ix), between the female self and the language within which it is inscribed, is the focus of *The Female Autograph* (New York Literary Forum, 1984), edited by Domna C. Stanton. The volume's contributors—among them Catharine R. Stimpson, Sandra Gilbert, and Susan Gubar—examine the practical and theoretical issues raised by the works of a wide range of female autobiographers, including Margery Kemp, women writers of Japan's Heian period, Artemisia Gentileschi, and Eva Perón. Julia Kristeva contributes her own autobiographical text. *Women's Personal Narratives: Essays in Criticism and Pedagogy,* edited by Leonore Hoffmann and Margo Culley (Modern Language Association of America, 1985), looks at diaries, letters, and oral testimonies by women. The essays are grouped into three sections: overviews of the issues involved in using nontraditional literature in the classroom; analyses of specific works; and suggested techniques for teaching women's autobiography.

594. Kamuf, Peggy, 1947- . **Fictions of Feminine Desire: Disclosures of Heloise.** Lincoln: University of Nebraska Press, 1982. 170p. bibliog. index. $15.95. LC 81-10290. ISBN 0803227051.

Kamuf examines writings "which stage the confrontation of a specific and active woman's desire with a social or symbolic order that represents no place for such a desire" (pp.xviii-xix). Kamuf begins with the letters of Heloise and Abelard, written in the twelfth century and published in the seventeenth. In them, she argues, Heloise struggles to articulate her erotic experience, while Abelard tries to reinscribe her passion in terms of Christian symbolism. Kamuf then moves on to seventeenth- and eighteenth-century texts— *The Portuguese Letters,* Mme. de Lafayette's *La Princesse de Clèves,* Rousseau's *Julie,* and Choderlos de Laclos's *Les Liaisons Dangereuses*—that show a similar strategy of arresting female desire. Blending psychoanalytic, feminist, and poststructuralist theory, Kamuf brilliantly demonstrates ways in which these works "appropriate and disguise the force of a woman's passion" (p.xvi) and "enclose women with their desire" (p.xvii).

595. Kelley, Mary, 1943- . **Private Woman, Public Stage: Literary Domesticity in Nineteenth-Century America.** New York: Oxford University Press, 1984. 409p. bibliog. index. $24.95. LC 83-17325. ISBN 0195033515.

Kelley's scholarly, provocative study draws on letters, journals, memoirs, economic history, publishing history, and literary criticism in examining the careers of twelve immensely popular nineteenth-century women novelists, among them Catharine Sedgwick, Sara Parton ("Fanny Fern"), and Harriet Beecher Stowe. Kelley argues persuasively that the same economic and social revolutions that created opportunities for women novelists in this period also created an ideology that belittled their accomplishments. Ten of the twelve writers profiled here used authorial pseudonyms; several pleaded economic hardship as their sole motive in writing; most trivialized their own artistic talent. All were what Kelley calls "literary domestics": they defended the "cult of true womanhood" in their fiction, even as they subverted it in their careers. A differing view of literary domesticity is provided by historian Mary P. Ryan in *The Empire of the Mother* (Haworth Press, 1982). Arguing that feminist historians have exaggerated the discontent felt by nineteenth-century women toward their gender role, Ryan uses popular novels to prove that women viewed the domestic role as bringing personal satisfaction and social respect. Ryan's earlier, prize-winning study, *Cradle of the Middle Class: The Family in Oneida County, New York, 1790-1865* (Cambridge University Press, 1981), depicts the historical relationship between the rise of domesticity, the emergence of the urban industrial family, and early revival and reform movements in the nineteenth century.

596. Kertesz, Louise, 1939- . **The Poetic Vision of Muriel Rukeyser.** Baton Rouge: Louisiana State University Press, 1980. 412p. bibliog. index. $35.00. LC 79-1131. ISBN 080710552X.

In this defensive literary study of Rukeyser (b.1913) that follows closely upon the publication of *The Collected Poems* (McGraw-Hill, 1978), the poet is evoked as "a woman Whitman." Kertesz asserts that Rukeyser has received short shrift from the literary establishment because "she didn't fit into critics' notions of what poetry should be, what poetry by a woman should be" (p.43). Her politics were misinterpreted, according to Kertesz, who examines Rukeyser's work and critical reaction to it in scrupulous detail, beginning with her first book, *Theory of Flight,* for which she won the Yale Series of Younger Poets award in 1935.

597. Keyssar, Helene. **Feminist Theatre: An Introduction to Plays of Contemporary British and American Women.** New York: Grove Press, 1985. 223p. bibliog. index. pbk. $7.95. LC 85-70226. ISBN 0394546318.

Keyssar's readable study is the best of the few published works on feminist theater. Keyssar sees "significant stage roles for women, a concern with gender roles in society, exploration of the texture of women's worlds and an urge towards the politicisation of sexuality" as the "essential characteristics" of feminist drama (p.xi). In contrast to conventional drama, feminist drama is more interested in the metamorphosis of contexts, actions, and characters than in the revelation of a fixed reality; Keyssar locates the immediate roots of feminist drama in the women's movement and the "new theatre" of the 1960s, and presents a history of twentieth-century plays by women. She then looks at the lives and careers of specific women playwrights (only some of whom define themselves as feminist). These include Megan Terry—one of the first American feminist playwrights; Caryl Churchill, Pam Gems, and Ntozake Shange—three of the most successful writers using experimental forms; Wendy Wasserstein, Beth Henley, and Marsha Norman—successful playwrights working in more conventional forms; and Myrna Lamb, Maureen Duffy, Maria Irene Fornes, and others currently working in regional and feminist theaters. Keyssar concludes that "feminist *scripts* are more subversive than the productions in ... large, commercial theatres" (p.148), and that most hit shows are on relatively safe terrain. She ends with a look at plays by collective and ensemble theaters, gay dramas, and feminist dramas by men. Not as well written as Keyssar's work, Elizabeth J. Natalle's *Feminist Theatre* (Scarecrow Press, 1985) explores the persuasive rhetoric of feminist theater to determine if it reflects the "radical ideology" of the women's movement. In *Feminist*

Drama: Definition & Critical Analysis (Scarecrow Press, 1979), Janet Brown uses Burkean theory to analyze five plays and the work of feminist theater groups. Although difficult to read and simplistic in its definition of feminist theater, Brown's work is notable for being the first full-length study in the field.

598. Lauter, Paul, ed. **Reconstructing American Literature: Courses, Syllabi, Issues.** Old Westbury, NY: Feminist Press, 1983. 249p. bibliog. pbk. $10.95. LC 83-20730. ISBN 0935312145.

A 1981 survey of college-level American literature courses found that of the thirty-seven writers most commonly included on syllabi, three (Wharton, Dickinson, Chopin) were white women, one (Ralph Ellison) was a black male — and the rest were white men. According to editor Paul Lauter, the purpose of this volume is to provide "practical assistance to the instructor interested in changing his or her teaching of American literature" (p.xi) — the instructor who would like to teach the works of Richard Wright, Mary Wilkins Freeman, or Zora Neale Hurston as well as those of Hawthorne, James, or Faulkner. The book thus becomes a tool in a larger effort to change "the definition of what we call American culture" (p.xi). It contains sixty-seven syllabi, plus paper assignments and bibliographies. The syllabi are drawn from introductory, period, genre, and thematic courses. Lauter's introduction discusses practical problems (mostly the availability of texts) as well as aesthetic issues involved in challenging the academic canon.

599. Leavitt, Dinah Luise. **Feminist Theatre Groups.** Jefferson, NC: McFarland, 1980. 153p. bibliog. index. $15.95. LC 80-10602. ISBN 0899500056.

Leavitt focuses on differences between feminist theater and establishment theater, the political theater of the 1930s, and the black theater movement; origins and current directions of feminist theater; and its impact on audiences, mainstream playwrights, and mainstream theaters. She examines many definitions of the words *feminist, feminist art, political,* and *theater* in the process of defining feminist theater. Feminist theater, in her view, is based on the assumption that all art is political and that personal experience belongs in the realm of art. In addition, feminist theater explores consciousness-raising and the possibilities of change for women, and provides opportunities for women to work in drama. Leavitt goes on to describe the structure, purpose, self-definition, works, reception, and problems of the Alive and Trucking Theatre Company, the Lavender Cellar Theatre, Circle of the Witch, and At the Foot of the Mountain, and then compares and contrasts the four Minneapolis groups.

600. Le Guin, Ursula K., 1929- . **The Language of the Night: Essays on Fantasy and Science Fiction.** Edited by Susan Wood. Hastings-on-Hudson, NY: Ultramarine, 1979. 270p. bibliog. $12.50. LC 78-24350. ISBN 0399123253.

In addition to being a prolific writer of fantasy fiction, Le Guin has contributed much to the critical literature on the genre. Most of the pieces here were written or delivered as speeches during the 1970s; others were first published as introductions to her own fiction. The writings speak to Le Guin's interest in finding new ways to express social and sexual relationships, in exploring the political aspects of aesthetics, and in reading and understanding the work of Eastern European writers. The bibliographic checklist by Jeff Levin included in this volume brings the reader up to 1978. Elizabeth Cummins Cogell's more recent bibliography, *Ursula K. Le Guin: A Primary and Secondary Bibliography* (G. K. Hall, 1983), includes over one thousand items. Still other secondary sources on Le Guin are the Twayne series' *Ursula K. Le Guin,* by Charlotte Spivack (1984); Joseph D. Olander and Martin Harry Greenberg's edited collection, *Ursula K. Le Guin* (Taplinger,

1979), which is not particularly illuminating for a feminst analysis; *Ursula K. Le Guin*, by Barbara J. Bucknall (Ungar, 1981), with readings of several of the novels and a useful chronology; and *Approaches to the Fiction of Ursula K. Le Guin* (UMI Research Press, 1984), by James Warren Bittner, an analysis of Le Guin's dominant themes. In *Ursula K. Le Guin: Voyager to Inner Lands and to Outer Space* (Kennikat Press, 1979), the essay by the book's editor, Joe De Bolt, is particularly worth reading for its discussion of the division between private and public that Le Guin has established in her life.

601. Lidoff, Joan. **Christina Stead.** New York: Ungar, 1982. 255p. bibliog. index. $15.50. LC 82-40283. ISBN 0804425205.

This volume is only the second full-length study of the work of Christina Stead (b.1902). Lidoff begins with a brief biography, presents extensive analyses of Stead's best-known works, and provides brief discussions of her other fiction. Lidoff also includes the text of an interview with Stead, a chronology, and a useful bibliography. She concludes that although "objective, ruthless, wholly unsentimental in her analysis of the human condition, Stead is not despairing"; instead, Lidoff argues, Stead "accepts a great variety of human idiosyncrasy — and delights in it," thus mitigating "the force of her dark vision of human nature" (p.129). Stead's literary reputation has been growing since the 1970s, evidenced by Virago Press' republication of two of her novels, *A Little Tea, A Little Chat* (1946; repr. 1981) and *The Beauties and Furies* (1936; repr. 1982).

602. Malpede, Karen, ed. **Women in Theatre: Compassion & Hope.** New York: Limelight Editions, 1985. 281p. bibliog. index. pbk. $9.95. LC 84-26138. ISBN 0879100354.

This anthology presents excerpts from many out-of-print and previously unpublished works by mostly well known women involved in the theater from the early nineteenth century to the present: among them, Ellen Terry, Eva Le Gallienne, Emma Goldman, Isadora Duncan, Katherine Dunham, Susan Glaspell, Hallie Flanagan, and Judith Malina. In her introduction, Malpede traces the roots of theater to ancient rites of worship in which women played a major role. She sees women's disappearance from the rituals, and the development of two separate forms of drama, tragedy and comedy, as supporting the developing patriarchal order. Although not all of the women in this collection discuss the relationship of gender to their art, Malpede believes they all contribute to the search for the roots of women's creativity. The selections range from Fanny Kemble's journal entries discussing the expression of real emotion on the stage; to Rosamond Gilder's biography of Hrotsvitha, "the first woman playwright"; to an interview with Barbara Ann Teer, founder and director of the National Black Theatre. Malpede provides biographical introductions for the excerpts, which are arranged by area: actors, critics, dancers, playwrights, and producers and directors. The book concludes with essays by Malpede and others on feminist theater.

603. Mann, Jessica. **Deadlier Than the Male: Why Are Respectable English Women So Good at Murder?** New York: Macmillan, 1981. 256p. bibliog. index. $12.95. LC 81-3760. ISBN 0025794604.

Readers looking for a source on English detective-story writers — Agatha Christie, Dorothy L. Sayers, Margery Allingham, Josephine Tey, and Ngaio Marsh — will find Mann a competent one. Mann identifies some of the ideological constraints placed on both detective writers and their heroines, specifically the necessity for a woman detective to appear "feminine" and to "reflect the prejudices and aspirations of the reader" (p.93) in order to gain a mass market. Mann's book, though somewhat crotchety, raises interesting questions about the genre. Earl F. Bargainnier's *10 Women of Mystery* (Bowling Green State University Popular Press, 1981) provides introductions to many of Mann's subjects. *The Web She Weaves: An Anthology of Mystery and Suspense Stories by Women,* edited by Marcia Muller and Bill Pronzini (Morrow, 1983), brings together the likes of Edith Wharton, Katherine Mansfield, Edna St. Vincent Millay, Dorothy Sayers, Agatha Christie, Joyce Carol Oates, and P. D. James.

604. Marks, Elaine, and Isabelle de Courtivron, eds. **New French Feminisms: An Anthology.** Amherst: University of Massachusetts Press, 1980. 279p. bibliog. index. $13.95. LC 79-4698. ISBN 0870232800.

This important volume encompasses over fifty selections by contemporary French feminists, among them such figures as Simone de Beauvoir, Hélène Cixous, Luce Irigaray, Marguerite Duras, Catherine Clément, Julia Kristeva, and Monique Wittig. The editors' introduction summarizes the history of feminism, antifeminism, and intellectualism in France. The volume opens with an excerpt from Beauvoir's *The Second Sex*; her concept of woman as the "Other" who is defined by a male subject provides the topic for debate in the other selections. Should women strive for an entirely new language that will allow them to become the subjects—rather than the objects—of discourse, as some writers, like Irigaray, propose? Or is feminism primarily a social and political movement, as others, like Clément, argue? Although the selections do touch on some issues familiar to U.S. feminists, such as pornography and abortion, the emphasis here is on language. Readers unfamiliar with Lacanian psychoanalysis and semiotic theory may find some of the essays opaque.

605. Martin, Wendy. **An American Triptych: Anne Bradstreet, Emily Dickinson, Adrienne Rich.** Chapel Hill: University of North Carolina Press, 1984. 272p. bibliog. index. pbk. $7.95. LC 83-6864. ISBN 0807841129.

Martin explores the lives and works of three quite different women poets to demonstrate "the evolution of female culture from Puritans to the present" (p.3). Combining biography with cultural history and literary criticism, Martin argues that Bradstreet, Dickinson, and Rich were all profoundly influenced by the Puritan tradition, though their responses to it have differed greatly, ranging from grudging acceptance (Bradstreet), to passive resistance (Dickinson), to open confrontation (Rich). More importantly, Martin asserts, their poetry creates an "alternative vision" to the prevailing ethos, one that is "grounded in the reality of their daily lives" (p.3). Based on "reverence for life," their female vision "radically challenges patriarchal ideology and politics" (p.6).

606. McClave, Heather, ed. **Women Writers of the Short Story: A Collection of Critical Essays.** Englewood Cliffs, NJ: Prentice-Hall, 1980. 171p. bibliog. $12.95. LC 79-22917. ISBN 0139624155.

Some of the twelve essays in this volume are dated; and editor Heather McClave seems more comfortable with traditional genre criticism than with the current feminist attempt to identify "a distinctive female sensibility" (p.3) in women's writing. Nevertheless, this is a significant volume both for the importance of the six authors it treats and for the prominence of its contributors. It includes essays on Willa Cather by Lionel Trilling and Katherine Anne Porter; on Sarah Orne Jewett by Warner Berthoff; on Porter by Eudora Welty and Robert Penn Warren; on Welty by Warren and Alun R. Jones; and on Flannery O'Connor by Thomas Meron, Robert Fitzgerald, Sister M. Bernetta Quinn, and Joyce Carol Oates.

607. Meyer, Doris, and Margarite Fernández Olmos, eds. **Contemporary Women Authors of Latin America: Introductory Essays.** Brooklyn, NY: Brooklyn College Press, 1983. 101p. bibliog. $9.50. LC 82-46046. ISBN 0930888200.

The writings of Spanish and Latin American women have only recently begun to receive serious critical attention. In this companion volume to their translations of Latin American women authors (see entry 656), editors Meyer and Olmos bring together seven studies by North American scholars of the writings of over a dozen contemporary Latin American women, along with "testimonial" essays by three women writers. The essays range from single-author analyses, such as Helen M. Anderson's "Rosa Castellanos and the Structures of Power," to broader studies of several writers, such as Gloria Feinman Waldman's "Affirmation and Resistance: Women Poets from the Caribbean." Though not comprehensive in scope, this volume does serve as an introduction to the study of Hispanic women writers. A more comprehensive but less detailed work is Lucía Fox-Luckert's *Women Novelists in Spain and Spanish America* (Scarecrow Press, 1979). Fox-Luckert presents a biography of, and analyzes one novel by, each of twenty-two women novelists from 1639 to the present, concentrating on how each author treats such issues as family, social class, and sexuality. In *Women in Colonial Spanish American Literature* (Greenwood Press, 1983), Julie Greer Johnson analyzes images of women in works written in Spanish between 1492 and 1800 by male colonial historians, poets, satirists, and dramatists, and compares them to the few works written by women during the same period.

608. Miller, Beth, ed. **Women in Hispanic Literature: Icons and Fallen Idols.** Berkeley: University of California Press, 1983. 373p. bibliog. index. $9.95. LC 81-14663. ISBN 0520043677.

In selecting the seventeen essays in this collection, editor Beth Miller aimed not at comprehensiveness, but at diversity—of time period (from the eleventh century to the 1970s); of place (Spain, Mexico, Chile, Argentina); and of genre (from medieval exempla to contemporary film). In her introduction, Miller argues that a feminist approach to Hispanic literature is long overdue, and outlines some of the important, and hitherto unasked, theoretical questions that need exploration. The essays themselves provide solid analyses of female characters in such standard works as Lorca's drama; examine the writings of well-known women like Ana María Matute and Gabriela Mistral; and bring to light neglected writers like Sara de Etcheverts and Gertrudis Gómez de Avallaneda. However, most of the essays don't live up to the theoretical concerns of Miller's introduction; even in Hispanic literature, the approaches taken here are hardly innovative in 1983.

609. Moi, Toril. **Sexual/Textual Politics: Feminist Literary Theory.** New York: Methuen, 1985. 206p. bibliog. index. $25.00. LC 85-11428. ISBN 0416353606.

In this short, brilliant study, Moi provides a concise introduction to Anglo-American and French feminist literary theory. She is critical of the major figures of Anglo-American theory—among them, Kate Millett, Ellen Moers, Elaine Showalter, Sandra Gilbert and Susan Gubar, and Annette Kolodny—arguing that their underlying assumption of a unified authorial "self," and of a text that can represent that self, reveals their affiliation with the theories and practices of "traditional humanist and patriarchal criticism" (p.87). Moi prefers the theoretical paradigms of the French feminists—Hélène Cixous, Luce Irigaray, and Julia Kristeva—who reject this metaphysical essentialism and argue that the "self" is constructed in and by language. Moi does, however, fault these French critics for ignoring how history, ideology, race, and class shape women's lives. For the reader bewildered by the multiplicity of current feminist theories, Moi's clear-sighted analysis of ideological underpinnings is essential reading.

610. Morley, Patricia A. **Margaret Laurence.** Boston: Twayne, 1981. 171p. bibliog. index. $14.50. LC 80-27501. ISBN 080576433X.

A reporter, literary critic, fiction writer, and essayist, Laurence (b.1926) is best known for five novels set in Africa, and especially for a five-novel cycle on the mythical Canadian prairie town of Manawaka. In both the African and Canadian novels, Laurence explores the dispossession and alienation that make up the psychology of colonialism. Morley concentrates on the social, political, and religious views of a writer who believes "the artist is necessarily *engagé*" (p.39). From her early anti-imperialist works to her later, more complex novels, Laurence's twin themes, "the search for freedom and the struggle for human communication," emphasize the relationship between the individual and the community (p.146). Morley includes a chronology of Laurence's life and writings, along with primary and secondary bibliographies. *A Place to Stand On,* edited by George Woodcock (NeWest Press, 1983), includes essays on Laurence by such well-known Canadian writers and critics as Margaret Atwood, George Bowering, and Marian Engel, as well as six essays by Laurence herself.

611. Newton, Judith Lowder. **Women, Power, and Subversion: Social Strategies in British Fiction, 1778-1860.** Athens: University of Georgia Press, 1981. 202p. bibliog. index. $17.00. LC 81-1068. ISBN 0820305642.

In this intelligent, closely argued study, Newton examines the ways in which four British novels—Fanny Burney's *Evelina,* Jane Austen's *Pride and Prejudice,* Charlotte Brontë's *Villette,* and George Eliot's *The Mill on the Floss*—covertly resist power inequities between men and women. Newton begins by arguing that the decrease in women's material power caused by the Industrial Revolution led to a compensatory ideology of women's "influence" in nineteenth-century England. Her chronological analyses of the novels document their growing rage against this ideology, culminating in Eliot's *The Mill on the Floss*; yet with this increased resistance came increased tension, ambivalence, and artistic confusion in the works. Newton argues for the social and artistic value of such fictional resistance, however covert, as "a form of struggle—and a form of power" (p.22). She depicts these four novels as moving from a protest against women's lot to an indictment of British society as a whole. Conversely in *Protest and Reform: The British Social Narrative by Women, 1827-1867* (University of Wisconsin Press, 1985), Joseph A. Kestner argues that fiction by women on the "Condition-of-England-Question" developed from an exploration of the economic and class inequities of industrialism to an examination of women's role in society. The twenty-three essays in *Fetter'd or Free? British Women Novelists, 1670-1815,* edited by Mary Anne Schofield and Cecilia Macheski (Ohio University Press, 1986), also look at politics, ideology, and subversion in British women's fiction.

612. Nussbaum, Felicity A. **The Brink of All We Hate: English Satires on Women, 1660-1750.** Lexington: University Press of Kentucky, 1984. 192p. bibliog. index. $20.00. LC 83-10181. ISBN 0813114985.

Feminist scholarship is belatedly making its way into eighteenth-century poetry criticism. Both Felicity Nussbaum, in *The Brink of All We Hate,* and Ellen Pollak, in *The Poetics of Sexual Myth* (University of Chicago Press, 1985), study the misogynist verse of the Age of Reason. Nussbaum confines herself to fairly conventional, albeit interesting, examination of the misogynist literary tradition as it appears in the works of such writers as Rochester, Butler, Addison, Steele, Swift, and Pope. Pollak, on the other hand, insists on the cultural context of literary art. Using the language and methods of contemporary theorists like Hélène Cixous and Roland Barthes, she examines Swift and Pope in terms of their "shared identity as writers inescapably committed to a common social text" (p.181).

613. Olauson, Judith. **The American Woman Playwright: A View of Criticism and Characterization.** Troy, NY: Whitston, 1981. 182p. bibliog. $12.50. LC 80-51605. ISBN 087875198X.

In what is unfortunately the only full-length study of American women playwrights to date, Olauson examines plays that had a run of at least thirty consecutive performances, either on- or off-Broadway, some of which have won the Pulitzer Prize. Olauson organizes her book by decades (1930-1970); in each chapter she gives brief plot synopses of a number of plays with, in some instances, short summaries or reviews. What analysis there is adds little to the simple plot descriptions. Her strongest conclusion—that women characters changed from "simple, passive women ... to complicated, active women who attempted ... to think and act on their own" (p.180)—is not borne out by her own plot summaries. While it is certainly true that change has occurred in the situation of women playwrights and in the characters they present, Olauson's poorly organized and generalized study does not provide the data or the analysis needed to accurately assess these changes.

614. Ostriker, Alicia. **Writing Like a Woman.** Ann Arbor: University of Michigan Press, 1983. 147p. bibliog. pbk. $8.95. LC 82-21959. ISBN 0472063472.

An admirable poet—her *A Woman Under the Surface* (Princeton University Press) appeared in 1982—Ostriker has shaped a formidable body of critical work on women poets as well. Collected in *Writing Like a Woman,* her essays take on the question of why fear governs women's poetry: Why does Walt Whitman write "I celebrate myself" while Emily Dickinson states "I'm nobody ... are you a nobody too?" Of her exploration of the work of H. D., Sylvia Plath, Anne Sexton, May Swenson, and Adrienne Rich, Ostriker writes "I have tried to understand what is unique in each writer ... I have tried to suggest the pain and fear confronted by each, the risks taken, the phases of her development" (p.5). During the process of working out what gendered writing might be, Ostriker defines "genderlessness" as "something like bisexual or androgynous or omnisexual, containing rather than excluding the two (or four or six) sexes latent in writers and readers" (p.147). Ostriker argues that great writers "are always approaching genderlessness" because all of their experience is subsumed in their art.

615. Pearson, Carol, 1944- , and Katherine Pope, 1939- . **The Female Hero in American and British Literature.** New York: Bowker, 1981. 314p. bibliog. index. $29.95. LC 81-10939. ISBN 0835214028.

Focusing on a large number of works—mostly novels, from Samuel Richardson's *Clarissa* to Margaret Atwood's *Surfacing*—Pearson and Pope describe the journey of the female hero, who refuses to support the patriarchal status quo by playing the part of a damsel in distress. Part I explains why the female hero has suffered literary and cultural neglect; Part II outlines the hero's psychological journey, as she slays inner dragons to achieve self-realization; Part III describes the transformed hero's return home, where she must slay the external dragons of patriarchal society. Other critics have taken a variety of approaches to the female hero. In *The Heroine's Text* (Columbia University Press, 1980), Nancy K. Miller uses the theories and vocabulary of French feminism to analyze a "grammar of possibilities" for the heroines of eighteenth-century French and English novels, and argues that the heroine's options—marriage or ruin—remain surprisingly consistent well into the twentieth-century. Rachel M. Brownstein, in *Becoming a Heroine* (Viking Press, 1982), interweaves critical analyses of nineteenth- and twentieth-century novels with an account of her own reactions to them as a young reader. While Brownstein's conclusion—that the traditional marriage plot ultimately perpetuates "a seductive reactionary dream" (p.296) in female readers—has provoked controversy, her use of a personal voice and her emphasis on how art affects life are significant. *A Portrait of the Artist as a Young Woman* (Ungar, 1983), by Linda M. Huf, examines six female *Künstlerromane* to delineate the distinctive qualities of the writer-heroine. In *Psyche as Hero* (Wesleyan University Press, 1984), Lee R. Edwards utilizes the myth of Psyche as a paradigm in her study of female heroes in seventeen English and American novels. Unlike Miller, Edwards sees an expansion in the heroine's possibilities, from Richardson's Clarissa, who is constrained within a plot that resists social reform, to Maxine Hong Kingston's woman warrior, who invokes a female deity to create a new social order.

616. Prenshaw, Peggy Whitman, ed. **Women Writers of the Contemporary South.** Jackson: University Press of Mississippi, 1984. 323p. bibliog. $20.00. LC 84-5165. ISBN 0878052224.

This uneven but very useful collection of essays examines the lives and works of seventeen Southern women who have published fiction since 1945. They include well-known figures like Alice Walker, Rita Mae Brown, Anne Tyler, and Elizabeth Spencer, as well as lesser-known writers like Bobbie Ann Mason, Beverly Lowry, and Mary Lee Settle. The essays range from general biographical treatments or overviews of major works to specific theme studies. A photograph and biographical data are provided for each writer, along with a checklist of her work and of secondary sources. In the final essay, Daphne Athas attempts to define what is characteristic of the writing of Southern women. In *Tomorrow Is Another Day: The Woman Writer in the South, 1859-1936* (Louisiana State University Press, 1981), Anne Goodwyn Jones examines the impact of the ideal of genteel Southern womanhood on seven white women writers, including Ellen Glasgow, Kate Chopin, and Margaret Mitchell. This ideal, Jones argues, "not only often conflicted with their actual human needs but also contained its own internal ambiguities and contradictions," exhorting "both intelligence and submission, both bravery and fragility" (p.xii).

617. Radway, Janice A., 1949- . **Reading the Romance: Women, Patriarchy, And Popular Literature.** Chapel Hill: University of North Carolina Press, 1984. 274p. bibliog. index. $25.00. LC 83-23596. ISBN 080781590X.

As feminism has opened up new possibilities for American women, the readership of romance novels has paradoxically skyrocketed. Of several feminist scholars who have tried to explain this apparent contradiction, Janice Radway is the only one who has asked the readers themselves. Radway interviewed forty-two dedicated romance readers from the Midwestern town of Smithton. She finds that these women are not simply unquestioning consumers of popular culture; rather, her readers choose works in which the male character is revealed to be gentle and nurturing at heart, and reject those works whose explicit sexuality emphasizes the hero's masculinity and the heroine's female dependence. Nevertheless, Radway concludes, "romances may still function as active agents in the maintenance of the ideological status quo by virtue of their hybrid status as realistic novels and mythic ritual" (p.17). Several other scholars have studied romance reading as a response to anxiety about gender roles within a patriarchal society. In *Loving With a*

Vengeance: Mass-Produced Fantasies for Women (Archon Books, 1982), Tania Modleski applies current psychoanalytic, feminist, and film theory to romance in order to define "a psychology of the interaction between feminine readers and texts" (p.31). Modleski argues that even mass-produced works "contain elements of protest and resistance underneath highly 'orthodox' plots" (p.25). Harlequin romances celebrate the heroine's dependence while serving as revenge fantasies against omnipotent men; gothic novels embody women's fear of victimization; and soap operas provide a surrogate family for the female viewer to mother, along with a villainess who provides an outlet for her anger. Kay Mussell, in *Fantasy and Reconciliation: Contemporary Formulas of Women's Romance Fiction* (Greenwood Press, 1984), argues, somewhat like Modleski, that romances offer readers both an escape from, and an affirmation of, patriarchal values; Mussell stresses, however, that romances do grant heroic stature to domestic values. Finally, Sally Allen McNall, in *Who Is in the House?* (Elsevier North Holland, 1981), provides a chronological overview of popular fiction for women in the United States from the eighteenth century to the present, using Freudian and Jungian concepts to analyze the heroine's relationships.

618.   Rice, Thomas Jackson. **Virginia Woolf: A Guide to Research.** New York: Garland, 1984. 258p. bibliog. index. $43.00. LC 83-48264. ISBN 0824090845.
Virginia Woolf scholarship has mushroomed in the last five years, commensurate with the growth of Woolf's reputation as a feminist and modernist. Rice's outstanding bibliography lists and annotates primary and secondary works from the 1920s to 1983. Rice is exhaustive in his coverage of books, dissertations, and foreign-language scholarship, and selective with periodical articles. The primary section covers Woolf's major works, editions and selections, letters, and concordances. The secondary section is divided into sixteen categories: bibliographies; biographical materials; critical books; critical articles; and criticism on Woolf's nine novels, short fiction, essays, and miscellaneous writings. The bibliography's four indexes, helpful annotations, and numerous cross-references make it indispensable to the student attempting to negotiate the maze of Woolf scholarship. Still, Rice's organization of the secondary works by format rather than by critical approach does obscure recent trends in Woolf studies, two of which deserve mention. The first is the recovery of unpublished or neglected writings by Woolf—her letters and diary, notebooks, early drafts of her fiction, and manuscripts—all of which have spurred discussion on her process of composition. There also has been a shift in critics' attention away from *Mrs. Dalloway* and *To the Lighthouse* to Woolf's essays and later works like *The Years* and *Between the Acts.* This shift is due in part to the recent reappraisal of the literary status of letters and biography—traditionally women's genres—and is related to the second trend in Woolf criticism: the application of feminist theory to her life and works. Two useful introductions to such criticism are *New Feminist Essays on Virginia Woolf* (University of Nebraska Press, 1981) and *Virginia Woolf: A Feminist Slant* (University of Nebraska Press, 1983), both edited by Jane Marcus. These collections apply historical, technical, mythological, and sociological approaches to shed new light on Woolf's individual works and on her identity as a woman writer, lesbian, and pacifist.

619.   Robinson, William Henry, 1922- . **Phillis Wheatley and Her Writings.** New York: Garland, 1984. 464p. bibliog. index. $61.00. LC 82-21027. ISBN 0824093461.
Robinson has brought together the most complete collection to date of Wheatley's writings: over eighty poems and their variants, and thirty-five prose pieces. Along with these primary works, Robinson provides a lengthy biography and a critical analysis of Wheatley's poems. Robinson attacks the view that Wheatley (1753-1784) was a mediocre neo-classical imitator of Alexander Pope, of historical interest only because she managed

to write even as an African-born slave in eighteenth-century Boston. Instead, he asserts, Wheatley was "more subtle, more intellectually substantive ... [and] more the original poet than has been recognized" (p.126). Robinson also edited *Critical Essays on Phillis Wheatley* (G. K. Hall, 1982)—which includes comments by the poet's contemporaries, reprinted essays, and five challenging original essays—and *Phillis Wheatley: A Bio-Bibliography* (G. K. Hall, 1981), the first comprehensive annotated bibliography of American and European references to Wheatley's life and works.

620. Russ, Joanna, 1937- . **How to Suppress Women's Writing.** Austin: University of Texas Press, 1983. 159p. bibliog. index. pbk. $7.95. LC 83-5910. ISBN 0292724454.

Joanna Russ is known as an original feminist theorist (see entry 433) and a Nebula Award-winning science fiction writer. Her recent SF titles include *The Zanibar Cat* (Arkham House, 1983) and *Extra (Ordinary) People* (St. Martin's Press, 1984). In this slim treatise, however, she wears the garb of the literary critic. Drawing on her wide-ranging knowledge of women's literary output in English over several centuries, Russ identifies and refutes patterns of misogynistic criticism. Among her numerous examples of critical "bad faith" are the denigration of women authors as mere regionalists or genre writers; the false categorization of women writers as sad spinsters, tragic suicides, and the like; and the dismissal of the artist or her work as anomalous or abnormal. This last ploy serves to devalue even those few women admitted to the established canon, such as Emily Dickinson, and to undermine the notion of a female literary tradition. Russ writes with imagination and verve, spicing her analysis with quotations from contemporary feminist writers and critics and with insights gained from teaching women's literature. Lynne Spender's *Intruders on the Rights of Men: Women's Unpublished Heritage* (Pandora Press, 1983), while less brilliantly styled, is a natural companion volume. Spender zeroes in on the sexual politics of publishing, documenting the male stake in "gatekeeping" to maintain the cultural status quo and to deny women the power of the printed word.

621. Sánchez, Marta Ester. **Contemporary Chicana Poetry: A Critical Approach to an Emerging Literature.** Berkeley: University of California Press, 1985. 377p. bibliog. index. $25.95. LC 84-8816. ISBN 0520052625.

Sánchez presents detailed analyses of the works of four poets: Alma Villanueva, Lorna Dee Cervantes, Lucha Corpi, and Bernice Zamora. Stating that "Chicana poetry is grounded in conflict" (p.9), Sánchez examines the writers' key poems, which she approaches as "strategies for articulating a sense of self arising from their conflicting social situation as women and as minority writers" (p.x). Each writer, Sánchez asserts, views her gender, ethnic, and artistic identities differently. Sánchez's introduction outlines the historical, social, and political contexts of Chicana literature. She supplies full texts of the shorter poems in each chapter, and three appendices provide selections of Villanueva's longer works. Somewhat reductive, Sánchez's approach does clarify the common concerns of stylistically diverse works.

622. Shapiro, Adrian M., et al. **Carson McCullers: A Descriptive Listing and Annotated Bibliography of Criticism.** New York: Garland, 1980. 315p. index. $48.00. LC 79-7909. ISBN 0824095340.

Lacking recent in-depth studies of Carson McCullers (1917-1967), researchers can benefit from this comprehensive annotated bibliography. Co-compilers Adrian M. Shapiro, Jackson R. Bryer, and Kathleen Field describe book, pamphlet, and periodical writings by McCullers, as well as books, sections of books, periodical articles, reviews, dissertations, and foreign-language materials about her life and works. For a succinct overview, see Margaret B. McDowell's *Carson McCullers* (Twayne, 1980).

623.   Showalter, Elaine, ed. **The New Feminist Criticism: Essays on Women, Literature, and Theory.** New York: Pantheon Books, 1985. 403p. bibliog. $22.95. LC 84-22625. ISBN 0394539133.

Showalter aims to show the range of feminist criticism employed by our best-known United States literary critics, with essays from Sandra Gilbert, Susan Gubar, Carolyn Heilbrun, Annette Kolodny, Nancy Miller, Lillian Robinson, Barbara Smith, and others. Many of these essays will be familiar to those who have worked with feminist literary theory; most of them have previously appeared in journals and/or anthologies. Kolodny's "Dancing Through the Minefield: Some Observations on the Theory, Practice, and Politics of a Feminist Literary Criticism" (1980) and Nina Baym's "Melodramas of Beset Manhood: How Theories of American Fiction Exclude Women Authors" (1981) both raise key questions about canons and the ideologies that shape them. Rachel Blau DuPlessis challenges the accepted forms of literary criticism in "For the Etruscans" (1981). Showalter's collection demonstrates the pluralism of feminist criticism, encompassing varied perspectives—lesbian, black, Anglo-American, what is termed "the new French feminisms," or a fusion. The anthology celebrates the project of feminist criticism whether it be pragmatic (recuperating and reinterpreting texts) or theoretical (raising questions of textuality and sexuality), stressing the diversity that distinguishes feminist criticisms from more narrowly defined critical approaches—Marxism, deconstruction, or structuralism.

624.   Squier, Susan Merrill, ed. **Women Writers and the City: Essays in Feminist Literary Criticism.** Knoxville: University of Tennessee Press, 1984. 306p. bibliog. index. $22.95. LC 83-17109. ISBN 0870494155.

The fifteen essays in this volume examine how French, British, and North American women writers of the past two centuries have used the city to explore female concerns. The contributors include such noted feminist scholars as Wendy Martin, Jane Marcus, and Louise DeSalvo, and their approaches range from historical and thematic to structuralist and socialist analyses. Some of the writers discussed here use the city to mirror women's imprisonment—such as Marguerite Duras, whose heroines are as trapped in patriarchal language as they are in the maze of city streets; or Vita Sackville-West, in whose *All Passion Spent* the city becomes the symbol of man's domination over women, the poor, and nature. For other women, however, the city represents their struggle for freedom and community—such as turn-of-the-century Chicago novelists, who viewed their city as an extended family; or Adrienne Rich, who creates a utopian vision of a women's "city upon a hill."

625.   Staicar, Tom, ed. **The Feminine Eye: Science Fiction and the Women Who Write It.** New York: Ungar, 1982. 148p. bibliog. $13.95. LC 81-70120. ISBN 0804428387.

Staicar's edited collection of essays by scholars of fantasy writing introduces and explores the work of some of the outstanding women writers of science fiction: Leigh Brackett, C. L. Moore, Andre Norton, C. J. Cherryh, Suzy Mckee Charnas, James Tiptree, Jr., Marion Zimmer Bradley, Suzette Haden Elgin, and Joan D. Vinge. Written for nonspecialists, Staicar's anthology identifies the writing of many of these prolific women in the accompanying bibliographies. Marlene S. Barr's *Future Females: A Critical Anthology* (Bowling Green State University Popular Press, 1981) similarly helps in gathering critical literature and bibliography, with essays by Joanna Russ and Suzy Mckee

Charnas, among others. Natalie M. Rosinksy's *Feminist Futures—Contemporary Woman's Speculative Fiction* (UMI Research Press, 1984) is a challenging work that explores how creative "seeing" by such fantasy writers as Virginia Woolf, Ursula K. Le Guin, Lois Gould, and Marge Piercy may change how society develops.

626. Staley, Thomas F., ed. **Twentieth-Century Women Novelists.** Totowa, NJ: Barnes and Noble, 1982. 224p. bibliog. index. $28.50. LC 82-1740. ISBN 038920272X.

This fine collection of essays examines the works of ten representative British writers of the 1960s and 1970s: Olivia Manning, Margaret Drabble, Muriel Spark, Edna O'Brien, Barbara Pym, Iris Murdoch, Susan Hill, P. D. James, Jennifer Johnston, and Doris Lessing. The essays focus on the influence of recent social and economic changes, especially the feminist movement, on the writers' works. Most, like Drabble and Pym, show "the ability to create women not in some image to conform or conflict with the masculine world, but clearly as themselves" (p.xiii). Yet some, like Murdoch, also indicate "a wider range of sensibility ... in their creation of male characters" (p.xiv) than earlier writers; and many demonstrate a new willingness to tackle larger human issues, as in Lessing's apocalyptic fiction. Other scholars have also studied the effects of social movements on fiction. In *Women and Fiction* (Barnes and Noble, 1979), Patricia Stubbs analyzes the works of such writers as H. G. Wells and Arnold Bennett to argue that images of women in novels from 1880 to 1920 reflect changes in social and sexual roles in British culture. Anne Z. Mickelson, in *Reaching Out* (Scarecrow Press, 1979), examines the impact of the women's movement on novels by contemporary American women writers, including Joyce Carol Oates, Erica Jong, Alice Walker, and Joan Didion.

627. Steedman, Carolyn. **The Tidy House: Little Girls Writing.** London: Virago Press, 1982. 263p. bibliog. index. $19.95. ISBN 0860683214.

This fascinating study examines the sociological, linguistic, and gender implications of a story written by three working-class eight-year-old girls during one week in 1976. In "The Tidy House," Carla, Melissa, and Lindie wrote about "romantic love, marriage and sexual relations, the desire of mothers for children and their resentment of them, and the means by which those children are brought up to inhabit a social world" (p.1). Thus, argues Steedman (their teacher), the story "served the children as investigation of the ideas and beliefs by which they themselves were being brought up, and their text can serve us too in this way" (p.1).

628. Sternburg, Janet, ed. **The Writer on Her Work.** New York: Norton, 1980. 265p. $14.95. LC 80-13613. ISBN 0393013618.

In this outstanding collection of essays, sixteen American women—among them Joan Didion, Toni Cade Bambara, Erica Jong, and Maxine Hong Kingston—discuss how and why they write. Though remarkably diverse in tone and emphasis, the essays are invariably articulate, and often moving. Two general themes emerge: gender and race limitations on the writer, and writing as a necessity for survival. *Women Writers Talking* (Holmes and Meier, 1983), edited by Janet Todd, includes fifteen interviews with such figures as Maya Angelou, Grace Paley, Margaret Drabble, and Luce Irigaray. Some of the interviews are clumsy or unenlightening; the volume's strength lies in its inclusion of U.S., British, and French writers. A more narrowly focused work is *Women Writers of the West Coast: Speaking of Their Lives and Careers* (Capra Press, 1983), edited by Marilyn Yalom. Ten edited public dialogues with authors as diverse as Judy Grahn, Ursula K. Le Guin, and Jessamyn West are supplemented by Margo Davis's superb photographs. The collection never succeeds in defining the "West Coast writer," but most of the authors do address both feminism and what it means to be a woman writer. *On Gender and Writing,* edited by Michelene Wandor (Pandora Press, 1983), includes thoughtful essays by twenty-two male and female writers from England. The contributors — among them, Margaret Drabble, Fay Weldon, and Eva Figes — explore the impact of feminism and heightened gender consciousness on their fiction and nonfiction.

629. Tate, Claudia, ed. **Black Women Writers at Work.** New York: Continuum, 1983. 213p. $14.95. LC 82-23546. ISBN 0826402321.

Claudia Tate offers us fascinating and informative interviews with fourteen writers. Some, like Gwendolyn Brooks, Toni Morrison, and Ntozake Shange, are well known; others, like Kristin Hunter and Gayl Jones, may be less familiar. Tate states that "no one can promote the black woman's literary well-being better than she can herself" (p.xxvi), and certainly the women interviewed here are uniformly articulate and compelling. Since Tate conducted all of the interviews herself, the volume is unified by common questions she raises — for example, on race, gender, the artist's responsibilities, and the craft of writing. Tillie Olsen has contributed a graceful foreword, while Tate's excellent introduction provides an overview of themes and techniques common to black women writers. *In the Memory and Spirit of Frances, Zora, and Lorraine: Essays and Interviews on Black Women and Writing* (Institute for the Arts and the Humanities, Howard University, 1979), edited by Juliette Bowles, collects the work of Frances Welsing, June Jordan, Barbara Smith, and Joyce Ladner, among others, along with interviews with Audre Lorde and Ntozake Shange.

630.* Toth, Emily, ed. **Regionalism and the Female Imagination: A Collection of Essays.** New York: Human Sciences Press, 1985. 205p. bibliog. index. LC 83-26546. ISBN 0898851688.

Countering the widely held view that regional literature is the province of "minor" women writers, Toth argues that our deepest emotions "are associated with and expressed in the private sphere — the sphere of home, women, region," so that "the work of women regionalists ... may be the most universal of all" (p.10). The eleven essays move well beyond standard discussions of well-known regionalists like Kate Chopin and Sarah Orne Jewett to pose questions about literary neglect, to bring to light lesser-known or unpublished writers, analyze regional typing and stereotyping, and suggest a new aesthetic for looking at regional literature. An interesting companion to this volume is *Teaching Women's Literature From a Regional Perspective* (Modern Language Association of America, 1982), edited by Leonore Hoffmann and Deborah Rosenfelt.

631. Wagner, Linda Welshimer. **Ellen Glasgow: Beyond Convention.** Austin: University of Texas Press, 1982. 150p. bibliog. index. $15.95. LC 82-2067. ISBN 0292720394.

Ellen Glasgow (1873-1945) has traditionally been approached as a regionalist who presented a spinster's view of the South. Wagner, however, sees Glasgow as a "chronicler of American women's lives" whose greatest works "came from her own responses to her thoroughly feminine identity" (p.123). In a graceful, intelligent blend of criticism and biography, Wagner argues that the gradual change in Glasgow's image is reflected in her nineteen novels — in the movement from a pseudomasculine to a feminine voice, from a didactic to an imagistic style, and from condescension to sympathy toward women. Wagner traces Glasgow's feminism to ambivalence about her native South, a patriarchal society to which she was emotionally attached but from which she longed to break free, and asserts that in her greatest heroines Glasgow celebrates female strength and self-reliance. Marcelle Thiébaux's *Ellen Glasgow* (Ungar, 1982) also stresses Glasgow's attitudes toward women and the South. A more comprehensive and cursory study than Wagner's, it is best read as an introduction to Glasgow and her work.

632. Walker, Cheryl, 1947- . **The Nightingale's Burden: Women Poets and American Culture Before 1900.** Bloomington: Indiana University Press, 1982. 189p. bibliog. index. $22.50. LC 81-48514. ISBN 0253340659.

Walker's purpose is to present "a theoretical framework for understanding particular poems as signs of women's culture" (p.2). She takes as her central image Philomena, the nightingale of the book's title, who was raped, silenced, and then transformed into a mournful singer. Due to social constraints, internalized patriarchal values, and alienation from the literary establishment — their "shared experience" (p.2) — women poets from Anne Bradstreet onward adopted Philomena's attitudes: a feeling of powerlessness and longing for power, ambivalence, and a sense of secret sorrow. To make her point, Walker conflates the lives of such minor figures as Lydia Sigourney, Frances Osgood, and Elizabeth Oakes-Smith into a "composite biography" that highlights their similarities — perhaps at the expense of their individuality. In a projected second volume, Walker promises to analyze the shared experience of twentieth-century women poets. The sixteen essays in *Coming to Light,* edited by Diane Wood Middlebrook and Marilyn Yalom (University of Michigan Press, 1985), discuss the relationship between twentieth-century women poets — among them H. D., Gertrude Stein, Louise Bogan, Sylvia Plath, Anne Sexton, and Adrienne Rich — and the American literary tradition. In *A Separate Vision* (Louisiana State University Press, 1984), Deborah Pope examines the theme of isolation and alienation in the works of Louise Bogan, Maxine Kumin, Denise Levertov, and Adrienne Rich.

633. Wilson, Katharina M., ed. **Medieval Women Writers.** Athens: University of Georgia Press, 1984. 366p. bibliog. $30.00. LC 82-13380. ISBN 0820306401.

This notable collection includes newly translated selections by fifteen women writers from the ninth to the fifteenth century, including Marie de France, Hildegard of Bingen, Margery Kempe, and Christine de Pizan. Wilson has chosen works from ten different geographical regions, eight languages, and a variety of genres; each writer's section features a critical biography and a bibliography by a noted scholar. Wilson's introduction considers the issue of the female imagination in a time when few women were literate. Peter Dronke's *Women Writers of the Middle Ages* (Cambridge University Press, 1984) is a scholarly study of the third to the thirteenth century. Dronke argues that medieval women writers' lives and works were bound up with the religious life of the period. In *God's Handiwork* (Greenwood Press, 1983), Richard J. Schrader examines images of women in early Germanic literature from England, Germany, and Scandinavia. Schrader moves well beyond the stereotypical Eve-Mary dichotomy to present a complex analysis of how Anglo-Saxon writers used images of women to convey social and religious concepts.

634. Woodbridge, Linda, 1945- . **Women and the English Renaissance: Literature and the Nature of Womankind, 1540-1620.** Urbana: University of Illinois Press, 1983. 364p. bibliog. index. $21.95. LC 82-24792. ISBN 0252010272.

In this erudite and entertaining work, Woodbridge examines whether the portrait of women in Renaissance literature reflects their actual lives. She begins with a study of the literary controversy about women's nature, looks at the pamphlet wars over women's cross-dressing and "mannish" behavior, and concludes with an analysis of the stock stage figure of the misogynist. Woodbridge's sources range from popular ballads to *The Duchess of Malfi* and *Much Ado About Nothing*; she incorporates fascinating historical details and has a clear grasp of classical rhetoric. Her conclusions, Woodbridge warns, are as paradoxical as the Renaissance itself, an age which "typically characterized womankind in general as weak and timid while portraying individual women as sturdy and aggressive" (p.8). In *Women of the English Renaissance and Reformation* (Greenwood Press, 1983), Retha M. Warnicke studies women's education over four generations, focusing on the acceptance or rejection of classical training for women. Carolly Erickson's *The First Elizabeth* (Summit Books, 1983) is a lively biography of the foremost woman of the English Renaissance. Unlike earlier biographers, Erickson emphasizes the private life of the Virgin Queen, a woman who, by refusing to marry, maintained her power in a social and political patriarchy.

635. Woolf, Virginia Stephen, 1882-1941. **Virginia Woolf, Women and Writing.** Edited by Michèle Barrett. New York: Harcourt, Brace, Jovanovich, 1980. 198p. pbk. $4.95. LC 79-3371. ISBN 0156936585.

This volume is especially welcome in light of recent interest in Virginia Woolf's own identity as a woman writer. Editor Michèle Barrett brings together twenty-five of Woolf's essays on women and literature — general essays such as "Women and Fiction" and "Women Novelists," as well as essays on a variety of women authors, from Mary Wollstonecraft to George Eliot to Katherine Mansfield. Barrett's excellent introduction relates these short works to Woolf's major analyses of women and literature, *A Room of One's Own* and *Three Guineas*.

636. Yourcenar, Marguerite. **With Open Eyes: Conversations With Mattieu Galey.** Boston: Beacon Press, 1984. 271p. bibliog. index. $19.95. LC 84-45074. ISBN 0807063541.

In 1981, at the age of seventy-seven, Marguerite Yourcenar became the first woman elected to the Académie Française. Best known for her historical novels — *Memoirs of Hadrian* (1951; Modern Library, 1984) and *The Abyss* (1968; Farrar, Straus, Giroux, `1976) — Yourcenar is also a poet, playwright, essayist, autobiographer, and translator. *With Open Eyes* consists of interviews conducted with Yourcenar over the course of several years by French critic Mattieu Galey. The conversations reveal Yourcenar's views on her childhood, education, and development of a literary voice, as well as on such topics as drugs, mysticism, politics, and feminism. After a biographical introduction, Galey wisely yields to Yourcenar, whose erudition, imagination, and passion are apparent throughout. Several of Yourcenar's earlier works have recently been translated, including her first novel, *Alexis* (1929; Farrar, Straus, Giroux, 1984), a letter from a homosexual to the wife he is leaving; *Oriental Tales* (1938; rev. ed. Farrar, Straus, Giroux, 1985), a collection of short stories; and *Fires* (1935; Farrar, Straus, Giroux, 1981), nine lyrical prose poems about such ancient characters as Sappho, Phaedra, and Mary Magdalene, overlaid with alternative versions and modern settings. Pierre L. Horn's *Marguerite Yourcenar* (Twayne, 1985) provides a biographical and critical study of the author and her work.

MIXED GENRES

637. Aichinger, Ilse, 1921- . **Selected Poetry & Prose.** Edited by Allen H. Chappel. Durango, CO: Logbridge-Rhodes, 1983. 141p. $16.00. LC 83-14867. ISBN 0937406252.

This volume brings together translations of a variety of works by one of Austria's best known postwar writers, including twenty-two poems (with their German originals); eleven prose pieces; and a radio play, *The Jouet Sisters.* Aichinger's style—difficult, lyrical, enigmatic—is a response to the corruption of language evident throughout the twentieth century, but especially Hitler's Germany. In his useful introduction, Lawrence L. Langer argues that Aichinger's "pursuit of controlled inaccuracy is not a willful transgression of clarity, but ... an assent to the partial collapse of traditional verbal power" (p.10)—a stance that will interest feminist critics of language. Aichinger searches for meaning, not in words, but in images, and she experiments with the power of the absurd to jolt us out of familiar ways of seeing and thinking—thus her kinship with Kafka, Beckett, and Ionesco.

638. Alexander, Maxine, 1944- , ed. **Speaking for Ourselves: Women of the South.** New York: Pantheon Books, 1984. 286p. pbk. $10.95. LC 84-7088. ISBN 0394722752.

The forty pieces collected in this anthology—poetry, personal narratives, interviews, short stories, oral history, a play—contribute to the emerging movement of Southern women who seek in their writings to articulate the complexity of their heritage, and in their activism to confront Southern injustice. A mixed group of women meet in these pages, including scholars, artists, journalists, activists, coal miners, and prostitutes; among the better known are Gloria Anzaldúa, hattie gosset, Anne Braden, Sara Evans, Rayna Green, and Mary Mebane. Black, white, Chicana, Indian, Appalachian—these writers reach back into their own pasts and those of their foremothers to describe coming of age in the South, women's work (paid and unpaid), home remedies, bawdy stories, women's consciousness. Mab Segrest, a contributor to this collection, is author of *My Mama's Dead Squirrel: Lesbian Essays on Southern Culture* (Firebrand Books, 1985). These writings reflect Segrest's perspective as an antiracist white Southern lesbian. Adrienne Rich wrote the introduction. Other recent works striving to redefine the Southern female identity include Rosemary Daniell's *Fatal Flowers: On Sin, Sex, and Suicide in the Deep South* (Holt, Rinehart and Winston, 1980), and Blanche McCrary Boyd's *The Redneck Way of Knowledge* (Knopf, 1982).

639.* Alta. **The Shameless Hussy: Selected Stories, Essays and Poetry.** Trumansburg, NY: Crossing Press, 1980. 238p. LC 80-15551. ISBN 0895940353.

It's not clear whether Alta speaks of male or female lovers, or both. Nor is it clear whether her voice is bitter or humorous. What hits the reader squarely are Alta's raw, vivid language and her considerable ability to transcribe unmediated experience, as in her True Story sequence. Alta doesn't back down from truth and ugliness; in fact, she subverts them by naming them. "i'm frigid when i wear see thru negligees./my almost good figure looks good half hidden,/nipples the only hard bumps on my body & men/are sposed to go sigh & go ooh & rub their hands/all over the filmy thing recalling norman mailer/& raquel welch & god knows who./it never occurred to me to dress that way for women" (p.18). Some of this work from 1969 to the present has been previously published by small presses.

640. Barolini, Helen, ed. **The Dream Book: An Anthology of Writings by Italian American Women.** New York: Schocken Books, 1985. 397p. bibliog. index. $19.95. LC 84-23503. ISBN 0805239723.

Barolini, a novelist and poet herself, has brought together fiction, drama, poetry, essays, and memoirs by fifty-six Italian-American women. Some of the writers—Mary Gordon, Dorothy Bryant, Louise DeSalvo, Sandra Gilbert—are widely published, but most are relative unknowns. Barolini's introduction addresses the barriers presented to Italian-American women writers, both by the publishing world's indifference to literature by Italians, and by the position of women in Italian culture. The quality of the selections varies widely, but at their best they convey a common ethnic experience, as in Maria Mazziotti Gillan's "Public School No. 18: Paterson, New Jersey": "I am proud of my mother,/dressed all in black,/proud of my father/with his broken tongue,/.... Remember me, ladies,/the silent one?/I have found my voice/and my rage will blow/your house down" (p.321).

641.   Bass, Ellen, and Louise Thornton, eds. **I Never Told Anyone: Writings by Women Survivors of Child Sexual Abuse.** New York: Harper and Row, 1983. 278p. bibliog. $17.26. LC 82-48655. ISBN 0060151498.

Thirty-three survivors of child sexual abuse testify, in poetry and prose, to the pain they endured and its lasting effect on them. Bass and Thornton group the contributions in four sections according to the perpetrators: fathers, other relatives, friends and acquaintances, and strangers. Each piece bears a short biographical introduction, revealing that the authors come from diverse class and racial backgrounds. Ellen Bass's introduction to the volume documents the extent of the sexual violation of girls and speaks movingly of her attempting to raise her daughter to be both self-confident and wary. In *Voices in the Night: Women Speaking About Incest* (Cleis Press, 1982), editors Toni A. H. McNaron and Yarrow Morgan gather another collection of stories, letters, poems, journal entries, essays, and the script for a ritual. The selections, many of them by lesbians, ring with a searing authenticity. Other volumes praised by critics for making a girl's experience of incest vivid include Katherine Brady's autobiographical *Father's Days* (Seaview Books, 1979); Michelle Morris's novel *If I Should Die Before I Wake* (J. P. Tarcher, 1982); and Louise Armstrong's "speak-out," *Kiss Daddy Goodnight* (Hawthorn Books, 1978).

642.   Blicksilver, Edith, ed. **The Ethnic American Woman: Problems, Protests, Lifestyle.** Dubuque, IA: Kendall/Hunt, 1978. 381p. bibliog. pbk. $14.95. LC 78-70677. ISBN 0840319517.

With this anthology, Blicksilver attempts to create a panorama of American women's experience, as seen through the prism of ethnicity. She defines ethnicity as broadly as possible to encompass the perspectives of Asian and Pacific American, Chicana, black, Puerto Rican, Indian, Jewish, and white-ethnic women. Blicksilver gathers nonfiction, letters, short stories, and poetry—many pieces reprinted from other sources—into thematic sections focused on the family, education, identity, work, religion and ritual, and the immigrant experience, among other topics. Two supplementary tables of contents sort the anthology material by literary form and ethnic group. Some of the better-known writers included here are Maxine Hong Kingston, Leslie Marmon Silko, Mary McCarthy, Ntozake Shange, Judith Plaskow, Joy Hargo, and Adrienne Rich.

643.   Brant, Beth, 1941- , ed. **A Gathering of Spirit: Writing and Art by North American Indian Women.** 2nd ed. Rockland, ME: Sinister Wisdom Books, 1984. 238p. bibliog. pbk. $7.95. LC 84-051751. ISBN 0931103002.

"I believe in each and every Indian woman whose words and pictures lie between the pages of this magazine. We are here. Ages twenty-one to sixty-five. Lesbian and heterosexual. Representing forty Nations. We live in the four directions of the wind" (p.13). Thus editor Beth Brant introduced the first edition of this unprecedented anthology, which appeared in 1983 as a special issue of the lesbian-feminist journal *Sinister Wisdom*. Sinister Wisdom Books has since issued a second edition, which supplements the poems, stories, personal histories, interviews, letters, essays, drawings, and photographs of the first edition with a new introduction, another essay, and a few additional poems and drawings. The power and breadth of this collection speak to Brant's determination to give voice to Indian women — women never before published, as well as established writers such as Paula Gunn Allen, Linda Hogan, Wendy Rose, and Joy Harjo. Brant has selected writings and graphics that express both loss and celebration, oppression and resistance. Buried heritage and mixed identity, destruction of the earth by the dominant non-Indian society, the ravages of alcohol, tradition and community — these are among the recurrent themes. Some of the specific references will escape the non-Indian reader, but the strength and the pain evoked here will not. Brant has recently published a collection of her own poems, stories, and reminiscences entitled *Mohawk Trail* (Firebrand Books, 1985).

644. Cliff, Michelle. **The Land of Look Behind: Prose and Poetry.** Ithaca, NY: Firebrand Books, 1985. 119p. $13.95. LC 85-16159. ISBN 0932379095.

Cliff's theme in these lyric prose and verse poems is the problem of her own mixed identity: as a Jamaican raised in the United States, a woman of color who can pass for white, a lesbian in a homophobic society, and a historian of the Italian Renaissance who seeks to unearth her African heritage. The volume opens with selections from Cliff's earlier work, *Claiming an Identity They Taught Me to Despise* (Persephone Press, 1980), poems marked by a sense of powerlessness, alienation, and self-accusation: "Passing demands a desire to become invisible. A ghost-life. An ignorance of connections" (p.21). In newer pieces like "If I Could Write This in Fire, I Would Write This in Fire," Cliff moves on to angry and acute observations on the social system that produced this internal division. She closes with a unifying poem that connects personal narrative and Yoruba myth, "I-tie-all-my-people-together." The issues of class, color, gender, and history also appear in Cliff's semi-autobiographical novel *Abeng* (Crossing Press, 1984). In this lyric, multi-layered work, Clare Savage is a light-skinned Jamaican girl who must come to terms with the contradictions of the past — her ancestors include an English slaveholder as well as the female leader of a black rebellion — in order to know her identity in the present.

645. Cooper, Jane, et al., eds. **Extended Outlooks: The Iowa Review Collection of Contemporary Women Writers.** New York: Macmillan, 1981. 381p. pbk. $9.95. LC 82-13032. ISBN 0025280805.

The efforts of the editors result in a splendid anthology of contemporary women's writing — poems, stories, short tributes to neglected writers, and other work that falls in the interstices between traditional literary forms. Agreeing from the outset that "academic women, Black and Third World women, lesbian women, politically committed women, women committed to an aesthetic vision" (p.xiii) would all be represented in the anthology, the editors successfully "reach beyond a purely literary audience" and create "a good feisty city" (p.xv) of talented writers. The rewarding reading here embraces the work of Canadians and Americans, some widely recognized and others less well known, including this sample: Margaret Atwood, Olga Broumas, Michelle Cliff, Carolyn Forché, Tess Gallagher, June Jordan, Jane Kenyon, Maxine Kumin, Audre Lorde, Cynthia Macdonald, Sharon Olds, Adrienne Rich, Elizabeth Spires, Ruth Stone, Eve Triem, and Nellie Wong. The collection originally appeared as a special issue of *The Iowa Review* (Spring/Summer, 1981).

646.   Fetterley, Judith, 1938- , ed. **Provisions: A Reader From 19th-Century American Women.** Bloomington: Indiana University Press, 1985. 467p. bibliog. $35.00. LC 84-42840. ISBN 0253170400.

Editor Judith Fetterley presents selections from the works of sixteen American women, beginning with Catharine Sedgwick's fictional analysis of a woman writer, "Cacoethes Scribendi" (1830), and concluding with Charlotte Forten Grimké's autobiographical account of her experience as a free black woman teaching Southern slave children, "Life on the Sea Islands" (1864). In between Fetterley includes fiction, letters, and essays by authors ranging from "Fanny Fern" to Harriet Beecher Stowe. In her cogent introduction, Fetterley considers why women's writings have been so "thoroughly eliminated from the map of nineteenth-century American literature" and explores how our "map" of American literature is altered by the inclusion of such works. She also provides a lengthy biographical and critical introduction, as well as a primary and secondary bibliography, for each writer.

647.   Fisher, Dexter, ed. **The Third Woman: Minority Women Writers of the United States.** Boston: Houghton Mifflin, 1980. 594p. bibliog. index. pbk. $17.50. LC 79-87863. ISBN 0395277078.

Intended as a textbook, Fisher's primer on American Indian, black, Chicana, and Asian American women writers foregrounds "the best of the literature written by contemporary minority women in the United States" (p.xxvii). Noting the invisibility of these writers in journals, anthologies, and curricula, Fisher organizes criticism, traditions, narratives, fiction, and poetry into separate sections for each minority, preceded by an introduction that places the literature in historical and cultural context. She appends substantial suggestions for discussion and for writing. Many well-known minority writers are published in Fisher, and the inclusion of first-rate work by lesser-known writers is equally impressive.

648.   Gilbert, Sandra M., and Susan Gubar, 1944- , comps. **The Norton Anthology of Literature by Women: The Tradition in English.** New York: Norton, 1985. 2457p. bibliog. index. pbk. $19.95. LC 84-27276. ISBN 0393019403.

By creating a gender-exclusive anthology, Gilbert and Gubar settle some questions and raise a host of others. Feminists will appreciate the remedy to the problem of the old unabashedly male-dominated Norton anthologies, which still give less than four percent of their pages to women. However, the separatist approach, compensatory treatment, and feminist interpretations that will make this text a natural for women's studies courses may, in the end, serve to further marginalize the woman writer's "tradition in English." Many of the writers collected in this massive volume will be familiar to feminists. Ama Ata Aidoo, Willa Cather, Isak Dinesen, Margaret Drabble, Margaret Fuller, Alice James, Denise Levertov, Doris Lessing, Toni Morrison, Dorothy Parker, Sylvia Plath, Leslie Marmon Silko, Mary Shelley, Stevie Smith, and Phillis Wheatley are but a sampling of the contents. In many cases, the selections do not so much reflect the most characteristic work of these writers as they do Gilbert and Gubar's thesis on women writers, so persuasively worked out in their controversial critical work *The Madwoman in the Attic: The Woman Writer and the Nineteenth Century Literary Imagination* (Yale University Press, 1979). In that ground-breaking volume, featuring Jane Austen and Emily Dickinson in pivotal roles as subversives, Gilbert and Gubar revise what critic Harold Bloom termed in male writers "the anxiety of influence." The authors diagnose the problem for female writers as one of "anxiety of authorship"; that is, in their view, women writers have anguished over the act of rebellion represented by their taking up the forbidden pen at all.

649. Goreau, Angeline. **The Whole Duty of a Woman: Female Writers in Seventeenth-Century England.** Garden City, NY: Dial Press, 1985. 344p. bibliog. pbk. $12.95. LC 84-12042. ISBN 0385278780.

Goreau's purpose in this collection of essays, poems, letters, and plays is to bring to light the work of many hitherto unfamiliar seventeenth-century women writers. The texts themselves reveal "the intricate web of impediments, both external and self-imposed, that so often entangled a woman who aspired to write"; yet they also demonstrate "a surprising degree of feminist feeling" (p.vii). Goreau emphasizes these themes in her first two sections. Part I includes seventeenth-century essays (mostly by men) that demonstrate societal limitations on women's character, education, and behavior, while Part II presents witty and impassioned replies by women to popular misogynist writings. Part III provides a selection of works by women, both well-known writers like the Duchess of Newcastle and Aphra Behn, and more obscure figures like Mary Astell and Penelope Aubin. Other seventeenth-century scholars have concentrated on women as they appear in writings by men. Suzanne W. Hull's *Chaste, Silent and Obedient* (Huntington Library, 1982), an annotated descriptive bibliography of books written for a female audience between 1475 and 1640, is a study of male ideology. In *Amazons and Warrior Women* (St. Martin's Press, 1981), Simon Shepherd examines a large number of mostly obscure seventeenth-century plays, finding two contrasting figures—the "warrior woman," whose verbal wit serves a moral purpose, and the "Amazon," who uses her strength for immoral, and often lustful, ends. Diane Kelsey McColley provides a fairly persuasive revisionist view of *Paradise Lost* in *Milton's Eve* (University of Illinois Press, 1983).

650. Green, Rayna, ed. **That's What She Said: Contemporary Poetry and Fiction by Native American Women.** Bloomington: Indiana University Press, 1984. 329p. bibliog. $29.95. LC 83-49002. ISBN 0253358558.

In her evocative introduction, Green affirms that native women have always told stories "in clay or reeds, in wool or cotton, in grass or paint or words to songs" (p.3). History has changed native women's lives materially, and with these changes have come new creative expressions—stories written down; traditions preserved, mingled, and transformed. The writers collected here are from many tribes and represent the diversity of Indian women's experience; they write of both tradition and change. Included are: Paula Gunn Allen, Diane Burns, Gladys Cardiff, Nora Dauenhauer, Charlotte de Clue, Louise Erdrich, Rayna Green, Joy Harjo, Linda Hogan, Wendy Rose, Carol Lee Sanchez, Mary TallMountain, Judith Mountain Leaf Volborth, Annette Areketa West, Roberta Hill Whiteman, and Shirley Hill Witt. A glossary explains unfamiliar terms. The bibliography lists works by and about native women writers, including some Green was unable to include in the anthology (e.g., Leslie Marmon Silko).

651. Hoffman, Nancy, and Florence Howe, eds. **Women Working: An Anthology of Stories and Poems.** Old Westbury, NY: Feminist Press; New York: McGraw-Hill, 1979. 271p. index. pbk. $8.95. LC 78-4636. ISBN 0070204314.

American women studies has long focused on the practical, in contrast to French women studies. In publishing this anthology that celebrates women working, the Feminist Press underscores the practical, goal-oriented women's studies approach used in many classrooms. Works of poetry and prose collected here are by Yezierska, Cather, Giovanni, Walker, Jewett, Hurston, Bambara, Le Sueur, Rich, and many others. More than half the selections treat women's unpaid work.

652. Hurston, Zora Neale, 1901-1960. **I Love Myself When I Am Laughing ... and Then Again When I Am Looking Mean and Impressive: A Zora Neale Hurston Reader.** Edited by Alice Walker. Old Westbury, NY: Feminist Press, 1979. 313p. pbk. $9.95. LC 79-17582. ISBN 0912670665.

Zora Neale Hurston—novelist, folklorist, journalist, and critic—is claimed as a foremother by many of today's black women writers. This anthology of short works and selections from longer ones (including a lengthy extract from her finest novel, *Their Eyes Were Watching God*) treats the reader to Hurston's vivid language, her easy command of Southern black dialect, her memorable characters, and her sometimes outrageous opinions and biting sarcasm. Selections are grouped by type: autobiography, folklore, and reportage; essays and articles; and fiction. Alice Walker provides a moving dedication and a humorous but touching afterword. Mary Helen Washington adds a perceptive critical introduction. This landmark anthology paved the way for other reissues, including *Spunk: The Selected Stories of Zora Neale Hurston* (Turtle Island Foundation, 1985) and *Dust Tracks on the Road: An Autobiography* (University of Illinois Press, 1984). When the latter was first published in 1942, the publisher cut many portions. The new edition restores the original text and adds a substantive critical introduction by Robert Hemenway, Hurston's biographer. In *Zora Neale Hurston* (Twayne, 1980), Lillie P. Howard ably surveys Hurston's life, works, and critical reception, with particular attention to her four novels.

653. Le Sueur, Meridel. **Ripening: Selected Work, 1927-1980.** Edited by Elaine Hedges. Old Westbury, NY: Feminist Press, 1982, 291p. bibliog. $14.95. LC 81-22063. ISBN 0912670983.

This comprehensive volume brings together a variety of Le Sueur's writings from the last six decades. Arranged chronologically, the selections include fiction (ranging from well-known stories like "Persephone" and "Annunciation" to *Memorial*, a novel-in-progress), poetry, journal entries, history, biography, and reportage (including "Women on the Breadlines" and "I Was Marching"). A radical who was involved in the worker's movements of the Depression Era and was blacklisted in the 1950s, Le Sueur takes as her subject the people of her native Midwest: farmers; laborers; immigrants; Native Americans; and, especially, women. An introduction by Elaine Hedges outlines Le Sueur's life and analyzes the themes and motifs of her writings. Photographs from Le Sueur's family album accompany the text. The Feminist Press has also published *Guardian Angel and Other Stories* (1984) by Le Sueur's girlhood friend Margery Latimer, who died in childbirth in 1932. Like Le Sueur, Latimer fills her tales with details of repressed Midwestern lives; yet her narrative style—spare, distanced, almost surreal—places her in the modernist tradition.

654. Levertov, Denise, 1923- . **Light Up the Cave.** New York: Published for J. Laughlin by New Directions, 1981. 290p. $15.95. LC 81-11295. ISBN 0811208133.

These prose writings by poet Denise Levertov attest to her intelligence, humanity, and common sense. The volume appears at first to be a random collection: it includes three short stories; a number of essays on "The Nature of Poetry" and "Poetry and Politics"; political commentary; remarks on writers as diverse as Anton Chekhov and Muriel Rukeyser; and autobiographical sketches. Yet *Light Up the Cave* is unified by two common themes. The first, stated most clearly in Levertov's title piece on Anne Sexton's suicide, is that self-destructiveness is not an inevitable part of creativity. The second is that political poetry is not only valid but necessary. Both themes reflect Levertov's belief in the importance of active engagement in the world, since the true poet is "passionately in love with life and art" (p.85). Four of the essays from this volume, along with seven others, appear in *Denise Levertov: In Her Own Province* (New Directions, 1979), edited by Linda Welshimer Wagner. The collection also includes two interviews with Levertov and eight critics' essays about her work.

655. Mazow, Julia Wolf, ed. **The Woman Who Lost Her Names: Selected Writings of American Jewish Women.** San Francisco: Harper and Row, 1980. 222p. $7.95. LC 79-2986. ISBN 0062505661.

The work of contemporary Jewish women writers marks "the beginning of a tradition," writes Mazow in her optimistic introduction: "While [the Jewish woman] may once have lost the power of naming, she is about to regain it" (p.xviii). Illustrating the many diverse perspectives among Jewish women writers, Mazow's collection gathers fictional and autobiographical pieces by both the famous and the more obscure. Anzia Yezierska's protagonist learns how to write about her roots in "My Own People." Emma Goldman recounts the story of her miserable first marriage and her sweatshop existence in an excerpt from *Living My Life*. Some selections qualify as classics—for example, Tillie Olsen's "I Stand Here Ironing" and E. M. Broner's "Birth" from her novel *A Weave of Women*. Norma Rosen raises gender, race, and class issues in her story about a Jewish intellectual's relationship to the Jamaican nursemaid she employs; and Grace Paley writes of similar matters. Perhaps most provocative is the title story of the collection by Nessa Rapoport. *Jewish Women Writers and Women in Jewish Literature* (State University of New York Press, 1983), edited by Daniel Walden, includes nine essays on women in the fiction of Jewish men (Bellow, Borges, Cahan, Lewishon, Malamud, and Roth) and eleven essays on fiction by Jewish women (Margolin, Ozick, Paley, Rosen, Yezierska). Livia Bitton-Jackson's *Madonna or Courtesan?* (Seabury Press, 1982) examines images of Jewish women in Christian literature from the sixteenth through the early twentieth century. Bitton-Jackson, a Holocaust survivor, argues that such stereotypes as the Wandering Jewess, the victim of ritual murder, the madonna, and the courtesan (*la belle Juive*) distorted the popular image of Jews and helped make the Holocaust possible.

656. Meyer, Doris, and Margarite Fernández Olmos, eds. **Contemporary Women Authors of Latin America: New Translations.** Brooklyn, NY: Brooklyn College Press, 1983. 331p. bibliog. pbk. $12.50. LC 82-46047. ISBN 0930888219.

In this companion volume to their collection of critical essays on contemporary Latin American women writers (see entry 607), editors Meyer and Olmos collect translations of poetry, fiction, and drama by twenty-four women writers from fifteen countries. The writers range from relative unknowns to women who are famous in their own countries, like Cuba's Belkis Cuza Malé and Chile's Gabriela Mistral. The editors include original versions of translated poems, a selected bibliography of works in English about each writer, and a short biography of each. Another useful anthology is *Open to the Sun,* edited by Nora Jaquez Wieser (Perivale Press, 1979), a collection of poems by nineteen twentieth-century Latin American women that presents Spanish and English versions of each work on facing pages. For each writer, Wieser includes a brief critical biography, a bibliography of critical works in English, and a list of the writer's publications. Lynn Ellen Rice Cortina's *Spanish American Women Writers* (Garland, 1983) is a comprehensive primary bibliography providing similar lists of publications by nearly two thousand writers from 1492 to 1980. However, Cortina's organization (by country rather than by genre) is confusing, and her annotations are often sketchy or nonexistent.

657. Moraga, Cherríe, 1952- . **Loving in the War Years: lo que nunca pasó por sus labios.** Boston: South End Press, 1983. 152p. bibliog. $20.00. LC 83-61474. ISBN 0896081958.

"So often in the work on this book I felt I could not write because I have a movement on my shoulder, a lover on my shoulder, a family over my shoulder. On some level you have to be willing to lose it all to write—to risk telling the truth that no one may want to hear, even you" (p.v). Moraga, who defines herself as "a Chicana poet and 'politica,'" has forged a reputation for herself as someone willing to risk telling the truth—the complex, contradictory truths of her life as a Chicana lesbian feminist. She gathers here poems, essays, stories, and journal entries written between 1976 and 1983. Her writings speak to the confusion of her tangled identities and her struggle to find acceptance without denial.

658. Olsen, Tillie, 1913- , ed. **Mother to Daughter, Daughter to Mother, Mothers on Mothering: A Daybook and Reader.** Old Westbury, NY: Feminist Press, 1984. 296p. bibliog. index. pbk. $9.95. LC 84-21038. ISBN 0935312374.

In honor of the fifteenth anniversary of the Feminist Press, Olsen has brought together a moving collection of poems, letters, short fiction, and diary excerpts on the concerns of mothers and daughters—their shared joys, disappointments, estrangements, and reconciliations. The social contexts of the pieces range from eighth-century Japan to rural Nigeria and contemporary America. Among the volume's 120 contributors are Simone de Beauvoir, Margaret Mead, Buchi Emecheta, Eudora Welty, Gloria Steinem, and Käthe Kollwitz. Complementing Olsen's anthology is *Real Mothers* (Talonbooks, 1981), which includes ten prize-winning stories by Audrey Thomas. From Greece to British Columbia, contemporary mothers are portrayed in a realistic, compassionate light—mothers with their children, mothers with their husbands or lovers, mothers alone.

659. Reese, Lyn, et al., eds. **I'm on My Way Running: Women Speak on Coming of Age.** New York: Avon Books, 1983. 363p. pbk. $4.95. LC 82-90544. ISBN 0380830221.

Lyn Reese, Jean Wilkinson, and Phyllis Sheon Koppelman are all experienced teachers of women's studies. They offer here a cross-cultural collection of prose and poetry that speaks to women's coming of age. The material is organized into five thematic sections: body changes, sexuality, appearance, mother-daughter relationships, and adventure. Some selections are from well-known authors such as Buchi Emecheta, Paule Marshall, Anne Frank, Nadine Gordimer, Anaïs Nin, and Alix Kates Shulman. Other selections are more obscure: a medieval European ballad, an Indonesian prayer, a poem from the *Book of Odes* (China, 500 B.C.). The title is taken from a traditional Papago song for a young girl's puberty ceremony.

660. Sanchez, Sonia, 1934- . **Homegirls & Handgrenades.** New York: Thunder's Mouth Press; distr. New York: Persea Books, 1984. 77p. pbk. $6.95. LC 84-8469. ISBN 0938410237.

The poetic voice of Sonia Sanchez, located "in the middle/of my biography/of dying drinking working dancing people/their tongues swollen with slavery" (p.76), expresses her range. She intersperses prose and verse in confessional and political pieces that record the harsh reality of life among the poor, the drug addicted, the marginalized elements of society, giving expression to those "simple" folk, "illiterate with juices/in a city where hunger/is passed around for seconds" (p.17). In *Homegirls,* she writes with more assurance than in *I've Been a Woman: New and Selected Poems* (Black Scholar Press, 1978).

661.* Sand, George, 1804-1876. **George Sand in Her Own Words.** Edited by Joseph Barry. Garden City, NY: Anchor Books, 1979. 475p. bibliog. index. LC 78-55845. ISBN 0385133464.

Sand's convictions, energy, and iconoclasm have revived interest in her work among contemporary readers; yet despite the enormous body of her writings—which would fill 150 volumes—few of her works have been translated into English. In this volume, editor and translator Joseph Barry has partially filled this void by providing selections from a variety of Sand's works, including the novels *Indiana, Valentine, Lélia, The Journeyman's Carpenter, Consuelo, The Countess de Rudolstadt,* and *The Devil's Pool*; autobiographical writings; political essays; and essays and letters on women, love, marriage, writing, and friends. Complementing *In Her Own Words* is *My Life* (Harper and Row, 1979), Dan Hofstadter's translation and condensation of Sand's twenty-volume autobiography. *My Life* begins with her family background and birth, and ends with her relationship with the composer Frederic Chopin. Hofstadter admits that the memoir, which was written to raise money, is often evasive and (in its original form) "mercilessly padded"; nevertheless, he asserts, it is "indeed 'her story,' the controversial woman's experience transformed by self-advocacy into melodrama" (p.vii). Sand wrote twenty-six plays that received professional productions, and numerous others for private productions, yet little has been written about her involvement in the theater. In *George Sand's Theatre Career* (UMI Research Press, 1985), Gay Manifold gives a history of Sand's work as a playwright, director, and producer.

662. Schipper, Mineke, ed. **Unheard Words: Women and Literature in Africa, the Arab World, Asia, the Caribbean, and Latin America.** New York: Allison and Busby; distr. New York: Schocken Books, 1985. 288p. bibliog. index. pbk. $8.95. ISBN 0850316391.

This inexpensive paperback provides a very general introduction to literature by and about Third World women. Each of its five sections—Africa, the Arab World, Asia, the Caribbean, and Latin America—includes a selection of regional proverbs, a bibliography, and one or more essays on women's oral and written literature, and on images of women in literature by men. Each section also features an in-depth interview with a woman writer: Miriam Tlali (South Africa), Etel Adnan (Lebanon), Nabaneeta Deb-Sen (India), Astrid Roemer (Surinam), and Christina Peri Rossi (Uruguay). Editor Mineke Schipper concedes that the essays' breadth precludes critical depth, but she points out that the book is "intended as an introduction to a subject on which much more could be said," and asserts that this is the first critical work to treat women's literature on an intercontinental scale (p.7). The reader may wish to consult the sectional bibliographies for more specialized sources.

663. Shimer, Dorothy Blair, ed. **Rice Bowl Women: Writings By and About the Women of China and Japan.** New York: New American Library, 1982. 390p. bibliog. pbk. $4.50. LC 81-85144. ISBN 0451620828.

Arranged chronologically by country, this useful collection includes memoirs by, and fiction about, Chinese and Japanese women from the seventh century to the present. The stories, mostly by women, range from fantasy and folk tale to an excerpt from Lady Murasaki's eleventh-century novel *The Tale of Genji*. Shimer's introduction sets Chinese and Japanese attitudes toward women in the context of the basic strands of Eastern thought: Confucianism, Taoism, Shintoism, and Buddhism. Also provided are short introductions on the social and literary characteristics of each historical period. Although there are no new translations here, Shimer does bring together works from a variety of sources into one fairly comprehensive volume. Readers especially interested in contemporary fiction may wish to examine *Born of the Same Roots* (Indiana University Press, 1981), edited by Vivian Ling Hsu, a collection of short stories by Chinese authors (mostly male) that documents the effects on Chinese women of sociopolitical changes from the 1920s to the 1970s. The woman's perspective appears in *Seven Contemporary Chinese Women Writers,* translated by Gladys Yang, et al. (Chinese Literature; distr. China Publications Centre, 1982). Many of the tales are marred by moralistic content and uneven translation. Nevertheless, in their criticism of the excesses of the Cultural Revolution, the stories attest to the greater freedom allowed to writers since 1976; and they do present a detailed portrait of the problems and desires of Chinese women.

664. Silko, Leslie Marmon, 1948- . **Storyteller.** New York: Seaver Books; distr. New York: Grove Press, 1981. 278p. $17.95. LC 80-20251. ISBN 0394515897.

Visually, *Storyteller* is a beautiful book, mixing folk tales, poetry, short fiction, reminiscences, and photographs of the author's family. ("Photographs have always had special significance/with the people of my family and the people at Laguna./A photograph is serious business and many people/still do not trust just anyone to take their picture" [p.1].) Silko draws on her early experiences at Laguna Pueblo in New Mexico, on her Pueblo and Mexican heritage, and on more recent experiences among Eskimo peoples in Alaska. A recent critical work on Silko is Per Seyersted's *Leslie Marmon Silko* (Boise State University, 1980).

665. Smith, Stevie, 1902-1971. **Me Again: Uncollected Writings of Stevie Smith.** Edited by Jack Barbera and William McBrien. New York: Farrar, Straus, Giroux, 1982. 360p. index. $15.95. LC 82-5062. ISBN 0374204942.

"Colors are what drive me most strongly," writes Smith in an essay on her creativity, included here to give us an "autobiographical profile" of a writer thought to be cheerful by some, childish by others. Her work, however, is preoccupied with death and loneliness, however wry the commentary. The essays, short stories, letters, book reviews, poems, and zany drawings in *Me Again* reveal a woman who lived a rather solitary life. Smith intuited that the single life was necessary for writing: "I do not know how people can manage to have animals, wives, and children and also write" (p.128). *Novel on Yellow Notepaper* (1936) was admired by the Bloomsbury Circle when it came out, and is now enjoying a renaissance along with two other early works, *Holiday* (1949) and *Over the Frontier* (1938), all reprinted in 1982 by Pinnacle Books. The recent appearance of *Stevie Smith: A Selection,* edited by Hermione Lee (Faber and Faber, 1983), is further evidence of the growing interest in this writer.

666. Stein, Gertrude, 1874-1946. **The Yale Gertrude Stein: Selections.** New Haven, CT: Yale University Press, 1980. 464p. $47.00. LC 80-5398. ISBN 0300025742.

Drawn from Yale's eight-volume *The Unpublished Works of Gertrude Stein* (1950-58), this collection includes Stein's major long poems, along with shorter poems, plays, and essays. Editor Richard Kostelanetz addresses the experimental rather than the modernist or postmodernist elements in Stein's work, viewing her fragmented syntax, repetition, and alliteration as strategies to capture "human dimensions that were ultimately beyond the capacities of language" (p.x). Stein's work is finally receiving the serious criticism it deserves. Marianne DeKoven's *A Different Language* (University of Wisconsin Press, 1983) defines Stein's experimental writing as an "obstruction" of reading—if reading requires "coherent, single, whole, closed, ordered, finite, sensible meanings" (p.5)—that escapes hegemonic (hence patriarchal) signification systems. DeKoven employs deconstructive criteria to judge the success or failure of Stein's "literary rebellions," and argues that Stein sought to assert lesbian identity "in language itself rather than in thematic content" (pp.149-150). In *The Making of a Modernist* (University of Massachusetts Press, 1984), Jayne L. Walker looks at Stein's early writings (from 1905 to 1912) and unpublished notebooks to argue that Stein moved from attempted realism to subjective description in her work as she increasingly found language inadequate to convey human character and experience. Randa K. Dubnick, in *The Structure of Obscurity* (University of Illinois Press, 1984), uses the terminology of structuralism and Cubism to analyze Stein's linguistic obscurity. *Gertrude Stein's Theatre of the Absolute,* by Betsy Alayne Ryan (UMI Research Press, 1984), is the first study to deal exclusively with Stein's theatrical works. For additional sources, readers may wish to consult Ray Lewis White's *Gertrude Stein and Alice B. Toklas: A Reference Guide* (G. K. Hall, 1984), an excellent comprehensive, annotated, secondary bibliography that covers popular and scholarly newspapers, journals, books, and monographs from 1909 to 1981.

667.   Tsui, Kitty. **The Words of a Woman Who Breathes Fire.** Argyle, NY: Spinsters, Ink, 1983. 70p. pbk. $5.95. LC 83-060254. ISBN 0933216068.

Tsui is a Chinese-American lesbian whose direct, powerful style suits her stand as "a warrior who grapples with three/many-headed demons: racism, sexism, homophobia" (p.52). This collection of poetry, prose, and dialogues stresses the power of words, especially for Asian-American women—"cutting the ropes/that bind us,/breaking from/ the silence of centuries/to write/our dreams into action" (p.3). Tsui also emphasizes the connections between women. She celebrates her ties not just with her lovers, but also with an old woman on the street in Chinatown, and with her grandmother, the Chinese opera singer Kwan Yin Lin, whom she takes as her model: "i am my grandmother's youngest daughter,/a warrior, a worker, a writer..../i am a woman who loves women,/i am a woman who loves myself" (pp. 51-52).

668.   West, Rebecca, Dame, 1892-1983. **The Young Rebecca: Writings of Rebecca West, 1911-17.** Selected by Jane Marcus. New York: Viking Press, 1982. 402p. index. $25.00. LC 81-52148. ISBN 0670794589.

Editor Jane Marcus has collected lively and quotable pieces from West's early days as a writer for feminist and socialist journals. Opening with an early review of a book on women in India, and concluding with a 1916 analysis of how West's socialist and feminist beliefs were affected by World War I, the volume includes literary reviews, social and political commentary, a short story, and a eulogy for Emmeline Pankhurst. West was often compared to George Bernard Shaw, and indeed her remarks do resemble his in their cutting wit and aphoristic conciseness: "Hatred of domestic work is a natural and admirable result of civilisation" (p.41). West's radicalism is apparent in her joyous call to readers to join "that splendid ... assault on the social system which calls itself the suffragist movement" (p.170). Nearly seventy years later, West was still thinking, analyzing, writing. *1900* (Viking Press, 1982) is her meditation on her childhood era, including comments on such events as the Boer War and on celebrities like Henry James and Albert Einstein. Motley F. Deakin's *Rebecca West* (Twayne, 1980), a basic study of West's life and work, examines her fiction as well as her views on feminism, literature, history, and treason.

669.   West Coast Editorial Collective, eds. **Women and Words: The Anthology/Les Femmes et Les Mots: Une Anthologie.** Madeira Park, British Columbia: Harbour, 1984. 264p. pbk. $10.95. ISBN 0920080537.

This bilingual anthology of Canadian women's literature was created for the first annual "Women and Words/les femmes et les mots" conference held in 1983. Some eighty writers are represented, a few of them widely recognized—like Louky Bersianik, Jane Rule, and Nicole Brossard—but most of them relative unknowns. The selections (generally short) include poems, essays, fiction, and one-act plays, and represent diverse cultural, racial, linguistic, and geographical backgrounds. Brief biographies of the writers are included. The seventeen critical essays in *Traditionalism, Nationalism, and Feminism: Women Writers of Quebec,* edited by Paula Gilbert Lewis (Greenwood Press, 1985), examine writings by women from 1884 to 1982 that explore women and their roles in Quebec's French-speaking culture. The essays consider the overlapping, and sometimes antithetical, concerns of traditionalism, nationalism, and feminism in the works of Laure Conan, Gabrielle Roy, Marie-Claire Blais, Anne Hébert, and other authors.

POETRY

670.* Aguilar, Mila D. **A Comrade Is as Precious as a Rice Seedling.** New York: Kitchen Table, Women of Color Press, 1984. 37p. ISBN 0913175048.

These are unabashedly political poems about the Philippines under the recently deposed Marcos dictatorship—"Damn the US-Marcos dictatorship./My people starve/While Imelda lives it up with Christina Ford" (p.28)—and feminist themes—"You are worried, you say,/About the eyebags, the glamour lost/And yet are glad about the hardening,/The learning of gut logic" (p.23). Under Marcos, Aguilar literally wrote at the peril of her life; she was imprisoned on subversion and conspiracy charges in 1984. When Corazon Aquino came to power in February 1986, Aguilar was among the political prisoners who were released. "You are not my mother," she writes, addressing herself to the wealthy women of her country. "My vision is not your vision./My lingo is not of creams that vanish scars/But of scars that vanish bourgeois dreams" (p.7). Audre Lorde has written an appreciative introduction to Aguilar's poems.

671. Alegría, Claribel, 1924- . **Flowers From the Volcano.** Pittsburgh, PA: University of Pittsburgh Press, 1982. 87p. pbk. $14.95. LC 82-70893. ISBN 0822953447.

In her preface, translator Carolyn Forché writes of Alegría's absence from her native El Salvador: "Her residencies in Mexico, Chile, and Uruguay have broadened her sense of geopolitical identity to embrace the continent" (p.xiii). This bilingual edition allows the English-speaking reader a glimpse of Alegría's rich poetic vision, one filled, as her capable translator writes, "with verdant jungles, volcanos, the glow of their craters, the spillage of black rock; with olive trees twisted by time, trees that are wisely neglected to assure that their fruit will be moist and firm" (p.xiii). Forché is right to describe Alegría as painterly in the style of Chagall and political in the tradition of Neruda, as the title poem, "Flores de volcán," admirably illustrates.

672. Allison, Dorothy. **The Women Who Hate Me.** Brooklyn, NY: Long Haul Press, 1983. 58p. pbk. $4.50. LC 84-121194. ISBN 096022842X.

The raw, searing power of Allison's first book of poetry comes from her refusal to prettify her life; she insists on claiming herself, and writing about herself, "not cleaned up, not lied about/stark, dirty, and hard" (p.37). She faces up to the women who hate her for her "no-count, low down" Southern working-class background, as well as those women, "God on their right shoulder/righteousness on their left," who hate her for being a lesbian—"as if my body, a temple of sin,/didn't mirror their own" (p.19). Through her own painful honesty in writing about her family, her lusts, her vulnerability, Allison concludes that a refusal to lie is the first step in accepting differences, and longs for the day when women "will sit knee to knee/finally listening/to the whole/naked truth/of our lives" (p.25). Laurie McLaughlin's drawings underscore the power and determination of these poems.

673. Atwood, Margaret Eleanor, 1939- . **Two-Headed Poems.** New York: Simon and Schuster, 1980. 115p. pbk. $6.95. LC 80-19276. ISBN 0671253700.

Published after a seven-year abstinence from poetry, this collection thematizes the poet's concerns about love's complications and dangerous dualisms, the nature of memory, history, and women's relationships. *True Stories* (Simon and Schuster, 1982), a collection of poetry that sets out to question the idea of consensual truth ("Don't ask for the true story; why do you need it?," p.9), has for its centerpiece "Small Poems for the Winter

Solstice," a meditative fourteen-poem series in which Atwood ponders her relationship with a lover. The poet does not shrink from creating images of brutality when these serve her. She is equally dexterous at intensely lyrical or oracular utterances, manipulating conventional imagery in startling ways. A critic as well as a poet and novelist, Atwood is increasingly gaining attention for her literary views, especially about Canadian women writers. *Second Words: Selected Critical Prose* (Beacon Press, 1984) brings together Atwood's essays, speeches, and reviews in a progression that sketches her development as a writer/critic. In "Writing the Male Character," Atwood critically explores a problem faced by the woman writer, returning to a thematic concern present in her fiction—the problem of Authority, or Author-ity. Sherrill Grace's *Violent Duality: A Study of Margaret Atwood* (Vehicule Press, 1980) considers *Surfacing* and *Lady Oracle* among pre-1980 works. Another critical collection on Atwood, *The Art of Margaret Atwood: Essays in Criticism* (Anansi, 1981), edited by Arnold E. and Cathy N. Davidson, gathers together scholarly work on Atwood and her relationship to the Canadian tradition, as well as essays on her novels, short stories, and poems. Among others, Sherrill Grace, Annis Pratt, and Judith McCombs contribute essays to this volume. In *Margaret Atwood* (Twayne, 1984), Jerome H. Rosenberg benefits from unpublished documents and long acquaintance with Atwood in useful analyses of her poetry, fiction, and criticism, and in an assessment of her place in Canadian and world literture.

674. Barnstone, Aliki, and Willis Barnstone, 1927- , eds. **A Book of Women Poets, From Antiquity to Now.** New York: Schocken Books, 1980. 612p. index. $29.95. LC 78 54391. ISBN 0805236937.

The inclusion of poets from many countries, careful translations, and a vast chronological scope distinguish this anthology. The volume begins with Enheduanna, a Sumerian moon priestess (c.2000 B.C.), and traces the tradition of women's poetry cross-culturally up to the present. A brief biography accompanies each selection. The editors of this immense project have also included thorough indexing for poets, translators, titles, and first lines. In *Women Poets of the World* (Macmillan, 1983), editors Joanna Bankier and Deirdre Lashgari respond to the "pressing need for a sense of ancestors that could lay the groundwork for an authentic female poetic tradition" (p.8) with four thousand years of poems, from ancient Sumeria to the present, many of them in new translations. The volume is organized by culture, with scholarly introductions to each section that relate the poets to their social and historical contexts.

675. Bishop, Elizabeth, 1911-1979. **The Complete Poems, 1927-1979.** New York: Farrar, Straus, Giroux, 1983. 287p. index. $17.50. LC 82-21119. ISBN 0374127476.

The poems here encompass the entire lifetime of a major American poet. This volume supersedes the 1969 collection *Complete Poems,* with fifty additional works, among them Bishop's youthful poems and many occasional poems probably never intended for publication. *Elizabeth Bishop and Her Art* (University of Michigan Press, 1983), edited by Lloyd Schwartz and Sybil P. Estess, a collection of general critical essays on Bishop, reviews of specific works, and critical comments by the poet herself, brings to light Marianne Moore's literary influence on Bishop. Like Moore, Bishop was a reticent poet; yet her personality shines through the seventeen autobiographical sketches and short stories of *The Collected Prose* (Farrar, Straus, Giroux, 1984)—most of them unpublished during her lifetime. Bishop appears here in plenty, as a child, as an adult traveler, as a poet— her life recorded with wit and grace, in precise, luminous detail. Especially powerful are the quasi-autobiographical short story "In the Village," about a little girl whose mother is going insane, and "Efforts of Affection," a loving tribute to Moore. Important to Bishop scholars is Candace W. MacMahon's *Elizabeth Bishop: A Bibliography, 1927-1979* (University Press of Virginia, 1980), a source that undoubtedly will be updated or superseded as scholarship on Bishop continues to grow.

676. Brontë, Anne, 1820-1849. **The Poems of Anne Brontë: A New Text and Commentary.** Edited by Edward Chitham. Totowa, NJ: Rowman and Littlefield, 1979. 217p. bibliog. index. $21.50. LC 78-16979. ISBN 0847661008.

In view of the wealth of Brontë scholarship, Anne Brontë's writings have suffered surprising neglect. There are still no authoritative texts of her novels *Agnes Grey* and *The Tenant of Wildfell Hall,* and it is only with Edward Chitham's impressive volume that we have a definitive edition of her poetry. Chitham's scholarly introduction sifts biographical fact from fiction, and analyzes the forms and themes of Anne Brontë's poetry. Biographical and literary allusions in the poems themselves are clarified by Chitham's commentary, and several appendices detail the extent of Anne Brontë's poetic output. *In Anne Brontë: A New Critical Assessment* (Vision Press/Barnes and Noble, 1983), P. J. M. Scott takes the writer on her own terms, as a thoughtful and sincere Christian whose novels and poems stress the need to maintain moral integrity in a flawed world. Despite her difficult, eccentric prose style, Scott presents a convincing argument that Anne initiated in *Agnes Grey* the sort of realistic, contemporary semi-autobiographical novel Charlotte used in *Jane Eyre* and *Villette*; and that *Tenant* is a theologically sophisticated, albeit artistically flawed, Christian response to the pantheism of Emily's *Wuthering Heights.*

677. Broumas, Olga. **Soie Sauvage.** Port Townsend, WA: Copper Canyon Press, 1979. 47p. $22.00. ISBN 0914742469.

Greek-born Broumas thematizes lesbianism as a sensual rather than a political experience expressed in word play: "nasturtium narcissus lily/dahlia crocus hyacinth sweet names/of bulbs I do not have my heart in any/language Friends/helping *Magnolia*/one drawled *Remember/me and the Dixie Dykes* I couldn't/lose magnolia all March" (p.39). Poet Gary Snyder has influenced Broumas's poetry; she emulates his verse disciplined by Buddhism in "Five Interior Landscapes," and she dedicates *Soie Sauvage* to Snyder and to Deborah Haynes, who illustrated the volume. Broumas has lived in Oregon and Provincetown, Massachusetts, though she does poetry readings throughout the United States, being widely in demand by feminist audiences who admired her award-winning first book, *Beginning With O* (Yale University Press, 1977). *Pastoral Jazz* (Copper Canyon Press, 1983), an ecstatic book celebrating woman loving herself and others, fuses music and mantra to amplify the poet's message of freedom and ardor.

678. Clampitt, Amy. **The Kingfisher.** New York: Knopf, 1983. 149p. $15.95. LC 82-47963. ISBN 0394528409.

Clampitt writes descriptive verse, presented from the standpoint of an engaged and intelligent observer. Her language is dazzling: so dense that it is sometimes difficult, it is vital, lyrical, and precise. The reader is continually struck by the aptness and originality of her metaphors. Clampitt employs a traditionally "feminine" vocabulary in nontraditional contexts: in "Gradual Clearing," the seaside fog lifts, disclosing "what had been wavering/fishnet plissé as a smoothness/of peau-de-soi or just-ironed/percale" (p.6). Although she opens the volume with poems about the seaside, Clampitt moves on to subjects as varied as Greece, Beethoven, quotidian love, and the nature of grief. Her most recent book of poems is *What the Light Was Like* (Knopf, 1985).

679. Clifton, Lucille, 1936- . **Two-Headed Woman.** Amherst: University of Massachusetts Press, 1980. 60p. $8.00. LC 80-5379. ISBN 0870233092.

Clifton pays homage to her womanhood and to strong women she has known. Of her body, she writes: "these hips are magic hips./i have known them /to put a spell on a man and/spin him like a top!" (p.6). Her hair generates a revivalist response: "when i feel her jump up and dance/i hear the music! my God/i'm talking about my nappy hair!" (p.5). The poet employs biblical cadences throughout, a language of prayer, of promise, and prophecy. To her unborn grandson, Clifton writes: "You will bloom/in a family of flowers./You are the promise/the Light made to adam ..." (p.32). It is her mother — long dead — who emerges as the most powerful presence in the book, however. To her, the poet promises: "i'm trying for the long one mama,/running like hell and if i fall/i fall" (p.14).

680. Cosman, Carol, et al., eds. **The Penguin Book of Women Poets.** New York: Viking Press, 1979. 399p. $14.95. LC 78-15342. ISBN 0670778567.

Comprising as it does poetry by women over a 3,500-year-span, this ambitious, scholarly volume is useful for its naming of names and dates, and pleasurable for the range of translated works. Editors Carol Cosman, Joan Keefe, and Kathleen Weaver include poems by Sappho, Ono no Komachi, Christine de Pizan, Louise Labe, Aphra Behn, Anne Bradstreet, Anna Akhmatova, Margaret Walker, and many more. Introductory notes accompany each group of poems. Space limitations have forced the editors to select relatively short poems of outstanding literary quality and, regrettably, to abbreviate the section of young, contemporary poets, whose work is more readily accessible elsewhere.

681.* Cowell, Pattie. **Women Poets in Pre-Revolutionary America, 1650-1775: An Anthology.** Troy, NY: Whitston, 1981. 404p. bibliog. index. LC 80-50492. ISBN 0878751920.

This excellent, scholarly collection makes accessible many out-of-print or unpublished works; only two of the thirty-nine writers — Anne Bradstreet and Phillis Wheatley — are frequently anthologized, and all but a few were obscure even in their own time. The poems vary in quality and include a variety of forms, from political satires, to religious meditations, to occasional pieces and elegies. Often centering on the family and domestic routine, the verses sometimes include sharp social analysis and even feminist rebellion. The most common, and moving, theme is the conflict experienced by many writers between a "ladylike" modesty and the desire, as Jane Turell put it, to "be worthy of a poet's name" (p.49). Cowell's introduction describes the opportunities and obstacles (both practical and ideological) facing colonial women poets, and analyzes the forms, themes, and motifs of their verse. Cowell has also edited, with Ann Stanford, *Critical Essays on Anne Bradstreet* (G. K. Hall, 1983), which includes criticism from Bradstreet's time to the present, as well as a bibliographic overview of Bradstreet scholarship.

682. Davis, Thulani. **Playing the Changes.** Middletown, CT: Wesleyan University Press; distr. Scranton, PA: Harper and Row, 1985. 64p. $16.00. LC 84-10456. ISBN 081951120X.

Davis's poems are marked by social commentary — on racism, male-female relationships, misogyny, and rape. She also writes knowingly of individuals such as Roslyn, who "couldn't name one desire/that is not someone else's" (p.12); of places such as Mecca Flats, a "landscape/like thin air/... behind God's back" (p.30); and of emotions such as a lover's loneliness, when "at night you try to make the knowledge of this love/show itself in the room and warm you" (p.51). These witty, slangy verses are sprinkled with references to contemporary politics, films, and music.

683. Derricotte, Toi, 1941- . **Natural Birth: Poems.** Trumansburg, NY: Crossing Press, 1983. 60p. $13.95. LC 83-2071. ISBN 0895941023.

Derricotte's sequence of narrative poems is powerful, often harrowing. A pregnant young black girl is sent by her family to a home for unwed mothers in a distant city. She longs for the experience to be "beautiful/like it's supposed to be." In staccato rhythms that reproduce the spasms of labor, the narrator recounts her feelings of terror, alienation, and pain — but power as well: "my face/contorted,/never/wore/such mask, so/rigid/and so dark/so/bright, un-/compromising/brave/no turning/back/no/no's" (p.43). Derricotte dissects and demythologizes a subject too long taboo in literature; yet she recognizes the joy as well as the pain of childbirth, and ends the volume with a love poem to her own son.

684. Doolittle, Hilda (H. D.), 1886-1961. **Collected Poems, 1912-1944.** Edited by Louis L. Martz. New York: New Directions; distr. New York: Norton, 1983. 629p. bibliog. index. $35.00. LC 83-6380. ISBN 0811208761.

Although H. D. was long dismissed as a minor Imagist poet, her status is now being reappraised, due both to interest by feminist critics and to the opening in 1980 of Yale University's H. D. archives. The *Collected Poems* is a landmark volume that brings together several works unavailable elsewhere: *Collected Poems* (1925) and *Red Roses for Bronze* (1931); uncollected and unpublished poems, many of them from H. D.'s supposed "fallow" period in the 1930s; and her masterpiece, *Trilogy* (1944), a long sequence on war. Two of H. D.'s autobiographical novels recently have been published for the first time — *The Gift* (New Directions, 1982), a mosaic of impressions from the poet's childhood; and *HERmione* (New Directions, 1981), whose protagonist, like H. D., experiences a broken engagement, a mental breakdown, and a lesbian relationship in her struggle to establish an identity. The third, *Bid Me to Live: A Madrigal* (1960; repr. Black Swan Books, 1983), has been reprinted. The most important recent study of H. D.'s work is Susan Stanford Friedman's *Psyche Reborn: The Emergence of H. D.* (Indiana University Press, 1981). Friedman blends biography, influence study, textual criticism, and history of ideas in a feminist analysis of how two apparently contradictory modes of perception — psychoanalysis and the occult — contributed to the "woman-centered mythmaking" (p.ix) of H. D.'s later poems. In her authorized biography *Herself Defined: The Poet H. D. and Her World* (Doubleday, 1984), Barbara Guest relies on H. D.'s unpublished works, along with the letters and recollections of her acquaintants, in an attempt to define the woman who was H. D. Janice S. Robinson's *H. D.: The Life and Work of an American Poet* (Houghton Mifflin, 1982) takes a psychoanalytic approach to H. D.'s life and art, stressing her experience as a patient of Sigmund Freud; her disastrous affairs with a number of literary men, including Ezra Pound, Richard Aldington, and D. H. Lawrence; and her lifelong relationship with the lesbian writer Bryher.

685. Doubiago, Sharon. **Hard Country.** Minneapolis, MN: West End Press, 1982. 263p. pbk. $9.95. ISBN 0931122252.

An ambitious, woman-centered exploration of the poet's revolutionary experience of America, *Hard Country* imagines in verse the blur of history, geography, and language. "I am five, I will never understand/why we are stranded in our selves/but in this moment I know/my own story/is understanding our singleness/that I am destined to move my body and time/into the body-time/the story/of others" (p.9), begins the poet autobiographically, as she sets off on her odyssey. Along the way, she invokes Mary Austin, Adrienne Rich, Jane Fonda, Rilke, Sitting Bull, newspaper archives, road signs, and gravestones. Quoted on the book's back cover, poet Carolyn Forché calls Doubiago's very American poetry "a brilliant response to Whitman ... free, spiritual, and gifted." A later collection is *Fatal Accident* (Black Mesa Press, 1984).

686. Flores, Angel, 1900- , and Kate Flores, eds. **The Defiant Muse: Hispanic Feminist Poems From the Middle Ages to the Present: A Bilingual Anthology.** New York: Feminist Press at the City University of New York, 1986. 145p. $29.95. LC 85-16294. ISBN 0935312471.

This is the first volume in the Feminist Press's ambitious and long-awaited series of international feminist poetry; later collections will present the works of French, German, and Italian writers. The volume includes eighty poems by thirty-two Spanish and Latin American women, mostly newly translated. The works range from thirteenth-century *canciones* and romances to contemporary free verse. Among the better-known authors are Florencia Pinar, Rosalía de Castro, Adela Zamudio, Alfonsina Storni, Gloria Fuertes, Claribel Alegría, Rosario Castellanos, Bertalicia Peralta, and Christina Peri Rossi. Although the editors include no bibliography, they do present brief biographies of the authors. The introduction provides a solid literary-historical background to the works, and discusses the need for a feminist reassessment both of the Hispanic literary canon and of individual women poets. The editors define a feminist as one who is not only "sensitive to the reality of women's lives, but courageous enough ... to speak out, to criticize" (p.xiii); and indeed, in spite of their diverse topics—family, work, love, war, religion, friendship—all of the poets in this volume are searching, in Rosario Castellanos's words, for "Another way to be human and free./Another way to be" (p.101).

687. Forché, Carolyn. **The Country Between Us.** New York: Harper and Row, 1981. 59p. $11.06. LC 81-47788. ISBN 0060149558.

Carolyn Forché won the Yale series of Younger Poets competition for *Gathering the Tribes* (Yale University Press, 1976). In *The Country Between Us,* selected for the prestigious Lamont Poetry award, she emerges as a major contemporary poet, whose recent work centers on El Salvador, Eastern Europe, and the dislocation of expatriation. Forché invokes the poets she admires—Claribel Alegría, Anna Akhmatova—her literary heroes because they wrote about explicitly political subjects. In "Ourselves or Nothing," she exhorts, "Go after that which is lost/and all the mass graves of the century's dead/will open into your waking hours:/Belson, Dachau, Saigon, Phnom Pehn/and the one meaning Bridge of Ravens,/Sao Paolo, Armagh, Calcutta, Salvador,/although these are not the same" (p.55-56). The choices in a world of mass graves and slaughter signal no less than "... the beginning or the end/of the world, and the choice is ourselves/or nothing" (p.59).

688. Fuertes, Gloria. **Off the Map: Selected Poems.** Edited by Philip Levine and Ada Long. Middletown, CT: Wesleyan University Press; distr. Scranton, PA: Harper and Row, 1984. 95p. $16.00. LC 83-23270. ISBN 0819551023.

One of very few volumes of translation devoted to the work of a single Hispanic woman writer, *Off the Map* presents Spanish and English versions of Fuertes's poems on facing pages. Fuertes is well known in her native Spain for her plain, concrete language, which clothes complex meditations on such issues as her working-class identity, God, and injustice. Despite a number of exuberant love poems and several half-serious prayers to God, the dominant tone of this collection is one of loneliness, frequently evoked by everyday objects: "a memory,/a letter,/a photo of my mother" (p.41).

689. Gilbert, Celia. **Bonfire.** Cambridge, MA: Alice James Books, 1983. 71p. $12.95. LC 82-074513. ISBN 0914086456.

"The Silence," one of the many outstanding poems in this collection, captures the mute dialogue behind the photograph of a child, her uncle, and grandmother in the garden. Gardens, cows, winter narcissi that "open their purses/and out fall stars" (p.11) stir Gilbert's imagination. In these unsentimental poems, Gilbert is the mistress of the riveting, often radiant image. A memory of her parents in bed recalls synesthetically the scene itself, "the pungent odor" of her parents' lovemaking "nails me to my flesh and bones" (p.34). Gilbert's poetry appears regularly in mainstream literary magazines and poetry reviews.

690. Glazer, Myra, ed. **Burning Air and a Clear Mind: Contemporary Israeli Women Poets.** Athens: Ohio University Press, 1981. 135p. $17.95. LC 80-22487. ISBN 0821405721.

This disturbing collection brings together the poetry of eighteen Israeli women. Glazer's excellent introduction sets a context for the poems in terms of both the Hebrew language and the Israeli experience. The Jewish tradition is patriarchal to begin with, and under constant threat of war, Israeli culture has embraced a strong, aggressive pioneering masculine ethic. Many of these poems portray women as outsiders in a male culture, whose voices go unheeded. The techniques and imagery of the poems depart from the male tradition of Israeli poetry: they are individualistic rather than nationalistic, personal in voice rather than detached; they identify woman with the land and frequently use nature imagery to explore women's sexuality; and their biblical allusions are often revisionist. Still, this is not a collection of feminist poetry; rather, the poems express the anguished ambivalence of women in living in a country where their perceptions and experience have been devalued.

691. Gordett, Marea. **Freeze Tag.** Middletown, CT: Wesleyan University Press; distr. Scranton, PA: Harper and Row, 1984. 55p. $15.00. LC 84-2250. ISBN 0819521175.

Her utilization of the "usable past" distinguishes Marea Gordett's poetry, which has been published in prestigious poetry journals, anthologized, and recognized by several poetry prizes. Gordett's subjects are memory and her Russian immigrant heritage. "We came over on the boat with the cheese," she recounts in "Songs of an Ordinary Woman," "... but don't misunderstand me/you were lucky to get out./There are no Litvaks now in Russia,/we had to leave and we came to Lowell" (p.10). Perhaps the most striking *tour de force* of Gordett's ironic poetry lies in the way she flattens the horrors of history as she observes the museumizing of the unspeakable. In "It Seemed a Shame," her subject is Auschwitz: "That's what they say about Auschwitz now./It seemed a shame not to preserve/the surroundings, so they called it The Museum./On fine days you can see the picnickers ..." (p.26).

692. Grahn, Judy, 1940- . **The Queen of Wands: Poetry.** Trumansburg, NY: Crossing Press, 1982. 111p. bibliog. $16.95. LC 82-17115. ISBN 0895940957.

In this first of four projected volumes centering on the queens of the suits of the Tarot, readers are treated to Grahn's particular genius—her nimble use of rhyme and near-rhyme, her ease with the rhythm of the storyteller's chant, and her ability to spin out the meaning of a single image and all its associations. Most of these rich but accessible poems link mythic female images—Helen of Troy, the spider, the weaver, the first mother—to the historical and present realities of women's lives. "Like a woman in childbirth wailing" echoes a refrain from the ancient Babylonian "Tablet of Lamentation" to illuminate women's alienation from the birth process. The poem "Helen you always were/the factory" alternates the voice of the omniscient spider with the words of a casualty of the Triangle Shirtwaist Fire, a slave, a woman seeing soldiers off to war, and a service worker. Several pages of notes recount folktales and myths from various cultures. The Crossing Press has reissued *The Work of a Common Woman* (1984), Grahn's collected poetry from 1964 to 1977. Grahn's commitment to literary redefinition and to "common women" is apparent as well in her decision to edit a two-volume series of stories by women, *True to Life Adventure Stories* (Diana Press, 1978, 1981). Writing in a deliberately nonacademic, nonliterary language, the authors redefine the "adventure" story by focusing on the experiences of ordinary working-class women.

693. Grilikhes, Alexandra. **On Women Artists: Poems 1975-1980.** Minneapolis: Cleis Press, 1981. 84p. pbk. $4.95. LC 81-65430. ISBN 093941600X.

The organizing principle of this interesting collection—to pay tribute to other women artists—works well for Grilikhes in the majority of poems here. She celebrates dance, photography, film, and painting, as well as particular artists and their work: Louise Nevelson, Joan Sutherland, and Marguerite Duras, among others. The black-and-white photographs of sculpture and fiber art serve the text poorly.

694. Grosholz, Emily, 1950- . **The River Painter.** Urbana: University of Illinois Press, 1984. 86p. pbk. $7.95. LC 83-4875. ISBN 0252010981.

This promising first book of poetry demonstrates the elegant, controlled versifying of philosopher Emily Grosholz. Grosholz's poetry spills over with regional rhythm from nature and art. Although lyrically beautiful, the verse inspired by Chinese nature poetry is neither feminist nor female-centered. Other poems do speak to women's experience. "To My Daughter" deliberately plays on some familiar Donne and Arnoldian lines and is a fine example of Grosholz's power: "Little one, though you and I/hold ourselves hard against/the tide of that great river/rounding continents,/we are fluid at our center" (p.84).

695. Hacker, Marilyn. **Assumptions.** New York: Knopf, 1985. 92p. $14.95. LC 84-48537. ISBN 0394542290.

Hacker's trademark is her ability to write poems that are traditional in form yet strikingly modern in tone; her colloquial, often blunt language both revitalizes and subverts the rigorous formality of her sonnets, sestinas, and villanelles. In this volume, Hacker reassesses her earlier assumptions about her identity as a mother, daughter, Jew, feminist, and lesbian. Most of the poems explore her relationship with her mother; in learning to forgive and accept her mother, the poet finds that she can come to terms with her relationship with her own daughter as well. In the concluding series of poems, Hacker moves from the personal to the mythic: she appropriates Hans Christian Andersen's story of "The Snow Queen," transforming it into a parable of a woman's quest for identity.

696. Hadas, Pamela White, 1946- . **Beside Herself: Pocahontas to Patty Hearst.** New York: Knopf, 1983. 241p. $14.95. LC 82-49003. ISBN 0394529936.

Most of the speakers in these seventeen remarkable poetic monologues are famous American women, public figures like Pocahontas, Carry Nation, Louisa May Alcott, the Watergate wives, Patty Hearst. Temperamentally, they range from Belle Starr, the Bandit Queen, to Pat Nixon. Yet public or private, outgoing or introspective, each speaker defines her femininity in disappearance, nonbeing—in Belle Starr's words, "I woke up missin" (p.73). Hadas captures each woman in an epiphanic moment when she is "beside herself." In this visionary moment, some women vanish altogether, like the anorexic girl who says, "I am revealed as I disappear" (p.137), or like convicted murderer Jean Harris, who describes herself as "a person in an empty chair" (p.174). Others, like Harriet Tubman, achieve self-affirmation: "I ain't like to disremember/a single thing what come to pass ... I done my best" (p.47). Hadas creates an astonishing variety of voices and poetic forms, from Pocahontas's dignified blank verse to Baseball Annie's breezy ballad stanzas. Extensively researched and skillfully executed, these poems provide a stunning articulation of the experience of American women.

697.   Harjo, Joy. **She Had Some Horses.** New York: Thunder's Mouth Press, 1983. 74p. $14.95. LC 82-17064. ISBN 0938410075.

In her third book of poetry, Joy Harjo of the Creek tribe explores the American Indian experience in cities like Anchorage, Kansas City, and Chicago. "The woman hanging from the 13th floor window/on the east side of Chicago is not alone./She is a woman of children, of the baby, Carlos,/and of Margaret, and of Jimmy who is the oldest./She is her mother's daughter and her father's son./She is several pieces between the two husbands/she has had ..." (p.22). The hanging woman's "mind chatters like neon and northside bars" (p.23). The poet finds dislocation in the urban experience. Often juxtaposed against the harsh city rhythms are the more natural rhythms of nature, meditation, and prayer. An earlier volume of verse, *What Moon Drove Me to This* (I. Reed Books, 1979), celebrates American Indian contemporary life, whether in "The Lost Weekend Bar" (p.14) or near home in "Oklahoma and the hungry prairie" (p.36).

698.   Head, Gwen, 1940- . **The Ten Thousandth Night.** Pittsburgh: University of Pittsburgh Press, 1979. 59p. $12.95. LC 78-21991. ISBN 0822933918.

Gwen Head is an important American poet who remains relatively obscure despite publishing in major poetry reviews. Her imagery is notable for its precision and crystalized elegance, as in "Recent Acquisitions": "Item: one tea bowl, Japanese *Oribe*/of a frozen porridge color/its rim marked/by three vertical lines/terminating in circular scrawls" (p.32). Her use of language, startling and original, results in lines that, camera-like, survey scenes: "Above her silken knees, the satin hem/hangs like a blade. It's nineteen twenty-nine" (p.3).

699.   Hogan, Linda. **Calling Myself Home.** Greenfield Center, NY: Greenfield Review Press, 1978. 33p. pbk. $3.00. LC 79-129720. ISBN 0912678372.

Hogan's poems grow out of her experiences on Chickasaw Indian "relocation land" in Oklahoma. She speaks of the Chickasaw's alienation in poems like "Heritage," where her family bequeaths her "the secrets/of never having a home" (p.17). Still, the dominant theme of the collection is one of unity and connectedness. Thus, although there is "a dry river bed/between them and us," Hogan feels at one with her ancestors, whose "bones are holding up the earth" (p.6). She also breaks down the barriers between humans and nature: "Everything speaks./Put your ear to the earth/and hear it, the trees speaking" (p.28). Like *Calling Myself Home,* Hogan's *Seeing Through the Sun* (University of Massachusetts Press, 1985) is filled with images of the Oklahoma landscape; it also features a sequence of poems on motherhood. *Daughters, I Love You* (Research Center on Women, Loretto Heights College, 1981) is a series of poems on nuclear war.

700. Jackson, Laura (Riding), 1901- . **The Poems of Laura Riding: A New Edition of the 1938 Collection.** New York: Random House, 1938; repr. New York: Persea Books, 1980. 419p. $20.00. LC 79-91169. ISBN 0892550449.

This volume reproduces the 1938 edition of Riding's complete poems, with a new introduction and notes by the author. Like Marianne Moore, Riding avoids the personal in her poetry; but unlike Moore's brilliant imagistic portraits, her verse is not descriptive but philosophical, musing on life, death, language, identity. In her introduction, Riding explains that she renounced poetry for philosophical and linguistic speculation because she viewed poetry as inadequate to express "human and linguistic universalness" (p.9). Indeed, her distrust of the language capabilities of poetry is apparent as early as the 1933 verse "Poet, a Lying Word": "It is a false wall, a poet: it is a lying word. It is a wall that closes and does not" (p.216). In *Laura Riding's Pursuit of Truth* (Ohio University Press, 1979), Joyce Piell Wexler combines textual criticism and biography to illuminate the linguistic, rhetorical, and philosophical complexities of Riding's Modernist verse. Wexler's *Laura Riding: A Bibliography* (Garland, 1981) includes full bibliographic descriptions of Riding's major works and a partially annotated list of secondary works.

701. Jacobsen, Josephine. **The Chinese Insomniacs: New Poems.** Philadelphia: University of Pennsylvania Press, 1981. 79p. $16.50. LC 81-40556. ISBN 0812278186.

The title poem in this collection sets the tone for these sometimes difficult, ironic meditations on the nature of time, memory, subjective experience, and history: "A date is only a mark/on paper—it has little to do/with what is long./It is good to have their company/tonight: a lady, awake/until birdsong; a gentleman who made/poems later out of frag-/ments of the dark" (p.11). Other poems in this eclectic volume deal with pigeons, the weather, Africa, and philosophy. Jacobsen's work spans a long career, beginning with *For the Unlost*, published in 1948. Her last book prior to *Chinese Insomniacs* was *The Shade Seller: New and Selected Poems* (1974).

702. Jong, Erica. **Ordinary Miracles: New Poems.** New York: New American Library, 1983. 141p. $12.95. LC 83-8222. ISBN 0453004520.

Jong's fifth volume of poetry epitomizes her desire "to write out of a naked female consciousness" (p.xiv). Deliberately unsophisticated and accessible, these intensely, and often painfully, personal poems recount not only the "ordinary miracles" of the writer's life—pregnancy, the birth of her daughter Molly, parenthood—but also the pain of her divorce from her beloved third husband, her consequent fear of life and love, and her confusion about the proper relationship between her life and art. Yet the volume closes with an insistence on the necessity of continued openness toward love. Many of the same autobiographical experiences reappear in a comic vein in Jong's 1984 novel *Parachutes and Kisses* (New American Library), an account of the latest adventures of *Fear of Flying* heroine Isadora Wing. In a change of pace, Jong has also produced a witty and ribald pastiche of an eighteenth-century picaresque, *Fanny: Being the True History of the Adventures of Fanny Hackabout-Jones* (New American Library, 1980), and a spinoff historical work, *Witches* (H. A. Abrams, 1981).

703. Jordan, June, 1936- . **Passion, New Poems, 1977-1980.** Boston: Beacon Press, 1980. 100p. $13.95. LC 80-66073. ISBN 0807032182.

Jordan is not only a poet, but also a teacher, political activist, journalist, film scenarist, novelist, and urban designer. The multiplicity of her interests, as well as her poetic abilities, is evident as she writes of U.S. imperialism in the Third World, racism, and sexism. Her poetry, like all her writings, grows out of her experience as a black woman and represents an attempt to change the world: as she writes in a poem about Sojourner Truth, "This hell has made me tough/I'm a strong Black woman/and Thank God!" (p.50). Aptly titled, *Passion* demonstrates Jordan's love for life and commitment to oppressed peoples in an unjust world. Injustice is also the subject of *Civil Wars* (Beacon Press, 1981), a collection of Jordan's essays, letters, journal entries, and articles from the sixties and seventies, which constitutes an intellectual and political autobiography of Jordan's life. Combative and provocative, Jordan takes on such subjects as black versus white English, and the portrayal of blacks in the media. In *On Call* (South End Press, 1985), a collection of political essays from the 1980s, and *Living Room* (Thunder's Mouth Press; distr. Persea Books, 1985), her latest book of poetry, she concentrates on recent examples of injustice in Central America, Lebanon, South Africa, and the United States.

704. Kaschnitz, Marie Luise, 1901-1974. **Selected Later Poems of Marie Luise Kaschnitz.** Princeton, NJ: Princeton University Press, 1980. 111p. $15.00. LC 80-7537. ISBN 0691064423.

A virtual unknown to Americans, Kaschnitz practiced her art with great success in Germany during her lifetime, turning out numerous volumes of verse, fiction, and journals. In the present collection, we find selections from four volumes of verse: *Neue Gedichte* (*New Poems,* 1957); *Dein Schweigen-meine Stimme* (*Your Silence—My Voice,* 1962); *Ein Wort weiter* (*One Word Further,* 1965); and *Kein Zauberspruch* (*No Magic Formula,* 1972). This edition provides the original German on the left facing a very competent translation on the right. Kaschnitz's poetic material derives from both public and private experience. For example, the poet recollects the horrors of war in the poems "Hiroshima" and "A Map of Sicily," while she mourns the death of her archaeologist husband in "More Terrible." She pits modernity against tradition, life against death in poems like "Broadcast for Women," in which she advises women to "smash the clocks in your washing machines," and "Who Would Have Thought It," which offers the prophecy "In a few decades/We will enter the world/Still between the legs of women/But so well designed/That we'll know how to do everything."

705. Kaye, Melanie, 1945- . **We Speak in Code: Poems and Other Writings.** Pittsburgh: Motheroot, 1980. 106p. pbk. $4.75. ISBN 0934238022.

Kaye explores the social and political implications of personal experience. After an opening highlighted by the essay "On Being a Lesbian Feminist Artist," the volume is divided into four sections. In "Jewish Food," the poet delves into her heritage. The poems in "Living With Chaos" speak about private love in the face of social disintegration. In "Naming," Kaye asks, "are we ready to name/with a common tongue?" (p.58), then renames the meaning of both her own life and the lives of such mythical women as Pandora and Cassandra. And in "We Speak in Code," Kaye's subject is communication between women. Kaye's poems are concrete, autobiographical, often angry, sometimes funny; all are written out of the evolving consciousness of a woman "who learns/how to season and stir/on one foot./and dance./sometimes the ground is not firm/sometimes no one/has stood this ground before" (p.4). Her writing is complemented by photographs of artwork by Paula King.

706. Kizer, Carolyn. **Mermaids in the Basement: Poems for Women.** Port Townsend, WA: Copper Canyon Press, 1984. 105p. $14.00. LC 84-71253. ISBN 0914742809.

Kizer was writing feminist poetry long before it was in fashion. *Mermaids in the Basement* brings together her poems for women from several earlier volumes arranged in thematic groups: mothers and daughters; female friends; mythic revisions; love poems based on Chinese models; a diary of a love affair; and poems of self-assessment. A separate section is devoted to "Pro Femina" (first published in 1965), a witty, angry discourse on the social and literary status of women: "I will speak about women of letters, for I'm in the racket./... we are the custodians of the world's best-kept secret:/Merely the private lives of one-half of humanity" (pp.43-44). Throughout, the poems shine with intelligence, luminous imagery, and formal elegance. Kizer's *Yin* (BOA Editions, 1984) won the 1985 Pulitzer Prize for poetry.

707.* Klepfisz, Irena, 1941- . **Different Enclosures.** London: Onlywomen Press, 1985. 183p. £3.95. ISBN 0906500176.

Different Enclosures brings together poems from two earlier volumes by Klepfisz. The first, *Periods of Stress* (1975), includes lesbian love poetry, poems on violence, and meditations on living alone. The second, and more powerful, volume is *Keeper of Accounts* (Persephone Press, 1982), a wrenching collection about Klepfisz's experience as an *outsider*: as a young girl in Warsaw who escaped the Holocaust only by denying her Jewishness; as a Pole uprooted and transplanted to America; as a lesbian in a heterosexual culture; and as an artist oppressed by the demands of everyday survival. In a variety of forms, Klepfisz explores the "different enclosures" in which we are entrapped, moving from monkeys in cages, to creative women stuck in deadening jobs, to Jews in ghettos and death camps. In the end, Klepfisz affirms the possibility of survival and renewal by recognizing her own Jewish roots: "Like these, my despised ancestors/I have become a keeper of accounts" (p.170).

708. Kumin, Maxine, 1925- . **Our Ground Time Here Will Be Brief.** New York: Viking Press, 1982. 224p. $7.95. LC 81-69995. ISBN 0670531081.

Drawing upon six previous volumes, this collection represents twenty years of Kumin's poetry. During that time, Kumin has taught, won a Pulitzer Prize, raised a family, and written prose fiction. Her perspective is womanly, not necessarily feminist. New England and its brisk, homey charms provide inspiration. Of children, the poet asks, "Where are the children/who ate their way through helpings/of cereals and stews/to designs of horse, pig,/sheep on view/at the bottom of the dish?" (p.7). The poet at sixty looks back on child-rearing, on friendships terminated by death, on fathers and great-grandfathers. In one poem, she likens her daughters to "woodsmoke, bee balm, heartsease/... concise as cats/fastidious as pearls...." While the poet "sing[s] in praise" of the girls, she contrasts them with the son who is "my monument, my stone" (p.178). In Kumin's latest poetry volume, *The Long Approach* (Viking Press, 1985), autobiographical poems about family and farm are framed by more overtly political verses that link empathy with the environment to the theme of survival in the nuclear age. Kumin writes creditable fiction, as well. Her first collection of stories, *Why Can't We Live Together Like Civilized Human Beings?* (Viking Press, 1982), chronicles the compromises and constrictions of marriage and love affairs. In "Another Form of Marriage," the protagonist wrestles with the slender line of difference between marriage and taking a lover: "What was this affair but another form of marriage?," Kumin asks. "Instead of being faithful to one man, she was faithful to two" (p.7).

709. Levertov, Denise, 1923- . **Candles in Babylon.** New York: New Directions, 1982. 117p. $12.95. LC 81-22289. ISBN 0811208303.

Candles in Babylon demonstrates the range of Levertov's poetic abilities, as well as the depth of her political commitment. She depicts both the horrors of the modern world — corruption, genocide, nuclear threat — and its beauties. Accordingly, she takes a wide variety of poetic stances: apocalyptic musings, meditations, love songs, satire, whimsy, and lyric. Although she recognizes the artist's need for solitude, Levertov calls for the poet to work for world change, so that "we may return/from this place of terror/home to a calm dawn" (n.p.). Readers can trace Levertov's growth as a poet, from the often flowery romanticism of her early verses, many of which are included in *Collected Earlier Poems, 1940-1960* (New Directions, 1979), to the spare, yet passionate maturity of her latest volume, *Oblique Prayers: New Poems With 14 Translations From Jean Joubert* (New Directions, 1984).

710. Lewis, Janet, 1899- . **Poems Old and New, 1918-1978.** Chicago: Swallow Press; Athens, OH: Ohio University Press, 1981. 112p. $15.95. LC 80-26209. ISBN 0804003718.

Lewis has established a solid reputation over the years for writing traditional verse. This collection gives the shape of her career — 1918-1927, Northern Michigan and Santa Fe, New Mexico; 1927-1930, Palo Alto; 1930-1944, Santa Clara County; and Later Poems, 1971-1978, Los Altos. Lewis is a Western American poet whose imagination has been strongly influenced by the American Indian experience and ecological concerns. Her skill in painting nature's brief moments is unexcelled among modern American poets, as when she evokes a hummingbird caught in its "Furious intent assault/Upon the honeyed blossom" (p.104).

711. Li, Ch'ing-chao, 1084-c.1151. **Li Ch'ing-chao, Complete Poems.** Edited by Kenneth Rexroth and Ling Chung. New York: New Directions, 1979. 118p. $12.95. LC 79-15596. ISBN 0811207447.

In that Li Ch'ing-chao is ranked by most scholars of Chinese literature as the greatest Chinese woman poet, the Rexroth and Chung edition is worth having. Li worked in the tz'u form, a lyric popular during the Sung dynasty; her subjects are loosely organized by Rexroth and Chung into thematic groups about youth, loneliness, exile, death, politics, mysticism, and old age. In his brief biography of Li, Ling Chung notes that her life was "colorful and versatile: other than a great poet, she was a scholar of history and classics, a literary critic, an art collector, a specialist in bronze and stone inscriptions, a painter, a calligrapher, and a political commentator" (p.83). In the poetry, her imagery is suffused with consciousness that she writes as a woman: "I wipe away my tears/And stain my silk sleeves with rouge and powder" (p.28).

712. Lifshin, Lyn. **Kiss the Skin Off.** Silver Spring, MD: Cherry Valley Editions; distr. Silver Spring, MD: Beach, 1985. 119p. $15.00. LC 84-17035. ISBN 0916156699.

Lifshin is known for her frank, casual, unacademic poetic style, for her strong personal voice, and for her satirical jabs at hypocrisy and pretension. Some of the poems in this volume are clever but shallow — wit for its own sake — and their unremitting sexual focus can get wearing. Still, Lifshin has a sharp eye for the nuances of contemporary culture, whether she is writing on Elvis Presley's Graceland, blues singer Alberta Hunter, the "women with dyed apricot hair" at a poetry reading who want to hear "poems about/marriage, limoge and baby/daughters" (p.66), or wolfish pedants at the Modern Language Association convention. Lifshin also writes of herself — her marriage, divorce, career, lovers, family—with an unstudied directness, as in "Mother and Daughter Photos": "I'm in several with/her standing in back her/arms around me her prize/melon a book she/would write" (p.98). Lifshin has published several other books of verse, among them *Blue Dust, New Mexico* (Basilisk Press, 1982) and *Madonna Who Shifts for Herself* (Applezaba Press, 1983).

713. Lorde, Audre. **Chosen Poems, Old and New.** New York: Norton, 1982. 115p. $12.95. LC 81-22484. ISBN 0393015769.

"For women, ... poetry is not a luxury. It is a vital necessity of our existence"—writes Audre Lorde in an essay in *Sister Outsider* (see entry 430). Lorde selects poems for this volume from five earlier collections: *Coal* (1976); *The First Cities* (1968); *Cables to Rage* (1970; second edition, 1973); *From a Land Where Other People Live* (1973); and *New York Head Shop and Museum* (1975). Seven new poems finish the volume. Lorde's poetry, like her prose, is strongly political, whether speaking of her own personal experience—raising children, falling in love—or events in the world. In "The Day They Eulogized Mahalia," Lorde juxtaposes the belated tribute paid by the city of Chicago to singer Mahalia Jackson—("Now she was safe/acceptable/that big Mahalia")—against the deaths that same day of six black children in a day care center housed in a condemned building on Chicago's South Side: "Small and without song/six black children found a voice in flame/the day the city eulogized Mahalia" (pp.50-51).

714. Loy, Mina, 1878-1966. **The Last Lunar Baedeker.** Edited by Roger L. Conover. Highlands: Jargon Society; distr. East Haven, CT: Inland Book Company, 1982. 334p. $25.00. LC 81-86061. ISBN 0942330465.

Mina Loy was a contemporary of Virginia Woolf, Gertrude Stein, and Djuna Barnes. A poet, artist, and playwright, she languished in undeserved obscurity until very recently, when scholars began to recognize the brilliance of her difficult, fragmented poetic style and her unsentimental explorations of female selfhood. This important volume will introduce readers to a variety of Loy's writings, including poems published between 1914 and 1950, unpublished poems, polemical writings, profiles and interviews, and prose fragments. Editor Roger L. Conover supplements Loy's works with a lengthy biographical introduction; photographs of her paintings, designs, and sculptures; and bibliographical notes. Virginia M. Kouidis's *Mina Loy: American Modernist Poet* (Louisiana State University Press, 1980) presents a detailed critical analysis of Loy's poems, stressing their "personal honesty and daring technical experiment" (p.2).

715. Maddock, Mary, trans. **Three Russian Women Poets: Anna Akhmatova, Marina Tsvetayeva, Bella Akhmadulina.** Trumansburg, NY: Crossing Press, 1983. 109p. $17.95. LC 83-14436. ISBN 089594121X.

Anna Akhmatova (1889-1966), Marina Tsvetaeva (1892-1941), and Bella Akhmadulina (b.1937) stand among the most important modern Russian poets. Maddock's selections from their works, sensitively translated, introduce these poets to Western readers and invite comparison of their distinctly female voices. The free verse English renderings preserve Akhmatova's dramatically personal and lyric tone, Tsvetaeva's staccato rhythms and elliptical meaning, and Akhmadulina's startling images of people and nature. Akhmatova, perhaps the most famous of the three, wrote in a classical form that is necessarily sacrificed here. Other translators have recently attempted to replicate Akhmatova's rhymes and meters, with mixed success. Among them are novelist and critic D. M. Thomas (*Way of All the Earth,* Ohio University Press, 1979) and poet Lyn Coffin (*Poems,* Norton, 1983).

716. McPherson, Sandra. **Patron Happiness.** New York: Ecco Press, 1983. 71p. $12.95. LC 82-11490. ISBN 0880010215.

McPherson has published in major poetry journals as well as in many little magazines. Her work is eclectic, ranging from a tribute to Elizabeth Bishop, a former teacher, to pornography in Nebraska; from marriage to a meditation on winter. These difficult poems have received much from Bishop's tutelage. In language spare and abstract, McPherson describes what most of us would overlook. The work of people in a natural history museum contains for her the stuff of poetry: "The dioramacist does not know/How the Creator shows emotion./So he flings the passenger pigeon across the sunset/As a guess. And the pigeons look joyous./In fact, he says, I could call it a sunrise,/no one will ever know" (p.62).

717. Miles, Josephine, 1911- . **Collected Poems, 1930-1983.** Urbana: University of Illinois Press, 1983. 260p. index. $17.50. LC 82-11014. ISBN 0252010175.

A first-rate poet, Miles is not widely known outside of poetry circles. Her published work marks a progression from her short, halting verse of the 1930s to the increasingly self-confident, philosophical voice of a Berkeley professor. This enduring poetic voice has uttered lyrics about nature, the seasons, items in the newspaper, the routine of college teaching, chance acquaintances, a lottery ticket, and hundreds of commonplace events. Of each poetic opportunity she makes "an enchantment/To be transformed also, so I might bend/Into the perilous shape not of my vague spirit/But of a friend" (p.245). Miles rarely writes about women; when she does, her poetry abstracts the topic, leaving no trace of feminism.

718.* Mohin, Lilian, ed. **One Foot on the Mountain: An Anthology of British Feminist Poetry, 1969-1979.** London: Onlywomen Press, 1979. 252p. £2.95. LC 80-454963. ISBN 090650001X.

This volume brings together poems by fifty-five British women, most of them previously unpublished. Editor Lilian Mohin comments that she has chosen works that are "clearly representative of feminist thinking," as well as "effective, moving, strongly put" (p.2). The result is a powerful, if uneven, collection. Angrily, often polemically, the poets write on such issues as abortion, body images, stereotypes of women, men's and women's language, and sexuality. Many of them emphasize the power of poetry as a liberating force and a means of redefinition. Each poet's works are accompanied by a short biography and a photograph. This collection provides U.S. readers with a provocative introduction to both political poetry and British feminism.

719. Moore, Marianne, 1887-1972. **The Complete Poems of Marianne Moore.** New York: Viking Press, 1981. 305p. index. $16.95. LC 82-6608. ISBN 0140423001.

This definitive edition of Moore's poetry replaces the 1967 volume of collected poems. It includes works published between 1935 and 1966, incorporating Moore's revisions, plus five poems written before her death in 1972. Moore's brilliant, oblique, apparently impersonal poetic style is the subject of Bonnie Costello's study, *Marianne Moore: Imaginary Possessions* (Harvard University Press, 1981). Unlike most critics, Costello concentrates on Moore's poetry rather than on the author as self-effacing eccentric. Her sensitive analyses should spark renewed appreciation of Moore's intellectual rigor, linguistic precision, and intense — if restrained — emotion.

720. Mora, Pat. **Chants.** Houston: Arte Público Press, 1984. 52p. pbk. $5.00. LC 83-070677. ISBN 0934770247.

These simple, stunning narrative poems, incantations, and love songs are set in El Paso, a town surrounded by desert. They capture the situation of Mexican-American women in whom the sensuality and magic of Mayan, Aztec, and Toltec legend, the rigid sexual taboos of Spanish Catholicism, and the materialism of modern America intersect. Mora sings of the Toltecs, who "made a castle of gleaming quetzal plumage" (p.14); of a mother who gives her daughter a golden ring for her wedding night so she can cut her finger and ensure the bloodstained sheets of a virgin; and of a Mexican maid who wants to lie in the moonlight and "wake to a new skin/that would glisten white" like her employer's (p.36). Dominating the collection is the image of the desert, the "strong mother" (p.9). Two other volumes of poetry in the Arte Público series are Ana Castillo's *Women Are Not Roses* (1984) and Sandra Cisneros's *The House on Mango Street* (1983).

721. Olds, Sharon. **The Dead and the Living.** New York: Knopf, 1984. 80p. $14.95. LC 83-47780. ISBN 0394530489.

Olds is often compared to Plath, perhaps because of the private sphere she makes horrifyingly public. There is a monster in the house, and in the segments of this book entitled "The Family" and "The Men," he takes over. "The Ideal Father"—the "one who threw up .../The one who passed out, the one who would not/speak for a week, slapped the glasses off a/young girl's face ..." (p.38)—is eerily close to something out of a case history. Ambivalence about the father pervades these technically adept poems. Olds addresses her husband: "As I see you/embracing me, in the mirror, I see I am/my father as a woman ..." (p.56). She ends this collection with a section on children that relieves the tension of some of the grimmer poems. *Satan Says* (University of Pittsburgh Press, 1980) was Olds's first book of verse.

722. Oliver, Mary Jane, 1935- . **Twelve Moons.** Boston: Little, Brown, 1979. 77p. $7.95. LC 79-10428. ISBN 0316650013.

A poet who has received wide recognition for her work in mainstream periodicals and the better-known little magazines, Oliver finds the material for her verse in nature. The Provincetown poet professes her poetics of nature-closely-observed in a small poem titled "Entering the Kingdom." "The dream of my life/Is to lie down by a slow river/And stare at the light in the trees—To learn something by being nothing/A little while but the rich/Lens of attention" (p.21). Other published collections by Oliver include *No Voyage and Other Poems* (1963), *The River Styx, Ohio and Other Poems* (1972), and *The Night Traveler* (1978). In *American Primitive* (1983), her latest book of poems, Oliver again celebrates the physical world. In clear, musical, and emotionally intense verse, she moves from the particulars of the natural world to such universal concerns as life and death, isolation and connectedness.

723. Parker, Pat, 1944- . **Jonestown and Other Madness.** Ithaca, NY: Firebrand Books, 1985. 75p. $11.95. LC 85-1679. ISBN 093237901X.

Parker has become well-known as a black lesbian poet who writes in a straightforward, no-nonsense style composed equally of humor and outrage. The poems in this volume are topical responses to such "madnesses" as the suicide of nine hundred blacks in Jonestown, Guyana and the murders of black children in Atlanta. Parker's anger burns hottest in "Jonestown," where she asserts that the nine hundred "did not commit suicide/they were murdered" (p.63) by indifferent teachers, welfare workers, the police, and politicians: "they went to Jonestown dead/convinced that America/and Americans/don't care" (p.64). Yet she closes the volume with "Legacy," a history of her family that ends with a hopeful expostulation to her daughter: "let the world stand screaming./You will mute their voices/with your life" (p.75).

724.* Pastan, Linda, 1932- . **Waiting for My Life.** New York: Norton, 1981. 72p. LC 80-20012. ISBN 039301441X.

Some of the most compelling poems in this collection wrestle with the tie between parent and child, especially as the child grows away from the closeness of the family bond. "Letter to a Son at Exam Time," to instance one, is an epistolary engagement of the mother with a son who "woke up/on the wrong side/of my life." "When you forget again/to call," she admonishes him, "it's poet and parent both/that you deny./This is what I didn't know/I knew" (p.15). Pastan, in her measured voice, is at "war between desire and dailiness." In a poem by that name, she domesticates military images of children with "spoons in the fists," and summons up "my only flag, a pillowcase/bleaching in the sun/on which no lover's head/has rested yet" (p.41).

725. Piercy, Marge. **Circles on the Water: Selected Poems of Marge Piercy.** New York: Knopf, 1982. 299p. $17.50. LC 81-17210. ISBN 0394520599.

Circles on the Water includes selections from seven volumes of poetry spanning twenty years, and provides an excellent introduction to Piercy's work. The poems in this volume treat women's issues such as rape, reproductive control, standards of beauty, and women's spirituality, along with nuclear war, ecological destruction, and the cycles of nature. Believing that writing should integrate the personal and the political, Piercy rejects the abstractions of men who would talk "of integrity and existential ennui/while the women ran out for six-packs and had abortions" (p.80). She thus emphasizes the concrete, both in her subjects — garden, friends, quilt-making — and in her style, where earthy, domestic similes abound. Belying the serenity of her title, Piercy's rage at women's oppression is evident thorughout the collection, since she believes "a good anger acted upon/Is ... swift with power" (p.88). This prolific writer's fusion of ideology and emotion is also apparent in two more recent volumes of poetry, *Stone, Paper, Knife* (Knopf, 1983) and *My Mother's Body* (Knopf, 1985); and in her novels, where each character's personal history is shaped by his or her sociopolitical context: *Vida* (Summit Books, 1979), about a revolutionary on the run in the 1970s; *Braided Lives* (Summit Books, 1982), a semi-autobiographical account of coming of age in the 1950s; and *Fly Away Home* (Summit Books, 1984), about the painful awakening of a comfortable housewife confronted with divorce in the 1980s. Though sometimes heavy-handed, Piercy's works remain compelling due to their narrative drive and emotional intensity. Readers interested in Piercy would do well to examine *Parti-Colored Blocks for a Quilt* (University of Michigan Press, 1982), a collection of essays and interviews in which she explains her philosophy as a writer and reviews such authors as Audre Lorde, Joanna Russ, Adrienne Rich, and Margaret Atwood.

726. Pratt, Minnie Bruce. **We Say We Love Each Other.** San Francisco: Spinsters, Ink, 1985. 98p. $5.95. LC 85-50991. ISBN 0933216130.

Pratt's poems concern her past experiences growing up in the South and her present love for women. The love poems are sandwiched between three longer, more ambitious pieces entitled "Reading Maps." In the first of these poems, Pratt reflects on the extent to which, in her involvement with another woman, she has broken out of "a map of someone else's world" to imagine "a place not marked yet on any map" (p.9). In the second, she searches for a "map for the past" (p.35) so that she can understand her relationship with her mother. And in the third, she connects past and present as she visits an island her mother has told her about, a place "marked by her words/in the map of her stories" (p.91), and imagines living there with her lover. Pratt's first volume of poetry, *The Sound of One Fork* (Night Heron Press, 1981), explores similar themes, evoking in particular the atmosphere of her Southern childhood.

727.* Raine, Kathleen, 1908- . **Collected Poems, 1935-1980.** Boston: Allen and Unwin, 1981. 312p. index. LC 82-126645. ISBN 0048210501.

Raine is a prominent British Blake scholar and poet whose work is largely unfamiliar to U.S. readers. This volume, which includes selections from ten earlier poetry collections, plus uncollected and occasional verses, shows her to be strongly in the mystical tradition of Blake and Yeats. Raine's theme is the incarnation of the metaphysical within the material world. Thus, many of her poems begin as meticulous observations of natural objects, but end up as meditations on love, loss, birth, death, God. Raine also employs mythic figures—often alienated women like Eve and Medea—to explore the mystical center of women's lives. The tension between Raine's Aristotelian intellect and her Platonic soul keeps the poems from sinking into prophetic bombast; stylistically, they are remarkable for the restrained lyricism of her language.

728. Reilly, Catherine W., ed. **Scars Upon My Heart: Women's Poetry and Verse of the First World War.** London: Virago Press, 1981. 144p. index. pbk. $7.50. ISBN 0860682269.

Of the two thousand or so Britons who published poetry about World War I during the period 1914 to 1918, over five hundred were women; yet anthologies of Great War poetry are almost exclusively male. *Scars Upon My Heart* fills that gap with 125 poems by 79 women, from anonymous writers to well-known figures like Vera Brittain and Alice Meynell. In so doing, it challenges stereotypes of the "women back home." The common thread in the poems is grief over the dead and injured, but the writers' attitudes vary widely. Several writers angrily critique the ideology of war, but the majority try desperately to find some meaning in the slaughter. The quality of the poems ranges from indifferent to superb; but it is as a testament of women's consciousness in wartime, rather than as a literary document, that this volume excels. Reilly has also edited a companion volume, *Chaos in the Night: Women's Poetry and Verse of the Second World War* (Virago Press, 1984).

729. Rich, Adrienne. **The Fact of a Doorframe: Poems Selected and New 1950-1984.** New York: Norton, 1984. 341p. index. pbk. $18.95. LC 84-6107. ISBN 0393019055.

This major collection brings together poems from nine volumes published between 1950 and 1984, plus uncollected works. Rich makes no secret of her political and poetic aim: "I have cast my lot with those/who age after age, perversely,/with no extraordinary power,/reconstitute the world" (p.264). Many of the later poems—especially those from *A Wild Patience Has Taken Me This Far* (Norton, 1981)—emphasize the connections between women (the "nets of telepathy contrived/to outlast the iron road" [p.282]) and women's courage. Not included in this collection are the twenty-three poems of *Sources* (Heyeck Press, 1983), in which Rich tries to rediscover and rename her own identity as a woman, Jew, white Southerner, adoptive New Englander, lesbian, and feminist. In the important and eloquent essays of *On Lies, Secrets, and Silence: Selected Prose 1966-1978* (Norton, 1979), Rich acts on her belief that "Re-vision—the act of looking back, of seeing with fresh eyes, ... —is for women ... an act of survival" (p.35). Here she turns a visionary eye on academia, motherhood, love, and literature. Both the prose and poetry collections document the pain and liberation of Rich's personal and artistic changes; as she says in *Sources*, "there is no finite knowing, no such rest" (p.35). *Reading Adrienne Rich* (University of Michigan Press, 1984), edited by Jane Roberta Cooper, is a useful collection of contemporary essays on Rich's poetry and prose, plus reviews of her poetry from 1951 to 1982.

730.   Rose, Wendy. **What Happened When the Hopi Hit New York.** New York: Contact II Publications, 1982. 41p. pbk. $3.50. ISBN 0936556080.

Wendy Rose writes intensely personal poetry about the American Indians' search for identity, especially as they move away from the tribal environment to punk parties in Brooklyn, Manhattan subways, Chicago's airport—experiences of fragmentation and of loss. Near the Hopi reservation in Arizona, the poet watches a Hopi family drive by in a pickup, smiling welcome. "I shout/I remember you/I am not one to forget" (p.4).

731.   Rossetti, Christina, 1830-1894. **The Complete Poems of Christina Rossetti. Vol. 1.** Edited by Rebecca W. Crump. Baton Rouge: Louisiana State University Press, 1979. $27.50. LC 78-5571. ISBN 0807103586.

Christina Rossetti was long dismissed by critics as a shy spinster "poetess" of the Victorian era, overshadowed by her famous brother Dante Gabriel. Recently, though, critics have begun to appreciate the artistic merit of her work, as indicated by this variorum edition of her complete poems. Volume I includes Rossetti's first two published works, *Goblin Market and Other Poems* (1862) and *Prince's Progress and Other Poems* (1866). The editor, R. W. Crump, promises that poems from *Sing-Song* (1872), *A Pageant and Other Poems* (1881), and *Verses* (1893) will appear in Volume II, while Volume III will include individually published and unpublished works. Although Crump's introduction and notes give extensive information on the printing history and textual variations of Rossetti's poems, they provide no information on her life, or on the themes and techniques of her lyrical, spiritually intense writings. This gap is partially filled by Georgine Battiscombe's biography, *Christina Rossetti: A Divided Life* (Holt, Rinehart and Winston, 1981), which explores the deep divisions in Rossetti's world: between her emotional nature and her devout, disciplined Anglo-Catholicism; and between her family obligations as a daughter and sister and her needs as an artist. However, Battiscombe is hampered by a lack of primary sources, so that her study remains tantalizing but incomplete. Edna Kotin Charles's *Christina Rossetti* (Susquehanna University Press, 1985) surveys 120 years of Rossetti criticism.

732.   Scott, Diana, comp. **Bread and Roses: An Anthology of Nineteenth- and Twentieth-Century Poetry by Women Writers.** London: Virago; distr. Salem, NH: Merrimac, 1982. 282p. index. pbk. $10.95. ISBN 0860682358.

Teachers who would like to include a range of nineteenth- and twentieth-century poets in their syllabi will find this a useful anthology. Emily Brontë, Elizabeth Barrett Browning, and Alice Meynell are among the better-known British, American, and European poets included here. Lesser lights appear also, among them Felicia Hemans, Frances Cornford, Penelope Shuttle, and Frankie Armstrong, along with many unrecognized names from the 1970s and 1980s. Brief biographical sketches appear at the head of each chronologically arranged section.

733.   Sexton, Anne, 1928-1974. **The Complete Poems.** Boston: Houghton Mifflin, 1981. 622p. index. $20.00. LC 81-2482. ISBN 0395294754.

"No other American poet in our time has cried aloud publicly so many private details," writes Maxine Kumin in her introduction to this collection of all eight published works of Sexton (p.xix). Sexton's candor won her an extensive female audience, but often offended male critics and fellow poets. It is difficult to separate this confessional poet's work from her troubled personal life between 1957 and 1974, the years that saw her writing, teaching, and giving readings—ending in her suicide. Kumin's essay deals with Sexton's habits of work and places her in a canon of American women poets—among them, Bogan, Levertov, Rukeyser, Swenson, Plath, and Rich—whose preoccupation with women's experience predates the second wave of feminism. Criticism of *The Complete Poems* has centered on the unedited presentation of the poet's work—the strong, authoritative poetry of the 1960s juxtaposed to her later and lesser work, including poems unpublished during her lifetime and written close to her death in 1974. A selection of Sexton's essays, interviews, and prose has been gathered by Steven E. Colburn into a volume entitled *No Evil Star* (University of Michigan Press, 1985).

734.   Song, Cathy, 1955- . **Picture Bride.** New Haven, CT: Yale University Press, 1983. 85p. $12.95. LC 82-48910. ISBN 0300029594.

Song's grandmother was the "picture bride" of the title poem: "a year younger/than I,/twenty-three when she left Korea" (p.3). At that age, Song was writing poetry evoking the immigrant experience of those women who came before her, as well as her own observations as an Asian-American daughter. Inspired by both Georgia O'Keeffe's paintings and Kitagawa Utamaro, a printmaker of the nineteenth century, Song writes poems of admiration on the works of each. In his introduction to the volume, which won the Yale Series of Younger Poets award, poet Richard Hugo terms Song "passive," missing perhaps O'Keeffe's lesson to this poet: to exploit precisionism for the purpose of drawing the eye to the canvas. In a letter the poet imagines sending to her mother, she writes, "When I stretch a canvas/to paint the clouds,/it is your spine that declares itself:/arching,/ your arms stemming out like tender shoots/to hang sheets in the sky" (p.48).

735.   Stetson, Erlene, 1949- , ed. **Black Sister: Poetry of Black American Women, 1746-1980.** Bloomington: Indiana University Press, 1981. 312p. bibliog. $22.50. LC 80-8847. ISBN 0253305128.

This is the most comprehensive volume to date of poetry by black American women, with fifty-eight writers spanning the years 1774 to 1980. Stetson argues that black women have shared neither a literary heritage nor a stylistic tradition; instead, their themes and subjects "have developed ... out of common historical experiences" (p.xvii). Stetson sees the major theme of these writers as "a compelling quest for identity"; their common approach as based on "a subversive perception of reality"; and their creative strategies as "subterfuge and ambivalence" (p.xvii). The poets represented include all the well-known figures, from Phillis Wheatley to Gwendolyn Brooks to Ntozake Shange, but also a number of neglected writers, especially those from early in this century, such as Rosalie Jonas, Lucy Ariel Williams, and Naomi Long Madgett. Although she gives no biographical information about the poets, Stetson does provide an excellent bibliography of anthologies, works by the poets, and critical works. *Confirmation* (Morrow, 1983), edited by Amiri and Amina Baraka, is an anthology of contemporary black women's writings, including fiction, essays, poetry, and drama. The writers range from the famous to the previously unpublished, and the quality of the works varies. Strongest are the prose writings, among them Faith Ringgold's unpublished autobiography and Vértàmàè Smart-Gròsvènòr's essay on standards of beauty, "Skillet Blonde." The only jarring note in this volume is Amiri Baraka's introduction, which displays an astonishing lack of understanding of feminism and its relation to black women.

736.   Tsvetaeva, Marina Ivanova Éfron, 1892-1941. **The Demesne of the Swans.** Edited by Robin Kemball. Ann Arbor, MI: Ardis, 1980. 211p. bibliog. index. $15.00. LC 80-12957. ISBN 088233493X.

Russian poet Marina Tsvetaeva's life was marked by political upheaval and personal tragedy. A supporter of the czar, she fled from Russia with her family after the 1917 Revolution, supported her tubercular husband and two children in Prague and Paris, endured her husband's execution, and committed suicide in 1941. Yet Tsvetaeva became one of the greatest Russian writers of the century. *Demesne of the Swans* is the first English translation of any of Tsvetaeva's major poetry cycles. Written between 1917 and 1920 about the Russian Revolution, the poems' concerns are family, Russian history, loyalty, bloodshed, and grief. Robin Kemball's translations capture Tsvetaeva's staccato, allusive, elliptical style. The bilingual text is accompanied by extensive notes. A less scholarly translation is Elaine Feinstein's *Selected Poems of Marina Tsvetayeva* (Oxford University Press, 1981), which includes works written from 1915 though 1938. *A Captive Spirit*, edited and translated by J. Marin King (Ardis, 1980), features Tsvetaeva's brilliant, experimental prose in essays on Russian literary figures, autobiographical writings, and literary criticism.

737.   Ullman, Leslie. **Natural Histories.** New Haven, CT: Yale University Press, 1979. 53p. $13.95. LC 78-25591. ISBN 0300023294.

Leslie Ullman, winner in 1978 of the Yale Series of Younger Poets competition, promises to be a major presence in American poetry, if this volume is a signal of things to come. In his introduction, poet Richard Hugo praises her for "her honest, quiet way" of tapping "the self-generating power that lies within her" (p.xiii). Ullman grounds her verse in women's concerns: "Why There Are Children"; "Midwife"; "Beyond Dreams"; and "On Vacation a Woman Mistakes Her Leg"—some memorable moments in the work.

738.   Van Duyn, Mona, 1921- . **Letters From a Father, and Other Poems.** New York: Atheneum, 1982. 63p. $11.95. LC 81-70060. ISBN 0689112866.

Published in major poetry journals and magazines and yet not widely known, Van Duyn's poetry is delightful to read. She has a fine eye for detail, and she listens for the quirky phrase, incorporating it into her verse. She keeps her sense of humor, as in "Speak, Memory!," a poem that depends on Nabokov's memoir of that title for its reference. She writes, "For once she gets to go with big Cousin Beatie,/who is starting her breasts. They're at Uncle Charlie's farm./Grandma says, 'Ach, Kind, what will they think of next/enahow, the town school? Hunt butterflies, yet!'/But Beatie says, 'It's an *Assignment* '" (p.8).

739.   Wakoski, Diane. **Cap of Darkness: Including "Looking for the King of Spain" & "Pachelbel's Canon."** Santa Barbara, CA: Black Sparrow Press, 1980. 117p. $14.00. LC 80-149. ISBN 0876854544.

Perhaps the most compelling verse in this, Wakoski's twelfth volume, speaks to us through a feminist optic. "It is hard to imagine women/not wearing black shawls down to their ankles,/standing on cliffs over the desert,/or the ocean,/wailing,/singing for their men, lost at sea, gone to war,/or simply away,/having walked out of those black shawled lives" (p.32), she writes in "Spending the New Year With the Man from Receiving at Sears."

In "Touching the King of Spain Under Water," the poet works toward grasping a central unresolved subject recurrent in her verse for several years now, that of women and men uneasily inhabiting the same space. Again and again Wakoski represents women and men betraying one another, but she now also acknowledges the gratifying aspects of their relationships. Wakoski's 1982 volume *The Magician's Feastletters* (another visually beautiful Black Sparrow Press publication) confirms that Wakoski is moving in new directions and expressing herself in new metaphors. *Toward a New Poetry* (University of Michigan Press, 1980) collects Wakoski's pre-1979 columns, lectures, essays, and interviews.

740.　Warn, Emily. **The Leaf Path.** Port Townsend, WA: Cooper Canyon Press, 1982. 57p. pbk. $5.00. LC 83-120219. ISBN 0914742612.

Warn takes nature as her subject in this, her first collection, chosen by Susan Griffin as the 1981 selection for the King County Arts Commission's Publication Project. The Northwest influences Emily Warn's poetic voice, as when she seeks to name "the white bloom under the eucalyptus" (p.15), or when she observes the bull moose "gone all summer from view/inland/feeding in the dying birch/swamps, where thimbleberry grows thick/as his matted shedding coat" (p.23).

741.　Whiteman, Roberta Hill. **Star Quilt.** Minneapolis: Holy Cow! Press, 1984. 79p. $13.00. LC 83 080591. ISBN 0930100166.

Although her work has often been anthologized, this is Whiteman's first collection of poems. In her foreword to this slim volume, Carolyn Forché praises Whiteman's luminous vision and spiritual guidance, calling the collection "a map of the journey each of us must complete ... as children and exiles of the Americas." Certainly these poems speak of exile and pain. In "A Nation Wrapped in Stone," Whiteman laments the plight of her people, the American Indians, who "Unlike dust/... cannot die from tears/... We are left with grief, sinking boneward/and time to watch rain soak the trees" (p.25). Yet Whiteman also writes lovingly of the land, friends, husband, and children, and invokes sky, wind, water, stars, coyote, mosquito. Like the star quilt of the title poem, which will "anoint us with grass and twilight air" (p.1), her poems are meant to heal.

742.　Williams, Sherley Anne. **Some One Sweet Angel Chile.** New York: Morrow, 1982. 112p. $11.50. LC 81-18752. ISBN 0688010121.

The most powerful verse in this volume is to be found in a sequence of a dozen or so epistolary poems, "Letters from a New England Negro." The poet captures the voice of a freed black teacher writing from August 1867 to March 1868. In one letter, the young woman writes: "I do not/recall, yet the memory/colors all that I am. I/know only that I was a/servant; now my labor is/returned to me and all my/waiting is upon myself" (p.34).

743.　Wilner, Eleanor. **Shekhinah.** Chicago: University of Chicago Press, 1984. 107p. $15.00. LC 84-2511. ISBN 0226900258.

The title of this collection is taken from the text "The Withdrawal of the Shekhinah from Her Home in the Temple," an early text that describes a residing female Hebraic spiritual presence. Wilner's project centers upon recovering a mythological past for women, to free the passive Penelopes of history—and, one supposes, any modern Penelope who conforms to the description, "that aging wife with a fixed idea ..." (p.20). In Wilner's version, she exhorts us: "Listen. The sound of scissors clicking./One by one, she cuts the threads/that strung the loom. The shroud/that she'd been weaving/becomes a cloud of falling/shreds, till the room is littered/with useless threads, like sentences/from which the sense has fled" (p.22). Overflowing with references to the early Church, to Vergil, Mayerling, Sartre, Donatello, and Michelangelo, Wilner's is a poetry of both substance and spirit that challenges scholarly readers. Her previous prize-winning volume, *Maya* (University of Massachusetts Press, 1979), demonstrates her dexterity with figurative language.

744.   **Woman Poet.** Reno, NV: Regional Editions for Women in Literature. 3v. Vol. 1: 1980; $16.95; LC 79-55988; ISBN 0935634010. Vol. 2: 1982; $16.95; LC 81-69793; ISBN 0935634037. Vol. 3: 1986; $16.95; LC 81-69793; ISBN 093563407X.

This series epitomizes the best that anthologies can achieve. Each volume features the poets of a specific region, both prominent and previously unpublished, with an emphasis on ethnic and stylistic diversity. Biographies, critical responses, and interviews supplement the work of selected writers. Volume One includes the poems of thirty poets, highlighting the work of Josephine Miles, Madeline De Frees, and Ann Stanford; Volume Two includes twenty-nine poets, among them Audre Lorde, Marie Ponsot, and June Jordan. The critical responses and biographies are useful and intelligent, and the interviews illuminating. Forthcoming volumes announced by the editors will feature poets of the Northwest, the Midwest, and the South.

MEDICINE, HEALTH, SEXUALITY, AND BIOLOGY

Recent feminist scholarship and the successful self-help movement have placed women's health in the limelight. The books cited below include general health guides and overviews of the health care system, as well as studies of particular problems and needs. A woman's reproductive capacity may lead her to raise specific queries about pregnancy, birth, infertility, abortion, the menstrual cycle, menopause, and contraception. These topics, and more, are covered in works in this chapter. Also highlighted are works on the biology of women, investigations of female sexuality, histories of women's experiences with the health care system, exposés of health hazards in traditional women's occupations, and studies of women's roles (past and present) as physicians, nurses, patients, and home care providers. *The New Our Bodies, Ourselves* (see entry 750) and *The Whole Birth Catalog* (see entry 747) serve as guides to the rich resources, print and organizational, available on women's health. The journal *Women & Health* (see entry 1207) offers updated information.

745.   Apfel, Roberta J., 1938- , and Susan M. Fisher, 1937- . **To Do No Harm: DES and the Dilemmas of Modern Medicine.** New Haven, CT: Yale University Press, 1984. 199p. bibliog. index. $15.95. LC 84-5089. ISBN 0300031920.

Hippocrates' medical rule of thumb was *primum non nocere* – "first of all, do no harm." Apfel and Fisher see the DES tragedy as just one instance of the drift of modern medicine away from Hippocratic conservatism and toward interventionist efforts to improve upon nature. DES, or diethylstilbestrol, was routinely prescribed to pregnant women for more than thirty years to prevent miscarriage. Not only has DES since been proven ineffective, but it has also been associated with significant medical problems, including cancer, in mothers who took the drug and the children exposed in utero. Apfel and Fisher, both psychiatrists, sensitively analyze the emotional as well as physical trauma that has been the legacy of DES, discussing the impact on the mother-child relationship, the doctor-patient relationship, and the affected adolescent child's sexual identity. Although they bend over backwards to avoid a "muckraking" approach, they do indict the reluctance of the medical profession to admit error. Cynthia Laitman Orenberg, a DES mother herself, is much more openly outraged in her book *DES: The Complete Story* (St. Martin's Press, 1981). A medical editor by profession, Orenberg writes the DES story for the layperson, describing the history of DES use, its physiological effects on mothers and their children, government response to DES, litigation, and contemporary drug use during pregnancy.

746.   Ashford, Janet Isaacs, 1949- . **The Whole Birth Catalog: A Sourcebook for Choices in Childbirth.** Trumansburg, NY: Crossing Press, 1983. 313p. bibliog. index. $32.95. LC 83-838. ISBN 0895941082.

In the tradition of the *Whole Earth Catalog*, this sourcebook offers an encyclopedic guide to the burgeoning literature and diverse products directed at prospective and new parents. Ashford is a strong advocate of homebirths; however, she attempts to cover the full spectrum of childbirth choices and experiences in this work. Sections on pregnancy, birth, the first few months of parenthood, and organizing for change present a mix of book reviews, excerpts, lists of organizations, fact sheets, descriptions of products, and personal accounts—all tied together by Ashford's commentary, and amply illustrated throughout. Ashford sets the subject in a broad context, incorporating works from psychology, sociology, and anthropology; depictions of childbirth in literature and art; and a special section on lesbian mothers. Packed with information, the *Catalog* is also consistently interesting and entertaining to read. In *Woman-Centered Pregnancy and Birth* (Cleis Press, 1984), Ginny Cassidy-Brinn, Francie Hornstein, and Carol Downer, of the Federation of Feminist Women's Health Centers, argue that childbirth alternatives have actually narrowed since the mid-1970s due to increasing legal pressure on midwives. Though basic information on pregnancy and birth is presented, the bulk of the book is devoted to a critical analysis of "the medical takeover of childbirth"; the tone is decidedly partisan. In *Silent Knife: Cesarean Prevention and Vaginal Birth after Cesarean, VBAC* (Bergin and Garvey, 1983), Nancy Wainer Cohen and Lois J. Estner speak to both the medical issues and the human emotions related to cesarean sections, which they believe are nearly always unnecessary.

747.   Asso, Doreen. **The Real Menstrual Cycle.** New York: Wiley, 1983. 214p. bibliog. index. $42.95. LC 83-5890. ISBN 0471900435.

The recent surge of interest in premenstrual syndrome (see entry 776) has in Asso's opinion distorted popular views of women's menstrual cycle. A psychologist at the University of London, Asso elects to highlight the normal functioning of the cycle, "considered in its broad biological context" (p.xiv). She reviews current knowledge of biological cycles; the menstrual cycle; systemic, psychological, and behavioral changes associated with the menstrual cycle; individual differences; menopause and its symptoms; causes (physiological and learned) and effects; and living with the cycle. Though this is not light reading, Asso does a good job of translating medical and social science literature for the lay reader. Even more technical and specialized discussions will be found in *The Menstrual Cycle*, the published proceedings of the first and second Interdisciplinary Menstrual Cycle Research Conferences. Volume I, edited by Alice J. Dan, Effie A. Graham, and Carol P. Beecher (Springer, 1980), presents thirty papers; volume II, edited by Pauline Komnenich, Maryellen McSweeney, Janice A. Noack, and Sister Nathalie Elder (Springer, 1981), brings together an additional twenty articles. The onset of menstruation is the focus of another set of conference papers, *Menarche: The Transition From Girl to Woman*, edited by Sharon Golub (Lexington Books, 1983). A much more accessible text, Dr. Kathryn Schrotenboer and Genell J. Subak-Sharpe's *Freedom From Menstrual Cramps* (Pocket Books, 1981) emphasizes the identification and treatment of menstrual problems—cramps, endometriosis, premenstrual tension, amenorrhea, and toxic shock syndrome. For readers concerned about toxic shock, feminist journalist Nancy Friedman has written a book for a lay audience that reveals *Everything You Must Know About Tampons* (Berkley Books, 1981).

748.   Borg, Susan Oransky, 1947- , and Judith N. Lasker, 1947- . **When Pregnancy Fails: Families Coping with Miscarriage, Stillbirth, and Infant Death.** Boston: Beacon Press, 1981. 252p. bibliog. index. $14.95. LC 80-28898. ISBN 0807032263.

Borg and Lasker, each of whom suffered the death of a baby, direct their book to both parents and professionals. Following a prologue detailing their own experiences, the authors discuss the grief of parents in child-loss experiences, including unwanted abortion due to prenatal diagnosis. In subsequent chapters, they examine the impact of child loss on parents'—including single mothers'—personal relationships; interaction between grieving parents and medical, religious, and legal institutions; possible environmental causes of infant death; the recovery process; and later pregnancies. Appendices list support groups and other resources. The work is enriched by quotations and anecdotes from the experiences of many bereaved parents, as are a number of other recent books on the topic. *Motherhood and Mourning: Perinatal Death,* by Larry G. Peppers and Ronald J. Knapp (Praeger, 1980), covers similar ground, but with greater detail on the stages of the grieving process and related communication problems between husbands and wives. Medical writer Hank Pizer and psychologist/mother Christine O'Brien Palinski cooperated on *Coping With a Miscarriage* (Dial Press, 1980) following Palinski's multiple miscarriages. Their book offers fairly detailed information on the causes, symptoms, and aftermath of miscarriage. *Maternal Bereavement,* by Linda Edelstein (Praeger, 1984), is a more scholarly work exploring the experiences of sixteen women who lost an older child through unexpected circumstances.

749.   The Boston Women's Health Book Collective. **The New Our Bodies, Ourselves: A Book By and For Women.** Rev. ed. New York: Simon and Schuster, 1984. 647p. bibliog. index. $19.95. LC 84-5545. ISBN 0671460870.

Since the second edition of *Our Bodies, Ourselves* was published in 1976, the book market has been flooded with new health guides for women (see entry 771). *The New Our Bodies, Ourselves* nonetheless remains *the* book to buy if one is able to buy only one. Increased in length by over 250 pages, the third edition has been completely rewritten and restructured, drawing on the contributions of writers and consultants from across the United States. There are expanded chapters on physical fitness and violence against women, and new chapters on alternatives to medical care; alcohol, mood-altering drugs, and smoking; environmental and occupational health; new reproductive technologies; growing older; and international issues. Following the format of earlier editions—which mixed medical information with personal testimony, and listed print, nonprint, and organizational resources—the new edition goes much further in addressing the complexity of feminist health politics and the diversity of women's experience, covering the perspectives of lesbians, bisexual women, disabled women, women of color, fat women, and older women in greater detail. Health professionals are the intended audience of *Women, Health, and Choice* (Prentice-Hall, 1981), a passionate feminist text on the double standard in the health delivery system, written by nursing professor Margarete Sandelowski. Sandelowski proposes a philosophy of health; profiles women's health status; reviews medical and psychological aspects of menstruation, menopause, and maternity; analyzes the ideas of the women's health movement and the potential of nursing as a women's profession; and indicts specific health hazards faced by women in a sexist society, such as estrogen therapy, rape, battering, and drug abuse.

750.   Chavkin, Wendy, ed. **Double Exposure: Women's Health Hazards on the Job and at Home.** New York: Monthly Review Press, 1984. 276p. bibliog. $26.00. LC 83-42525. ISBN 0853456321.

Part I of this thorough and up-to-date guide centers on health hazards — stress as well as physical dangers — in "female" occupations. Opening with a harsh critique of the electronics industry, this section moves on to examine the risks faced by nurses, office workers, and migrant workers; the exceptional risks confronting minority women; sexual harassment; and the misuse of protective legislation. Work hazards related to women's reproductive role are examined in Part II. Contributors point out that risks to male workers' reproductive functions are often ignored, while women's fertility is used to exclude them from high-paying jobs or working conditions that should be made safer for all workers. Part III documents the physical dangers and stress associated with women's work in the home. The concluding chapter describes successful organizing campaigns around environmental issues in which women often had major roles. A much smaller volume that covers similar ground, but with a nonacademic, self-help focus, is *Our Jobs, Our Health: A Woman's Guide to Occupational Health and Safety.* copublished by the Massachusetts Coalition for Occupational Safety and Health and the Boston Women's Health Book Collective (1983). *Women, Work, and Health: Challenges to Corporate Policy,* edited by Diana Chapman Walsh and Richard E. Egdahl (Springer-Verlag, 1980), is an uneven collection of papers aimed at representatives of industry, education, the medical and legal professions, and consumer health groups.

751. Edwards, Margot, and Mary Waldorf. **Reclaiming Birth: History and Heroines of American Childbirth Reform.** Trumansburg, NY: Crossing Press, 1984. 223p. bibliog. index. $19.95. LC 84-1859. ISBN 0895941295.

Edwards and Waldorf's excellent study profiles U.S. childbirth reform movements and their women leaders over the last fifty years. An overview of natural vs. drugged childbirth begins the work, focusing on Margaret Gamper, pioneer childbirth educator. Chapter Two explains the Read and Lamaze methods, and features the contributions of Elisabeth Bing, Marjorie Karmel, and Lester Hazell. Edwards and Waldorf next survey the decline and resurrection of breastfeeding in this century, highlighting Niles Newton's pioneering work on the "science" of breastfeeding which supported the newly founded La Leche League. In their fourth chapter, the authors review the history of obstetrical technology and the accomplishments of childbirth educators Doris Haire and Sheila Kitzinger. Chapter Five is devoted to the history and contemporary practice of midwifery, specifically the work of California lay midwife Raven Lang. Although *Childbirth: Alternatives to Medical Control,* edited by Shelly Romalis (University of Texas Press, 1981), and *Women, Health, and Reproduction,* edited by Helen Roberts (Routledge and Kegan Paul, 1981), overlap to a degree with *Reclaiming Birth,* emphasis and detail differ in the three volumes. Roberts's contributors, for example, examine the contraceptive Depo-Provera, reproductive technologies, and a feminist abortion collective, among other topics. Romalis's collection includes a review of anthropological research on childbirth, the history of an alternative birthing center, and a discussion of the medical socialization of obstetricians. In *Pain, Pleasure, and American Childbirth: From the Twilight Sleep to the Read Method, 1914-1960* (Greenwood Press, 1984), Margarete Sandelowski traces the "shift in emphasis from conquest of pain to quest for pleasure" (p.xi) that accompanied the transition from drugged to natural childbirth in this country.

752.* Federation of Feminist Women's Health Centers. **How to Stay Out of the Gynecologist's Office.** Culver City, CA: Peace Press, 1981. 136p. bibliog. index. LC 81-2983. ISBN 0915238519.

The dedication of this volume well expresses its philosophy: "This book is dedicated to the lay health workers in the women's health movement who have challenged the monopoly of the male-dominated medical profession and who have revived the tradition of women healers, providing information, care, and support in a respectful and nonjudgmental way." This book and its companion volume, *A New View of a Woman's Body: A Fully Illustrated Guide* (Simon and Schuster, 1981), serve as valuable adjuncts to the more encompassing *Our Bodies, Ourselves* (see entry 749). Suzann Gage's remarkably informative illustrations appear in both volumes. *How to Stay Out of the Gynecologist's Office* presents the reader with the basic tools of self-help for consistent care of the sexual and reproductive organs. It also demystifies the procedures of a routine gynecological examination. *A New View* is best known for its radical redefinition of the clitoris, and for what the authors claim is the first cross section of the clitoris. In addition, the volume describes and illustrates vaginal and breast self-examination, female reproductive anatomy as a whole, the typical clinical "well-woman" exam, universal health problems of women, birth control, menstrual extraction, feminist abortion care, and surgical procedures such as mastectomy and hysterectomy. Both volumes conclude with glossaries of medical terminology.

753. Gold, Ellen B., ed. **The Changing Risk of Disease in Women: An Epidemiologic Approach.** Lexington, MA: D. C. Heath, 1984. 330p. bibliog. index. $35.00. LC 81-48270. ISBN 0669053198.

Originally presented at a 1981 symposium, these state-of-the-art reviews are by now somewhat dated. They nonetheless offer an excellent starting point for research into health risks facing women — among them, coronary heart disease, smoking, widowhood, alcohol, oral contraceptives, pelvic inflammatory disease, environmental exposures, cancer, hypertension, diabetes mellitus, and osteoporosis. The opening article assesses sex differences in disease risk; the closing piece summarizes the data's implications for health policy. Although the conference was convened in part to gauge risk factors possibly associated with women's changing roles, feminist perspectives do not shape the analyses offered here. Feminist treatments of women's health problems are, however, beginning to appear. Recent examples include Julia Older's *Endometriosis* (Scribner, 1984); Susanne Morgan's *Coping With a Hysterectomy* (Dial Press, 1982); and Bobbie Jacobson's *The Ladykillers: Why Smoking Is a Feminist Issue* (see entry 1029).

754. Greenwood, Sadja, 1930- . **Menopause, Naturally: Preparing for the Second Half of Life.** San Francisco: Volcano Press, 1984. 201p. bibliog. pbk. $10.00. LC 84-7333. ISBN 091207874X.

This delightful book lays out in clear language the basic facts about menopause. Greenwood, a physician, became intrigued with the subject after going through her own menopause. Her approach is reassuring, holistic, and very positive. While she emphasizes good nutrition, relaxation, and physical exercise as essential components of continuing good health, she is also informative and nonjudgmental about pharmaceutical remedies for menopause symptoms. In Part I, Greenwood discusses menopausal bleeding, hot flashes, sex after menopause, appearance, osteoporosis, hormones and emotions, premature menopause, and estrogen replacement therapy. In the second part, she outlines a strategy for maintaining "post-menopausal zest." An annotated list of suggested readings concludes the volume. Cartoons by Marcia Quackenbush add an entertaining touch. For an anthology of research conducted in the 1970s, consult *Changing Perspectives on Menopause,* edited by Ann M. Voda, Myra Dinnerstein, and Sheryl R. O'Donnell (University of Texas Press, 1982).

755.*   Hosken, Fran P., 1919- . **The Hosken Report: Genital and Sexual Mutilation of Females.** 3rd ed. Lexington, MA: Women's International Network News, 1982. 327p. bibliog. LC 83-122206. ISBN 0942096053.

Fran Hosken has campaigned against female genital mutilation since the early 1970s. Here she surveys the nature and extent of the practice in East and West Africa, the Arab peninsula, Asia, Europe, and the United States, viewing it within the context of economic development. Female "circumcision" — which varies from removal of the clitoris to complete excision of the clitoris and labia and stitching of the vaginal opening — is a practice deeply embedded in broader cultural restrictions on women's sexuality and reproduction. As such, it is often defended within the Third World against what is seen as the cultural imperialism of Western feminist criticism. Hosken critically examines "the reasons given" for genital mutilation; compares the practice to male circumcision; indicts the "conspiracy of silence" surrounding the custom; and reviews the outlook for women's health. For a detailed case study of genital mutilation in the Sudan, see *Woman, Why Do You Weep? Circumcision and Its Consequences,* by physician Asma el Dareer (Zed Press, 1982).

756.   Howe, Louise Kapp. **Moments on Maple Avenue: The Reality of Abortion.** New York: Macmillan, 1984. 209p. bibliog. $13.95. LC 84-12244. ISBN 0025551701.

"All in all, I'm told it was just an ordinary Thursday at the clinic on Maple Avenue. One false alarm, one follow-up pelvic exam, one IUD insertion, and twenty-three abortions were attended to without a single medical complication during the course of clinic hours" (p.3). Thus Howe opens *Moments on Maple Avenue,* a work that vividly recreates "a day in the life" of a contemporary abortion clinic in White Plains, New York. Through Howe's eyes, we meet the variety of women who seek help from the clinic; observe the counseling given to abortion patients, as well as the different abortion procedures themselves; take in the reactions of the few men in attendance; and stand by as the patients recover and consider birth control options. Howe gracefully intersperses bits and pieces of abortion history throughout the narrative and appends some statistical data. In *Thinking About Abortion* (Dial Press, 1984), Beryl Lieff Benderly offers a well-written compendium of information on abortion. Approaching the subject from a clearly feminist perspective, Benderly combines medical fact, social science research, and interview material into a readable text. *A Woman's Guide to Safe Abortion* (Holt, Rinehart and Winston, 1983), by Maria Corsaro and Carole Korzeniowsky, is a very slim, down-to-earth handbook addressed directly to the woman who is pregnant and has opted for an abortion.

757.   Jay, Karla, and Allen Young. **The Gay Report: Lesbians and Gay Men Speak Out About Sexual Experiences and Lifestyles.** New York: Summit Books, 1979. 816p. LC 78-24056. ISBN 0671400134.

This massive tome reports responses from some five thousand lesbians and gay men to a lengthy questionnaire on sexual practices, lifestyles, and backgrounds. Statistics are clearly presented, but far more fascinating are the answers to open-ended essay questions. For the most part, lesbians and gay men are treated in separate chapters.

758.   Kirkpatrick, Martha, ed. **Women's Sexual Experience: Explorations of the Dark Continent.** New York: Plenum Press, 1982. 298p. bibliog. index. $25.00. LC 82-482. ISBN 0306407930.

Women's Sexual Experience is, in the words of the editor, "a potpourri of ideas, not campaign literature to promote a particular point of view" (p.xi). While it is an interesting collection, one regrets that Kirkpatrick didn't provide an introduction to pull the "potpourri" together. Some of the papers are scholarly; others are journalistic or experiential. The nearly thirty contributors represent a variety of fields—medicine, psychiatry, psychology, social work, sociology, health activism—and write on a range of topics: women's sexual response; the sexual experience of black women; sexual consequences of the acculturation of American Indian women; aging; incest; teenage motherhood; pregnancy; voluntary childlessness; wife beating; prostitution; and venereal disease. Most articles are accompanied by a short "discussion" authored by another contributor. Kirkpatrick has also edited a "companion volume," *Women's Sexual Development: Explorations of Inner Space* (Plenum Press, 1980).

759. Kitzinger, Sheila. **Woman's Experience of Sex.** New York: Putnam, 1983. 320p. bibliog. index. $17.95. LC 83-3403. ISBN 0399128565.

"Most books about sex talk *about* women, but do not speak from women's experience," writes Kitzinger in her foreword. Rejecting the sex manual emphasis on technique and performance, Kitzinger views sexuality in its relationship to self-worth, relationships, emotions, and life circumstances. First guiding the reader through an exploration of her own body and its feelings, Kitzinger moves on to discuss sexual lifestyles (heterosexuality, lesbianism, celibacy); relationships (including those of the disabled); children and sex; transitions (growing up, contraceptives, infertility, pregnancy and birth, breastfeeding, menopause and aging); sexual difficulties; sex and power (sexual harassment, sexual assault, pornography); and loss and grieving (death of a loved one, death of a baby, mutilating operations). Nancy Durrell McKenna's many photographs add a frank and moving accompaniment to the sensitive, well-written text. Two new surveys of women's sexuality have recently joined the ranks of the Hite and Kinsey reports. *The Cosmo Report* (Arbor House, 1981), by Linda Wolfe, is based on the largest sample ever (although an unrepresentative one): 106,000 *Cosmopolitan* readers who filled out the seventy-nine-question survey printed in the magazine's January 1980 issue. Wolfe organizes the results by topic ("The First Time," "Sexual Practices"), first citing major findings, then continuing with her own analysis liberally spiced with quotations. Lonnie Barbach and Linda Levine interviewed 120 women for their book *Shared Intimacies: Women's Sexual Experiences* (Anchor Press/Doubleday, 1980).

760. Leavitt, Judith Walzer, ed. **Women and Health in America.** Madison: University of Wisconsin Press, 1984. 526p. bibliog. index. $32.50. LC 83-40267. ISBN 0299096408.

Recent scholarship on women and health draws on new perspectives in social history and medical history, as well as contemporary feminism, as reflected in this invaluable collection. Among the twenty articles in Part I, "The Health of Women," we find a number of classics: Carroll Smith-Rosenberg's "The Female World of Love and Ritual"; Leila J. Rupp's "Imagine My Surprise"; Linda Gordon's "Voluntary Motherhood"; and Judith Leavitt's "Birthing and Anesthesia." Rima D. Apple's pictorial essay in Part II visually dramatizes many of the topics discussed here. In Part III, "Women in the Health Professions," Nancy Schrom Dye recounts the history of the Frontier Nursing Service; Regina Markell Morantz looks at the participation of middle-class women in nineteenth-century health reform; Barbara Melosh analyzes the nature of twentieth-century hospital-based nursing; and Darlene Clark Hine relates the history of efforts to integrate black nurses into the armed forces during World War II. Leavitt has written an introductory overview and short introductions to each subsection. The collection successfully reflects the vitality of this emerging field. That the factors of class and race are not yet adequately treated in the literature is acknowledged by Leavitt, who expresses the hope that scholars will soon close this gap, bringing the field closer to "a thorough analysis of the experiences of all women ..." (p.6).

761. Lewin, Ellen, and Virginia Olesen, eds. **Women, Health, and Healing: Toward a New Perspective.** New York: Tavistock, 1985. 317p. bibliog. index. $12.95. LC 84-16214. ISBN 0422780200.

Editors Lewin and Olesen bring to this interdisciplinary collection of essays British and American perspectives on women's health issues. Many of the contributors go beyond delineation of the problems themselves to investigate the social and political context within which women's health policy is hammered out. The essays are: "Women, Health, and Healing: A Theoretical Introduction" (Virginia Olesen and Ellen Lewin); "Providers, Negotiators, and Mediators: Women as the Hidden Carers" (Hilary Graham); "Occupational Health and Women: The Case of Clerical Work" (Ellen Lewin and Virginia Olesen); "The Frail Elderly Woman: Emergent Questions in Aging and Women's Health" (Helen Evers); "Estrogen Replacement Therapy: The Production of Medical Knowledge and the Emergence of Policy" (Patricia A. Kaufert and Sonja M. McKinlay); "Abortion in the 1980s: Feminist Morality and Women's Health" (Rosalind Pollack Petchesky); "Struggle Between Providers and Recipients: The Case of Birth Practices" (Shelly Romalis); "Women and Sports: Reflections on Health and Policy" (Mary Boutilier and Lucinda SanGiovanni); "Women and the National Health Service: The Carers and the Careless" (Lesley Doyal); and "Women and Health: The United States and the United Kingdom Compared" (Margaret Stacey).

762. Lorber, Judith. **Women Physicians: Careers, Status, and Power.** New York: Tavistock, 1984. 149p. bibliog. index. $22.00. LC 84-16213. ISBN 0422790400.

Lorber's aim is to document and explain differences in the careers of men and women physicians practicing in the United States between 1940 and 1979. The book's first segment, an analysis of data from a longitudinal study, demonstrates the failure of women physicians to attain the status their early accomplishments would have predicted. Lorber's subsequent interviews with sixty-four male and female doctors locate the reasons for men and women's differential achievement in the limited sponsorship available to women and the imbalanced sexual division of labor in the family. Women physicians, Lorber demonstrates, face tremendous informal discrimination as "sisters in the brotherhood." Where Lorber looks to the structure of the medical profession for insight into the careers of women physicians, in *Work, Marriage, and Motherhood: The Career Persistence of Female Physicians* (Praeger, 1981), Dorothy Rosenthal Mandelbaum examines her subjects' backgrounds. Factors such as early development, personality, marital status, parenthood, role priorities, and work behavior are correlated with career patterns in an effort to determine why some women physicians persist in their careers and others withdraw.

763. Loulan, JoAnn. **Lesbian Sex.** San Francisco: Spinsters, Ink, 1984. 309p. bibliog. pbk. $9.95. LC 84-52008. ISBN 0933216130.

This book is as straightforward as its title. Loulan leaves no aspect of lesbian love unexplored—physiology, fantasies, sexual techniques, and "the issues in our lives and how they affect our sexuality" (p.xiii). In one set of chapters, "To Learn and Unlearn," she deals with such concerns as coming out, being single, long-term relationships, sex and disability, and sex and motherhood. The text is keyed throughout to a series of "homework exercises" for individuals and couples. Based on counseling sessions with thousands of lesbians, Loulan charts a female sexual response cycle more complex than that outlined by sexologists Masters and Johnson. Quotes from her clients demonstrate the wide range of lesbian sexual expression. Always nonjudgmental and reassuring, *Lesbian Sex* complements other feminist books on sex and relationships (see entry 759).

764.　Marieskind, Helen I. **Women in the Health System: Patients, Providers, and Programs.** St. Louis: Mosby, 1980. 329p. bibliog. index. pbk. $15.95. LC 80-19961. ISBN 0801631068.

Though somewhat dated by now, this volume remains a valuable text for the classroom or the general reader, taking a broad view of women's experience as both providers and consumers in the health care system. Marieskind presents the material in nine sections: women's health status; ambulatory health care; governmental programs and women's health; women in the health care work force; women and occupational health; health care for young women; impact of technology on women's health care; women's health activism; and toward a national health policy for women's health. Each section concludes with extended references and a list of suggested topics for discussion, further reasearch, and field projects. A brief bibliography of bibliographies appears at the end of the volume. Tables and photographs illustrate the text throughout.

765.　Mazor, Miriam D., and Harriet F. Simons, eds. **Infertility: Medical, Emotional and Social Considerations.** New York: Human Sciences Press, 1984. 239p. bibliog. index. $32.95. LC 83-10872. ISBN 0898851408.

About one in six couples in the United States has difficulty conceiving or completing a pregnancy. Mazor and Simons's collection of papers by infertility specialists covers the subject well, and often in depth. Medical language occasionally interferes with clarity, but in general, articles are readable and informative. Section I details male and female medical workups for infertility, emotional reactions to infertility, counseling by professionals and peer groups, and policy implications. The papers in Section II look at the adoption alternative, and Section III discusses artificial insemination — its medical and psychological aspects, legal implications, and the nurse's role in the procedure. Problems related to use of DES are explored in Section IV, and amniocentesis in Section V. Concluding the collection is a paper on *in vitro* fertilization and a list of potentially helpful organizations.

766.　Melosh, Barbara. **"The Physician's Hand": Work Culture and Conflict in American Nursing.** Philadelphia: Temple University Press, 1982. 260p. bibliog. index. $29.95. LC 82-10537. ISBN 0877222789.

Melosh opens this elegantly written social history of nursing with the provocative assertion that "nursing is not and cannot be a profession" (p.15). In Melosh's view, the sexual division of labor in medicine, which subordinates (primarily female) nurses to the authority of (primarily male) doctors, deprives nurses of the autonomy that is a defining characteristic of the professions. Melosh traces the tension throughout this century between nursing leaders striving for professionalization, and rank and file nurses operating in an apprenticeship culture. Evaluating the move from home- to hospital-based nursing, Melosh concludes that hospital nursing represents an improvement in working conditions and an expansion in opportunities for organizing. *The New Nightingales: Hospital Workers, Unions, New Women's Issues* (Enquiry Press, 1982), by Patricia Cayo Sexton, offers an unusually intimate glimpse into the conflicts and struggles of contemporary hospital workers, based on a study of the Service Employees International Union (SEIU).

While Sexton is attentive to the racial dimensions of the medical division of labor, most studies of nursing gloss over the specific experiences of women of color. Darlene Clark Hine's *Black Women in the Nursing Profession* (Garland, 1985) pulls together a variety of sources documenting the little-known history of black nursing.

767. Mintz, Morton. **At Any Cost: Corporate Greed, Women, and the Dalkon Shield.** New York: Pantheon Books, 1985. 308p. bibliog. index. $17.95. LC 85-6389. ISBN 0394548469.

Mintz, a reporter for the *Washington Post,* reconstructs the infuriating and grisly history of the Dalkon Shield. Prior to its removal from the market in 1974, the Shield was the leading intrauterine device (IUD). Mintz documents in horrifying detail how the Shield manufacturer, the A. H. Robins Company, destroyed documents and resorted to fraud and perjury throughout the 1970s and early 1980s in an effort to conceal the mounting toll of Shield-related septic spontaneous abortions, pelvic inflammatory disease, premature births, deformed babies, and infertility. In the words of Miles W. Lord, the outspoken judge who presided over Shield litigation in Minnesota, the device was "a deadly depth charge in [women's] wombs, ready to explode at any time" (p.267). In the epilogue, Mintz asks the reader to ponder the astonishing gap between personal and corporate morality in the United States. Two other recent accounts of the Shield story are *Nightmare: Women and the Dalkon Shield,* by Susan Perry and Jim Dawson (Macmillan, 1985), and *Lord's Justice,* by Sheldon D. Engelmayer and Robert Wagman (Anchor Press/Doubleday, 1985).

768. Morantz, Regina Markell, et al., eds. **In Her Own Words: Oral Histories of Women Physicians.** Westport, CT: Greenwood Press, 1982. 284p. bibliog. index. $29.95. LC 81-13349. ISBN 0313226865.

Women considering a career in medicine will find in this collection the rich legacy of nine physicians who have forged the way over the course of this century. These are stirring stories, based on interviews designed to elicit each woman's thoughts on her own background, how she chose medicine, her medical education and practice, her personal life, and feminism. The volume opens with the story of Katharine Sturgis, a pioneer in the field of preventive medicine who gained her medical degree in 1935, and closes with the open-ended self-portrait of Vanessa Gamble, a young black M.D./Ph.D. candidate. Editors Regina Markell Morantz, Cynthia Stodola Pomerleau, and Carol Hanson Fenichel attempt to pull together the diverse experiences represented here — including specializations in plastic surgery, public health, Indian health care, academic medicine, administration, obstetrics, and ophthalmology — in brief discussions concluding each of three sections organized by generation. Morantz provides the substantial introduction, "From Art to Science: Women Physicians in American Medicine, 1600-1980." She has more recently authored a book-length study entitled *Sympathy and Science: Women Physicians in American Medicine* (Oxford University Press, 1985), published under her new name, Regina Markell Morantz-Sanchez. The historical role of separate women's institutions is the subject of Virginia G. Drachman's carefully documented study, *Hospital With a Heart: Women Doctors and the Paradox of Separatism at the New England Hospital, 1862-1969* (Cornell University Press, 1984).

769. Rothman, Barbara Katz. **In Labor: Women and Power in the Birthplace.** New York: Norton, 1982. 320p. bibliog. index. $14.95. LC 81-19027. ISBN 039301584X.

Rothman counterposes two models for handling pregnancy and childbirth. The medical model, she argues, treats childbearing as a disease requiring medical management.

The midwifery model, which Rothman favors, views birthing as a normal process and gives authority to the woman's own body and sensations. In her first section, Rothman looks at childbirth politically, theoretically, and historically, and describes the consumer movements that have challenged contemporary obstetrical practice. The stages of maternity care — conception and infertility, pregnancy, birth, newborn care, and maternal bonding — are explored in the second section from the contrasting perspectives of the medical and midwifery models. Rothman devotes her third section to a discussion of the practice and recent radicalization of midwives. In a legal treatise on midwifery — *Regulating Birth: Midwives, Medicine, and the Law* (Temple University Press, 1985) — Raymond G. DeVries concludes that women and their midwives stand the best chance of regaining control over the birth process by remaining outside the law. Three recent works offer a glimpse into the personal experience of the practicing midwife. *Wide Neighborhoods: A Story of the Frontier Nursing Service,* by Mary Breckinridge (University Press of Kentucky, 1981), is rich with autobiographical detail, as well as organizational and case study material about the nurse midwives who worked in rural Kentucky during the second quarter of this century. Fran Leeper Buss's *La Partera* (University of Michigan Press, 1980) is presented largely in the words of its subject, Jesusita Aragon, one of the few midwives still practicing in New Mexico. In *Wives and Midwives: Childbirth and Nutrition in Rural Malaysia* (University of California Press, 1983), Carol Laderman tells of her apprenticeship to a traditional midwife in a Malaysian fishing village. Addressed to the aspiring midwife, Elizabeth Davis's *A Guide to Midwifery: Heart and Hands* (J. Muir Publications, 1981) explains how to set up a practice, and outlines procedures for prenatal care, problems with pregnancy, normal birthing and complications, and postpartum care.

770.* Scully, Diana. **Men Who Control Women's Health: The Miseducation of Obstetrician-Gynecologists.** Boston: Houghton Mifflin, 1980. 285p. bibliog. index. LC 79-27503. ISBN 0395291372.

Scully is a sociologist, but she pretends to no "objective" or dispassionate viewpoint: "The women's health movement provided the motivation to write this book and continues to be among the more salient influences in my thinking on health care" (p.vii). In preparing this well-researched book, Scully spent three years in intensive observation of ob/gyn residents at two teaching hospitals, with a primary focus on surgical training. Having gained the trust and respect of the residents, Scully followed up with in-depth interviews, eliciting remarkably candid — and often chilling — statements that offer insight into the problematic nature of male ob/gyn care for female patients, the epidemic of unnecessary gynecological surgery, and class inequalities in health care delivery. The reader will find a strikingly similar analysis embedded in the personal account of a woman ob/gyn resident in *A Woman in Residence* (Random House, 1982), by Michelle Harrison.

771. Shephard, Bruce D., 1944- , and Carroll A. Shephard, 1944- . **The Complete Guide to Women's Health.** Tampa, FL: Mariner, 1982. 419p. bibliog. index. $19.95. LC 82-14802. ISBN 093616607X.

For a politically sensitive, *feminist* treatment of women's health issues, *Our Bodies, Ourselves* (see entry 749) has no peer. Yet for simple reference, several other works are worthy of mention. *The Complete Guide to Women's Health* is a lavishly illustrated, well-documented, and accurate source written by a physician and nursing Ph.D. Weighted toward gynecology and obstetrics, the guide covers health strategies, birth control, pregnancy and childbirth, sexual issues, menopause, drugs, diseases of the reproductive system, gynecologic surgery, healthy lifestyles, and the meaning of different symptoms. The Shephards are careful to include information on medical issues of current concern (e.g., PMS, DES, and toxic shock syndrome) and on alternative health care such as home birthing. However, differences between women—of race, class, sexual preferences, or disability—are not treated as important determinants of health care. Other recent guides follow this pattern, even the feminist *The Ms. Guide to a Woman's Health*, by Cynthia W. Cooke, M.D., and Susan Dworkin (Doubleday, 1979; Berkley Books, 1981), which is now quite dated. *Everywoman's Health: The Complete Guide to Body and Mind* (Doubleday, 1980), by June Jackson Christmas and sixteen other women physicians, is another good, basic guide, with chapters on nutrition and weight, fitness, rape and spouse abuse, and emotional health, as well as on the usual ob/gyn subjects. Two recent titles are arranged as encyclopedias: Christine Ammer's *The A to Z of Women's Health* (Facts on File, 1983), which emphasizes ob/gyn but also discusses smoking, diet, patients' rights, drug use, exercise, and alternative remedies; and Emrika Padus's *The Woman's Encyclopedia of Health and Natural Healing* (Rodale Press, 1981), a well-written, amply illustrated, and carefully indexed work. Two final titles are also encyclopedic in coverage, though organized thematically. *Woman's Health and Medical Guide*, edited by Patrica J. Cooper and packaged by Better Homes and Gardens Books (Meredith Corporation, 1981), is a slick production, plentifully illustrated, that covers the gamut of general health topics, in addition to ob/gyn topics. In *Being a Well Woman* (Holt, Rinehart and Winston, 1982), British physician/journalist Miriam Stoppard brings an unusually thoughtful and personal voice to her broadly focused discussion. Some feminist readers may balk, however, at her uncritical attitude toward conventional standards of "feminine" beauty.

772.   Sloane, Ethel. **Biology of Women.** 2nd ed. New York: Wiley, 1985. 656p. bibliog. index. $18.95. LC 84-25726. ISBN 0471879398.

Sloane, a professor of zoology, gracefully mixes the facts of women's biology with the politics of women's lives and health care in a way that is sure to awaken the interest of undergraduates—and the general reader. The second edition is revised and updated, with two new chapters and additional material throughout. Opening and closing the volume with chapters on how knowledge can empower women confronting the health care system, Sloan integrates a feminist perspective into each of her fourteen other chapters as well, covering: reproductive anatomy; the menstrual cycle and its hormonal relationships; menstrual problems; the basis of biological differences; female sexuality; the mammary glands; the gynecological exam; gynecological difficulties; pregnancy, labor, and delivery; infertility; contraception; menopause; health and the working woman; and the cosmetics industry. The volume is packed with diagrams, drawings, and photographs that enliven and humanize the text. Each chapter is fully referenced. Intended for the undergraduate classroom, *Biology of Women,* by Eileen S. Gersh and Isidore Gersh (University Park Press, 1981), is strictly limited to biological topics—specifically, the genetic aspects of sex and the female genital system—and presents these in more intricate detail (and flatter prose) than does Sloane.

773.   Sorel, Nancy Caldwell. **Ever Since Eve: Personal Reflections on Childbirth.** New York: Oxford University Press, 1984. 388p. bibliog. $14.95. LC 84-916. ISBN 0195034600.

A wide range of anecdotes about pregnancy and the birth experience fills the pages of this volume, many by or about such well-known figures as Mary Tudor, Margaret Mead, Leo Tolstoy, and Maya Angelou. Grouped under sixteen headings ("Conceiving," "Labor/Delivering," "Fathering," "Mourning," etc.) are more than 140 accounts, including

Colette's "Having a Masculine Pregnancy," a black midwife's recollection of her midwife grandmother, and a brief description of "Transporting Infants on the Santa Fe Trail." More detailed accounts of childbirth will be found in Janet Isaacs Ashford's *Birth Stories: The Experience Remembered* (Crossing Press, 1984). These twenty-seven first-person accounts and six poems by mothers, grandmothers, and fathers describe a variety of experiences, including hospital births in the early part of this century, a recent homebirth, the stillbirth of an anencephalic infant, a lesbian birth, and the birth of a child given up for adoption.

774.* Stage, Sarah. **Female Complaints: Lydia Pinkham and the Business of Women's Medicine.** New York: Norton, 1979. 304p. bibliog. index. LC 78-14414. ISBN 039301178X.

"AT THE COUNTRY CLUB. Barbara: 'I wish I could go in for sports like the rest of the crowd.' Louise: 'Have you tried Lydia E. Pinkham's Vegetable Compound?'" So ran a typical advertisement for Lydia E. Pinkham's remedy for "PROLAPSUS UTERI or falling of the Womb, and all FEMALE WEAKNESSES..." (p.90). First produced in 1875, the "cure" became phenomenally successful, riding the crest of popular preoccupation with women's health, and distrust of medicine in general, and gynecology in particular. Stage writes a lively social history of the Lydia E. Pinkham Medicine Company, and of the woman whose name it made famous. Lydia Pinkham (1819-1883) was an abolitionist and a feminist who viewed her patent medicine business as an outgrowth of her wider reform commitments. Her story, Stage believes, epitomizes "the transition from female domestic practitioner to dispenser of patent medicine" (p.250), while the history of Pinkham advertising allows one "to view in microcosm changing attitudes toward women and medicine" (p.10) over the last century.

775. Watson, Rita Esposito, and Robert C. Wallach. **New Choices, New Chances: A Woman's Guide to Conquering Cancer.** New York: St. Martin's Press, 1981. 273p. bibliog. index. $13.95. LC 81-16746. ISBN 0312566034.

Watson, a science writer, and Wallach, a gynecologic oncologist, present a feminist, nontechnical introduction to the subject of women and cancer. The tone is decidedly upbeat. Watson and Wallach discuss prevention and treatment, and cover the facts on specific cancers of the breasts and reproductive organs. Their final chapter, "The Holistic Approach," considers alternative treatments and the hospice movement. U.S. cancer centers, cancer programs, and support groups are listed in the appendices. Although the lungs have recently outdistanced the breasts as the leading site for cancer in women, breast cancer remains foremost in the popular consciousness, as evidenced by the number of books on the subject. Rose Kushner, a breast cancer survivor herself, is an activist for the rights of breast cancer victims, and a medical writer who has published widely on the subject. Her latest book, *Alternatives: New Developments in the War on Breast Cancer* (Kensington Press, 1984), challenges many current standards of medical practice, from surgery to radiation to chemotherapy. In *A Woman's Choice: New Options in the Treatment of Breast Cancer* (Beacon Press, 1982), science writer Mary Spletter (another survivor of breast cancer) provides a well-written synopsis of current knowledge on breast cancer detection, psychological response to diagnosis, treatment options, and breast reconstruction.

776. Witt, Reni L., 1953- . **PMS: What Every Woman Should Know about Premenstrual Syndrome.** New York: Stein and Day, 1983. 252p. bibliog. index. $14.95. LC 82-42724. ISBN 0812829034.

Discussions of premenstrual syndrome (PMS) are often volatile. Women who define themselves as PMS sufferers are caught between misogynists who believe women's "raging hormones" disqualify them for positions of responsibility, and misogynists who assert that the "syndrome" exists only in a woman's head. The controversy notwithstanding, women themselves are now demanding diagnosis and treatment for PMS, and a number of recent books aim to provide the sought-after guidance. Witt addresses her book to the lay reader, discussing the definition of PMS, self-diagnosis (charting symptoms on a PMS calendar), physiology and causation, the psychology of PMS, the social context, natural and medical treatments, and living with PMS. Witt brings a healthy dose of skepticism to her examination of new treatments such as progesterone therapy and the care offered in for-profit PMS clinics. Other comparable books geared to the general reader include: *Dr. Susan Lark's Premenstrual Syndrome Self-Help Book,* by Susan Lark, M.D. (Forman, 1984); *PMS: Premenstrual Syndrome*, by Ronald V. Norris, M.D., with Colleen Sullivan (Rawson Associates, 1983); *PMS: Premenstrual Syndrome and You: Next Month Can Be Different*, by Niels H. Lauersen, M.D., and Eileen Stukane (Simon and Schuster, 1983); and *Pre-Menstrual Tension,* by Judy Lever with Dr. Michael G. Brush (McGraw-Hill, 1981). In *Premenstrual Tension: A Multidisciplinary Approach*, edited by Charles H. Debrovner, M.D. (Human Sciences Press, 1982), five specialists share perspectives on gynecological, endocrinological, psychiatric, and nutritional approches to PMS, with a final note on the effect of placebos. In contrast to more recent titles, Dr. Katharina Dalton's pioneering work, *Once a Month* (1979; rev. ed., Hunter House, 1983), offers primarily a dismaying litany of symptoms.

POLITICS AND POLITICAL THEORY

Most of the works in this chapter treat women's participation in mainstream politics—as elected officials, candidates, policymakers, lobbyists, and the voters who created the "gender gap." A secondary focus is political movements, including socialism, conservatism, and the peace movement. Critiques of traditional political philosophies appear here or in the Religion and Philosophy chapter; newer feminist perspectives on politics cluster in the chapter on Women's Movement and Feminist Theory. Most of the works covered here explore the political process in the United States; for books about other countries, consult the subject index. Look to the History chapter for relevant historical materials, and to Law for discussions of legislative reform. Mari Jo Buhle's bibliography *Women and the American Left* (see entry 303) is an exemplary research guide; and Barbara J. Nelson's *American Women and Politics: A Selected Bibliography and Resource Guide* also proves helpful (see entry 884). Esther Stineman profiles women in politics in *American Political Women* (see entry 911); other recent biographical volumes such as *Who's Who of American Women* provide further data on women leaders.

777. Abzug, Bella S., with Mim Kelbar. **Gender Gap: Bella Abzug's Guide to Political Power for American Women.** Boston: Houghton Mifflin, 1984. 257p. pbk. $6.95. LC 83-22854. ISBN 0395354846.

The "gender gap" hit the American political scene in the aftermath of the 1982 congressional and gubernatorial elections. Post-election analyses confirmed a measurable difference in how men and women voted. Abzug's book, written as the 1984 presidential race was getting underway, is perhaps best seen as a campaign tool. Abzug takes the risk of predicting the election's outcome—"I believe that in 1984, women will defeat President Reagan or any stand-in for the policies he represents" (p.200)—as she entreats women to register and vote. Displaying her familiar and delightful irreverence, Abzug reviews women's activism in the seventies and eighties, analyzes the results of the 1980 and 1982 elections, lambastes the policies of the Reagan administration, and offers a blueprint for defeating Reagan in 1984. The E.R.A., abortion, childcare, the economy, military spending, and the environment are pinpointed as gender-gap issues. An appendix lists organizations active in gender-gap politics. *Why and How Women Will Elect the Next President* (Harper and Row, 1984), by the former president of the National Organization for Women, Eleanor Smeal, covers similar territory, with somewhat better documentation.

778. Azari, Farah, ed. **Women of Iran: The Conflict With Fundamentalist Islam.** London: Ithaca Press; distr. N. Hollywood, CA: Evergreen, 1983. 225p. bibliog. pbk. $8.00. ISBN 0903729954.

The fate of human rights in Iran over the last decade presents the observer with a welter of contradictions, raising many difficult questions about the course of women's liberation in an Islamic context (see also entry 29). Since the revolution of 1979 and the subsequent Islamic revival, many writers have attempted to interpret the experience of Iranian women. Three socialist feminists from the London-based Iranian Women's Solidarity Group contribute articles to this volume on Islam's appeal to women in Iran, the economic foundations of the Iranian Islamic revival, sexuality and women's oppression in Iran, the Iranian Left, and the Iranian women's movement before and after the revolution. *In the Shadow of Islam: The Women's Movement in Iran* (Zed Press; distr. Lawrence Hill, 1982), edited by Azar Tabari and Nahid Yeganeh, opens with interpretive essays on women's divergent responses to the struggle against the Shah, Iranian Marxist feminism, and Khomeini's position on women. "Documents on the Question of Women" follow, with statements by Islamic leaders, political parties, and women's organizations. Part III summarizes the history, aims, and objectives of women's organizations (Islamic, nationalist, and Marxist) formed after the revolution. A historical chronology, 1905-1981, completes the volume. One journalist and thirteen scholars contribute essays on women in prerevolutionary Iran, women's contributions to the revolution, and their fate under Khomeini, to the volume *Women and Revolution in Iran* (Westview Press, 1983), edited by Guity Nashat. One of the contributors to this collection, Eliz Sanasarian, has herself written a monograph on Iranian women's history entitled *The Women's Rights Movement in Iran: Mutiny, Appeasement, and Repression From 1900 to Khomeini* (Praeger, 1982). Sanasarian critically analyzes the rise and decline of women's demands under the Shah, women in the anti-Shah movement, and women's oppression under the new Islamic Republic. Readers can view the immediate postrevolutionary period through the eyes of Kate Millett and photographer Sophie Keir in *Going to Iran* (Coward, McCann and Geoghegan, 1982).

779. Baxter, Sandra, 1945- , and Marjorie Lansing, 1916- . **Women and Politics: The Visible Majority.** Rev. ed. Ann Arbor: University of Michigan Press, 1983. 259p. bibliog. index. $19.95. LC 82-6555. ISBN 0472100432.

The first edition of this work was subtitled "The Invisible Majority." When the second edition appeared three years later, the subtitle was changed to "The Visible Majority." In the intervening period, the authors — and the nation — had discovered the "gender gap" (an observable difference in men's and women's voting patterns) and had taken it as a portent of women's future power at the polls. One additional chapter on the gender gap, reviewing the election results of 1980 and 1982, is in fact the only substantial change in this second edition, which, like the first, analyzes women's attitudes towards politics, the political parties, candidates, and specific issues; black women's voting patterns; women's political participation at both grassroots and national levels; and comparative data on women's political participation in other countries. In another book entitled *Women and Politics* (St. Martin's Press, 1982), Vicky Randall offers a helpful and critical introduction to the political science literature on women's political participation, women's status among political elites, the impact of public policies on women, the politics of the women's movements in Britain and the United States, and feminism and policymaking.

780. Cambridge Women's Peace Collective, ed. **My Country Is the Whole World: An Anthology of Women's Work on Peace and War.** Boston: Pandora Press, 1984. 306p. bibliog. $8.95. LC 83-17201. ISBN 0863580041.

The title is taken from Virginia Woolf's *Three Guineas,* and as this anthology shows, Woolf is only one of a multitude of women who have spoken out about war and peace over the centuries. Sappho, Christine de Pizan, Aphra Behn, Harriet Martineau, Sarah

Bernhardt, Margaret Mead, and Helen Caldicott are among the more than two hundred women writers and artists included in this chronological survey. The quotations are often brief, the biographical data sketchy, but the cumulative effect is powerful. Perhaps because of the women's camp at Greenham Common (see entry 1111), British women have been particularly outspoken on the issue of peace in recent years. Most of the contributors to *Over Our Dead Bodies: Women Against the Bomb*, edited by Dorothy Thompson (Virago Press, 1983), reside in Great Britain, while another British-produced anthology — *Keeping the Peace: A Women's Peace Handbook*, edited by Lynne Jones (The Women's Press, 1983) — includes material on other European nations, the United States, and Japan.

781.   Cantarow, Ellen, et al. **Moving the Mountain: Women Working for Social Change.** Old Westbury, NY: Feminist Press; New York: McGraw-Hill, 1980. 166p. bibliog. index. pbk. $8.95. LC 79-11840. ISBN 0912670614.
Part of the "Women's Lives/Women's Work" series, a collection of texts designed for the secondary or college classroom, this book presents the oral histories of three veteran activists to demonstrate that "behind-the-scenes organizers — especially women — have been as important ... as the leaders whose names make the front pages of newspapers" (p.xiii). Sharon Hartman Strom wrote the chapter on Florence Luscomb (b.1887), an architect turned suffrage, labor, and peace organizer. Ellen Cantarow and Susan Gushee O'Malley have recorded the story of Ella Baker (b.1903), seasoned civil rights activist. Ellen Cantarow also contributed the third chapter, in which Jessie Lopez de la Cruz (b.1919) tells of her years organizing for the United Farmworkers. Cantarow's introduction briefly surveys the history of U.S. movements for social change over the last century.

782.   Dworkin, Andrea. **Right-Wing Women.** New York: Putnam, 1983. 255p. bibliog. index. pbk. $8.95. LC 82-9784. ISBN 0399506713.
What explains the attraction of right-wing politics for women? Dworkin is audacious, eloquent, and harsh as she tries to answer this question. She leads the reader on a nightmarish journey through the starkest reality of misogyny — woman hatred; forced intercourse and pregnancy in marriage; rape; prostitution; the denigration of women's intelligence. Then in a *tour de force* of reasoning, she argues that the views of rank-and-file right-wing women are grounded in an accurate appraisal of the woman-hating society in which they live. "Facing the true nature of the sex-class system," Dworkin asserts, "means ultimately that one must destroy that system or accommodate to it" (p.236). Feminists, though sharing in all women's powerlessness, strike out to destroy the system. Right-wing women accommodate to it; convinced of the permanence of the system, they are attracted more to promises of order, shelter, safety, rules, and love in exchange for compliance, than to the feminist call to rebellion. Where Dworkin views the Right through the eyes of its rank-and-file recruits, several other authors have recently turned their critical gaze to the movement leadership and its backing. In *The Right to Lifers: Who They Are, How They Operate, Where They Get Their Money* (Summit Books, 1983), journalist Connie Paige describes the origins of the "right-to-life" movement in the Catholic Church, and its later adoption by forces in the New Right seeking an expanded, national power base. Journalist Andrew H. Merton covers similar ground in *Enemies of Choice: The Right-to-Life Movement and Its Threat to Abortion* (Beacon Press, 1981). In *The Invisible Woman: Target of the Religious New Right* (Delacorte Press, 1983), Shirley Rogers Radl subjects the Right as a whole to her scathing critique. The highly visible leader of the anti-E.R.A.

movement, Phyllis Schlafly, is sympathetically profiled in *The Sweetheart of the Silent Majority*, by Carol Felsenthal (Doubleday, 1981).

783. Fulenwider, Claire Knoche. **Feminism in American Politics: A Study of Ideological Influence.** New York: Praeger, 1980. 165p. bibliog. $31.95. LC 79-25131. ISBN 0030534615.

Fulenwider analyzes national electoral surveys conducted between 1972 and 1976 to investigate the structure of feminism as a political ideology, and its influence on the political attitudes and behavior of its supporters. In doing so, she distinguishes between the feminism of women and men, and of whites and minorities. Her major finding is that feminism does affect the political attitudes and behavior of women; interestingly, the effect she found was stronger for minority women than for white women. By contrast, she concludes that feminism is a more "peripheral" belief system for men.

784. Klein, Ethel, 1952- . **Gender Politics: From Consciousness to Mass Politics.** Cambridge, MA: Harvard University Press, 1984. 209p. bibliog. index. $16.50. LC 84-8992. ISBN 0674341961.

Seeking an understanding of the origins of the current women's movement, Klein asks "how women's personal problems became politicized and why women—and even men—now demand equal social and economic opportunities when they did not do so in the past" (p.2). Klein's focus is hardly novel. What distinguishes her treatment is its empirical grounding in public opinion surveys and census data. Klein analyzes changes in women's domestic, work, and political lives over the course of this century, concluding that "although the resources, organization, and leadership for a women's movement were around for a long time, the feminist movement could not emerge until the 1970s when there was a constituency which believed that women should have the same opportunities as men ..." (p.31). Key factors in the growth of this constituency, in Klein's estimation, were the increasing labor force participation of women, the decline in fertility, and the increase in marital instability—which, taken together, altered traditional expectations of women's roles. Klein also looks at election results from 1972, 1976, and 1980, tracing the emergence of the "gender gap."

785. Lovenduski, Joni, and Jill Hills, eds. **The Politics of the Second Electorate: Women and Public Participation.** Boston: Routledge and Kegan Paul, 1981. 332p. bibliog. index. pbk. $16.95. LC 81-199239. ISBN 0710008066.

Thirteen articles outline the political status of women in Britain, the United States, Canada, Australia, France, Spain, West Germany, Italy, Sweden, Finland, Eastern Europe, the USSR, and Japan in this valuable contribution to the comparative study of women and politics. The editors greatly enhance the utility of the collection by imposing a common framework on each of the articles. Although the essays treat women's participation in the formal political arena (including their voting behavior) in some depth, they transcend "a pursuit of the political science of the measurable" (p.2) by discussing forms of feminist activism as well. Studies of the industrialized nations predominate among other recent cross-cultural sources on women and politics, as they do in the Lovenduski and Hills volume. In *Comparative Women's Rights and Political Participation in Europe* (Transnational Publishers, 1983), Gisbert H. Flanz surveys women's political involvement during this century in the thirty-four countries of Eastern and Western Europe. Walter S. G. Kohn presents extensive data on women's representation in the legislatures of the United States, Britain, Canada, Germany, Austria, and Switzerland in

Women in National Legislatures: A Comparative Study of Six Countries (Praeger, 1980), covering the period from women's enfranchisement in each country through 1980. Recent area studies offer more detailed discussions of women and politics in Japan (*Political Women in Japan: The Search for a Place in Political Life* [University of California Press, 1981], by Susan J. Pharr); Latin America (*Supermadre: Women in Politics in Latin America* [University of Texas Press for Institute of Latin American Studies, 1979], by Elsa M. Chaney); Australia (*A Woman's Place: Women and Politics in Australia* [Allen and Unwin, 1984], by Marian Sawer and Marian Simms, and *Women in Australian Politics* [Fontana/Collins, 1983], by Jocelyn Clarke and Kate White); and India and Pakistan (see entry 315).

786. Mandel, Ruth B. **In the Running: The New Woman Candidate.** New Haven, CT: Ticknor and Fields, 1981; repr. Boston: Beacon Press, 1983. 280p. bibliog. index. $9.95. LC 83-70746. ISBN 0807067156.

At the time of this book's writing, Mandel was director of the Center for the American Woman and Politics at Rutgers University, where she had a wealth of data to work with. She reports here on a survey of 102 women candidates conducted during the 1976 elections. Mandel begins with a portrait of the candidates themselves and their motivations for seeking office. She goes on to outline the tyranny of image-making, candidates' loss of privacy, the campaigns, and support received from the women's movement. Mandel spices her discussion with real-life examples, quotes, and small details that bring her topics alive. Susan J. Carroll also studied women who ran for office in the 1976 elections. In *Women as Candidates in American Politics* (Indiana University Press, 1985), she reports her findings on the candidates' recruitment, why they won or lost, and their views on policies related to women. *Congressional Women: Their Recruitment, Treatment, and Behavior* (Praeger, 1984), by Irwin N. Gertzog, is a detailed examination of changing patterns in the experiences of women who have served in the U.S. House of Representatives since Jeannette Rankin took her seat in 1917.

787. Mullaney, Marie Marmo. **Revolutionary Women: Gender and the Socialist Revolutionary Role.** New York: Praeger, 1983. 401p. bibliog. index. $34.95. LC 82-22437. ISBN 0030619270.

Mullaney rejects psychohistory's model of *the* revolutionary personality, asserting that it reflects solely the experience of men. The lives of women revolutionaries, she finds, diverge sharply from those of men. Here Mullaney draws brief portraits of five women socialists: Eleanor Marx (1855-1898), daughter of Karl Marx and activist in the British labor movement; Alexandra Kollontai (1872-1952), the "Red Rose of the Russian Revolution"; Rosa Luxemburg (1871-1919), brilliant theorist and activist in the German socialist movement; Angelica Balabanoff (1878-1965), Russian-born revolutionary who chose Italy as her terrain of struggle; and Dolores Ibarruri (b.1895), the famed "Pasionaria" of the Spanish Civil War. In each of her biographies, Mullaney seeks to demonstrate how gender shaped the revolutionary experience. She writes in her conclusion: "The humanizing element that these women brought to the socialist movement, their tender kindness, passionate fervor, and sensitive reluctance to utilize power for destructive ends have all, unfortunately, been drastically undervalued" (p.264).

788. Okin, Susan Moller. **Women in Western Political Thought.** Princeton, NJ: Princeton University Press, 1979. 371p. bibliog. index. $35.00. LC 79-84004. ISBN 0691076138.

Okin seeks to define the vision of women in the thought of Plato, Aristotle, Rousseau, and Mill. She analyzes these philosophers' ideas about women in relation to their larger political theories (and particularly their concepts of the family) to test "whether the existing tradition of political philosophy can sustain the inclusion of women in its subject matter" (p.4). She concludes that women *cannot* be admitted as equals into these four theoretical systems without fundamentally undermining their structure and logic. In *Public Man, Private Woman: Women in Social and Political Thought* (Princeton University Press, 1981), Jean Bethke Elshtain uses the concepts of public and private "as a conceptual prism through which to see the story of women and politics from Plato to the present" (p.xiv). First turning a feminist critical eye on the body of Western political thought, Elshtain proceeds to bring the concerns of the political theorist to bear on radical, liberal, Marxist, and psychoanalytic feminism. She defends the sanctity of the biological family and calls upon feminists to make the public, not the private, world "the target of social rebellion" (p.333). In *Women in the History of Political Thought* (Praeger, 1985), Arlene W. Saxonhouse's aim is to rescue political thinkers from Plato to Machiavelli from androcentric interpretation. In her view, these theorists did not emphasize the public world to the neglect of the private, but rather stressed the interdependence of the sexes. Scholars are beginning to scrutinize the political systems of individual philosophers from a feminist angle. Two such works are Joel Schwartz's *The Sexual Politics of Jean-Jacques Rousseau* (University of Chicago Press, 1984) and Hanna Fenichel Pitkin's *Fortune Is a Woman: Gender and Politics in the Thought of Niccolò Machiavelli* (University of California Press, 1984).

789. Randall, Margaret, 1938- . **Sandino's Daughters: Testimonies of Nicaraguan Women in Struggle.** Edited by Lynda Yanz. Seattle, WA: Left Bank Books, 1981. 220p. pbk. $7.95. LC 82-127147. ISBN 0919888348.

On July 19, 1979, the Nicaraguan Sandinist National Liberation Front (FSLN) achieved its victory against the dictatorship of Anastasio Somoza. By the time of the final offensive, women accounted for thirty percent of the FSLN army. Randall, whose earlier books brought alive the Cuban revolution for English-speaking readers, presents the testimony of a diverse group of Nicaraguan women who were active in the revolution: peasant women as well as women from more privileged backgrounds; rank-and-file women as well as army commanders. Randall elicits specific comments on women's experience *as women* in the revolution; most of them manage to integrate motherhood and a profound revolutionary commitment. One particularly moving theme is the politicization of mothers and daughters: mothers drawn into the revolution through the activity of their daughters, and vice versa.

790. Sahgal, Nayantara, 1927- . **Indira Gandhi: Her Road to Power.** New York: Ungar, 1982. 260p. bibliog. index. $15.95. LC 81-70116. ISBN 0804418276.

Given India's continuing conflicts of caste, class, and religion—exacerbated by the legacy of colonialism—it is not surprising that assessments of Indira Gandhi (1917-1984) should vary wildly in point of view. A well-known novelist, Sahgal is Gandhi's cousin, and the daughter of Jawaharlal Nehru's sister, Mrs. Pandit. Sahgal takes a sharply critical view of Gandhi in this book. She views Gandhi as having made a decisive break with the democratic values of her two predecessors, Nehru and Lal Bahadur Shastri, in the interests of building a one-party system and a dynastic succession. The Emergency of 1975-1977, in Sahgal's view, served these purposes. Tariq Ali, in a newer work, *An Indian Dynasty: The Story of the Nehru-Gandhi Family* (Putnam, 1985), writes from a similar perspective, singling out Indira Gandhi for particularly searing criticism. Two more sympathetic biographies are Mary C. Carras's *Indira Gandhi: In the Crucible of Leadership* (Beacon Press, 1979) and *Mrs. Gandhi*, by Dom Moraes (J. Cape, 1980). In the aftermath of Gandhi's assassination in October 1984 and her son Rajiv's immediate succession as prime minister, it is clear that more definitive accounts of Indira Gandhi's life and politics remain to be written. *Indira Gandhi: Letters to an American Friend* (Harcourt, Brace, Jovanovich, 1985), selected, with commentary, by Dorothy Norman, yields a glimpse into Gandhi's private character.

791. Sapiro, Virginia. **The Political Integration of Women: Roles, Socialization, and Politics.** Urbana: University of Illinois Press, 1983. 205p. bibliog. index. $16.95. LC 82-2672. ISBN 0252009207.

"... [T]he private roles women are expected to perform as adults promote political marginality" (p.138), Sapiro finds in her study of the relationship between women's private lives and their integration into politics. Sapiro's empirical conclusions are drawn from a database of 676 women interviewed as teenagers in 1965, and then again in 1973, as part of the Michigan Socialization Panel Study—women who came of age during the emergence of the contemporary women's movement. The Michigan study measured both attitudes toward political involvement and reported behavior. Sapiro argues that policies that help to maintain the traditional sexual division of labor must be held at least partly responsible for women's political marginalization: "Analysis of women and politics shows ... the profoundly interlocked character of the public and private domains ..." (p.10). In *Women, Power, and Politics* (Tavistock, 1981), British sociologists Margaret Stacey and Marion Price define politics more broadly to encompass both the public and private realms, arguing that women lost substantial domestic power with the capitalistic transformation of work and the household. While they agree with Sapiro that in our own time privatization diminishes women's access to political power, Stacey and Price conclude their wide-ranging historical survey with a positive assessment of women's political progress in this century.

792. Siltanen, Janet, and Michelle Stanworth, eds. **Women and the Public Sphere: A Critique of Sociology and Politics.** New York: St. Martin's Press, 1984. 251p. bibliog. index. $25.00. LC 93-40290. ISBN 0312887345.

Siltanen and Stanworth extract fifteen articles from books, and from journals such as *Social Problems, New Socialist, Politics and Society,* and the *British Journal of Political Science,* to construct "an argument against traditions of political analysis which fail to consider seriously women's capacity for political thought and action, and an argument for the reconstruction of political analysis in ways that take into account the importance of gender" (pp.9-10). They add a general introduction, section introductions, and a conclusion to enhance the coherence of the volume as a whole. Dating from 1972 to 1981, the articles look at women's participation in work-based and electoral politics.

793. Stewart, Debra W., 1943- , ed. **Women in Local Politics.** Metuchen, NJ: Scarecrow Press, 1980. 232p. bibliog. index. $17.50. LC 80-14526. ISBN 0810813122.

"Clearly, the most dramatic gains in women's elective political participation have taken place at the local level.... Still, the local level remains a relatively unexplored arena for female activism, while researchers set their sights on the more distant national and state arenas" (pp.4-5). Stewart begins filling this gap in the research with a collection of nine scholarly articles that addresses two questions: How do women attain public office at the local level, and how do they perform once in that public role? Stewart herself has authored a study titled *The Women's Movement in Community Politics in the U.S.: The Role of Local Commissions on the Status of Women* (Pergamon Press, 1980). Another related collection of articles is *Political Women: Current Roles in State and Local Government* (Sage Publications, 1984), edited by Janet A. Flammang. The volume presents research on women as political activists and government officials, and on women and public policy.

794.   Tinker, Irene, ed. **Women in Washington: Advocates for Public Policy.** Beverly Hills: Sage Publications, 1983. 327p. bibliog. index. $28.00. LC 83-7761. ISBN 0803920695.

Contributors to this volume claim years of experience with organizations such as the National Council for Research on Women, the National Women's Political Caucus, the Coalition of Labor Union Women, the National Women's Health Network, the Women's Equity Action League, and the Women's Legal Defense Fund. These twenty Washington-based activists write on a range of policy issues, including the E.R.A., equal employment, sex equity in education, health, unions, development, the military, science and technology, domestic violence, and women's business enterprises. Two other recent titles evaluate feminist efforts to influence policy: *Women, Power and Policy* (Pergamon Press, 1982), a collection of sixteen articles edited by Ellen Boneparth that analyzes policies related to economics, motherhood, sexuality and crime, and foreign and military affairs; and Joyce Gelb and Marian Lief Palley's *Women and Public Policies* (Princeton University Press, 1982), a detailed assessment of credit, education, abortion, and pregnancy disability policies. Both volumes suggest that the most successful policies are those that seek incremental advances in role equity, rather than sweeping role change. The policy consequences of sexist research are the focus in *Taking Sex Into Account*, a collection of thirteen articles edited by Jill McCalla Vickers (Carleton University Press, 1984).

795.*   United States. National Commission on the Observance of International Women's Year. **What Women Want: From the Official Report to the President, The Congress and the People of the United States.** Compiled by Caroline Bird, et al. New York: Simon and Schuster, 1979. 192p. index. LC 78-8602. ISBN 0671242520.

This volume reprints the National Plan of Action adopted by the National Women's Conference held in Houston, Texas in November 1977. Originally published as part of the official report entitled *The Spirit of Houston* (National Commission on the Observance of International Women's Year, 1978), the twenty-six-plank Plan specifies the conference's proposals on battered women, childcare, disabled women, education, homemakers, minority women, sexual preference, and more. In addition to the Plan, this volume includes a summary of the state meetings, a narrative account of the conference, a description of the 2,600-mile torch relay, and interviews with delegates and observers. Alice S. Rossi, a member of the National Commission, reports on the results of her study of the conference in *Feminists in Politics* (Academic Press, 1982). Rossi surveyed over twelve hundred delegates, alternates, commissioners, and staff both before and after the conference to determine their political aspirations, their feminist beliefs, and the impact of the conference itself.

PSYCHOLOGY

Both theoretical and applied works find a home in this chapter. Important works draw on the psychoanalytic models of Freud and Jung — sometimes to demolish them, sometimes to mine them for useful insights into women's experiences. Other core studies look at the stages of women's lives, reassessing such areas as moral development, sex-role socialization, the parent-child bond, and male-female intimacy. Some researchers zero in on specific deviant behaviors — studying, for example, the effects of rape and battery, or examining evidence of female psychopathology. (There is overlap here with the Sociology chapter, especially.) Lastly, psychologists turn a critical eye on their own professional methods and the history of women in the discipline. The *Psychology of Women Quarterly* (see entry 1190) and *Sex Roles* (see entry 1194) remain the leading journals in this field.

796.* Al-Issa, Ihsan. **The Psychopathology of Women.** Englewood Cliffs, NJ: Prentice-Hall, 1980. 390p. bibliog. index. $15.95. LC 79-20257. ISBN 0137368275.

Al-Issa follows in the footsteps of Phyllis Chesler's pathbreaking *Women and Madness*, exploring the ways in which women's relative powerlessness makes them "vulnerable to the accusation of madness" (p.viii). Al-Issa brings this critical perspective to bear on his assessment of the psychological literature on psychosis, neurosis, sexual dysfunctions, homosexuality, alcoholism, drug abuse, criminality, and psychophysiological disorders. The sixteen articles in *Sex Roles and Psychopathology*, edited by Cathy Spatz Widom (Plenum Press, 1984), look at a similar range of disorders, with an emphasis on the contribution of sex roles to their etiology. By contrast, *Gender and Disordered Behavior,* a collection of seventeen articles edited by Edith S. Gomberg and Violet Franks (Brunner/Mazel, 1979), seeks to document sex differences in psychopathology. Readers may be offended by the editors' inclusion of obesity and homosexuality under the heading "Problem Behaviors."

797. Allgeier, Elizabeth Rice, and Naomi B. McCormick, eds. *Changing Boundaries: Gender Roles and Sexual Behavior.* Palo Alto, CA: Mayfield, 1983. 347p. bibliog. index. $13.95. LC 82-60885. ISBN 087484536X.

The impact of gender roles on sexual behavior is the focus of this nicely designed collection of articles. Contributors to Part I, "Developmental Perspective," look at gender roles in relation to childhood sexual socialization, adolescent sexuality, courtship, sexual response, men's and women's expectations of love and sex, and sexuality in the second half of life. Articles in Part II, "Contemporary Perspective," examine the impact of gender roles on reproduction and parenting, sexual harassment at work, singles' lifestyles, lesbian and gay relationships, sexual violence, and response to erotica. Allgeier and McCormick's introductions and headnotes, and the clear exposition throughout, make this an excellent text for the undergraduate classroom.

798.   Arcana, Judith. **Every Mother's Son.** Garden City, NY: Anchor Press/Doubleday, 1983. 322p. bibliog. index. $16.95. LC 82-12912. ISBN 0385156405.

What does it mean to a woman to mother a son in a misogynist society? Arcana is driven to grapple with this question because of her own experience with her son Daniel. "Mothers need to understand," she asserts, "that we are creating and nurturing the agents of our own oppression ..." (p.3). By far the most compelling part of the book is the first chapter, in which Arcana shares portions of a diary she kept between Daniel's fourth and tenth years. In the balance of the book, Arcana draws on her interviews with sixty mothers and sixty sons as she ponders the passage from male infant to boy to man, seeking clues as to where in the process feminist mothers might make a difference. Arcana's previous book is *Our Mother's Daughters* (Shameless Hussy Press, 1979), also based on extensive interviews. In this work, Arcana attempts to identify the many ways in which patriarchal culture estranges mothers and daughters.

799.   Baruch, Grace, et al. **Lifeprints: New Patterns of Love and Work for Today's Woman.** New York: McGraw-Hill, 1983; repr. New York: New American Library, 1984. 291p. bibliog. index. pbk. $8.95. LC 83-22045. ISBN 0452255333.

Combining a survey with in-depth interviews, Grace Baruch, Rosalind Barnett, and Caryl Rivers look at the lives of U.S. white women between the ages of thirty-five and fifty-five. Their study differs from much earlier social science research on midlife women by focusing not on the problems of aging, but on the factors that contribute to a woman's sense of well-being. Other books that detail the lives of middle-aged women (although somewhat less optimistically) are Lillian B. Rubin's *Women of a Certain Age: The Midlife Search for Self* (Harper and Row, 1979) and Elissa Melamed's *Mirror, Mirror: The Terror of Not Being Young* (Linden Press/Simon and Schuster, 1983), both based on interviews. Jane Porcino's *Growing Older, Getting Better* (Addison-Wesley, 1983) is a popular handbook for aging women, but its comprehensive coverage of psychological, economic, and health issues, plus its resource listings of publications and organizations, makes it a useful guide for younger researchers as well.

800.   Benedict, Helen. **Recovery: How to Survive Sexual Assault for Women, Men, Teenagers, Their Friends and Families.** Garden City, NY: Doubleday, 1985. 293p. bibliog. index. $15.95. LC 84-13821. ISBN 0385192061.

Threading her text with personal accounts from survivors of rape and their friends and families, Benedict offers warm reassurance and practical advice. After demolishing the common myths about rape, the author turns her attention in Part One to the woman victim, counseling short-term strategies for coping with the police, hospital staff, and rape crisis services, and long-term approaches to psychological recovery. A second group of chapters focuses on special groups: women raped by their husbands; men; older victims; teenagers; incest survivors; and lesbians and gay men. Up-to-date listings of rape crisis programs and other resources conclude the volume. When a more concise source is called for, *Surviving Sexual Assault*, edited by Rochel Grossman with Joan Sutherland (Congdon and Weed, 1983), proves ideal. Its question-and-answer format is straightforward, its advice sound, and its overall message empowering. Other recent books on the effects of rape speak to different audiences. Among them are *The Rape Crisis Intervention Handbook* (Plenum Press, 1980), a collection of articles by medical, legal, and counseling professionals, edited by Sharon L. McCombie; *The Aftermath of Rape* (Lexington Books, 1979), by Thomas W. McCahill, Linda C. Meyer, and Arthur M. Fischman, a longitudinal study of fourteen-hundred rape survivors that focuses on post-rape adjustment and experiences in the criminal justice system; and *The Second Assault: Rape and Public Attitudes* (Greenwood Press, 1981), a dual study of rape victims and public opinion, in which researchers Joyce E. Williams and Karen A. Holmes pay special attention to differences among Anglos, blacks, and Mexican-Americans.

801. Beneke, Timothy. **Men on Rape.** New York: St. Martin's Press, 1982. 174p. $12.95. LC 82-5628. ISBN 0312529503.

In the mushrooming body of literature on sexual assault, the male viewpoint has been noticeably absent. Beneke interviewed twenty-seven men from many walks of life, including lawyers, doctors, and policemen, as well as husbands, lovers, and friends of women who were raped. They describe their experiences, fantasies, and attitudes about rape. Beneke's introduction analyzes the language of the interviews, discusses the process of "pornographizing" (i.e., objectifying) women, and explicates the dynamics of blaming the victim. Andrea Rechtin, a rape counselor and the final interviewee, voices her anger that so many of the men see rape not as a violent crime but merely as an extreme strategy of seduction. The interviews reported by journalists Les Sussman and Sally Bordwell are even more chilling. The authors traveled to penitentiaries in three states to compile *The Rapist File* (Chelsea House, 1981), in which fifteen convicted rapists recount their crimes with surprising candor and little remorse.

802. Block, Jeanne Humphrey, 1923-1981. **Sex Role Identity and Ego Development.** San Francisco: Jossey-Bass, 1984. 327p. bibliog. index. $21.95. LC 84-7918. ISBN 0875896073.

This posthumous collection of previously published articles represents Block's "principal contributions to understanding sex role differences" (p.ix), written between 1973 and 1980. Block was rigorously critical of the developing field of sex-role socialization, as is evident in her review (included here) of the widely cited *The Psychology of Sex Differences,* by Eleanor Maccoby and Carol Jacklin. In other chapters, Block formulates her own perspective on topics such as parental and societal influences on sex roles, psychological development of female children and adolescents, gender differences and children's orientations to the world, and differential sex-role socialization and psychological functioning. Ravenna Helson has written an appreciative memoir of Block.

803. Boskind-White, Marlene, and William C. White, Jr. **Bulimarexia: The Binge/Purge Cycle.** New York: Norton, 1983. 219p. bibliog. index. $16.95. LC 82-14374. ISBN 0393016501.

Marlene Boskind-White was one of the first clinicians to identify the eating disorder she and William C. White have named "bulimarexia." They define the syndrome as habitual gorging and purging behavior, related to "perfectionism, low self-esteem, and a strong commitment to please others, often at the individual's expense" (p.20). White and Boskind-White consider bulimarexia a *learned* behavior, and therefore a behavior that can be unlearned. The authors analyze the disorder—which affects women almost exclusively—from a feminist perspective, describing their extensive experience with treatment in a readable, accessible style. With increased public awareness, a rash of books has appeared on the subject of bulimarexia and other eating disorders, primarily anorexia nervosa, a form of self-starvation. *Bulimia: The Binge-Purge Compulsion* (Doubleday, 1983), by Janice M. Cauwels, is based on interviews with medical specialists and sufferers.

The Binge-Purge Syndrome: Diagnosis, Treatment, and Research (Springer, 1984), edited by Raymond C. Hawkins, II, William J. Fremouw, and Pamela F. Clement, is a collection of papers from a 1980 professional symposium. *New Hope for Binge Eaters* (Harper and Row, 1984), by Harrison Pope and James Hudson, reviews evidence suggesting that bulimia may be related to what psychiatry terms "major affective disorders," and reports on experience with drug therapy. *Anorexia Nervosa: A Guide for Sufferers and Their Families* (Penguin Books, 1980), by British psychiatrist R. L. Palmer, is a fairly technical clinical discussion. Counterbalancing Palmer's account, *The Art of Starvation: A Story of Anorexia and Survival* (Schocken Books, 1982) relates the personal history of British novelist Sheila MacLeod. Three additional titles look at bulimia and anorexia nervosa together: *When Food Is a Four-Letter Word* (Prentice-Hall, 1984), by Paul Haskew and Cynthia H. Adams; *The Eating Sickness* (Harvester Press, 1984), by Jill Welbourne and Joan Purgold; and *When Will We Laugh Again?* (Columbia University Press, 1984), edited by Barbara P. Kinoy. Readers wanting a self-help approach to the problem of compulsive eating can turn to Susie Orbach's *Fat Is a Feminist Issue II: A Program to Conquer Compulsive Eating* (Berkley Books, 1982).

804.   Cox, Sue, ed. **Female Psychology: The Emerging Self.** 2nd ed. New York: St. Martin's Press, 1981. 494p. bibliog. $21.95. LC 80-52382. ISBN 0312287429.

Unusually well designed, with quotations, cartoons, poetry, and striking artwork enhancing the text, this popular anthology is notable for going beyond a psychology of white, middle-class, heterosexual women. Twenty-seven articles—many new to the second edition—are gathered in seven thematic sections: "Biological and Cultural Perspectives"; "Psychological Sex Differences"; "Ethnic Diversity of Female Experience" (including black, Asian-American, Chicana, and Native American women); "Psychological Oppression"; "Relationships: Sexuality and Intimacy"; "Mental Illness or Social Problem?"; and "Toward Change and Liberation." Such notable scholars as Eleanor Emmons Maccoby, Carol Nagy Jacklin, Jeanne H. Block, Nancy Henley, Jo Freeman, Nancy Felipe Russo, and Phyllis Chesler contribute to the volume. Cox provides a substantial introduction to the volume, and briefer introductions to each section. Another valuable reader for the undergraduate psychology classroom is Juanita H. Williams's *Psychology of Women: Selected Readings* (2nd ed., Norton, 1985), designed to accompany Williams's introductory text, *Psychology of Women: Behavior in a Biosocial Context* (2nd ed., Norton, 1983). Among the authors are Sharon Golub, Rhoda Kesler Unger, Carol Gilligan, Barbara Grizzuti Harrison, Del Martin and Phyllis Lyon, Alice S. Rossi, and Pamela Daniels.

805.   Eichenbaum, Luise, and Susie Orbach, 1946- . **Understanding Women: A Feminist Psychoanalytic Approach.** New York: Basic Books, 1983. 212p. bibliog. index. $15.50. LC 82-72545. ISBN 0465088643.

Luise Eichenbaum and Susie Orbach take a psychoanalytic approach to therapy. They discuss consciousness-raising, object relations theory, gender identity, and the construction of feminity, emphasizing the pivotal role of the mother-daughter relationship in women's psychological development. They also cover individual and group therapy situations, the interactions between women clients and women therapists, and particular issues such as phobias, somatic symptoms, and couples counseling. In a related book, *What Do Women Want?* (Coward-McCann, 1983), Eichenbaum and Orbach again draw on their experiences at the Women's Therapy Centre in London. The co-authors counter the premise advanced by Colette Dowling in *The Cinderella Complex* (Summit Books, 1981)—that female dependency is a debilitating learned behavior—with the opposite view that emotional dependency is a basic human need that goes unfulfilled in women, who are socialized to give rather than to receive emotional care.

806. Gallop, Jane, 1952- . **The Daughter's Seduction: Feminism and Psychoanalysis.** Ithaca, NY: Cornell University Press, 1982. 164p. bibliog. index. $19.95. LC 81-70709. ISBN 0801414938.

With this difficult, critical work, Gallop hopes to "seduce" feminism (the daughter) "out of her resistance to psychoanalysis (the father)" (p.xv) by creating a dialogue between contemporary feminist theory and the psychoanalysis of Jacques Lacan. Gallop begins with the work of Juliet Mitchell, who urged feminists to reconsider their repudiation of Freud back in the early 1970s, and who has more recently edited a collection of Lacan's writings (see entry 1129). In later chapters, Gallop creates "encounters" between the texts of different authors—e.g., Lacan and Ernest Jones; Luce Irigary and Freud; Lacan, Eugénie Lemoine-Luccioni, and Julia Kristeva; Hélène Cixous and Catherine Clément and Freud—in an effort to break through their seeming oppositions. Psychoanalysis, Gallop argues, "can unsettle feminism's tendency to accept a traditional, unified, rational, puritanical self—a self supposedly free from the violence of desire" (p.xii). Feminism, in turn, can disabuse psychoanalysis of its claim to be apolitical. Gallop's final chapter, "Keys to Dora," is reprinted in a recent volume of essays entitled *In Dora's Case: Freud—Hysteria—Feminism* (Columbia University Press, 1985), edited by Charles Bernheimer and Claire Kahane. The volume includes Felix Deutsch's follow-up report on this famous patient who so befuddled Freud; interpretations by Erik Erikson, Steven Marcus, and Jacques Lacan; and a number of feminist rereadings.

807. Gilbert, Lucy, and Paula Webster. **Bound by Love: The Sweet Trap of Daughterhood.** Boston: Beacon Press, 1982. 175p. bibliog. pbk. $8.95. LC 81-65760. ISBN 0807032506.

Gilbert and Webster's work with battered women brought them face to face with the difficult question: Why do abused women stay with their abusers? Seeking answers in the childhood socialization of daughters, they came to the conclusion that "the cultural requirements for femininity ensure that all women will be vulnerable to victimization whether or not they are in fact violated by men" (p.x). Gilbert and Webster begin by detailing "the dangers of femininity," then move into an analysis of mothers, fathers, daughters, and "the family romance." They see the cultural mandate of femininity as dividing women into Good Girls, Princesses, or Bad Girls. The psychology of incest, rape, and battering victims is explored, and Gilbert and Webster finish with a call to women to reject daughterhood and seek autonomy with the support of other women. It is intriguing that Susan Brownmiller, who pioneered a feminist analysis of rape in her book *Against Our Will,* should also have moved from the topic of violence against women to that of *Femininity* (Linden Press/Simon and Schuster, 1984). Published to very mixed reviews, her well-written book stands in sharp contrast to Gilbert and Webster's. Although Brownmiller certainly identifies femininity with constraint in chapters on body, hair, clothes, voice, skin, movement, emotion, and ambition, she also admits to the seductions of a "powerful esthetic that is built upon a recognition of powerlessness" (p.19). Both of these books tend to sweeping generalizations and give scant attention to differences of race, class, and ethnicity.

808. Gilligan, Carol, 1936- . **In a Different Voice: Psychological Theory and Women's Development.** Cambridge, MA: Harvard University Press, 1982. 184p. bibliog. index. $15.00. LC 81-13478. ISBN 0674445430.

Gilligan offers a radical revision of prevailing theories of moral development as exemplified in the work of Freud, Piaget, and, more recently, Harvard psychologist Lawrence Kohlberg. Within these theories, Gilligan argues, the male experience has unconsciously been taken as normative, the female as deviant. Kohlberg, for example, has postulated a series of stages in moral development through the life cycle culminating in adherence to abstract absolute principles such as justice and equality. From his viewpoint, women's countervailing concern with human relationships and responsibility interferes with their attainment of full moral maturity. Gilligan shows how the different moral sensitivities of men and women correspond to other gender differences — for example, their response to separation vs. attachment, autonomy vs. interdependence, rights vs. responsibilities. She presents the results of three different studies that used interviews to explore conceptions of self and morality, and experiences of conflict and choice. She quotes at length from this material to draw out women's "different voice." Though Gilligan's work has made waves both within and outside academia, there is in fact a long tradition — embraced at different times by both feminists and conservatives — that takes women's moral difference as moral *superiority*. Gilligan takes pains to assert her independence from this tradition, arguing instead that true moral maturity would entail an integration of both masculine and feminine, rights and responsibilities. Nel Noddings draws on Gilligan's work in her book *Caring: A Feminine Approach to Ethics and Moral Education* (University of California Press, 1984).

809. Greenspan, Miriam. **A New Approach to Women & Therapy.** New York: McGraw-Hill, 1983. 355p. bibliog. index. $16.95. LC 82-14851. ISBN 0070243492.

Drawing on her own experiences as a patient, student, and therapist, Greenspan exposes the failure of traditional psychotherapy and the newer humanist therapy to address women's needs. She illustrates how feminist therapy can change women's perceptions of themselves and their options. Susan Sturdivant's *Therapy With Women* (Springer, 1980) likewise takes a lucid look at feminism as the foundation of a new "philosophy of treatment." Sturdivant covers the theoretical and historical development of feminist therapy and such central concerns as the nature of women, the interpretation of symptoms, and the role of the therapist. Mary Ballou and Nancy W. Gabalac attempt to move thinking about feminist therapy to a new stage in *A Feminist Position on Mental Health* (C. C. Thomas, 1985). They review and synthesize existing theories and positions, and sketch their own model for a therapeutic process that advances women from harmful adaptation in a sexist cultural context to corrective action and health maintenance. Two recent titles are addressed specifically to the consumer. *A Woman's Guide to Therapy* (Prentice-Hall, 1979), by Susan Stanford Friedman, with co-authors Linda Gams, Nancy Gottlieb, and Cindy Nesselson, arms clients with information about the therapist/client relationship, psychological theories and terminology, and typical policies and procedures. Sheila Ernst and Lucy Goodson's *In Our Own Hands: A Woman's Guide to Self-Help Therapy* (J. P. Tarcher, 1981) suggests exercises from a variety of therapies (psychodrama, gestalt, bodywork, dream analysis, etc.) for use by individuals and leaderless groups.

810. Hall, Nor. **The Moon and the Virgin: Reflections on the Archetypal Feminine.** New York: Harper and Row, 1980. 283p. bibliog. index. $12.45. LC 78-2138. ISBN 0060117036.

Delving into myth, fairy tale, modern poetry, and dreams, therapist Nor Hall explores archetypal images of the feminine and their use to women on the quest for self-discovery. She builds upon a four-pointed model proposed by Toni Wolff, an early Jungian who conceptualized the components of the feminine principle as the Mother, the Amazon, the

Hetaira, and the Medium. Hall is quick to distinguish the "primoridal patterns" embodied in archetypes from negative stereotypes of women. In *The Goddess: Mythological Images of the Feminine* (Crossroad, 1981), Christine Downing examines images from Greek mythology, women's poetry, anthropology, and psychology. In autobiographical accounts of dreams and actions, she demonstrates the enduring influence of ancient images. *Goddesses in Everywoman: A New Psychology of Women* (Harper and Row, 1984) presents an up-to-date typology of female personalities. Author Jean Shinoda Bolen categorizes her archetypes as "virgin," "vulnerable," or "alchemical" goddesses, spotlights the strengths and difficulties of each, and encourages readers to identify and develop their own inner goddesses. Ann Belford Ulanov brings a Christian perspective to archetypal theory in *Receiving Woman: Studies in the Psychology and Theology of the Feminine* (Westminster Press, 1981), charting a careful path between male chauvinists who "would subtract from woman her physical power, her intellect, her ambition, her capacity for free assertion" and "hard-line feminists" who create new stereotypes by denying sex differences (p.16). All of the above writers develop concepts first articulated by C. G. Jung. Readers wishing to go straight to the source can consult Jung's own writings on women and the *anima/animus,* recently brought together under the title *Aspects of the Feminine* (Princeton University Press, 1982).

811. Howell, Elizabeth, and Marjorie Bayes. **Women and Mental Health.** New York: Basic Books, 1981. 654p. bibliog. index. $27.50. LC 81-66982. ISBN 0465092020.

Howell and Bayes direct this well-designed reader primarily to mental health practitioners, but it is accessible to a broader readership. Reprinted here are fifty-one articles — most originally published in books or academic journals during the 1970s — divided into six thematic sections: theoretical views; general issues of sexism in mental health; diagnosis and psychopathology; women's particular treatment needs; therapies; and future directions. Many topics of current interest are treated, among them diagnostic sexism, depression and phobias, eating disorders, addiction, teenage pregnancy, lesbian families, abortion, incest, and rape. A feminist perspective, evident in most of the selections, shapes the authors' section introductions and suggestions for supplementary reading. In *Sex-Role Issues in Mental Health* (Addison-Wesley, 1980), Kay F. Schaffer seeks to acquaint professionals and students in the mental health field with recent literature on sex roles. Although similar in many respects to other social psychology texts (see entry 1057), Schaffer's book is tailored throughout to her specific readership. Articles in *The Stereotyping of Women: Its Effects on Mental Health,* edited by Violet Franks and Esther D. Rothblum (Springer, 1983), attempt to track the impact of sex-role stereotypes on, for example, language use, women's depression, agoraphobia, female sexual dysfunction, assertiveness, and weight and health.

812. Hyde, Janet Shibley. **Half the Human Experience: The Psychology of Women.** 3rd ed. Lexington, MA: D. C. Heath, 1985. 482p. bibliog. index. pbk. $14.95. LC 84-80246. ISBN 0669067547.

Now in its third edition, Janet Hyde's *Half the Human Experience* may well become *the* core text for psychology of women courses. It is readable, comprehensive, up to date, and assumes no prior background in psychology. Hyde attempts to respond to current directions in feminist scholarship, incorporating material on lesbians and black women. This latest edition adds discussions of men, sociobiology, eating disorders, sexual harassment, and incest to her previous presentations on images of women in mythology and religion; theoretical perspectives; femininity, masculinity, and androgyny; gender differences in personality behavior; the life cycle; abilities and achievement; language; biological influences; psychology and health; sexuality; mental illness; and rape. Readers may find that Hyde's comprehensiveness occasionally is achieved by sacrificing depth. Two other books praised as more advanced texts are now somewhat dated: *Female and Male: Psychological Perspectives,* by Rhoda K. Unger (Harper and Row, 1979) and Joanna Bunker Rohrbaugh's *Women: Psychology's Puzzle* (Basic Books, 1979).

813. Kaufman, Debra R., and Barbara L. Richardson. **Achievement and Women: Challenging the Assumptions.** New York: Free Press; London: Collier Macmillan, 1982. 188p. bibliog. index. $24.95. LC 81-68324. ISBN 0029167809.

Kaufman and Richardson combine sociology, social psychology, and intellectual history in an effort to make sense of the substantial literature on the subject of achievement. This literature is not only male-biased; it is also skewed toward a "stress on individual ambition and personal attributes" (p.x) as determinants of achievement. In contrast, Kaufman and Richardson begin with the assumption "that women are forced to relate to the educational and occupational world ... first as members of a subordinate sex and only secondarily as individuals" (p.x). Organizing their discussion around life stages (childhood, adolescence, young adulthood, and maturity), they combine critical analysis of the literature with a revisionist view of women and achievement.

814. Leifer, Myra. **Psychological Effects of Motherhood: A Study of First Pregnancy.** New York: Praeger, 1980. 291p. bibliog. index. pbk. $14.95. LC 79-26179. ISBN 003055781X.

Leifer looks at the attitudes of "normal" women toward pregnancy and early motherhood, and analyzes the complex of social and psychological factors that surround childbearing in this culture. Leifer followed nineteen white, first-time mothers from the early second trimester of pregnancy through seven months postpartum. She presents her findings in topical chapters: pregnancy; emotional changes during pregnancy and the postpartum period; development of maternal feelings; nursing; childbirth; and motherhood as dream vs. reality. *Psychology and Human Reproduction*, by James W. Selby, Lawrence G. Calhoun, Albert V. Vogel, and H. Elizabeth King (Free Press, 1980), provides a very thorough, if occasionally jargon-laden, review of the literature based on a view of childbearing as a "critical life problem."

815. Lewin, Miriam, 1931- , ed. **In the Shadow of the Past: Psychology Portrays the Sexes, a Social and Intellectual History.** New York: Columbia University Press, 1984. 336p. bibliog. index. $32.00. LC 83-10072. ISBN 0231053029.

Thirteen provocative essays scrutinize psychology in the twentieth century in an attempt to ferret out its "'apparently innocent suppositions' about women and men" (p.vii). The general finding is that by unconsciously absorbing prevailing gender stereotypes, psychology has given nineteenth-century prescriptions the status of twentieth-century "science." In representative articles, Barbara J. Harris turns a critical eye on Freud's legacy; Rosalind Rosenberg profiles early women psychologists who challenged the field's gender assumptions; Ben Harris resurrects John B. Watson's popular advice on childrearing, women, and the family; and Miriam Lewin critically dissects psychological measures of femininity and masculinity.

816. Malamuth, Neil M., and Edward Donnerstein, eds. **Pornography and Sexual Aggression.** Orlando, FL: Academic Press, 1984. 333p. bibliog. index. $35.00. LC 84-3086. ISBN 0124662803.

The relation of sexually explicit stimuli (including violent pornography) to aggressive sexual behavior is the subject of this anthology assembled by two leading investigators. The introductory survey of past research, plus the eleven papers (several reporting on original studies and their theoretical and policy implications), will help concerned readers evaluate the adage that pornography is the theory and rape is the practice. The collection is important background reading for the more emotional and theoretical feminist discussions of pornography.

817. Masson, Jeffrey Moussaieff, 1941- . **The Assault on Truth: Freud's Suppression of the Seduction Theory.** New York: Farrar, Straus, Giroux, 1984. 308p. bibliog. index. $16.95. LC 83-20806. ISBN 0374106428.

Early in his career, Sigmund Freud expounded his "seduction theory," declaring that female hysteria could be traced to instances of childhood sexual abuse. Later he publicly abandoned the theory and focused instead on children's sexual fantasies. Jeffrey Masson asserts that Freud suppressed the evidence of actual sexual trauma in his patients' backgrounds and developed his Oedipal theory (a theory that became the linchpin of psychoanalysis) because he could not bear the condemnation of his colleagues. Masson had unprecedented access to Freud's unpublished letters and other documents. Although discredited by the psychoanalytic establishment, his revelations mesh with the findings of feminist researchers that incest is far more widely practiced than most suspect, and that the psychological consequences for the victims can be severe. (See entries 641 and 1025.)

818. O'Connell, Agnes N., and Nancy Felipe Russo, 1943- . **Models of Achievement: Reflections of Eminent Women in Psychology.** New York: Columbia University Press, 1983. 338p. bibliog. index. $28.00. LC 82-23583. ISBN 0231053126.

O'Connell and Russo provide supplementary readings for psychology and women's studies courses, as well as inspiration for women psychologists in search of their foremothers. Seventeen psychologists, born between 1897 and 1922, share recollections of their backgrounds, education, and careers; each autobiographical sketch is accompanied by a photograph and a list of the individual's publications. Russo's historical essay on the field of psychology sets these accounts in perspective, while O'Connell's concluding piece attempts to tease out similarities and differences in the women's patterns of achievement. Russo and O'Connell earlier edited a special issue of *Psychology of Women Quarterly,* "Eminent Women in Psychology: Models of Achievement," which gathered biographies of seven additional women (1980; repr. Human Sciences Press, 1980). *The Women of Psychology,* a two-volume set by Gwendolyn Stevens and Sheldon Gardner (Schenkman, 1982), offers brief biographies of more than 130 psychologists. Volume I, "Pioneers and Innovators," looks at women born between 1849 and 1890; Volume II, "Expansion and Refinement," documents the lives of women born between 1891 and 1940. Occasional sideswipes at feminism and feminists mar what is otherwise a valuable sourcebook and lively critique of the field of psychology.

819. O'Leary, Virginia E., 1943- , et al., eds. **Women, Gender, and Social Psychology.** Hillsdale, NJ: L. Erlbaum, 1985. 381p. bibliog. index. $39.95. LC 84-23114. ISBN 0898594472.

Virginia E. O'Leary, Rhoda Kesler Unger, and Barbara Strudler Wallston invited scholars in a number of substantive areas in social psychology to submit original essays on "the ways in which the study of women and gender have enhanced theory and research" in their areas of expertise (p.2). Included here are "Integrating the Feminist Critique and the Crisis in Social Psychology: Another Look at Research Methods," by Barbara Strudler

Wallston and Kathleen F. Grady; "Images of Masculinity and Femininity: A Reconceptualization," by Janet T. Spence and Linda L. Sawin; "Sex-Determined Attributions," by Ranald D. Hansen and Virginia E. O'Leary; "Achievement Motivation and Sex Roles," by Elyse Sutherland and Joseph Veroff; "From Theories of Equity to Theories of Justice: The Liberating Consequences of Studying Women," by Arnold S. Kahn and William P. Gaeddert; "The Helpful but Helpless Female: Myth or Reality?," by Jane Allyn Piliavin and Rhoda Kesler Unger; "Adding Gender to Aggression Research: Incremental or Revolutionary Change?," by Jacqueline Macaulay; "Gender and Influence-ability: Stereotype Versus Behavior," by Alice H. Eagly and Wendy Wood; "Women and Men in Love: Gender Differences in Close Heterosexual Relationships," by Letitia Anne Peplau and Steven L. Gordon; "Sex, Gender, and Groups: Selected Issues," by Kenneth L. Dion; and "Epilogue: Toward a Synthesis of Women, Gender, and Social Psychology," by Rhoda K. Unger.

820. Pogrebin, Letty Cottin. **Growing Up Free: Raising Your Child in the 80s.** New York: McGraw-Hill, 1980. 641p. bibliog. index. $15.95. LC 80-13054. ISBN 0070503702.

A founding editor of *Ms.,* Pogrebin wrote this handbook for parents in the breezy style of that magazine. Her aim is to open minds and dispel fears, to convince parents that they "do not have to choose between raising children to be 'sex-typed' and raising children to be 'the same'" (p.29). Her emphasis is on providing children with equal chances and choices, regardless of sex. She elaborates this perspective in chapters on nonsexist infancy, sharing tasks, family relationships and feelings, nonsexist sexuality, play, media ("television is sexistvision"), and education. In a chapter entitled "Homosexuality, Hysteria, and Children: How Not to Be a Homophobic Parent," Pogrebin confronts parental anxieties about changing sex roles and prejudices about homosexuality head-on. The volume is documented with extensive notes but lacks a bibliography. Academic rather than popular in approach, *Boys and Girls at Play: The Development of Sex Roles*, by Evelyn Goodenough Pitcher and Lynn Hickey Schultz (Praeger, 1983), documents the effects of sexist childrearing as observed in a study of preschool children in the Boston area.

821.* Romer, Nancy. **The Sex-Role Cycle: Socialization From Infancy to Old Age.** Old Westbury, NY: Feminist Press, 1981. 167p. bibliog. index. LC 80-17211. ISBN 091267069X.

This introductory text for the high school or undergraduate classroom lives up to the high standards established by other volumes in the Feminist Press series "Women's Lives/ Women's Work." Distilling a wide range of recent research on sex roles, the book is well organized, clearly written, and attractively designed. Romer, a psychologist, elects a developmental approach, with separate chapters on each stage of the life cycle: infancy; early childhood; adolescence; young adulthood; middle adulthood; later adulthood. While the existing research literature emphasizes the experiences of the middle-class, white, heterosexual population, Romer strives to make distinctions by race, class, and sexual preference. Two older texts also attempt to translate social science theory and research on sex-role socialization into everyday language. Jeanne Brooks-Gunn and Wendy Schempp Matthews's *He and She: How Children Develop Their Sex-Role Identity* (Prentice-Hall, 1979) is geared to the undergraduate classroom, covering sex-role development from infancy through adolescence. Lenore J. Weitzman's *Sex Role Socialization: A Focus on Women* (Mayfield, 1979) is a concise overview of the field through the late 1970s.

822. Rosenbaum, Marsha, 1948- . **Women on Heroin.** New Brunswick, NJ: Rutgers University Press, 1981. 196p. bibliog. index. $25.00. LC 80-29566. ISBN 0813509211.

The ratio of women to men addicts has increased dramatically over the past decade, yet Rosenbaum's is the first full-length study of the lives of female heroin users. (Earlier research dwelled on the hazards to the fetus of heroin use during pregnancy and the relation of drug abuse to female crime and pathology.) Drawing on interviews with one hundred women addicts, Rosenbaum outlines a typical "career of narrowing options" in the areas of work, family, social life, and psychological outlook. Her text is readable and enlightening; statistics and the explication of her methodology are relegated to appendixes. *Women and Drugs,* edited by Thomas J. Glynn, Helen Wallenstein Pearson, and Mollie Sayers (National Institute on Drug Abuse, 1983), offers lengthy abstracts of psychosocial and physiological research on the use of heroin and other controlled substances. Additional publications are listed in an unannotated bibliography.

823. Rosewater, Lynne Bravo, and Lenore E. Λ. Walker, eds. **Handbook of Feminist Therapy: Women's Issues in Psychotherapy.** New York: Springer, 1985. 352p. bibliog. index. $34.95. LC 85-4782. ISBN 0826149707.

The thirty-two chapters in this volume testify to the spectrum of theories and techniques that engage practicing feminist psychotherapists. Although based on presentations at the first Advanced Feminist Therapy Institute held in 1982, the collection serves as a fine state-of-the-art overview for nonspecialists. The papers are grouped by topic: a feminist philosophy of treatment; psychotherapeutic techniques and practices; women's issues across the lifespan; violence against women; power and advocacy issues; feminist ethics; the training of feminist therapists. An earlier collection, likewise spawned by a conference, was edited by Annette M. Brodsky and Rachel T. Hare-Mustin— *Women and Psychotherapy: An Assessment of Research and Practice* (Guilford Press, 1980). The contributors address the influence of gender on research, disorders of high prevalence (depression, anxieties, eating disorders, and marital and family conflicts), traditional and alternative therapeutic approaches, and crisis intervention. The editors wrap up the volume by recommending priorities for research. Several themes from these two books are echoed in the more narrowly focused *Behavior Modification With Women,* edited by Elaine A. Blechman (Guilford Press, 1984).

824. Rubin, Lillian B. **Intimate Strangers: Men and Women Together.** New York: Harper and Row, 1983. 222p. index. $14.37. LC 82-48678. ISBN 0060149221.

Rubin is exceptionally skilled at rendering social science scholarship meaningful and accessible to the general reader. In this well-written book, she draws on her fifteen years as a researcher and psychotherapist and interviews with 150 couples to describe and interpret "the deep-seated internal differences" between women and men "on such issues as dependency, intimacy, sexuality, work, and parenting" (p.12). Acknowledging her considerable debt to Nancy Chodorow and Dorothy Dinnerstein, Rubin follows their lead, seeking clues to the origin of men's and women's differences in "the fact that only women mother" (p.49). She concludes that women's monopoly on mothering means that boys and girls confront very different developmental tasks, which leave a legacy of personality differences making women and men "strangers" even when intimate. Rubin uses her interview material to great advantage, liberally intermingling quotes with her text.

825. Sanford, Linda Tschirhart, and Mary Ellen Donovan. **Women and Self-Esteem: Understanding and Improving the Way We Think and Feel About Ourselves.** Garden City, NY: Anchor Press/Doubleday, 1984; repr. New York: Penguin Books, 1985. 454p. bibliog. index. pbk. $7.95. LC 85-6490. ISBN 0140082255.

In this work geared to a popular audience, Sanford (a psychotherapist) and Donovan (a freelance writer) work from a set of four assumptions: 1) that low self-esteem in women largely results from — and is itself a form of — female oppression; 2) that low self-esteem underlies many other common psychological problems, such as eating disorders and alcoholism; 3) that low self-esteem contributes to the continuing oppression of women; and 4) that individual women must enhance their self-esteem if women as a group are to fight male domination. Their analysis moves from a consideration of interpersonal relationships to the larger world of education, religion, government, the media, and the helping professions, examining how each contributes to women's problems with self-esteem. In their final section, the authors tally the many costs of low self-esteem.

826. Scarf, Maggie, 1932- . **Unfinished Business: Pressure Points in the Lives of Women.** New York: Ballantine, 1980. 581p. bibliog. index. pbk. $3.95. LC 78-22352. ISBN 0385122489.

Scarf brings her skills as a science writer to bear on this discussion of women and depression, interweaving technical information and case studies of ten women. Each chapter focuses on a single decade in the life cycle, from the teens through the sixties, pinpointing notable "pressure points." Scarf views women as predisposed by both genetics and socialization to value attachment, affiliation, and nurturance. In a world in which "Rupture and disintegration ... are cultural norms" (p.536), this predisposition makes women more susceptible to depression than men, Scarf argues. Feminist reviewers have faulted Scarf for embracing psychotherapy and drug treatment too uncritically.

827. Seidenberg, Robert, and Karen DeCrow. **Women Who Marry Houses: Panic and Protest in Agoraphobia.** New York: McGraw-Hill, 1983. 224p. bibliog. index. $15.95. LC 82-14934. ISBN 0070162840.

"Agoraphobics may well be the most completely uncompromising feminists of our times," declare Seidenberg and DeCrow at the outset of their provocative book (p.7). In the authors' view, agoraphobics (mostly women) are "living and acting metaphor[s]" (p.209), refusing to leave home for a public space that is hostile to them. This refusal can also be interpreted as a strike against domestic responsibilities, since agoraphobics cannot shop, chauffeur, or attend their husbands' social functions. Presenting numerous case studies of agoraphobics, including Emily Dickinson, Carolyn Wyeth, and Queen Victoria, Seidenberg and DeCrow attack contemporary treatments — psychotherapeutic and biochemical — for treating "metaphor" as disease. Reviewers, including feminists, have judged the argument here insightful but overstated.

828. Van Herik, Judith. **Freud on Femininity and Faith.** Berkeley: University of California Press, 1982. 216p. bibliog. index. $27.50. LC 81-3413. ISBN 0520043685.

Van Herik's concern is with the nature of Freud's thought as a "theory of culture," not with its clinical utility. The author's intention is "to read Freud's theory of religion through his theory of gender ..." (p.2). Van Herik discovers linkages in Freud's thought between the renunciation of wishes, acceptance of the reality principle, moral sense, the scientific attitude, and masculinity. Femininity, on the other hand, Van Herik finds intertwined with wish fulfillment, the pleasure principle, and religious faith. More specifically, Van Herik argues, Freud "discerned similar mental structures in (a) femininity and Christian 'illusion'; [and] (b) masculinity and Jewish renunciation of wish ..." (p.2).

829. Walker, Lenore E. **The Battered Woman Syndrome.** New York: Springer, 1984. 256p. bibliog. index. $21.95. LC 84-1324. ISBN 0826143202.

Building on her earlier work (*The Battered Woman,* 1979), Walker delineates the psychosocial characteristics of battered women, as well as the traits of their husbands and children. She draws two theoretical conclusions from her data: that battered women suffer from "learned helplessness" and that battering incidents conform to a cycle of escalating tension and violence, ending with displays of loving contrition by the batterer. This last phase, Walker contends, provides the positive reinforcement that keeps women in abusive relationships. In her closing chapters, Walker outlines directions for future research and recommends therapeutic and legal approaches to changing violent relationships. Walker interviewed and tested some four hundred battered women to arrive at her findings; an eighty-two page appendix presents statistical charts and an extremely detailed (and interesting) account of her methodology. Mildred Daley Pagelow's *Woman-Battering: Victims and Their Experiences* (Sage Publications, 1981) demands from the reader greater patience and a sophisticated appreciation of the perils and rewards of social science research methods. Pagelow attempts to answer the puzzling question, why do battered women stay in destructive relationships? Despite the inconclusiveness of the findings, the work is valuable for its thorough review of the literature, its case studies, and its examination of myths and stereotypes of battered women through the lens of social learning theory.

830. Williams, John E., and Deborah L. Best. **Measuring Sex Stereotypes: A Thirty-Nation Study.** Beverly Hills, CA: Sage Publications, 1982. 368p. bibliog. index. $29.95. LC 82-3291. ISBN 0803918372.

Williams and Best report the results of their ambitious thirty-nation study of sex stereotypes among adults and children. The study utilized a three-hundred-adjective checklist (ACL) designed to elicit subjects' beliefs about men's and women's psychological characteristics. The authors' findings emphasize substantial pancultural similarities, with the male stereotype "characterized by higher needs for dominance, autonomy, aggression, exhibition, achievement, and endurance, and the female stereotype [revealing] higher needs for abasement, deference, succorance, nurturance, affiliation, and heterosexuality" (pp.244-245). Skeptical readers might question the validity of cross-cultural research based on a single instrument. Designed and standardized in the United States, the ACL has been widely used in American sex-role studies. In *Human Sex-Role Behavior* (Pergamon Press, 1981), clinical psychologist Alfred B. Heilbrun, Jr. reviews the findings of his own research over twenty years using the ACL. Heilbrun discusses myths and misconceptions about sex-role behavior, measurement issues and commonly used instruments, androgyny, sex roles and personal competence, lifestyle and cultural differences in sex-role behavior, and parent identification and sex-role behavior of the child.

831. Wittig, Michele Andrisin, and Anne C. Petersen, eds. **Sex-Related Differences in Cognitive Functioning: Developmental Issues.** New York: Academic Press, 1979. 378p. bibliog. index. $47.50. LC 79-9827. ISBN 0127611509.

As the editors note in their preface, this collection of articles on sex-related cognitive differences "is 'biased' in the direction of biological factors" (p.xvi). Petersen and Wittig's overview of the subject is followed by twelve articles divided into five topical sections:

genes; brain organization; hormones; socialization; and measurement. Carol Nagy Jacklin contributes an epilogue. As the volume is intended as a vehicle for communication among specialists, its level of discussion is quite advanced. An earlier source that nonspecialist readers may find more accessible is Julia A. Sherman's *Sex-Related Cognitive Differences: An Essay on Theory and Evidence* (C. C. Thomas, 1978).

REFERENCE

Reference materials appear under four major divisions: Audiovisual, Bibliographies, Biographical Materials, and General.

The Audiovisual section is disappointingly slim, considering the widespread reliance on films, videotapes, and other media presentations in both classroom and community settings. This is an area still desperately in need of improved bibliographic control and more accessible current awareness tools.

The Bibliographies subchapter, on the other hand, is highly selective, because here the literature has grown tremendously. Many narrowly focused bibliographies are mentioned in the annotations to other works—especially critical guides to writings by and about individual authors, which are covered in Literature. By contrast, those works included here are of general importance. They are notable for addressing topics previously neglected (e.g., Sahli's annotated guide to works on sexuality [see entry 889], or Green's contextual bibiography on Native American women [see entry 869]), for offering authoritative bibliographic overviews (e.g., Harrison's *Women in American History* [see entry 873]), or for providing clues to sources in areas that defy categorization by discipline (e.g., Ballou's bibliography of bibliographies [see entry 843]). The smaller the library, the more central bibliographies must be to the information-seeking process. With handy tools like *Women's Periodicals and Newspapers from the 18th Century to 1981* (see entry 872), researchers can use interlibrary loan to access a larger universe of resources.

The section on Biographical Materials complements the Autobiography chapter. Here we highlight collective biographies and biographical dictionaries, often treating specific subgroups of women—black women, women in politics, women of Great Britain, and so forth. Indexes to biographical writings also appear here.

The final Reference subchapter, labeled General, is a potpourri of handbooks, manuals, directories, quotation dictionaries, and other miscellaneous factual sources.

To keep abreast of new materials, we advise readers to consult the review column "New Reference Works in Women's Studies," appearing quarterly in *Feminist Collections* (see entry 865), and the standard reviewing sources such as *Choice, Library Journal, RQ,* and *Wilson Library Bulletin.*

AUDIOVISUAL

832. Cohen, Aaron I., comp. **International Discography of Women Composers.** Westport, CT: Greenwood Press, 1984. 254p. index. $35.00. LC 83-26445. ISBN 0313242720.

Claiming near-comprehensive coverage of "classical or serious music," this guide to recordings lists the works of 468 women composers. The alphabetical listing notes the dates and nationalities of the composers, the record company and record number, and (in most cases) the names of performers and conductors and the length of the piece. A similar volume by Jane Frasier, *Women Composers: A Discography* (Information Coordinators, 1983), covers 337 composers, including some not mentioned in Cohen's discography. Both volumes have title indexes; Cohen additionally offers an index to composers by country, while Frasier provides a record company index. Cohen's index to instruments and music forms uses more precise categories than does Frasier's index to musical genres. Both treat a wide range of vocal and instrumental music; solo, ensemble, and orchestral works; and electronic pieces as well as traditional forms.

833.   Foreman, Alexa L. **Women in Motion.** Bowling Green, OH: Bowling Green State University Popular Press, 1983. 248p. bibliog. $19.95. LC 83-72435. ISBN 0879722665.

Unlike other filmographies listing films *about* women, Foreman's guide is limited to films *by* women. Foreman provides annotations only for films still available for sale or rental; distributors are indicated. Complete filmographies for seventeen of the filmmakers appear at the back of the volume. By including "representative women involved with motion pcitures from the birth of films to the present" (Introduction) and highlighting editors and screenwriters as well as independent filmmakers and directors, Foreman lays the groundwork for exploring women's contributions to the film industry.

834.   Nordquist, Joan. **Audiovisuals for Women.** Jefferson, NC: McFarland, 1980. 145p. index. $15.95. LC 80-14691. ISBN 0899500110.

This guide to women-oriented materials contains separate sections on 16mm films, videotapes, filmstrips, slides, and recordings, with a subject index. The compiler excludes materials designed primarily for use in elementary school classrooms. Most of the 876 entries have brief annotations, consisting mostly of citations to reviews and occasional excerpts from critical comments. Every entry includes title, producer, distributor, release date, and a technical description. Because of the exhaustive coverage of films in Sullivan's *Films For, By and About Women* (see entry 836), Nordquist's slimmer listing is most useful for identifying videotapes and recordings.

835.   Oshana, Maryann. **Women of Color: A Filmography of Minority and Third World Women.** New York: Garland, 1985. 338p. index. $30.00. LC 82-49143. ISBN 082409140X.

Feminist film critics have ably demonstrated that the stereotyped portrayal of female characters in popular movies mirrors women's oppression in society at large; that this is doubly true for women of color should surprise no one. Oshana has documented the screen roles to which women of color have been relegated, noting that minority and Third-World characters are often played by white women. Films, largely produced in the United States between 1930 and 1983, are cited alphabetically by their titles. Each entry includes the year of release, running time, director, principal cast members, screenwriter, other key personnel, and a short description or synopsis. Oshana includes many films in which a woman of color is merely a supporting or token character. There are indexes to actors, directors, and minority/Third-World content classifications (e.g., Asian, Latin American, Black, and more subtle distinctions such as Chinese, Mexican, and American Black).

836.   Sullivan, Kaye, 1921- . **Films For, By and About Women.** Metuchen, NJ: Scarecrow Press, 1980. 552p. bibliog. index. $30.00. LC 79-26830. ISBN 0810812797.

Sullivan's aims are twofold: to provide access to films helpful in the analysis of sex roles, and to present the works of women filmmakers. Approximately 2,800 films are listed alphabetically in this first volume, and another 3,200 in the supplement, *Films For, By and*

About Women, Series II (Scarecrow Press, 1985). Each entry provides the following information: running time; black and white or color; production or release date; brief synopsis; directors, producer, etc.; and distributor. A complete list of film sources, with addresses, is appended. The main listing is indexed by subject (including, in the second volume only, the names of individuals) and by women filmmakers. Most of the films Sullivan describes are available in 16mm, but videotapes and slide sets also appear. Documentaries, full-length features, educational films, cartoons, and short films all fall within the filmography's scope. There are no indications of price or assessments of technical quality.

837.   Vedder-Shults, Nancy, comp. **The Music of Women: A Selection Guide.** Madison: Wisconsin Women Library Workers, 1984. 18p. $3.00.

The Music of Women presents a basic record collection in four categories: concert music; jazz, blues, and gospel; folk music; and the new "women's music" of the feminist counterculture. Providing brief evaluative annotations and listing prices for most items, the discography serves both librarians and listeners well.

BIBLIOGRAPHIES

838.   Addis, Patricia K. **Through a Woman's I: An Annotated Bibliography of American Women's Autobiographical Writings, 1946-1976.** Metuchen, NJ: Scarecrow Press, 1983. 607p. index. $37.50. LC 82-10813. ISBN 0810815885.

Addis's bibliography gathers together more than two thousand personal narratives by women published between 1946 and 1976, including autobiographies, journals, letters, diaries, travel narratives, and memoirs. The book covers much the same ground as Mary Louise Briscoe's *American Autobiography 1945-1980: A Bibliography* (University of Wisconsin Press, 1982), which is not restricted to works by women but does highlight them with asterisks. In her introduction, Addis notes that listing a work does not imply that it has literary worth; her clearly written annotations address the content of each book without analysis. She supplies the writer's dates when possible and gives complete bibliographic information. Three indexes—an author index that identifies writers by category (i.e., ichthyologist, immigrant), a subject index, and a title index—assist in locating less recognized women. Yet another volume covers the same general time period, citing a mere 224 works but offering longer, critical annotations: *First Person Female American: A Selected and Annotated Bibliography of the Autobiographies of American Women Living After 1950,* edited by Carolyn H. Rhodes (Whitson, 1980).

839.*   Arthur and Elizabeth Schlesinger Library on the History of Women in America. **The Manuscript Inventories and the Catalogs of Manuscripts, Books, and Periodicals.** 2nd ed. Boston: G. K. Hall, 1984. 10v. LC 84-202313. ISBN 0816104255.

The Schlesinger Library at Radcliffe houses the premier collection of printed and archival materials on American women's history. Its holdings, which have tripled since the first three-volume catalog (1973), now total some eighteen thousand books, more than four hundred manuscript collections, and thousands of photographs. Long dedicated to preserving materials on notable U.S. women and their achievements in such areas as politics, social reform, and the professions, the library has recently sought to document the lives and experiences of "anonymous" women, women of color, and working-class women. Books are listed by author, title, and subject, while photographs are indexed by subject and proper name. Manuscript inventories describe in detail the contents of family papers, organizational archives, and oral histories; among the treasures are unpublished writings of Susan B. Anthony, Amelia Earhart, Charlotte Perkins Gilman, and Betty Friedan. Historians interested in primary and secondary works on American women since 1800 will need to access this set.

840.   August, Eugene R., 1935- . **Men's Studies: A Selected and Annotated Interdisciplinary Bibliography.** Littleton, CO: Libraries Unlimited, 1985. 215p. index. $30.00. LC 84-28894. ISBN 0872874818.

Men's studies, August asserts, is "the logical complement to women's studies and a necessary component of any balanced gender-related scholarship" (p.xi). In this unique bibliography, he selects nearly six hundred books about male experience, sorting them into twenty-one chapters by topic, discipline, and type of material. "Men in Families," "Masculinity," and "Men's Awareness" figure among the longest chapters. August treats both scholarly and popular literature, and gears his evaluative annotations to the nonspecialist. There are author and title indexes but no subject index; cross-referencing between chapters somewhat fills the gap. While the bibliography documents a growing interest over the past decade and a half in fresh perspectives on men's lives, it also reveals a substantial backlash to the women's movement. August's annotations, though exceptionally well written, too often lash out defensively at traces of "feminist bias" (e.g., p.94) and at "militant feminists" (e.g., p.106). The bibliography remains valuable as an overview of the full spectrum of current writings on men. Researchers seeking additional leads can consult *The Male Sex Role: A Selected and Annotated Bibliography,* by Kathleen E. Grady, Robert Brannon, and Joseph Pleck (National Institute of Mental Health, 1979), which emphasizes empirical and theoretical works among its listings.

841.   Bailey, Susan F., 1944- . **Women and the British Empire: An Annotated Guide to Sources.** New York: Garland, 1983. 185p. index. $46.00. LC 82-49161. ISBN 0824091620.

India, Australia, New Zealand, the Americas, and Africa—all once lived under British rule. In this unique work, Bailey draws attention to primary sources and scholarly writings from the seventeenth century to the mid-twentieth century concerning women settlers, missionaries, wives of colonial administrators, and native women. Not unexpectedly, the chapter on native women is the shortest. Each chapter opens with an extensive review of the literature, making this a valuable guide to women's roles in the history of British imperialism.

842.*   Bakerman, Jane S., and Mary Jean DeMarr. **Adolescent Female Portraits in the American Novel, 1961-1981.** New York: Garland, 1983. 254p. index. LC 82-49139. ISBN 0824091361.

Focusing on society's changing views of women and teenagers as reflected in the fiction of a twenty-year period, this bibliography provides plot summaries for 579 novels. The citations are in alphabetical order by author, but the subject index allows the reader to locate works on particular themes: family, friendship, historical periods, racism, sexual activity, and other topics. In their introduction, Bakerman and DeMarr outline fourteen recurrent female images—among them aspiring artists, friends, heroes, mates, rebellious daughters, victims, and villains—and provide a checklist of the novels in which these images stand out.

843. Ballou, Patricia K. **Women: A Bibliography of Bibliographies.** Boston: G. K. Hall, 1980. 155p. index. $18.00. LC 80-21042. ISBN 0816182922.

Encompassing 557 citation lists, bibliographic essays, literature reviews, library catalogs, and guides to archives and manuscript repositories—whether issued separately, as journal articles, or within books—this bibliography of bibliographies is nonetheless selective. All of the items described were published (or scheduled to be published) between 1970 and 1979. Ballou can be commended for her descriptive annotations and her well-thought-out subject arrangement. A contemporaneous source—Jane Williamson's *New Feminist Scholarship: A Guide to Bibliographies* (Feminist Press, 1979)—is even more straightforward in its topical organization, but cites fewer bibliographies and provides annotations only for separately published works. There is less overlap between the two than might be expected. Both rightly belong in any basic reference collection for women's studies. Unfortunately, no recent sources update these volumes; for bibliographies of the 1980s, researchers must turn to standard tools such as the *Bibliographic Index.*

844. Benjamin N. Cardozo School of Law, Yeshiva University. **Women's Annotated Legal Bibliography.** New York: Clark Boardman, 1984. 331p. $45.00. LC 83-15219. ISBN 0876323492.

This very useful bibliography is the first volume of what is promised to be a continuing project. The bibliography furnishes a meticulously organized guide to professional articles and student notes and comments published in over 150 journals from 1978 to 1983. (Unfortunately, there is no comprehensive list of journals abstracted.) The citations are sorted into twelve subject areas: abortion; battered women; DES; employment discrimination; Equal Rights Amendment; pornography; prostitution; rape; the draft; health; international law; and taxation. All cases and statutes mentioned in a section are listed and described at the beginning of that section; a complete table of cases concludes the volume. While this bibliography will undoubtedly find its heaviest use among practicing attorneys and legal scholars, its careful organization, clearly written annotations, consistent explanation of abbreviations, and review of pertinent cases and statutes ensure its usefulness to the layperson as well. In contrast, nonspecialists are the intended audience for *Women's Legal Rights in the United States: A Selective Bibliography* (American Library Association, 1985). Joan Ariel, Ellen Broidy, and Susan Searing compiled this concise guide to nontechnical works on women and the law, highlighting economic issues, education, employment, family and relationships, health, lesbians, reproductive rights, sexual harassment, and violence against women. In addition, there are references to state-specific legal guides and national organizations.

845.* Bettison, Margaret, and Anne Summers, comps. **Her Story: Australian Women in Print 1788-1975.** Sydney, Australia: Hale and Iremonger, 1980. 181p. index. $24.95. ISBN 0908094515.

This bibliography, the best guide to materials on the sociology and history of Australian women, lists over three thousand items in its main classified section. Work, public life, and biography stand out as the fullest categories. Bettison and Summers cite (and occasionally annotate) books, chapters, articles from periodicals, parliamentary papers, theses, and manuscripts through 1975. They append an alphabetical list of book titles from 1976 to 1978.

846. Block, Adrienne Fried, and Carol Neuls-Bates, eds. **Women in American Music: A Bibliography of Music and Literature.** Westport, CT: Greenwood Press, 1979. 302p. index. $39.95. LC 79-7722. ISBN 0313214107.

Following the successful model of the *RILM Abstracts of Music Literature*, Block and Neuls-Bates have compiled an impressive aid to the study of American women and music. There are over five thousand entries, including articles, books, dissertations, and reviews, as well as many published musical works and recordings by American women composers. Vernacular music is covered from colonial times to 1920 only, but the treatment of art music extends to 1978. After short sections devoted to reference materials, collected works, and historical studies, entries are grouped in five chronological sections, with further subdivisions by genre (vernacular or art), medium (chamber music, vocal music, etc.), and women's roles (as composers, performers, and so on). Written materials are fully abstracted. The volume concludes with an author-subject index to literature and a composer-author index to music.

847. Bogenschneider, Duane R., ed. **The Gerritsen Collection of Women's History, 1543-1945: A Bibliographic Guide to the Microform Collection.** Sanford, NC: Microfilming Corporation of America; distr. University Microfilms International, 1983. 3 vols. in 2. index. ISBN 0667006834.

Although the microform set was produced and marketed in 1976, the printed catalog to the Gerritsen Collection did not appear until 1983. The computer-created guide vastly improves upon the interim short title lists hitherto available, for it offers a variety of approaches—by subject, author, title, language, and date—to the materials in microform. Gathered in the late nineteenth century by Aletta H. Jacobs (the first woman doctor in the Netherlands and founder of the world's first birth control clinic) and added to by later owners, the Gerritsen Collection comprises books, pamphlets, and periodicals, with a particular emphasis on women's rights and suffrage movements. Other subject strengths, according to the introduction, include "the nature and role of women, the historical and legal status of women, prostitution, the education of girls and women, biography and autobiography, and secondary materials on women writers, marriage and the family, employment of women, women and religion, and women's voluntary associations" (p.vi). Although few libraries can afford the expensive microform set, the guide stands alone as a useful bibliographical tool for the identification of nineteenth-century and early-twentieth-century works on women's status.

848. Borenstein, Audrey, 1930- , comp. **Older Women in 20th-Century America: A Selected Annotated Bibliography.** New York: Garland, 1982. 351p. index. $48.00. LC 82-6082. ISBN 0824093968.

In lengthy, objective annotations, Borenstein describes nearly nine hundred works about women over the age of forty. Included are books, articles, government publications, conference proceedings, and position papers. Social science literature is well represented in sections devoted to gerontology, housing, life-span development, middle age, psychology, social and economic issues, and sociological perspectives. However, the bibliography is exceptional for its equal coverage of the humanities. Borenstein offers a section on "Creativity and Productivity in Later Life," plus sections listing novels, short stories, literary history and criticism, published primary sources (both oral history and personal documents), and cross-cultural studies. Borenstein's analysis of this large and interdisciplinary body of scholarship and creative writing appears in her *Chimes of Change and Hours: Views of Older Women in Twentieth-Century America* (Fairleigh Dickinson University Press, 1983).

849. Bracken, Jeanne, and Sharon Wigutoff. **Books for Today's Young Readers: An Annotated Bibliography of Recommended Fiction for Ages 10-14.** Old Westbury, NY: Feminist Press, 1981. 52p. $4.95. LC 81-19532. ISBN 093531203X.

Surveying realistic fiction for readers aged ten to fourteen published between 1977 and 1980, Bracken and Wigutoff select seventy-three junior novels that offer engaging stories free of stereotyping of the sexes, racial and cultural minorites, the disabled, the aged, and nontraditional families. The annotations point out the strengths and weaknesses of each book, while the introductions to the volume and the chapters survey and analyze themes in children's literature. Similar in intent is Joan E. Newman's annotated guide, *Girls Are People Too! A Bibliography of Nontraditional Female Roles in Children's Books* (Scarecrow Press, 1982). Newman describes 540 books that "exhibit active, adventurous, persistent, self-confident, independent, creative, proud, courageous, and individualistic females" (p.v), covering both fiction and nonfiction, and paying special attention to books on blacks, Native Americans, the handicapped, and other minorities. Titles are graded for primary or intermediate readers. The second edition of Mary-Ellen Siegel's *Her Way: A Guide to Biographies of Women for Young People* (American Library Association, 1984) cites some seventeen hundred works. In the section devoted to individual biographies (the bulk of the volume), a short synopsis of the subject's life precedes annotated references to works about her. Siegel provides indexes to nationality, ethnic group, and vocation/avocation, as well as an author/title index.

850. Byerly, Greg, and Rick Rubin. **Pornography, the Conflict Over Sexually Explicit Materials in the United States: An Annotated Bibliography.** New York: Garland, 1980. 152p. $24.00. LC 80-14336. ISBN 0824095146.

Similar in scope and methodology to the co-compilers' more recent work on incest (see entry 888), this bibliography cites key court cases and government documents, as well as books and articles. The strict criteria for selection and the emphasis on mainstream sources—plus a cut-off date of 1979—mean that the current debate within the women's movement over the issue of pornography is not covered. At this time, unfortunately, there is no comprehensive guide to feminist writings on pornography.

851. Byrne, Pamela R., and Suzanne R. Ontiveros, eds. **Women in the Third World: A Historical Bibliography.** Santa Barbara: ABC-Clio, 1986. 152p. index. $28.00. LC 85-19968. ISBN 0874364590.

Covering six hundred articles published in journals and anthologies between 1970 and 1985, this bibliography is a good starting point for research on women in developing countries. Byrne and Ontiveros group the abstracts by region—General, Africa, Middle East, Asia, the Pacific Region, and Latin America and the West Indies—and furnish an exceptionally useful subject index. Most of the cited articles are in English, though a few are in other Western languages; all abstracts are in English. Many contemporary surveys and reports of recent field research are included, in addition to historical studies. Because it is limited to articles, this bibliography cannot aid in unearthing the vast literature on women's status in the Third World in the form of United Nations documents, government publications, and reports from nongovernmental international agencies.

852.* Cantor, Aviva, comp. **The Jewish Woman: 1900-1980.** Rev. ed. Fresh Meadows, NY: Biblio Press, 1981. 88p. LC 81-67447. ISBN 096020363X.

The body of scholarly and creative work by and about Jewish women is rapidly growing; this partially annotated bibliography draws attention to the many directions writing about Jewish women takes. Separate sections treat history, religious life and law, and the Holocaust and resistance, and additional chapters focus on Jewish women in the United States and Canada, in Israel, and in other countries. Nonfiction, fiction, poetry, biography, and autobiography are all included, whether published as books, periodical articles, or contributions to anthologies. The annotations have a strong feminist flavor, especially when evaluating works written from a traditionalist viewpoint on such matters as women rabbis and alternative religious rituals. Biblio Press has issued two other related books: *The Jewish Women's Studies Guide* (1982), an inspiring collection of syllabi and reading lists by Ellen Sue Levi Elwell and Edward R. Levenson; and *Jewish Women and Jewish Law Bibliography* (1980), compiled by Ora Hamelsdorf and Sandra Adelsberg.

853. Cardinale, Susan. **Anthologies by and About Women: An Analytical Index.** Westport, CT: Greenwood Press, 1982. 822p. $49.95. LC 81-13423. ISBN 0313221804.

Since many pathbreaking articles by and about women have now been anthologized, and with the publication of women-related readers emerging as a minor industry, librarians and researchers need the increased access that Cardinale's exemplary bibliographic work provides. The interdisciplinary index covers 375 anthologies, most of them published in the 1960s and 1970s. Special issues of journals are excluded. A title list provides the full table of contents for each volume. There are two modes of subject access: a subject/genre index that groups anthologies by broad topics; and a keyword index based on the titles of the essays, short stories, plays, and documents contained in the indexed anthologies. Contributor and editor indexes further assist the user. Cardinale's introduction puts the anthologies into historiographic and topical perspective in a most interesting, informative way.

854. Conway, Jill K., 1934- . **The Female Experience in Eighteenth- and Nineteenth-Century America: A Guide to the History of American Women.** New York: Garland, 1982; repr. Princeton, NJ: Princeton University Press, 1985. 290p. bibliog. index. pbk. $14.50. LC 85-42665. ISBN 0691005990.

The first work in a projected two-volume set, this unusual guide treats the theories and assumptions that have shaped secondary writing on the history of women in the United States. Conway pairs short critical reviews of the literature with unannotated bibliographies that emphasize primary sources. The basic outline of the volume employs six categories: I. American Culture and Society, 1750-1840; II. Industrialization, Women's Work, and the Transformation of the Household, 1810-1910; III. Cultural Roles of Middle-class Women in Industrializing America: Schools, Literacy, and Women's Intellectual Work; IV. Women's Religious Life and the Reform Tradition, 1790-1860; V. Women and Politics, 1776-1920; VI. Biology and Domestic Life: Evolutionary Thought and Its Impact, 1830-1900. These categories are further subdivided, creating over fifty sections (each with an essay and reading list) on such topics as child rearing, prostitution, urbanization, women writers, antislavery, and health reform. The commentaries summarize many of the key concerns in the field of American women's history. Yet there are gaps; little appears on women of color, for example. Because the references themselves carry no annotations, researchers should plan to spend some unhurried time digesting the essays.

855.* Cotera, Martha P., comp. **Latina Sourcebook: Bibliography of Mexican American, Cuban, Puerto Rico and Other Hispanic Women Materials in the U.S.** Austin, TX: Information Systems Development, 1982. 61p. pbk.

The growth of the literature on Latinas in the United States is evidenced in this selective annotated listing of books, pamphlets, research reports, journal articles, government publications, and films. The bibliography is in four sections, treating general references, Cuban Americans, Mexican Americans, and Puerto Ricans. Background readings and materials suitable for grades K-12 are included, in addition to recent writings on the history, status, and opportunities of Latinas. A lengthy directory of publishers and periodicals concludes the volume. There are, unfortunately, no indexes. Cotera is also the author of *Mujer: Conquistadoras, Generales and Plain Old Hispanic Sisters in the United States* (Information Systems Development, 1980) and *Multicultural Women's Sourcebook: Materials Guide for Use in Women's Studies and Bilingual/Multicultural Programs* (Women's Educational Equity Act Publishing Center, 1982).

856. Coven, Brenda, 1940- . **American Women Dramatists of the Twentieth Century: A Bibliography.** Metuchen, NJ: Scarecrow Press, 1982. 237p. index. $16.00. LC 82-5942. ISBN 0810815621.

All 133 playwrights included in this bibliography have had at least one play successfully produced on the New York stage. Among the better-known names are Edna Ferber, Lorraine Hansberry, Lillian Hellman, Anita Loos, Ntozake Shange, Gertrude Stein, Elizabeth Swados, Megan Terry, and Mae West. Each unannotated entry cites biographical sources, plays with dates of production, and reviews. A short general bibliography on women's theater and women dramatists introduces the volume. Decidedly selective, this is nonetheless the single best guide available to materials by and about U.S. women playwrights.

857. Crippen, Cynthia, ed. **The New York Times Cumulative Subject and Personal Name Index: Women, 1965-1975.** Glen Rock, NJ: Microfilming Corporation of America, 1978. 1150p. index. $75.00. LC 79-100443. ISBN 0667006052.

The decade covered by this large volume was a critical one in the reemergence of feminism as a social and political force. Gathered here are citations from *The New York Times Index,* organized by subject. In addition to coverage of women's liberation actions, nearly every story about women has been included—reports of medical discoveries affecting women's health, predictions of fashion trends, profiles of entertainers and athletes, campaign and election news, and reports of crimes, to name just a few examples. The volume concludes with a bibliography on women's issues, and four indexes: geographic, name, organization, and subject.

858. Daims, Diva, and Janet Grimes. **Toward a Feminist Tradition: An Annotated Bibliography of Novels in English by Women, 1891-1920.** New York: Garland, 1982. 885p. index. $91.00. LC 82-15496. ISBN 0824095235.

Daims and Grimes have selected over 3,400 works from their comprehensive volume *Novels in English by Women, 1891-1920: A Preliminary Checklist* (Garland, 1981). The criterion for inclusion is not literary merit but rather unconventional treatment of women characters "which focuses attention either on the efforts of women to control their lives or on social attitudes and conditions functioning as counterforces to that achievement" (p.vii). These turn-of-the-century novels deal with such themes as marriage, career, rebellion, suffrage, and relationships between women—themes still of crucial interest to present-day readers. The lack of a subject index, however, makes it exceedingly difficult to sift out works with thematic similarities. The bibliography is arranged alphabetically by author, with a title index. Daims and Grimes painstakingly searched out reviews from the period, from which they distilled their annotations; some are merely plot summaries, while others provide succinct critical commentary. *Women Novelists, 1891-1920: An Index to Biographical and Autobiographical Sources* (Garland, 1984), by Doris Robinson, is a companion work that offers citations to biographical background on some 1,565 authors drawn from Grimes and Daims's database. Robinson's tome is notable for its careful cross-referencing of variant names, and for its inclusion of obituaries, entries in collective biographies, and book-length biographies and autobiographies.

859. Davis, Nanette J., and Jone M. Keith. **Women and Deviance: Issues in Social Conflict and Change: An Annotated Bibliography.** New York: Garland, 1984. 236p. index. $35.00. LC 82-49164. ISBN 0824091655.

"Deviance" is a tricky concept for feminists, who have frequently called into question the social norms against which women's behavior is measured. Davis and Keith take a bold, multidisciplinary approach to the topic, with an eye to documenting how deviance takes different forms and carries different consequences for women and men. Annotations are long, evaluative, and exceptionally well written. Most of the topically organized references treat social deviance by women — criminal behavior, alcohol and drug abuse, lesbianism, teenage pregnancy, and mental illness, among other concerns. Other sections focus on deviant behaviors that affect women, such as battering and pornography. Subject and name indexes provide the researcher with additional access points.

860. DeCaro, Francis A. **Women and Folklore: A Bibliographic Survey.** Westport, CT: Greenwood Press, 1983. 170p. index. $29.95. LC 83-12837. ISBN 0313238219.

The materials DeCaro treats in this volume reinforce two truths: first, that "folklore is a fundamental source of stereotypes, of images of women, positive and negative"; and second, that "women, who have often been denied full access to many of the expressive media, have always created their own folklore" (p.xii). DeCaro's interdisciplinary survey of the field is useful to students of anthropology, literature, psychology, history, and popular culture, as well as to general readers. A forty-five page "Essay Guide" is keyed to an unannotated, alphabetical bibliography of 1,664 items. Although this is not a happy arrangement for quick reference, the comparative perspective in DeCaro's thematically organized text is invaluable. The essay covers such topics as female folk heroes, women's speech, courtship and marriage customs, healers, sexual lore, and material culture. The volume concludes with a subject index.

861. Diner, Hasia R. **Women and Urban Society: A Guide to Information Sources.** Detroit: Gale Research, 1979. 138p. bibliog. index. $60.00. LC 78-13109. ISBN 0810314258.

Observers of the processes and effects of urbanization and urban life look most often to Third-World countries, as this international and interdisciplinary bibliography documents. Annotated references to books, articles, reports, and conference papers fall into six categories: Women and Urbanization; Women in Urban Families; Urban Fertility; Employment of Urban Women; Women's Roles in Urban Society: Social and Psychological Implications; and a small section, Views of Urban Women. Diner completes the guide with lists of abstracts, indexes, and periodicals for more up-to-date research, and with author, title, and subject indexes.

862. Duke, Maurice, et al., eds. **American Women Writers: Bibliographical Essays.** Westport, CT: Greenwood Press, 1983. 434p. index. $39.95. LC 82-6156. ISBN 0313221162.

The bibliographical essays assembled here cover twenty-four major women writers: Anne Bradstreet, Mary Rowlandson, Sarah Kemble Knight, Sarah Orne Jewett, Mary E. Wilkins Freeman, Mary N. Murfree, Kate Chopin, Edith Wharton, Gertrude Stein, Djuna Barnes, Anaïs Nin, Ellen Glasgow, Katherine Anne Porter, Eudora Welty, Flannery O'Connor, Carson McCullers, Zora Neale Hurston, Constance Rourke, Pearl Buck, Marjorie Kinnan Rawlings, Margaret Mitchell, Marianne Moore, Anne Sexton, and Sylvia Plath. To date, only a handful of them have been the subject of full critical bibliographies. The contributing scholars follow a standard format, discussing bibliographies, editions of the authors' works, sources for unpublished manuscripts and letters, biographies, and (in greatest depth) critical studies. Current through 1981, the essays are excellent introductions for students of American literature and women's writing. Maurice Duke, Jackson R. Bryer, and M. Thomas Inge shared in the editing.

863. Fairbanks, Carol, and Sara Brooks Sundberg. **Farm Women on the Prairie Frontier: A Sourcebook for Canada and the United States.** Metuchen, NJ: Scarecrow Press, 1983. 237p. $17.50. LC 83-4498. ISBN 0810816253.

Pioneer women are the subject of much recent scholarship, and many of their rediscovered writings have been published anew. The second half of *Farm Women on the Prairie Frontier* is a selective but much-needed guide to this body of literature. The annotated, interdisciplinary bibliography embraces social history, works of fiction, literary criticism, first-person accounts, and natural history. The sourcebook also offers historical and literary analyses of the experiences of women on the frontier. Sundberg's opening essay surveys the environmental conditions that faced settlers—the landscape, the climate, and the agricultural uses of the prairies. Fairbanks's article, "A Usable Past," draws on letters, diaries, and memoirs of prairie women, arguing that such sources permit us to rewrite American history, to challenge male-created images of long-suffering pioneer wives, and to locate inspiring role models. The two remaining essays treat the concept of women as helpmates in the settling of the Canadian grasslands, and the images of pioneer women in fiction.

864. Farr, Sidney Saylor. **Appalachian Women: An Annotated Bibliography.** Lexington: University Press of Kentucky, 1981. 187p. $20.00. LC 80-5174. ISBN 0813114314.

Farr, who herself hails from the mountains of eastern Kentucky, lists and annotates over thirteen hundred books, short stories, magazine articles, oral histories, and other items, all touching on the lives of women in the southern Appalachian mountains. She cites regional and national publications from 1825 to 1979, including both accurate portrayals of mountain women and those she judges prejudicial. Her annotations are well written but rarely evaluative. Autobiography and biography, fiction and drama, and oral history chapters account for over eight hundred of the entries. Additional chapters cover: coal mining; education; health conditions and health care; industry; life styles; migrants; music; poetry; religion and folklore; and a catch-all category, "studies and surveys." Farr provides a single index to authors, titles, and subjects. There are too few bibliographies devoted to regions or states of the United States; Farr's is a model of diligent research and thoughtful organization.

865. **Feminist Periodicals: A Current Listing of Contents.** 1981- . University of Wisconsin Women's Studies Librarian, 112A Memorial Library, 728 State St., Madison, WI 53706. Quarterly. Free to individuals and organizations affiliated with the University of Wisconsin; others inquire. ISSN 0742-7433.

Periodicals for and about women have multiplied mightily in the last half-decade, yet standard indexing tools still cover only a handful. *Feminist Periodicals*, a current awareness service, partially compensates for these omissions by regularly reproducing the tables of contents from over eighty English-language periodicals. Both scholarly and popular titles are included, among them such core periodicals as *Signs, Feminist Studies,* and *Ms.,* as well as special-interest publications like *Broomstick: A Periodical By, For, and About Women Over Forty, Women and Therapy,* and *Sage: A Scholarly Journal on Black Women.* Introductory matter provides current addresses, prices, and other details, plus brief statements of each periodical's purpose and scope. Researchers can scan *Feminist Periodicals* to keep abreast of trends in women's studies and the wider women's movement, or use it to supplement mainstream indexes and abstracts for systematic bibliographical retrieval. Subscribers to *Feminist Periodicals* also receive *Feminist Collections: A Quarterly of Women's Studies Resources,* which features reviews and articles about new print and nonprint materials, library and archival collections, and the women-in-print movement; *New Books on Women and Feminism,* a semiannual, indexed comprehensive bibliography; and other occasional publications produced by the women's studies librarian.

866. Frey, Linda, et al., comps. **Women in Western European History: A Select Chronological, Geographical, and Topical Bibliography.** Westport, CT: Greenwood Press. 2v. index. LC 81-20300. Vol. 1: 1982; $49.95; ISBN 0313228582. Vol. 2: 1984; $55.00; ISBN 0313228590.

With over seventeen thousand entries, this ambitious bibliography is the most extensive guide yet to writings on the political, economic, religious, social, and cultural history of women in Western Europe. Joint compilers Linda Frey, Marsha Frey, and Joanne Schneider emphasize readily available books and articles; primary sources and literary works are excluded. All cited materials are in English or other major Western languages. Naturally, such a massive work has flaws. Specialists in particular fields may find the selections inadequate. (The sections on contemporary literary art and criticism, for example, are surprisingly brief.) The keys to using the volumes are their detailed tables of contents, which run to over thirty pages each. The outline first follows traditional historical periods and then geographic/political divisions. Within these sections the compilers employ complex topical hierarchies, thus permitting the careful researcher to locate specific subjects (including individuals) by consulting the tables of contents. Both volumes have name and author indexes and skimpy subject indexes. Despite the complicated arrangement and lack of annotations, this set performs the invaluable service of assembling references on all of Western European women's history.

867. Gelfand, Elissa D., 1949- , and Virginia Thorndike Hules. **French Feminist Criticism: Women, Language and Literature: An Annotated Bibliography.** New York: Garland, 1985. 318p. index. $36.00. LC 82-48275. ISBN 082409252X.

Gelfand and Hules's subject is "the textuality/sexuality of women," as treated in works by and about French feminist theorists and their Francophone colleagues in Quebec and Belgium. Books, essays, and articles in French and English, published between 1970 and 1982, make up the citations. There are extensive listings for such well-known writers as

Hélène Cixous, Luce Irigarary, Julia Kristeva, and Monique Wittig, as well as their critics. Hules's introduction, "A Topography of Difference," does a remarkable job of orienting the American nonspecialist to the historical development of French feminist theory, outlining the positions of its major figures and comparing it to American approaches. The bibliography itself is in two parts: a section labeled "The General Problematics of a Feminist Criticism" and the major portion of the book, which lists works by and about individual French thinkers. All entries receive lengthy annotations, which frequently end with evaluative comments. Gelfand and Hules list special issues of journals in an appendix and provide indexes to titles and subjects. Oddly, there is no index to the authors of secondary literature, making it tedious to identify critical writings by key U.S. feminist theorists who have responded to French ideas.

868. Gilbert, Victor Francis, and Darshan Singh Tatla, comps. **Women's Studies: A Bibliography of Dissertations 1870-1982.** New York: Basil Blackwell, 1985. 496p. index. $75.00. LC 85-6192. ISBN 0631137149.

Gilbert and Tatla identify over twelve thousand dissertations on a full range of topics: arts, criminology, demography, education, employment, family dynamics, feminism, health, history, language, law, literature, media, philosophy, physiology, politics, psychology, religion, reproduction, sexuality, sociology, sport, and women in the Third World. Representing dissertations emanating from British, Irish, Scotch, Welsh, U.S., and Canadian universities—and thus written mainly in English—the entries list author, title, university, and year of submission. Although Gilbert and Tatla have tried to include all dissertations and theses related to women, some important materials have inevitably eluded the bibliographic net. The book is exceptionally attractive and well organized, with each of the topic chapters analyzed closely. One major drawback, however, is the lack of an author index.

869. Green, Rayna. **Native American Women: A Contextual Bibliography.** Bloomington: Indiana University Press, 1983. 120p. index. $19.50. LC 82-48571. ISBN 0253339766.

Green has been at the forefront of the emerging field of native women's studies, beginning with her incisive and comprehensive review essay in *Signs* in 1980. Her opening chapter here (a revised version of that essay) reviews the literature chronologically, assessing trends from the late seventeenth century to the present with a critical and vigilantly political eye—from European tales of "princesses" and "saints" to ethnographic accounts of rites and customs; from autobiographies and narratives to endless studies of native "pathology." Little of this literature, Green writes, "treats of real Native women or real Native categories of significance.... Little is written about the women who most mattered to Native people" (pp.14-15). The annotated bibliography includes 672 citations to books, articles, films, dissertations, reports, tapes, documents, and records, the bulk of them from the last twenty years. Green lists both scholarly and popular sources, writings from native and non-native perspectives; her sharply evaluative annotations will help the researcher to find her way through the diverse literature. Date and subject indexes follow. While the coverage here is heavily weighted toward history and anthropology—essentially omitting creative literature—Green achieves a balance with her most recent book, *That's What She Said: Contemporary Poetry and Fiction by Native American Women* (see entry 650).

870. Grier, Barbara. **The Lesbian in Literature.** 3rd ed. Tallahassee, FL: Naiad Press, 1981. 168p. pbk. $7.95. LC 81-82859. ISBN 0930044231.

In this third edition of what has become the standard guide to literary treatments of lesbianism, Grier continues her coding scheme: letters to symbolize the degree of emphasis on lesbian characters and action; and asterisks to convey her judgment of the quality of the lesbian material. Included are fiction, poetry, drama, biography, and selected nonfiction.

871. Guy, Patricia A. **Women's Poetry Index.** Phoenix: Oryx Press, 1985. 174p. index. $65.00. LC 84-42816. ISBN 0897741730.

The standard *Granger's Index to Poetry* has meager coverage of women-focused anthologies, so this index (which omits books indexed in *Granger's*) is a necessary complement. Guy covers the years 1945 through 1983 and pointedly includes anthologies with ethnic perspectives, as well as collections of translations. Citations appear under the poet's name, with title and first-line indexes. Lacking a subject index, *Women's Poetry Index* is nevertheless immensely useful for locating known poems.

872. Hady, Maureen E., et al., comps. **Women's Periodicals and Newspapers From the 18th Century to 1981: A Union List of the Holdings of Madison, Wisconsin, Libraries.** Edited by James P. Danky. Boston: G. K. Hall, 1982. 376p. index. $40.00. LC 82-11903. ISBN 0816181071.

Listing 1,461 titles, this monumental work is the most complete bibliography of U.S. women's periodicals and newspapers yet compiled. It encompasses literary, political, and historical journals, as well as general newspapers and feature magazines aimed at women, both past and contemporary. The entries are models of full bibliographic data; in addition to the usual information, they include physical descriptions, indexing sources, and names of previous editors. Holdings for seventy-seven Madison-area libraries are described in detail, and other repositories across the country are also noted. (Librarians will appreciate the provision of both NUC and OCLC holding symbols and the listing of all periodicals contained in the *Herstory* microfilm collection.) Chronological charts indicating each periodical's lifespan are a boon to researchers of specific periods, events, and historical trends. The subject index serves anyone searching for coverage of particular social issues, subgroups of women, or literary genres. Other indexes cover places of publication, foreign languages, editors, publishers (which in most cases are women's organizations), and key words from the titles and subtitles. Maureen E. Hady, Barry Christopher Noonan, and Neil E. Strache were the team that labored on this landmark volume, under James P. Danky's editorship.

873. Harrison, Cynthia Ellen, ed. **Women in American History: A Bibliography.** Santa Barbara, CA: ABC-Clio Books, 1979. 2v. index. LC 78-26194. Vol. 1: 1979; $58.00; ISBN 0874362601. Vol. 2: 1985; $64.00; ISBN 0874364507.

By culling abstracts from the standard reference tool *America: History and Life,* this important series surveys over seven thousand articles on American and Canadian women's history from 1964 to 1977 (volume 1) and 1978 to 1984 (volume 2). Volume One roughly follows the pattern of the parent series. After short sections on methods, sources, and general works, the bulk of the abstracts are arranged by historical period. Within chronological divisions, article summaries are grouped by subject, covering economic, social, political, religious, and cultural topics and subtopics. Separate sections for regional U.S. history and Canadian history follow. In Volume Two, a different scheme is introduced, without editorial comment, but in keeping with feminist criticism of traditional approaches to periodization. About one-quarter of the entries appear in general or chronological categories. The remainder are assigned to subject chapters and subchapters, in the following major groupings: Domestic, Social, and Personal Roles; Women and Religion; Women and Education; Women and Ethnicity; Women in American Culture; Women in the Work Force; Women and Politics; Women and Violence; and Women and Biology. Some of the categorization seems forced — prostitution under the violence heading, for example. Nonetheless, the subject approach makes for pleasurable browsing. Both volumes utilize the "Subject Profile Index" system developed by ABC-Clio. Each document is assigned a list of generic and specific subject terms, personal names, geographic descriptors, and an indication of time period. A typical entry in the index is: "Legislation. Jarvis, Anna Reeves. Mother's Day. West Virginia. 1905-14," followed by the page reference. The string of descriptors acts as a document profile, and is repeated in the index under each term. The benefits of such carefully analyzed indexing are obvious when one skims the large clusters of references under terms like "feminism" or "the South."

874. Heys, Sandra, comp. **Contemporary Stage Roles for Women: A Descriptive Catalogue.** Westport, CT: Greenwood Press, 1985. 195p. index. $35.00. LC 84-19218. ISBN 0313244731.

Heys created this catalog to "spotlight published, accessible plays with strong female roles" (p.xi). The main title listing of approximately 250 plays includes playwrights, dates, publishers (or agents), one-sentence plot summaries, and brief descriptions of the female characters. Because of their brevity, the descriptions sometimes reduce the characters to a list of stereotypical traits, using terms for personalities (e.g., common, girlish, softer) and appearances (e.g., pretty, plain, dowdy) that feminists may find troublesome. In addition to the main listing, female characters are indexed by age range, by character type (heroic, kind and nurturing, comic, villainous, etc.), by unusual physical characteristics, and by race. An appendix classifies plays by gender distribution (all-female vs. mixed casts). A directory of agents and publishers, indexes to playwrights and characters, and a bibliography round out the volume. Although this catalog serves as a starting point to identify stage roles for women, Hays inexplicably omits many excellent plays and recent works by well-known playwrights.

875. **History of Women: Guide to the Microfilm Collection.** Woodbridge, CT: Research Publications, 1983. 408p. $100.00. LC 78-68793. ISBN 0892350407.

The *History of Women* collection reproduces, on nearly a thousand reels of microfilm, the treasures of several libraries and archives. Materials from the Sophia Smith Collection at Smith College and the Schlesinger Library at Radcliffe form the core of the collection. The scope is international; the cut-off date is 1920. This printed guide to the set consists of four sections: a main-entry index, listing books, pamphlets, and manuscripts alphabetically by author; a periodical-title index; a subject/added-entry index; and a name index to photographs. The subject/added-entry index is woefully incomplete and is not keyed to the main-entry index, where full bibliographic entries appear. To use the subject/added-entry index, one must work directly with the microform reels; this greatly diminishes the volume's value as a stand-alone reference tool.

876.* Hurst, Marsha, and Ruth E. Zambrana. **Determinants and Consequences of Maternal Employment: An Annotated Bibliography, 1968-1980.** Washington, DC: Business and Professional Women's Foundation, 1981. 85p. pbk.

Books, journal articles, chapters from books, unpublished papers, theses, and technical and government reports are reviewed in this bibliography of recent literature on mothers in paid employment. With the exception of the reports, all citations are annotated (213 in all). Annotations are unusually well written; descriptive, critical, and often comparative, they will greatly aid the beginning researcher in sifting through these sources, as will the authors' introductory review of the literature. Hurst and Zambrana organize the citations by genre: popular books on working mothers; professional and clinical studies (further divided by subject area); popular childrearing guides; bibliographies; children's books; and technical and government reports. While these subject categories divide up the literature in a sensible way, users will undoubtedly wish the authors had taken the extra step to provide author, title, and subject indexing.

877.   Jarrard, Mary E. W., and Phyllis R. Randall. **Women Speaking: An Annotated Bibliography of Verbal and Nonverbal Communication, 1970-1980.** New York: Garland, 1982. 478p. index. $73.00. LC 82-15737. ISBN 0824092813.

Focusing on the settings, characteristics, and means of interpersonal communication, this bibliography surveys a decade of scholarship on women. The compilers describe over thirteen hundred studies of both spoken and nonverbal communication, primarily reported in journals and from a wide range of disciplines. Works on the mass media, the development of speaking skills, and literary expression—all large and diverse fields in themselves—are not cited. The subject index and the topical organization of entries allow for the exploration of particular topics; there is no author index. Linguists will also be interested in an extensive bibliography included in *Language, Gender, and Society,* edited by Barrie Thorne, Cheris Kramarae, and Nancy Henley (see entry 387).

878.   Kanner, Barbara, 1925- , ed. **The Women of England From Anglo-Saxon Times to the Present: Interpretive Bibliographical Essays.** Hamden, CT: Archon Books, 1979. 429p. index. $30.00. LC 78-32166. ISBN 0208016392.

Kanner gathers together twelve strong bibliographical essays, interdisciplinary in nature, each followed by a substantial bibliography on a specific period of English history. The sources cited are a happy blend of the primary and secondary, including letters, official records, private papers, standard historical studies, and new feminist scholarhip. Arranged chronologically, the essays include both general overviews of women's position at various points over the centuries since 600 A.D. and specific examinations of law, politics, demography, and literature.

879.   King, Betty, 1948- . **Women of the Future: The Female Main Character in Science Fiction.** Metuchen, NJ: Scarecrow Press, 1984. 273p. bibliog. index. $18.50. LC 83-20130. ISBN 0810816644.

Science fiction and fantasy have proved exceptionally fertile genres for feminist writers, as this guide demonstrates. King devotes her first chapter to the years between 1818 and 1929; subsequent chapters examine every decade through the 1980s. Selected stories and novels receive in-depth treatment, with descriptions of the characters and plot summaries, while others are merely cited. Indexes identify stories by the physical and personality traits of the characters, by such devices as location and time setting, by major theme, and by author and title. Perhaps the most complete bibliography of women-written science fiction is *Urania's Daughters: A Complete Checklist of Women Science-Fiction Writers, 1692-1982* (Starmont House, 1983). In this unannotated list, Roger C. Schlobin covers over 375 authors of over 830 works, all in English. Indicative of the growing critical interest in speculative fiction by and about women are a number of recent author-focused bibliographies. Rosemarie Arbur's *Leigh Brackett, Marion Zimmer Bradley, Anne McCaffrey: A Primary and Secondary Bibliography* (G. K. Hall, 1982) is one example.

880.   Leavitt, Judith A., comp. **Women in Management: An Annotated Bibliography and Sourcelist.** Phoenix: Oryx Press, 1982. 197p. bibliog. index. $29.95. LC 82-2190. ISBN 0897740262.

Covering scholarly, professional, and popular publications, this bibliography is an essential guide to the fast-growing body of literature for and about women managers. Leavitt cites and succinctly describes over eight hundred books, papers, newspaper and journal articles, and dissertations, all published between 1970 and 1981. The citations are grouped in twenty subject categories, including: mentors and networking; management training; sex-role stereotypes; education; career and family; obstacles; and the psychology of women in management. There is an index of authors.

881.   McCaghy, M. Dawn. **Sexual Harassment: A Guide to Resources.** Boston: G. K. Hall, 1985. 181p. index. $25.00. LC 84-25148. ISBN 0816186693.

Since the term "sexual harassment" was coined in 1975, the literature on the subject has mounted. McCaghy presents nearly three hundred references—books, chapters of books, organizational and advocacy publications, government reports, dissertations, periodical articles, and audiovisual materials. General newspaper accounts are omitted. Covering sexual harassment "in employment, in education, on the street, and on the telephone" (p.ix), the bibliography's scope is interdisciplinary, and the long annotations descriptive but uncritical. Chapters are devoted to general works (including writings from a feminist perspective, general overviews, surveys and research reports, studies of specific occupations and settings, and bibliographies); the academic setting; coping strategies (both legal and personal); the legal perspective; and management response. Each chapter opens with a cogent and concise analysis of the major streams of thought and significant findings in the citations that follow. The volume concludes with an author/title and a subject index.

882.   McFeely, Mary Drake. **Women's Work in Britain and America From the Nineties to World War I: An Annotated Bibliography.** Boston: G. K. Hall, 1982. 140p. index. $26.00. LC 82-9281. ISBN 0816185042.

It is a major strength of McFeely's bibliography that it aims to encompass both paid and unpaid work by women—from farm labor to union organizing, medicine to retail sales, domestic service to settlement work. McFeely includes books (fiction and nonfiction), pamphlets, and articles—549 in all—dating from the period under examination through 1980, providing annotations that are both descriptive and evaluative. She omits unpublished works, but does cite guides to manuscript collections and archives. Titles are listed alphabetically by author in two sections, Great Britain and America. Separate author, title, and subject indexes close the volume.

883.   Meghdessian, Samira Rafidi, comp. **The Status of the Arab Woman: A Select Bibliography.** Westport, CT: Greenwood Press, 1980. 176p. index. $32.50. LC 80-1028. ISBN 0313225486.

Over 1,600 publications are listed in this unannotated bibliography, which is based on the collection at the Institute for Women's Studies in the Arab World at Beirut University College in Lebanon. Most of the cited materials were published between 1950 and 1978, primarily in English and French. Entries are arranged under broad topics (e.g., "Women in

Islam and the Law") and under individual countries. In Michelle Raccagni's similar work, *The Modern Arab Woman: A Bibliography* (Scarecrow Press, 1978), which also includes Arabic titles, entries total nearly three thousand. About one-fourth have brief annotations.

884. Nelson, Barbara J., 1949- . **American Women and Politics: A Selected Bibliography and Resource Guide.** New York: Garland, 1984. 255p. index. $42.00. LC 82-49142. ISBN 0824091396.

In light of feminist involvement in political arenas in the United States, the paucity of current bibliographic guides is surprising. In this regrettably unannotated bibliography, Nelson takes a broad view of what is "political." She cites books, articles, government publications, and research reports on women's history, the nature-versus-nurture debate, feminist theory, and women's employment, in addition to writings on political socialization, campaigns and elections, social policy, and leadership. Over sixteen hundred entries are grouped in thirteen topical chapters. The progression of topics reflects a model syllabus for a course on women and politics. Most references date between 1970 and 1982. Author and subject indexes complete the volume.

885. Potter. Clare, comp. **The Lesbian Periodicals Index.** Tallahassee, FL: Naiad Press, 1986. 413p. pbk. $29.95. LC 85-21798. ISBN 0930044746.

A testament to the breadth and depth of lesbian culture, this index provides unprecedented author and subject access to some twenty-four thousand articles, letters, reviews, stories, poems, and graphics. Forty-two lesbian periodicals are covered, from the late 1940s to the early 1980s. Many of the titles were short-lived, but others—including *Feminary, The Lesbian Tide, Lavender Woman,* and *So's Your Old Lady*—had long and successful publishing histories. The index is ideal for topical searching because Potter incorporates terms that signal some of the main themes of lesbian life and politics: "Butch and femme"; "Coffeehouses, women's"; "Coming out"; "Fat oppression"; "Lesbian straight splits"; "Male presence at women's events"; "Politically correct and incorrect positions"; "Sexuality, lesbian"; and many, many more. The index also points to writings by and about individuals, organizations, and events, and highlights (in separate sections) creative writing, book reviews, and visual art.

886. Reardon, Joan, and Kristine A. Thorsen. **Poetry by American Women, 1900-1975: A Bibliography.** Metuchen, NJ: Scarecrow Press, 1979. 674p. index. $32.50. LC 78-11944. ISBN 0810811731.

By striving for comprehensiveness and making no judgments of literary value, the compilers of this bibliography have provided unprecedented access to the works of women poets in the twentieth-century United States. More than 5,500 poets are listed alphabetically, with their works sublisted chronologically, for a total of some 9,500 citations. All references are to separately published volumes of poetry, many of them from small presses or feminist publishers. Individual poems are not indexed.

887. Resnick, Margery, and Isabelle de Courtivron. **Women Writers in Translation: An Annotated Bibliography, 1945-1982.** New York: Garland, 1984. 272p. $50.00. LC 80-9039. ISBN 0824093321.

Working with a network of contributors and a shoestring budget, Resnick and de Courtivron created a milestone work in the field of women's literature. Well organized and thorough, the bibliography aids teachers, scholars, and librarians in identifying and evaluating in-print English translations of literature by women. Over a third of the volume is devoted to recent works by French, French-Canadian, and other Francophone authors.

Other chapters treat materials originally in Portuguese, German, Italian, Japanese, Russian, and Spanish. Chapter introductions highlight important works that remain untranslated. Except for the chapter on German literature, which contains some works published in journals and anthologies, only books are listed. The brief annotations fulfill the editors' promise to "acquaint readers with the theme, genre, literary significance, and quality of translation of each work" (p.viii), and introductory comments place each author in historical and literary context.

888.* Rubin, Rick, and Greg Byerly. **Incest, the Last Taboo: An Annotated Bibliography.** New York: Garland, 1983. 169p. LC 82-49181. ISBN 082409185X.

As an introductory, highly selective guide to recent writings on incest, Rubin and Byerly's annotated bibliography serves well. Two chapters cover monographs, dissertations, and audiovisual materials. Six more chapters cite journal and magazine articles by type: psychological; sociological and legal; anthropological; medical and scientific; popular; and literary. The authors emphasize readily available English-language sources; they exclude fictional works, general treatments of child abuse or child pornography, and general works on sexual relations. These restrictions, coupled with the reliance on standard indexing and abstracting tools, cause the authors to overlook recent feminist analyses, including many moving first-person accounts from victims. *Incest: An Annotated Bibliography* by Mary de Young (McFarland, 1985), complements Rubin and Byerly's efforts. De Young aims her volume at clinicians and researchers, omitting popular literature and pamphlets issued by treatment centers and prevention agencies. There is less overlap with *Incest, The Last Taboo* than one would anticipate. De Young's subject arrangement is easy to use, and her introductions to chapters and subchapters highlight recurring themes and prevailing theories.

889. Sahli, Nancy Ann. **Women and Sexuality in America: A Bibliography.** Boston: G. K. Hall, 1984. 404p. index. $49.95. LC 84-10751. ISBN 0816180997.

Sahli selects published writings from the nineteenth and twentieth centuries to document changing concepts of female sexuality in the United States. She emphasizes the professional literature of such fields as medicine, psychiatry, history, sociology, and women's studies. She excludes literary pieces, biographies, heavily scientific or technical studies, and popular publications. Separate chapters cover historical interpretations; social and political analysis and theory; legal and ethical questions; contributions of psycho-analysis; medical and scientific writings; prescriptive literature; and studies of sexual behavior and attitudes. Sahli also devotes several chapters to more specific populations and concerns: children and adolescents; masturbation; nymphomania; lesbians; older women; disabled women; women prisoners and girl delinquents; transsexuals; and sexual dysfunction. Each chapter opens with a short note on the literature, followed by annotated entries for books and pamphlets, and an unannotated checklist of journal articles. The lengthy annotations frequently suggest a work's usefulness to particular lines of inquiry. Sexuality is a key theme in women's studies scholarship, and Sahli's bibliography provides a much-needed historical, cross-disciplinary synthesis.

890. Sakala, Carol. **Women of South Asia: A Guide to Resources.** Millwood, NY: Kraus International Publications, 1980. 517p. index. $30.00. LC 79-28191. ISBN 0527785741.

This exhaustive guide covers both contemporary and historical materials on the women of India, Pakistan, Bangladesh, Sri Lanka, and Nepal. The compiler admits a dual purpose: to spur feminist scholars to incorporate "the richness of nonwestern experiences and traditions" into their research (p.xi); and to encourage South Asian specialists to study women. Part I, "Published Resources," contains over 4,600 citations, mostly annotated, to materials primarily in English. Serving as the key to this section, the "Outline of Headings" fills fourteen single-spaced pages. Although the outline is designed to be "both referential and provocative" (p.xii), beginning researchers may find it more intimidating than inspiring. Part II, "Libraries, Archives, and Other Local Resources," will be of interest only to advanced scholars contemplating research on site in South Asia or England. Because of its panoramic perspective, this is the single best guide to information on the women of South Asia. Included are materials on general topics (such as religious traditions, the life cycle, and sexuality); on specific events, people, and themes in religious, cultural, and political history; and on numerous aspects of the current status of women in South Asian societies. Author and subject indexes add to the usefulness of this volume. Harshida Pandit's *Women of India: An Annotated Bibliography* (Garland, 1985) is far less exhaustive and more simply arranged, though the overlap with Sakala is considerable.

891. Schwartz, Narda Lacey, 1948- . **Articles on Woman Writers, 1976-1984: A Bibliography.** Santa Barbara, CA: ABC-Clio, 1985. 305p. index. $50.00. LC 85-7484. ISBN 0874364388.

The first volume of Schwartz's bibliography highlighted literary criticism from 1960 to 1975; the second updates the listings through 1984. More than a thousand novelists, essayists, poets, dramatists, diarists, letter writers, and short-story writers are covered, including women from the United States, Great Britain, Ireland, Australia, Canada, and New Zealand, plus others who write in English, regardless of their nationality. The attractive layout facilitates use. Both popular and scholarly articles are cited, including many from feminist academic journals. Totaling nearly 7,800 unannotated entries, this volume is testimony to the tremendous surge of interest in women writers. Another early bibliographer of feminist literary criticism, Carol Fairbanks, documented the same growth phenomenon in *More Women in Literature: Criticism of the Seventies* (Scarecrow Press, 1979).

892. Searing, Susan E., 1950- . **Introduction to Library Research in Women's Studies.** Boulder, CO: Westview Press, 1985. 257p. index. $17.95. LC 85-3162. ISBN 0865312672.

Searing's handbook follows the classic pattern of library research guides. The opening chapters offer a brief introduction to the field of women's studies, discuss the organization of library resources (including catalogs and indexes), and present model research strategies. Annotated citations to major reference works fill the bulk of the volume. Six chapters present bibliographies and indexes to types of materials: books, periodical articles, newspapers, government publications, conference proceedings, and dissertations. Another seventeen chapters address research tools in particular fields of study, covering all the major disciplines as well as selected interdisciplinary areas. The final chapters highlight other specialized materials: guides to special collections, biographical sources, directories of organizations and services, microforms, online databases, and periodicals. The volume concludes with author, title, and subject indexes. Searing's purpose throughout the work is to illustrate how the library and its collections can be used most effectively in feminist research.

893. Sims, Janet L., 1945- , comp. **The Progress of Afro-American Women: A Selected Bibliography and Resource Guide.** Westport, CT: Greenwood Press, 1980. 378p. index. $35.00. LC 79-8948. ISBN 0313220832.

Citing over four thousand publications, Sims draws on a wide range of nineteenth- and twentieth-century sources, including scholarly books and articles, dissertations, audiovisual materials, and the popular press. Thirty-four chapters treat such diverse topics as the armed services, the arts, biographies, education, employment, family life, health, history, literature, organizations, psychology, sports, and women's rights. Some of the longer chapters are organized by subtopics—the chapter on employment is divided into sections for various occupations, for example—but to discover these sections one must browse through the entire chapter or consult the index, where subchapter headings constitute the only subject terms. The lack of annotations is also a drawback, but the sheer scope of this ambitious work offsets such inadequacies. Sims's work serves to introduce the researcher to many aspects of black women's studies; fortunately, other in-depth specialized bibliographies are slowly appearing. Especially notable are Marilyn Richardson's *Black Women and Religion: A Bibliography* (G. K. Hall, 1980) and JR Roberts's *Black Lesbians: An Annotated Bibliography* (Naiad Press, 1981). For additional bibliographic guidance, researchers should consult the inspiring anthology *All the Women Are White, All the Blacks Are Men, But Some of Us Are Brave: Black Women's Studies* (see entry 1115).

894.   Stineman, Esther, 1947- , with Catherine Loeb. **Women's Studies: A Recommended Core Bibliography.** Littleton, CO: Libraries Unlimited, 1979. 670p. index. $45.00. LC 78-13679. ISBN 0872871967.

The first major interdisciplinary guide to women's studies, this selective bibliography critically describes some 1,750 English-language books and 15 periodicals published through 1979. The bibliography incorporates many rediscovered older works, and directs readers to both scholarly monographs in the humanities and social sciences and more popular treatments of current feminist issues. Stineman represents both commercial and small press offerings; her generous samplings of autobiography, biography, fiction, and poetry are particularly valuable. Like the present five-year supplement, the volume is organized by discipline and genre, and indexed by author, title, and subject.

895.   Swanson, Kathryn. **Affirmative Action and Preferential Admissions in Higher Education: An Annotated Bibliography.** Metuchen, NJ: Scarecrow Press, 1981. 336p. index. $20.00. LC 81-45. ISBN 0810814110.

Swanson draws a distinction between "affirmative action" in academic employment and promotion, and "preferential admissions" of minority and women students; she treats both topics in depth. Citations fall into three major sections: "The Law and the Courts" (containing a sizeable subsection on the Bakke ruling); "The Academic Community Response"; and "The Philosophical Debate." Cogent essays introduce each section and outline the legal, professional, and philosophical arguments for and against affirmative action. Within the sections, the 1,181 entries are grouped by form: government publications, legal sources, bibliographies, books and articles. Without a subject index, one cannot easily identify materials specifically about women, racial minorities, the disabled, laws such as Title IX, or concepts such as reverse discrimination—although all are well covered in the works cited. A much briefer work, notable for its full, evaluative abstracts, is Jennie Farley's *Academic Women and Employment Discrimination: A Critical Annotated Bibliography* (New York State School of Industrial and Labor Relations, 1982). Farley limits her attention to faculty, selecting 179 works (primarily books and journal articles) from the fields of law, sociology, psychology, education, economics, and business. Another information-packed volume is Joan Bartczak Cannon and Ed Smith's *Resources for Affirmative Action: An Annotated Directory of Books, Periodicals, Films, Training Aids, and Consultants on Equal Opportunity* (Garrett, 1982). Unique for its coverage of nonprint sources, the guide's utility is weakened by the lack of a subject index. Moreover, many citations to general works on women and minorities dilute the content.

896.   Tufts, Eleanor. **American Women Artists, Past and Present: A Selected Bibliographic Guide.** New York: Garland, 1984. 340p. $43.00. LC 83-48201. ISBN 0824090705.

Five hundred U.S. women artists, from the seventeenth century to the present, are covered in this handy guide. Tufts has included painters, sculptors, graphic artists, photographers, and conceptual artists, but omitted those working in craft media (such as pottery or fiber). Set forth alphabetically by the artists' names, the information given is brief and non-evaluative: birth and death dates (about half are still living); an identification by medium; and a list of unannotated references to books, articles, newspaper articles, reviews of exhibits, and exhibit catalogs. Published works *by* the artists are also noted, as are entries in standard reference guides, biographical dictionaries, and surveys. This is a sensible first stop for research on individual American women artists.

897.   Unesco. **Bibliographic Guide to Studies on the Status of Women: Development and Population Trends.** Edited by Janet Holland. Epping, Essex: Bowker; New York: Unipub, 1983. 292p. index. $33.00. LC 84-164667. ISBN 0890590281.

Six experts contribute annotated reading lists to this volume on Africa, the Arab region, Asia, Eastern Europe, Latin America, and the United Kingdom, the United States, and Western Europe. Coverage by country is, not surprisingly, somewhat uneven. Largely reflecting materials issued between 1975 and 1980, the nearly six hundred entries focus on labor-force participation by women, women's role in economic development, education, family and home life, and demographic features. English-language publications are emphasized, although sources in other languages are also frequently cited; criteria for selection are not spelled out. The lengthy and substantive annotations are all in English, and when foreign materials are cited, an English translation of the title is given. (The chapter on Eastern Europe, unfortunately, gives *only* the English versions of titles.) Entries are indexed by country, subject, and author.

898.   Wei, Karen T. **Women in China: A Selected and Annotated Bibliography.** Westport, CT: Greenwood Press, 1984. 250p. index. $35.00. LC 84-10863. ISBN 0313242348.

This masterful interdisciplinary bibliography cites over 1,100 published English-language sources on the past and present of both mainland China and Taiwan. References are grouped in fourteen chapters addressing such topics as: biography, autobiography, and memoirs; economics and employment; female roles; social status and customs; feminism and the women's movement; literature and the arts; marriage and the family; and politics and government. Wei emphasizes nineteenth- and twentieth-century materials. With the increasing attention to non-Western societies in women's studies teaching and research, it is gratifying to have bibliographies like *Women in China* finally available. Students of the Orient will also appreciate Fan Kok-Sim's *Women in Southeast Asia* (G. K. Hall, 1982), an impressive listing of 3,865 items on women in Brunei, Burma, Indonesia, Malaysia, the Philippines, Singapore, and Thailand. Its unannotated entries are arranged by subject.

899.   Wilkins, Kay S. **Women's Education in the United States: A Guide to Information Sources.** Detroit: Gale Research, 1979. 217p. $60.00. LC 79-54691. ISBN 081031410X.

It is puzzling that no single selective bibliography on women's education adequately serves the undergraduate researcher, let alone the advanced scholar. Wilkins's guide remains the best starting point for research on many aspects of girls' and women's schooling in the United States. It emphasizes publications from 1968 to 1978, although historical materials are also cited. The briefly annotated entries are organized by topic, with author, title, and subject indexes. Renee Feinberg's *Women, Education, and Employment: A Bibliography of Periodical Citations, Pamphlets, Newspapers, and Government Documents, 1970-1980* (Library Professional Publications, 1982) covers roughly the same time frame, but less than a third of its entries concern education. Feinberg selects the most accessible and substantive writings (yet books are completely excluded) and provides an easy-to-use topical index and a well-thought-out subject arrangement. The entries, unfortunately, carry no annotations. Franklin and Betty June Parker's set, *Women's Education—A World View* (Greenwood Press, 1979-1981), is an exhaustive bibliography, the first volume devoted to dissertations and the second to books and reports. Citations total nearly six thousand. However, the arrangement of entries by author, coupled with poor subject indexing, makes the set frustrating to use. Because as yet no one-stop source for references on women's education exists, researchers consulting the works described here must still resort to the standard indexes in the field.

900.   Wilson, Carolyn F. **Violence Against Women: An Annotated Bibliography.** Boston: G. K. Hall, 1981. 111p. index. $23.00. LC 81-6232. ISBN 0816184976.

Battered women, rape, sexual abuse of children, and pornography are the major concerns of this well-wrought bibliography. Wilson emphasizes books and articles published between 1975 and 1980. Selecting over two hundred titles from both scholarly and popular sources, she presents historical, legal, medical, psychological, and cultural perspectives. The annotations are lengthy and informative. Chapter introductions discuss the issues and review the literature from a feminist stance. Joseph J. Costa's thick volume, *Abuse of Women: Legislation, Reporting, and Prevention* (Lexington Books, 1983), contains a three-hundred-page, partially annotated bibliography. Unfortunately, it lacks a subject index, although the main themes of the cited works are coded in the right-hand margin for readers willing to scan the pages. Costa also provides extensive listings of programs and services, annotated references to films and videotapes, comparative data on state legislation, and background papers by such recognized experts as Richard Gelles and Lisa Lerman.

901.   **Women Studies Abstracts.** 1972- . Rush Publishing Co., P.O. Box 1, Rush, NY 14543. Quarterly. $36.00 (individuals); $72.00 (institutions). ISSN 0049-7835.

Issued for over a decade by editor/publisher Sara Stauffer Whaley, *Women Studies Abstracts* is a flawed but essential bibliograhic resource. Despite the title, few of its entries are abstracted. Nearly a thousand articles from both scholarly and popular periodicals are listed in each quarterly issue, yet lacking a full list of source journals, readers cannot judge the thoroughness of coverage. The arrangement is by subject (e.g., education, employment, mental and physical health) and type of material (e.g., biography, book reviews)—twenty-four categories in all. Each issue has a subject index, and cumulative subject and author indexes appear annually. Indexing terminology was inconsistent in the initial years of publication, but recent volumes show marked improvement. *Women Studies Abstracts* was the sole periodical index devoted to women's studies until 1983, when *Studies on Women Abstracts* first appeared. Lengthy, evaluative summaries are the strong point of this British bibliographic service, which covered only nine hundred books and journal articles in 1985. The unorthodox ordering of article entries by journal title inhibits browsing, but the author and keyword subject indexes in each bimonthly issue compensate for this. Indexes are cumulated annually. The scope is interdisciplinary, encompassing both women-focused monographs and serials, and mainstream academic journals. However, the list of "Journals Covered by the Service" is greatly exaggerated, and the section treating books emphasizes British imprints. Thus, while *Studies on Women Abstracts* has the potential to become *the* basic bibliographic tool for the field, *Women Studies Abstracts* at this point still offers a much wider lens on the literature.

902.* Zukerman, Elyse. **Changing Directions in the Treatment of Women: A Mental Health Bibliography.** Rockville, MD: National Institute of Mental Health, 1979. 494p. index. LC 79-603203.

Feminists have been vocal in their criticism of traditional psychotherapy, as this hefty bibliography of works from 1960 to 1977 reveals. Except for a brief concluding list of self-help readings, the bibliography stresses theoretical writings and research reports. There are over 400 entries, each with a page-long abstract. Among the topics covered are: Freudian psychoanalysis and recent critiques; sexism in psychiatric counseling; sex as a factor in the process and outcome of treatment; feminist therapists, women's groups, and other new approaches; specific problems (such as alcohol and drug abuse, depression, and work-related difficulties); special populations (lesbians, minorities, and prisoners); and new alternative therapies. This final category includes assertiveness training, consciousness-raising, crisis intervention, and general principles of feminist therapy.

BIOGRAPHICAL MATERIALS

903. Banks, Olive. **The Biographical Dictionary of British Feminists. Vol. One: 1800-1930.** New York: New York University Press, 1985. 239p. bibliog. index. $55.00. LC 85-3110. ISBN 0814710786.

More specialized than the *Europa Biographical Dictionary of British Women* (see entry 905), this volume provides biographical background on one hundred women and nineteen men. Entries average two pages in length and include cross-references and notes on sources. The selection is consistent with Banks's broad view of feminist activity, as explicated in her earlier work, *Faces of Feminism: A Study of Feminism as a Social Movement* (St. Martin's Press, 1981). In that book, she traces the history of British and U.S. feminism from 1840 to the present, identifying three concurrent strands: equal-rights feminism, rooted in Enlightenment philosophy; communitarian social feminism, born among the Owenites; and evangelical feminism, derived from nineteenth-century religious thinking.

904. Blashfield, Jean F. **Hellraisers, Heroines, and Holy Women: Women's Most Remarkable Contributions to History.** New York: St. Martin's Press, 1981. 204p. index. $14.95. LC 80-27889. ISBN 0312367368.

In the tradition of the classic reference volume *Famous First Facts,* this compendium is both informative and fun. A sampling of entries reveals such enticements as "Only Ex-Dancer to Become a President" (Isabel Perón), "First Woman to Serve as a Regular American Soldier" (Deborah Sampson, disguised as a man in 1782), "Woman to Do the Most Phsyical Labor for an Intellectual Achievement" (Marie Curie), and "Only Woman to Form an Important Club Because She Couldn't Meet Charles Dickens" (Jane Croly, founder of Sorosis). In a more serious vein, Susan Raven and Alison Weir highlight women's accomplishments in *Women of Achievement: Thirty-Five Centuries of History* (Harmony Books, 1981). Some five hundred biographical entries are divided into ten chapters: "Politics and Power"; "Education and Social Reform"; "Religion"; "The Written Word"; "The Performing Arts"; "The Visual Arts"; "Science and Medicine"; "Money and Management"; "Travel and Exploration"; "Sport." The scope is international, the writing crisp, and the illustrations plentiful.

905. Crawford, Anne, et al., eds. **The Europa Biographical Dictionary of British Women: Over 1000 Notable Women From Britain's Past.** Detroit: Gale Research, 1983. 436p. $55.00. LC 84-162865. ISBN 0810317893.

Signed biographies of over one thousand women, all deceased, span the history of the British Isles from the earliest times to the twentieth century. In addition to the expected "household names"—Anne Boleyn, Agatha Christie, Emmeline Pankhurst—the browsing reader discovers women of all walks of life who influenced the society, politics, and culture of their times: medieval nuns, witches, suffragists, royalty, writers and artists, social reformers, and many others. Entries average three paragraphs in length; they are accurate, written in a lively style, but necessarily lack depth. Most cite further references. Unfortunately, the compilers provide no indexes to occupations, time periods, or other identifying characteristics.

906. Herman, Kali. **Women in Particular: An Index to American Women.** Phoenix: Oryx Press, 1984. 740p. index. $95.00. LC 84-1019. ISBN 0897740882.

Herman aims to foster research on the history of women in the U.S. by indexing entries in biographical dictionaries. Her work replaces Norma Ireland's *Index to Women of the World From Ancient to Modern Times* (1970), itself one of the fifty-four sources Herman draws upon. Each entry gives the woman's names (including maiden name, nicknames, and pseudonyms), her birth and death dates, a few words describing her career, and abbreviated references to information in standard biographical dictionaries. In many cases there is additional data: religious affiliation; place of residence and/or work; and racial or ethnic identification. Full entries are repeated as necessary in each of the four major indexes: field and career; religious affiliation; ethnic and racial; and geographical. An alphabetical name index rounds out the volume.

907. Leavitt, Judith A. **American Women Managers and Administrators: A Selective Biographical Dictionary of Twentieth-Century Leaders in Business, Education, and Government.** Westport, CT: Greenwood Press, 1985. 317p. bibliog. index. $45.00. LC 84-12814. ISBN 0313237484.

Leavitt documents the lives and achievements of 226 successful women managers, drawing information from published sources and questionnaires. From politician Bella Abzug to Ella Flagg Young, appointed superintendent of the Chicago school system in 1909 and elected president of the National Education Association in 1910, the volume emphasizes the women who accomplished "firsts" in their fields. Other women warrant inclusion because they founded businesses or colleges, served as presidents of corporations, colleges, or universities, or held other positions of national prominence, primarily in government. Each entry averages a page in length, highlighting the usual biographical facts (degrees, work history, accomplishments, and honors) and concluding with bibliographic references. Wherever possible, Leavitt inserts a brief quotation concerning the subject's philosophy of management or of life in general.

908. Petteys, Chris, et al. **Dictionary of Women Artists: An International Dictionary of Women Artists Born Before 1900.** Boston: G. K. Hall, 1985. 851p. bibliog. $49.95. LC 84-22511. ISBN 0816184569.

Working with art librarians and scores of informants worldwide, Petteys compiled this monumental biographical dictionary of women painters, sculptors, printmakers, and illustrators. More than twenty-one thousand artists, all born before the turn of the century, are listed, even those about whom very little is known. The alphabetically arranged entries provide the following data: name (including married name and pseudonym); dates and places of birth and death; media; place of residence or activity; other artists in the same family; schools and teachers; and exhibitions. In addition, Petteys provides references to the sources of information; these are keyed to a lengthy bibliography in the back of the volume. Although lacking indexes, this volume serves as a standard reference tool for students, art historians, women's studies scholars, museum curators, and art dealers and collectors. *The International Dictionary of Women Workers in the Decorative Arts,* compiled by Alice Irma Prather-Moses (Scarecrow Press, 1981), complements Petteys's listing by covering ceramics, interior design, metalwork, textiles, and other crafts.

909. Sicherman, Barbara, and Carol Hurd Green, eds. **Notable American Women: The Modern Period.** Cambridge, MA: Belknap Press of Harvard University Press, 1980. 773p. index. $45.00. LC 80-18402. ISBN 0674627326.

A companion to the classic *Notable American Women, 1607-1950,* this biographical dictionary profiles 442 U.S. women who died between 1951 and 1975. Four basic criteria governed selection: "the individual's influence on her time or field; the importance and significance of her achievement; the pioneering or innovative quality of her work; and the relevance of her career for the history of women" (p.x). A diverse group of women appears here, including conservationist Rachel Carson, businesswoman Elizabeth Arden, birth control advocate Margaret Sanger, novelist Zora Neale Hurston, psychiatrist Karen Horney, musician Janis Joplin, and Indian activist Alice Lee Jemison. Like its parent set, the volume offers signed articles by specialists, each about a page and a half in length. The biographical and critical assessments are followed by short bibliographies of primary and secondary sources. The classified list at the back of the volume indexes the women by the professions, disciplines, or causes in which they were active.

910. Siegel, Patricia Joan, and Kay Thomas Finley. **Women in the Scientific Search: An American Bio-Bibliography, 1724-1979.** Metuchen, NJ: Scarecrow Press, 1985. 399p. index. $32.50. LC 84-20290. ISBN 0810817551.

This first-of-its-kind resource assembles 1,517 biographical and bibliographical entries on some 160 women scientists, all deceased by 1979. Fewer than half the women are represented in *Notable American Women.* After a listing of general biographies, information on individuals is arranged by scientific field; astronomers, botanists, chemists and biochemists, mathematicians, medical researchers, psychologists, and zoologists predominate. The first entry for each woman is a two-to-three-paragraph biography that emphasizes her career and the significance of her work, followed by a chronological bibliography of writings about her with evaluative annotations. (Except for the most prominent women, the sources cited are obituaries, newspaper and periodical articles, and entries in biographical dictionaries.) The index is limited to proper names, organizations, colleges, journal titles, and a very few selected subject terms.

911. Stineman, Esther, 1947- . **American Political Women: Contemporary and Historical Profiles.** Littleton, CO: Libraries Unlimited, 1980. 228p. bibliog. index. $27.50. LC 80-24478. ISBN 0872872386.

Stineman captures sixty high-level office holders—members of Congress, ambassadors, Cabinet members, special presidential assistants, governors, lieutenant governors, and mayors—in brief portraits of their political careers. These women—most of them prominent in the late 1970s and early 1980s—have taken diverse paths to power; they occupy many points on the political spectrum. Each profile pays particular attention to the subject's accomplishments, her views on the women's movement, and her career preparation and development, and cites selected speeches and writings, honors, and publications about her. A separate annotated bibliography highlights additional sources for the study of women in U.S. politics, including reference materials, books, periodicals, dissertations, indexes, and selected libraries and organizations. Appendices identify women who served in Congress (1917-1980), chiefs of mission (1933-1980), and women serving, as of spring 1980, as federal judges and in other key posts. Shirley Temple Black, Nancy Dick, Sissy Farenthold, Dianne Feinstein, Patricia Roberts Harris, Barbara Jordan, Clare Booth Luce, and Dixy Lee Ray are among the remarkable women who come to life on the pages of this volume.

912. Todd, Janet M., 1942- , ed. **A Dictionary of British and American Women Writers, 1660-1800.** Totowa, NJ: Rowman and Allanheld, 1985. 344p. index. $48.50. LC 84-2123. ISBN 0847671259.

Nearly five hundred bio-critical essays, written by specialists in Restoration and eighteenth-century studies, are gathered in this landmark reference volume. Among those featured are a few well-known women—Abigail Adams, Fanny Burney, Mary Wollstonecraft, Phillis Wheatley. "But it is rare to find even a student of literature who has heard of more than half a dozen of them," laments Todd. "This book is a plea for notice" (p.25). The entries are arranged alphabetically; they reveal what is known of the writer's life and career and cite her published works. In her lengthy introduction, Todd examines patterns of class, location, education, politics, marriage, motives for authorship, occupation, and membership in formal and informal female networks. She also discusses the authors' choices of genres and themes. The entries lack bibliographical references to biographical or critical studies, but Todd does suggest some sources in the preface.

913. Uglow, Jennifer S., ed. **The International Dictionary of Women's Biography.** New York: Continuum, 1982. 534p. index. bibliog. $35.00. LC 82-7417. ISBN 0826401929.

Some 1,500 women of achievement from all time periods and all fields of activity are spotlighted in this very useful volume. Although the scope is international, women of North America and Western Europe predominate. Entries average a half column in length; references to published biographies or autobiographies are usually included. A subject index groups women by their primary field of activity. Necessarily highly selective, this compendium is nonetheless a readable and inspiring source for information on outstanding women's lives.

914. **The World Who's Who of Women.** 7th ed. Cambridge, England: International Biographical Centre, 1984. 800p. $125.00. ISBN 0900332689.

With this type of directory, one should always be suspicious of coverage and selection. "Inclusion is entirely by invitation and achievement," claims the editor in the foreword, yet many notable names are missing. It is good, however, to see "ordinary women" granted

granted worldwide recognition for their accomplishments. Up-to-date and offering over five thousand biographies, this volume is a welcome addition to the reference shelves, in light of the steady demand for biographical information and the dearth of sources. It should also prove a useful database for current and future sociological analysis of women's interests and achievements.

GENERAL

915.   Beere, Carole A. **Women and Women's Issues: A Handbook of Tests and Measures.** San Francisco: Jossey-Bass, 1979. 550p. index. $37.95. LC 78-88106. ISBN 0875894186.

Behavioral scientists in various fields can turn to this handy volume for detailed descriptions of 235 instruments used through 1977 in research on or about women. Rating scales, true-false quizzes, toy preference tests, and projective storytelling are examples of research tools profiled. The topical chapters cover sex roles, sex stereotypes, sex-role prescriptions, children's sex roles, gender knowledge, marital and parental roles, employee roles, multiple roles, attitudes toward women's issues, and somatic and sexual issues. Each entry includes notes on the development, reliability, and validity of the measure, plus a bibliography of reported research in which the instrument was utilized. Entries are indexed by title, name, and the variables measured. Beere's short cautionary chapter titled "Measurement Problems" should be read both by researchers and by those who make use of their findings.

916.*   Chaney, Elsa M. **Women of the World: Latin America and the Caribbean.** Washington, DC: U.S. Bureau of the Census, 1984. 173p. bibliog. LC 84-601056.

The first of four reference volumes based on the Census Bureau's Women in Development Data Base, this handbook presents and discusses statistical evidence of women's socioeconomic position in twenty-one nations of Central America, South America, and the Caribbean. Various measures are grouped under the headings "Population Distribution and Change," "Literacy and Education," "Women in Economic Activity," "Marital Status and Living Arrangements," and "Fertility and Mortality." The graphs and charts are easy to interpret; the written analyses signal important trends and national differences, while warning of inconsistencies and gaps in the available data. Other volumes in the series are subtitled *Sub-Saharan Africa* (by Jeanne S. Newman, 1984), *Asia and the Pacific* (by Nasra M. Shah, 1985), and *Near East and North Africa* (by Mary Chamie, 1985).

917.   Cohen, Aaron I. **International Encyclopedia of Women Composers.** New York: Bowker, 1981. 597p. $145.00. LC 81-12233. ISBN 0835212882.

This remarkable volume lists some five thousand women composers from seventy countries. A typical entry provides basic biographical data, a list of musical works and other publications by the composer, and references to writings about her. Among the appendices are an index by country and century, and a bibliography. Cohen has also compiled the *International Discography of Women Composers* (see entry 832). In addition to these comprehensive sources, there are several recent specialized reference books on women composers. Some exemplary titles are: *Keyboard Music by Women Composers: A Catalog and Bibliography* (Greenwood Press, 1981), by Joan M. Meggett; *Women Composers: A Checklist of Works for the Solo Voice* (G. K. Hall, 1980), by Miriam Stewart-Green; and *Contemporary Concert Music by Women: A Directory of the*

Composers and Their Works (Greenwood Press, 1981), by Judith Lang Zaimont and Karen Famera. Jane Weiner LePage's two-volume set, *Women Composers, Conductors, and Musicians of the Twentieth Century* (Scarecrow Press, 1980-1983), covers thirty-four contemporary women in music, offering lengthy biographies and lists of works and recordings.

918.   The Feminist Writers Guild. **Words in Our Pockets: The Feminist Writers Guild Handbook on How to Gain Power, Get Published & Get Paid.** Edited by Celeste West. Paradise, CA: Dustbooks, 1985. 368p. index. $15.95. LC 81-2106. ISBN 0913218014.

A veteran of the women-in-print movement who is also savvy about corporate publishing, Celeste West is perfectly placed to serve as editor of this entertaining anthology aimed at the aspiring feminist writer. Establishment publishing is the topic in Part I, where readers will learn the basics of book proposals, self-promotion, author law, taxes for freelancers, grant writing, and more. Part II presents the alternative of women's publishing, with profiles of *off our backs,* the now defunct Persephone Press, Dorothy Bryant's self-publishing ventures, and Alice James Books (a publishing cooperative), along with advice on time management and a somber warning about feminist censorship. In Part III, writers in a number of genres share their experience – among them, Elsa Gidlow (poet), Karen Malpede (playwright), Margaret Cruikshank (lesbian studies), and Joanne Genet (children's literature). The final section draws in a broader support network, including feminist printers, women's bookstores, libraries, and writers' support groups. With its mix of idealism and nitty-gritty detail, this book will inform and inspire not just writers, but all women interested in the word trade.

919.   Fishburn, Katherine, 1944- . **Women in Popular Culture: A Reference Guide.** Westport, CT: Greenwood Press, 1982. 267p. bibliog. index. $29.95. LC 81-13421. ISBN 0313221529.

"Reference guide" is a somewhat misleading label for this readable collection of review essays, although each chapter concludes with a bibliography of works discussed and several appendices provide researchers with additional leads. Fishburn's focus is on images of women the popular media of the United States. She devotes a chapter each to histories of American women and theoretical writings. The remaining chapters treat genres: popular literature; magazines and magazine fiction; film; television; and advertising, fashion, sports, and comics. In her introduction, Fishburn traces the relation of our nation's complex iconography of women to changing social and political mythologies, from colonial times to the present. Whereas Fishburn is largely concerned with images of women, other scholars have begun to study women as creators and consumers of popular culture, particularly romance fiction. Kay Mussell's *Women's Gothic and Romance Fiction: A Reference Guide* (Greenwood Press, 1981), like Fishburn's volume, provides review essays and lists of works.

920.   Howe, Florence, et al., eds. **Everywoman's Guide to Colleges and Universities.** Old Westbury, NY: Feminist Press, 1982. 512p. index. $12.95. LC 82-15402. ISBN 0935312099.

Profiling nearly 600 institutions, both public and private, *Everywoman's Guide* is an important and unique supplement to the standard descriptive directories of colleges and universities. The volume is packed with information on curriculum, campus security, childcare facilities, health care and counseling, sports, career services, and much more. Included are telling statistics: the percentage of female students on each campus; the faculty/student gender ratio; the percentage of female students in nontraditional fields of study; and the proportionate enrollment of racial minorities. The entries are arranged by states. Symbols highlight such desirable characteristics as evening and/or weekend classes, sexual harassment policies, women's studies programs, and women's centers; these signals, plus a consistent ordering of the textual information, make comparison between colleges easy. Joint compilers Florence Howe, Suzanne Howard, and Mary Jo Boehm Strauss have also rated institutions in three areas: women in leadership positions (as students, faculty, and administrators); women and the curriculum; and women and athletics. Inclusion in the guide hinged on the completion of a lengthy questionnaire, and regrettably some major schools are not covered.

921. Kramarae, Cheris, and Paula A. Treichler. **A Feminist Dictionary: In Our Own Words.** Boston: Pandora Press, 1985. 587p. bibliog. $28.95. LC 85-9278. ISBN 0863580602.

In this entertaining and enlightening reference work, Kramarae and Treichler demonstrate the centrality of language to women's position. They explicate feminist neologisms (comparable worth, gender gap, herstory, Ms., supermom, etc.) and provide definitions with a feminist (often satiric) twist for familiar words. (See, for example, the entries for girl, man, menstruation, sexual revolution, and writing.) Not simply words, but concepts, events, even book and journal titles are accorded entries. Thus one finds Christmas, class, and Cinderella; gothic novel, Gray Panthers, and Greenham Common; sob sisters, socialization, and *Spare Rib* — not to mention a variety of proposed nonsexist pronouns. While they occasionally invent their own definitions, Kramarae and Treichler usually quote words and phrases in context, thereby granting feminist writers and speakers the stature of authorities on language. At seventy-plus pages, their source bibliography attests to the extent of their research. The dictionary succeeds in documenting women's linguistic contributions and highlighting areas of language use and research where inequalities still exist.

922. Mainiero, Lina, ed. **American Women Writers: A Critical Reference Guide From Colonial Times to the Present.** New York: Ungar. 4v. bibliog. LC 78-20945. Vol. 1: 1979; $60.00; ISBN 0804431515. Vol. 2: 1981; $60.00; ISBN 0804431523. Vol. 3: 1981; $60.00; ISBN 0804431531. Vol. 4: 1982; $60.00; ISBN 0804431558.

The collaborative work of many scholars, *American Women Writers* serves as an indispensable guide to the lives and writings of more than a thousand woman authors. Each critical biography assesses the writer's contribution; provides the basic biographical information, including married and maiden names, pseudonyms, and aliases that often elude even diligent searchers; and offers a checklist of the writer's works (the first such compilations for many of the women included). Selected secondary literature is also cited. The signed entries average about two pages in length. Elizabeth Bishop, Louisa May Alcott, and Elizabeth Cady Stanton are, not surprisingly, here, but so are newer names — Olga Broumas, E. M. Broner, Barbara Tuchman, Cynthia Ozick. Coverage is not limited to poets and fiction writers but embraces writers on social, political, scholarly, and popular topics as well. Yet the thin coverage of minority authors is disappointing. The fourth volume contains a comprehensive index to names and subjects. About four hundred entries were selected for inclusion in a paperback abridgement (Ungar, 1983).

923. McPhee, Carol, and Ann FitzGerald, comps. **Feminist Quotations: Voices of Rebels, Reformers, and Visionaries.** New York: Thomas Y. Crowell, 1979. 271p. index. $12.95. LC 78-3308. ISBN 0690017707.

Noting that "even the earliest feminists still speak for the present," McPhee and FitzGerald assemble more than fifteen hundred quotations "to provide for the women of our time – particularly those who rebel and are isolated by rebellion – a consciousness of sisterhood with the women who have gone before, and a sense of reassurance and reaffirmation in the multitude of voices encouraging us to become a force in history" (p.xii). Abigail Adams, Mary Wollstonecraft, Elizabeth Cady Stanton, Betty Friedan, and Adrienne Rich are representative of the nearly three hundred feminist writers and speakers from England and North America whose insightful and inspiring words ring out from these pages. The volume is in two parts: "The Feminist As Critic" and "The Feminist As Rebel and Visionary," each further divided into several thematic sections with titles like "The Business of Marriage," "Sisterhood," and "Liberation of the Body." Within sections, quotations are ordered chronologically. Author and subject indexes offer other approaches for research.

924. Navaretta, Cynthia, comp. **Guide to Women's Art Organizations and Directory for the Arts.** 2nd ed. New York: Midmarch Associates, 1982. 174p. bibliog. pbk. $8.50. LC 82-80588. ISBN 0960247637.

Both practicing artists and students of the arts will uncover a wealth of information in this compendium. Navaretta emphasizes the visual arts, providing descriptions of art centers, national and state organizations, women-run galleries, artists' support groups, slide registries, exhibitions, conferences, and other resources and events. Bibliographic sections list books and periodicals. Topics such as financial aid, health hazards, and business management are also covered. In addition to the visual arts, there is information on dance, music, theater, architecture and design, crafts, film and electronic print media, and writing. Despite the lack of an index, this is a useful guide.

925.* Partnow, Elaine, ed. **The Quotable Woman: From Eve to 1799.** New York: Facts on File, 1985. 533p. index. LC 82-15511. ISBN 0871963078.

A companion to Partnow's *The Quotable Woman: 1800-1975* (1977; revised to cover 1800-1981 in 1982), this volume presents pithy quotations and literary lines from over eight hundred women. Following a section of biblical sayings, quotations are arranged chronologically by date of birth, from Enheduanna (a Sumerian moon priestess, c.2300 B.C.) to Madame de Launay (a French actress popular in the 1820s). Partnow identifies the women in an alphabetical biographical index at the back of the volume, with full cross-referencing of variant names and brief notes on nationality, profession, and important relatives. A well-constructed subject index provides a topical approach, but many readers will no doubt prefer to browse. The selections are by no means limited to feminist concerns; there are as many entries listed in the index under "God" as under "woman/women." Notable for its international scope, the compendium benefits from Partnow's scrupulous documentation of sources and her inclusion of footnotes to explain archaic words and obscure references.

926. Rubin, Mary, 1957- , and the Business and Professional Women's Foundation. **How to Get Money for Research.** Old Westbury, NY: Feminist Press, 1983. 78p. bibliog. index. pbk. $6.95. LC 83-1444. ISBN 0935312188.

Aimed at individual women researchers, this affordable guide is full of good advice on identifying funding agencies and submitting proposals. Rubin describes eighty-one sources for grants covering research by and about women, general fellowships, and nontraditional pursuits by women. A section titled "resources" lists publications and organizations that can provide further guidance. Anyone in women's studies preparing a grant application for the first time will find this booklet a valuable aid.

927.   Schmidt, Peggy J. **Making It Big in the City: A Woman's Guide to Living, Loving, and Working There.** New York: Putnam, 1983. 287p. bibliog. $16.95. LC 82-25264. ISBN 0698112288.

An avid champion of big-city life, Schmidt delivers pragmatic advice to the new city dweller. She draws on over fifty interviews, a survey sponsored by *Mademoiselle,* and her own experience in explaining how to land a job, find housing, make friends, live on one's own, and cope with fear and the threat of crime. By addressing the reader directly and incorporating anecdotes on nearly every page, Schmidt produces a readable and reassuring guide that is ideal for graduating women students moving out into a wider urban world.

928.   Sivard, Ruth Leger. **Women ... A World Survey.** Washington, DC: World Priorities, 1985. 44p. pbk. $5.00. ISBN 0918281008.

The year 1985 marked the close of the International Decade for Women and the fortieth anniversary of the founding of the United Nations—an apt time to survey the position of women worldwide and to assess their modest progress toward equality. Through statistical charts, color maps and graphs, and readable analytic text, Sivard facilitates comparisons of nations and regions, while illuminating global trends. She begins with a page of revealing facts that document women's inequality and then offers a quick overview of major world developments since World War II, highlighting population growth, economic development, and social changes. A more detailed examination of women's status in work, education, health, and government and law follows. The concluding charts reformat and amplify the data in profiles of 140 countries. Sivard draws her data primarily from the United Nations, UNESCO, the World Health Organization, and the International Labor Office.

929.   United States. Department of Labor. Women's Bureau. **Time of Change: 1983 Handbook on Women Workers.** Washington, DC: U.S. Women's Bureau, 1983. 192p. bibliog. $6.50. LC 84-231013.

Superseding the *1975 Handbook on Women Workers,* this edition continues its basic organization and updates statistical data through the early 1980s. Part 1 covers women's labor market activity, the occupations and industries in which they are employed, their income and earnings, educational attainment, and job training. Chapters in this part are about equally divided between statistical charts and explanatory text. Part 2 spells out federal and state laws governing women's employment and status in such areas as equal pay, sex discrimination, occupational safety and health, and social security. Somewhat older data on working women are available in a publication of the Bureau of Labor Statistics, *Perspectives on Working Women: A Databook*, prepared by Howard Hayghe and Beverly L. Johnson (1980). The federal Census Bureau has not yet issued a new edition of its general guide, *A Statistical Portrait of Women in the United States, 1978* (1980), but the two works noted above, although focused on employment, include much demographic data.

930.   Walker, Barbara G. **The Woman's Encyclopedia of Myths and Secrets.** San Francisco: Harper and Row, 1983. 1124p. bibliog. $28.80. LC 83-47736. ISBN 0062509268.

Mythology, anthropology, history, religion, and linguistics mix in this attractive and readable volume to present an engrossing overview of ancient female-centered knowledge and of the cultural origins of sexism. Many of the 1,350 entries are names—gods and goddesses, creatures of folklore and myth, saints and martyrs—but events, places, symbols, and customs are also covered in treatments ranging from single sentences to several pages. The breadth of Walker's research is evident; still, reviewers have faulted her for presenting theory and speculation as fact. A feminist perspective strongly flavors her commentary. Patricia Monaghan's *The Book of Goddesses and Heroines* (Dutton, 1981) is less ambitious but equally absorbing. Monaghan identifies over a thousand female deities in alphabetical order. Some of the entries are quite short; others retell myths and legends. In *Ancient Mirrors of Womanhood* (Beacon Press, 1979), Merlin Stone recounts the legends of 115 female deities and mythic heroines from various cultures of Europe, the Middle East, Asia, Africa, Oceania, and the Americas.

931.   Warren, Mary Anne. **The Nature of Woman: An Encyclopedia and Guide to the Literature.** Pt. Reyes, CA: Edgepress, 1980. 708p. bibliog. index. $16.00. LC 79-55299. ISBN 0918528070.

In this unusual survey, the works of two hundred individual theorists are discussed. Warren turns a critical feminist eye on such influential shapers of Western thought as Aristotle, Darwin, and Freud, as well as modern writers such as Mary Daly, Norman Mailer, and Susan Brownmiller. Interspersed among the articles on individuals are short entries on diverse subjects—abortion, androgyny, the Bible, language and women, menstruation, and patriarchy, among others. Students will find these evaluative essays a fascinating introduction to the ideas of feminists and male supremacists alike. Teachers may appreciate the additional annotated listing of women-focused anthologies and sourcebooks in twenty-five fields and the full bibliography of works cited in the text. Other features are a glossary of key terms, a selected (and outdated) list of periodicals, and a well-wrought index.

932.*   Women's Action Alliance. **Women's Action Almanac: A Complete Resource Guide.** Edited by Jane Williamson, et al. New York: Morrow, 1979. 432p. index. LC 79-16326. ISBN 0688035256.

As a source for quick facts and as a jumping-off point for further research, nothing quite equals the *Women's Action Almanac,* edited by Jane Williamson, Diane Winston, and Wanda Wooten. Eighty-four issue-oriented chapters cover such pressing topics as abortion, battered women, career development, disabled women, the Equal Rights Amendment, labor unions, older women, rape, sex discrimination, and women's arts and media. Each chapter offers a brief essay, names and addresses of concerned organizations, and publications recommended for further reading. The volume includes a directory of over 250 national women's organizations that outlines the goals and programs of each. The Women's Action Alliance has also issued *Women Helping Women: A State-by-State Directory of Services* (distr. Neal-Schuman, 1981), which lists battered women and rape victim services, career counseling services, displaced homemaker programs, Planned Parenthood clinics, skilled trades training centers, women's centers, state and local women's commissions, and women's health centers.

933.   **The Women's Annual: The Year in Review.** Boston: G. K. Hall. 5v. bibliog. index. LC 82-641994. Vol. 1: 1981; $35.00; ISBN 0816185301. Vol. 2: 1982; $35.00; ISBN 0816186146. Vol. 3: 1983; $35.00; ISBN 0816186413. Vol. 4: 1984; $35.00; ISBN 0816187037. Vol. 5: 1985; $35.00; ISBN 0816187177.

The auspicious debut of *The Women's Annual* heralded the growing stature of women's studies as a distinct field of inquiry, a field diverse and vital enough to merit its own yearbook. The series admirably realizes its dual objectives—to survey recent scholarship on women and to report on feminist activity in the public sphere. The librarian-editors (Barbara Haber of the Schlesinger Library for volumes 1-3, Sarah M. Pritchard of the Library of Congress for volume 4, and Mary Drake McFeely of Smith College for volume 5) are uniquely situated to compile authoritative overviews of the vast arena of feminist writing and action, and to corral some first-rate contributors. The five volumes published to date each contain ten or eleven essays, accompanied by references to publications, nonprint media, organizations, and other resources. Some topics appear consistently: education, health, politics and law, the humanities, psychology, and work. Other concerns—among them domestic life, feminist theory, popular culture, religion, violence against women, women of color, lesbians, and international issues—have been included as reader interest and the shape of the literature dictate. Researchers seeking a quick, evaluative introduction to feminist thought in the eighties need only consult *The Women's Annual.*

RELIGION AND PHILOSOPHY

For the researcher's convenience, works on religion and philosophy are grouped together in this chapter. The two fields share a focus on values, morality, and the nature of humanity. For example, both philosophers and theologians are defining a new feminist ethics, one that dovetails with the findings of psychologist Carol Gilligan and others (see entry 808).

In the literature on women and religion, one finds books on the ordination of women, the status of women in mainstream Jewish and Christian denominations, the tenets of radical feminist theology, the image of women in the Bible, and the role of women throughout church history—as preachers, churchgoers, nuns, missionaries, devout mothers, and clergymen's wives. Alongside these studies are titles that describe "women's spirituality" as a compelling experience of individual and community growth. This emergent women-focused spiritual movement incorporates goddess worship, witchcraft, and self-awareness as strands of a broader "new age" religious awakening.

Additional books on political philosophy appear in the Politics and Political Theory chapter, and several titles in Women's Movement and Feminist Theory have a philosophical bent. Religious and spiritual motifs surface in a number of the writings cited in the Literature chapter. A new annotated bibliography by Anne Carson—*Feminist Spirituality and the Feminine Divine* (Crossing Press, 1986)—aids in identifying further readings on women's spirituality. A comparable book-length guide to women's perspectives on mainstream religious traditions is sorely needed.

934. Atkinson, Clarissa W., et al., eds. **Immaculate & Powerful: The Female in Sacred Image and Social Reality.** Boston: Beacon Press, 1985. 330p. bibliog. index. $19.95. LC 85-70448. ISBN 0807062245.

A dozen participants in Harvard's Women's Studies in Religion Program contributed to this volume. Their topics are diverse—women's status in ancient Israel, Paul's views on female homoeroticism, the relevance of black women's literature to feminist theology, female symbolism in Tibetan Buddhism, and the nineteenth-century Marian revival, to name a few. By examining intersections of religion and culture, the authors shed light on both theological questions and the history of social roles and institutions. The volume is co-edited by Clarissa W. Atkinson, Constance M. Buchanan, and Margaret R. Miles.

935. Bell, Linda A., ed. **Visions of Women: Being a Fascinating Anthology With Analysis of Philosophers' Views of Women From Ancient to Modern Times.** Clifton, NJ: Humana Press, 1983. 489p. $39.50. LC 82-48866. ISBN 089603044X.

Bell's introductory text pulls together passages from the writings of fifty Western philosophers, among them, Plato, Aristotle, Thomas Aquinas, Thomas More, Hobbes,

Spinoza, Locke, Voltaire, Rosseau, Mary Wollstonecraft, Hegel, John Stuart Mill, Engels, Nietzsche, Lenin, Emma Goldman, and Simone de Beauvoir. Noting that it is the more sexist ideas that have tended to be canonized, Bell attempts to bring out the contradictions in these writers' thoughts by recovering little known or previously untranslated passages. The philosophers are presented chronologically, with short biographical headnotes provided for each. For readers interested in approaching the material topically, Bell furnishes an extended problem-oriented discussion in her introduction, which lists relevant selections from the volume on each particular topic (e.g., "The Education of Women"; "Love and Sex"; "Political Rights and Responsibilities"), along with a comparative discussion. Martha Lee Osborne uses a similar approach in her text *Woman in Western Thought* (Random House, 1979), presenting a succession of philosophers chronologically, supplemented by a syntopicon. While her coverage of the classics is much less complete than Bell's, Osborne follows each selection with a response by a modern or contemporary commentator — including feminist writers such as Rosemary Radford Ruether and Shulamith Firestone — and provides lengthier and more substantive headnotes.

936.* Campbell-Jones, Suzanne, 1941- . **In Habit: A Study of Working Nuns.** New York: Pantheon Books, 1978. 229p. bibliog. index. LC 78-20410. ISBN 0394506669.

Inaugurated by Pope John in 1959, Vatican II spurred momentous changes in the Roman Catholic Church. Campbell-Jones, a British sociologist, explores the impact of Vatican II on women's religious communities. She gained permission to conduct interviews and engage in participant observation in two very different British congregations, a progressive teaching order and a conservative, Franciscan nursing order. She brings to the study not so much feminist questions as an interest in how organizations relying on normative compliance respond to social change. The most dramatic change in recent decades has been the mass exodus from religious communities. According to Gerelyn Hollingsworth, in *Ex-Nuns: Women Who Have Left the Convent* (McFarland, 1985), the number of nuns in American convents decreased from more than 180,000 in 1966 to fewer than 120,000 in 1985. Part I of her slim volume presents excerpts from interviews with ex-nuns; Part II is a very brief overview of American communities. Mary Gilligan Wong gives a personal account of her own transformation from nun to wife, mother, and clinical psychologist in her memoir *Nun* (Harcourt, Brace, Jovanovich, 1983).

937. Christ, Carol P., and Judith Plaskow, eds. **Womanspirit Rising: A Feminist Reader in Religion.** San Francisco: Harper and Row, 1979. 287p. bibliog. pbk. $5.95. LC 78-3363. ISBN 0060613858.

The list of contributors to this anthology reads like a who's who of feminist writers on religion: Rosemary Radford Ruether, Mary Daly, Phyllis Trible, Elisabeth Fiorenza, Elaine Pagels, Rita Gross, Aviva Cantor, Naomi R. Goldenberg, Starhawk, Zsuzsanna E. Budapest, and ten others, including the editors. Christ and Plaskow have assembled key articles from 1960 to 1978, including scholarly theological studies, well-reasoned and passionate opinion pieces, and alternative rituals. The introduction sketches the "creative tensions in feminist theology" (p.15), which the articles — on diverse aspects of religious experience in Christianity, Judaism, and goddess worship — reflect and celebrate.

938. Clark, Linda, 1937- , et al. **Image-Breaking/Image-Building: A Handbook for Creative Worship With Women of Christian Tradition.** New York: Pilgrim Press, 1981. 144p. bibliog. pbk. $7.95. LC 80-28896. ISBN 0829804072.

Christian feminists have struggled to make worship meaningful for women by insisting on nonsexist liturgical language and alternatives to the masculine image of God. Written by Linda Clark, Marian Ronan, and Eleanor Walker, this handbook grows out of an ecumenical seminar. It recommends a variety of exercises to increase religious awareness and to aid participants in envisioning God in new ways. It also presents model worship services, rituals, prayers, and poems, plus essays that were used in or inspired by the workshop. In *Faithful and Fair: Transcending Sexist Language in Worship* (Abingdon Press, 1981), Keith Watkins speaks directly to the planners of worship services, offering justification for language reform and practical examples of changed wording.

939. Curb, Rosemary, 1940- , and Nancy Manahan, 1946- , eds. **Lesbian Nuns: Breaking Silence.** Tallahassee, FL: Naiad Press, 1985. 383p. bibliog. $16.95. LC 84-29594. ISBN 0930044630.

In this unprecedented anthology, editor Rosemary Curb makes the point that many contemporary lesbian-feminist activists are ex-nuns. Going further, she speculates about the parallels between lesbian communities and convents, viewing both as providing "refuge from heterosexuality, Catholic marriage, and exhausting motherhood" (p.xxii). Nearly fifty past and present nuns "break silence" in this book; they are mostly white women, ranging in age from the late twenties to the mid-sixties. Some write anonymously; others are exhuberant about their transformations. The women both exorcise the stifling aspects of cloistered life and celebrate the memory of religious ecstasy and community. A recurrent theme is the pull of "particular friendships," forbidden by the religious orders. In *Immodest Acts* (Oxford University Press, 1986), Stanford historian Judith C. Brown reconstructs the life of a lesbian nun in Renaissance Italy, a woman who was sentenced to prison for both religious crimes and her passionate affair with a sister nun.

940. Daly, Mary. **Pure Lust: Elemental Feminist Philosophy.** Boston: Beacon Press, 1984. 471p. bibliog. index. $18.95. LC 83-71944. ISBN 0807015040.

In *Pure Lust,* "Nag-Gnostic" philosopher and theologian Mary Daly continues the spiraling journey she charted in *Gyn/Ecology: The Metaethics of Radical Feminism* (Beacon Press, 1978). Using dazzling wordplay, Daly reconceptualizes patriarchal categories of knowledge; she reclaims and redefines familiar terms (e.g., lust, hag, spinning, remembering) and invents new words and meanings (e.g., biophilia, bore-ocracy, crone-ology, fembot). The title itself contrasts the traditional deadly sin of phallic lust with an elemental passion for life. Although the book defies summary, one can highlight its more original points: Daly's attack on "sadosociety" and its ascetic legitimators, from Gandhi to Robert Oppenheimer; her study of the symbolic use of the Virgin Mary; her exposing of "plastic or potted passions" (including guilt, anxiety, depression, and resentment) that inhibit true "E-motion"; her naming women as the "touchable caste"; her call to "be-long," "be-friend," and "be-witch." Even critics of Daly's difficult style and her extreme conclusions acknowledge her brilliance and her important contributions to feminist theory.

941. Demetrakopoulos, Stephanie, 1937- . **Listening to Our Bodies: The Rebirth of Feminine Wisdom.** Boston: Beacon Press, 1983. 199p. bibliog. index. $13.50. LC 81-70489. ISBN 0807067040.

Combining interdisciplinary scholarship and personal insights, Demetrakopoulos attempts to reveal the sources of feminine spirituality and "matriarchal wisdom." In Part I, "The Physical Body," she explores the ego formation and early adulthood of women and the spiritual potential of birthing, breast-feeding, aging, and dying. Greek mythology,

Jungian archetypes, and contemporary literature by women figure prominently in Demetrakopoulos's ruminations. In Part II, "The Faces of the Matriarchy," she examines fiction and autobiography by Margaret Laurence, Toni Morrison, and Colette, with particular attention to images of older women. The final group of chapters, "Knowledge From the Bodies of Women," delves into symbolism and occult traditions (especially reincarnation) and posits a distinctly feminine ethic of love and caretaking.

942. Falk, Nancy Auer, and Rita M. Gross, eds. **Unspoken Worlds: Women's Religious Lives in Non-Western Cultures.** San Francisco: Harper and Row, 1980. 292p. bibliog. pbk. $5.95. LC 79-2989. ISBN 0060634928.

Seventeen original case studies by anthropologists, area specialists, and historians document the diversity of women's models of religious expression. The collection balances portraits of women who have experienced extraordinary religious callings—an African diviner, an Indian guru, and Buddhist nuns, for example—with descriptions of everyday religious practices relating to childbirth, menstruation, mourning, and domestic concerns. It also contrasts male-dominated religious systems with egalitarian religious traditions. For a systematic comparative overview, see Denise Lardner Carmody's *Women and World Religions* (Abingdon Press, 1979). Carmody surveys the position of women in Judaism, Christianity, Islam, archaic religions, and the religions of India and East Asia, concluding with her own theological reflections on the data. Penelope Washbourn's *Seasons of Woman* (Harper and Row, 1979) takes a very different angle on women's spiritual experiences across cultures and centuries, blending "song, poetry, ritual, prayer, myth, story" to trace the life cycle and sexuality of women.

943. Fiorenza, Elisabeth Schüssler, 1938- . **Bread Not Stone: The Challenge of Feminist Biblical Interpretation.** Boston: Beacon Press, 1984. 182p. bibliog. index. $17.95. LC 84-14669. ISBN 0807011002.

Acknowledging that many women suffer from "theology anxiety," Fiorenza does not shrink from employing technical terms and concepts to justify the development of a "feminist biblical hermeneutics." Consequently, readers unschooled in traditional academic theology may find her carefully documented arguments difficult at first. Grounding her analysis in the experiences of women and a vision of a "women-church," Fiorenza rejects irredeemably patriarchal passages, yet continues to find in the Bible a "vision of freedom and wholeness" (p.xiii). Fiorenza is one of twelve contributors to *Feminist Interpretation of the Bible,* edited by Letty M. Russell (Westminster Press, 1985). Among the other better-known contributors (academic theologians all) are Rosemary Radford Ruether, Katie Geneva Cannon, Phyllis Trible, and Margaret A. Farley. The anthology traces the development of feminist critical consciousness; offers examples of biblical interpretation on such themes as motherhood, female sexual imagery, and women battering; and sets forth models and methods for scriptural criticism. In another anthology, *Feminist Perspectives on Biblical Scholarship* (Scholars Press, 1985), editor Adela Yarbro Collins gathers eight essays that reveal the creative tension between historical criticism and feminism. Two other recent books on the Bible stand in stark contrast to each other. Phyllis Trible's *Texts of Terror* (Fortress Press, 1984) retells four horrifying Hebrew narratives in which women are banished, raped, killed, and dismembered. In *The Divine Feminine* (Crossroad, 1984), Virginia Ramey Mollenkott celebrates biblical images of God as nursing mother, midwife, homemaker, mother eagle, and Dame Wisdom, among other examples. She points to these female metaphors as a basis for gender-inclusive language in Christian worship.

944.   Fiorenza, Elisabeth Schüssler, 1938- . **In Memory of Her: A Feminist Theological Reconstruction of Christian Origins.** New York: Crossroad, 1983. 351p. bibliog. $22.50. LC 82-19896. ISBN 0824504933.

Fiorenza undertakes a historical-critical reconstruction of women's contributions to early Christianity in light of the new feminist scholarship. An expert in biblical exegesis, she devotes the first three chapters to theoretical and methodological problems in the interpretation of androcentric texts. The remaining chapters describe the Jesus movement within Judaism and the missionary movement in Hellenistic cities as discipleships of equals, gradually modified by the patriarchal Greco-Roman culture of the times. Christian feminism, Fiorenza concludes, calls women to gather in an *ekklēsia* (independent religious assembly) to create a post-patriarchal and ecumenical model for church.

945.   French, Marilyn. **Beyond Power: On Women, Men, and Morals.** New York: Summit Books, 1985. 640p. bibliog. index. $19.95. LC 85-2718. ISBN 0671499599.

In the opinion of several critics, Marilyn French's intellectual reach exceeds her grasp in this panoramic overview of patriarchal values across cultures and millennia. Novelist *(The Bleeding Heart*, Summit Books, 1980) and literary critic (see entry 592), here French dives into anthropology, history, sociology, political science, psychology, and philosophy to ponder the origins of male dominance, the consequences (to women and men) of masculine power from the Stone Age to the present, and the grim totalitarian future that patriarchy's moral path portends. In feminism and "feminine" values French discerns a glimmer of hope for humanity.

946.   Goldenberg, Naomi R. **Changing of the Gods: Feminism and the End of Traditional Religions.** Boston: Beacon Press, 1979. 152p. bibliog. index. pbk. $7.95. LC 78-19602. ISBN 080701110X.

"Every woman working to improve her own position in society or that of women in general is bringing about the end of God," Goldenberg triumphantly announces (p.10). She condemns religious reformists for denying the sexist foundations of Jewish and Christian traditions; explores Freud's criticism of established religion as "father worship"; and draws on Jungian psychology to argue against rigid archetypal (often stereotypical) images of divinity, and for a shared *process* of symbol creation. Patriarchal theology, Goldenberg maintains, is being replaced by multiple approaches to religious image-making: visions of God as woman, adrogyne, or non-oppressive male; feminist witchcraft and goddess worship; mysticism grounded in experience; and dream analysis.

947.   Greaves, Richard L., ed. **Triumph Over Silence: Women in Protestant History.** Westport, CT: Greenwood Press, 1985. 295p. bibliog. index. $35.00. LC 85-961. ISBN 0313247994.

Nine specialists assess the contributions of women to various Protestant denominations. Greaves's introduction notes the scriptural justifications for doctrines limiting female participation in worship, the gradual progress toward ordination of women, and the other vital roles played by church women. The essays, ranging over European and American Protestantism, discuss women in the Lutheran and Calvinist movements; Anabaptist women of the sixteenth century; early English women Nonconformists; sectarian women in England from 1641 to 1700; women and religion in Puritan New England; women in the Methodist movement; Protestant women abolitionists; American Presbyterian women, 1870-1980; and women's past and present role in the public life of the Anglican Communion.

948. Greenberg, Blu, 1936- . **On Women and Judaism: A View From Tradition.** Philadelphia: Jewish Publication Society of America, 1981. 178p. pbk. $5.95. LC 81-11779. ISBN 0827601956.

Greenberg, an Orthodox Jew, tries to conjoin feminist values with the structure of traditional Judaism and the teaching of the *Halakhah* (Jewish religious law). Speaking candidly of her own experiences and conflicted feelings, Greenberg also writes knowledgeably of the Torah and Talmudic interpretations. She tackles the crucial issues of divorce, abortion, working mothers, and women's status in religious observations. Rachel Biale, author of *Women and Jewish Law: An Exploration of Women's Issues in Halakhic Sources* (Schocken Books, 1984), argues that women must take upon themselves the study of the *Halakhah*—which, because of its complex methods of argumentation and the sheer volume of sources and commentaries, is inaccessible to untrained readers. Biale organizes her analysis by topic, treating women and the *mitzvot* (commandments), marriage, divorce, sexuality (within and outside marriage), menstruation, procreation and contraception, abortion, and rape. Each chapter takes a historical approach, highlighting majority and dissenting voices.

949. Harding, Sandra, 1935- , and Merrill B. Hintikka, 1939- , eds. **Discovering Reality: Feminist Perspectives on Epistemology, Metaphysics, Methodology, and Philosophy of Science.** Boston: D. Reidel; distr. Hingham, MA: Kluwer Boston, 1983. 332p. bibliog. index. $54.50. LC 82-16507. ISBN 9027714967.

The sixteen articles in this collection "pursue two complementary projects": the feminist "deconstructive project" of identifying "how masculine perspectives on masculine experience have shaped the most fundamental and most formal aspects of systematic thought in philosophy and in the social and natural sciences"; and the feminist "reconstructive project" of building toward a "more representatively human understanding" (p.x). Several contributors scrutinize the philosophy of Aristotle, the relation of its sexist elements to the whole, and its continuing influence within philosophy. Several others take issue with the claims of the natural and social sciences to be "value-free," and even with the idea that they need be. In other essays, the prevailing adversary method within philosophy comes under attack, and philosophy's famous dualisms (mind/body, reason/sense, etc.) are alleged to derive from masculine infantile experience. Two final essayists call for a new feminist methodology and epistemology. Included in this lineup of well-known feminist scholars are Ruth Hubbard, Janice Moulton, Kathryn Pyne Addelson, Evelyn Fox Keller, Jane Flax, and Nancy Hartsock. In *The Man of Reason: "Male" and "Female" in Western Philosophy* (University of Minnesota Press, 1984), Genevieve Lloyd explores the philosophies of Plato, Aquinas, Descartes, Rousseau, Hegel, and de Beauvoir, among others, to demonstrate that the "maleness of the Man of Reason ... lies deep within our philosophical tradition" (p.ix).

950. Harrison, Beverly Wildung, 1932- . **Making the Connections: Essays in Feminist Social Ethics.** Boston: Beacon Press, 1985. 312p. bibliog. index. $22.95. LC 84-45718. ISBN 0807015245.

Harrison, a theologian, gathers thirteen scholarly essays on both theoretical topics and social issues. Collaborator Carol S. Robb supplies an introduction that situates feminist ethics in the tradition of Christian ethical thought, and praises Harrison's "simultaneous commitments to historical research, social analysis, philosophical integrity, the Christian community and ministry, and a socialist vision of human community" (p.xxi). Robb is herself a contributor to a reader in feminist ethics titled *Women's Consciousness, Women's*

Conscience (Winston Press, 1985), along with Margaret Farley, Judith Plaskow, Elisabeth Schüssler Fiorenza, Rosemary Radford Ruether, Janice Raymond, and others. Barbara Hilkert Andolsen, Christine E. Gudorf, and Mary D. Pellauer are the anthology's editors.

951. Hellman, John, 1940- . **Simone Weil: An Introduction to Her Thought.** Philadelphia: Fortress Press, 1984. 111p. bibliog. index. pbk. $6.95. LC 83-48917. ISBN 0800617630.

Everyone who writes of Simone Weil (1909-1943) acknowledges the impossibility of studying her works separately from her life. Ascetic mystic, political philosopher, social activist, and member of the French Resistance, Weil published no books in her lifetime. She left behind a group of essays, letters, and notebooks, and the legend of a woman so desiring to share in human suffering that she left the academy to labor in factories, begged for dangerous wartime assignments, and starved herself to death at the age of thirty-four. Hellman's readable overview situates Weil's evolving religious and political ideas in the context of her life and times. John M. Dunaway's *Simone Weil* (Twayne, 1984) acquaints the nonspecialist with Weil's "holistic" vision as revealed in her writings. The eight contributors to *Simone Weil: Interpretations of a Life,* edited by George Abbot White (University of Massachusetts Press, 1981), present fresh insights that readers already familiar with Weil will appreciate.

952. Heschel, Susannah, ed. **On Being a Jewish Feminist: A Reader.** New York: Schocken Books, 1983. 288p. bibliog. $20.00. LC 81-16543. ISBN 0805238379.

Part One of this anthology, "Old Myths and Images," examines traditional views of women—in Jewish law and worship, within the family, and within Jewish culture—and contrasts these images to the reality of Jewish women's lives. Part Two, "Forging New Identities," presents essays by and about women who have moved beyond the stereotypes to participate in services, for example, or to seek a place for single women and lesbians in the family-oriented Jewish community. Part Three, "Creating a Feminist Theology of Judaism," goes to the root of Jewish religion, liturgy, and ritual. Reviewers have consistently singled out a few of the twenty-four contributions for particular praise, among them Cynthia Ozick's "Notes Toward Finding the Right Question" and Judith Plaskow's response, "The Right Question Is Theological"; and Rachel Adler's classic, "The Jew Who Wasn't There." Heschel's introduction surveys the challenges feminism poses to Judaism and the varied reactions of the major U.S. denominations (Orthodox, Reform, Conservative, Reconstructionist). Heschel situates women's issues within larger theological quandaries created by opposing forces of modernity and Jewish tradition.

953. Heyward, Carter. **Our Passion for Justice: Images of Power, Sexuality, and Liberation.** New York: Pilgrim Press, 1984. 264p. bibliog. pbk. $10.95. LC 84-4936. ISBN 0829807055.

Heyward, among the first women ordained in the Episcopal church, speaks to readers "as a woman, a lesbian feminist, a socialist, and a Christian priest" (p.230). She composed the essays, sermons, lectures, and liturgical poetry in this collection between 1977 and 1983; their chronological presentation highlights the development of her political and theological views. Many of the pieces treat the theme of sexuality, which Heyward sees as central to a constructive feminist faith. Others discuss women in the priesthood, the church's response to homosexuality, Latin American liberation theology, U.S. involvement in El Salvador, and the limits of liberal feminism. Heyward addresses head-on the problems of racism, anti-Semitism, misogyny, class exploitation, homophobia, and cultural imperialism. A number of pioneering feminist theologians are now bringing out collections of their writings. Nelle Morton, for example, gathers ten insightful essays on feminist imagery, consciousness raising, and other topics in *The Journey Is Home* (Beacon Press, 1985).

954. Hill, Patricia. **The World Their Household: The American Woman's Foreign Mission Movement and Cultural Transformation, 1870-1920.** Ann Arbor: University of Michigan Press, 1985. 231p. bibliog. index. $19.50. LC 84-13206. ISBN 0472100556.

"The interdenominational woman's foreign mission movement," Hill notes, "... was substantially larger than any of the other mass woman's movements of the nineteenth century" (p.3). It involved thousands of women in the field, and hundreds of thousands at home in the United States. Opening with a look at images of missionaries in popular novels of the period, Hill proceeds to document the rise and decline of women's foreign mission societies. By analyzing the changing rhetorical content of *Woman's Work for Women, Heathen Woman's Friend,* and similar magazines, Hill sheds light on the role the foreign mission movement "played in the cultural imperialism that aimed at transforming the non-Western world and its [the movement's] symbiotic relationship with changing cultural paradigms of ideal womanhood in America" (p.3). Using the private papers of forty women, archival records, and photographs, Jane Hunter concentrates on the experiences of women missionaries in turn-of-the-century China. In *The Gospel of Gentility* (Yale University Press, 1984), she examines the lives and motives of both married and single missionaries, their status as Westerners in a colonized society, and their impact on Chinese women students and converts.

955. Iglehart, Hallie. **Womanspirit: A Guide to Woman's Wisdom.** San Francisco: Harper and Row, 1983. 176p. bibliog. pbk. $6.68. LC 83-47724. ISBN 0060640898.

Iglehart's personal spiritual quest has led her to a synthesis of feminism and spirituality that she terms "Womanspirit." In this warmly encouraging book, Iglehart shares her experiences and suggests techniques for meditation, dreamwork, mythmaking, healing, and creating rituals. Diane Mariechild takes a similar approach in *Mother Wit: A Feminist Guide to Psychic Development* (Crossing Press, 1981), with additional attention to psychic communication, reincarnation, witchcraft, and psychic skills for children.

956. Jagger, Alison M. **Feminist Politics and Human Nature.** Totowa, NJ: Rowman and Allanheld, 1983. 408p. bibliog. index. $24.95. LC 83-3402. ISBN 084767181X.

Jaggar offers a systematic exposition of four feminist paradigms—liberal, Marxist, radical, and socialist—and of their conceptions of human nature and politics. Jaggar's intent is not simply to clarify but also to evaluate: she argues from the outset that "socialist feminism is the most adequate of the feminist theories formulated to date" (p.9). While feminists of every stripe are likely to find something to disagree with in this work, Jaggar's key contribution lies in her careful demonstration of the fact that "organized feminism has not spoken with a single voice" (p.4). Construing feminism as a single, consistent belief system is in fact a weakness of several other recent works. In *The Sceptical Feminist* (Routledge and Kegan Paul, 1980), Janet Radcliffe Richards subjects the ideas and slogans of "feminists" (or even more vaguely, "some feminists") to unrelenting criticism, arguing for the paramount importance of *reason* against what she perceives as "*a new breed of anti-rational feminist*" (p.16). Richards distinguishes between what she sees as feminist and nonfeminist issues in discussions of nature, freedom, sexual justice, femininity, work, fashion, abortion and contraception, and motherhood. In *Equality and the Rights of Women* (Cornell University Press, 1980), Elizabeth H. Wolgast seemingly equates "feminism" with egalitarianism, arguing that equality is an inadequate concept to undergird women's rights, since men and women are manifestly different. Wolgast suggests we replace the notion of strict equality with a combination of equal rights and special rights. Two other works pursuing similar lines of thought are *Women's Choices: Philosophical Problems Facing Feminism,* by Mary Midgley and Judith Hughes (St. Martin's Press, 1983), and *Women, Reason and Nature: Some Philosophical Problems With Feminism*, by Carol McMillan (Princeton University Press, 1982).

957.   Jewett, Paul King. **The Ordination of Women: An Essay on the Office of Christian Ministry.** Grand Rapids, MI: Eerdmans, 1980. 148p. bibliog. index. pbk. $5.95. LC 80-15644. ISBN 0802818501.

Jewett, a professor of systematic theology, presents a scholarly argument for the presence of women in the Christian ministry. He states, and then responds to, the major rationales used to exclude women: women's own nature; the nature of the ministerial office; and, most crucially, the supposed masculinity of God.

958.   Johnson, Sonia. **From Housewife to Heretic.** New York: Doubleday, 1981. 406p. index. pbk. $8.95. LC 82-45960. ISBN 0385174942.

As the title suggests, this is a story of transformation. Excommunicated from the Mormon church in 1979 for her feminist views, Sonia Johnson rails against the church strictures (especially its opposition to the Equal Rights Amendment), against her former husband, and against patriarchy at large. The role of heretic seems congenial to her, however; her ordeal with the church has resulted in finding "in myself untapped sources of energy and strength" (p.387). Having earned a doctorate in education and gone on to become the 1984 presidential candidate of the Citizens' Party, Johnson lectures widely on the topic of her uneasy relationship with Mormonism and her conversion to radical feminism. She professes to remain an adherent to the essential tenets of Mormonism, and as such, finds herself facing the theoretical dilemma common to devout Catholic and Jewish women: how to reconcile political convictions with patriarchally defined matters of dogma and doctrine.

959.   Lehman, Edward C., Jr. **Women Clergy: Breaking Through Gender Barriers.** New Brunswick, NJ: Transaction Books, 1985. 307p. bibliog. $24.95. LC 84-5644. ISBN 0887380719.

Lehman, a sociologist, surveyed nearly three thousand laypersons and clergy in the United Presbyterian church on their attitudes toward women in the ministry and supplemented this data with interviews. Sex discrimination and its causes are carefully documented, but, encouragingly, Lehman discovers that personal contact with women clergy noticeably increases church members' receptivity. Lehman does a superb job of explaining the sociopsychological concepts on which his arguments hinge, and of demystifying his analytic methods. Sociologists Jackson W. Carroll, Barbara Hargrove, and Adair T. Lummis have also studied the recent dramatic rise in the numbers of women clergy. In *Women of the Cloth* (Harper and Row, 1983), they compare the experiences of male and female pastors in nine leading Protestant denominations in the United States. The authors detail their subjects' family backgrounds, their experiences in seminaries and in the job market, their lives as parish ministers, their interpersonal relationships on the job, and their difficulties in balancing personal lives and pastoral commitment. Thirteen women ministers (and one dual-career clergy couple) discuss the role of women in church work and share their personal and professional experiences in *Women Ministers*, edited by Judith L. Weidman (2nd ed., Harper and Row, 1985).

960. Maitland, Sara, 1950- . **A Map of the New Country: Women and Christianity.** Boston: Routledge and Kegan Paul, 1983. 218p. bibliog. index. pbk. $8.95. LC 82-13142. ISBN 0710093268.

From her Anglican perspective, Maitland charts the shifting terrain of modern Christianity for feminists who have not broken with the faith. The opening chapter traces the historical struggles over women's role in the churches, and subsequent chapters explore laywomen's religious organizations, communities of nuns, the issue of ordination, women's place in denominational bureaucracies, and the movement toward gender-inclusive worship. Judith L. Weidman's anthology *Christian Feminism: Visions of a New Humanity* (Harper and Row, 1984) likewise surveys theological and practical feminist concerns within Christianity and presents Christian feminist viewpoints on sexuality, work, and social change. The contributors are Rosemary Radford Ruether, Elisabeth Schüssler Fiorenza, Rita Nakashima Brock, Letty M. Russell, Nanette M. Roberts, Clare B. Fischer, Beverly Wildung Harrison, and Constance F. Parvey. Other recent books by Christian women include: *Woman: Survivor in the Church,* by Joan Ohanneson, a collection of inspirational essays written from a Roman Catholic vantage point (Winston Press, 1980); and *Faith, Feminism, and the Christ,* Patricia Wilson-Kastner's reconstruction of Christology and the doctrine of the Trinity (Fortress Press, 1983).

961. Massey, Marilyn Chapin, 1942- . **Feminine Soul: The Fate of an Ideal.** Boston: Beacon Press, 1985. 219p. bibliog. index. $22.95. LC 84-28312. ISBN 0807067202.

Massey analyzes in detail three German stories from the late eighteenth and early nineteenth centuries that both expressed and influenced the romantic ideology of a distinct, spiritually superior female soul. Turning to present-day feminism, Massey uses a historical/literary framework to explore the polarization between those who celebrate women's unique spiritual and moral character (among them Adrienne Rich, Mary Daly, and some French writers) and those who reject such beliefs as apolitical, even reactionary. Drawing on de Beauvoir and Marx, her conclusion speaks of a "divinizing mirror," in which God has been reflected as the "essential" or best qualities of *men*. Women-centered feminists, Massey declares, view the wholeness of women in their divinizing mirror, not merely the image of the good mother, to discover "a completely new, transformative ethic" (p.183).

962. Ochs, Carol. **Women and Spirituality.** Totowa, NJ: Rowman and Allanheld, 1983. 156p. bibliog. index. pbk. $9.95. LC 83-3397. ISBN 0847672328.

The Western spiritual tradition, Ochs believes, can and should be transformed by women seeking fulfillment in their own, real-world experience of mothering. Ochs challenges the common image of the spiritual quest as a lonely, linear journey, suggesting that women's spirituality is process-oriented, rather than goal-oriented. She reinterprets the notions of circumstance, conflict, suffering, guilt, and death (aspects of existence that make an other-worldly spirituality attractive) and adds to them the positive women's "boundary situations" of love, unity, joy, contribution, and birth. The Old Testament characters Hagar and Leah serve as role models. Although her vision of mothering is idealized, Ochs's emphasis on everyday experience and relationships as the source of spiritual development is provocative.

963. Ochshorn, Judith, 1928- . **The Female Experience and the Nature of the Divine.** Bloomington: Indiana University Press, 1981. 269p. bibliog. index. $17.50. LC 81-47012. ISBN 025331898X.

Using ancient and biblical texts, Ochshorn documents a dramatic shift in religious ideas about gender as Near Eastern civilization passed from a polytheistic outlook to a monotheistic one. Her evidence points to widespread participation by both women and men in early polytheistic cults, and to a remarkable lack of stereotyped sex roles among the deities. Gods and goddesses shared many of the same attributes and exercised equivalent power. The active sexuality of goddesses (and their priestesses) was central to polytheistic religions. Ochshorn finds that the Bible, by contrast, exaggerates the differences between the sexes and conveys an ambivalent and fearful attitude toward women's sexuality. Although she stops short of concluding that polytheistic societies were more egalitarian than the monotheistic societies that evolved later, Ochshorn does suggest that, contrary to popular assumption, gender and power have not been inextricably linked throughout cultural history.

964. Olson, Carl, ed. **The Book of the Goddess, Past and Present: An Introduction to Her Religion.** New York: Crossroad, 1983. 261p. bibliog. $14.95. LC 82-23606. ISBN 0824505662.

The seventeen essays gathered here—from Anne L. Barstow's "The Prehistoric Goddess" to Carol P. Christ's "Symbols of Goddess and God in Feminist Theology"—introduce Western readers schooled in monotheism to the many manifestations of goddess worship. Judith Ochshorn, Christine R. Downing, and Rita M. Gross are among the contributors. Historical and cross-cultural, the collection treats female deities as portrayed in Greek, Egyptian, Roman, Hebrew, Christian, Hindu, Chinese, Japanese, African, and Native American sources.

965. Phillips, John A. **Eve: A History of an Idea.** San Francisco: Harper and Row, 1984. 200p. bibliog. index. $12.95. LC 83-48424. ISBN 0060665521.

"If one would understand Woman, one must come to terms with Eve," Phillips asserts (p.xiii). For the myth of Eve "remains deeply imbedded in both male and female ideas about the nature and destiny of women, and the attitudes it has engendered are embodied in the psychology, laws, religious life, and social structures of the Western world—not to mention the most intimate of human activities" (p.172). Illustrating his survey with black-and-white reproductions of images of Eve in art, Phillips traces the treatment of Eve in Western culture. He compares Eve's tale to Middle Eastern creation myths and the Roman tale of Pandora; explores the theological and psychoanalytic interpretations of Eve's sin; and discusses her identification with the Virgin Mary and "heretical Eves" in Shi'ite Islam, Jewish mysticism, and Gnosticism. He concludes by positing the future meanings of Eve for religion and feminism.

966. Porterfield, Amanda, 1947- . **Feminine Spirituality in America: From Sarah Edwards to Martha Graham.** Philadelphia: Temple University Press, 1980. 238p. bibliog. index. $16.50. LC 80-12116. ISBN 0877221758.

Examining the lives of exemplary women and the images of women in eighteenth- and nineteenth-century fiction and poetry, Porterfield traces a uniquely American "domestic consciousness" linked to spiritual transformation and beauty. "The receptivity to change and the capacities to see one's environment as a home and oneself as a maker of a home characterize a tradition of spirituality that has played a powerful role in the history of

American culture," she states (p.4). Sarah Edwards, Victoria Woodhull, Elizabeth Seton, Catharine Beecher, Emily Dickinson, Mary Baker Eddy, Jane Addams, and Martha Graham are some of the women whose lives and works express a spiritual transformation.

967.   Ruether, Rosemary Radford. **Sexism and God-talk: Toward a Feminist Theology.** Boston: Beacon Press, 1983. 289p. bibliog. index. $18.95. LC 82-72502. ISBN 0807011045.

A working paradigm for a feminist theology emerges from Ruether's wide-ranging study. Grounding her analysis in women's experience, Ruether addresses the major themes of Christian theology — images of the divine; nature and creation; the anthropology of sex differences; Christology; Mariology; the consciousness of evil; ministry and community; and eschatology. Her brilliant insights are drawn from "usable traditions" culled from scriptures of the Old and New Testaments; marginalized or counter-cultural Christian traditions, such as Gnosticism and Quakerism; dominant classical theology (Orthodox, Catholic, and Protestant); non-Christian Near Eastern and Greco-Roman religions and philosophy; and the critical post-Christian world views of liberalism, romanticism, and Marxism. All these traditions are sexist, she admits, but they provide "intimations of alternatives" (p.22). From such alternative traditions Ruether has assembled an anthology of texts and interpretive essays titled *Womanguides: Readings Toward a Feminist Theology* (Beacon Press, 1985) as a first step toward a new religious canon.

968.   Ruether, Rosemary Radford, and Rosemary Skinner Keller, eds. **Women and Religion in America.** San Francisco: Harper and Row. 2v. bibliog. index. LC 80-8346. Vol. 1: 1981; pbk. $10.95; ISBN 0060668288. Vol. 2: 1983; $23.99; ISBN 0060668326.

The first two volumes of this projected triology introduce readers to women's religious experiences in nineteenth-century America (vol. 1) and during colonial and revolutionary periods (vol. 2). Each chapter presents a short interpretive essay, a handful of illustrations or photographs, and about a dozen primary documents. Revivalism, utopian movements, the leadership of nuns in immigrant Catholicism, Jewish women's encounters with American culture, the struggle for the right to preach, laywomen in the Protestant tradition, and social reform movements are all covered in the first volume. Volume Two is notable for its attention to American Indian, Spanish, French, and black traditions in the New World, as well as the more-often-studied Puritan, Wesleyan, and sectarian Protestant influences. Women of New England and women of the South are accorded separate chapters. The twelve scholarly articles in *Women in American Religion,* edited by Janet Wilson James (University of Pennsylvania Press, 1980), nicely complement the original sources spotlighted by Ruether and Keller. Ranging widely over the experiences of Protestant, Catholic, and Jewish women, the contributors examine both women's participation in religion (as churchgoers, missionaries, nuns, and ministers) and the ideas about women embodied in religious thinking.

969.   Ruether, Rosemary Radford, and Eleanor McLaughlin, eds. **Women of Spirit: Female Leadership in the Jewish and Christian Traditions.** New York: Simon and Schuster, 1979. 400p. bibliog. index. pbk. $10.95. LC 78-11995. ISBN 0671228439.

Thirteen essays in this anthology trace women's influential roles in the Church from the beginning of the Christian era to the present. A single essay treats women in Judaism. Taken together, these scholarly pieces demonstrate a long history of female leadership in the Western religious tradition. Knowledge of women's "alternative tradition," Ruether and McLaughlin claim, can be used "to reshape and enlarge the vision and life of the church today" (p.28). Although considerably narrower in its scope, Leonard I. Sweet's *The*

Minister's Wife (Temple University Press, 1982) convincingly documents one aspect of women's historical contributions to Christianity. Sweet focuses on nineteenth-century evangelicalism, digging deeply into both primary and secondary sources to derive a typology of pastors' wives. His four models, illustrated with case histories, are the Companion, the Sacrificer, the Assistant, and the Partner.

970. Schaef, Anne Wilson. **Women's Reality: An Emerging Female System in a White Male Society.** New ed. Minneapolis: Winston Press, 1985. 169p. pbk. $7.95. LC 80-53560. ISBN 0866837531.

A practicing psychotherapist, Anne Wilson Schaef divides society into the White Male System (which is easily mistaken for reality) and the Female System. She delineates the strategies women employ to cope with the "original sin of being born female," the "stoppers" used to keep women in their place (e.g., guilt), and the rage that women experience as a result of being branded inferior. Further, Schaef explicates the opposing male and female conceptions of time, relationships, power, communication, morality, and other key constructs, culminating in a description of the White Male System as dualistic and the Female System as grounded in paradox. A final chapter introduces the tenets of "female system theology." Sprinkled with anecdotes — and with frequent admonitions that neither system is inherently "right" — *Women's Reality* has touched a responsive chord among general readers and therapists.

971. Schneider, Susan Weidman. **Jewish and Female: Choices and Changes in Our Lives Today.** New York: Simon and Schuster, 1984. 640p. bibliog. index. $19.95. LC 84-5344. ISBN 0671421034.

As editor of *Lilith* (see entry 1183), Schneider is well situated to survey the changes in Jewish women's lives since the advent of the women's movement. Her encyclopedic volume is divided into three major sections: "Women and Religious Judaism"; "Defining and Transforming Our Relationships"; and "Power and Participation in the Jewish Community." Throughout the book, Schneider highlights the diversity of Jewish women's experiences. The closing chapter speaks of the difficulty of "reconciling Jewish and female" in order "to create a community that values all Jews, women as much as men" (p.513). Richly illustrated with black-and-white photographs, and drawing frequently on first-person accounts, the book makes enjoyable reading but also has significant reference value. The text is liberally peppered with the names and addresses of resource organizations, and an eighty-page "Jewish Women's Networking Directory" is appended. Using the directory, one can locate women rabbis and cantors, women's prayer and study groups, Jewish family service agencies, and a host of specialized support and advocacy organizations.

972. **Spinning a Sacred Yarn: Women Speak From the Pulpit.** New York: Pilgrim Press, 1982. 230p. pbk. $8.95. LC 82-569. ISBN 0829806040.

Thirty-six sermons — by Protestant, Catholic, and Jewish women — are gathered in this inspirational collection. While some address traditional religious themes, many others clearly evince a woman's (even a feminist's) perspective. The titles are indicative: "The Wait of Pregnancy," "Women: Living Wholly/Holy in a Fractured World," "It's Hard to Sing the Song of Deborah," and "Chafing Dish, Apron Strings," for example. This is a unique and multidenominational sourcebook of women's spirituality.

973.   Spretnak, Charlene, 1946- , ed. **The Politics of Women's Spirituality: Essays on the Rise of Spiritual Power Within the Feminist Movement.** Garden City, NY: Anchor Books, 1982. 590p. bibliog. pbk. $12.95. LC 80-2876. ISBN 0385177704.

This reader in the diverse roots and manifestations of "postpatriarchal" holistic spirituality reveals a powerful facet of contemporary feminism. Spretnak, who as editor provides a provocative introduction, afterword, and headnotes, sums up the basic premise of the volume: "Both politics and spirituality are concerned with power" (p.349). Many of the forty-plus pieces gathered here are feminist classics by such visionary thinkers as Merlin Stone, Adrienne Rich, Starhawk, Carol P. Christ, Phyllis Chesler, Gloria Steinem, Judy Chicago, Judy Grahn, Mary Daly, E. M. Broner, and Robin Morgan. Nearly half the contributions, however, appear for the first time in print. The essays grouped in Part One, "Discovering a History of Power," document prepatriarchal goddess worship and meditate on the myths of strong and wise women—from ancient amazons and Chinese swordsmen to the comic-book heroine Wonder Woman. Part Two, "Manifesting Personal Power," explores consciousness-raising, spiritual renewal, witchcraft, and ritual, as well as the expression of female spirituality in the martial arts, healing, theater, art, fiction, and other arenas. Part Three offers two sections, one consisting of theoretical pieces on "The Unity of Politics and Spirituality" and the other describing "Applications of Spirituality as a Political Force." Among the examples of spiritual practice are ecological activism, anti-nuclear work, counseling survivors of sexual assault, and countering the Christian right-wing backlash against feminism.

974.   Starhawk. **Dreaming the Dark: Magic, Sex, & Politics.** Boston: Beacon Press, 1982. 242p. bibliog. $15.95. LC 81-70485. ISBN 0807010006.

Self-avowed witch, feminist, and anti-nuclear activist, Starhawk delineates the woman-centered principle of "immanence" or "power-from-within" as symbolized in the goddess and manifested in rituals, organizational structures, and "magic." Starhawk's spiritual vision is inextricably entwined with political and ecological protest. An appendix titled "The Burning Times" links the persecution of witches during the sixteenth and seventeenth centuries to land enclosures, the "expropriation of knowledge" by physicians, and the triumph of a mechanistic world view. Starhawk's earlier writings include *The Spiral Dance: A Rebirth of the Ancient Religion of the Great Goddess* (Harper and Row, 1979).

975.   Welch, Sharon D. **Communities of Resistance and Solidarity: A Feminist Theology of Liberation.** Maryknoll, NY: Orbis Books, 1985. 102p. bibliog. index. pbk. $7.95. LC 85-4809. ISBN 0883442043.

As a white, middle-class, American woman, theologian Sharon Welch identifies herself as both oppressor and oppressed. In this thoughtful study, she draws on the ideas of Michel Foucault and other contemporary thinkers, erecting a complex critique of Christian theology in remarkably understandable language. For additional insights into liberation theology, see *The Strength of the Weak: Toward a Christian Feminist Identity,* the diverse and provocative translated writings of German theologian Dorothee Soelle (Westminster Press, 1984).

SCIENCE, MATHEMATICS,
AND TECHNOLOGY

The first volume of *Women's Studies* did not devote a chapter to science and technology because feminist scholarship in the seventies had made few inroads into the male-dominated scientific disciplines. Today, by contrast, there is a sizeable and thought-provoking body of literature on women and science. The books described in this chapter offer several angles on the subject: biographies of influential women researchers; surveys of women's roles in the scientific establishment; critiques of scientific theories about gender; and inquiries into the effects of technological change on women's lives. Coverage of the biological sciences overlaps the Medicine chapter. Reference works on women's studies in science and technology are still scant. In addition to the bibliography in *Biological Woman—The Convenient Myth* (edited by Ruth Hubbard, et al. [see entry 983]), *Women in the Scientific Search* (see entry 910) is a useful source.

976.   Arditti, Rita, 1934- , et al., eds. **Test-Tube Women: What Future for Motherhood?** Boston: Pandora Press, 1984. 482p. bibliog. index. LC 84-4282. ISBN 0863580300.
This heft anthology examines the ethical, political and legal implications of reproductive technologies, raising unsettling questions about current medical practice and scientific research on conception and birth. Under the editorship of Rita Arditti, Renate Duelli Klein, and Shelley Minden, thirty-two authors contribute perspectives on contraception, *in vitro* fertilization, genetic engineering, surrogate mothering, sex selection, abortion, sterilization, and other subjects. The writing is nontechnical, the tone decidedly feminist, the information often alarming. Gena Corea furthers the feminist critique of reproductive technologies in her full-length analysis, *The Mother Machine: Reproductive Technologies from Artificial Insemination to Artificial Wombs* (Harper and Row, 1985). Corea contrasts the glowing promises of the "pharmocrats" to the underlying potential for stricter social control of women; she links her empirical evidence to Mary O'Brien's theory of reproduction (see entry 1135). *Test-Tube Women* and *The Mother Machine* sound harsh warnings about the not-so-distant medical future, while an earlier work—*Birth Control and Controlling Birth: Women-Centered Perspectives* (Humana Press, 1980)—looks closely at technologies already in use, including birth control methods, abortions, Depo-Provera (a long-term, injected contraceptive drug), surgical sterilization, electronic fetal monitoring, and childbirth techniques. The volume, edited by Helen B. Holmes, Betty B. Hoskins, and Michael Gross, presents conference papers, responses, and transcripts of discussions.

977.   Bleier, Ruth, 1923- . **Science and Gender: A Critique of Biology and Its Theories on Women.** Elmsford, NY: Pergamon Press, 1984. 220p. bibliog. index. $25.00. LC 83-22054. ISBN 0080309720.

Bleier, a neurophysiologist and professor of women's studies, takes issue with theories of biological determinism—theories that postulate a genetic, evolutionary, and hormonal basis for sex differences, and hence explain as "natural" the inferior status of women. She convincingly illustrates how social values and political biases underlie "objective" scientific ideas and practice. She denounces in particular sociobiology, as propounded by E. O. Wilson and his followers, for the weaknesses of its basic premises and for its tainted methodologies. The influence of environmental factors on brain anatomy and development, the Man-the-Hunter theory of human cultural evolution, the presumption of the universal subordination of women, and the ideological control of sexuality are among the other subjects Bleier tackles. Her concluding chapter, "Patriarchal Science, Feminist Visions," asserts that the very concepts of objectivity and dualism—the keystones of traditional scientific thinking—must be overthrown and replaced with modes of truth-seeking that are change-oriented, contextual, and interactive. In *Myths of Gender: Biological Theories About Women and Men* (Basic Books, 1985), developmental geneticist Anne Fausto-Sterling similarly questions the validity of biological explanations of sex differences. *Women, Biology, and Public Policy* (Sage Publications, 1985), a collection of ten articles edited by Virginia Sapiro, examines the implications of recent debate about sociobiology for public policy concerning sex education, abortion, occupational safety and health, crime, and military recruitment of women, among other issues.

978.   D'Onofrio-Flores, Pamela M., and Sheila M. Pfafflin, eds. **Scientific-Technological Change and the Role of Women in Development.** Boulder, CO: Westview Press, 1982. 206p. bibliog. index. $29.00. LC 81-10463. ISBN 0865311455.

Scientific "advances" and Western-style technological "progress" often disrupt the lives and diminish the status of women in developing countries. Prepared by women scholars and policy analysts for the 1979 U. N. Conference on Science and Technology for Development, the six papers in this collection document women's exclusion from decision-making in development processes, and explore women's roles in both agricultural and industrial economies. *Women and Technological Change in Developing Countries* (Westview Press, 1981) complements the work of D'Onofrio-Flores and Pfafflin. Editors Roslyn Dauber and Melinda L. Cain gather fifteen papers from a session on women and technology held at the 1979 annual meeting of the American Association for the Advancement of Science. The papers develop theoretical approaches to the study of women and technology, present case studies on the impact of economic development on women, and offer reflections on policy implications. "Women must be allowed to define their own needs," the editors conclude. "If the developed world wishes to act as a partner in development, it must learn to listen to those who traditionally have had the least access to sources of power" (p.255).

979.   Easlea, Brian. **Fathering the Unthinkable: Masculinity, Scientists, and the Nuclear Arms Race.** London: Pluto Press, 1983. 230p. bibliog. index. pbk. £5.95. LC 83-126528. ISBN 086104391X.

A number of feminist thinkers and peace activists view the "nuclear mentality" as a reflection of male values taken to their extremes. Easlea's analysis, grounded in the philosophy and history of science, is surely the most sustained treatment of this theme to date. Starting with Mary Shelley's *Frankenstein*, presented as the paradigmatic tale of masculine science penetrating the secrets of female nature, Easlea offers a socio-historical reading of scientific practice that looks closely at male/female imagery in the language of prominent scientists. *Fathering the Unthinkable* focuses on nuclear weapons technology, an area relatively unexplored by feminist scholars; students seeking a more wide-ranging critique of the male culture of science may prefer Easlea's lengthier work, *Science and Sexual Oppression: Patriarchy's Confrontation with Woman and Nature* (Weidenfeld and Nicolson, 1981), and Carolyn Merchant's *The Death of Nature* (see entry 1127).

980. Fox, Lynn H., 1944- , et al. **Women and the Mathematical Mystique: Proceedings of the Eighth Annual Hyman Blumberg Symposium on Research in Early Childhood Education.** Baltimore: Johns Hopkins University Press, 1980. Now available from Books-on-Demand. 211p. bibliog. index. $55.80. LC 79-3655. ISBN 031720484X.

By the seventh grade, striking differences between the sexes emerge in measures of mathematics achievement and enjoyment, lending credence to the "mathematical mystique"—the belief that mathematics is a masculine domain. Fox and her co-editors, Linda Brody and Dianne Tobin, present twelve papers from a 1976 symposium that bypass questions of biological sex differences to focus on socio-environmental influences. Parents, teachers, peers, and school policy all reinforce traditional notions about girls' inferior math ability. The summary chapter suggests directions for further research and recommends strategies for change that include remediation, intervention, and prevention. In a related book, *Encouraging Girls in Mathematics: The Problem and the Solution* (Abt Books, 1980), Lorelei R. Brush zeroes in on student attitudes to determine why girls avoid elective math courses in high school. After reporting on her longitudinal study of nearly two thousand sixth-, ninth-, and twelfth-graders, she proposes a multi-faceted solution that involves livelier and more meaningful classes, career-focused programs, new courses, and four years of required mathematics.

981. Gornick, Vivian. **Women in Science: Portraits From a World in Transition.** New York: Simon and Schuster, 1983. 172p. bibliog. index. $15.95. LC 83-4742. ISBN 067141738X.

In this self-described work of "impressionistic journalism" (p.21), Gornick details the lives and feelings of contemporary women scientists. She interviewed over a hundred women engaged in basic research, women ranging in age from twenty-four to seventy-eight, working in a variety of settings, and possessing a wide range of personal and class backgrounds. Gornick takes pains to convey the intense dedication and intellectual excitement they share. An inspirational thread runs through the interviewees' revelatory tales of discrimination in graduate school and on the job, struggles to combine marriage and motherhood with a scientific career, and the impact of feminism on their lives.

982. Haas, Violet B., and Carolyn Cummings Perrucci, eds. **Women in Scientific and Engineering Professions.** Ann Arbor: University of Michigan Press, 1984. 246p. bibliog. index. $24.00. LC 83-23575. ISBN 0472100491.

Several books on women's status and opportunities in the sciences have emerged from benchmark conferences. This volume, which collects papers from a conference held at Purdue in 1981, provides an excellent overview. Its thirteen contributors (among them Betty M. Vetter, Jewel Plummer Cobb, and Donna J. Haraway) offer personal, pragmatic, and theoretical perspectives on the issues facing women scientists and engineers. Part I features cross-cultural and historical data on women and professional employment, as well as occupational forecasts and strategies to increase female involvement in the sciences.

Part II focuses on academe, while Part III assesses alternative science-based careers. Part IV offers a taste of feminist thinking on math anxiety, women engineers in history, male models of scientific achievement, and the intersection of class, race, and sex with the politics of knowledge. Anne M. Briscoe and Sheila M. Pfafflin, editors of *Expanding the Role of Women in the Sciences* (New York Academy of Sciences, 1979), bring together thirty-three contributions by scientists and policy-makers in government, higher education, and industry, originating from a 1978 conference co-sponsored by the Association for Women in Science and the New York Academy of Sciences. The volume is no. 323 in the Academy's *Annals*. *Women and Minorities in Science: Strategies for Increasing Participation* (Westview Press, 1982), edited by Sheila M. Humphreys, draws on presentations made at the 1980 meeting of the American Association for the Advancement of Science and covers high school curricula, college-level recruitment and retention, career conferences, and more. In sharp contrast to these three titles — all of which document pervasive sexism — in *Fair Science: Women in the Scientific Community* (Free Press, 1979), sociologist Jonathan Cole concludes that "the academic scientific community distributes its resources and rewards in an equitable fashion" (p.300), and that individual recognition and reward are based purely on productivity, quality of work, and reputation among peers. Feminist critics counter that Cole's empirical measures of a scientist's status merely incorporate the effects of sexist education and employment practices.

983. Hubbard, Ruth, et al, eds. **Biological Woman — The Convenient Myth: A Collection of Feminist Essays and a Comprehensive Bibliography.** Cambridge, MA: Schenkman, 1982. 376p. bibliog. $18.95. LC 82-10781. ISBN 0870737023.

Joint editors Ruth Hubbard, Mary Sue Henifin, and Barbara Fried undertake to debunk some of the myths about women and their bodies — ideas grounded, they argue, in the supreme myth of scientific objectivity. Six articles are reprinted from a previous collection, *Women Look at Biology Looking at Women* (Schenkman, 1979): Ruth Hubbard's critique of evolutionary theory, "Have Only Men Evolved?"; Barbara Fried's "Boys Will Be Boys Will Be Boys," a study of sex and gender in scientific language; "Taking the Men Out of Menopause," by psychologist Marlyn Grossman and sociologist Pauline Bart; Datha Clapper Brack's historical essay, "Displaced — The Midwife by the Male Physician"; Mary Roth Walsh's "The Quirls of a Woman's Brain," a study of the exclusion of women from medical schools; and Naomi Weisstein's autobiographical (and marvelously sarcastic) "Adventures of a Woman in Science." New articles address lesbianism, occupational hazards, sterilization abuse, the menstrual cycle, black women's health, and the interaction of culture and biology. The volume concludes with an eighty-four-page bibliography on women, science, and health. Although unannotated, the bibliography is the most complete and most recent guide to further reading on these topics. From England comes a similar anthology, *Alice Through the Microscope* (Virago, 1980), compiled by the Brighton Women and Science Group. Its eleven papers address the larger issue of masculine values in science, as well as specific instances of the impact of science and technology on women's lives and health.

984. Keller, Evelyn Fox, 1936- . **A Feeling for the Organism: The Life and Work of Barbara McClintock.** New York: W. H. Freeman, 1983. 235p. bibliog. index. $17.95. LC 82-21066. ISBN 0716714337.

Barbara McClintock won a Nobel Prize in 1983 for her pioneering work in genetics. As Keller illustrates in this probing biography, McClintock's path to worldwide acclaim was not an easy one. For years she labored in relative isolation, persisting in her research on chromosomal transposition in maize, while her peers in the scientific community turned to studies of DNA structure in bacteria and forged the new discipline of molecular biology. In interviews related here, McClintock intrigues the reader with her insights into a different form of science, an almost mystical "feeling for the organism." On the scientific method, Keller quotes McClintock: "It gives us relationships which are useful, valid, and technically marvelous; however, they are not the truth" (p.201). Quite aside from the implication that women may bring new ways of seeing and doing to science, the story of McClintock's education and career documents the typical obstacles women face and the sacrifices they make to work as scientists. Other recent biographies of women scientists, though less provocative than Keller's work, likewise convey the excitement of scientific discovery. Among them are G. June Goodfield's intimate portrait of five years in the life of a cancer researcher, *An Imagined World* (Harper and Row, 1981); Richard S. Baldwin's *The Fungus Fighters* (Cornell University Press, 1981), which recounts the collaboration of microbiologist Elizabeth Hazen and chemist Rachel Brown; and Deborah Jean Warner's study of nineteenth-century naturalist and social reformer, *Graceanna Lewis: Scientist and Humanitarian* (National Museum of History and Technology, 1979).

985. Keller, Evelyn Fox, 1936- . **Reflections on Gender and Science.** New Haven, CT: Yale University Press, 1985. 193p. bibliog. index. $17.95. LC 84-17327. ISBN 0300032919.

Keller, a mathematical biophysicist and biographer of Nobel laureate Barbara McClintock (see entry 984), gathers nine pieces here, some previously published. From their multiple perspectives—historical, psychoanalytic, scientific, philosophical—the essays taken together "begin to chart a terrain that amounts to a psychosociology of scientific knowledge" (p.13). Keller's central concern is the equation of objectivity with the male and subjectivity with the female. Her investigations range from Plato's and Bacon's world views, to psychology's object relations theory, to quantum physics and cellular biology. Eloquently conveying her vision of a "gender-free science" that will be "premised on a transformation of the very categories of male and female, and correspondingly of mind and nature" (p.178), Keller has emerged as a leading feminist critic of Western scientific ideology and practice.

986. Lowe, Marian, and Ruth Hubbard, 1924- , eds. **Woman's Nature: Rationalizations of Inequality.** New York: Pergamon Press, 1983. 155p. bibliog. index. $27.50. LC 83-4066. ISBN 0080301436.

The nine contributors to this anthology—all professors in the natural or social sciences—convincingly argue that generalizations about the nature of women have no scientific basis. Several chapters, particularly those on black and Indian women, underscore related truths: that race, age, and class compound gender stereotypes; and that rationalizations for sexual inequality have varied over the course of history. This provocative and interdisciplinary sampler not only analyzes the myths about female behavior and their far-reaching political, social, and cultural effects, but also critiques the very notion of scientific "objectivity" that supports such myths. Papers were contributed by the editors along with Elizabeth Fee, Dorothy Burnham, Beatrice Medicine, Karen Messing, Joan Smith, Eleanor Leacock, and Lila Leibowitz.

987. Newman, Louise Michele, ed. **Men's Ideas/Women's Realities: Popular Science, 1870-1915.** New York: Pergamon Press, 1985. 337p. bibliog. index. $32.50. LC 84-1072. ISBN 0080319300.

Because primary sources for the study of women in the history of scientific thought are not widely available, this is a pathbreaking anthology. The "woman question" was hotly debated in the pages of *Popular Science Monthly* between 1870 and 1915; the articles and editorials chosen for this volume present a stimulating range of views, from men and women, liberals and conservatives, scientists and the general public. Taken as a whole, the collection demonstrates how ideologies of women's nature and duties were closely tied to scientific inquiries into the evolution of sex differences. Newman arranges her selections into seven chapters, treating biological determinism, education, the birth rate, homemakers, suffrage, waged work, and the "new woman." Within chapters, items are chronologically ordered. Newman provides historical background in her introductions to each chapter and to the volume as a whole as well as lists of other relevant articles.

988. Richter, Derek, ed. **Women Scientists: The Road to Liberation.** London: Macmillan, 1982. 219p. index. £2.95. ISBN 0333324684.

The international perspective of this anthology makes it unique. Among its thirteen papers are essays on India, the United States, Japan, France, Italy, Iran, Sweden, the Soviet Union, the United Kingdom, and Kenya. Each author combines facts about women's status in scientific practice in her country with an autobiographical account of her childhood, education, and work. Noticeably missing from this volume is a critique of science itself. Both Derek Richter in his introduction and Nancy Seear in her conclusion laud modern science as a means for liberating individual women to use their full talents, and as a force "to free us all from the oppressive influence of outmoded forms of traditional thinking" (p.13).

989. Rossiter, Margaret W. **Women Scientists in America: Struggles and Strategies to 1940.** Baltimore: Johns Hopkins University Press, 1982. 439p. bibliog. index. $35.00. LC 81-20902. ISBN 0801824435.

In this richly detailed history, Rossiter traces the roles of women in the development of science in the United States. After examining the crucial function of women's colleges in providing scientific education in the nineteenth and twentieth centuries, and the struggles of women to attain doctorates, she turns her attention to the problems of employment. Academic, government, and industrial career opportunities were all restricted throughout the period under scrutiny. Rossiter highlights two causes of occupational segregation: "territorial" discrimination, which relegated women to fields such as home economics; and "hierarchical" discrimination, which kept women in low- or middle-level positions, in workplaces and scientific associations alike. Thus women occupied their own niche in the American scientific community—a niche determined by a complex of forces, including the economy, the feminist movement, and the turn-of-the-century trend toward the professionalization of science. Despite the barriers, a surprising number of women became scientists prior to 1940; their names and stories lend a lively immediacy to Rossiter's study. A sequel will follow the fate of women scientists since 1940. Recent biographies of women scientists—notably Lois Arnold's *Four Lives in Science: Women's Education in the Nineteenth Century* (Schocken Books, 1984) complement Rossiter's overview. Arnold writes of the careers of naturalist and illustrator Maria Martin Bachman (1796-1863), science educator Almira Hart Lincoln Phelps (1793-1884), home economist Louisa C. Allen Gregory (1848-1920), and geologist Florence Bascom (1862-1945).

990. Rothschild, Joan, ed. **Machina Ex Dea: Feminist Perspectives on Technology.** New York: Pergamon Press, 1983. 233p. bibliog. index. $27.50. LC 83-8353. ISBN 0080294049.

The twelve papers in this anthology document the omission of women from scholarly writings on technology and culture, and demonstrate how feminist perspectives strengthen the emerging discipline of technology studies. Part I looks at the positive role of women as producers of technology (both historically and in the present), as well as the mixed effects of technological innovations on women in the home and in the workplace. Part II presents three contrasting views of gender dualism in science. Part III explores feminist values in discussions of technology assessment, reproductive technology, and science and technology as envisioned in feminist utopian novels. Sally M. Gearhart's essay in this section, "An End to Technology: A Modest Proposal," defends the extreme position of the anti-technologist with exceptional cogency. *The Technological Woman: Interfacing With Tomorrow* (Praeger, 1983), edited by Jan Zimmerman, is an even more eclectic, interdisciplinary sampler of feminist writings. Thirty-one contributions fall into four broad categories: "New Technology, Old Values," which examines the interplay of gender, race, and class differences with technical development; "Ladies' Home Technology," which covers not only household devices but also transportation, energy, electronic media, and abortion; "A Living Wage," about women working in technical environments, from blue-collar workers to upper managers; and "The Politics of Tomorrow," about reproductive options, health care, science fiction, computer training, office automation, and feminist agendas for the future.

991. Tobach, Ethel, 1921- , and Betty Rosoff, eds. **Genes and Gender: I.** Staten Island, NY: Gordian Press, 1978. 90p. pbk. $5.00. LC 78-50640. ISBN 0877522154.

Presenting six papers from a 1977 conference, *Genes and Gender* denounces "hereditarianism" (now commonly labeled "biological determinism"), the scientific dogma that an individual's genetic make-up largely decides her destiny. The pathbreaking volume spawned a series of the same title. Second in the series, *Pitfalls in Research on Sex and Gender* (1979) is noteworthy for its introductory and concluding chapters, in which Ruth Hubbard and Marian Lowe erect the framework of a feminist critique of the theories and methods of research on sex differences, and place such research in its social, political, and historical contexts. Other numbers in the series are *Genetic Determinism and Children* (vol. 3, 1980) and *The Second X and Women's Health* (vol. 4, 1983).

992. Trescott, Martha Moore, 1941- , ed. **Dynamos and Virgins Revisited: Women and Technological Change in History: An Anthology.** Metuchen, NJ: Scarecrow Press, 1979. 280p. bibliog. index. $18.00. LC 79-21404. ISBN 0810812630.

Trescott has assembled eleven analyses of women's relation to technology, eight of which derive from papers delivered to the Society for the History of Technology in the mid-1970s. The papers in Part I look at women as active participants in technological change, through their contributions as industrial workers, inventors, engineers, scientists, and entrepreneurs. Part II assesses the effect of technological change within the domestic sphere: two papers treat women's work as homemakers; two others, women's relation to technology as bearers and rearers of children.

SOCIOLOGY AND SOCIAL ISSUES

Many of the books treated in this chapter are issue-oriented. Among the social problems studied by feminist scholars are woman-battering, racism, poverty, rape, alcoholism, incest, and reproductive choice. All constitute objects of research and theory-building, as well as rallying points for women's activism. Sociologists also look at the experiences of groups and classes of women: mothers, lesbians, homemakers, older women, women in the military, and women from a variety of racial, ethnic, and religious backgrounds, for instance. They observe women in a range of social environments and institutions, charting women's contributions to family and workplace, and their portrayal by the media. Many of these topics, of course, overlap with materials cited in other chapters (for example, see the Law chapter for books on crime and female prisoners), and with items assigned to Periodicals and Reference. The subject index is the key to specific topics that cross disciplines.

993. Acosta-Belén, Edna, with Elia Hidalgo Christensen, eds. **The Puerto Rican Woman.** New York: Praeger, 1979. 169p. bibliog. index. $29.95. LC 79-17638. ISBN 0030524660.
  Research on Puerto Rican women is hard to come by, as is research on Latinas in general. The eleven academic articles gathered in this multidisciplinary collection examine the lives of Puertorriqueñas in Puerto Rico and in the mainland United States. Among the essays are: "The Development of Capitalism in Puerto Rico and the Incorporation of Women into the Labor Force," by Marcia Rivera Quintero; "The History of Women's Struggle for Equality in Puerto Rico," by Isable Picó de Hernández; "The Educational and Professional Status of Puerto Rican Women," by Edna Acosta-Belén and Barbara R. Sjostrom; "Ideology and Images of Women in Contemporary Puerto Rican Literature," by Edna Acosta-Belén; "The Puerto Rican Cultural Response to Female Homosexuality," by Hilda Hidalgo and Elia Hidalgo Christensen; "Puertorriqueñas in the United States," by Lourdes Miranda King; and "The Black Puerto Rican Woman in Contemporary American Society," by Angela Jorge. A brief bibliography completes the volume.

994. Aldous, Joan, ed. **Two Paychecks: Life in Dual-Earner Families.** Beverly Hills, CA: Sage Publications, 1982. 247p. bibliog. $24.00. LC 82-10538. ISBN 0803918828.
  As feminism entered the professions, and professional women attempted to forge more egalitarian relationships with professional partners, social scientists identified what they saw as a new phenomenon: the "dual-career couple." Aldous quite consciously elects to use the term "dual-*earner* family" in order to encompass a broader population. Her collection brings together twelve articles by sociologists, psychologists, and economists on both professional and nonprofessional dual-earner families—their demographic characteristics; the impact of work schedules; effects of occupational attainment; domestic

interaction of family members; and work allocation in the household. Much of the recent literature on working couples is not academic in orientation. *The Two-Career Couple* (Addison-Wesley, 1979), by Francine S. Hall and Douglas T. Hall, is a practical guide for couples, replete with inventories and checklists designed for reader self-analysis. *Sharing Caring: The Art of Raising Kids in Two-Career Families* (Prentice-Hall, 1982), by Margaret B. White, has a similar self-help bent but focuses exclusively on the challenges of balancing children and work in an egalitarian relationship. In *Commuter Marriage: A Study of Work and Family* (Guilford Press, 1984), Naomi Gerstel and Harriet Gross report on their studies of couples whose work commitments require residences in different locations. After discussing the decision to commute and factors such as long-distance emotional support, division of labor, friendships, and independence and dependence, the authors conclude: "Commuting represents an extension of the separation of work and family, [and of] the male model of careers to women ..." (p.201).

995.* Andersen, Margaret L. **Thinking About Women: Sociological and Feminist Perspectives.** New York: Macmillan, 1983. 334p. bibliog. index. LC 82-14030. ISBN 0023033703.

Andersen's thoughtfully organized and well-written introduction to sociology is distinctive for its emphasis on social organization rather than social psychology, its more-than-token attention to underrepresented women (women of color, lesbians, poor women), and its substantial discussion of feminist theory. Andersen begins by introducing her reader to the "sociological imagination" in the tradition of C. Wright Mills, revealing the radical impulse in a field that looks at the "relationship between personal troubles and public issues" (p.7). She subsequently reviews current theory and research—feminist and nonfeminist—on sex, biology, and culture; sex-role socialization; work and the economy; the family; health and reproduction; and crime and deviance. In her last section, Andersen outlines the foundations of the sociology of knowledge subfield and the critique of scientific objectivity, then lays out the essential ideas of liberal, socialist, and radical feminism. Detached Andersen is not; she concludes by arguing that developing an analysis of race is "the most important task of feminist theory" (p.292).

996. André, Rae. **Homemakers: The Forgotten Workers.** Chicago: University of Chicago Press, 1981. 299p. bibliog. index. $20.00. LC 80-21258. ISBN 0226019934.

André challenges her readers to reexamine their views of homemaking and to consider the part played by the American work ethic, in addition to sexism, in the cultural devaluation of homemakers. Even as she documents the hazards and liabilities of this unwaged, insecure occupation, André highlights the positive values attached to loving care for home and children, associating these with fledgling movements for enhanced quality of home and work life, decentralist philosophies, and the "small is beautiful" perspective. She proposes strategies for change at all levels, from the individual and her family to the community, the state, the federal government and (somewhat tentatively) the world. André's discussions are enlivened by excerpts from her interviews with homemakers. Interviews also form the basis of Meg Luxton's study of housewives in a Canadian mining town. *More Than a Labour of Love: Three Generations of Women's Work in the Home* (The Women's Press, 1980) attempts "to locate domestic labor within the development of industrial capitalism in North America ... [and] to illustrate the actual work process as women experience it ..." (p.24).

997.   Barcus, Francis Earle, 1927- . **Representations of Life on Children's Television: Sex Roles, Minorities, and Families.** New York: Praeger, 1983. 217p. bibliog. index. $25.95. LC 83-4131. ISBN 0030638836.

Sponsored by Action for Children's Television, Barcus's work is based on content analysis of some fifty hours of network and independent programming for children during one week in 1981. His findings largely confirm those of earlier research: male characters outnumber female characters by about four to one, and all characters generally exhibit traditional sex-role characteristics. Barcus found similar stereotyping in television's treatment of minorities and families. "Freestyle," an experimental 1970 television series designed to alter children's stereotypes about sex roles, gave rise to two related volumes. *Positive Images: Breaking Stereotypes With Children's Television,* by Jerome Johnston and James S. Ettema (Sage Publications, 1982), describes the development of the series from conception to production and evaluation, and includes some program synopses. A more scholarly work that draws on research used in developing the series is *Children, Television, and Sex-Role Stereotyping,* by Frederick Williams, Robert LaRose, and Frederica Frost (Praeger, 1981). Both studies conclude that children's sex-role stereotypes can be modified by strong alternative role portrayals.

998.   Barry, Kathleen. **Female Sexual Slavery.** Englewood Cliffs, NJ: Prentice-Hall, 1979; repr. New York: New York University Press, 1984. 274p. bibliog. index. $30.00. LC 84-16505. ISBN 0814710100.

In this passionate and often painful exposé, Barry documents the extent of sexual terrorism practiced against women. Part I outlines the difficulties in studying a phenomenon that is widespread but largely invisible, recounts nineteenth-century campaigns to abolish sexual slavery, and sets forth Barry's definitions of victimism and survival. Part II documents the international traffic in women and the suppression of evidence about it, reveals the methods of procuring and pimping, spotlights the state's role in legitimizing prostitution, and, most daringly, takes the experiences of kidnapped heiress Patricia Hearst as paradigmatic of the victimization of enslaved women, and of their survival strategies. In Part III, Barry indicts the patriarchal family structure and pornography for promoting an "ideology of cultural sadism." Barry's final chapter raises a stirring call for new sexual values of intimacy and respect.

999.   Baruch, Grace, and Jeanne Brooks-Gunn, eds. **Women in Midlife.** New York: Plenum Press, 1984. 404p. bibliog. index. $35.00. LC 84-3374. ISBN 0306414449.

In their brief introduction, Baruch and Brooks-Gunn attribute negative stereotypes of middle-aged women in theory and research to two sources: past studies of aging based on a male model; and the inordinate attention paid to the supposedly distressing life events of menopause and the "empty nest." The seventeen papers in this volume paint a different picture, drawing on recent studies in a number of disciplines to demonstrate that, "although midlife is not without its difficulties, it is, for many women, a time of unexpected pleasure, even power" (p.1). The contributions are arranged in three sections: "Conceptual Approaches to Midlife"; "Roles and Relationships" (including studies of women's roles in the family and in the labor force); and "Enhancing Well-Being" (covering health care, menopause, reentry students, therapy, and sexuality). Another anthology, *Older Women: Issues and Prospects* (Lexington Books, 1983), covers similar ground. Editor Elizabeth W. Markson offers fifteen viewpoints on the diverse experiences and lifestyles of aging women, in areas of "Changing Bodies, Changing Selves," "Older Women in Labor," "Without and Within the Family," and "Health Issues in Later Life." For a multidisciplinary review of the research on older women in the 1960s and 1970s, consult *Women Over Forty: Visions and Realities*, by Marilyn R. Block, Janice L. Davidson, and Jean D. Grambs (Springer, 1981). This comprehensive overview treats demographics, images of older women, menopause and sexuality, mental health, life situations, family relations, employment and retirement, and ethnic and racial variations in older women. A brief concluding chapter suggests avenues for further research.

1000.   Berk, Sarah Fenstermaker, ed. **Women and Household Labor.** Beverly Hills, CA: Sage Publications, 1980. 295p. bibliog. $28.00. LC 78-23003. ISBN 0803912110.

In introducing this collection of eleven articles, Berk identifies "three disturbing tendencies in the extant research on women and household labor" (p.17): its defensiveness about the legitimacy of household labor as a topic for scholarly inquiry; its preference for theory-building over empirical research; and its efforts to squeeze housework conceptually into existing social science frameworks. Contributors to this multidisciplinary volume share a commitment to the kind of empirical research Berk has heretofore found lacking. A majority of the authors report on studies using sophisticated quantitative methods; the reader lacking training in this area will find the statistical tables and discussions challenging. Eclectic in focus, the articles address the impact of technology on household labor, the social status of the homemaker, the new home economics, time allocation, and women's class position, among other topics. In her most recent work, *The Gender Factory: The Apportionment of Work in American Households* (Plenum Press, 1985), Berk reports on her research on the division of labor among 335 U.S. couples.

1001.   Bernard, Jessie Shirley. **The Female World.** New York: Free Press, 1981. 614p. bibliog. index. $27.50. LC 80-69880. ISBN 0029030005.

Bernard, a sociologist and a prolific writer, begins with the theoretical argument that "most human beings live in single-sex worlds ... that ... are different from one another in a myriad of ways, both subjectively and objectively" (p.3). She then proceeds with a wide-ranging, eclectic survey of the "female world": demographic characteristics; group structure (kinship, friendship, associations, collective behavior); culture (language, technology, fine arts, folk culture); and relation to the economy and the polity. This survey seems overambitious ("... I am fully aware that I have spread myself too thin," Bernard writes in her preface) and yields little that is new. On the other hand, her theoretical stance, while not original, is controversial and intriguing; one wishes that it shaped her discussion more consistently. Unfortunately, with the exception of chapter five, where she explores what the nineteenth-century "woman's sphere" looked like from the inside, Bernard does little to elucidate the "subjective" differences between the male and female worlds.

1002.   Bowker, Lee Harrington. **Beating Wife-Beating.** Lexington, MA: Lexington Books, 1983. 154p. bibliog. index. $22.00. LC 82-48603. ISBN 0669063452.

Studies of battered women generally address the problem of temporarily sheltering them, or helping them to rebuild independent lives. Bowker looks at wife-beating from a different angle, by interviewing women who have eliminated the problem of abuse and remained with their husbands or partners. The solutions include personal strategies and techniques (for example, talking, hiding, self-defense), informal help-sources (family, neighbors, friends, shelters), and formal help-sources (police, social service agencies, lawyers, clergy, women's groups). A number of variables, including demographic characteristics and personal backgrounds of the couples, are examined, as are factors present at the times of attack—use of alcohol or drugs, assault of children, pregnancy, and the like.

The data reveal no consistent correlations. Bowker concludes that "the crucial factor is not always the nature of the strategy or help-source; what really matters is the woman's showing her determination that the violence *must stop now*" (p.131). He recommends wider distribution of information about the options available to battered women, additional training for police officers and staff of service agencies, and self-help groups for men who batter.

1003. Bryan, Beverly, 1949- , et al. **The Heart of the Race: Black Women's Lives in Britain.** London: Virago Press, 1985. 250p. bibliog. index. £4.50. LC 85-23473. ISBN 0860683613.

Acknowledging the pioneering efforts of black women in the United States to break the silence about their lives, Beverly Bryan, Stella Dadzie, and Suzanne Scafe seek here to document the specific experience of Afro-Caribbean women in Britain. In so doing, they add an important dimension to American black women's history as we know it. The authors trace their roots back to Africa via the Caribbean, asserting that slave labor in the Americas fueled European development and fortified European domination. "When, a century later, Black people began to enter Britain as immigrants," they write, "we came to a country we had already helped to build" (p.7). Focusing especially on the past forty years, Bryan, Dadzie, and Scafe survey black women's experiences with work, education, health, and welfare services; trace the history of their organizing and resistance; and describe their efforts to reclaim their culture, quoting liberally from interviews throughout the text.

1004. Burgess, Ann Wolbert, ed. **Rape and Sexual Assault: A Research Handbook.** New York: Garland, 1985. 433p. bibliog. index. $50.00. LC 83-48217. ISBN 0824090497.

Burgess, herself a prolific researcher in the field of rape treatment, assembles twenty-five up-to-date reports and analyses from a range of disciplines. The contributors are affiliated with universities, hospitals and clinics, research institutes, treatment centers, and advocacy organizations. Part I examines past and present anti-rape efforts. Part II focuses on victims of rape and sexual assault, with special attention to incest, sexual abuse of children and adolescents, handicapped victims, and marital rape. Part III explores family and legal responses to the victim, while Part IV takes a look at the aggressor. The final section, "Mass Media, Prevention, and the Future," places rape and sexual assault in a broader societal context. Bibliographies accompany most of the papers. In *Stopping Rape: Successful Survival Strategies* (Pergamon Press, 1985), Pauline B. Bart and Patricia H. O'Brien examine actual cases in which women resisted rape and conclude that some common advice on how to avoid rape is both wrong and dangerous.

1005. Buss, Fran Leeper, 1942- , comp. **Dignity: Lower Income Women Tell of Their Lives and Struggles.** Ann Arbor: University of Michigan Press, 1985. 290p. bibliog. $22.00. LC 85-990. ISBN 0472100610.

Having herself known poverty, single motherhood, and ill health, Buss brought an unusual degree of sensitivity and respect to her seventy-two interviews with lower-income women. She selected the stories of ten women for inclusion in this book: four white women, three blacks, one American Indian, and one Japanese-American. Buss directed the women to speak of their backgrounds, their childhoods, menarche and adolescence, marriage and motherhood, sexual abuse, working, and aging. Her own responses are edited out of these lengthy and moving narratives, but she provides brief headnotes for each, as well as an introduction to the volume as a whole. Though poor, these women are survivors, Buss emphasizes. In *Shopping Bag Ladies: Homeless Women Speak About*

Their Lives (Pilgrim Press, 1981), we get a rare glimpse of another set of poor women who survive, but barely, on the very margins of society. Anne Marie Rousseau presents the stories of eighteen women living on the streets of New York City, Boston, and San Francisco. Her accompanying photographs add a painfully graphic view into the lives of these women—"the ulcerated feet, the endless search for food, the weariness, the waiting, ... the invisibility...," as Alix Kates Shulman expresses it in her preface to the volume.

1006. Butler, Matilda, and William Paisley. **Women and the Mass Media: Sourcebook for Research and Action.** New York: Human Sciences Press, 1980. 432p. bibliog. index. $34.95. LC 79-16271. ISBN 0877054096.

In this overview of research on sexism in mass media, Butler and Paisley's findings are not surprising: women are underrepresented in all media and in media industries; women are generally portrayed in stereotyped roles; this skewed portrayal does affect audience perceptions of women; and things haven't changed much during the last fifteen years. Part I provides background on women's rights in the United States, sexism in language and image, and mass media institutions. Part II reviews sexism in media content; Part III looks at employment practices within the media industry; and Part IV discusses composition of, and effects on, audiences. Suggestions for research and action complete the volume. A more international perspective is provided by *Unequal Opportunities: The Case of Women and the Media,* by Margaret Gallagher (Unesco Press, 1981). Reviewing mass media research by region, Gallagher arrives at conclusions similar to those of Butler and Paisley.

1007. Coles, Robert, and Jane Hallowell Coles. **Women of Crisis II: Lives of Work and Dreams.** New York: Delacorte Press/Seymour Lawrence, 1980; New York: Dell, 1980. 237p. pbk. $6.95. LC 79-25210. ISBN 0550096359.

In this second "women of crisis" volume, as in the first, Robert Coles and Jane Hallowell Coles combine biography and oral history to render what they call "a reading" of individual lives. One of the most impressive "readings" here is of the life of a Pueblo woman. The authors also profile a corporate executive, a nurse, a bank teller, and a civil rights activist. Representing diverse regional and racial experiences, these women's responses to externally and internally imposed pressures are studies in the complexity of American women's lives.

1008.* Conference on the Educational and Occupational Needs of Asian-Pacific-American Women, San Francisco, CA, 1976. **Conference on the Educational and Occupational Needs of Asian-Pacific-American Women, August 24 and 25, 1976.** Washington, DC: National Institute of Education, 1980. 390p. bibliog. LC 81-600532.

Between 1975 and 1978, the National Institute of Education held a series of five conferences on the educational and occupational needs of Asian and Pacific American, black, Hispanic American, American Indian, and white ethnic women. For each of the conferences, a volume was published reprinting the conference papers, along with individual and group recommendations of the participants. The conferences brought together community organizers and researchers, catalyzing discussion on issues such as health and mental health, childrearing, political organizing, education, immigration, economic and employment status, and cultural identity.

1009. Courtney, Alice E., and Thomas E. Whipple. **Sex Stereotyping in Advertising.** Lexington, MA: Lexington Books, 1983. 239p. bibliog. index. $26.00. LC 80-8115. ISBN 0669039551.

Following extensive review of research from the 1970s and early 1980s, Courtney and Whipple conclude that the advertising industry has largely ignored consumer preference and scholarship on the portrayal of women in advertising and is only very slowly incorporating new images of women. Part I looks at how both sexes are portrayed in ads, the attitudes of audiences and advertisers, and the social and economic effects of stereotyping. The discussion of advertising techniques in Part II examines women as a new market segment, the effectiveness of sex-role and decorative/sexual portrayals, and the use of male vs. female authority voices. Part III reviews the possibilities for change through research and regulation, and offers suggestions for educating the advertiser. Erving Goffman, in *Gender Advertisements* (Harper and Row, 1979), uses numerous photographic illustrations to support his thesis that commercial advertising presents highly ritualized expressions of male-female roles and relationships.

1010. Darty, Trudy, and Sandee Potter, eds. **Women-Identified Women.** Palo Alto, CA: Mayfield, 1984. 316p. bibliog. $11.95. LC 83-062837. ISBN 0317265504.

In this anthology designed for classroom use, Darty and Potter have created a useful introduction to the lesbian experience and the lesbian-feminist movement in the United States. Section One, "Identity," covers the development of lesbian identity, the coming-out process, partner relationships, and the special perspectives of older, Indian, and Puerto Rican lesbians. Section Two, "Oppression," opens with Adrienne Rich's classic essay "Compulsory Heterosexuality and Lesbian Existence" and proceeds to explore the subjects of law, motherhood, childbirth and conception, health care, and employment. Section Three, "Culture and Community," addresses politics, literature, and women's music. The papers are an eclectic blend of empirical research, opinion, criticism, and personal revelation. A well-chosen bibliography of books and articles from 1972 to 1983 and a list of lesbian periodicals conclude the book.

1011. Davis, Angela Y., 1944- . **Women, Race and Class.** New York: Random House, 1981. 271p. bibliog. $15.95. LC 81-40243. ISBN 0394510399.

Angela Davis traces the ebb and flow of solidarity and antagonism along lines of race, class, and sex in U.S. women's history of the last century. Her discussion of racism concentrates primarily but not exclusively on relations between whites and blacks. Davis depicts the history of racism in the woman suffrage movement, identifying instances of personal anti-racism on the part of white suffragists at the same time as she portrays their mounting public appeal to racism and class prejudice. She retrieves the lost history of black women's strivings for education, black women's part in the club movement (and the racism of the white club movement), and the contributions of a number of black communist women. Davis brings her account of racist and classist elements in white feminism into the present with penetrating analyses of contemporary feminist movements concerned with rape, reproductive rights, and housework. An introduction and index—both missing here—would have enhanced the volume's cohesiveness.

1012. Deegan, Mary Jo, 1946- , and Nancy A. Brooks, 1943- , eds. **Women and Disability: The Double Handicap.** New Brunswick, NJ: Transaction Books, 1985. 144p. bibliog. $24.95. LC 84-2618. ISBN 0887380174.

This collection had its beginnings in a special issue of *The Journal of Sociology and Social Welfare* (July 1983). It brings together current research by scholars and other professionals on the lives of women with disabilities. Editors Deegan and Brooks identify three unifying themes that run through the eleven articles: "the 'double' jeopardy of disabled women, the lack of information available about their lives and experiences, and the need to alleviate the conditions that perpetuate structured inequality" (p.2). Some of the researchers study specific disabilities (deafness, spinal-cord injury, visual impairment, chronic renal failure, and breast cancer). Other speak to more general issues, such as multiple minority status, benefits for the disabled, peer counseling, and motherhood. Michelle Fine and Adrienne Asch's article "Disabled Women: Sexism without the Pedestal" is often cited as one of the first and most articulate statements on the topic. For a concise statistical overview of the U.S. population of disabled women, based on census data from 1981 to 1982, turn to *Disabled Women in America,* by Frank Bowe (President's Committee on Employment of the Handicapped, 1984).

1013.   Dobash, R. Emerson, and Russell Dobash. **Violence Against Wives: A Case Against the Patriarchy.** New York: Free Press, 1979. 339p. bibliog. index. $19.95. LC 79-7181. ISBN 0029073200.

Like most writers on wife abuse, Dobash and Dobash look at the causes and characteristics of battering, the actions taken by victims, and the responses of the helping professions, the legal system, refuges, and other services. Their text, like many, is filled with personal accounts by survivors. What sets their work apart is their refusal to subsume the particularity of wife abuse under the broader rubric of family violence or violence in society at large. They offer a historical analysis of the subordinate role of women in the family and a compelling critique of the institution of marriage. Their research is based on interviews with residents of women's refuges in Scotland and on examination of police court records. "The problem lies in the domination of women," they conclude. "The answer lies in the struggle against it" (p.243).

1014.   Ehrenreich, Barbara. **The Hearts of Men: American Dreams and the Flight From Commitment.** Garden City, NY: Anchor Press/Doubleday, 1983. 206p. bibliog. index. pbk. $6.95. LC 82-45104. ISBN 0385176155.

Ehrenreich is an elegant and witty writer, and in this book she achieves a *tour de force* of feminist argument. The kind of critical rethinking of men's breadwinner role we associate with the contemporary men's movement is not new at all, she tells us. Rather, men's rebellion against their responsibilities took shape thirty years ago. What is more, it is this rebellion, she argues, this flight from commitment to dependent women and children, that fueled both feminism and antifeminism. There is many a barb in Ehrenreich's narrative as she pursues her theme from the early rebels against corporate conformity, "the gray flannel dissidents," to the *Playboy* mavericks and, finally, the Beats. Doctors and psychologists are also targeted for their role in providing "scientific" justification for men's flight, under the guise of alarm about the unhealthiness of "the masculine script" and the "Type A" personality. Whether Ehrenreich's historical logic holds remains to be determined by future research and debate. Her work will in any case stand as an original and provocative essay that forces us to look at the past thirty years in new ways.

1015.   Elsasser, Nan, 1945- , et al. **Las Mujeres: Conversations From a Hispanic Community.** Old Westbury, NY: Feminist Press, 1980. 163p. index. $14.95. LC 80-20200. ISBN 0912670843.

Oral history is a particularly powerful tool for the reclamation of Chicana history and the documentation of contemporary Chicana reality. In this volume, Nan Elsasser, Kyle MacKenzie, and Yvonne Tixier y Vigil present the stories of twenty-one women from the Albuquerque region. The accounts make for compelling reading and clearly illustrate the considerable changes this century has brought to the Chicano community, and to Chicanas in particular. Most striking is the shift from a land-based, deeply religious, family-centered, and Spanish-speaking way of life to increasingly urban, better educated, but less close-knit communities. Both the young and the older women whose stories are included here express deeply ambivalent feelings about these changes. Alfredo Mirandé and Evangelina Enríquez reach back further in history to document the colonial heritage of Chicanas in Mexico and the United States in *La Chicana: The Mexican-American Woman* (University of Chicago Press, 1979). In addition, the authors review the status of contemporary Chicanas in the family, work, and education; images of Chicanas in literature; and Chicana feminism, past and present.

1016.   Enloe, Cynthia. **Does Khaki Become You? The Militarisation of Women's Lives.** Boston: South End Press, 1983. 262p. bibliog. index. $20.00. LC 84-164990. ISBN 0896081842.

Military forces past and present have depended on women's as well as men's labor but have been loath to admit it, Enloe argues. Enloe looks to the contradictions between the military's need for female "manpower" and its masculine ideology for insights into militarization and gender. In chapters on camp followers, military wives, nurses, official and guerrilla soldiers, and women in defense industries in the United States and abroad, she shows how the military seeks to control the women it needs for its maintenance and reproduction — by manipulating the sexual division of labor, by defining the "front" as where women are *not* — in order to preserve the military's image as a male bastion. Enloe's critical perspective calls into serious question the "equal rights" approach that sees sexual integration of the military as an important component of women's liberation. An earlier collection, to which Enloe is a contributor, also explores the contradictions opened up by women's recruitment into the armed forces. *Loaded Questions: Women in the Military,* edited by Wendy Chapkis (Transnational Institute, 1981), presents fourteen brief essays written by feminist antimilitarists who attended a 1981 international conference on women in the militaries of NATO nations. *Minerva: Quarterly Report on Women and the Military* publishes news, reviews, commentary, and letters reflective of diverse perspectives on the military, war, and peace.

1017.   Faux, Marian. **Childless by Choice: Choosing Childlessness in the Eighties.** Garden City, NY: Anchor Press/Doubleday, 1984. 196p. bibliog. index. $13.95. LC 83-2038. ISBN 0385158459.

During the last twenty years, the number of women choosing to remain childless or to postpone motherhood has increased significantly, and several recent books document and attempt to explain the phenomenon. Although Faux's work leans toward a childless bias, it covers the topic well. Having thoroughly researched the scant literature and interviewed forty-three women, she discusses the childbearing decision from the perspectives of family background, the marriage relationships, cost of rearing children, conflict with career, "maternal instinct," and the cultural mandate to have children. A survey of working- and middle-class women undergirds another scholarly book, Kathleen Gerson's *Hard Choices: How Women Decide About Work, Career, and Motherhood* (University of California Press, 1985). Gerson shows that childbearing decisions are shaped more by adult life experience than by childhood environment and aspirations. More popular in approach but quite informative is *Up Against the Clock,* by Marilyn Fabe and Norma Wikler (Random House, 1979). The authors present interviews with three groups of women — working mothers, single mothers, and childless women — followed by a summary discussion. *Sooner or Later: The Timing of Parenthood in Adult Lives,* by Pamela Daniels and Kathy Weingarten (Norton, 1982), draws on in-depth interviews with eighty-six couples. Finally, in *Why Children?* (Harcourt, Brace, Jovanovich, 1980), Stephanie Dowrick and Sibyl Grundberg offer eighteen first-person accounts of women's childbearing decisions. Among those represented are single, adoptive, and lesbian mothers, and those childless by choice and chance.

1018.* Forisha, Barbara L., and Barbara H. Goldman, eds. **Outsiders on the Inside: Women & Organizations.** Englewood Cliffs, NJ: Prentice-Hall, 1981. 312p. bibliog. index. LC 80-39705. ISBN 0136453821.

As the title suggests, this collection of twenty-one articles takes a critical, yet ultimately integrationist approach to the question of women's relationship to organizations. The unifying theme of the volume is the separation of love ("women's sphere") and power ("men's sphere"). In essays on a range of organizational settings — business, science, law, academia — contributors show how the "power dimension" holds sway in organizations, reinforcing women's outsider status and dehumanizing the workplace. In their concluding essay, Forisha and Goldman speak to the possibility of "integrating love and power." One of the articles included here is excerpted from an earlier classic in the field, Rosabeth Moss Kanter's *Men and Women of the Corporation* (Basic Books, 1977). Kanter is also author of the whimsical but astute *A Tale of "O": On Being Different in an Organization* (Harper and Row, 1980).

1019. Fowlkes, Martha R. **Behind Every Successful Man: Wives of Medicine and Academe.** New York: Columbia University Press, 1980. 223p. bibliog. index. $25.00. LC 79-24901. ISBN 0231047762.

Fowlkes, a sociologist, interviewed twenty wives of university professors and twenty wives of doctors to investigate the impact of the husbands' careers on the women's lives and, more broadly, the structure of American professional life with its gender-based expectations. Fowlkes documents that for these forty couples, medicine and academia essentially constitute "two-person careers," with the wives serving in every imaginable capacity to enhance the husbands' professional success: as hostesses to their colleagues, as secretaries, as collaborators. In addition, she demonstrates how the women organize their domestic responsibilities so as to minimize interference with their husbands' commitments. A corollary of this study — which Fowlkes touches on in her preface — is that women seeking advancement in these professions will be significantly disadvantaged compared to their married male colleagues.

1020. Friedland, Ronnie, and Carol Kort, eds. **The Mothers' Book: Shared Experiences.** Boston: Houghton Mifflin, 1981. 363p. $15.95. LC 80-24938. ISBN 0395305276.

Concerned about the uncertainty and isolation experienced by many new mothers, Friedland and Kort collected a fascinating variety of personal accounts to convey "what it *feels* like to be a mother today" (p.xv). The stories are consistently well written and told with unusual candor. Many are extremely moving. The twenty-one themes give a sense of the breadth of experience shared here: pregnancy; postpartum changes; breast or bottle; staying home; going to work; changes in self-concept; redefining relationships; friends; sexuality and motherhood; ambivalence, anger, and shame; the only child; becoming a single mother; becoming a stepmother; foster, adoptive, and natural mothers; teenage mothers; feelings about surgical deliveries; mothering children with special needs; when things go wrong; dealing with death; dealing with the future. For a work that looks at the contemporary reality of motherhood against a backdrop of other cultures, see *Women as Mothers*, by social anthropologist Sheila Kitzinger (Random House, 1978). *The Mother Mirror: How a Generation of Women Is Changing Motherhood in America*, by Nancy Rubin (Putnam, 1984), reviews current trends, including single motherhood, late motherhood, surrogate motherhood, and "the new fathers."

1021.   Gottlieb, Naomi, 1925- , ed. **Alternative Social Services for Women.** New York: Columbia University Press, 1980. 391p. bibliog. index. $31.50. LC 80-164. ISBN 0231042124.

Gottlieb's purpose here is not to document institutionalized sexism in the helping professions (which she takes as a given), but rather to survey nonsexist alternatives. Gottlieb organizes the anthology around problems (mental health, health care, chemical dependency) and client groups (battered women, rape victims, single parents, older women, displaced homemakers, ethnic minority women) and discusses research related to each topic. Most of the case studies are written by women actively involved in alternative services. Two other recent titles bring similarly feminist perspectives to their examinations of social work practice. In *Women, Power, and Change* (National Association of Social Workers, 1982), editors Ann Weick and Susan T. Vandiver present selected papers from the First National Conference on Social Work Practice with Women, held in 1980. The collection is especially strong in its coverage of women of color; a final section considers issues of power confronting social work practitioners. The twelve articles in *Women's Issues and Social Work Practice*, edited by Elaine Norman and Arlene Mancuso (F. E. Peacock, 1980), consider social service systems as well as particular problems and populations. Susan T. Vandiver contributes an article on the history of women in social work. The eight articles by British social scientists in *A Labour of Love: Women, Work and Caring,* edited by Janet Finch and Dulcie Groves (Routledge and Kegan Paul, 1983), shift the focus from women as social service consumers to women as *unpaid providers* of services to others, primarily disabled or chronically ill children and adults, and old people.

1022.   Grahn, Judy, 1940- . **Another Mother Tongue: Gay Words, Gay Worlds.** Boston: Beacon Press, 1984. 324p. bibliog. index. $19.95. LC 83-45953. ISBN 0807067164.

In this dizzying amalgam of folklore, history, myth, scholarly word play, and insightful observations of modern sexual mores, Grahn offers a prodigious amount of information on the lives of lesbians and gay men in many cultures and many centuries. At times she is boldly speculative, particularly when tracing the derivations of words and customs. Her central thesis is that gay people throughout history have served powerful ceremonial functions in their societies—functions associated with religion, healing, and community self-definition. The mannerisms and labels that adhere to gay people today, she argues, manifest a rich unwritten tradition. Grahn, a fine poet and author of fiction (see entry 692), writes movingly and inventively, blending truths she has gained through personal experience and spiritual visions with the fruits of years of scholarly research. Grahn's *The Highest Apple: Sappho and the Lesbian Poetic Tradition* (Spinsters, Ink, 1985) was originally intended as a chapter in *Another Mother Tongue.* In it Grahn discusses the lives and works of Emily Dickinson, Amy Lowell, H. D., Gertrude Stein, Adrienne Rich, Audre Lorde, Olga Broumas, and Paula Gunn Allen.

1023. Guttentag, Marcia, 1932-1977, and Paul F. Secord. **Too Many Women? The Sex Ratio Question.** Beverly Hills, CA: Sage Publications, 1983. 277p. bibliog. index. $28.00. LC 82-19192. ISBN 0803919182.

"This book is generated from a simple but powerful idea: that the number of opposite-sex partners potentially available to men or women has profound effects on sexual behaviors and sexual mores, on patterns of marriage and divorce, childrearing conditions and practices, family stability, and certain structural aspects of society itself" (p.9). The authors pursue the effects of high and low sex ratios in classical Athens and Sparta, medieval Europe, among orthodox Jews, in colonial North America, and among contemporary whites and blacks in the United States. In doing so, they distinguish between what they call dyadic power (belonging to the sex in short supply) and structural power (which they believe to be universally held by men).

1024. Hansson, Carola, and Karin Lidén, 1941- . **Moscow Women.** New York: Pantheon Books, 1983. 194p. bibliog. $16.45. LC 82-18841. ISBN 0394523326.

In the spring of 1978, Swedish journalists Hansson and Lidén conducted unauthorized interviews with thirteen women in Moscow. Their conversations reveal common problems: the struggle to balance work and family responsibilities; sex discrimination in education and employment; the inadequacy of state-run daycare facilities; the prevalence of divorce; the glaring lack of birth control; shortages of housing and consumer goods. Although diverse in background and personality, these Soviet women concur that biological differences between men and women lead to unequal treatment, and they cling to a romantic ideal of femininity and motherhood. Paradoxically, they accept the official Soviet ideology that men and women are equal. As the interviewers point out, this "split perception of reality" (p.186) causes a chord of resignation that echoes through the book. *Moscow Women* spells out the paramount issues in the lives of contemporary Soviet women, which more scholarly studies also explore. *Women in Eastern Europe and the Soviet Union* (Praeger, 1980), edited by Tova Yedlin, brings together fourteen papers, primarily by North American academics, covering both historical and current concerns. *Women, Work, and Family in the Soviet Union* (M. E. Sharpe, 1982), edited by Gail Warshofsky Lapidus, provides translated works by Soviet researchers on the levels and patterns of female employment, the impact of women's employment on the family, and policies for the 1980s. In *Women and State Socialism* (Macmillan, 1979), Alena Heitlinger builds a theoretical and historical context for understanding women's situation in the present-day USSR and in Czechoslovakia. And finally, a collection edited by Barbara Holland and titled *Soviet Sisterhood* (Indiana University Press, 1985) offers eight studies on topics ranging from Soviet women's magazines to the absence of women from political leadership in the USSR.

1025. Herman, Judith Lewis, 1942- , with Lisa Hirschman. **Father-Daughter Incest.** Cambridge, MA: Harvard University Press, 1981. 282p. bibliog. index. $16.50. LC 81-2534. ISBN 0674295056.

Addressing victims of incest and the professionals who work with them, Herman develops a feminist analysis of father-daughter incest and examines the possibilities for healing and prevention. Part One, "The Incest Secret," evaluates existing theories about the causes and effects of incest, sharply diverging from the viewpoints of Freud and Kinsey by asserting that incest is real and inflicts lasting damage. Part Two, "Daughters' Lives," draws on interviews with incest victims and with women whose fathers were seductive but stopped short of genital contact. Part Three, "Breaking Secrecy," reports on legal, clinical, and self-help approaches to dealing with incest. Herman's study is well documented, insightful, and makes skillful use of case histories and interviews. In *The Best Kept Secret: Sexual Abuse of Children* (Prentice-Hall, 1980), Florence Rush presents a scathing indictment of a society that condones the sexual exploitation of children. Her wide-ranging analysis takes in the biblical and Talmudic traditions, Christianity, ancient Greek pedophilia, Victorian double standards, Freudian psychology, child marriage in India, fairy tales, films, and "kiddy porn." Rush concludes by exposing modern-day advocates of child-adult sexual relationships. Jean Renvoize's *Incest: A Family Pattern* (Routledge and Kegan Paul, 1982) is another good overview of both theoretical and practical concerns.

1026.   Hertz, Susan Handley. **The Welfare Mothers Movement: A Decade of Change for Poor Women?** Washington, DC: University Press of America, 1981. 193p. bibliog. $23.50. LC 81-40358. ISBN 0819117803.

Hertz defines welfare as a women's issue as well as an economic one in this study of the history of the welfare mothers movement based on research conducted in Minneapolis during the early 1970s. Hertz's frame of reference is the sociology of social movements as she analyzes the organization, ideology, recruitment practices, and commitment of the movement for welfare rights, and the opposition to it. In contrast to earlier studies that emphasized class factors, Hertz highlights "the impact of traditional female gender roles on the opportunities and constraints experienced by groups of welfare mothers" (p.16). While Hertz's study embraces a network of organizations working on welfare issues, Guida West's *The National Welfare Rights Movement: The Social Protest of Poor Women* (Praeger, 1981) details the history of the National Welfare Rights Organization (NWRO) specifically. West emphasizes that while the NWRO "was officially labeled by all a poor people's movement, it was in fact a movement of poor women, mostly black" (p.xiii).

1027.   Holm, Jeanne, 1921- . **Women in the Military: An Unfinished Revolution.** Novato, CA: Presidio Press, 1982. 434p. bibliog. index. $16.95. LC 82-12324. ISBN 0891410783.

A major general, retired from the U.S. Air Force, Holm provides a detailed overview of the utilization of women by the U.S. military from the time of the Revolutionary War, devoting the bulk of the volume to the post-World War II era. Combining a concern with women's rights with a promilitary stance, Holm terms the Second World War the "breakthrough," as the military's need for "manpower" paved the way for the establishment of the women's auxiliaries. Once the all-volunteer force was instituted in 1973, "manpower" needs could be met only by substantially increasing the number of women recruits, a development that brought sex inequities and men's resistance into sharper relief. The 1978 merger of the Women's Army Corps (WAC) with the Army provoked intensified opposition. It is the post-integration era that magazine writer Helen Rogan emphasizes in her book *Mixed Company: Women in the Modern Army* (Putnam, 1981). Rogan portrays the new integrated Army as a "gender laboratory" (p.63), in an account based largely on her observations at a basic training camp and at West Point. For an in-depth analysis of the integration process at one of the service academies, see Judith Hicks Stiehm's *Bring Me Men and Women: Mandated Change at the U.S. Air Force Academy* (University of California Press, 1981).

1028.   Inglis, Kate. **Living Mistakes: Mothers Who Consented to Adoption.** Sydney: Allen and Unwin, 1984. 195p. bibliog. $22.50. LC 83-73460. ISBN 0868616400.

Adoption is often touted as the alternative to abortion by the "Right to Life" movement, and as a blessing for infertile couples. Yet the experience of the mothers who do relinquish their children has remained a virtual unknown. In *Living Mistakes*, fifteen Australian women speak of the humiliation, confusion, and coercion that contributed to their decision, and of the grief of losing a child to adoption. At least some of this distress may be attributed to the universal and potent condemnation noncustodial mothers experience from family, friends, and strangers. In *Absentee Mothers* (Allanheld, Osmun/Universe Books, 1982), Patricia Paskowicz — an "absentee mother" herself — documents through personal experience and survey results the reality of mothers who relinquish custody of their children after having lived with them for some time.

1029. Jacobson, Bobbie. **The Ladykillers: Why Smoking is a Feminist Issue.** New York: Continuum, 1982. 136p. bibliog. pbk. $6.95. LC 81-17358. ISBN 0826401856.

"Why a book on women and smoking?" Because, Jacobson says, although smoking still kills more men than women each year, "... women are rapidly gaining ground, each year coming closer to an equality in death that most never achieve in life" (p.vi). In Part I of this book, "The Sexual Politics of Smoking," Jacobson, a British medical journalist, examines some of the ways in which the smoking habit differs for women and men. Jacobson concedes that the aura of liberation may entice more women to begin smoking, but, she argues, it is continuing sexual inequality that keeps them smoking. Women maintain the habit as a way of keeping the lid on emotions, from fear of getting fat, and out of lack of confidence that they can in fact stop. Jacobson also surveys the sexual politics of cigarette advertising in the United States and Britain, and the campaigns of health educators and political activists against smoking. She decries the absence of anti-smoking action in the women's movement. In Part II, Jacobson advises the would-be nonsmoker on how to quit. For a wealth of medical data, the reader can turn to *The Health Consequences of Smoking for Women: A Report of the Surgeon General* (U.S. Department of Health and Human Services, 1980).

1030. Krieger, Susan. **The Mirror Dance: Identity in a Women's Community.** Philadelphia: Temple University Press, 1983. 199p. bibliog. $19.95. LC 82-19424. ISBN 0877223041.

In the late 1970s, Krieger, a sociologist, spent a year as a member of a loosely knit lesbian community in an unnamed Midwestern college town, where she conducted the seventy eight interviews on which this book draws. Her central theme is that of merging and separation — the recurring dilemma faced by women in a community that held out "a strong promise of identity affirmation stemming from what its members had in common" while suffering from "a lack of established mechanisms for dealing with the differences between members" (p.xiv). Krieger's method of presentation is as intriguing as her content. She deliberately uses only the paraphrased words of those she interviewed, never inserting herself as interpreter or theorizer. The interplay of many voices, often fraught with ambivalence, challenges the reader "to adopt these women temporarily as a peer group, to muddle through their difficulties with them ..." (p.xvii). Deborah Goleman Wolf's sympathetic study, *The Lesbian Community* (University of California Press, 1979), makes an interesting comparison to Krieger's effort, since it conforms more closely to traditional social science reporting. Wolf, a heterosexual anthropologist, similarly used the methods of participant observation and interviewing to compose a picture of the San Francisco lesbian-feminist community in the early seventies. In *Sunday's Women: A Report on Lesbian Life Today* (Beacon Press, 1979), journalist Sasha Gregory Lewis relies on both in-depth interviews and existing research reports to counter conservative misrepresentations of lesbian lifestyles.

1031.   Luker, Kristin. **Abortion and the Politics of Motherhood.** Berkeley: University of California Press, 1984. 324p. bibliog. index. $14.95. LC 83-47849. ISBN 0520043146.

In the first half of this scrupulously balanced book, sociologist Kristin Luker turns to written records from the last century to trace how physicians gained control over abortion and maintained this hegemony until their own consensus on the issue began to disintegrate in the 1960s. She then depicts the emergence of two political camps in the aftermath of the 1973 Supreme Court decision in *Roe v. Wade,* drawing on her extensive interviews with "prolife" and "prochoice" activists in California. This interview material enables Luker to achieve an unusually sympathetic portrayal of the concerns of anti-abortion women. Yet she has been criticized by at least one reviewer for reducing the very complex networks of abortion politics to two opposing world views, as expressed in the words of her interviewees. Luker's central argument is that the abortion controversy turns on their sharply contrasting definitions of motherhood. Fred M. Frohock sets his interviews with "prolife" and "prochoice" abortion activists in the context of political philosophy in *Abortion: A Case Study in Law and Morals* (Greenwood Press, 1983), demonstrating that the abortion issue eludes "standard tests for deciding between state regulation and private choice" (p.viii) and ultimately transforms political theory itself. Sidney Callahan and Daniel Callahan, editors of *Abortion: Understanding Differences* (Plenum Press, 1984), sought to achieve a broader context for their own opposing views on abortion by soliciting thoughtful papers from scholars in both camps. Opening with a survey of research data from public opinion polls, and a summary of Kristin Luker's research, the volume moves on to a selection of articles representing "prolife" and "prochoice" positions on four topics: women and feminism, the family, children, and social and cultural life.

1032.   Macdonald, Barbara, with Cynthia Rich. **Look Me in the Eye: Old Women, Aging, and Ageism.** San Francisco: Spinsters, Ink, 1983. 115p. bibliog. pbk. $5.95. LC 83-82554. ISBN 0933216092.

Barbara Macdonald turns an uncompromising, angry eye on ageism in our society, and within the feminist/lesbian movement in particular. In her seventies at the time these essays were collected, Macdonald speaks movingly of the isolation and invisibility she has experienced, of younger women's stereotyping of the aged, and of accepting the inevitability of death. Macdonald's five essays are complemented by those of Cynthia Rich. One of Rich's contributions is a favorable review of Sarah H. Matthews's *The Social World of Old Women: Management of Self-Identity* (Sage Publications, 1979). Matthews employed two research methods—participant observation in a senior citizens' center and intensive interviewing of white widowed mothers over seventy years of age—to probe the self-definition of the "old woman" as she interacts with her peers, family members, and service providers, and as she confronts death. Quotations from old women enliven the otherwise somewhat dull academic prose.

1033.   Mora, Magdalena, and Adelaida R. Del Castillo, eds. **Mexican Women in the United States: Struggles Past and Present.** Los Angeles: Chicano Studies Research Center Publications, University of California, 1980. 204p. bibliog. pbk. $14.95. LC 80-10682. ISBN 0895510227.

Gathering some original pieces, and others previously published in difficult-to-access sources, this anthology aims to document and evaluate "Mexican women's participation in the struggle against national oppression, class exploitation, and sexism" (p.1). Part I analyzes contemporary Chicana activism in the Chicano and women's movements. The two articles in Part II address the issue of Chicana sterilization. Part III presents case studies of recent Chicana labor history, while Part IV looks back to earlier struggles. Part V offers profiles of four Chicanas. A statistical fact sheet concludes the volume. More academic and less political in orientation is the collection *Twice a Minority: Mexican American Women*, edited by Margarita B. Melville (Mosby, 1980). The twenty-two contributors to the volume—men and women, Anglos and Mexican Americans—represent a range of backgrounds in the social sciences, social work, and medicine. Melville arranges the seventeen articles in three thematic sections: Matrescence (family planning, abortion, childbirth, breastfeeding); Gender Roles (the Chicana women's movement, Chicana innovators, women and traditional medicine); and Cultural Conflict (acculturation, health and illness perceptions, Chicana and Anglo feminism, sterilization, aging).

1034. NiCarthy, Ginny. **Getting Free: A Handbook for Women in Abusive Relationships.** Seattle, WA: Seal Press, 1982. 272p. bibliog. pbk. $8.95. LC 82-80723. ISBN 093118813X.

NiCarthy's self-help manual is directed to battered women themselves, although counselors and shelter staff will find it immensely useful. The handbook discusses the dynamics of family violence, the pro's and con's of leaving an abusive partner, and guidelines for emotional recovery and life on one's own. Practical information on shelters, legal options, counseling, and protection of children abounds. Throughout the volume, NiCarthy uses quizzes and checklists to aid the reader in clarifying her values and choices. An earlier manual—*Stopping Wife Abuse* (Anchor Press, 1979), by Jennifer Baker Fleming—runs to over five hundred pages and might intimidate a woman seeking help. Subtitled "A Guide to the Emotional, Psychological, and Legal Implications ... for the abused woman and those helping her," the volume comprehensively covers options for battered women and counselors, the legal system, legislative reform, treatment for abusers, and the myriad details of establishing shelter and support services. Chapter VII is a succinct overview of research, which, like the listings of programs that conclude the volume, is now out of date.

1035. Oakley, Ann. **Subject Women.** New York: Pantheon Books, 1981. 406p. bibliog. index. $17.95. LC 81-47208. ISBN 0394521706.

Viewing the world through the lens of women's studies, Oakley muses, is something like being on the other side of Alice's looking glass: one finds "a familiar, yet also oddly contradictory, reality" (p.ix). Oakley attempts an ambitious overview of women's status in late twentieth-century industrialized society, using Britain as her primary case study. In her opening section, Oakley briefly traces the history of women's movements in the last two centuries. Subsequent sections take up socialization; paid and unpaid work; relationships with children, men, and women; class, politics, and power; and the field of women's studies.

1036. O'Donnell, Lydia N., 1949- . **The Unheralded Majority: Contemporary Women as Mothers.** Lexington, MA: Lexington Books, 1985. 170p. bibliog. index. $20.00. LC 83-49530. ISBN 0669082740.

O'Donnell interviewed seventy-four working- and middle-class women from the Boston metropolitan area in order "to learn how the rhetoric, ideologies, and realities of recent social changes, and specifically changing women's roles, have filtered through and been experienced by mainstream U.S. families" (p.4). In her view, these women are achieving a "new synthesis" of motherhood, paid employment, and community involvement, rejecting "either/or" options. The women attest outspokenly to the importance of their contributions, and the gratification they derive from them. British sociologist Ann Oakley presents a somewhat contrasting picture in *Women Confined: Towards a Sociology of Childbirth* (Schocken Books, 1980), a report on her interviews with fifty-five first-time mothers in London. The women she interviewed speak of the losses as well as the gains that come with a new child. Oakley provides lengthy verbatim accounts from these interviews in her book *Becoming a Mother* (Schocken Books, 1979). Mary Georgina Boulton, another British researcher, reports on her study of fifty middle- and working-class women with preschool children in *On Being a Mother* (Tavistock Publications, 1983). She analyzes her interviews in terms of both the women's immediate frustrations or satisfactions and their long-term sense of meaning and purpose.

1037.   Ostrander, Susan A. **Women of the Upper Class.** Philadelphia: Temple University Press, 1984. 183p. bibliog. $16.95. LC 83-18214. ISBN 0877223343.

Ostrander opens a door into the lives of thirty-six married women from the upper class of a major Midwestern city. Her focus is "the day-to-day *activities* of upper-class women, with an emphasis on their *meaning* and *consequence*" (p.3). Drawing on her interviews with these women, Ostrander describes their roles as wives, mothers, club members, and community volunteers, concluding that the upper-class woman's "work serves largely to uphold the power and privilege of her own class in the social order of things" (p.3).

1038.   Palgi, Michal, et al. **Sexual Equality: The Israeli Kibbutz Tests the Theories.** Darby, PA: Norwood Editions, 1983. 337p. bibliog. $32.50. LC 83-2133. ISBN 084825676X.

In the contest between proponents of "nature" and "nurture," the Israeli kibbutz has been seen as an invaluable "social laboratory" in which to investigate conflicting claims about the character of sexual inequality. The fifteen articles in this collection, most previously published between 1973 and 1981, consider the kibbutz controversy from a number of different angles. For example, Melford Spiro, author of *Gender and Culture: Kibbutz Women Revisited* (Duke University Press, 1979), sees the drift toward increasingly rigid and traditional sex roles as a "counterrevolution" brought about by "precultural motivational dispositions" (p.57). On the other hand, in a close critique of Spiro's arguments, Joseph Blasi questions just how "revolutionary" the original kibbutz sex-role experiments really were. Part I presents conflicting approaches to the general controversy. Part II examines work and public activity in the kibbutz, and Part III looks at education and family. The final chapter, in Part IV, attempts an integration of the issues.

1039.   Pleck, Joseph H. **The Myth of Masculinity.** Cambridge, MA: MIT Press, 1981. 229p. bibliog. index. $27.50. LC 81-6058. ISBN 0262160811.

Pleck, a leading theoretician in the new field of "mens studies," demolishes the premises of what he terms the Masculine Sex-Role Identity (MSRI) paradigm and presents an alternative—the Sex-Role Strain (SRS) paradigm. The prevailing theory since the 1930s, the MSRI "holds that the fundamental problem of individual psychological development is establishing a sex role identity" (p.3); thus, many social ills can be blamed on men's insecurities about their masculinity. In contrast, Pleck's SRS paradigm holds that societal pressures, not innate psychological need, create problems for those who violate or overconform to traditional sex roles. Clyde Franklin likewise summarizes recent research and offers his own theories in *The Changing Definition of Masculinity* (Plenum Press, 1984), while James A. Doyle brings a feminist perspective to historical, biological, anthropological, sociological, and psychological views of manhood in his excellent overview, *The Male Experience* (W. C. Brown, 1983). Two other works on male roles are worth noting here: *The American Man* (Prentice-Hall, 1980), an anthology of historical studies edited by Elizabeth H. Pleck and Joseph H. Pleck; and *Men in Difficult Times* (Prentice-Hall, 1981), edited by Robert A. Lewis, an eclectic anthology focused on men's personal responses to traditional sex role socialization and the changes wrought by feminism.

1040. Pogrebin, Letty Cottin. **Family Politics: Love and Power on an Intimate Frontier.** New York: McGraw-Hill, 1983. 278p. bibliog. index. $14.95. LC 83-9818. ISBN 0070503869.

Pogrebin synthesizes recent feminist thinking about the family for a broad audience, including policymakers. Her objective is twofold: "to explore the use and misuse of family issues in American politics, and to examine ... the power relations that exist among women, men, and children who live together" (p.ix). She states her perspective simply: "... it won't do to just trash the family; we must transform it" (p.25). In discussions of children, economics, family power struggles, conflicts between home and work, housework, pregnancy and motherhood, and fatherhood, Pogrebin is quick to identify the hypocrisy of supposedly pro-family public policy, and to outline the very different kinds of measures we might see "if we really cared about families." While she stresses that the "Dick-and-Jane nuclear households" of right-wing propaganda are a distinct minority, race and class differences between American families are not a primary focus here.

1041. Renvoize, Jean. **Going Solo: Single Mothers by Choice.** Boston: Routledge and Kegan Paul, 1985. 318p. bibliog. $19.95. LC 84-2244. ISBN 071020065X.

Renvoize interviewed single mothers in Britain, the United States, and Holland. While not all these women are feminists, Renvoize credits the women's movement with having made single motherhood a positive choice. The interviewees describe the reasons they chose to become mothers, the difficulties in finding a father, the question of family, methods of getting pregnant, problems and joys of the single-parent family, and relationships with men. Several of the women interviewed are lesbian. Oddly, lesbian experience is completely neglected by Nancy L. Peterson in her work *The Ever-Single Woman: Life Without Marriage* (Quill, 1982). Peterson presents the stories of women ranging in age from their twenties to their seventies — with and without children — who have chosen not to marry, having instead developed "lives of positive autonomy."

1042. Roberts, Albert R., with Beverly J. Roberts. **Sheltering Battered Women: A National Study and Service Guide.** New York: Springer, 1981. 227p. bibliog. index. pbk. $17.95. LC 80-19827. ISBN 0826126901.

Roberts, a professor of sociology and social work, conducted a national survey of battered women's emergency shelters, hotlines, and counseling services in the summer of 1978. Here he reports the responses he received to questions about these programs' goals, activities, funding, organizational structures, and interaction with criminal justice agencies. In addition, Roberts offers direct advice to abused women, police, and church workers; examples of shelter procedures; and prevention strategies. Appendices describe the eighty-nine programs included in the survey and list community funding sources. Betsy Warrior's *Battered Women's Directory* (9th ed., Terry Mehlman, 1985) presents the fullest and most current lists of services for battered women in the United States, Canada, and abroad, along with practical suggestions for service providers and a mixed bag of background readings from feminist perspectives.

1043. Roberts, Helen, ed. **Doing Feminist Research.** Boston: Routledge and Kegan Paul, 1981. 207p. bibliog. index. $9.95. LC 80-42164. ISBN 0710007728.

The eight contributions to this anthology focus on the discipline of sociology, but the principles set forth and the problems described will resonate for researchers in other fields as well. The papers point to theoretical, methodological, practical, and ethical issues raised by feminist investigators. Among the contents are Helen Roberts's "Women and Their Doctors: Power and Powerlessness in the Research Process," Ann Oakley's "Interviewing Women: A Contradiction in Terms," Christine Delphy's "Women in Stratification Studies," and Dale Spender's "The Gatekeepers: A Feminist Critique of Academic Publishing." *Breaking Out: Feminist Consciousness and Feminist Research* (Routledge and Kegan Paul, 1983) can be profitably read along with Roberts's volume. In it, Liz Stanley and Sue Wise present a readable critique of social science theory and methodology and argue for their own deeply felt belief that "the analytic use of feeling and experience in an examination of 'the personal' should be the main principle on which feminist research is based" (p.178).

1044. Rodgers-Rose, La Frances, ed. **The Black Woman.** Beverly Hills: Sage Publications, 1980. 316p. bibliog. $28.00. LC 79-28712. ISBN 0803913117.

In her preface, Rodgers-Rose laments the paucity of good research on black women. To counterbalance prevailing characterizations of black women as "matriarchal, domineering, aggressive, permissive, superstrong, [and] overly religious" (p.11), Rodgers-Rose gathers original research and theory papers by black women trained almost exclusively in the social sciences, among them Christina Brinkley-Carter, Bonnie Thornton Dill, Gloria Wade-Gayles, and Harriet Pipes McAdoo. The nineteen articles are arranged in four thematic sections: "Social Demographic Characteristics"; "The Black Woman and Her Family"; "Political, Educational, and Economic Institutions and the Black Woman"; and "Social Psychology of the Black Woman."

1045. Rossi, Alice S., 1922- , ed. **Gender and the Life Course.** New York: Aldine, 1985. 368p. bibliog. index. pbk. $14.95. LC 84-12335. ISBN 020230311X.

Aiming "to provide a good sampler of what is occurring in gender and age research" (p.xvii), Rossi pulls together revised versions of eighteen papers originally presented at the annual conference of the American Sociological Association in 1983. Half the authors are sociologists; the others represent the fields of history, political science, anthropology, psychology, demography, and economics. The disciplinary mix makes for a lively and thought-provoking volume. Part I includes four chapters on gender and the life course in historical perspective, while the four contributions to the third and final part look at contemporary aged populations. The middle and longest section, "Gender Differentiation and Social Institutions," offers ten essays on such topics as individual development, deviant behavior, fertility and parenthood, women and men in the labor force, love, and the welfare state.

1046. Russell, Diana E. H. **Rape in Marriage.** New York: Macmillan, 1982. 412p. bibliog. index. $16.95. LC 82-7824. ISBN 0026061902.

Rape in Marriage broke the silence on the subject of marital rape, and it remains a landmark study. Russell interviewed a random sample of over nine hundred women in San Francisco; she found that fourteen percent of those who were or had been married had been raped by their husbands. Quoting extensively from the interviews, Russell details the women's experiences, examines the husbands' motivations and the lasting effects on the wives, and outlines strategies women use to stop the violence. The penultimate chapter adds an international perspective, with many first-hand accounts from other countries related in letters. Russell concludes that the first and most important tactic to combat marital rape is to make it illegal everywhere. She further insists that wife rape must be studied in the broader context of violence and sexuality within marriage; rape, she declares, is an extreme expression of the unequal power relationship enshrined in the traditional family. David Finkelhor and Kersti Yllo's more recent survey of Boston-area women (*License to Rape: Sexual Abuse of Wives,* Holt, Rinehart and Winston, 1985) confirms some of Russell's findings.

1047. Russell, Diana E. H. **Sexual Exploitation: Rape, Child Sexual Abuse, and Workplace Harassment.** Beverly Hills, CA: Sage Publications, 1984. 319p. bibliog. index. $29.00. LC 84-6950. ISBN 0803923546.

Russell takes on an ambitious task: to document the prevalence of rape, child sexual abuse, and sexual harassment; and to draw connections among various theories of causation. In achieving her goal, she provides a thorough and systematic survey of existing literature. She also takes pains to elucidate the findings of her own research, the first large-scale survey in this area to utilize random sampling techniques. In *Intimate Intrusions: Women's Experience of Male Violence* (Routledge and Kegan Paul, 1985), Elizabeth A. Stanko synthesizes British and American studies of incest, rape, wife battering, and sexual harassment. She shows how "men's threatening, intimidating, and violent behavior" (p.1) causes all women to lead lives of fear and silence, and how those who handle women's complaints within the criminal justice system and places of employment become "second assailants." *Rape and Inequality*, by Julia R. Schwendinger and Herman Schwendinger (Sage Publications, 1983), also bears comparison to Russell's volume. The Schwendingers critique prevailing theories of rape, both androcentric and feminist, basing their interpretations on anthropological and historical evidence.

1048. Sandmaier, Marian. **The Invisible Alcoholics: Women and Alcohol Abuse in America.** New York: McGraw-Hill, 1980. 298p. bibliog. index. pbk. $5.95. LC 79-17819. ISBN 0070546614.

"Our current body of knowledge on alcoholism derives almost wholly from male experience," Sandmaier observes. "But far from duplicating male reality, the alcoholic woman lives out a nightmare uniquely shaped by her cultural role and status" (p.xvi). Sandmaier supplements a thorough review of existing research and theory with case studies gleaned from interviews with recovering alcoholic women, including housewives, employed women, minority women, teenagers, lesbians, and women on skid row. Her feminism, always close to the surface, shines most visibly in the final chapters, which critique professional and self-help treatment options and recommend as sources of help not only groups and agencies specifically focused on problem drinking but also women's organizations and services. *Women Who Drink*, by John Langone and Dolores deNobrega Langone (Addison-Wesley, 1980), also documents the social stigmatization of women alcoholics, stringing together long quotes from alcoholism experts and interviewed drinkers. In *Broken Promises, Mended Dreams* (Little, Brown, 1984), Richard Meryman creates a riveting composite case history of a housewife who undergoes treatment for alcoholism. Recovery is also the theme of an anthology edited by Jean Swallow — *Out From Under: Sober Dykes and Our Friends* (Spinsters, Ink, 1983). Written by and for lesbians, the collection covers the struggles and triumphs of alcoholics, co-alcoholics (those who are affected by another's drinking), adult children of alcoholics, and lesbians dependent on other drugs. Swallow's and Sandmaier's volumes contain brief bibliographies; for additional references, consult *Social and Behavioral Aspects of Female Alcoholism: An Annotated Bibliography*, by H. Paul Chalfant and Brent S. Roper (Greenwood Press, 1980).

1049. Schur, Edwin M. **Labeling Women Deviant: Gender, Stigma, and Social Control.** Philadelphia: Temple University Press, 1983. 286p. bibliog. index. $24.95. LC 83-10942. ISBN 0877223327.

Schur, who has written many books on deviance and social control, here brings a critical feminist perspective to bear on the sociology of deviance, and uses the concepts of labeling theory to argue that "women have served as 'all-purpose deviants' within our society" (p.7). Two central themes govern his analysis: 1) that stigma is inversely related to social power; and 2) that deviance labeling is a form of social control. Schur first surveys the many ways women are stigmatized (e.g., in relation to appearance, maternity, and sexuality). He then shifts the focus to male behavior, showing how a society eager to stigmatize women is reluctant to label as deviant acts committed by men, such as sexual harassment, rape, woman-battering, and the buying of female sexuality (prostitution, pornography). Next, he attempts to explain how female deviance is produced, focusing particularly on mental illness and crime. Schur concludes by considering the implications of his analysis for the sociology of deviance and for social change. A lengthy and up-to-date bibliography rounds out the volume.

1050.* Scott, Hilda, 1915- . **Sweden's "Right to Be Human": Sex-Role Equality: The Goal and the Reality.** Armonk, NY: M. E. Sharpe, 1982. 191p. bibliog. index. LC 81-5239. ISBN 0873321820.

Author of an insightful, widely read study of women and socialism, Scott here turns her attention to the experience of Sweden. Scott has visited Sweden three times since 1969 and interviewed well over a hundred people. She examines policies adopted in the last decade and a half to transform the roles of both men and women in many areas of life: employment, trade unions, the family, education, childcare, housing, and politics. While carefully documenting "the areas where women and men have conflicting interests that cannot be reached by such reforms," Scott believes her study "illustrates how much can be accomplished in a welfare state that is prepared to invest in equality" (p.xi). In *The State and Working Women: A Comparative Study of Britain and Sweden* (Princeton University Press, 1984), Mary Ruggie argues that differences in the status of British and Swedish working women are attributable much less to gender-specific policy than to the role of the state in the two countries. Specifically, it is the willingness of the state to intervene in the economy, in Ruggie's view, that has made possible Swedish women's "greater relative equality" (p.xiv).

1051. Scott, Hilda, 1915- . **Working Your Way to the Bottom: The Feminization of Poverty.** Boston: Pandora Press, 1984. 192p. bibliog. index. pbk. $8.95. LC 84-15913. ISBN 0863580114.

The recently coined catchphrase "the feminization of poverty" has provoked controversy. Critics of the concept say that the narrow emphasis on the increasing correlation of *gender* and poverty obscures the considerable impact of race and class. Scott responds to these criticisms but defends her woman-centered focus in this wide-ranging study of women's impoverishment worldwide. Tapping history, anthropology, and psychology, Scott argues that women's poverty is fundamentally linked to their large share of unpaid and undervalued labor, and she calls for a new political economy that would make "unpaid work and the values it represents at least as central to our planning as paid work ..." (p.147). Women's unpaid labor in the home and their underpaid labor in the workforce are also addressed in the pamphlet *Poverty in the American Dream: Women and Children First* (Institute for New Communications/South End Press, 1983). Authors Karin Stallard, Barbara Ehrenreich, and Holly Sklar critically review U.S. women's employment status, inadequate childcare, federal poverty policy, and Reaganomics, emphasizing that for many women, "poverty may be a divorce away" (p.9). For a closer look at the statistics behind the analysis, readers can turn to *A Growing Crisis: Disadvantaged Women and Their Children* (U.S. Commission on Civil Rights, 1983). *Lives in Stress: Women and Depression,* edited by Deborah Belle (Sage Publications, 1982), reports the findings of an intensive field study on the mental health consequences of the "feminization of poverty."

1052. Shapiro, Thomas M. **Population Control Politics: Women, Sterilization, and Reproductive Choice.** Philadelphia: Temple University Press, 1985. 221p. bibliog. index. $24.95. LC 84-8681. ISBN 0877223653.

An activist with the Committee to End Sterlization Abuse, Shapiro writes that he was drawn to study reproduction rights "because it was a concrete way to analyze the theoretical and political dynamics among class, race, and gender" (p.ix). Shapiro is careful from the outset to distinguish between birth control (voluntary planning by individuals), family planning (state programs for reproductive control), and population control (eugenics-inspired programs). After tracing population control history in the United States, and examining the programs and influence of the contemporary Population Council, Shapiro undertakes a detailed empirical analysis of recent patterns of female sterilization and sterilization abuse, and describes the movement against such abuse. In his final chapter, he attempts to define what his study has to say about the functions of the modern welfare state and reproductive freedom.

1053. Shields, Laurie. **Displaced Homemakers: Organizing for a New Life.** New York: McGraw-Hill, 1981. 272p. index. pbk. $5.95. LC 80-15336. ISBN 0070568022.

A displaced homemaker is "an individual who has, for a substantial number of years, provided unpaid service to her family, has been dependent on her spouse for her income but who loses that income through death, divorce, separation, desertion, or the disablement of her husband" (p.ix). Author Laurie Shields (and Tish Sommers, who wrote the epilogue to this book) founded the Alliance for Displaced Homemakers in 1975. Here Shields gives a history of the movement in the years since then; documents the patterns of discrimination suffered by homemakers; gives an account of lobbying efforts for national displaced homemaker bills; offers ideas on "organizing for a new life"; and describes programs set up across the United States to aid former homemakers. Nancy C. Baker's *New Lives for Former Wives: Displaced Homemakers* (Anchor Press/Doubleday, 1980) alternates practical advice and profiles of displaced homemakers in chapters on loss and loneliness; self-esteem; finding new relationships; establishing independence; motherhood; relationships with family and the former spouse; poverty; and work skills and employment opportunities.

1054. **Social Science Research and Women in the Arab World.** Dover, NH: F. Pinter, 1984. 175p. bibliog. $20.95. LC 84-8941. ISBN 0861873874.

Women scholars from Algeria, Egypt, Iraq, Libyan Arab Jamahiriya, Morocco, Saudi Arabia, Tunisia, and Sudan contributed papers to this volume; seven out of the eight articles were originally prepared for a UNESCO conference held in Tunis in 1982. The first five articles survey the status of social science research on women in the Arab Gulf region, North Africa, Morocco, Algeria, and the Sudan. The following two pieces attempt to formulate a theoretical framework for the study of women in the Arab world, and to specify the conditions necessary for Arab women to conduct such research. A final essay surveys trends in social science research on women in the Arab region from 1960 to 1980. The studies call for future research to be undertaken not by "outsiders," but by women from the region themselves, and urge that the research attend to questions of human rights.

1055. Staines, Graham L., and Joseph H. Pleck. **The Impact of Work Schedules on the Family.** Ann Arbor: Institute for Social Research, University of Michigan, 1983. 166p. bibliog. $22.00. LC 83-8451. ISBN 0879442840.

Most recent studies of dual-earner families are based on intensive interviews with very small, nonrepresentative samples. Staines and Pleck's work departs from this pattern. Using a large national sample and a sophisticated research design, the authors investigate the effects of alternative work schedules on families (both dual- and single-earner). Their findings reveal workers' control over work schedules to be of major importance in mitigating stress. Joel C. Moses introduces a comparative framework in *The Politics of Women and Work in the Soviet Union and The United States: Alternative Work Schedules and Sex Discrimination* (Institute of International Studies, University of California, Berkeley, 1983), illuminating the paradoxical finding that Soviet women reject the alternative work schedules sought by women in the United States. In *Professional Work and Marriage* (St. Martin's Press, 1981), Marilyn Rueschemeyer conclues, on the basis of interviews with American, Soviet Jewish emigré, and East German dual-career and single-career couples, that some of the tension between family and professional work inheres in the very nature of the work. Yet, she adds, government policy does make a difference.

1056. Stimpson, Catharine R., 1936- , and Ethel Spector Person, eds. **Women — Sex and Sexuality.** Chicago: University of Chicago Press, 1980. 345p. bibliog. index. $20.00. LC 80-51587. ISBN 0226774767.

In 1980, *Signs: Journal of Women in Culture and Society* published two special issues on women and sexuality. Reprinted here are nine articles: "Who is Sylvia? On the Loss of Sexual Paradigms," by Elizabeth Janeway; "Sex and Power: Sexual Bases of Radical Feminism," by Alix Kates Shulman; "Sexuality as the Mainstay of Identity: Psychoanalytic Perspectives," by Ethel Spector Person; "Compulsory Heterosexuality and Lesbian Existence," by Adrienne Rich; "Reproductive Freedom: Beyond 'A Woman's Right to Choose,'" by Rosalind Pollack Petchesky; "Menstruation and Reproduction: An Oglala Case," by Marla N. Powers; "Pornography and Repression: A Reconsideration," by Irene Diamond; "The Politics of Prostitution," by Judith Walkowitz; and "The Front Line: Notes on Sex in Novels by Women, 1969-1979," by Ann Barr Snitow. In addition, the collection includes seven review essays on: biological influences on human sex and gender; behavior and the menstrual cycle; pregnancy; maternal sexuality and asexual motherhood; the biology of menopause; social and behavioral constructions of female sexuality; and couples advice books of the late 1970s. Book reviews and archival notes complete the text.

1057. Stockard, Jean, and Miriam M. Johnson. **Sex Roles: Sex Inequality and Sex Role Development.** Englewood Cliffs, NJ: Prentice-Hall, 1980. 331p. bibliog. index. pbk. $23.95. LC 78-23286. ISBN 0138075603.

In this introductory social psychology text, Stockard and Johnson argue that "sex roles and sex differences cannot be studied without reference to sex inequality" (p.xv). Accordingly, Part One introduces the reader to the literature on sex inequality in cultural symbolism, interpersonal relations, politics, the economy, the family, and education — in the United States and cross-culturally. In Part Two, the authors turn to sex-role development, touching on biological influences, psychological sex differences, psychological and psychoanalytic theories of sex-role development, the role of parents and peers, and the life cycle. Reinforcement learning theory — which Stockard and Johnson criticize for its victim-blaming implications — is the theoretical model forming Bernice Lott's somewhat more advanced text, *Becoming a Woman: The Socialization of Gender* (C. C. Thomas, 1981). Lott adopts a life-cycle approach, discussing a range of topics including work and sexual abuse as well as marriage and motherhood. A topical approach is taken by British psychologists Barbara Lloyd and John Archer in *Sex and Gender* (1982; rev. ed., Cambridge University Press, 1985). In cogent discussions of physical sex differences, sexuality, aggression and power, mental health, the family, intelligence and achievement, the development of gender differences, and social change, the authors strive to show how "commonsense" views of sex and gender have influenced social science. Although Lloyd and Archer draw on British literature to a degree, the United States is the predominant focus in all three of these works. In contrast, a Canadian perspective shapes the presentation in Marlene Mackie's *Exploring Gender Relations* (Butterworths, 1983). None of these texts makes more than fleeting mention of differences of race, class, or sexual preference among women.

1058. Straus, Murray A., et al. **Behind Closed Doors: Violence in the American Family.** Garden City, NY: Anchor Press/Doubleday, 1980. 301p. bibliog. index. pbk. $8.95. LC 78 22741. ISBN 0385142595.

Noting the burgeoning body of literature on child abuse and wife battering, the authors of this highly readable study advocate focusing more broadly on violence in the family as a whole. Thus they also observe intra-sibling violence, husband abuse, and children's attacks on parents in their population of 2,143 families. Their research measured the incidence of different types of violence in U.S. families (from spanking to murder), surveyed participants' attitudes toward violence, and assessed its causes. Murray A. Straus, Richard J. Gelles, and Suzanne K. Steinmetz skillfully blend statistical interpretation and quotations from interviews to illuminate internal family dynamics and broader social patterns. They close by recommending a number of short-term solutions (shelters, daycare, counseling, and the like) and cautioning that only "long-term changes in the fabric of a society which now tends to tolerate, accept, and even encourage the use of violence in families" (p.244) will break the cycle of violence from one generation to the next.

1059. Swerdlow, Amy, et al. **Household and Kin: Families in Flux.** Old Westbury, NY: Feminist Press, 1981. 183p. bibliog. index. $14.95. LC 80-17038. ISBN 0912670916.

One of twelve volumes in the Feminist Press series "Women's Lives, Women's Work," *Household and Kin* exemplifies the series' commitment to create feminist texts for the undergraduate classroom. Amy Swerdlow, Renate Bridenthal, Joan Kelly, and Phyllis Vine are all notable historians. Their presentation here is beautifully concise and free of technical language, yet it incorporates much of the latest feminist thinking on the family.

Their aim is, first of all, to impress upon their readers the wide variability of family forms, and, secondly, to demonstrate how the family shapes, and is shaped by, social patterns of production, reproduction, and consumption. Throughout the work, the authors attend to race and class as key determinants of family relationships and quality of life. Joan Kelly places the family in historical and cross-cultural context in Part I; Renate Bridenthal surveys contemporary family patterns in the United States in Part II; and Amy Swerdlow and Phyllis Vine consider alternatives to the family—utopian and real; past, present, and future—in Part III. Carefully chosen photographs further bring home the authors' message that there is no such thing as the normative family.

1060.* Tsuchida, Nobuya, ed. **Asian and Pacific American Experiences: Women's Perspectives.** Minneapolis: Asian/Pacific American Learning Resource Center and General College, University of Minnesota, 1982. 255p. bibliog. LC 81-86586.

Nobuya Tsuchida compiled this anthology for use in a course she developed on Asian American women at the University of Minnesota. Twenty-four contributions—some written for this volume, others previously published elsewhere—address a wide range of topics concerning Asian and Pacific American women, past and present. There are historical pieces on California's anti-miscegenation laws, Chinese immigrant women in nineteenth-century California, Japanese prostitution in Hawaii, Japanese immigrant women in the United States, and Korean women in Hawaii. Among a number of biographical and autobiographical selections, five in particular stand out—moving testimonies by Japanese American women presented to the Commission on Wartime Relocation and Internment of Civilians. Finally, there are essays on the contemporary status of Filipinas in Hawaii and in Minnesota, on family structure and acculturation in the Chinese community in Minnesota, and on Japanese American interracial marriage, nursing care for Indochinese refugees, Asian women and the law, and Asian women in Hawaiian politics.

1061. Wagner, Jon, ed. **Sex Roles in Contemporary American Communes.** Bloomington: Indiana University Press, 1982. 242p. bibliog. $20.00. LC 81-47571. ISBN 0253351871.

The six case studies comprising this volume seriously call into question the belief that communalism is necessarily linked to the ideal of sex-role equality. In fact, for each of the communes profiled here, sex roles are reported to be very traditional in character, and, in some cases, downright misogynist. The communities range from the Black Hebrew Israelites, to the Mormon Levites, to The Farm, Tennessee's utopian offshoot of the late sixties' Haight-Ashbury movement. Editor Jon Wagner opens the volume with an introductory survey of communal utopias in the United States, past and pesent, using the opportunity to constrast sexually egalitarian and inegalitarian ventures.

1062. Weitzman, Lenore J. **The Divorce Revolution: The Unexpected Social and Economic Consequences for Women and Children in America.** New York: Free Press, 1985. 504p. bibliog. index. $19.95. LC 85-6868. ISBN 0029347106.

Weitzman spent ten years interviewing judges, lawyers, and divorced persons, and examining court records to try to assess the impact of the "divorce revolution," a phenomenon she attributes to three current trends: the mounting divorce rate; passage of no-fault divorce laws in all but two states; and the destigmatization of divorce. While she found that liberalized divorce laws have, as intended, lessened the acrimony traditionally associated with divorce proceedings, Weitzman was surprised to discover their other "unexpected consequences"—such as "the systematic impoverishment of women and children" (p.xiv). No-fault divorce, along with new gender-neutral rules for allocating property and child support, unrealistically assumes an economic equality between husband and wife. Weitzman found that newly divorced women with young children experience on average a seventy-three percent decline in their standard of living, while their former husbands' standard rises by forty-two percent. Older homemakers and mothers of young children are especially victimized. Weitzman also analyzes what the new divorce laws tell us about changing marriage norms, especially the drift toward a more individualistic ethos. In a final chapter, she proposes a series of possible reforms. *Separated and Divorced Women* (Greenwood Press, 1982), by Lynne Carol Halem, documents similarly bleak legal, emotional, and economic effects of separation and divorce on middle-class American women. A related title is Phyllis Chesler's *Mothers on Trial: The Battle for Children and Custody* (McGraw-Hill, 1986), which indicts the effects of new family law on custody decisions.

1063.   Willenz, June A. **Women Veterans: America's Forgotten Heroines.** New York: Continuum, 1983. 252p. bibliog. index. $19.50. LC 83-7850. ISBN 0826402410.

When Willenz, Executive Director of the American Veterans Committee, resolved to learn something about the 1,218,000 women veterans in the United States, she was shocked to discover that neither academic research nor government statistics were available. The story she eventually uncovered is one of gross inequities. After a brief historical recap of American women's military involvements, Willenz presents brief profiles of seventeen World War II veterans and nine veterans from the postwar period. (Several in the latter group served in Vietnam.) She goes on to review government and Veterans Administration policies, women's participation in veterans' organizations, and recent policy initiatives. Repetition and an infelicitous style mar this work, which must nonetheless be recommended as a unique source on the topic. For a riveting personal account—the first—by a woman Vietnam veteran, turn to *Home Before Morning,* by Lynda Van Devanter, with Christopher Morgan (Beaufort Books, 1983). Van Devanter served one year as a surgical nurse in one of the most dangerous areas of Vietnam. The horror of her war account is matched only by the grimness of her subsequent ten years at home, marked by severe post-traumatic stress syndrome. At the time this book appeared, Van Devanter was director of the Women's Project of the Vietnam Veterans of America.

1064.   Women and Geography Study Group of the IBG. **Geography and Gender: An Introduction to Feminist Geography.** Dover, NH: Hutchinson, 1984. 160p. bibliog. index. pbk. $4.95. LC 84-12871. ISBN 0091566711.

Intended as a text for undergraduates, *Geography and Gender* is a lucid introduction to some of the new theoretical questions being explored within feminist geography, written by the women's group of the Institute of British Geographers. The authors analyze women's relation to urban spatial structure; the reorganization and relocation of industry and employment in postwar Britain; access to facilities; and the organization of social life and production in Third World countries. They conclude with a chapter on feminist pedagogy and methodology in geography. Less concerned with questions of theory, *Making Space: Women and the Man-Made Environment* (Pluto Press, 1984) documents how narrow and prescriptive conceptions of gender are embedded in the built environment, and discusses the consequences for women. (The picture on the front cover shows a woman struggling up a long set of stairs with a baby in a stroller.) The book is written by the members of Matrix, a British architectural collective committed to developing feminist approaches to design.

SPORTS

The literature on women and sport is sparse but varied. It bridges the disciplines (including sociology, physical education, biology, medicine, and even philosophy) and spans genres, from serious scholarly studies, to fitness manuals, to biographies and first-person accounts. Although not every field of athletic endeavor is covered, a sampling of sports and outdoor activities is presented in the references below. Now somewhat out of date, Mary L. Remley's *Women in Sport: A Guide to Information Sources* (Gale, 1980) provides annotated listings of books, periodicals, sports organizations, and other resources.

1065. Averbuch, Gloria, 1951- . **The Woman Runner: Free to Be the Complete Athlete.** New York: Cornerstone Library, 1984. 213p. bibliog. index. $9.95. LC 84-9528. ISBN 0346126444.

In the last decade, the popularity of running has skyrocketed among men as well as women. For women, however, the change is part of a fundamental reorientation in women's attitudes toward athletics. Averbuch's emphasis here is on this change in consciousness, and how running changes women's lives, rather than on questions of technique. "Being fit is a feminist issue," she writes; "it has to do with being strong and in control, not just being thin" (p.18). In Part I, "The Woman Athlete," Averbuch surveys women's athletic progress and profiles six top women runners. In "A Runner's Body," she offers very brief comments about the effects of running on menstruation, pregnancy, breasts, and bone disorders, among other topics. Part III, "Running and Winning," examines issues raised by competition, describes major women's races, and furnishes tips about safety and running gear. In the final section, Averbuch speculates about the future of women's running. For more on the health effects of women's running, readers may turn to *Running Free: A Book for Women Runners and Their Friends,* by Joan L. Ullyot, M.D. (Putnam, 1980).

1066. Blum, Arlene, 1945- . **Annapurna: A Woman's Place.** San Francisco: Sierra Club Books, 1980. 256p. bibliog. index. $16.95. LC 80-13288. ISBN 0871562367.

Blum writes a personal account of the 1978 American Women's Himalayan Expedition to Annapurna, a tale that alternately entertains, inspires, and terrifies. At the time the expedition was planned, no woman had ever reached the summit of an eight-thousand-meter peak, and the ten-woman team faced daunting prejudice and lack of support. In fact, only four of thirteen earlier male expeditions had reached Annapurna's peak, and nine climbers had died in the attempt. Blum not only relays the facts of the climb—the route, the equipment, conflicts with the sherpas, storms and avalanches, the ascent to the summit—but also recreates conversations and quotes from diaries, conveying a vivid sense of the personalities and their unusual intimacy as a team. Numerous photographs document every stage of the journey. Though part of the team did achieve Annapurna's summit, two women fell to their deaths, and the expedition concluded in an uneasy spirit of celebration and mourning. Where the Annapurna team tested themselves against mountains of snow and ice, in *Tracks* (Pantheon Books, 1980), Robyn Davidson writes the account of one woman's seventeen-hundred-mile trek across the Australian desert. *Women of the Four Winds*, by Elizabeth Fagg Olds (Houghton Mifflin, 1985), profiles four American women explorers from the turn of the century.

1067.   Boutilier, Mary A., and Lucinda SanGiovanni. **The Sporting Woman.** Champaign, IL: Human Kinetics, 1983. 289p. bibliog. index. $22.95. LC 82-83147. ISBN 0931250358.

Boutilier and SanGiovanni ground their ambitious and provocative analysis in the sociology of sport, feminist theory, and their own experiences as athletes and coaches. In Part I, they establish their theoretical stance, a mix of humanist sociology and socialist feminism; review American women's sporting history; and examine the social context of women in sport. In addition, Susan Birrell contributes a chapter on the psychological dimensions of women's athletic participation. In Part II, "Institutional Analyses," the authors (joined by contributor Susan Greendorfer in one chapter) bring their theoretical perspective to bear on discussions of how the family, education, the mass media, and government shape women's athletic participation. Women's sporting achievement is curtailed, in their view, not only by male dominance of sports institutions and masculine prescriptions for athletic behavior, but also by homophobia: "The fear of being labeled a lesbian serves to keep heterosexual women out of sports or to assure that they will play sports in socially acceptable ways" (p.120). The substantial bibliography reflects the authors' interdisciplinary approach.

1068.   Dyer, Kenneth Frank, 1939- . **Challenging the Men: The Social Biology of Female Sporting Achievement.** New York: University of Queensland Press, 1982. 271p. bibliog. index. $14.95. LC 81-21846. ISBN 0702216526.

Australian social biologist Kenneth Dyer undermines many popular assumptions about women's athletic potential. He first outlines the biological, psychological, social, material, and cultural requirements of successful sporting performance, then turns his attention to the thorny question of sex differences, both biological and cultural. Finally, he assesses women's athletic record in specific sports: swimming, track and field, cycling, skating, rowing and canoeing, and skiing. Just how closely women's athletic performance could match men's cannot be known, Dyer asserts, "until sporting opportunities are more nearly equal" (p.3). His own judgment is that there are few if any sports in which women won't one day equal or nearly equal men.

1069.   Green, Tina Sloan, et al. **Black Women in Sport.** Reston, VA: AAHPERD Publications, 1981. 75p. bibliog. $6.95. LC 81-209212. ISBN 0883140365.

In this slim volume, Tina Sloan Green, Carole A. Oglesby, Alpha Alexander, and Nikki Franke provide an overview of black women's athletic achievements. The longest chapter, "Her Story of Black Sportswomen," presents biographical data on seventeen "outstanding" athletes, among them authors Alexander, Franke, and Green. Other chapters survey the limited research on this topic, racism and other obstacles to black women's participation in sport, consciousness-raising and other white antiracisim work, the achievements of Nigerian women in sport, and future opportunities for black women athletes.

1070. International Congress on Women and Sport (1980: Rome, Italy). **Women and Sport: An Historical, Biological, Physiological and Sportsmedical Approach: Selected Papers of the International Congress on Women and Sport, Rome, Italy, July 4-8, 1980.** Edited by Jan Borms, et al. New York: Karger, 1981. 229p. bibliog. index. $53.00. ISBN 3-8055-2725-X.

Included in this volume are thirty-one selected papers presented at the International Congress on Women and Sport, held in Rome in 1980. The Congress attracted scholars from all over the world, as is evident from the contributors represented here. Reflecting the sessions convened at the conference, four subject areas group the articles: "Historical Aspects"; "Biology and Biochemistry of Exercise"; "Physiology of Exercise"; and "Sportsmedical Aspects." Some of the papers are extremely technical. The Congress also produced a companion volume, *The Female Athlete* (Karger, 1981), with twenty-one papers from the fields of sociology, sports psychology, kinanthropometry, and biomechanics. Jan Borms, Marcel Hebbelinck, and Antonio Venerando edited both volumes.

1071. Levin, Jenifer. **Water Dancer.** New York: Poseidon Press, 1982. 368p. $15.50. LC 82-479. ISBN 0671447645.

This first novel vividly captures the driving ambition, grueling training, pain, and triumph of the serious athlete's life. Dorey Thomas is a long-distance swimmer who decides to do what no one has ever successfully done before: to cross the thirty-two mile San Antonio Strait off the coast of Washington State. She chooses as a coach a man whose son died attempting the same feat. Though many themes play a part here — estrangement between the coach and his wife as they grieve over their son; the love they each grow to feel for Dorey — critics agree that Levin's real forte is her ability to make the reader enter the athlete's world.

1072. Lumpkin, Angela. **Women's Tennis: A Historical Documentary of the Players and Their Game.** Troy, NY: Whitston, 1981. 193p. bibliog. $15.00. LC 79-57328. ISBN 0878751890.

Lumpkin recounts the history of women's tennis from the 1870s, when it was first introduced in the United States as a country-club pastime, to the 1970s, by which time it had expanded into a competitive professional sport. Helen Wills Moody, May Sutton, Hazel Hotchkiss Wightman, Maureen Connolly, Billie Jean King, and Chris Evert Lloyd are among the tennis luminaries profiled here. Lumpkin devotes one-third of the volume (the appendices) to lists of U.S. women's tennis champions during the period. Though the book is packed with information, it is poorly written and edited. Two tennis superstars have recently published autobiographies. In *Billie Jean* (Viking Press, 1982), Billie Jean King (with Frank Deford) goes public with her own account of her controversial life — her feminism, her match with Bobby Riggs, her affair with Marilyn Barnett. Martina Navratilova tells of her Czech childhood, her defection to the United States, and her rise to tennis fame in *Martina* (Knopf, 1985), written with George Vecsey.

1073. Markel, Robert, et al. **For the Record: Women in Sports.** New York: World Almanac; distr. New York: Ballantine Books, 1985. 195p. index. pbk. $8.95. LC 85-167253. ISBN 0345321928.

This handy reference volume fills a gap in the literature on women's athletic achievements. Co-authors Robert Markel, Nancy Brooks, and Susan Markel cover twenty-six competitive sports, from badminton to volleyball. Each chapter opens with a short historical overview, followed by selected biographies and chronological lists of champions in Olympic events and other major contests through 1984.

1074.   Maughan, Jackie Johnson, 1948- , with Kathryn Collins. **The Outdoor Woman's Guide to Sports, Fitness, and Nutrition.** Harrisburg, PA: Stackpole Books, 1983. 288p. bibliog. index. $15.95. LC 83-355. ISBN 0811711579.

Maughan and Collins take a feminist approach, viewing physical fitness as "a literal application of 'taking control of your own body'" (p.13). They take women's physiological capacity (whether biologically or culturally determined) into account in advising readers on how to gain proficiency in a range of outdoor activities: backpacking, hiking, and snowshoeing; climbing and mountaineering; paddle sports; Nordic skiing and ski mountaineering. In addition, they discuss women's strength, training, fitness testing, nutrition, adaptation to the environment, and ob-gyn concerns. Similarly feminist in tone, but offering far less specific guidance, *Women in Motion*, by Sandy Hayden, Daphne Hall, and Pat Stueck (Beacon Press, 1983), seeks to break through women's resistance to the idea of an active lifestyle, and to assist women in developing a personal regimen of activity. For counsel on actual fitness programs, readers may turn to *Diana Nyad's Basic Training for Women,* by Diana Kyad and Candace Lyle Hogan (Harmony Books, 1981), or *The Sports Doctor's Fitness Book for Women,* by John L. Marshall, M.D., with Heather Barbash (Delacorte Press, 1981).

1075.   Murray, Mimi. **Women's Gymnastics: Coach, Participant, Spectator.** Boston: Allen and Bacon, 1979. 289p. index. $29.29. LC 78-11569. ISBN 0205061621.

Murray, a gymnastics teacher and coach, provides a step-by-step guide to proficiency in gymnastics. Following two introductory chapters on the sport, she discusses each of the four basic gymnastics skills at length, from the easiest to the most advanced: floor exercise; side horse vaulting; balance beam; and uneven bars. Coaching suggestions are interspersed throughout, and the final chapter sums up Murray's coaching philosophy. Photographs and line drawings illustrate virtually every page.

1076.*   Parkhouse, Bonnie L., and Jackie Lapin. **Women Who Win: Exercising Your Rights in Sport.** Englewood Cliffs, NJ: Prentice-Hall, 1980. 256p. bibliog. index. LC 80-10248. ISBN 0139623655.

"It is well-documented that nowhere in society has discrimination been so rampant and blatant as in athletics," Parkhouse and Lapin state baldly in their opening chapter. Despite occasional sideswipes at "extremist feminists" and the "Ultra-Lib Female," the authors are full of righteous indignation about inequality in college athletics in this guide to the legal methods, court decisions, and persuasive techniques women may use in fighting for support for women's athletic programs. Parkhouse and Lapin survey provisions of Title IX, the Equal Pay Act, the Civil Rights Act, the Equal Rights Amendment, and other relevant legislation, and review individual and collective methods of gaining compliance. Their message throughout is that "change will not come until women begin demanding change" (p.5). Useful for its overview of the issues through 1980, this guide is already considerably dated; readers will need to turn elsewhere for information on more recent developments in the battle for equality in sports.

1077.   Postow, Betsy C., 1945- , ed. **Women, Philosophy, and Sport: A Collection of New Essays.** Metuchen, NJ: Scarecrow Press, 1983. 315p. bibliog. index. $21.50. LC 83-10146. ISBN 0810816385.

Representing the fields of philosophy, law, education, physical education, linguistics, psychology, and women's studies, the contributors to this volume bring the methods of philosophical inquiry to bear on issues relating to feminism and sports. Postow divides the articles into three general themes: "What Constitutes Fairness to Women in Sports?"; "What Is the Proper Place of Competition in Sports?"; and "What Can the Theory of Education Teach Us About Physical Education for Women?" Among the contributors are Mary Anne Warren, Janice Moulton, Mary Vetterling-Braggin, and Kathryn Pyne Addelson.

1078.   Sabo, Donald F., and Ross Runfola. **Jock: Sports and Male Identity.** Englewood Cliffs, NJ: Prentice-Hall, 1980. 365p. bibliog. index. $14.95. LC 80-11147. ISBN 0135101492.

Written from a "men's liberation" perspective, and addressed primarily to men, this anthology sees sports as both metaphor and breeding ground for masculinity in a sexist society. The work is critical of the aggressiveness, competitiveness, and obsession with winning that are the hallmarks of American sports and masculinity; in their preface, editors Sabo and Runfola argue that "contrary to popular sentiment, men have much to gain from sexual equality" (p.xvi). The volume is divided into six thematic sections: "Sports and Sexism"; "Male Identity and Athletics: Rites of Passage"; "Violence, Sport, and Masculinity"; "High From the Game: Spectators and the Spectacle"; "Women, Sex-Role Stereotyping and Sports"; and "Alternatives for the Future." Among the contributors are Paul Hoch, Warren Farrell, Marc Feigen Fasteau, and Lucy Komisar.

1079.* Stanek, Carolyn. **The Complete Guide to Women's College Athletics: Includes Over 10,000 Women's Athletic Scholarships and Recruiting Rules and Regulations.** Chicago: Contemporary Books, 1981. 244p. bibliog. index. LC 80-70635. ISBN 0809259869.

Stanek addresses her book to the high school or college student who is considering combining athletics with academic study during her college years. Written in a folksy style, the guide encourages girls to take advantage of the increased funding now available for women's athletic scholarships at many campuses. Stanek outlines the provisions of Title IX; answers questions about the difficulties of combining athletics and academics; offers advice to the young athlete who is recruited, and to the one who is not; argues for the value of visiting college campuses and meeting coaches before making a final selection; and recommends considering a summer sports camp. Two appendices provide directories to sports scholarships and sports camps—invaluable information that is undoubtedly already becoming dated.

1080.   Twin, Stephanie L. **Out of the Bleachers: Writings on Women and Sport.** Old Westbury, NY: Feminist Press; New York: McGraw-Hill, 1979. 229p. bibliog. index. pbk. $9.95. LC 78-16531. ISBN 0070204292.

Like other texts in the Feminist Press series "Women's Lives/Women's Work," this reader is thoughtfully designed with the high school or undergraduate classroom in mind. Articles both contemporary and historical address three broad themes: physiology and social attitudes; the lives of sportswomen; and the structure of women's sports. Stephanie Twin's historical introduction, the section introductions and headnotes, and several photographic essays combine with the interesting selections to create a volume that both informs and entertains. High points of the anthology include Dr. Arabella Kenealy's 1899 treatise on the threat physical activity poses to womanhood; Frances Willard's enthusiastic memoir of how she learned to ride a bicycle; Louise Bernikow's critical reflections on her cheerleader past; and Jack Scott's proposal for a radical ethic in sports. More encyclopedic in scope is the hefty volume *Her Story in Sport*, edited by Reet Howell (Leisure Press, 1982). Howell gathers forty-two essays written during the 1970s; together, they constitute a beginning history of American women's experience in sports, from pre-colonial Indian societies through the present.

1081. Wells, Christine L., 1938- . **Women, Sport & Performance: A Physiological Perspective.** Champaign, IL: Human Kinetics, 1985. 333p. index. $20.00. LC 84-25255. ISBN 0931250870.

Wells provides a broad, scholarly introduction to the physiology of women's sports throughout the life cycle, written in a style accessible to the lay reader or undergraduate student. She begins by outlining the physiological differences between the sexes, then moves on to discuss the relationship between exercise and the menstrual cycle, pregnancy, menopause, postmenopause, nutrition, and weight control. The final chapter reviews training principles and common injuries specific to women. Of course, many of the concerns of women athletes are not dissimilar from those of men. *Sports Medicine for the Athletic Female* (1980; repr., Perigee Books, 1984), an anthology edited by Christine E. Haycock, combines articles on topics of specific interest to women (e.g., gynecological and endocrinological factors, pregnancy) with many others on the most general subjects (ear, nose, and throat problems; dental problems), all written by specialists.

WOMEN'S MOVEMENT AND
FEMINIST THEORY

In one sense, this entire volume treats the women's movement and feminist theory in their varied scholarly manifestations. But many recent works transcend the boundaries of traditional disciplines; they are grouped in this chapter. The result is a grab bag of theoretical, historical, and visionary writing.

As throughout the volume, the emphasis is on diverse political and theoretical perspectives. Included here are reprinted statements by pioneers in the long battle for women's rights (Harriet Martineau, Lucretia Mott, Florence Nightingale, Dora Russell), as well as the collected works of key "second wave" thinkers (Gloria Steinem, Juliet Mitchell, Susan Griffin).

We begin to see feminist actions from the angle of "current history" in a number of works that recount and evaluate the struggles of the past two decades, and in other books that focus on key social issues: abortion, violence against women, racism within the women's movement, class differences, homophobia, and the changing nature of the family. This chapter also references general works on feminist methodology, introductory textbooks in women's studies, and multidisciplinary readers. The purely theoretical writings cited here are complemented by different critical viewpoints in the chapters devoted to Politics and Political Theory, Literature: History and Criticism, Religion and Philosophy, and other fields. Indeed, the themes of the current women's movement have become so numerous that no one bibliography (let alone a single chapter) can fully encompass them. Turn to sources in the Reference and Periodicals chapters for further guidance.

1082. Abel, Elizabeth, and Emily K. Abel, eds. **The Signs Reader: Women, Gender, & Scholarship.** Chicago: University of Chicago Press, 1983. 297p. bibliog. $25.00. LC 83-5781. ISBN 0226000745.

Signs: A Journal of Women in Culture and Society has been the leading interdisciplinary forum for feminist scholarship since its founding in 1975. Reprinted here are thirteen influential articles selected from its first thirty issues: Joan Kelly-Gadol's "The Social Relation of the Sexes: Methodological Implications of Women's History"; Carroll Smith-Rosenberg's "The Female World of Love and Ritual: Relations Between Women in Nineteenth-Century America"; Fatima Mernissi's "Women, Saints, and Sanctuaries"; Myra Jehlen's "Archimedes and the Paradox of Feminist Criticism"; Elaine H. Pagels's "What Became of God the Mother? Conflicting Images of God in Early Christianity"; Evelyn Fox Keller's "Feminism and Science"; Donna Haraway's "Animal Sociology and a Natural Economy of the Body Politic, Part I: A Political Physiology of Dominance"; Adrienne Rich's "Compulsory Heterosexuality and Lesbian Existence"; Diane K. Lewis's

"A Response to Inequality: Black Women, Racism, and Sexism"; Heidi Hartmann's "Capitalism, Patriarchy, and Job Segregation by Sex"; Catharine A. MacKinnon's "Feminism, Marxism, Method, and the State: An Agenda for Theory"; Judith Herman and Lisa Hirschman's "Father-Daughter Incest"; and Hélène Cixous's "The Laugh of the Medusa." The articles by MacKinnon, Keller, and Jehlen are included in another anthology drawn from *Signs — Feminist Theory: A Critique of Ideology* (University of Chicago Press, 1982). Editors Nannerl O. Keohane, Michelle Z. Rosaldo, and Barbara C. Gelpi have also selected a wide-ranging group of writings by Julia Kristeva, Temma Kaplan, Zilla R. Eisenstein, Mary O'Brien, Jean Bethke Elshtain, Ann Ferguson, Jacquelyn N. Zita, Kathryn Pyne Addelson, Jane Marcus, Marilyn J. Boxer, and Susan Griffin. The result is a stimulating overview of liberal, Marxist, socialist, and radical feminist perspectives on theoretical issues, including power, sexuality, language, and scientific thought.

1083. Altbach, Edith Hoshino, et al, eds. **German Feminism: Readings in Politics and Literature.** Albany: State University of New York Press, 1984. 389p. bibliog. index. $39.50. LC 83-17849. ISBN 0873958403.

Editors Edith Hoshino Altbach, Jeanette Clausen, Dagmar Schultz, and Naomi Stephan lament the obliviousness of U.S. feminists to feminist writing from outside the English-speaking world. Determined to overcome their readers' resistance to translated works, they provide ample introductory matter that gracefully explicates the historical and cultural background of the German women's movement, and its current tendencies. The editors draw on literary and political writings originally published in commercial, Left, and feminist presses and journals, representing the work of more than forty contributors from East and West Germany and Austria. While there is much in the volume that is familiar — writings on abortion, lesbianism, sexuality, and battered women, for example — readers will discover more distinctive German perspectives in discussions of motherhood and housework, the ecology and peace movement, and armed resistance. Accessible to a broad range of readers, this text makes an invaluable contribution to the internationalization of feminism. Volume One of the *Women in German Yearbook*, titled *Feminist Studies and German Culture* (University Press of America, 1985), is a collection of eight feminist essays on German literature and culture. The volume is edited by Marianne Burkhard and Edith Waldstein. *Sexism: The Male Monopoly on History and Thought* (1976; Farrar, Straus, Giroux, 1982) is an ambitious work by German theorist Marielouise Janssen-Jurreit. Janssen-Jurreit draws on the work of both European and U.S. social scientists and feminist theorists in formulating an analysis of the foundations of male dominance and the potential for women's liberation.

1084. Barrett, Michèle, 1949- , and Mary McIntosh, 1936- . **The Anti-Social Family.** New York: Schocken Books, 1983. 164p. bibliog. index. $18.50. LC 82-184232. ISBN 0805271341.

"The model of family life has pervaded our society in its public institutions to such an extent that, far from speaking of the decline of the family, we should be speaking of the familial character of society," argue British sociologists Barrett and McIntosh (p.8). In their view, the economic and social institution of the family and its reinforcing ideology serve to maintain class and gender inequality. Furthermore, the family's antisocial nature intensifies the antisocial character of the society as a whole "... in privileging the intimacy of close kin [family] has made the outside world cold and friendless, and made it harder to sustain relations of security and trust except with kin" (p.80). The authors advocate fighting to broaden the range of alternatives to family life, and to devise collectivist (rather than family-based) policies in the areas of income maintenance, housework, childcare, and nursing.

1085. Beck, Evelyn Torton, 1933- , ed. **Nice Jewish Girls: A Lesbian Anthology.** Watertown, MA: Persephone Press, 1982; repr. Trumansburg, NY: Crossing Press, 1984. 286p. $20.95. ISBN 0895941384.

"Why is this book different from all other books?," asks its editor. Because "according to Jewish law, this book is written by people who do not exist" (p.xiii). As the twenty-five contributors from varied ethnic backgrounds make painfully clear, Jewish lesbians are doubly invisible — subject to homophobia in their Jewish communities, and to anti-Semitism in lesbian and feminist circles. The anthology blends essays, journals, letters, poems, stories, personal testimony, and photographs in moving explorations of Jewish lesbian identity, the legacy of the Holocaust, family relationships, the situation of lesbians in Israel, and other themes. Several pieces by Jewish lesbians of color are especially eye-opening.

1086. Bell, Susan Groag, and Karen M. Offen, eds. **Women, the Family, and Freedom: The Debate in Documents.** Stanford, CA: Stanford University Press, 1983. 2v. bibliog. index. LC 82-61081. Vol.1: $32.50; ISBN 0804711704. Vol.2: $32.50; ISBN 0804711720.

As proof positive that "the woman question has recurred with cyclical regularity" and that "women have, in fact, a true intellectual heritage on which they can call when considering their situation" (p.11), this two-volume set has no equal. Bell and Offen bring together 264 European and American documents that illustrate the historical debate over women's roles and rights. Their sources include philosophers, politicians, scientists, novelists, religious leaders, and other public figures; their framework is both chronological and thematic, covering marriage, motherhood, employment, education, legal rights, political action, and other topics, from the Englightenment to 1950. The arrangement of sources is guaranteed to stimulate: sharing chapters are Flora Tristan and Friedrich Engels; Olive Schreiner and George Bernard Shaw; and Jung, Freud, and Virginia Woolf. In addition to the arguments advanced by individuals, the collection includes public documents — sections of the Napoleonic Code, for example, and newspaper accounts of the Seneca Falls Convention. The compilers introduce each major section with a lucid critical essay and provide contextual notes for the selections. Many foreign documents appear here in English for the first time. Each volume concludes with a lengthy bibliography and an index. The set is a milestone in the documentation of women's history, political philosophy, and the history of ideas.

1087. Brody, Michal, ed. **Are We There Yet? A Continuing Story of Lavender Woman, A Chicago Lesbian Newspaper, 1971-1976.** Iowa City: Aunt Lute Book Company, 1985. 188p. $8.95. ISBN 0918040078.

The *Lavender Woman* published twenty-six issues from November 1971 to July 1976. Brody, one of the founding members of the collective, uses fifty selections from the newspaper and seven recent interviews with former *LW* collective members to document not just the history of the publication but, more importantly, the history of lesbian-feminism in the early 1970s. The *LW* articles, editorials, and letters are full of passion, argument, energy, and vision, bringing to life the major issues and debates of the day: lesbian separatism; racism; gay oppression; exploitation by the gay bars. The contemporary interviews, interspersed through the volume, help to put the raw history into perspective, as do Brody's two admittedly subjective background chapters. "Where Some of Us Are Now" furnishes current information on an additional nineteen former *LW* collective members.

1088.   Browne, Susan, et al. **With the Power of Each Breath: A Disabled Women's Anthology.** Pittsburgh: Cleis Press, 1985. 354p. pbk. $9.95. LC 85-71206. ISBN 0939416069.

Editors Susan E. Browne, Debra Connors, and Nanci Stern intend this anthology as "a work of resistance against institutionalized silence" (p.10). They succeed in representing tremendous diversity in these pages. The women are lesbian and heterosexual, single and married, old and young, black and white. Their disabilities are many: not just physical impairments like polio, muscular dystrophy, diabetes, blindness, and multiple sclerosis, but also agoraphobia, mental retardation, learning disabilities, obesity, and simple old age. The forms the contributions take are also diverse, including personal histories, poetry, interviews, journals, drama, and theory. The pieces are divided into chapters on the themes of survival, anger, family, identity, body, motherhood, friendship, and unity. The cumulative message of the writings is well summarized by the editors: "We claim our bodies and our integrity as disabled women.... We do not have good parts, bad parts, or inner beauty. We come in many sizes, shapes, and colors.... We are *whole, beautiful and sexy women!*" (p.247). This volume follows close on the heels of three other recent works documenting the experience of disabled women. In *Images of Ourselves: Women With Disabilities Talking* (Routledge and Kegan Paul, 1981), Jo Campling gathers the personal statements of twenty-five disabled women living in England. Gwyneth Ferguson Matthews tells her own story and draws on those of forty-five other Canadian women in *Voices From the Shadows: Women With Disabilities Speak Out* (The Women's Press, 1983). In ... *All Things Are Possible* (A. J. Gavin, 1981), Yvonne Duffy writes about the sexuality of (mostly heterosexual) orthopedically disabled women, based on her own experience and a small survey.

1089.   Bulkin, Elly, et al. **Yours in Struggle: Three Feminist Perspectives on Anti-Semitism and Racism.** Brooklyn, NY: Long Haul Press, 1984. 233p. bibliog. pbk. $7.95. LC 84-80956. ISBN 0960228438.

Elly Bulkin, Minnie Bruce Pratt, and Barbara Smith bring much-needed clarity to the contentious issues of racism and anti-Semitism. Pratt writes of her coming to political consciousness in a Southern white Christian context. Smith addresses the complex tensions between black and Jewish women in the women's movement. Bulkin, in the longest piece, tries to break through the webs of anger and bias to come to a realistic depiction of Jewish oppression, Jewish privilege, Jewish survival in the world. In doing this, she discusses the complexity of Jewish lives in the United States, then goes further to dissect Jewish/Arab relations in the Middle East. The notes to Bulkin's article comprise a thorough and up-to-date bibliography on these issues. The overall message of the volume is that activists of different persuasions must veer away from the politics of accusation and strive for a politics of coalition.

1090.   Caldecott, Léonie, and Stephanie Leland, eds. **Reclaim the Earth: Women Speak Out for Life on Earth.** London: The Women's Press, 1983. 245p. bibliog. $7.95. LC 83-112040. ISBN 0704339080.

This eclectic anthology gathers essays, poems, and interviews by women primarily from Britain and the United States, but also from Canada, Japan, Africa, Italy, New Zealand, and India. Though their specific concerns are diverse—nuclear weapons and power; childbirth; environment and health; urban geography; food—they are united by an ecofeminist perspective that seeks to transform the relationship of human beings to nature. Among the pieces included here are "Feminism: Healing the Patriarchal Dis-ease," by Jill Raymond and Janice Wilson; "Feminism and Ecology: Theoretical Connections," by Stephanie Leland; "Against Nuclearisation and Beyond," a statement by Sicilian women; "He Wanine, He Whenua: Maori Women and the Environment," by Ngahuia Te Awekotuku; "Alternative Technology: A Feminist Technology?," by Chris Thomas; and "Saving Trees, Saving Lives: Third World Women and the Issue of Survival," by Anita Anand; along with poetry by Marge Piercy, Susan Saxe, Rosalie Bertell, and Susan Griffin.

1091.   Cavin, Susan, 1948- . **Lesbian Origins.** San Francisco: Ism Press, 1985. 288p. bibliog. index. $28.00. LC 85-18158. ISBN 0910383162.

In Cavin's "grand theory" of human social origins, empirical data about sex ratios, sexuality, and sex segregation in a wide range of cultures serve as indicators of prehistoric social and sexual organization, and as clues to the cause of women's oppression. Cavin posits that female society (gynosociety) "is the constant base of all societies, even patriarchies" (p.4) and that "female homosocial relations are critical to the formation and maintenance of the family, community, and society" (p.6). Her evidence argues against classical Marxist theories of societal development and other ideologies advanced by "patriscientists." The final chapter, "Women's Liberations," proposes a number of lesbian-feminist strategies for ending women's oppressions and defining female power. Originally a dissertation, the book sports voluminous footnotes and statistical appendices.

1092.   Chernin, Kim. **The Obsession: Reflections on the Tyranny of Slenderness.** New York: Harper and Row, 1981. 206p. bibliog. $12.98. LC 81-47224. ISBN 0060148845.

There is a growing body of clinical literature on the eating disorders that affect a disturbing number of contemporary women (see entry 803). Chernin brings to the subject her considerable gifts as a writer, her knowledge of literature, and her own personal experience. She begins with memories of her twenty-year struggle against hunger and the twin obsession with food and slenderness. She then follows the course of her own gradually acquired understanding of the conflict, threading fiction, poetry, interviews, and social science into a passionate argument. "The body holds meaning," Chernin states in her prologue, and she reminds us that in other times and places the voluptuous rather than the anorexic woman has been idealized. On a general level, she connects the struggle against hunger to the age-old battle of mind against body, to the denial of human sensual existence. Yet today, self-loathing and fear of fat are problems that especially afflict women. In Chernin's view, hatred of large women derives from patriarchal fear of women's power. The last twenty years, Chernin argues, have sparked both the movement toward women's power (women's liberation) and the flight from it (anorexia, bulimia, the expanding diet industry). In her latest book, *The Hungry Self: Women, Eating, and Identity* (Times Books, 1985), Chernin explores these themes further, focusing particularly on the troubled relationship between mother and daughter in sexist society.

1093.   **Coming to Power: Writings and Graphics on Lesbian S/M.** 2nd ed. Boston: Alyson Publications, 1982. 281p. bibliog. pbk. $7.95. ISBN 0932870287.

In recent years, the lesbian-feminist community has been rocked by the so-called "sex wars." The debates range from the "politically correct" feminist stance on pornography to the philosophy and psychology of female desire. The practice and ideology of lesbian sadomasochism, however, is perhaps the most controversial and difficult of the topics. *Coming to Power* and *Against Sadomasochism: A Radical Feminst Analysis* (Frog in the

Well, 1982) anthologize the opposing camps. In *Coming to Power,* woman-to-woman S/M is celebrated as "a form of eroticism based on a consensual exchange of power," a definition proclaimed on the title page. The contributions include personal testimony, drawings, photographs, a long theoretical piece by feminist Gayle Rubin, and a history of the lesbian S/M movement by Pat Califia. The bulk of the writing, however, is erotic fiction. *Against Sadomasochism*—edited by Robin Ruth Linden, Darlene R. Pagano, Diana E. H. Russell, and Susan Leigh Star—is, by contrast, a collection primarily of essays and personal accounts. Most are thoughtful and moderate in their criticism; they argue that lesbian sadomasochism "is firmly rooted in patriarchal sexual ideology" (p.4) and is inconsistent with feminist politics. Ti-Grace Atkinson, Kathleen Barry, Susan Griffin, Audre Lorde, Robin Morgan, and Alice Walker are among the contributors. Taken together, these books raise challenging questions about the nature of power in personal relations, and the implications of sexual expression for the liberation or continued oppression of women in both public and private spheres.

1094.* Coote, Anna, and Beatrix Campbell. **Sweet Freedom: The Struggle for Women's Liberation.** Oxford: Basil Blackwell, 1982. 257p. bibliog. index. LC 82-126415. ISBN 0631125558.

Coote and Campbell, both journalists, want to record the history of the contemporary British women's movement lest it be forgotten in the conservative climate of the eighties. In their first chapter, they present an overview of the movement's history, its catalyzing conferences and demonstrations, its issues, and its political factions (radical and socialist feminism). In subsequent chapters, they review women's status in and feminist campaigns around work, the family, law, the unions, education, culture, and sex. In their final chapter, the authors speculate about future strategies for the movement. Feminist critics have challenged Coote and Campbell's interpretation of British radical feminism and of the movement's debates over sexuality, and reproached the authors for not addressing the question of racism. Clearly, Coote and Campbell's is only one of many versions of British feminist history that could be written.

1095. Coward, Rosalind. **Patriarchal Precedents: Sexuality and Social Relations.** Boston: Routledge and Kegan Paul, 1983. 326p. bibliog. index. pbk. $9.95. LC 82-12206. ISBN 0710093241.

British theorist Rosalind Coward seeks the conceptual roots of contemporary feminist theory in nineteenth- and early twentieth-century anthropological debates about the family and kinship. Feminist theorists who draw on the ideas of writers like Bachofen and Engels would do well, Coward argues, to first identify these theorists' submerged ideological assumptions, particularly their "absolutely fixed ideas about sex and sexual identity" (p.254). Marxist and Freudian theories of the family—additional key sources for feminist thought—have also, in Coward's view, been shaped by the limiting assumptions of the early kinship debates. Finding concepts like "patriarchy" and "the relations of reproduction" similarly problematic, Coward advises feminists to build a theory of male domination around the idea of "sexual identity," as expressed not simply through kinship and the family but also through public institutions and policies. Readers lacking familiarity with the theories discussed here, or unversed in the language of Coward's deconstructionist methodology, will find this work heavy going.

1096. Cruikshank, Margaret, ed. **Lesbian Studies: Present and Future.** Old Westbury, NY: Feminist Press, 1982. 286p. bibliog. index. $9.95. LC 82-4972. ISBN 0935312064.

"As long as lesbian issues are kept at the fringe of women's studies or treated in a fragmentary, cursory way, none of us in the field will understand the constraints imposed on us by heterosexist thinking," warns Cruikshank (p.xiii). Her rich sourcebook urges academic feminists to incorporate lesbian perspectives into their research and teaching, and gives them the tools to do so. Five autobiographical accounts are grouped in the first section, "Lesbians in the Academic World: The Personal/Political Experience." The second section, "In the Classroom," focuses on pedagogical strategies. "New Research/New Perspectives" is the third and longest section in the volume; its fourteen contributions will be of equal interest to teachers and students. Brief reports on content and method address such areas as lesbian history, feminist literary criticism, biography, periodical indexing, and black lesbians. Two bibliographies – one of books and one of articles – close the book. The sourcebook also presents model syllabi and a potpourri listing of "Resources," including archives, groups, slide shows, conferences, publishers, and works in progress. Many leading lesbian scholars are represented in the pages of *Lesbian Studies*, among them Doris Davenport, Toni McNaron, Elly Bulkin, Evelyn Torton Beck, Estelle Freedman, Lillian Faderman, and Marilyn Frye.

1097. Davies, Miranda, comp. **Third World – Second Sex: Women's Struggles and National Liberation; Third World Women Speak Out.** London: Zed Press; distr. Westport, CT: Lawrence Hill, 1983. 257p. bibliog. $21.95. ISBN 0862320178.

"There is no single road to women's liberation," writes Miranda Davies in her preface to this collection of brief articles and interviews on women's activism in twenty Third World countries. Not all of the women who contribute to this volume identify as feminists – some associate feminism exclusively with its Western expressions, which they repudiate – but they are all directly involved in organizing around women's concerns, from dowries, work, and health to rape and revolution. Yolla Polity Sharara writes of Lebanese women's efforts to overcome sectarian divisions. Miriam Galdemez is interviewed about women's lives in El Salvador. A statement by the National Union of Eritrean Women describes women's part in the Eritrean national liberation struggle, while two women from a Nicaraguan women's organization recount women's continuing contributions to the Nicaraguan revolution. This volume documents not only the many roads to women's liberation, but also that feminism has indigenous roots outside the Western world.

1098. Delacoste, Frédérique, and Felice Newman, eds. **Fight Back! Feminist Resistance to Male Violence.** Minneapolis: Cleis Press, 1981. 398p. pbk. $13.95. LC 81-68220. ISBN 0939416018.

Delacoste and Newman create a powerful sourcebook to inspire women to actively resist, whether by fighting off an attacker or by protesting the violence inherent in pornography. The contributions include: first-person accounts by survivors of rape, beating, and incest; guidelines for offering victim services; analytical reports on the successes (and some failures) of shelters, protests, and other programs; interviews; essays; literary work in the form of fiction, poetry, and dramatic scripts; and photography and other artwork. The special perspectives of women of color and lesbians are highlighted. The final section is a state-by-state directory of rape crisis centers, shelters for battered women, services for incest victims, karate and self-defense instructors, legal resources, and political organizations.

1099. Delphy, Christine. **Close to Home: A Materialist Analysis of Women's Oppression.** Edited by Diana Leonard. Amherst: University of Massachusetts Press, 1984. 237p. bibliog. index. $18.00. LC 84-40285. ISBN 0870234536.

Simone de Beauvoir named Delphy France's most exciting feminist theorist. This collection brings together ten articles published between 1970 and 1981; Delphy's introduction places her work in context for English-speaking readers. Her writing is brilliant, dialectical, full of paradox. She advocates separating Marx's method — historical materialism — from his analysis of capitalism, and sees feminist materialism as representing "an epistemological revolution, not just a new discipline with women as its object... " (p.215). Delphy makes her most original contribution in discussing domestic labor; refreshingly, her interpretation breaks free of the conceptual logjams that have stymied the "housework debates" within U.S and British Left-feminism. She also delivers insightful analyses of women and class, family consumption, marriage and divorce, and the relationship between the women's movement and the Left. Delphy takes socialist feminists to task for subordinating feminist analysis to class analysis and for evincing "a religious attitude to the writings of Marx ..." (p.154). In striking contrast, in *Marxism and the Oppression of Women: Toward a Unitary Theory* (Rutgers University Press, 1983), U.S. theorist Lise Vogel "remain[s] convinced that the revival of Marxist theory, not the construction of some socialist-feminist synthesis, offers the best chance to provide theoretical guidance in the coming battles for the liberation of women" (p.x). Vogel first offers a rather sketchy review of socialist feminism in the seventies, then moves on to an examination of the Marx/Engels opus and of the nineteenth-century socialist movement, and closes with the presentation of her own perspective on women's oppression. The goal of English sociologist Michèle Barrett, in *Women's Oppression Today: Problems in Marxist Feminist Analysis* (NLB, 1980), is precisely to explore the possibilities for "a genuine synthesis of Marxist and feminist perspectives" (p.1). She begins by laying out conceptual problems in Marxist-feminist analysis, then continues with discussion of sexuality, ideology, education, paid labor, the family, the state, and women's liberation.

1100. DuBois, Ellen Carol, 1947- , et al. **Feminist Scholarship: Kindling in the Groves of Academe.** Urbana: University of Illinois Press, 1985. 227p. bibliog. index. $19.95. LC 84-2589. ISBN 0252009576.

Writing in a single, eloquent voice, Ellen Carol DuBois, Gail Paradise Kelly, Elizabeth Lapovsky Kennedy, Carolyn W. Korsmeyer, and Lillian S. Robinson assess the impact of the women's movement on American scholarship. To explore "how feminist scholarship both challenges and is shaped by disciplinary inquiry" (p.1), they take a close comparative look at their own specialties — history, literature, education, anthropology, and philosophy. The opening chapters trace the initial process of identifying male bias in the disciplines, and the next step of building new, women-centered conceptual frameworks. The middle chapters take a different and complementary approach, singling out the concepts of oppression and liberation as central to research that transcends disciplinary boundaries and fosters an integrated body of knowledge about women. Among the subjects of feminist inquiry highlighted in this section are the origins of oppression, elements of sexist ideology, public and domestic spheres, notions of equality, and the impact of modernization and socialism on women. The final chapter turns again to the disciplines, evaluating their response to the new feminist scholarship as manifest in major academic journals.

1101. Eichler, Margrit, and Hilda Scott, eds. **Women in Futures Research.** New York: Pergamon Press, 1982. 117p. bibliog. index. $19.00. LC 81-83021. ISBN 0080281001.

Feminists should take an interest in futures research, Eichler and Scott contend, because "it is a way of breaking the time and space barrier and creating a weightless state in which propositions can be judged on their merits and not according to socially weighted criteria of 'reasonableness'" (Editorial). Furthermore, feminist models are needed to counterbalance or replace male models for the future. Contributors to this volume, which originally appeared as a special issue of *The Women's Studies International Forum* (see entry 1210) address a number of themes: the failure of futures research to take into account changing gender relations; the character of women's research on disarmament, national security, and world order; how women scientists might transform scientific inquiry; feminist science fiction; feminist perspectives on technology; how women architects might redesign the environment; and how changing gender relations might contribute to a more human and ecological future.

1102.   Eisenstein, Hester. **Contemporary Feminist Thought.** Boston: G. K. Hall, 1983. 196p. bibliog. index. $17.95. LC 83-11867. ISBN 0816190429.

Eisenstein's focus in this well-written and brilliantly argued work is primarily on radical feminism since 1970. She examines the evolution of feminist thought chronologically, beginning with writers such as Shulamith Firestone, Juliet Mitchell, and Kate Millett who located the source of women's oppression in socially constructed female difference. Partly in reaction, later writers (e.g., Adrienne Rich, Susan Griffin) began to explore a woman-centered perspective, seeking to revalue female difference. More recently, the woman-centered perspective has taken a reactionary turn, Eisenstein argues, in the work of theorists such as Mary Daly, sparking "a renewal of essentialism, a feminist version of the eternal female" (p.106) that asserts "the intrinsic moral superiority of women" (p.xii). In Eisenstein's view, the insights gained from the woman-centered perspective must be wedded to a feminist theory and practice that rejects both the integrationism of liberal feminism and the political retreat and biological determinism of metaphysical feminism. This newly radical feminism would instead engage with the patriarchal world and fight to change it. In *Feminist Theory: The Intellectual Traditions of American Feminism* (Ungar, 1985), Josephine Donovan provides an extended discussion of the historical sources of feminist ideas in chapters on Enlightenment liberal feminism, nineteenth-century "cultural feminism" (Margaret Fuller, Elizabeth Cady Stanton, and others), Marxism, Freudianism, existentialism, radical feminism, and "the new feminist moral vision."

1103.*   Eisenstein, Zilla R. **The Radical Future of Liberal Feminism.** New York: Longman, 1981. 260p. bibliog. index. LC 80-19464. ISBN 0582282055.

Zillah Eisenstein analyzes liberal feminism's potential to expose and subvert the premises of capitalist patriarchy. Liberal feminism takes the ideology of liberalism seriously, with its commitment to individualism and equality of opportunity. Yet, Eisenstein claims, the demands of liberal feminism cannot be met by the capitalist patriarchal state because it is built on women's subordination. This reevaluation of the potential of liberal feminism is imperative, Eisenstein argues, given the conservative drift of the eighties. The bulk of the volume is given to a critical interpretation of the historical origins of liberal feminism (Locke, Rousseau, Mary Wollstonecraft, J. S. Mill and Harriet Taylor, and Elizabeth Cady Stanton), and of the contemporary practice of liberal feminism (Betty Friedan, the E.R.A., NOW, reproductive rights, and the Houston Women's Conference). Eisenstein carries her line of argument further in *Feminism and Sexual Equality: The Crisis in Liberal America* (Monthly Review Press, 1984). Here she examines the crisis of welfare-state liberalism, the ideas of revisionist liberalism, New Right anti-feminism, and the rise of revisionist feminism. As represented in the recent writings of

Betty Friedan, Jean Elshtain, and others, revisionist feminism asserts the importance of sexual difference as a qualification on sexual equality. Eisenstein calls for a new feminist theory that would demand recognition of women as "sexually particular, equal, and free."

1104. Ferguson, Kathy E. **The Feminist Case Against Bureaucracy.** Philadelphia: Temple University Press, 1984. 286p. bibliog. index. $24.95. LC 84-221. ISBN 0877223572.

Ferguson brings radical critiques of modern bureaucratic organization (especially the work of Michel Foucault) face to face with contemporary radical feminist theory. Since domination is built into the very structure of bureaucracy, she aruges, a feminist organization that adopts bureaucratic structure ceases to be feminist. Ferguson likens women's subordination within patriarchy to the subordination of workers and clients within bureaucracies. She rejects emphatically the liberal view that women's integration into existing bureaucratic structures can bring meaningful change, offering a hard-hitting critical dissection of the recent spate of "success manuals" for women. Drawing on the work of Carol Gilligan and Nancy Chodorow, she theorizes that women's outsider status and their ethics of connectedness and responsibility hold the potential for a feminist discourse of opposition to bureaucracy.

1105. Ferree, Myra Marx, and Beth B. Hess, 1928- . **Controversy and Coalition: The New Feminist Movement.** Boston: Twayne, 1985. 215p. bibliog. index. $17.95. LC 84-22421. ISBN 0805797076.

In this introductory overview, diversity is embraced as the central theme, and the authors reject "narrow and defensive definitions of what a good feminist should be and want" (p.165). As they trace the evolution of the movement, Ferree and Hess identify its bureaucratic and collectivist "strands" and describe painful conflicts over such issues as lesbianism, pornography, reproductive rights, and anti-Semitism and racism. They introduce a typology of feminists—career, liberal, radical, and socialist—based on differing orientations to *means* and *ends*, and evaluate the aims, issues, and accomplishments of each tendency. Grounded in the sociology of social movements and presented in a lucid style, this text would be useful in the undergraduate classroom. Diversity is also a key theme of Leah Fritz's *Dreamers and Dealers: An Intimate Appraisal of the Women's Movement* (Beacon Press, 1979), a very personal account of women's movement conflicts over lesbianism, class, race, and the Left. David Bouchier's *The Feminist Challenge* (Schocken Books, 1984) is primarily a history of the contemporary women's movement in Britain, but it takes the United States as a point of comparison and shows familiarity with feminist literature from both sides of the Atlantic.

1106. FitzGerald, Maureen, 1942- , et al., eds. **Still Ain't Satisfied! Canadian Feminism Today.** Toronto: The Women's Press, 1982. 318p. bibliog. pbk. $10.95. LC 82-246383. ISBN 0889610746.

Editors Maureen FitzGerald, Connie Guberman, and Margie Wolfe intend this anthology not as "a history or survey of the women's movement in Canada but rather [as] an evaluation of feminist activities over the last ten years" (pp.13-14). Following Naomi Wall's introductory overview of the decade, more than forty contributors review Canadian feminist activism on a broad spectrum of issues: reproductive rights, pornography, rape, lesbianism, childcare, unions, sexual harassment, occupational hazards, clerical work, the trades, immigrant women, and native women, among them. Three articles in the final section, "Tools for Politicization," describe developments in Canadian feminist publishing, education, and art. *Feminism in Canada: From Pressure to Politics* (Black Rose Books,

1982) makes a perfect companion volume, supplementing the activist view of *Still Ain't Satisfied!* with a survey of feminist academic ferment in Canada. Contributors to Part I, "Scholarship: Theory and Practice," report on feminist challenges to the traditional disciplines. The five articles in Part II grapple with questions of feminist political practice. Editors Angela R. Miles and Geraldine Finn draw the collection together thematically in the introduction and conclusion.

1107.   Friedan, Betty. **The Second Stage.** New York: Summit Books, 1982. 352p. pbk. $6.95. LC 81-14345. ISBN 0671459511.

Friedan addresses her book to "the daughters," whom she perceives as burdened by the legacy of feminist expectations, the "feminist mystique" (p.27). The "first stage" of the women's movement, in her view, bought the male model of success. Yet circumstances have changed little in the world of work, and thus women who want families and careers often face insurmountable conflicts. "I think we must at least admit and begin openly to discuss feminist denial of the importance of family, of women's own needs to give and get love and nurture ..." (p.22), writes Friedan. In the "second stage," she argues, a movement of women *and* men must fight to "restructure institutions and transform the nature of power itself" (p.28). Friedan's work has met with very mixed reviews; many feminists find distortion and too little documentation in her arguments.

1108.   Frye, Marilyn, 1941- . **The Politics of Reality: Essays in Feminist Theory.** Trumansburg, NY: Crossing Press, 1983. 176p. bibliog. $18.95. LC 83-2082. ISBN 0895941007.

Frye offers nine essays from the 1970s and 1980s—some originally lectures, others reprinted from the journal *Sinister Wisdom*—which combine the philosopher's clarity of thought and precision of language with the politics of lesbian feminism. Her first three essays grapple with the meanings of the terms "oppression," "sexism," and "male chauvinism" or "phallism." Other essays take up topics of vital concern to feminists: love and enslavement; anger; separatism and power; the racism of white feminists; lesbian feminism and the gay rights movement; and lesbian invisibility.

1109.   Greer, Germaine, 1939- . **Sex and Destiny: The Politics of Human Fertility.** New York: Harper and Row, 1984. 541p. bibliog. index. $19.18. LC 83-48349. ISBN 0060151404.

Writing in her usual fluent style, Greer takes on a range of topics—attitudes toward children, fertility, sterility, sexuality, birth control, abortion and infanticide, the family, eugenics—which she discusses in an international context. Pondering the relationship of the highly industrialized and the developing nations, she finds it ironic that the rich, who consume the largest share of the world's resources, are so intent on lowering the birth rate of the poor, whose rate of consumption is so much lower. Furthermore, she argues that population planners, imbued with what she sees as a generalized Western antipathy toward children, cannot possibly understand the resistance of Third World peoples, whose cultures and economies welcome large families. The industrialized West's low birth rate, its mounting environmental problems, and its arms build-up are all symptoms, in Greer's view, of a death culture. With her contrasting descriptions of pronatalist Third World cultures as life-affirming, Greer has been interpreted by feminist critics as mourning a lost world in which reproduction *was* destiny for women. Although difficult to pin down on this point, Greer does raise provocative questions that go to the heart of feminist ideas about fertility, sexuality, childbearing, and human oppression.

1110. Griffin, Susan. **Made From This Earth: An Anthology of Writings.** New York: Harper and Row, 1982. 344p. $14.37. LC 82-48229. ISBN 0060151188.

In this selection of her material from 1967 to 1982, Susan Griffin pulls her work into three sections (essays and theory; writings on women and literature; and poetry, plays, and stories), prefacing each with her reflections on the personal, social, and historical context of the writings. Few readers will be familiar with the interviews on abortion and early articles on feminism and motherhood in Part I, "Made From This Earth." The other selections in the first part are excerpted from Griffin's better-known published works: *Woman and Nature: The Roaring Inside Her* (Harper and Row, 1978); *Rape: The Power of Consciousness* (Harper and Row, 1979); and *Pornography and Silence: Culture's Revenge Against Nature* (Harper and Row, 1981). In each piece, Griffin demonstrates her commitment to find a personal voice. Her essay "The Politics of Rape," for example, begins, "I have never been free of the fear of rape" (p.39). Throughout this section she is working on a theme pursued by many feminist thinkers of the last decade: that the association of men with the idea of "culture," and of women with "nature," is key to understanding male supremacy. Griffin attacks this problem head-on in the selection from *Women and Nature* by delving into the history of science. She then follows the path of these dualisms—nature and culture, female and male—through analyses of rape and pornography, interpreting men's debasement of women as an attempt to conquer nature, fear, vulnerability. Women and the creative process is the unifying theme of Part II, "Every Woman Who Writes is a Survivor." Part III, "Poetry as a Way of Knowledge," presents stories, poems, and plays, including Griffin's acclaimed 1974 drama, "Voices." Griffin's poems rove the territory between the personal and the political, from the intensely felt "I Like to Think of Harriet Tubman" to the satiricial "Is the Air Political Today?"

1111. Harford, Barbara, and Sarah Hopkins, eds. **Greenham Common: Women at the Wire.** London: The Women's Press; distr. Salem, NH: Merrimack, 1984. 171p. bibliog. pbk. $7.95. LC 84-132596. ISBN 0704339269.

The peace camp established by women at the U.S. missile base in Greenham Common, England in 1981 became a rallying point for feminist action on disarmament, intensified debates over theory and tactics within both the women's movement and anti-war groups, and inspired similar camps around the world. Harford and Hopkins blend the voices of over fifty women who participated at Greenham Common in a chronological insiders' look at the camp from the summer of 1981 to the spring of 1984. They are eloquent on the significance of women's organizing: "Traditionally men have left home for the front-line of war. Now women are leaving home to work for peace" (p.3). Caroline Blackwood provides a well-written journalistic account of the camp in *On the Perimeter* (Penguin Books, 1985); and *Greenham Women Everywhere,* edited by Alice Cook and Gwyn Kirk (South End Press, 1983), brings together powerful personal statements by participants with analytical commentary on feminism, nonviolence, and civil disobedience.

1112. Hartsock, Nancy C. M. **Money, Sex, and Power: Toward a Feminist Historical Materialism.** New York: Longman, 1983; Boston: Northeastern University Press, 1985. 310p. bibliog. index. pbk. $10.95. LC 85-5076. ISBN 0930350782.

This is an ambitious and difficult work, with far-reaching concerns that impose, as Hartsock admits, "a complicated logic on the book" (p.3). Her ultimate interest is in a "retheorization of power on the basis of women's as well as men's activity ..." (p.12). Hartsock's pursuit of this goal takes her on a lengthy journey, through a critical exposition of the exchange theories of power dominant in the social sciences, their implied theories of community, and their underlying epistemology; an assessment of the way a Marxist perspective upsets the exchange theorists' view of the world; an exploration of the linkages between masculinity, violence, and domination; and an examination of women theorists of power, such as Hannah Arendt. Hartsock's concluding chapters attempt to rethink power at the level of reproduction, and suggest questions for future research. Hartsock relegates to her appendices interesting discussions of Lévi-Strauss, Simone de Beauvoir, and Gayle Rubin.

1113. Heide, Wilma Scott, 1921-1985. **Feminism for the Health of It.** Buffalo, NY: Margaretdaughters, 1985. 164p. bibliog. pbk. $8.95. LC 85-15363. ISBN 093191101X.

Nurse, scholar, and an early president of NOW, Heide was an outspoken advocate of feminist issues. In this volume she expounds her views on higher education, health care, feminist scholarship, welfare reform, communications, language, and international affairs.

1114. Hooks, Bell. **Ain't I a Woman: Black Women and Feminism.** Boston: South End Press, 1981. 205p. bibliog. index. $20.00. LC 81-51392. ISBN 0896081303.

Hooks strives to articulate the experience and perspectives of black women, from slavery through the present. In doing so, she makes strong arguments about the sexism of black men and the racism of white women. Widely reviewed, *Ain't I a Woman* provoked intense controversy, especially for its harsh depiction of the women's movement. Critics pointed out that Hooks seemed to equate the movement as a whole with its least progressive (white, middle-class, professional) elements, glossing over emerging feminisms of women of color and antiracist white women and omitting any mention whatsoever of lesbians, black or white. In her more recent book, *Feminist Theory: From Margin to Center* (South End Press, 1984), Hooks attempts to respond to some of these criticisms, although continuing to build on the themes introduced in *Ain't I a Woman*. Feminist theory, she argues, is formulated primarily by "privileged women who live at the center, whose perspectives on reality rarely include knowledge and awareness of the lives of women and men who live in the margin" (Preface). Hooks follows this line of argument through discussions of sisterhood, men, power, work, education, violence against women, parenting, and sexual oppression. In both works, Hooks stresses the persistent barriers between black and white women. *Common Differences: Conflict in Black and White Feminist Perspectives*, by Gloria I. Joseph and Jill Lewis (2nd ed., South End Press, 1986), is the product of several years' collaborative discussion and writing by two professors—one black, one white—at Hampshire College. The process of their mutual learning and the reality of their differences are currents throughout the book. Each of the authors contributes chapters on black women's and white women's liberation, mothers and daughters, and sexuality and sexual attitudes.

1115. Hull, Gloria T., et al., eds. **All the Women Are White, All the Blacks Are Men, But Some of Us Are Brave: Black Women's Studies.** Old Westbury, NY: Feminist Press, 1982. 401p. bibliog. index. pbk. $9.95. LC 81-68918. ISBN 0912670959.

The title of this pathbreaking volume speaks to the unconscious assumptions that have conspired to keep the lives of black women hidden. "Merely to use the term 'Black women's studies' is an act charged with political significance," write Gloria T. Hull and Barbara Smith in an introduction that advocates the establishment of the subdiscipline as "an autonomous academic entity" (p.xxviii). Coeditors Hull, Smith, and Patricia Bell Scott have compiled a volume that will serve as both reference work and pedagogical tool.

Articles on black feminism, racism, social science myths about black women, black women's literature, health, education, and religion are supplemented by a substantial number of bibliographies, bibliographic essays, and syllabi. Notable contributors include Michele Wallace, the Combahee River Collective, Alice Walker, Erlene Stetson, Elizabeth Higginbotham, Lorraine Bethel, and Mary Helen Washington. Barbara Smith carries forward the vision articulated here in her other edited volume, *Home Girls: A Black Feminist Anthology* (Kitchen Table, Women of Color Press, 1983). Some of the anthology's material originally appeared in *Conditions: Five, The Black Women's Issue* (Autumn 1979). In her introduction, Smith outlines the rudiments of black feminism with clarity and passion, arguing that it is "on every level ... organic to Black experience" (p.xxiii). She intermingles poetry, fiction, interviews, essays, reviews, and photographs by contributors such as Michelle Cliff, Audre Lorde, Pat Parker, June Jordan, Alice Walker, and Bernice Johnson Reagon to address four themes: blood ties and the meaning of family; artistic identity; lesbianism; and feminist issues and organizing. Though focused on the experience of black women in particular, the volume reflects a commitment to the growing connection among U.S. feminists of color, and to a politics of coalition.

1116. Hunter College Women's Studies Collective. **Women's Realities, Women's Choices: An Introduction to Women's Studies.** New York: Oxford University Press, 1983. 621p. bibliog. index. $24.95. LC 82-8059. ISBN 0195032276.

Eight scholars from diverse fields avoid the usual discipline-by-discipline survey of female experience, substituting instead an exciting and thoroughly interdisciplinary exploration of key areas in feminist studies. Part I begins with the individual, and treats images of women, ideas about women's "nature," women's bodies, their personalities, and their social roles. Part II explores the situations of women as daughters, wives, and mothers, and devotes a chapter to alternative relationships. In Part III the focus broadens to examine women in public life and their interactions with social institutions. Religion, education, health, work, and politics are all covered. Each chapter concludes with discussion questions and an annotated selection of recommended readings. The book's final chapter reviews the accomplishments of feminism in the past and present and speculates about the future. Anthologies also work well as texts for introductory classes. Sheila Ruth's *Issues in Feminism* (Houghton Mifflin, 1980) gathers a stimulating set of readings from both feminist and patriarchal thinkers, linked by an analytical narrative outlining major concepts—the dynamics of patriarchy, images of women, the notion of gender asymmetry, and feminist activism. In *Feminist Frontiers: Rethinking Sex, Gender, and Society* (Addison-Wesley, 1983), Laurel Richardson and Verta Taylor mix scholarly essays, personal statements, poems, cartoons, news stories, and other items in a volume sure to appeal to undergraduates. The topics they cover are: language, images, and ideas; socialization; religion; law; science; medicine; violence against women; sex-based inequality; intimacy; occupational and political inequality; the feminist movement; racism; spirituality; and feminism in the future.

1117. Irigaray, Luce. **Speculum of the Other Woman.** Ithaca, NY: Cornell University Press, 1985. 365p. bibliog. $42.50. LC 84-45151. ISBN 0801416639.

The works of philosopher-psychoanalyst Luce Irigaray, enormously important to French feminist theory, are only now being translated into English. This volume is divided into three parts. In the first, "The Blind Spot of an Old Dream of Symmetry," Irigaray systematically criticizes Freud's account of the nature and development of female sexuality, including his analyses of the castration complex, Oedipal anxiety, penis envy, clitoral and vaginal orgasm, and female homosexuality. In "Speculum," Irigaray argues that the Western philosophical tradition has defined "woman" so as to exclude her from subjectivity. In "Plato's Hysteria," she equates Plato's cave with hysteria ("the woman's disease") in order to examine the relationship between self and other. Irigaray's erudite, elliptical, punning style is dazzling but difficult; readers unfamiliar with Freudian, Lacanian, and Derridean concepts may have trouble following her argument, despite Gillian C. Gill's careful translation. More accessible are the eleven essays in Irigaray's *This Sex Which Is Not One* (Cornell University Press, 1985), translated by Catherine Porter with the assistance of Carolyn Burke. Among the more useful pieces are the title essay, which attempts to describe female desire, and "Psychoanalytic Theory: Another Look," a cogent summary of Irigaray's objections to androcentric psychological models. In her famous manifesto, "When Our Lips Speak Together," Irigaray exhorts her female readers to move outside of the masculine structures that divide women.

1118. Kanter, Hannah, et al., eds. **Sweeping Statements: Writings From the Women's Liberation Movement, 1981-1983.** London: The Women's Press; distr. Salem, NH: Merrimack, 1984. 307p. bibliog. pbk. $9.95. LC 84-132543. ISBN 0704339307.

This anthology is a treasure trove for U.S. feminists, who continue to have little access to feminist writings from other countries. Editors Hannah Kanter, Sarah Lefanu, Shaila Shah, and Carole Spedding gather short articles not only from the better-known British periodicals like *Spare Rib* and *Feminist Review*, but also from an exciting array of smaller publications, which are listed with address and subscription information at the back of the volume. Arranged in eight thematic sections—Violence Against Women; Forever Working; Racism; No Nukes; Up Against the State; Sex and Sexuality; Our Bodies; and Challenges—the writings convey the immediacy of feminist activism, theory-building, and controversy in Britain in the early eighties. The Women's Press has made a substantial commitment to bringing such ephemeral writings to a wider readership, having published an earlier companion anthology entitled *No Turning Back: Writings From the Women's Liberation Movement 1975-80,* edited by the Feminist Anthology Collective (1981); and *On the Problem of Men,* edited by Scarlet Friedman and Elizabeth Sarah (1982), an exciting compendium of articles drawn from two British feminist conferences.

1119. Kimball, Gayle, ed. **Women's Culture: The Women's Renaissance of the Seventies.** Metuchen, NJ: Scarecrow Press, 1981. 296p. bibliog. index. $16.00. LC 81-9004. ISBN 0810814552.

Celebrating a present-day "women's renaissance," Kimball assembles twenty original essays and interviews on the theme of creativity. The first section features an introduction by Kimball and an interview with Robin Morgan, both arguing that cultural feminism—criticized in some circles for fostering ineffective separatism and political apathy—in truth holds great revolutionary potential. The following sections focus on the visual arts, music, literature and dreams, religion, and organizations. Artist Judy Chicago, composer Kay Gardner, poet Marge Piercy, and witch Z. Budapest are among the contributors. Few other volumes take such an inclusive approach to the impact of the women's movement on creative expression. In *Women, the Arts, and the 1920s in Paris and New York* (Transaction Books, 1982), editors Kenneth W. Wheeler and Virginia Lee Lussier gather fifteen short, lively conference papers on an earlier period of cultural flowering.

1120.   Koen, Susan, and Nina Swaim. **Ain't Nowhere We Can Run: A Handbook for Women on the Nuclear Mentality.** Rev. ed. Norwich, VT: Women Against Nuclear Development (WAND); distr. Trumansburg, NY: Crossing Press, 1982. 74p. bibliog. pbk. $3.00. ISBN 03173161457.

The authors state their eco-feminist position on the very first page of this emotionally charged but tightly argued tract: "We feel strongly that the attitude held by nuclear proponents is directly related to the discriminatory attitudes towards women in this world, to the prevalence of rape and violence against individuals, and to the steady annihilation of life on this planet. It is our intent to demonstrate these interconnections...." Koen and Swaim detail the risks of continued development of atomic power plants and weapons, the role of women in the nuclear industry, and the accomplishments of well-known women in the anti-nuclear movement—Rosalie Bertell, Grace Paley, Winona La Duke, Karen Silkwood, Helen Caldicott, Dolly Weinhold, and Holly Near—as well as women active at the grassroots level. The book concludes with specific suggestions for education and action. The life and death (murder?) of Karen Silkwood (1946-1974) inspired Richard Rashke's compelling book, *The Killing of Karen Silkwood* (Houghton Mifflin, 1981); a feminist biography remains to be written.

1121.   Lederer, Laura, ed. **Take Back the Night: Women on Pornography.** New York: Morrow, 1980. 359p. bibliog. index. $14.95. LC 80-23701. ISBN 0688037283.

Some of the women's movement's most insightful writers penned the thirty-five contributions to this anthology—Diana E. H. Russell, Susan Brownmiller, Gloria Steinem, Alice Walker, Robin Morgan, Susan Griffin, Andrea Dworkin, Adrienne Rich, and others. All have come "to make the connections between media violence to women and real-life violence to them, to recognize the threat which pornography poses to our lives and livelihood ..." (p.16). The authors define pornography, assess its destructive consequences for women and its appeal to men, review the research on its effects, examine pornography's status under the First Amendment, suggest anti-pornography actions, and articulate the centrality of pornography to women's oppression. Andrea Dworkin emerges as the most vocal and passionate feminist critic of pornography. In *Pornography: Men Possessing Women* (Putnam, 1981), Dworkin argues that pornography is the ultimate instrument of male power. Her ideas are forceful, and she shocks the reader with graphic descriptions of violent, sexually explicit materials. In the six years since the publication of *Take Back the Night*, the feminist debate over pornography has intensified, threatening to divide the women's movement into two hostile camps. In *Women Against Censorship* (Douglas and McIntyre, 1985), editor Varda Burstyn presents eleven essays, written from a variety of theoretical and personal vantage points, that caution against a simplistic view of pornography as *the* central problem for women, warning that laws to outlaw obscene media might be used to suppress feminist materials as well.

1122.   Leghorn, Lisa, and Katherine Parker. **Woman's Worth: Sexual Economics and the World of Women.** Boston: Routledge and Kegan Paul, 1981. 356p. bibliog. index. $22.95. LC 82-106360. ISBN 0710008368.

"In virtually all existing cultures, women's work, though usually invisible to the male eye, sustains the economy and subsidizes the profits, leisure time and higher standard of living enjoyed by individual men, private corporations, and male-dominated governments" (p.3). The question pursued by these two feminist theorists, neither of them academics, is one that has challenged critics of Western economic development: why, given their extensive economic contributions, do women lack "corresponding economic, political and social control over their lives"? (p.3). Leghorn and Parker evaluate women's status by assessing (a) the valuation of women's fertility and physical integrity; (b) women's access to and control over crucial resources; and (c) women's networks. They conclude that women have at most three limited forms of power — minimal, token, or negotiating power — and give examples of societies where each is practiced. In their final chapter, the authors attempt to envision a "matriarchal economy."

1123. Malos, Ellen, ed. **The Politics of Housework.** London: Allison and Busby; distr. New York: Schocken Books, 1980. 286p. bibliog. index. $16.00. LC 79-41427. ISBN 0850313279.

Few issues create the fireworks housework has between competing theoretical camps — not to mention between cohabiting individuals. Malos surveys the history of the housework debates in her valuable introduction to this collection, summarizing arguments both theoretical (over the relation of domestic labor to capital) and activist (over the wages for housework campaigns). The collection makes available movement classics previously dispersed in periodicals and pamphlets by such authors as: Pat Mainardi; Margaret Benston; Peggy Morton; Mariarosa Dalla Costa and Selma James; Margaret Coulson, Branka Magas, and Hilary Wainwright; and Jean Gardiner, Susan Himmelweit, and Marueen Mackintosh. Another collection on the topic, *Hidden in the Household: Women's Domestic Labor Under Capitalism* (Women's Educational Press, 1980), edited by Bonnie Fox, brings together articles by Fox, Wally Seccombe, Emily Blumenfeld, Bruce Curtis, Susan Mann, and Linda Briskin.

1124. Mamonova, Tatyana, 1943- , ed. **Women and Russia: Feminist Writings From the Soviet Union.** Boston: Beacon Press, 1984. 273p. $21.95. LC 82-73963. ISBN 0807067083.

"In 1979, a group of extraordinarily brave women in the Soviet Union, knowing virtually nothing about the Women's Movement in the rest of the world, reinvented feminism" (p.ix). Thus Robin Morgan, in her foreword, signals the importance of the unprecedented underground anthology *Woman and Russia* (*Zhenschina i Rossia*), from which the twenty-nine translated pieces in this volume are drawn. Mamonova's introduction describes the repression of feminist writing and the harassment of the editorial staff by the KGB, while bravely condemning the sexism of both the Party elite and the dissident movement. Organized thematically into sections devoted to "Working Women," "Everyday Life," "Foremothers," "Upbringing," and other familiar topics, the selections confirm the facts of modern life for women in the USSR (already documented in other sources, notably Hansson and Lidén's *Moscow Women*, entry 1024). In addition, the Westerner reads here for the first time of Soviet lesbians and women prisoners and, more movingly, of the desire of feminists in the USSR to unite with women around the globe in the causes of equality and peace.

1125. Martineau, Harriet, 1802-1876. **Harriet Martineau on Women.** Edited by Gayle Graham Yates. New Brunswick, NJ: Rutgers University Press, 1985. 283p. bibliog. index. $29.00. LC 84-4827. ISBN 0813510570.

Harriet Martineau was a prolific English writer, radical thinker, positivist, and influential commentator on economics, politics, and society. Gayle Graham Yates rightly declares that "an overview of Martineau's writings and the issues and campaigns she fought for with her pen gives a contemporary reader both a profile of the emergence of feminism in nineteenth-century England and America and a theoretical foundation for the feminist social philosophy still dominant today" (p.18). Following an introduction that traces

Martineau's life and work, and honors her contributions to feminist and liberal thought, are thirty-two pieces of nonfiction. These include: memoirs; letters; essays on equal rights and female education; reports on American women; sketches of prominent women of Martineau's day; and discussions of such issues as women's wages, the abolition of slavery, harmful fashions in dress, and the Contagious Diseases Act (an attempt to control prostitution that middle-class English feminists staunchly opposed). Valerie Kossew Pichanick has written a scholarly biography titled *Harriet Martineau: The Woman and Her Work, 1802-76* (University of Michigan Press, 1980); and Martineau's own *Autobiography* (written in 1855 but not published until the year after her death) has been reprinted in two volumes by Virago Press (1983).

1126.   McAllister, Pam, ed. **Reweaving the Web of Life: Feminism and Nonviolence.** Philadelphia: New Society Publishers, 1982. 440p. bibliog. index. $19.95. LC 82-81879. ISBN 0865710171.

Essays, poems, short stories, plays, interviews, songs, speeches, photographs, and original artwork by more than fifty contributors celebrate a range of feminist viewpoints on pacifism. Editor Pam McAllister describes nonviolent feminism as "the merging of our uncompromising rage at the patriarchy's brutal destructiveness with a refusal to adopt its ways" (p.iii). Among the topics addressed in this thought-provoking anthology are civil disobedience, sexism and militarism, racism, male sexuality, draft resistance, abortion, and self-defense. The late Barbara Deming, a leading thinker on issues of civil rights, feminism, and peace, is represented here only by a short poem. Fortunately, readers have ready access to her writings in *We Are All Part of One Another* (New Society Publishers, 1984), compiled by Jane Meyerding. Gathered together are essays, speeches, poems, letters, and autobiographical pieces from a forty-year period, including excerpts from *Prison Notes* (1966), *Running Away From Myself* (1969), *Revolution and Equilibrium* (1971), *We Cannot Live Without Our Lives* (1974), and *Remembering Who We Are* (Pagoda Publications; distr. Naiad Press, 1981).

1127.   Merchant, Carolyn. **The Death of Nature: Women, Ecology, and the Scientific Revolution.** San Francisco: Harper and Row, 1980. 348p. bibliog. index. pbk. $8.95. LC 79-1766. ISBN 0062505726.

"The world we have lost was organic," writes Merchant (p.1), in this analysis of changing orientations to women and nature over the last five centuries. Medieval society viewed nature as a living organism, placing strictures on the freedom to exploit natural resources. Merchant shows how the emergence of capitalism and science during the sixteenth and seventeenth centuries created implacable demands for resources such as minerals and lumber. This industrial transformation of society and the natural world produced in its wake a new world view that "sanctioned the domination of both nature and women" (p.xvii). (Merchant interprets the witch hunts of the period as a case in point.) The women's movement and the ecology movement therefore share many of the same interests and goals, according to Merchant. In the course of her analysis, Merchant critically reinterprets the ideas of Bacon, Descartes, Hobbes, and Newton, as well as those of early feminist philosopher Anne Conway. For a very different treatment of similar themes, see Susan Griffin's *Woman and Nature* (discussed in entry 1110). *Nature, Culture and Gender* (entry 28) provides cross-cultural comparisons that call into question the universality of the association of women with nature.

1128.   Meulenbelt, Anja, et al., eds. **A Creative Tension: Key Issues of Socialist-Feminism.** Boston: South End Press, 1984. 152p. bibliog. $20.00. LC 84-209289. ISBN 0896082377.

The six articles collected in this slim volume all originally appeared in the Dutch series "Socialisties-Feministiese Teksten" (Socialist Feminist Texts). While the editorial collective selected articles with an international rather than a Dutch focus, their introduction will acquaint the reader with the history of the women's movement in the Netherlands. Reflecting close readings of European and U.S. socialist-feminist theory, the articles offer articulate discussions of key issues: the women's movement and motherhood; the split between domestic and public spheres cross-culturally; the "dual heritage" of Marxist and feminist thought; feminism and psychoanalysis; the controversial work *The Policing of Families* (Pantheon Books, 1979), by Jacques Donzelot; and women's struggles in the Third World.

1129.   Mitchell, Juliet, 1940- . **Women: The Longest Revolution: Essays on Feminism, Literature and Psychoanalysis.** New York: Pantheon Books, 1984. 335p. bibliog. index. pbk. $9.95. LC 83-43144. ISBN 0394725743.

The title essay of this volume was first published in the *New Left Review* in 1966. Mitchell's highly original effort in this piece to define the "separate structures" of "woman's condition" — production, reproduction, sexuality, and socialization — still stands as a milestone of feminist theory. This collection of Mitchell's writing over two decades enables the reader to trace the evolution of her intellectual preoccupations, from the literary criticism of the 1960s, to the essays on feminism, to her later immersion in psychoanalysis. The author's headnotes to each selection provide background, and attempt — not altogether successfully — to trace thematic continuities. One of Mitchell's essays on psychoanalysis, "Freud and Lacan: Psychoanalytic Theories of Sexual Difference," first appeared in a volume she edited with Jacqueline Rose, entitled *Feminine Sexuality: Jacques Lacan and the Ecole Freudienne* (1982; Norton/Pantheon Books, 1985). The book presents a selection from the writings of Jacques Lacan and his followers "to show the relevance of Lacan's ideas for the continuing debate on femininity within both psychoanalysis and feminism" (p.vii).

1130.   Moraga, Cherríe, and Gloria Anzaldúa, eds. **This Bridge Called My Back: Writings By Radical Women of Color.** 2nd ed. New York: Kitchen Table, Women of Color Press, 1983. 261p. bibliog. $17.95. ISBN 091317503X.

A book that has catalyzed significant changes in the United States women's movement, this anthology is stirring testimony to the coming together of women of color in the eighties. Black, Chicana, Asian-American, American Indian, and Puerto Rican women — lesbian and "straight" — speak here in their many voices of the differences that could divide them, and of the commonalities they hope will unite them. They also provide a critical perspective on the women's movement, reminding us that different heritages give birth to different feminisms, and that sisterhood is not a simple matter. Contributions to the volume include poems, letters, a variety of first-person accounts, and a selected bibliography on Third World women in the United States. This essential anthology has recently been joined by another that takes a regional approach to collecting the work of U.S. women of color. Edited by Jo Cochran, J. T. Stewart, and Mayumi Tsutakawa, *Gathering Ground* (Seal Press, 1984) brings us artwork and writing in several genres by women of color from the Pacific Northwest, organized around three themes: self-discovery, community perspectives, and cultural awareness.

1131. Morgan, Robin. **The Anatomy of Freedom: Feminism, Physics, and Global Politics.** Garden City, NY: Anchor Press/Doubleday, 1982. 365p. bibliog. index. pbk. $8.95. LC 81-43730. ISBN 0385177933.

In this dazzling and controversial amalgam of feminist theory, social commentary, parable, and polemic, Morgan meditates on the meaning of freedom. She chooses quantum physics, with its central tenets of relativity and interconnectedness, as a framing analogy. Each chapter presents an "anatomy" or dissection of a basic social/ideological construct; "woman," dreams, sexual passion, marriage, family, death, art and technology, and politics. Some readers will find Morgan's most personal passages self-indulgent (her nine-page examination of her own body, for example). Others may resent her mean-spirited attacks on feminists who oppose the anti-pornography movement, or her witty arguments for child suffrage. No one can deny that her prose is exuberantly poetic, her metaphors original, her feelings passionately genuine. Morgan's inimitable style is also evidenced in *Depth Perception: New Poems and a Masque* (Anchor Press/Doubleday, 1982).

1132. Morgan, Robin, ed. **Sisterhood Is Global: The International Women's Movement Anthology.** Garden City, NY: Anchor/Press Doubleday, 1984. 815p. bibliog. index. $24.95. LC 82-45332. ISBN 0385177978.

Feminists from seventy nations furnish essays here that are informative, often opinionated, and richly diverse in perspective and tone, recounting women's lives and struggles around the globe. The contributors are an eclectic mix, including grass-roots organizers, political leaders, writers, and revolutionaries. Third World countries predominate here, as they do on the map. The volume has considerable reference value, for Robin Morgan and her research staff have assembled in the preface to each chapter statistics and other background information, including a brief introduction to the country's demography, government, and economy. Many issues of particular concern to feminists fall under the heading "Gynography." Attempts are made to differentiate between official policies and actual practices, although comparative data are often unavailable. Brief notes on history and mythology are also offered. Morgan's inspiring introduction, "Planetary Feminism: The Politics of the 21st Century," traces the recurring themes of the collection: reproduction, the family, and sexuality; women in the paid (and unpaid) labor force; the experiences that unite women despite barriers of race, class, and caste; violence against women; nationalism and anti-nationalism; the challenge feminism presents to both the Right and the Left; the oppression of women by organized religions; and the struggles of women to redefine power, while creating and preserving their cultures. Although this work has its flaws—a few major countries are not covered, and some of the facts and figures are quite out of date—it heralds an expanding awareness of international women's issues and seems destined, like Morgan's earlier anthology, *Sisterhood Is Powerful*, to become a classic.

1133. Mott, Lucretia, 1793-1880. **Lucretia Mott: Her Complete Speeches and Sermons.** Edited by Dana Greene. New York: Edwin Mellen Press, 1980. 401p. index. $69.95. LC 80-81885. ISBN 0889469687.

Mott was a Philadelphia Quaker active in many of the foremost reform movements of the nineteenth century. Her contributions to women's rights were such that when the E.R.A. was first introduced in 1923, it was called the "Lucretia Mott Amendment." However, according to editor Dana Greene, little scholarly attention has been directed to Mott's reformist philosophy, for which the sermons and speeches collected here constitute the primary source. The publication of this book will serve not only to encourage research, but also "to counter the hagiography which has grown up around [Mott]" (p.2). Greene judges Mott to have been "above all a religious woman" (p.3), and indeed this collection is full of sermons on traditional Christian ideals. Alongside these religious pieces, however, are speeches on political and feminist themes: for example, "The Principles of the Co-Equality of Woman With Man" (1853), "A Faithful Testimony Against Bearing Arms" (1875), and "Place Woman in Equal Power" (1878).

1134. Nightingale, Florence, 1820-1910. **Cassandra: An Essay.** Old Westbury, NY: Feminist Press, 1979. 60p. bibliog. pbk. $3.50. LC 79-15175. ISBN 091267055X.

"What women suffer — even physically — from the want of ... work no one can tell. The accumulation of nervous energy, which has had nothing to do during the day, makes them feel every night, when they go to bed, as if they were going mad ..." (p.43). This strongly worded passage is from "Cassandra," written by Nightingale in 1852, when she herself was struggling against the restrictive lifestyle of the privileged Victorian woman. In this brief essay, Nightingale is relentless in her attack on the sexist conventions that directed the elite woman to move from the suffocating domesticity of her birth home to a similarly constricting vocation as wife and mother, while bestowing on elite men the privilege of meaningful work. That Nightingale did succeed in her personal effort to free herself for purposeful work is common knowledge. While nineteenth-century biographical assessments of Nightingale tended to eulogize the famed "Lady with the Lamp," revisionist interpretations in our own century have leaned toward character assassination, bringing out the power-seeking and manipulative elements in her personality.

1135. O'Brien, Mary. **The Politics of Reproduction.** Boston: Routledge and Kegan Paul, 1981. 240p. bibliog. index. pbk. $10.95. LC 81-203741. ISBN 0710094981.

For more than a decade, feminist theorists have labored to develop a theory of reproduction. O'Brien's widely acclaimed book greatly advances this project. A practicing midwife before undertaking her studies in political theory, O'Brien argues "... that reproductive process is not only the material base of the historical forms of the social relations of reproduction, but that it is also a dialectical process, which changes historically" (p.21). Men's and women's different roles in the reproductive process create male and female reproductive consciousness; most of political philosophy as we know it (or what O'Brien calls "male-stream thought") in her view reflects male reproductive consciousness. In the course of developing her argument about the centrality of reproduction to a feminist materialist theory, O'Brien critically scrutinizes the work of Plato, Hegel, Marx, Freud, and other male thinkers. She goes on to review the writings of feminist theorists such as de Beauvoir, Millett, Firestone, and Rowbotham, building on their insights and identifying their shortcomings. Lorenne M. G. Clark and Lynda Lange's earlier collection, *The Sexism of Social and Political Theory: Women and Reproduction From Plato to Nietzsche* (University of Toronto Press, 1979), develops related themes. Seven contributors (of whom O'Brien is one) examine the theories of Plato, Locke, Rousseau, Hume, Hegel, Marx, and Nietzsche in relation to their "failure to recognize that the manner of reproduction in human societies requires as thorough an understanding as do other matters with which political philosophy has traditionally been concerned ..." (p.vii).

1136. Petchesky, Rosalind Pollack. **Abortion and Woman's Choice: The State, Sexuality, and Reproductive Freedom.** Boston: Northeastern University Press, 1984. 404p. bibliog. index. $22.95. LC 83-11342. ISBN 0582282152.

Petchesky's significant contribution in this book is to develop a feminist materialist analysis of abortion. Abortion has, in her view, "become the cutting edge of reproductive and sex-gender politics" (p.vii). In Part I, Petchesky traces the history of abortion practice and state regulation of abortion to illustrate the social and historical—rather than biological or technological—determination of reproductive relations. In Part II, she surveys U.S. abortion practice in the 1970s, outlining differences by class and race and analyzing with particular sensitivity the issue of teenage sexuality and pregnancy. The focus in Part III is sexual politics in the 1980s: how the New Right has exploited the abortion issue, along with sexuality and the family, in its bid for power. Petchesky concludes by advancing a socialist-feminist theory of reproductive freedom, including a discussion of morality and "personhood." She decries the "historical amnesia" of most "current literature on the morality of abortion ..." (p.328). Theologian Beverly Wildung Harrison, author of *Our Right to Choose: Toward a New Ethic of Abortion* (Beacon Press, 1983), would agree with Petchesky on the imperative to view moral issues in historical context. Harrison critically examines the history of Christian teaching on abortion, then elaborates a vision of the conditions necessary for an ethic of procreative choice. She argues that it is "intrinsically sexist" to view the status of fetal life as "*the* determining issue in the moral debate about abortion" (p.16), countering that "noncoercion in childbearing is a foundational social good" (p.17). In *Not an Easy Choice: A Feminist Re-Examines Abortion* (South End Press, 1984), Kathleen McDonnell challenges feminists to address ambivalent feelings about abortion and to acknowledge the right of the fetus as well as women's rights to control their own bodies.

1137.   The Quest Staff. **Building Feminist Theory: Essays from Quest.** New York: Longman, 1981. 280p. bibliog. index. pbk. $14.95. LC 80-28842. ISBN 0582282101.

Quest: A Feminist Quarterly was founded in 1974 by twelve women active in Washington, D.C. feminist politics. The founders—who included Rita Mae Brown, Charlotte Bunch, Alexa Freeman, Nancy Hartsock, and Karen Kollias—envisioned the national journal as "a tool for the already committed" (p.xvi) that would contribute to the development of strategies for political change. *Quest* distinguished itself among feminist publications by consistently publishing essays that attended to questions of class, race, and lesbian-feminism. This retrospective anthology draws essays from *Quest's* first three volumes, among them: "Fundamental Feminism: Process and Perspective," by Nancy Hartsock; "Beyond Either/Or: Feminist Options," "Not for Lesbians Only," and "The Reform Tool Kit," by Charlotte Bunch; "Who Wants a Piece of the Pie?," by Marilyn Frye; "An Open Letter to the Academy," by Michelle Russell; "Class Realities: Create a New Power Base," by Karen Kollias; "Patriarchy and Capitalism," by Linda Phelps; and "Put Your Money Where Your Movement Is," by Beverly Fisher-Maniak. Charlotte Bunch recounts the history of the journal in her introduction. *Quest* ceased publication not long after this anthology appeared.

1138.   Reardon, Betty A. **Sexism and the War System.** New York: Teachers College Press, 1985. 111p. bibliog. index. $17.95. LC 85-12619. ISBN 0807727709.

Betty A. Reardon addresses women's studies educators and researchers, and their counterparts in peace research and world order studies. She argues persuasively that militarism and sexism are "two interdependent manifestations of a common problem: social violence" (p.5). Achievement of world disarmament requires not only structural change (political, economic, and social), but a fundamental transformation of the human psyche, she declares. Reardon probes the underlying psychological and ideological supports for oppression, violence, and misogyny; criticizes the absence of feminine values and skills in policy-making and peace research; and shares her vision of a world transformed by a shift in human relations toward equality, mutuality, and emotional maturity. Birgit Brock-Utne covers many of the same points in *Educating for Peace: A Feminist Perspective* (Pergamon Press, 1985), giving greater emphasis to women's peace activities and women's role in peace education, and less attention to theory. She issues a strong warning against women entering military service. Other recent scholarly works include a special issue of *Women's Studies International Forum* (vol. 5, no. 3/4) on "Women and Men's Wars," and Anne Wiltsher's study of British opposition to World War I, *Most Dangerous Women: Feminist Peace Campaigners of the Great War* (Pandora Press, 1985).

1139. **Report of the World Conference of the United Nations Decade for Women: Equality, Development and Peace; Copenhagen, 14-30 July 1980.** New York: United Nations, 1980. 238p. $18.00. ISBN 0686714547.

The United Nations Decade for Women was inaugurated in 1975; plans were subsequently made for a mid-decade world conference to be held in Copenhagen in July 1980. This volume provides documentation on the Copenhagen conference, including official decisions and resolutions, origins of the conference, attendance and organization of work, summary of the general debate, reports of subsidiary bodies and action taken on these reports, adoption of the report of the conference, and a list of conference documents. The Decade's close in 1985 was marked by a final conference in Nairobi.

1140. Root, Jane. **Pictures of Women: Sexuality.** Edited by Jane Hawksley. Boston: Pandora Press, 1984. 128p. bibliog. index. $8.95. LC 83-21932. ISBN 0863580238.

The text of this book is based on a series of six programs produced for British television by the Pictures of Women Cooperative. The series and its resulting book aim "to serve as an introduction to a way of looking at sexuality which has developed within feminism over the past decade ..." (p.7), with critical discussions on sexual relationships, pornography, advertising, prostitution, sexual harassment, and the law. Rosalind Coward, a scriptwriter for the TV series, along with Carol Smart and Annette Kuhn, looks specifically at cultural representations of female pleasure and desire in *Female Desires: How They Are Sought, Bought, and Packaged* (Grove Press, 1985). The brief essays in this volume consider the symbols and codes embedded in a range of cultural forms—the Royal Family, "food pornography," Harlequin romances, fashion.

1141. Rowbotham, Sheila. **Dreams and Dilemmas: Collected Writings.** London: Virago Press, 1983. 379p. bibliog. index. pbk. $8.95. LC 83-149314. ISBN 0860683427.

Rowbotham assembles in this volume her writings, published and unpublished, from the 1960s through the early 1980s. The collection will greatly interest those who have followed the development of socialist-feminist theory in the United States and abroad, including Rowbotham's own widely read earlier writings. There is an abundance here of astute commentary on the evolution of the British women's movement and feminist theory, interspersed with Rowbotham's poetry. One of the last selections, "The Women's Movement and Organizing for Socialism," is excerpted from Rowbotham's contribution to *Beyond the Fragments: Feminism and the Making of Socialism* (Alyson Publications, 1981), a critical feminist analysis of political organization on the Left co-authored with Lynne Segal and Hilary Wainwright. In thoughtful introductions to the volume as a whole, each thematic section, and every selection, Rowbotham reflects on her earlier thinking and provides contextual background for the reader. These significant documents of the contemporary women's movement convey a stirring sense of history.

1142.   Rowland, Robyn, ed. **Women Who Do and Women Who Don't Join the Women's Movement.** Boston: Routledge and Kegan Paul, 1984. 242p. bibliog. index. pbk. $8.95. LC 83-24502. ISBN 0710202962.

Rowland, an Australian professor of social psychology and women's studies, wanted to know "*why* some women can have similar experiences, yet one becomes a feminist and the other an antifeminist" (p.xi). To answer this question, she invited twenty-four women to submit short essays on their views of feminism and the women's movement; their feelings about themselves, women, and men; and their assessments of women's status. It is a diverse group of women – married and unmarried, mothers and non-mothers, white and black – ranging in age from seventeen to seventy-five, and living in several English-speaking countries. In her introduction, Rowland provides brief sketches of the women's movement and its opposition. Her conclusion identifies differences and similarities between the feminists and the antifeminists, and speculates about the source of the differences. Not surprisingly, the most contentious issues prove to be motherhood, children, family, work, abortion, and religion.

1143.   Russell, Dora Winifred Black, 1894-1986. **The Dora Russell Reader: 57 Years of Writing and Journalism, 1925-1982.** London: Pandora Press, 1983. 242p. bibliog. index. pbk. $7.95. LC 83-209668. ISBN 0863580203.

"We, who in a sense are the children of the feminist pioneers, ... we at least will pay our tribute to those who lit the sacred fires, before we take up pen and paper to criticize" (p.11). This homage to the first-wave feminists is taken from Dora Russell's first book, *Hypatia,* published in 1925 and reprinted here in full. Contemporary feminists will likely acknowledge Russell herself as an inspiring foremother after reading the work gathered here – nearly sixty years' worth of sharply worded opinion on feminism, racism, militarism, and industrialism. Dale Spender wrote the foreword and provided brief introductions to the selections. In her own life, Russell struggled to live out many of the ideals she articulated in her writings: traveling to Soviet Russia in the 1920s; creating a non-monogamous marriage with Bertrand Russell; founding a progressive school; working as a peace activist. Two volumes of Russell's autobiography, *The Tamarisk Tree,* have been published – the first in 1975, and the second in 1980. The third volume, bringing her account into the eighties, is forthcoming from Virago Press. Russell is one of five "elder stateswomen" whose contributions to (mostly) British feminism are celebrated in *There's Always Been a Women's Movement This Century* (Pandora Press, 1983), edited by Dale Spender. The others are Hazel Hunkins Hallinan (1890-1982), Rebecca West (1892-1983), Mary Stott (b.1907), and Constance Rover (b.1910).

1144.   Sargent, Lydia, ed. **Women and Revolution: A Discussion of The Unhappy Marriage of Marxism and Feminism.** Boston: South End Press, 1981. 373p. bibliog. $20.00. LC 80-54829. ISBN 0896080625.

Heidi Hartmann's essay "The Unhappy Marriage of Marxism and Feminism" has circulated in feminist circles since the mid-seventies, inspiring heated discussion. Arguing that "the 'marriage' of marxism and feminism has been like the marriage of husband and wife depicted in English common law: marxism and feminism are one, and that one is marxism" (p.2), Hartmann calls for a more progressive union – or a divorce. Sargent's invaluable collection brings together – in addition to Hartmann's piece – twelve critical responses representing radical-, socialist-, Marxist-, and anarchist-feminist perspectives. Together, these essays offer the reader an accurate glimpse of feminist theoretical debates during the seventies—on the nature of the historical relationship between patriarchy and capitalism; on the neglect of racism and heterosexism in feminist theory; on the relative analytical power of Marxism and feminism in explaining women's oppression. Contributors include Gloria Joseph, Sandra Harding, Lise Vogel, Carol Ehrlich, Azizah Al-Hibri, and Zilla Eisenstein. Hartmann writes a final rejoinder to the discussion. Sargent's introduction places these debates in historical context and summarizes the different arguments.

1145.   Schechter, Susan. **Women and Male Violence: The Visions and Struggles of the Battered Women's Movement.** Boston: South End Press, 1982. 367p. bibliog. index. $20.00. LC 82-61150. ISBN 0896081605.

In the first half of this important book, Schechter chronicles the growth of the battered women's movement—its rapid success in establishing shelters; the struggles over internal structure, funding, and legitimacy; the forging of coalitions on local, state, national, and international levels; and the contradictions of working with the criminal justice system and the federal government. Schechter records the vital contributions of radical feminists at the earliest stages, contributions now overlooked as services for battered women become increasingly professionalized. Had Schechter written only this chapter of feminism's recent history, the book would be well worth the price. But she proceeds to tackle thornier questions in the second half of the volume. Speaking as a socialist feminist and a pragmatic activist, she refutes a number of theories about family violence. She insists that only by understanding the dynamics of oppression in capitalist society (instead of narrowly focusing on individual behavior) can we envision a violence-free future. Calling for a dual focus on service and politics within the battered women's movement, she outlines an agenda of pressing issues: men in the movement; heterosexism and homophobia; race and racism; and the role of battered women themselves in the movement. She makes sound suggestions for organizing in the face of right-wing attacks and fiscal cutbacks, emphasizing alliances and community education. In her final chapter, Schechter optimistically assesses the battered women's movement as a "laboratory" offering "important insights for the future of feminist theory and practice" (p.312).

1146.   Schoenfielder, Lisa, and Barb Wieser, eds. **Shadow on a Tightrope: Writings by Women on Fat Oppression.** Iowa City: Aunt Lute Book Company, 1983. 243p. bibliog. pbk. $8.95. ISBN 0918040028.

This is a powerful book, guaranteed to turn the reader's head around. Some of the articles, personal stories, interviews, and poems were originally part of a packet distributed by the Fat Underground in the seventies; others were written more recently. The point of view expressed by many of these contributors stands in sharp contrast to widely accepted (and unexamined) ideas about weight, health, and well-being. For example, in her foreword, Vivian F. Mayer argues that biology rather than eating habits causes fat; that stress deriving from stigmatization causes the health problems of fat people; that dieting almost never succeeds, and in fact causes food binging; and that the role of the therapist is "to help fat women feel good about themselves as fat women and stop trying to lose weight" (p.xii). Writings are arranged topically: myths about fat; memories of growing up fat; the struggle to exercise and participate in sports; living with harassment and isolation; "medical crimes and the dieting war against women"; and fat women as survivors. The survivors who speak out in this collection attest to the extremity of fat oppression, whether young or old, black or white, lesbian or heterosexual. Narrower in focus, *Such a Pretty*

Face: Being Fat in America (Norton, 1980) is a sociological study of "the meanings of being overweight" (p.ix). Drawing on interviews with a sample of white, middle-class, urban fat women, author Marcia Millman discusses organizations such as Overeaters Anonymous; summer diet camps; the isolation of fat people; sexuality and obesity; and compulsion and control in eating. Photographs by Naomi Bushman illustrate the text.

1147. Snitow, Ann, 1943-   , et al., eds. **Powers of Desire: The Politics of Sexuality.** New York: Monthly Review Press, 1983. 489p. bibliog. $25.00. LC 82-48037. ISBN 0853456097.

Snitow and co-editors Christine Stansell and Sharon Thompson have shaped a provocative collection of scholarly inquiries, poems, short stories, oral histories, and a dialogue that raises compelling questions about women's experience of sex and sexual fantasy. The lucid introduction outlines the history of sexual issues within the socialist and feminist movements of the nineteenth and twentieth centuries, and the brief notes at the beginning of each section and each piece identify recurring themes. The contributions are divided into six sections: "The Capitalist Paradox: Expanding and Contracting Pleasures"; "Sexual Revolutions"; "The Institution of Heterosexuality"; "Domination, Submission, and the Unconscious"; "On Sexual Openness"; and "Current Controversies." Among the pieces most often singled out by reviewers are: "Master and Slave: The Fantasy of Erotic Domination," by psychoanalyst Jessica Benjamin; "Is the Gaze Male?," by film critic E. Ann Kaplan; three analyses of the historical experiences of black American women, by Rennie Simson, Jacquelyn Dowd Hall, and Barbara Omolade; "I Just Came Out Pregnant," an oral history by Felicita Garcia; "Feminism, Moralism, and Pornography," by journalist Ellen Willis; and "What We're Rolling Around in Bed With: Sexual Silences in Feminism," a dialogue between Amber Hollibaugh and Cherríe Moraga. Overall, the volume furthers the belief that sex is socially constructed, and that the time has come for the women's movement to explore the varieties and roots of desire, rather than promoting a sanitized feminism drained of sexual content. *Pleasure and Danger: Exploring Female Sexuality* (Routledge and Kegan Paul, 1984) continues this project. Carole S. Vance edited the anthology, which originated in the controversial "The Scholar and the Feminist" IX conference at Barnard in 1982. The collection reproduces keynote papers by Carole S. Vance, Ellen DuBois and Linda Gordon, Alice Echols, and Hortense J. Spillers; papers from nineteen workshops, many of them substantial contributions (for example, Gayle Rubin's "Thinking Sex: Notes for a Radical Theory of the Politics of Sexuality"); and materials from the closing session, including poems.

1148. Spender, Dale, ed. **Feminist Theorists: Three Centuries of Key Women Thinkers.** New York: Pantheon Books, 1983. 402p. bibliog. $22.45. LC 83-47747. ISBN 0394534387.

Women are forced to "reinvent rebellion" cyclically, Spender asserts, because women's knowledge has been rendered invisible by the patriarchy. In this anthology, she gathers short critical pieces by contemporary scholars on twenty-one past feminists—among them, Mary Astell, Mary Wollstonecraft, Margaret Fuller, Lucy Stone, Emma Goldman, Christabel Pankhurst, Vera Brittain, and Simone de Beauvoir—to document a tradition of questioning male power. Ellen DuBois's short introduction to the U.S. edition provides a historical perspective and Spender concludes the volume with a brief essay on modern feminist theorists and an eighteen-page bibliography. A prolific writer and editor, Spender reveals her powers of feminist analysis in her major work, *Women of Ideas and What Men Have Done to Them* (Routledge and Kegan Paul, 1982). In nearly six hundred pages, she calls the reader's attention to myriad women, from Aphra Behn to Adrienne Rich, whose ideas have been erased by men and male scholarship. Thoroughly researched, the volume is a central reference work in the history of feminist thought. Spender continues her project of reclaiming past women's writing in *Time and Tide Wait for No Man* (Pandora Press, 1984), a collection of articles from the British feminist weekly of the 1920s *Time and Tide*. In *For the Record* (The Women's Press, 1985), Spender illuminates "the making and meaning of feminist knowledge" by surveying the key texts of the modern women's movement. Pivotal works by Betty Friedan, Kate Millett, Germaine Greer, Robin Morgan, Shulamith Firestone, Eva Figes, Alice Rossi, Juliet Mitchell, Ann Oakley, Phyllis Chesler, Adrienne Rich, and Mary Daly come under Spender's careful scrutiny, along with many other books that she treats in less depth.

1149. Steinem, Gloria. **Outrageous Acts and Everyday Rebellions.** New York: Holt, Rinehart and Winston, 1983. 370p. bibliog. index. $14.95. LC 83-222. ISBN 0030632366.

Steinem is a leading spokesperson for the U.S. women's movement and a favorite of the media. Consequently, her name and appearance are perhaps more familiar to most Americans than are her ideas. This collection of essays and journalistic writings spanning more than twenty years reclaims her as one of feminism's most articulate proponents. Steinem is outspoken and uncompromising, and her words can sparkle with wit ("If Men Could Menstruate"), move the reader to sharp anger ("The Real Linda Lovelace"), or lift her to new places of understanding ("Why Young Women Are More Conservative" and "If Hitler Were Alive Today, Whose Side Would He Be On?"). Several pieces profile individual women, including Marilyn Monroe, Pat Nixon, Jackie Onassis, and Alice Walker. Other pieces treat such topics as sexist language, the beautiful diversity of women's bodies, the politics of food, and erotica versus pornography. The autobiographical pieces — which range from the classic "I Was a Playboy Bunny" to the extraordinarily moving story of her mentally ill mother, "Ruth's Song (Because She Could Not Sing It)" — are among the best in the volume.

1150.* Swerdlow, Amy, and Hanna Lessinger, eds. **Class, Race, and Sex: The Dynamics of Control.** New York: Barnard College Women's Center; Boston: G. K. Hall, 1983. 362p. bibliog. index. LC 82-21270. ISBN 0816190399.

Initiated in 1974, the Barnard College Women's Center's "The Scholar and the Feminist" conferences have attracted scholar/activists at the forefront of new feminist inquiry. Swerdlow and Lessinger have selected papers presented at the seventh (1980) and eighth (1981) conferences, among them: "Notes Toward a Feminist Dialectic," by Renate Bridenthal; "The Social Enforcement of Heterosexuality and Lesbian Resistance in the 1920s," by Lisa Duggan; "Feminism, the Family, and the New Right," by Jan Rosenberg; "Issues of Race and Class in Women's Studies: A Puerto Rican Woman's Thoughts," by Angela Jore; "Women's Role in Economic Development: Practical and Theoretical Implications of Class and Gender Inequalities," by Lourdes Benería and Gita Sen; "Reproduction and Class Divisions Among Women," by Rosalind Pollack Petchesky; "Women, Media, and the Dialectics of Resistance," by Lillian S. Robinson; and "The Challenge of Profamily Politics: A Feminist Defense of Sexual Freedom," by Ellen Willis. Selected papers from the sixth Barnard conference were published in a volume entitled *The Future of Difference*, edited by Hester Eisenstein and Alice Jardine (Barnard College Women's Center/G. K. Hall, 1980). Among the contributors to this earlier volume are Nancy Chodorow, Jane Flax, Jessica Benjamin, Jane Gallop, Audre Lorde, Carol Gilligan, and Elizabeth Janeway.

1151. Thorne, Barrie, and Marilyn Yalom, eds. **Rethinking the Family: Some Feminist Questions.** New York: Longman, 1982. 246p. bibliog. index. pbk. $13.95. LC 81-2427. ISBN 0582282659.

Under attack from the Right as "anti-family," feminists have attempted to replace the simplistic "pro" and "con" of the family debate with a more sophisticated analysis. The twelve scholarly articles in this collection critically evaluate prevailing ideologies; break down the monolithic concept of "The Family" into its different components (sexual division of labor, regulation of sexuality, socialization); distinguish between the experiences and relative power of household members; modify the popular conception of the isolated modern family by demonstrating that state intervention into the "private realm" is on the rise; and identify the conflicting pulls of individualist and family-based values. The articles address a range of topics, including birth control, motherhood, marital property reform, the relation of home and market, and the welfare state. Among the contributors are Michelle Z. Rosaldo, Linda Gordon, Nancy Chodorow, Sara Ruddick, Rayna Rapp, Eli Zaretsky, and Renate Bridenthal. Equally scholarly in approach are the twenty-two articles in *Families, Politics, and Public Policy: A Feminist Dialogue on Women and the State,* edited by Irene Diamond (Longman, 1983). Articles in Part I establish a theoretical and historical context for understanding the changing reality of the family, gender relations, and the state. In Part II, contributors zero in on specific areas of family policy, such as housing, childcare and child custody, incest, and wife abuse. Part III opens up the question of change, with essays on China and Scandinavia as well as on the United States. A less academic collection, rooted in the experience of the British "Thatcherist" state, is *What Is to Be Done About the Family?*, edited by Lynne Segal (Penguin Books, 1983).

1152. Trebilcot, Joyce, ed. **Mothering: Essays in Feminist Theory.** Totowa, NJ: Rowman and Allanheld, 1983. 336p. bibliog. $26.50. LC 83-4517. ISBN 0847671151.

Eighteen essays by philosophers and social scientists reflect a spectrum of feminist viewpoints—liberal, radical, socialist, lesbian—and raise some key issues regarding motherhood in patriarchal society. In the first section, "Who Is to Look After Children?," contributors assess men and women's unequal responsibility for childraising, and the promise of attempts to achieve a more even balance. In one provocative essay, Susan Rae Peterson dispatches a vigorous critique of the faddish new expression "parenting," contending that it obfuscates the reality of women's mothering. Part II, "Mothering and the Explanation of Patriarchy," is the theoretical heart of the collection, weighing the role of mothering in the generation of male supremacy. Essays in Part III explore woman-centered "Concepts of Mothering," from the maternal instinct to nurturing to peace-making. In Part IV, "Pronatalism and Resistance," Martha E. Gimenez advances a Marxist-feminist analysis of pronatalism, while Jeffner Allen advocates women's wholesale rejection of motherhod on the grounds that it represents their "annihilation." Lacking in this collection is any attention to the diversity of women's choices and experience depending on their race, class, ethnicity, or national background.

1153. Treichler, Paula A., et al., eds. **For Alma Mater: Theory and Practice in Feminist Scholarship.** Urbana: University of Illinois Press, 1985. 450p. bibliog. $32.50. LC 84-16346. ISBN 0252011783.

Paula A. Treichler, Cheris Kramarae, and Beth Stafford present a stimulating mix of research reports, critical essays, and personal accounts of feminist scholars' experiences in academia. The subjects are diverse, and the editors have organized them provocatively.

"On Women and the Academy" offers a historical view of women at the University of Illinois, by way of introduction to current concerns. "On Language," the largest section, groups six articles on feminist discourse and linguistic theory. The three papers under "On Boundaries" explore the divisions between black and white women, between the past and the present, and among the disciplines, while the four papers in "On Methodologies" address the fundamental assumptions of patriarchal versus feminist research. The remaining sections are titled "On the Body," "On the Relationship Between the Personal and the Professional," and "On Resources." With topics ranging from Chicana poetry to female obesity to library research tools, and with such distinguished contributors as Gayatri Chakravorty Spivak, Marilyn Frye, and Pauline B. Bart (as well as several promising younger scholars), this volume is a compelling state-of-the-art look at academic feminism. But *For Alma Mater* is hardly the only such anthology. *Feminist Visions,* edited by Diane L. Fowlkes and Charlotte S. McClure (University of Alabama Press, 1984), combines surveys of feminist scholarship in selected disciplines with more complex theoretical explorations. *Women's Worlds: From the New Scholarship* (Praeger, 1985) brings together thirty papers from the First International Interdisciplinary Congress on Women, held in Israel in 1981. Scholars from many nations address a wide spectrum of topics, primarily in the social and behavioral sciences. Marilyn Safir, Martha T. Mednick, Dafne Israeli, and Jessie Bernard are the editors.

1154. Whitelegg, Elizabeth, et al., eds. **The Changing Experience of Women.** Oxford: M. Robertson, 1982; repr. Oxford: Basil Blackwell in association with the Open University, 1985. 406p. bibliog. index. $29.95. LC 82-184218. ISBN 0855205172.

Designed to accompany a women's studies course taught through the British Open University, this volume emphasizes studies of Britain in the postwar period and offers an introduction to contemporary British feminist scholarship. The articles—some commissioned, some reprinted—are arranged under five broad themes: "The Historical Separation of Home and Workplace"; "Employment and Training"; "The Domestic Sphere"; "Constructing Gender"; and "Feminism and the Production of Knowledge."

PERIODICALS

Since it is in periodicals that most new feminist writing and theory first appear, we chose to be generous in our standards for inclusion in this chapter, admitting a large selection of English-language publications covering nearly every broad subject area represented in our other chapters. Periodicals from the United States, Great Britain, and Canada predominate (in that order). *Connexions,* the *Isis International Women's Journal*, and *Women's Studies International Forum* offer a window on women's lives and scholarship in other lands.

For women's studies scholarship, the premier journals remain *Signs* and *Feminist Studies. Sojourner, off our backs,* and *New Directions for Women,* all high-quality, national feminist newspapers, keep readers up to date on the women's movement, feminist issues, and current art and literature. For scholarly reviews of recent feminist works, *The Women's Review of Books* has no peer.

Sadly, most of the periodicals listed in this chapter are still omitted from standard indexing sources. *Women's Studies Abstracts, Studies on Women Abstracts*, and *Feminist Periodicals* (see entries 901 and 866) provide some access to this valuable literature. To stay abreast of new feminist periodical titles, consult "Periodical Notes," a regular column appearing in *Feminist Collections* (see entry 865).

1155. **Atlantis: A Women's Studies Journal/Journal d'études sur la femme.** 1976- . Mount Saint Vincent University, 166 Bedford Highway, Halifax, Nova Scotia B3M 2J6, Canada. Semiannual. $10.00 (indiv.); $16.00 (inst.). ISSN 0702-7818.

Celebrating its tenth anniversary in 1985, *Atlantis* is a refereed Canadian scholarly journal intended as "a forum for all feminist perspectives." *Atlantis* publishes English and French critical and creative writing representing the many disciplines. Articles, review essays, reports on Canadian women's archives, poems, short fiction, and book reviews will be found in most issues. Contributors are primarily faculty from Canadian universities. Topics explored in recent issues of the journal include feminist biography, the work of Marguerite Duras, Canadian abortion policy, Zola's women, affirmative action, reproductive labor and the creation of value, education, and women and rock music.

1156. **Belles Lettres: A Review of Books by Women.** 1985- . P.O. Box 987, Arlington, VA 22216. Bimonthly. $18.00 (indiv.); $30.00 (inst.). ISSN 0884-2957.

Belles Lettres publishes reviews of scholarly and popular books by women; trade, university, and small press publishers are represented. Although the editors state their interest in reviewing nonfiction, literature predominates in the first issues, complementing nicely the emphasis in *The Women's Review of Books* (see entry 1208). In addition to reviews, *Belles Lettres* publishes interviews, essays and commentaries, poetry, and letters to the editor in issues averaging twelve to sixteen pages. Contributors to the first three issues include Claudia Tate, Evelyn Torton Beck, Susan Koppelman, and Doris Grumbach.

1157. **Broomstick: By, For, and About Women Over Forty.** 1978- . 3543 18th St., San Francisco, CA 94110. Bimonthly. $15.00 (indiv.); $25.00 (inst.). ISSN 0883-9611.

Broomstick is committed to presenting authentic images of women over forty, and solicits material largely from its subscribers: "Our readers, not professional writers, are our authors" (Editorial Policy). *Broomstick* publishes articles, poetry, short fiction, cartoons and other graphics, personal narratives, letters, editorials, reviews, and news in issues averaging forty to fifty pages. Some issues are devoted to specific themes—e.g., "Allergies and Other Disabilities"; "Feminism and Older Women." Ageism, community, illness and death, pride, life planning, and economic and spiritual survival are among the recurring issues explored in *Broomstick*.

1158. **Calyx: A Journal of Art and Literature by Women.** 1976- . P.O. Box B, Corvallis, OR 97339. 3/year. $18.00 (indiv.); $22.50 (inst.). ISSN 0147-1627.

Originally subtitled "A Northwest Feminist Review," *Calyx* is achieving an increasingly national presence within feminist publishing, although the journal still takes pride in being "the ONLY WEST COAST PUBLICATION OF ITS KIND" (subscription ad). Marge Piercy, Olga Broumas, Sandra Gilbert, Marilyn Hacker, Margaret Randall, Ellen Bass, Joan Larkin—these are some of the writers represented in this beautifully produced journal. *Calyx* is primarily but not exclusively literary in focus, publishing poetry, fiction, interviews, drama, essays, reviews, and art work. *Calyx* has also published a few thematic issues; "Bearing Witness/Sobreviviendo: An Anthology of Writing and Art by Native American/Latina Women" and "Women and Aging" are two recent noteworthy examples.

1159. **Camera Obscura: A Journal of Feminism and Film Theory.** 1976- . P.O. Box 25889, Los Angeles, CA 90025. 3/year. $13.50 (indiv.); $27.00 (inst.). ISSN 0270-5346.

An elegant and sophisticated journal, *Camera Obscura* refers to its "project" as the examination of "the various ways in which the representation of sexual difference is determined—physically, socially and historically" (no.11, p.4). Recognizing the changing nature of film studies as a field, the journal is open to discussions of video, television, photography, and art, in addition to classical and avant-garde film. *Camera Obscura* publishes theory, criticism, and book reviews.

1160. **Canadian Woman Studies/les cahiers de la femme.** 1978- . 212 Founders College, York University, 4700 Keele St., Downsview, Ontario, M3J 1P3, Canada. Quarterly. $18.00 (indiv.); $28.00 (inst.). (Outside Canada add $3.00). ISSN 0713-3235.

CWS/cf has accurately described itself as "a bilingual, interdisciplinary, feminist journal that brings exciting scholarship about women to non-scholars, broadcasts our diverse experiences and bridges the gap between Canada's languages and cultures." It is an ambitious and beautifully designed publication, averaging some 120 pages per quarterly issue, and testifying to the vitality of women's studies in Canada. Articles, book reviews, fiction, and poetry appear regularly in the journal's pages, in French or (more often) in English. Abstracts introduce each contribution—in French, if the piece is in English; in English, if it is in French. Contributors are primarily, but not exclusively, Canadian academics and other professionals. Each issue of the journal focuses on a particular theme; affirmative action, the future, women's studies conferences, women internationally, science and technology, aging, religion, sport, belles lettres, and violence figure among recent topics.

1161. **Common Lives/Lesbian Lives: A Lesbian Quarterly.** 1981- . P.O. Box 1553, Iowa City, IA 52244. Quarterly. $12.00 (indiv.); $20.00 (inst.).

Edited by a collective, *Common Lives/Lesbian Lives* has established a remarkably consistent publication record in its first five years. The journal appears regularly, each issue running over one hundred pages; it is tastefully designed; and—more importantly—it is lively, brimming with material, and obviously beloved by its readers. *CL/LL* publishes writing in several genres, emphasizing short fiction and poetry by new writers. The desire to make lesbian life, literature, and culture visible is powerfully evident in contributions exploring a full range of lesbian concerns—coming out; relationships; fat and other oppressions; family; motherhood; illness and disability; separatism; work. Photographs scattered through each issue add visual documentation of lesbian ties, past and present.

1162. **Conditions: A Feminist Magazine of Writing by Women with an Emphasis on Writing by Lesbians.** 1976- . P.O. Box 56, Van Brunt Station, Brooklyn, NY 11215. Irregular. 3 issues: $15.00 (indiv.); $25.00 (inst.). ISSN 0147-8311.

Conditions has been, since the mid-1970s, one of two major journals publishing lesbian-feminist poetry, fiction, and essays. (The other is *Sinister Wisdom*, see entry 1196.) Founding editors Elly Bulkin, Jan Clausen, Irena Klepfisz, and Rima Shore—all significant authors in their own right—established *Conditions* as a journal of provocative ideas and fine writing, publishing women such as Jane Rule, Toi Derricotte, Judy Grahn, Melanie Kaye/Kantrowitz, Cherríe Moraga, Maureen Brady, and Michelle Cliff. *Conditions: Five: The Black Women's Issue* was a major publishing event, helping to spark the emergence of black feminism in the United States. (The issue became the core of an anthology of black feminist writings; see entry 1115). Many other classics of lesbian-feminist writing originally appeared in *Conditions,* among them Audre Lorde's "Man Child: A Black Lesbian Feminist's Response," Paula Gunn Allen's "Beloved Women: Lesbians in American Indian Cultures," and Elly Bulkin's "Hard Ground: Jewish Identity, Racism, and Anti-Semitism."

1163. **Connexions: An International Women's Quarterly.** 1981- . 4228 Telegraph Ave., Oakland, CA 94609. Quarterly. $12.00 (indiv.); $24.00 (inst.). ISSN 0884-7002.

"*Connexions* is the collective product of feminists of diverse nationalities and political perspectives committed to contributing to an international women's movement" (editorial statement). *Connexions* publishes articles, interviews, and personal narratives written by women the world over, translated into English where necessary. Each issue focuses on a specific theme—e.g., "Media: Getting to Women"; "Changing Technology"; "Women and Prostitution." One recent issue featured excerpts from the British feminist newspaper *Outwrite*; *Women's World,* published in Geneva, Switzerland (see entry 1179); *Iris*, an Irish Republican publication; *Colección Comunicación Alternativa de la Mujer,* published by the Latin American Institute of Transnational Studies; the Canadian *Resources for Feminist Research* (see entry 1191); and the New Zealand quarterly *Alternative Cinema*—among others. *Connexions* also includes letters to the editor and an international list of periodicals and publishers. *Women's International Network News* (*WIN News*) is another source for information on women worldwide. A quarterly, *WIN* prints excerpts from books, documents, and articles with an emphasis on international agencies, development issues, health, and female circumcision. (Editor Fran P. Hosken is author of a book on genital mutilation; see entry 755.) Unfortunately, *WIN* presents its wealth of data in such a dense format as to discourage all but the most determined of readers.

1164. Feminary: Lesbian Feminist Magazine of Passion, Politics and Hope. 1969- . San Francisco Women's Center, 3543 18th St., San Francisco, CA 94110. 3/year. $12.00 (indiv.); $22.00 (inst.).

This resilient periodical has weathered three changes in identity. It began in 1969 as the *Female Liberation Newsletter of Durham-Chapel Hill.* It metamorphosed from newsletter to journal in 1974, becoming for the next decade *Feminary: A Feminist Journal for the South Emphasizing Lesbian Visions.* During this period, *Feminary* broke new ground in exploring the nature of Southern women's experience and articulating a distinctly Southern progressive vision. Minnie Bruce Pratt, Mab Segrest, and Cris South, each of whom has gone on to publish works of her own, were key members of the Southern editorial collective. When in the early 1980s this group decided to give up the journal, a new collective based in San Francisco took over, giving *Feminary* its third incarnation as a national "lesbian feminist magazine of passion, politics and hope." The new *Feminary* publishes articles, short fiction, poetry, interviews, photo essays, and book reviews on diverse topics — among them, racism, lesbian identity, Latin America, motherhood, work, alcoholism and recovery, ageism, and sports.

1165. Feminist Bookstore News. 1976- . P.O. Box 882554, San Francisco, CA 94188. Bimonthly. $35.00. ISSN 0741-6555.

Though both the title and the editorial statement of this newsletter describe it as a communications vehicle for feminist bookstores, *Feminist Bookstore News* is in fact indispensable to anyone interested in the world of feminist publishing: students, teachers, librarians, publishers, and the "common reader," as well as booksellers. Compiled and published by Carol Seajay (formerly with Old Wives Tales, San Francisco's feminist bookstore), *FBN* is the place to get the inside word on the status of feminist bookstores nationwide, feminist publishers new and old, and feminist printers, along with lengthy annotated listings of new books and periodicals from women's and other small presses, university presses, and trade publishers. *FBN* also provides a forum for discussion of political questions currently being debated within the women-in-print network — from the merits of a gay and lesbian book club to the ethics of lesbian-feminist publishing.

1166. Feminist Issues: A Journal of Feminist Social and Political Theory. 1980- . Transaction Periodicals Consortium, Dept. 8010, Rutgers — The State University, New Brunswick, NJ 08903. Semiannual. $15.00 (indiv.); $25.00 (inst.). ISSN 0887-5480.

Conceived originally as the English-language edition of the French theoretical journal *Questions Féministes, Feminist Issues* soon came to see itself more broadly as a forum for "an international exchange of ideas" between English-language feminists and feminists from other countries. Judging by recent issues, the journal is publishing more English-language articles than translations at this point, and most translations are still from the French. The geographic focus, however, is broad: women heads of family in a Brazilian fishing village, the development of feminism in Japan, and the emancipation of Tunisian women are some recent topics. The journal continues to be edited by founders Mary Jo Lakeland, Susan Ellis Wolf, and Monique Wittig.

1167.   **Feminist Review.** 1979- . 11 Carleton Gardens, Brecknock Rd., London N19 5AQ, England. 3/year. $18.00 (indiv.); $50.00 (inst.). ISSN 0141-7789.

Describing itself in a recent editorial as "a journal committed to the development of socialism and feminism" (no.20, p.4), *Feminist Review* publishes scholarly articles, reviews, and letters. The range of topics is broad—theory, social and political analysis, criticism of art and literature—but the contributions tend to share an underlying interest in further defining women's movement theory and strategy, and to reflect *FR*'s British context. The journal occasionally publishes thematic issues—for example, "Cultural Politics" (no.18); "Many Voices, One Chant: Black Feminist Perspectives" (no.17). Recent contributors include Maxine Molyneux, Michèle Barrett, Mary McIntosh, Sheila Rowbotham, and Annette Kuhn.

1168.   **Feminist Studies.** 1972- . c/o Women's Studies Program, University of Maryland, College Park, MD 20742. 3/year. $19.50 (indiv.); $39.00 (inst.). ISSN 0046-3663.

"We wish not just to interpret women's experiences but to change women's condition," reads the statement of purpose on the inside cover of *Feminist Studies. Feminist Studies* has a distinguished history of publishing fine scholarship informed by a political perspective and commitment. Many of the most innovative feminist thinkers have tried out new ideas and published early versions of scholarly projects in the pages of *Feminist Studies*—among them Ellen DuBois, Mary Jo Buhle, Gerda Lerner, Carroll Smith-Rosenberg, Blanche Wiesen Cook, Rosalind Pollack Petchesky, Helene Vivienne Wenzel, and Linda Gordon. *FS* has welcomed not only academic work from the many disciplines (particularly history), but also poetry, art, and reports from the women's movement. The journal is edited by a collective whose membership reads like a who's who of socialist-feminist scholarship, including Barbara Christian, Heidi Hartmann, Ruth Milkman, Rayna Rapp, and Martha Vicinus, among others. Readers may find interesting the retrospective overview of *Feminist Studies* by Emily K. Abel and Margaret K. Nelson recently published in *The Women's Review of Books* (January 1985).

1169.   **Feminist Teacher.** 1984- . 442 Ballantine Hall, Indiana University, Bloomington, IN 47405. Quarterly. $12.00 (indiv.); $20.00 (inst.). ISSN 0882-4843.

Dubbing itself a "reader-developed magazine," *Feminist Teacher* aims to provide a forum for the exchange of ideas about the theory and practice of nonsexist teaching at all levels, preschool through graduate school. In its first year of publishing, however, *Feminist Teacher* was more successful in attracting contributions from high school and college teachers than from teachers of young children. Topics examined include science and math teaching, sexual harassment in academia, making students aware of ableism, teaching about women in introductory courses in American politics, and celebrating women's history. In addition to feature articles, the quarterly publishes a directory of Feminist Teacher Network members, news reports, resource lists and bibliographies, calls for papers, and conference notices.

1170.   **Frontiers: A Journal of Women Studies.** 1975- . Women Studies, University of Colorado, Boulder, CO 80309. Irregular. 3 issues: $14.00 (indiv.); $28.00 (inst.). ISSN 0160-9009.

"The continuing goal of *Frontiers* is to publish a journal that bridges the gap between university and community women; to find a balance between academic and popular views on issues common to women" (Editorial Statement). *Frontiers* publishes articles, experiential essays, photography, film and book reviews, criticism, and, occasionally, creative work. The journal encourages an interdisciplinary approach geared to a general readership. Most issues focus on a single theme; notable examples are "Women and Peace," "Women on the Western Frontier," "Women's Oral History," "Native American Women," "Chicanas in the National Landscape," and "Lesbian History."

1171. **Harvard Women's Law Journal**. 1978- . Subscription Manager, Publications Center, Harvard Law School, Cambridge, MA 02138. Annual. $7.00. ISSN 0270-1456.

Modeled in format after the traditional law reviews, the *Harvard Women's Law Journal* serves as a corrective to the male-centeredness of those publications. The journal provides a forum for the creation of a feminist jurisprudence, exploring the law's impact on women and women's impact on the law. To this end, *HWLJ* publishes not solely legal articles, but also political essays and writing from the social sciences on topics related to women's legal standing in society. For example, the opening essay in the spring 1985 issue was "Against the Male Flood: Censorship, Pornography and Equality," by feminist critic and visionary Andrea Dworkin. Other topics recently covered include battered women, female circumcision, black women under apartheid, and discrimination by religious institutions. Case comments, notes about recent legal developments, and book reviews round out the typical issue. *HWLJ* is not the only publication of its kind. The *Women's Rights Law Reporter,* issued by the Rutgers Law School, the *Women's Law Reporter,* out of Loyola, the *Wisconsin Women's Law Journal,* from the University of Wisconsin, and the University of California *Berkeley Women's Law Journal* also publish legal scholarship on women's topics.

1172. **Hecate: A Women's Interdisciplinary Journal**. 1975- . P.O. Box 99, St. Lucia, Brisbane, Queensland 4067, Australia. Semiannual. $8.00 (indiv.); $15.00 (inst.). ISSN 0311-4198.

An Australian women's studies publication, *Hecate* emphasizes writing that "employs a feminist, Marxist or other radical methodology to focus on the situation of women in any given area." *Hecate* reflects a mix of feminist concerns transcending geographic boundaries and preoccupations specific to its Australian context. The journal publishes articles, reviews, creative writing, and graphics.

1173. **Helicon Nine: The Journal of Women's Arts and Letters**. 1979- . P.O. Box 22412, Kansas City, MO 64113. 3/year. $15.00. ISSN 0197-3371.

Helicon Nine astonishes the reader new to its exquisite format. Supported by grants, the journal has attained an aesthetic standard well beyond the financial reach of most struggling feminist periodicals. An editorial in the winter 1983 issue speaks of the editors' insistence — in the face of skepticism from funders — on achieving the desired "feel" for the journal, making "the body ... worthy of the soul." Attracting contributions from contemporary women writers and artists, the journal publishes poetry, essays, interviews, journal excerpts, fiction and criticism, along with a wealth of photographs and fine art reproductions in color and black and white. In addition, each issue includes a brief tear-out recording of music or readings. At fifteen dollars per year, *Helicon Nine* is a real bargain.

1174. **Heresies: A Feminist Publication on Art and Politics**. 1977- . P.O. Box 766, Canal Street Station, New York, NY 10013. Semiannual. Four issues: $15.00 (indiv.); $24.00 (inst.). ISSN 0146-3411.

The best-known and most controversial of the several serials covering women and art, *Heresies* is "an idea-oriented journal devoted to the examination of art and politics" from multiple feminist perspectives. An ongoing collective is responsible for publishing the journal and developing themes, while a different editorial staff referees, edits, and designs each issue. Although all illustrations are in black and white, *Heresies* is visually provocative, offering a patchwork of graphic art and prose that stimulates the reader to see new connections among women's lives, art, and ideology. The "Sex Issue" (no.12) has become a feminist classic. Other notable issues have focused on class, film and video, racism, mass media, ecology, architecture, music, Third World women, violence, the great goddess, traditional arts, and lesbians.

1175. **Hot Wire: The Journal of Women's Music and Culture.** 1984- . Not Just a Stage, 1321 W. Rosedale, Chicago, IL 60660. 3/year. $14.00 (indiv.); $19.00 (inst.). ISSN 0747-8887.

Hot Wire is a vital new journal that fills the gap left by *Paid My Dues*, its predecessor from the 1970s. *HW*'s debut was greeted with excitement: volume one, number one sold out the first week. Each sixty-five page issue is packed with news, analysis, reviews, and photographs relating to the ever-expanding world of women's music and culture, including performers (past and present) in a wide range of genres, music festivals, recording companies, and production companies, plus the broader network of women in print (writers, publishers, printers, bookstores), women's coffeehouses, and so on. In addition to articles, poetry, and news, each issue includes a sound sheet of selected women's music.

1176. **Hurricane Alice: A Feminist Review.** 1983- . 207 Lind Hall, 207 Church St., Minneapolis, MN 55455. Quarterly. $9.00. ISSN 0882-7907.

Hurricane Alice evinces both its Midwestern roots and the ambition to become a national presence. Its pages have been frequented by writers such as Sandy Boucher, Meridel LeSueur, Valerie Miner, and Grace Paley, as well as by new, aspiring writers. A twelve-page tabloid, *HA* publishes reviews of books and the arts, poetry, personal narratives, conference presentations, and editorials in three full-scale issues and one brief newsletter per volume.

1177. **Hypatia: A Journal of Feminist Philosophy.** 1983- . Department of Philosophical Studies, Southern Illinois University at Edwardsville, Edwardsville, IL 62026-1001. Semiannual. $20.00 (indiv.); $40.00 (inst.). ISSN 0887-5480.

Named after a fourth-century Egyptian philosopher, mathematician, and astronomer, *Hypatia* was founded in 1983 as a "journal within a journal," published as annual special issues of *Women's Studies International Forum* (see entry 1210). Beginning in 1986, *Hypatia* became an autonomous journal. The publication is the brainchild of the Society for Women in Philosophy, which planned for more than a decade to create a forum explicitly dedicated to feminist philosophy. Writers who appeared in *Hypatia*'s first three issues include Alison M. Jaggar, Ann Ferguson, Claudia Card, Marilyn Frye, and Margaret A. Simons.

1178. **Ikon: Creativity and Change.** Second series. 1982/83- . P.O. Box 1355, Stuyvesant Station, New York, NY 10009. Irregular. 2 issues: $9.50 (indiv.); $15.00 (inst.).

Published and edited by Susan Sherman, the original *Ikon* first appeared in February 1967 and became, at its height, a significant journal of art and politics with a national circulation of 10,000. Sherman launched the second series of the journal in 1982, with a focus on work by women. Beautifully produced, the journal blends poetry, fiction and nonfiction prose, personal narrative, and photographs and other graphics, attracting fine writers such as Audre Lorde, Michelle Cliff, Irena Klepfisz, June Jordan, Margaret Randall, Valerie Miner, Vickie Sears, Marilyn Hacker, and Gloria Anzaldúa. Some issues feature special thematic sections, for example, on women and the computer, or photography. Political struggle is a recurrent, underlying theme, particularly as it takes shape in the United States and in Latin America.

1179. **Isis International Women's Journal.** 1984- . Via Santa Maria dell-Anima 30, 00186 Rome, Italy. Semiannual. $15.00 (indiv.); $25.00 (inst.).

Isis International, a women's organization based in Rome and Geneva, published a bulletin documenting international feminist resources, networks, and exchanges from 1974 to 1984. The *Isis International Women's Journal* continues that bulletin. Each issue is produced jointly by the Rome office and one or more Third World women's groups. The first issue, co-produced with a Peruvian collective, reported on the Second Latin American and Caribbean Feminist Meeting held in Lima in 1983. The Pacific and Asian Women's Forum (New Delhi) collaborated with Isis on the second issue of the *Journal*, a special report on women and media in the Asian and Pacific region. The *Journal* is supplemented twice a year by *Women in Action*, which surveys women's movement developments around the world. In 1984, the Geneva contingent of Isis became Isis-WICCE (Women's International Cross-Cultural Exchange), initiating exchanges of feminist activists worldwide, and publishing a quarterly report on WICCE programs entitled *Women's World*.

1180. **Kalliope: A Journal of Women's Art.** 1979- . 3939 Roosevelt Blvd., Jacksonville, FL 32205. 3/year. $9.00 (indiv.); $15.00 (inst.). ISSN 0735-7885.

Beautifully produced, *Kalliope* publishes women's art and writing. Issues average seventy pages in length and typically include short fiction, poetry, an interview, and black-and-white photographs and other visual art. The editorial collective keeps an unusually low profile, rarely contributing editorials or other introductory remarks. Nina Kiriki Hoffman, Ruth Moon Kempher, Carole Dine, Barbara Goldberg, Claire Keyes, Jame Somerville, and Judith Sornberger are among the writers represented in *Kalliope*'s pages; E. M. Broner, Alice Walker, Barbara Deming, May Sarton, and Margaret Atwood have been featured in *Kalliope* interviews.

1181. **Legacy: A Journal of Nineteenth-Century American Women Writers.** 1984- . Department of English, Bartlett Hall, University of Massachusetts, Amherst, MA 01003. Semiannual. $15.00 (indiv.); $18.00 (inst.). ISSN 0748-4321.

As the present women's studies bibliography amply demonstrates, nineteenth-century studies constitute a flourishing area within feminist literary scholarship. Founded as a newsletter, with the fall 1985 issue *Legacy* became a full-fledged journal, quadrupling in length. In its first issue as a journal, *Legacy* published critical articles by Nina Baym, Suzanne Gossett and Barbara Ann Bardes, and Carolyn L. Karcher; a reprint of a short story by Lydia Maria Child; profiles of Fanny Fern and Frances Ellen Watkins Harper; a bibliography of women's utopian writing; and book reviews. A future issue of the journal will commemorate the Emily Dickinson centenary. Founded the same year, *Turn-of-the-Century Women*, another semiannual, draws on the lively scholarship focusing on the period from 1880 to 1920, in Europe and the United States. Interdisciplinary in approach, the journal publishes articles, reprints, short notes, and book reviews.

1182. **Lesbian Ethics.** 1984- . P.O. Box 943, Venice, CA 90294. 3/year. $12.00 (indiv.); $16.00 (inst.). ISSN 8755-5352.

Lesbian Ethics is intended as "a forum for lesbian feminist ethics and philosophy, with an emphasis on how lesbians behave with each other." In her introduction to the first issue, editor Jeanette Silveira argues that the lesbian-feminist community, free of the oppressive relationships characterizing the "straight" world, is building "the first true ethics." Articles appearing in *Lesbian Ethics*'s initial two issues include "The Mystery of Lesbians," by Julia Penelope; "A Call for an End to Ageism in Lesbian and Gay Services," by Barbara Macdonald; "Rule Making," by Jane Rule; "Lesbian Origins," by Susan Cavin; and "The Tired Old Question of Male Children," by Anna Lee.

1183. **Lilith: The Jewish Women's Magazine.** 1976- . Suite 1328, 250 West 57th St., New York, NY 10019. Irregular. 4 issues: $14.00 (indiv.); $20.00 (inst.). ISSN 0146-2334.

Named "for the legendary predecessor of Eve who insisted on equality with Adam," *Lilith* is a forum for American Jewish feminism. The magazine averages thirty to fifty pages and is professional in appearance. Pluralist in approach, *Lilith* publishes fiction and nonfiction prose, poetry, photos, and art work reflective of a range of perspectives—from Orthodox Judaism to Jewish lesbian-feminism. Topics recurrently explored in *Lilith* include Jewish women's history, sexism in the Jewish community, Israel, anti-Semitism, and the feminist transformation of Jewish religious practice.

1184. **m/f.** 1978- . 24 Ellerdale Rd., London NW3 6BB, England. Semiannual. $7.50 (indiv.); $14.00 (inst.). ISSN 0141-948X.

"m/f" in the title of this scholarly journal stands for "marxist/feminist." In the first issue, the editors describe *m/f* as "a contribution to the development of political and theoretical debate within what is loosely called the Women's Movement," a forum for the critical examination of both Marxist and feminist theories. Though based in England, the journal strives to be a part of international socialist-feminist dialogue; for example, no. 10, 1985, presents proceedings from a conference sponsored by *m/f*, with participants from Britain, France, the United States, Holland, and Italy. That issue featured articles on philosophy in feminist thought, the feminine super-ego, feminism and film theory, the women's liberation movement in socialist France and women's employment.

1185. **Media Report to Women.** 1972- . Women's Institute for Freedom of the Press, 3306 Ross Place, N.W., Washington, DC 20008. Bimonthly. $15.00 (indiv.); $20.00 (inst.). ISSN 0145-9651.

As its subtitle indicates, *Media Report to Women* reports "What Women Are Doing and Thinking to Build a More Democratic Communications System." Twelve pages in length, the newsletter publishes notices of employment opportunities in journalism and the communications field; news about journalism schools, journalists, and the treatment of women in the media; announcements of new publications; and excerpts from relevant literature.

The Women's Institute for Freedom of the Press also issues the annual *Index/Directory of Women's Media,* which offers short descriptions of a wide range of feminist media projects in the U.S. and elsewhere—from periodicals and presses to radio and television programs; from theater groups to library collections. A list of "individual media women and media-concerned women" rounds out the directory.

1186. **Ms.** 1972- . 123 Garden St., Marion, OH 43302. Monthly. $16.00. ISSN 0047-8318.

Ms. holds a controversial place in American feminist politics, its consistent publication record, professional appearance, and mass circulation underwritten by aggressive marketing and heavy corporate advertising (for cosmetics, diet products, cigarettes, etc.) that offend many feminists. There are those who argue that *Ms.*'s politics—soft-pedaling the more contentious issues in the movement—result from the magazine's dependence on corporate grants and advertising revenue. There is no denying, however, that *Ms.* reaches a far larger and more diverse readership than any other U.S. feminist periodical, and that it consistently features quality writing. Moreover, the magazine is an important vehicle for popularizing and disseminating women's studies scholarship. Contributors to *Ms.* include writers such as Elaine Showalter, Molly Haskell, Robin Morgan, Marilyn French, Alice Walker, Barbara Ehrenreich, and Rita Mae Brown, along with regulars like Gloria Steinem and Lindsy Van Gelder. Covering politics, economics, health, literature, film, and personal lifestyles, *Ms.* clearly remains a "must-buy" for any women's studies collection.

1187. **New Directions for Women.** 1972- . 108 Palisade Ave., Englewood, NJ 07631. Bimonthly. $10.00 (indiv.); $16.00 (inst.). ISSN 0160-1075.

New Directions for Women began as a fourteen-page, mimeographed newsletter reporting on issues of interest to women in New Jersey; continuously expanding, it went national in 1975, and in 1980 switched from a quarterly to its present bimonthly publication schedule. Paula Kassell, founder and editor, shaped its character from the beginning. In contrast to *off our backs* (see entry 1188), another pioneering feminist newspaper, *NDW* reflects an older and more mainstream constituency and devotes less space to political theory and debate. *NDW* does provide regular, quality reporting on health issues, the arts, employment and pay equity, law, and the media, along with feature articles, film and book reviews, photographic essays, and a calendar of upcoming events. The *NDW Ten Year Cumulative Index* (1972-1981) documents not only the newspaper's impressive publishing record, but also the history of the U.S. women's movement as reflected in *NDW* during this period.

1188. **off our backs: a women's news journal.** 1970- . 1841 Columbia Rd., N.W., #212, Washington, DC 20009. 11/year. $11.00 (indiv.); $25.00 (inst.). ISSN 0030-0071.

One of the oldest feminist newspapers, *off our backs* has an astonishingly consistent publishing record dating back to 1970, and subscriptions remain a bargain in 1986. It not only offers good news coverage about women in the United States and internationally, with regular reporting on work, health, education, law, lesbians, prisoners, and women of color; it also serves as a national feminist forum, publishing articles, interviews, and letters to the editor in which topics and issues of current concern are presented and hotly debated. Although at any one time it may be perceived by some women as biased in one direction or another, on the whole the newspaper has a history of opening its pages to controversy. Complete collections of *off our backs* serve as an excellent documentary source on the growth and evolution of the contemporary U.S. women's movement. *oob* recently inherited the readership of a high-quality sister newspaper, the *New Women's Times,* which ceased in 1985 after a decade of publishing.

1189. **On Campus With Women.** 1971- . Project on the Status and Education of Women, Association of American Colleges, 1818 R St., N.W., Washington, DC 20009. Quarterly. $15.00 (indiv.); $25.00 (inst.). ISSN 0734-0141.

On Campus With Women is the publication of the Project on the Status and Education of Women, a clearinghouse for information concerning women and education.

OCWW publishes short notices of new publications, pertinent research findings, news of university programs, assessments of women's status at colleges and universities, and excerpts from the literature. Subscribers also receive special reports prepared by PSEW on topics such as reentry women, Title IX, and the classroom climate for women.

1190. **Psychology of Women Quarterly.** 1976- . Cambridge University Press, 32 E. 57th St., New York, NY 10022. Quarterly. $30.00 (indiv.); $72.00 (inst.). ISSN 0361-6843.

Psychology of Women Quarterly is the journal of Division 35 of the American Psychological Association. It publishes empirical studies, critical reviews, theoretical articles, and book reviews in the broad areas of sex-related differences, psychobiological factors, role development and change, career choice and training, management, education, discrimination, therapy, social processes, and sexuality. Specific topics recently examined in the quarterly have included rape, narcissism, support networks of black women, rural mothers, achievement motivation, tokenism, and depression.

1191. **Resources for Feminist Research/Documentation sur la recherche féministe.** 1972- . Ontario Institute for Studies in Education, 252 Bloor St. West, Toronto, Ontario M5S 1V6, Canada. Quarterly. $30.00 (indiv.); $50.00 (inst.). ISSN 0707-8412.

International, interdisciplinary, and bilingual in scope, *Resources for Feminist Research* (the *Canadian Newsletter of Research on Women*, 1972-1978) is an invaluable aid to students and researchers struggling to stay abreast of women's studies scholarship. In any given year, subscribers receive a book review issue (with some forty reviews), an annual index, and two thematic issues. (Some recent themes are "Women and Disability," "Women and Language," "Women and Education," and "Quebec Women's Writings.") Every issue is packed with information, including abstracts of Canadian and international research, bibliographies, reports of archival holdings, syllabi, and periodical and resource guides, along with feature articles, occasional poetry, and reviews.

1192. **Sage: A Scholarly Journal on Black Women.** 1984- . P.O. Box 42741, Atlanta, GA 30311-0741. Semiannual. $15.00 (indiv.); $25.00 (inst.). ISSN 0741-8639.

Sage is an interdisciplinary forum for research by and about black women. With black women's studies emerging as a distinct and vital field, there is a clear need for such a journal; *Sage* more than doubled in length from its first to its third issue. *Sage* publishes brief feature articles, interviews, reviews, research reports, photographic essays, personal narratives, documents, resource lists, letters, conference announcements, and bibliographies. Each of the first three issues focuses on a theme: education, mothers and daughters, women as writers. *Sage* contributors have included Patricia Bell-Scott, Beverly Guy-Sheftall, Janet Sims-Wood, Gloria Wade-Gayles, Gloria Joseph, Joyce A. Ladner, and Bell Hooks.

1193. **Samya Shakti: A Journal of Women's Studies.** 1983- . Centre for Women's Development Studies, B-43, Panchsheel Enclave, New Delhi-110017, India. Annual. $18.00.

"Equality/Power" is how *Samya Shakti* translates, the title of a new journal of women's studies in the Third World. The publication reflects an interest both in specific studies of Third World women and in the development of women's studies as a discipline internationally. The contributors are primarily though not exclusively Indian scholars writing on Indian society. Each issue has a thematic focus; the two themes to date are the relevance and future of women's studies, and the women's role in people's movements. Topics explored in the first two issues include women and the Indian independence movement, women's responses to Gandhi, women's movement in Iran, women's studies in the People's Republic of China, and Third World perspectives on Western women's studies.

1194.   **Sex Roles: A Journal of Research.** 1975- . Plenum Publishing Corp., 233 Spring St., New York, NY 10013. Monthly. $25.00 (indiv.); $137.50 (inst.). ISSN 0360-0025.

This cross-disciplinary journal publishes empirical research and theory "concerned with the basic processes underlying gender-role socialization in children and its consequences" (editorial statement). Contributors come from the fields of psychology, psychiatry, sociology, anthropology, education, political science, and social work. Topics recently examined in *Sex Roles* include children's perceptions of male and female principals and teachers, the effects of sex-role identity and sex on definitions of sexual harassment, sex differences in the clinical expression of depression, the independence of masculine and feminine traits, fear of success, and sex-role stereotyping in the Sunday comics.

1195.   **Signs: Journal of Women in Culture and Society.** 1975- . The University of Chicago Press, Journals Division, P.O. Box 37005, Chicago, IL 60637. Quarterly. $27.50 (indiv.); $55.00 (inst.). ISSN 0097-9740.

Signs is the premier journal of women's studies scholarship; interdisciplinary in scope, it is *the* journal to follow to stay abreast of new developments in feminist research across the disciplines. In addition to the scholarly articles that lead off each issue, *Signs* regularly publishes essays on the field of women's studies itself, broad review essays of the disciplines and key topics, brief research reports, book reviews (typically comparing several related titles), archival documents, and letters and comments. While *Signs* does accept the work of young researchers, many of its contributors are scholars at the forefront of their fields. For example, one recent issue featured writing by Gerda Lerner, Maxine Baca Zinn, Bonnie Thornton Dill, Linda K. Kerber, Eleanor E. Maccoby, Carol Gilligan, Leila J. Rupp, Martha Vicinus, and Elizabeth Janeway, among others. A number of *Signs* thematic issues are also available as monographs (see entries 1056 and 1082).

1196.   **Sinister Wisdom.** 1976- . P.O. Box 1023, Rockland, ME 04841. Quarterly. $14.00 (indiv.); $26.00 (inst.). ISSN 0196-1853.

Founding editors Harriet Desmoines and Catherine Nicolson launched *Sinister Wisdom* following the demise of *Amazon Quarterly* in 1975. Like its sister journal, *Conditions,* founded in the same year, *Sinister Wisdom* hoped to provide a consistent outlet for lesbian-feminist creative writing, art, and theory, and to appeal, in the words of its former subtitle, to "the lesbian imagination in all women." Many lesbian writers now known to a broad feminist reading public first published classic pieces in *Sinister Wisdom* — Judith Schwarz on lesbian history, Marilyn Frye on separatism, Irena Klepfisz on lesbian literature and criticism, Audre Lorde on her experience with breast cancer, Elly Bulkin on racism and writing. Two special issues on lesbian writing and publishing edited by Beth Hodges (1976, 1980) contributed substantially to the ideas and the network of the women-in-print movement. "A Gathering of Spirit: North American Indian Women's Issue," edited by Beth Brant (Degonwadonti) in 1983 (see entry 643), was another major thematic issue. Michelle Cliff and Adrienne Rich served as editors from 1981 to 1984. Currently edited by Melanie Kaye/Kantrowitz, *Sinister Wisdom* publishes poetry, narratives, essays, drama, interviews, reviews, and art.

1197.   **Sojourner: The Women's Forum.** 1975- . 143 Albany St., Cambridge, MA 02139-4298. Monthly. $15.00. ISSN 0191-8699.

Small press periodicals frequently fall victim to poverty and burnout, and feminist publications are no exception. *Sojourner* entered its tenth year in a state of crisis but managed to attract enough support from women in the Boston area and nationally to turn the situation around. The newspaper emerged financially stronger, spiritually revitalized, and with an intensified political commitment to increase the diversity of voices represented in its pages. *Soj* (as the publication refers to itself) carries feature articles; reviews of books, film, dance, theater, the visual arts, and music; news; and poetry. Recent contributors have included Audre Lorde (on sisterhood and survival), Margorie Agosín (on Chile), Vera Laska (on women in the resistance and the Holocaust), Cynthia Enloe (on black women in the U.S. military), Ellen Cantarow (on Jewish women and Nairobi), and Lisa Leghorn (on the shelter movement).

1198. **Spare Rib: A Women's Liberation Magazine.** 1972- . 27 Clerkenwell Close, London EC1, England. Monthly. $23.00 (indiv.); $36.00 (inst.). ISSN 0306-7971.

As Britain's only national feminist magazine, *Spare Rib* makes for an interesting contrast with *Ms.* As recounted by Katie Campbell in her fascinating retrospective essay in the June 1984 issue of *The Women's Review of Books,* at its inception *Spare Rib* more closely mirrored *Ms.*'s corporate-supported glossy format and liberal politics. By the mid-1970s, however, *Spare Rib*'s readership had shrunk. The magazine became a collective, dropped its slick image and big-name authors, and began publishing material by and for grass-roots British feminists. Today, *Spare Rib* is unlike anything published in the United States — approximating a blend of the *Ms.* magazine format (it still sports a slick cover) and *off our backs*'s politics and reporting. Feature articles, domestic and international news, letters, fiction, reviews, and announcements crowd each issue. The magazine is open to political controversy, and demonstrates a heightened commitment to represent the true diversity of British women. *Spare Rib Reader,* edited by *Spare Rib* founder Marsha Rowe (Penguin Books, 1982), offers a selection from the first one hundred issues of the magazine.

1199. **13th Moon: A Feminist Literary Magazine.** 1973- . Box 309, Cathedral Station, New York, NY 10025. Semiannual. 2 volumes: $13.00. ISSN 0094-3320.

Originally a graduate school women's poetry magazine, *13th Moon* has grown to become a hefty literary journal, acquiring an increasingly feminist identity along the way. *13th Moon* publishes poetry, short fiction, essays, translations, reviews, and artwork by both new and established writers and artists. A recent editorial affirms the publication's "special interest in the perspectives of women of color, working-class women, and lesbians." Among the writers whose work has appeared in *13th Moon* are June Jordan, lyn lifshin, Marge Piercy, Robin Morgan, Toi Derricotte, Marilyn Hacker, and Joanna Russ. Other North American small press, feminist literary magazines include *Black Maria* (Chicago), *Moving Out* (Detroit), *Room of One's Own* (Vancouver), and *Backbone* (Seattle).

1200. **Trivia: A Journal of Ideas.** 1982- . P.O. Box 606, N. Amherst, MA 01059. 3/year. $12.00 (indiv.); $18.00 (inst.). ISSN 0736-928X.

Having considered both "scholarly" and "radical feminist" as possible descriptions of their new publication, and rejected both as too narrow, the editors of *Trivia* hit upon the simple subtitle "A Journal of Ideas." The ideas published here are both scholarly and feminist — often lesbian-feminist — with an emphasis on theory. Writers who contributed to the first eight issues include Janice Raymond, Kathleen Barry, Andrea Dworkin, Cynthia Rich, Mary Daly, and Paula Gunn Allen. In addition to essays and reviews, each issue features at least one profile of a woman whose work has been neglected. Some representative recent articles are "Lesbian Economics," by Jeffner Allen; "Against the

Male Flood: Censorship, Pornography, and Equality," by Andrea Dworkin; and "The View From Over the Hill: Notes on Ageism Between Lesbians," by Baba Cooper.

1201. **Tulsa Studies in Women's Literature.** 1982- . University of Tulsa, Tulsa OK 74104. Semiannual. $12.00 (indiv.); $14.00 (inst.). ISSN 0732-7730.

Tulsa Studies in Women's Literature publishes scholarship on women and writing, with an emphasis on "the specific links between the woman writer and her work" ("Notes to Contributors"). Within that broad focus, the journal accepts studies of literature in any time period or genre. It has attracted scholars who are at the forefront of developing feminist critical and literary theory—among them, Elaine Showalter, Nina Baym, Jane Marcus, Josephine Donovan, Nina Auerbach, Lillian S. Robinson, and Catharine R. Stimpson. Issues typically include critical articles, reviews, notes and queries, and letters.

1202. **WLW Journal: News, Views, Reviews for Women and Libraries.** 1976- . 2027 Parker St., Berkeley, CA 94704. Quarterly. $15.00. ISSN 0272-1996.

Women Library Workers is a national organziation of feminists working in libraries; WLW admits as members library workers both credentialled and uncredentialled functioning in public, school, university, or corporate library settings. The *WLW Journal* publishes articles on issues such as comparable worth and feminist library programming; profiles library services and collections; surveys research on women in librarianship; reviews books, periodicals, and records; and reports on news of interest to the WLW membership.

1203. **Woman of Power: A Magazine of Feminism, Spirituality, and Politics.** 1984- . P.O. Box 827, Cambridge, MA 02238. Semiannual. $9.00 (indiv.); $12.00 (inst.). ISSN 0743-2356.

Woman of Power was launched in 1984, coincidentally the year that *WomanSpirit* ceased after a decade of publishing. Although the spiritual and activist strains of feminism often seem to be tugging in opposite directions, *Woman of Power* smoothly incorporates both. The first three issues—each some one hundred pages in length—are ambitious, packed with interviews, profiles, articles, fiction, poetry, photography, and artwork, and designed with care and taste. The list of contributors demonstrates the breadth of the journal's vision and outreach: among them are Helen Caldicott, Starhawk, Susan Griffin, Marge Piercy, Rita Arditti, Sonia Johnson, Melanie Kaye/Kantrowitz, and Paula Gunn Allen. Each issue is organized around a theme—to date, "Womanpower," "EnVisioning a Feminist World," and "Woman as Warrior." *Woman of Power* promises to become a quarterly in 1987.

1204. **Woman's Art Journal.** 1980- . Woman's Art, Inc., 7008 Sherwood Dr., Knoxville, TN 37919. Semiannual. $10.00 (indiv.); $14.00 (inst.). ISSN 0270-7993.

Each issue of this handsome journal now follows a standard format: two or three scholarly articles; several shorter pieces on individual women artists, past and present; and a book review section. Maintaining high standards of historical scholarship and critical perspective, recent articles have covered such diverse topics as nude photography, the sexual division of labor in the arts and crafts movement, the image of the "modest maiden" in nineteenth-century art, women artists in Sweden, and Eastern European embroidery. Except for the cover, the numerous illustrations are in black and white. Other journals covering women and art include *Heresies* (see entry 1174) and *Women Artists News*. The latter is a bimonthly magazine for and about contemporary women in the arts. In addition to articles on feminist criticism, creative expression, and surviving as an artist, *Women Artists News* features reviews of exhibitions and books, and a national "almanac" of solo and group shows, job opportunities, and other useful information.

1205.   **Women & Health: The Journal of Women's Health Care.** 1976- . The Haworth Press, 75 Griswold St., Binghamton, NY 13904. Quarterly. $28.00 (indiv.); $82.00 (inst.); $95.00 (libraries). ISSN 0363-0242.

Women and Health publishes academic research relating to the health concerns of women. The journal defines these concerns fairly broadly, encompassing social and psychological as well as medical factors related to health. Sexuality, disability, drugs, pregnancy and childbirth, the feminist health movement, public health policy, contraception, nutrition, aging, and health education are some of the topics explored in recent issues. Issues average 120 pages in length, and carry articles, book and film reviews, and news and notes. The Haworth Press issues two other women's studies journals in similar format. *Women and Politics,* a quarterly launched in 1980, publishes new feminist scholarship from the field of political science, covering women's political participation, political roles, professional power, and public policy issues. Both psychological research and clinical experience are reflected in *Women and Therapy: A Feminist Quarterly,* which began in 1982. The Haworth price structure makes these three journals expensive buys for libraries and other institutions. Thematic issues from the journals are often published simultaneously by Haworth as separately priced monographs.

1206.   **Women and Language.** 1975- . University of Illinois at Urbana-Champaign, 244 Lincoln Hall, 702 South Wright St., Urbana, IL 61081. 2-3/year. $6.00. ISSN 8755-4550.

Women and Language serves as an interdisciplinary clearinghouse for information and research related to language and gender. It publishes short articles, bibliographies, book reviews, conference papers, comments on language use in the media, notices of upcoming conferences, and abstracts of research in progress. Some issues have a thematic focus—for example, "Women and Organizational Communication." *Women's Studies in Communication,* a semiannual that began in 1977, publishes descriptive and empirical studies, book reviews, and syllabi pertaining to gender and interpersonal, small group, and organizational communication; the mass media; and rhetoric.

1207.   **Women & Performance: A Journal of Feminist Theory.** 1983- . New York University/Tisch School of the Arts, Performance Studies Department, 51 W. 4th St., Rm. 300, New York, NY 10012. Semiannual. $9.00 (indiv.); $15.00 (inst.). ISSN 0740-770X.

Women & Performance was founded to establish "an ongoing dialogue among women performers and theorists" (editorial, vol.1, no.1). The journal publishes articles, interviews, photoessays, reviews, and announcements relating to a range of performance genres. Representative articles from the first three issues include: "Notes Toward a Feminist Performance Aesthetic," by Martha Roth; "Why Do We Need a Feminist Theatre?," by Clare Coss, Sondra Segal, and Roberta Sklar; "Theories of Melodrama: A Feminist Perspective," by E. Ann Kaplan; "Filmmaker Lizzie Borden: An Interview," by Anne Friedberg; "Jane Chambers: In Memoriam," by Penny Landau; "Locating the Language of Gender Experience," by Linda Walsh Jenkins; and "Presencias: Latin American Filmmakers in the Feminine Plural," by Susan Resnick.

1208.   **The Women's Review of Books.** 1983- . Wellesley College Center for Research on Women, 828 Washington St., Wellesley, MA 02181. Monthly. $14.00 (indiv.); $25.00 (inst.). ISSN 0738-1433.

"... [F]eminist but not restricted to any one conception of feminism" *The Women's Review of Books* publishes reviews of works representing diverse disciplines and perspectives. The publication distinguished itself from the outset by covering the very latest publications and by attracting as contributors some of the most respected feminist scholars and writers — Rayna Rapp, Dale Spender, Carolyn Heilbrun, Valerie Miner, Blanche Wiesen Cook, Joan Hoff-Wilson, Vivian Gornick, and other luminaries. By virtue of both its astute selection of books and the length and substantiveness of its reviews, *WRB* keeps readers abreast of current feminist issues and debates, both scholarly and political. Published in newspaper format, *WRB* averages twenty pages and ten reviews per issue, and also features letters to the editor, poems, and retrospective profiles of feminist writers, periodicals, and publishers. *The Women's Studies Review,* a bimonthly review of feminist scholarship published by the Ohio State University Center for Women's Studies, draws its contributors primarily from that university.

1209. **Women's Studies: An Interdisciplinary Journal.** 1972- . Gordon and Breach Science Publishers, c/o STBS Ltd., 1 Bedford St., London, WC2E 9PP, England. 3/year. $55.00 (indiv.); $138.00 (inst.). ISSN 0049-7878.

Women's Studies welcomes scholarship about women from across the disciplines, along with poetry, short fiction, and film and book reviews. It is strongest in the area of literature. Recent issues have featured literary criticism by Suzanne Juhasz on Emily Dickinson and Margaret Atwood, by Susan M. Squier on Virginia Woolf, and by Elaine Hedges on Susan Glaspell; film criticism by Leslie Fishbein; and poetry by Alicia Ostriker. Issues are often developed around specific themes; recent examples are Canadian and American women writers, Willa Cather, women in the Middle Ages, bias in feminist anthropology, and women in classical antiquity (see entry 319).

1210. **Women's Studies International Forum.** 1978- . Pergamon Press, Maxwell House, Fairview Park, Elmsford, NY 10523. Bimonthly. $40.00 (indiv.); $110.00 (inst.). ISSN 0277-5395.

The *Women's Studies International Forum* (formerly the *Women's Studies International Quarterly*) is "a multidisciplinary journal for the rapid publication of research communications and review articles in women's studies." As its title suggests, the journal publishes work from the international community of women's studies scholars; recent issues have featured writing by women from the United States, Canada, England, Ireland, Australia, New Zealand, Sweden, Norway, Finland, West Germany, the Netherlands, Kenya, and South Africa. Many of the journal issues are devoted to a single theme — e.g., "Rethinking Sisterhood"; "Reproductive and Genetic Engineering." Subscribers also receive a bimonthly newsletter, *Feminist Forum,* providing reports on conferences, news, announcements, calls for papers, lists of new publications, and letters. The *International Journal of Women's Studies,* published in Canada five times a year, also tries to tap an international women's studies readership. Like *WSIF,* the *Journal* is multidisciplinary in scope, but it concentrates on empirical research in the social sciences.

1211. **Women's Studies Quarterly.** 1982- . The Feminist Press at the City University of New York, 311 E. 94th St., New York, NY 10128. Quarterly. $25.00 (indiv.); $35.00 (inst.). ISSN 0732-1562.

In its second decade of publishing, the *Women's Studies Quarterly* (formerly the *Women's Studies Newsletter*) is an indispensable resource. Publisher Florence Howe, founder the The Feminist Press, has pioneered the development of feminist materials for the secondary and undergraduate classroom. *WSQ* provides a forum for on-going dialogue and debate about feminist pedagogy and women's studies growth worldwide. The teachers and students who contribute to *WSQ* propose new ideas for classroom teaching, report on their pedagogical approaches to specific subjects, debate the merits of the curriculum integration movement, and exchange syllabi and bibliographies. In addition, each year the quarterly prints up-to-date lists of women's studies research centers belonging to the National Council for Research on Women and of women's studies programs across the United States. *Index to the First Ten Years, 1972-1982,* by Jo Baird, Shirley Frank, and Beth Stafford (Feminist Press, 1985), includes (in addition to subject and author indexes) a retrospective essay by Florence Howe and a chronology charting the evolution of women's studies over the course of the decade.

APPENDIX
PUBLISHERS' ADDRESSES

Addresses for lesser-known book and periodical publishers appear below. Publishers included in *Books in Print* (1985-1986) or *Ulrich's International Periodicals Directory* (1985) are not covered here. Periodicals accorded main entries in the Periodicals chapter have addresses included in their citations.

Al Saqi Books
26 Westbourne Grove
London W2 5RH England

Allison and Busby, Ltd.
6a Noel St.
London W1V 3RB England

American Jewish Archives
3101 Clifton Ave.
Cincinnati, OH 45220

American Place Theatre
111 West 46th St.
New York, NY 10036

Anansi (*see* House of Anansi Press)

Anglo-Chinese Educational Institute
152 Camden High St.
London NW1 0NR England

Arlen House
The Women's Press
69 Jones Road
Dublin 3 Ireland

Asian/Pacific American Learning
    Resource Center and General College
University of Minnesota
Minneapolis, MN 55455

Australian Institute of Aboriginal Studies
P.O. Box 553
Canberra City, ACT 2601 Australia
(distr. by Humanities Press)

Backbone
P.O. Box 95315
Seattle, WA 98145

Barnard College Women's Center
3009 Broadway
New York, NY 10027

Basilisk Press
P.O. Box 71
Fredonia, NY 14063

Beach and Company, Publishers
3510 Olympic St.
Silver Spring, MD 20906

Berkeley Women's Law Journal
Boalt Hall, School of Law
University of California
Berkeley, CA 94720

Black Maria
P.O. Box 25187
Chicago, IL 60625-0187

Black Rose Books
3981 boulevard St. Laurent
Montreal, QUE H2W 1YS Canada

The Blatant Image
2000 King Mountain Trail
Sunny Valley, OR 97497

Boston Women's Health Book Collective
465 Mt. Auburn St.
Watertown, MA 02172

Canadian Women's Educational Press
    (*see* The Women's Press)

Carleton University Press
Carleton University
Colonel By Dr.
Ottawa, ONT K1S 5B6 Canada

Chicano Studies Research Center
    Publications
University of California, Los Angeles
405 Hilgard Ave.
Los Angeles, CA 90024

China Publications Centre
P.O. Box 399
Beijing, People's Republic of China

Chinese Literature
Baiwanzhang St.
Beijing, People's Republic of China

Clarity Educational Productions
4560 Horton St.
Emeryville, CA 94608

CORD (Congress on Research on Dance,
    Inc.)
New York University, Dance and Dance
    Education Dept.
35 West Fourth St., Room 675
New York, NY 10003

Coward, McCann and Geoghegan, Inc.
51 Madison Ave.
New York, NY 10010

Croom Helm, Ltd.
St. John's Chambers
2-10 St. John's Road
London SW11 1PN England

J. M. Dent and Sons, Ltd.
33 Welbeck St.
London W1M 8LX England

ECW Press
307 Coxwell Ave.
Toronto, ONT M4L 3B5 Canada

Edinburgh University Press
22 George Sq.
Edinburgh EH8 9LF Scotland

Elizabeth Cady Stanton Foundation
P.O. Box 227
Seneca Falls, NY 13148

Fontana Paperbacks
14 St. James Place
London SW1A 1PF England

Forman Publishing, Inc.
11661 San Vincente Blvd.
Los Angeles, CA 90049

A. J. Gavin
P.O. Box 7525
Ann Arbor, MI 48107

Glad Hag Books
P.O. Box 2934
Washington, DC 20013

Hale and Iremonger
P.O. Box 2552
Sydney, NSW 2001 Australia

Harbour Publishing Co., Ltd.
P.O. Box 219
Madeira Park, BC V0N 2HO Canada

Harvester Press
17 Ship St.
Brighton, Sussex BN1 1AD England

House of Anansi Press, Ltd.
35 Britain St.
Toronto, ONT M5A 1R7 Canada

Index/Directory of Women's Media
Women's Institute for Freedom of the
    Press
3306 Ross Place NW
Washington, DC 20008

Inland Book Company
22 Hemingway Ave.
East Haven, CT 06512

Institute for Research on Public Policy
2149 rue MacKay, Suite 102
Montreal, QUE H3G 2J2 Canada

Institute for the Arts and the Humanities
Howard University
2400 Sixth St. NW
Washington, DC 20059

Jonathan Cape, Ltd.
30 Bedford Square
London WC1B 3EL England

Journeyman Press
17 Old Mill Road
West Nyack, NY 10994

Kennikat Press and National University
    Publications
90 South Bayles Ave.
Port Washington, NY 11050

Kitchen Table: Women of Color Press
P.O. Box 2753
Rockefeller Center Station
New York, NY 10185

Latin American Perspectives
P.O. Box 5703
Riverside, CA 92517

Lester and Orpen Dennys, Ltd.
78 Sullivan St.
Toronto, ONT M5T 1C1 Canada

Library Professional Publications
P.O. Box 4327
Hamden, CT 06514

Manchester University Press
Oxford Road
Manchester M13 9PL England

Moving Out: Feminist Literary and Arts
    Journal
P.O. Box 21249
Detroit, MI 48221

National Computing Centre
Oxford Road
Manchester M1 7ED England

National Women's Studies Association
University of Maryland
College Park, MD 20742

New Hogtown Press
c/o University of Toronto
12 Hart House Circle
Toronto, ONT M5S 1A1 Canada

New Press
30 Lesmill Road
Don Mills, ONT M3B 2T6 Canada

NeWest Publishers, Ltd.
No. 204, 8631-109 St.
Edmonton, ALTA T6G 1E8 Canada

Night Heron Press
P.O. Box 3103
West Durham Station
Durham, NC 27705

NLB (see Verso Editions)

Onlywomen Press
38 Mount Pleasant
London WC1 England

Ontario Institute for Studies in Education
252 Bloor St. W.
Toronto, ONT M5S 1V6 Canada

Pagoda Books
30 Museum St.
London WC1A 1LH England

Peace Press, Inc.
3828 Willat Ave.
Culver City, CA 90230

Pluto Press, Ltd.
Unit 10 Spencer Ct.
7 Chalcot Road
London NW1 8LH England

Port Nicholson Press
P.O. Box 838
Manners St.
Wellington, New Zealand

Press Gang Publishers
603 Powell St.
Vancouver, BC V6A 1H2 Canada

Ravan Press, Ltd.
23 O'Reilly Road, Berea
P.O. Box 31134
2017 Braamfontein, South Africa

D. Reidel Publishing Co., Inc.
160 Old Derby St.
Hingham, MA 02043

Research Center on Women
Loretto Heights College
P.O. Box 706
Loretto Station
Denver, CO 80236

M. E. Robertson
160 Forest Road
Loughton
Essex 1G10 1EG England

Rosegarden Press
701 Keasbly
Austin, TX 78751

Seabury Press
815 Second Ave.
New York, NY 10017

Subterranean Co.
P.O. Box 10233
Eugene, OR 97440

Swallow Press
Scott Quadrangle
Athens, OH 45701

Talonbooks, Ltd.
201/1019 East Cordova St.
Vancouver, BC V6A 1M8 Canada

Transnational Institute
1901 Q St. NW
Washington, DC 20009

Trident Press
630 Fifth Ave.
New York, NY 10020

Véhicule Press
P.O. Box 125
Station La Cité
Montreal, QUE H2W 2M9 Canada

Verso Editions
15 Greek St.
London W1V 5LF England

Vision Press
15781 Sherbeck
Huntington Beach, CA 92647

Weidenfeld and Nicolson, Ltd.
91 Clapham High St.
London SW4 7TA England

Wheatsheaf Books, Ltd. (*see* Harvester
    Press)

Wideview Books
c/o Putnam Publishing Group
200 Madison Ave.
New York, NY 10016

Wisconsin Women Library Workers
P.O. Box 1425
Madison, WI 53701

Wisconsin Women's Law Journal
c/o University of Wisconsin Law School
975 Bascom Mall
Madison, WI 53706

Women Against Nuclear Development
    (WAND)
P.O. Box 421
Norwich, VT 05055

Women's Educational Press (*see* The
    Women's Press)

Women's Law Reporter
Loyola University School of Law
One East Pearson
Chicago, IL 60611

The Women's Press
229 College St.
Suite 204
Toronto, ONT M5T 1R4 Canada

Women's Studies in Communication
Dept. of Speech Communication
Humboldt State University
Arcata, CA 95521

Women's Studies Review
Center for Women's Studies
207 Dulles Hall
230 West 17th Ave.
Columbus, OH 43210

Zed Press
57 Caledonian Road
London N1 9BU England

AUTHOR INDEX

Reference is to entry number. Names in boldface are referred to in the annotations; others are main entries.

Abakanowicz, Magdalena, 50
Abdullah, Tahrunnessa A., 1
Abel, Elizabeth, 553, 1082
Abel, Emily K., 1082
Abzug, Bella S., 777
Achtenberg, Roberta, 391
Acker, Sandra Sue, 262
Acosta-Belén, Edna, 993
Adams, Alice, 436
Adams, Carolyn Teich, 213
Adams, Cynthia H., 803
Adams, Kathleen J., 28
Addis, Patricia K., 838
Adelsberg, Sandra, 852
Adler, Freda, 389
Adler, Renata, 437
Aguilar, Mila K., 670
Aichinger, Ilse, 637
Akers, Charles W., 119
Albers, Patricia, 2
Aldous, Joan, 994
Alegría, Claribel, 671
Alexander, Alpha, 1069
Alexander, Maxine, 638
Alexander, Paul, 182
Ali, Tariq, 790
Al-Issa, Ihsan, 796
Allen, Margaret Vanderhaar, 150
Allen, Paul Gunn, 438
Allende, Isabel, 439
Allgeier, Elizabeth Rice, 797
Allison, Dorothy, 672
Alpers, Antony, 120
Alta, 639
Altbach, Edith Hoshino, 1083
American Civil Liberties Union, 391
Ammer, Christine, 51, **771**

Ammons, Elizabeth, 554-55
Amsden, Alice H., 236
Andersen, Margaret L., 995
Anderson, Judith, 289
Anderson, Karen, 290
Anderson, Laurie, 105
Anderson, Mary B., 6
Andors, Phyllis, 42
André, Rae, 996
Andreas-Salomé, Lou, 556
Angelou, Maya, 121
Anker, Richard, 3
Anscombe, Isabelle, 52
Anshen, Frank, 379
Anthony, Susan B., 198
Anzaldúa, Gloria, 1130
Apfel, Roberta J., 745
Appelbaum, Eileen, 252
Aptheker, Bettina, 291
Arbur, Rosemarie, 879
Arbus, Diane, 59
Arcana, Judith, 798
Archer, John, 1057
Ardener, Shirley, 4
Arditti, Rita, 976
Ariel, Joan, 844
Armstrong, Louise, 641
Arnold, Eve, 53
Arnold, Lois, 989
Arnold, Marilyn, 185
Arthur and Elizabeth Schlesinger Library
    on the History of Women in
    America, 839
Asbell, Bernard, 165
Aschenbrenner, Joyce, 89
Ascher, Carol, **191**, 557
Ashford, Janet Isaacs, 746, **773**

TITLE INDEX

Reference is to entry number. Italicized titles are referred to in the annotations; others are main entries.

SUBJECT INDEX

Reference is to entry number.

Abakanowicz, Magdalena, 50
Abbott, Berenice, 96
Abbott, Edith, 136
Abbott, Grace, 136
Abolition Movement and abolitionists
    (U.S.), 140, 291, 368, 1011. *See*
    also Reform movements
letters, 134, 198-99
Aboriginal women, 18, 377
Abortion, 401, 756, 782, 976, 1031, 1136.
    See also Birth control; Reproductive
    rights
bibliography, 844
Abstracting services, 901
Academia. *See* Universities and colleges
Achievement motivation, 813
Actresses, 55, 114, 117, 565, 590, 602. *See*
    also Drama
directories, 924
Actresses' Franchise League, 590
Adams, Abigail, 119, 212
Adams, Henry, 158-59
Adams, Marian Hooper, 158-59
Administration. *See* Management
Adolescence, 821. *See also* Girls and young
    women
bibliography, 842
in literature, 194, 500, 529, 535
Adoption, 765, 1028
Adult education, 287
Adultery
in literature, 499
Advertising, 919, 1009
Affirmative action, 225
bibliography, 895

Africa, 13, 25, 29, 33, 36, 39-40, 43, 755
anthologies, 19
bibliography, 851, 897
liberation movements, 25, 45
in literature, 202, 473, 561, 564
literature of, 662
statistics, 916
writers, 454, 561, 564
African diaspora, 43
Afro-American women. *See* Black women
Aging, 1032, 1045. *See also* Middle age;
    Older women
in literature, 146
periodicals, 1157
Agoraphobia, 827
Agricultural workers, 10, 34, 329
Akhmadulina, Bella, 715
Akhmatova, Anna, 715
Alcohol and drug abuse, 749, 822, 1048
bibliography, 822, 859, 1048
in literature, 527
Alcott, Louisa May, 575
Allingham, Margery, 603
Amazons, 337
American Civil Liberties Union,
    404
American Indian women. *See* Indian
    women
American Woman Suffrage Association,
    199
Ames, Jessie Daniel, 306
Amniocentesis. *See* Reproductive
    technologies
Anarchists, anarchism, and anarcha-
    feminism, 143

Civil War (U.S.) 133, 305
Cixous, Hélène, 569, 806
Class and feminism, 223, 230, 291, 1011, 1099, 1150
  in literature, 463
Clergy. *See* Ministers
Clerical workers. *See* Office workers
Coeducation, 273
Cognition, 831
Colette, Sidonie Gabrielle, 68, 462
Colleges. *See* Universities and colleges
Collett, Camilla, 489
Collins, Wilkie, 559
Colombia, 10
Colonial period (U.S.), 128, 298, 350-51, 372
  in literature, 681
Colonialism and anti-colonial struggles. *See* Imperialism and anti-imperialist struggles
Commissions on the status of women, 793
Communal life, 1061
  in literature, 486
Communes. *See* Utopian communities
Communications. *See also* Mass media
  periodicals, 1185, 1206
Communist and socialist nations, 8, 42, 330, 1024. *See also names of individual countries*
Communist Party (U.S.), 132
Commuter relationships, 994
Comparable worth, 229
Composers, 51, 60, 63, 71, 94, 832, 846, 917
Computers. *See* Information technology; Technology and automation
Conductors, 51, 94
Congress (U.S.), 786
Conjugal violence. *See* Domestic violence; Marital rape; Violence against women
Consciousness, 223, 230
Contagious Diseases Acts, 374
Continuing education. *See* Adult education
Contraception. *See* Birth control; IUDs; Population trends and population control
Convents. *See* Nuns
Cooper, James Fenimore, 578
Corinne, Tee, 58
Corpi, Lucha, 621

Corporations, 225
Courtship, 356
Craft, Ellen, 368
Craig, Edith, 590
Crandall, Prudence, 285
Credit, 217
Crime, 389-90, 392, 397, 400, 405, 998. *See also* Juvenile delinquency; Prisons and prisoners
  bibliography, 859
Criminal justice, 390, 392-93, 400, 405, 409. *See also* Prisons and prisoners
Cross-cultural literature, 659, 662-63
Cross-cultural studies, 4, 6, 13, 15, 19, 23, 26-28, 30, 37, 44, 46, 48-49, 216, 224, 928, 1054, 1091, 1122, 1132. *See also* Anthropology; *names of individual countries or continents*
  aging, 11
  art, 87
  bibliography, 897
  demography, 1023
  development, 8
  education, 262
  employment, 219, 244
  history, 325
  mass media, 1006
  motherhood, 1020
  religion, 942
  sex-role stereotypes, 830
  slave systems, 33
Cuba, 32. *See also* Caribbean
Cuban-American women, 32. *See also* Women of color
  bibliography, 855
Culture, 28, 37, 1001, 1110, 1119, 1127
Cunningham, Imogen, 65
Cunningham, Mary, 233
Curriculum and instruction, 273, 277, 281, 283, 598. *See also* Pedagogy
Curriculum integration, 281
Czechoslovakia, 1024

DES (Diethylstilbestrol), 745, 765
  bibliography, 844
Dalkon Shield, 767
Dance and dancers, 67, 89, 93, 113
  directories, 924
Daughters. *See* Fathers: and daughters; Mothers: and daughters